BUBBLEGUM MUSIC

is the Naked Truth

BUBBLEGUM MUSIC

is the Naked Truth

Kim Cooper and David Smay, editors

With contributions from Jake Austen, Peter Bagge,
Keith Bearden, Derrick Bostrom, Mary Burt,
Carl Cafarelli, Don Charles, Chinta Cooper,
Morgan Cooper, Chris Davidson, Katrina Dixon,
Brian Doherty, Becky Ebenkamp, Chuck Eddy,
Dennis P. Eichhorn, Peter Geiberger, Chas Glynn,
Gary Pig Gold, Margaret Griffis, Bill Holmes,
Elizabeth Ivanovich, Gloria Keeley, P. Edwin Letcher,
Steve Mandich, Mike McPadden, Alec Palao,
The Partridge Family Temple, Robrt L. Pela,
Bill Pitzonka, James Porter, Domenic Priore,
Glenn Sadin, Metal Mike Saunders, Gene Sculatti,
Greg Shaw, Jack Stevenson, Vern Stoltz,
Lisa Sutton, Dave Thompson, Tom Walls,
Glynis Ward and J.R. Williams

FERAL HOUSE

"Raiding Hannah's Stash: An Appreciation of late '90s Bubblegum Music" by Peter Bagge appeared in a different form in *Scram* #10.

"An Informal History of Bubblegum Music" by Carl Cafarelli appeared in a longer version in *Goldmine* on April 25 1997.

"Jeff Barry's Bubblegum Blues" interview by Don Charles appeared in a longer version in *Discoveries* magazine, issue #120, May 1998.

"Boyce & Hart" by Kim Cooper appeared in a different form in Scram #4 and in the anthology *Having a Rave Up with Scram Magazine*.

"Bubblegum Music is the Naked Truth" by Kim Cooper appeared in a different form in *Scram* #5.

"The Partridge Family + The Manson Family = The Poppy Family" by Kim Cooper appeared in a different form in *Scram* #3 and in the anthology *Having a Rave Up with Scram Magazine*.

"Toomorrow" by Kim Cooper appeared in a different form in *Scram* #12.

"Bubblegum Never Died! It's Just That Nobody Ever Writes About It!" by Chuck Eddy appeared in a different form in *Creem* magazine in 1987.

"1999: The Year Bubblegum Snapped" by Mike McPadden appeared in a different form in *New York Press* in October 1999.

"Kasenetz-Katz and their Super-Duper Rock & Roll Kavalcade" by James Porter appeared in a different form in *Roctober* magazine, 1998

"Never Mind the Bollocks, Here's the Banana Splits" by James Porter appeared in a different form in *Roctober* magazine, 1994

The Gary Zekley and Yellow Balloon stories appear courtesy Domenic Priore and Sundazed Records.

"All Ears: Disney Dreams Up the Best Radio Station in 30 Years" by Metal Mike Saunders originally ran in a different form *Village Voice* on March 15, 2000.

"The Candy Ass Charisma of the Archies" by David Smay appeared in a different form in *Scram* #8 and in the anthology *Having a Rave Up with Scram Magazine*.

"The Brady Bunch" by Lisa Sutton appeared in a different form in *Goldmine*.

Kim Cooper would like to thank Sean Carrillo, Phil Drucker, Gary Morris, Lynn Peril, and all the contributors.

David Smay would like to thank Colleen Kingston, Keith Davidheit, Laura Pinto, Andrew Bergey, Zax and the all the authors and Yummy listers whose lively contributions to the Bubblegum 100 debate were a treat.

Feral House wishes to thank the following, and particularly Lisa Sutton, for sharing their Bubblegum collection: Derrick Bostrom, Kim Cooper, Margaret Griffis, Hitomi Ishikawa, P. Edwin Letcher, Glenn Sadin, Mike Saunders, The Partridge Family Temple, Tom Walls and Glynis Ward.

Our belated thanks to Scott Sookman for providing photos seen on pages 72, 81, 116, 132, 229, 237, 240 and 241.

ISBN 0-922915-69-5

Feral House
P.O. Box 13067
Los Angeles, CA 90013

www.feralhouse.com

Design by Linda Hayashi

10 9 8 7 6 5 4 3 2

For Lester Bangs and Joey Ramone

Contents

INTRODUCTION Bubble Entendres by Kim Cooper & David Smay

Once upon a time the AM radio dial grew sticky with a sickly sweet confectionery masquerading as rock 'n' roll. DJs, promotion men, executives and songwriters greedily conspired to tap the vast and largely untouched pre-pubescent music market, and the results were more successful—commercially and artistically—than they could have hoped.

It didn't take much to entice the tykes who'd been spending their allowances on comic books, candy bars, and baseball cards into throwing some of that cabbage towards vinyl 45s. Most homes had turntables, and anyone with an older sibling already thought buying records was a cool thing to do. All that was required was that rock be revamped into something that would appeal to this new market. Tone down the lovey-dovey stuff and the blatant aggression, and substitute lyrics that were just half a step away from kindergarten. Nursery rhymes are good, so are repetitions of baby-talk phrases. Kids love to dance, so give 'em a backbeat that even the klutziest infant can't miss. And churn it all out at lightning speed direct from the Bubblegum Factory—young songwriters knocking out lyrics to five songs before lunch, interchangeable singers and backing musicians racing into the studio, visionary producers stage-managing the whole shebang, while the kids wait eagerly for the next kinderpop sensation to hit the airwaves.

Did we say once upon a time? This formula was true in 1968, and as we go to press in 2001 it remains a very good description of the machinations behind many of the top charting acts worldwide. The twenty-first century version may be sexier—kids grow up faster nowadays, after all—but it's still the same old gumball when you cut it open.

Bubblegum Is . . .

Defining bubblegum is a tricky proposition as the term variously describes: 1. the classic bubblegum era from 1967–1972; 2. disposable pop music; 3. pop music contrived and marketed to appeal to pre-teens; 4. pop music produced in an assembly line process—driven by producers and using faceless singers; 5. pop music with that intangible, upbeat "bubblegum" sound.

A very strict definition of bubblegum insists on faceless bands, either shifting studio groups or music fronted by a television presence (usually a cartoon) with, as Bill Pitzonka describes it, "a contrived innocence that transcends its contrivance." This is the music of the Kasenetz and Katz bands (Ohio Express, 1910 Fruitgum Co.) and cartoon groups like the Archies within the first era of bubblegum chart dominance.

In this book we take a broader approach to the subject. Without compromising our core notions of what constitutes "Bubblegum," we investigate any number of borderline cases with varying degrees of gumminess. Sometimes we applied a diagnostic model to the question, charting how many symptoms a band presents. Was the group assembled by an outside producer? Did the producer fire the lead singer, or steal the lead singer and fire the group? Was the group dependent on outside songwriters/producers for its singles? Was the music produced by a faceless studio group? Were cartoons or a live TV show used to sell the music? Are the lyrics kid-slanted, referencing children's games, nursery rhymes, candy? Were teenagers themselves making the music?[1] Was it marketed to pre-teens?[2] Does the music have that sweet, sunny, upbeat danceable, entirely subjective bubblegum sound? Were canonical bubblegum creators involved?[3] No single factor defines bubblegum—though that slippery, indefensibly tautological, "Bubblegum Sound" comes close.

We also contend that a band can be bubblegum for part of their career. The Monkees' first two albums satisfy every bubblegum criteria we've got (though some would dispute that assessment: see Gary Pig Gold's and Carl Cafarelli's chapter). After the *Headquarters* coup, they emerged as a middling folk/country rock band. Then with the *Changes* album they fell squarely back into bubblegum mode. Paul Revere & the Raiders clearly begin at the other end of the spectrum as a hard-rocking garage band. After pulling in some Brill Building songwriting (Mann/Weil), outside production (Terry Melcher), TV show stardom (*Where the Action Is*), cartoony costumes and studio musicians (their last few albums) then you've got a band moving into bubblegum. When a group starts cutting ads for Mattel's groovy mod Barbie doll, Swingy, then you have to assume they're seriously catering to a pre-teen fan base. Or consider Tommy James' career arc. He launched with a crude frat rocker ("Hanky Panky"), turned out a stretch of essential bubblegum hits with Ritchie Cordell and Bo Gentry ("I Think We're Alone Now," "Mirage"), after which Tommy resumed control of his career and charted with the pop-psych of "Crimson and Clover" and such barely-gum as "Sweet Cherry Wine." Finally, look at how closely early Jackson 5 songs are modeled after bubblegum, with recess-ready lyrics on songs like "ABC," "2-4-6-8," "Ready Or Not Here I Come," "Stop the Love You Save" and "Sugar Daddy" (the all important "Sugar/Candy" title giveaway). Factor in a Saturday morning cartoon and the usual hallmarks Motown shared with bubblegum production (outside producers, Svengali lead, studio musicians) which indicate that we should consider the J-5 as bubblegum born.

Clearly we've got a flexible notion of what makes bubblegum, but we'll make it easy on you from the start and tell you what isn't included. Teen idols aren't bubblegum. Not usually anyway. Sometimes Boy Bands are bubblegum, but definitely not when they're crooning a ballad. Shaun Cassidy isn't bubblegum, but *David* Cassidy is, particularly when fronting the Partridge Family. Bobby Sherman's choker made our Bubblegum 100, but he just squeaked in since he's really a Teen Idol from the High Bubblegum era. That string of '70s Bathos-Pop one-shots? Not Bubblegum: "Billy Don't Be a Hero," "The Night Chicago Died," "One Tin Soldier," "Shannon," "Wild Fire."

We're interested in the causes of bubblegum too. But instead of asking why bubblegum happens, it's almost more interesting to ask why bubblegum isn't the norm. If it works at all, why doesn't it always work? One simple answer is that it runs in cycles. Whenever rock abandons its mandate for fun, danceable bubblegum (or its near equivalents) will fill that gap. When rock went psychedelic and larded down with social statement, up popped bubblegum. It happened in the '90s again after a stretch of "complaint rock." There will always be a market catering to 12-year-old girls who wanna dance. When disco was around the need for bubblegum wasn't as acute. Similarly, the early new wave days of MTV scratched the bubblegum itch nicely and broke out genres of music that weren't getting radio play. Notably, most of the icons of the '80s worked the dance-pop vein: Michael Jackson, Madonna, Prince. Michael and Madonna were particularly adept at selling their music to pre-teens.

1. Consider this: Tommy James, Toni Wine, Alex Chilton, Annabella, Peter Noone and Debbie Gibson were all in their mid-teens when they first hit. That's not even counting family groups and boy bands, which have always traded on the novelty of young performers.
2. Through cereal boxes—surely the major print medium for pre-teens; or, the Disney Channel or Nickelodeon; or through pre-to-early-teen magazines like *16*, *Tiger Beat, or Smash Hits*.
3. Look for: Jeff Barry, Jerry Kasenetz and Jeff Katz, Max Martin and Denniz Pop, Tony Burrows, Mike Chapman and Nicky Chinn, Boyce & Hart.

Bubblegum Precursors

Humorous songs have always been a part of the popular folk tradition. Although superficially aimed at a juvenile audience, adults take different pleasures from wacky numbers ripe with double entendres and inspired nonsense. In some respects, bubblegum fits tidily in the line of American novelty music that proceeds from "I Scream, You Scream, We All Scream For Ice Cream" (1927) to "(Boop-Boop Dit-em Dat-em What-em Choo!) Three Little Fishies (Itty Bitty Poo)" (1939) to "Mairzy Doats" (1943) to "Surfin' Bird" (1963). There was even an obscure strain of Doo-Wop music that specialized in adapting nursery rhymes and fairy tales to the style, apparently for a teen audience.

Apply the ten commandments of gum to helium-toned cartoon sensations Alvin & the Chipmunks, and they are revealed as a quintessential bubblegum act, emerging a full decade before the style exploded. Fuse the goofball lyricism of the novelty song with the deliberate prurience of under-the-counter "blue" party recordings like Doug Clark's "Hot Nuts," bring it all up to date with electric guitars and psychedelic imagery, and you've got a recipe for a teenybopper treat so tasty we had to write a book about it.

Other important precursors to bubblegum include the Brill Building, the British Invasion, the West Coast Sound, Motown and garage rock—all major commercial genres of the '60s. Just to cite one group, every major figure associated with the Archies graduated from the Brill Building scene (with honors): Don Kirshner, Jeff Barry, Ron Dante, Andy Kim, and Toni Wine.

Listening to Jeff Barry and Ellie Greenwich's recordings as the Raindrops, you can actually catch a whiff of the bubblegum to come. It's no coincidence that a 13-year-old Tommy James flipped over a Raindrops single and recorded his first hit, "Hanky Panky." Jeff Barry always had a knack for the rhythm track, and was one of the earliest pop producers to assimilate the backbeat coming out of Motown and Memphis. Motown returned the favor by launching the Jackson 5 in 1970, in belated response to bubblegum's success. Dan Penn in Memphis was more prescient when he decided he could make his own Monkees and had the Box Tops on the charts by 1967.

The British Invasion has been rewritten to emphasize the achievements of the Beatles, Rolling Stones, the Who and the Kinks (all loitering around the Olympian heights bumming fags off each other) while the

Ten Commandments of Bubblegum

Thou shalt dance to the groovy beat and the beat shall be within thee.

Thou shalt be animated, or if that is physically impossible, aspire to that condition.

Thou shalt fixate on the oral stage, honey thy words with the lip-smacking treats, candy-coat thy innuendo and make with the bubble entendre.

Honor thy Producer, for he is King of Kings, and maker of shiny sounds and keeper of the royalty checks.

Thou shalt market unto the pre-teen and yet render unto the teen what is due the teen.

Thou shalt make unto the compilation, which begat the K-Tel, which begat the Ronco, which begat the Rhino, which begat the Varèse Sarabande, which begat *Totally Hits*, which begat *Now That's What I Call Music Volume 4*.

Thou shalt come pre-assembled with batteries included and thy choreography shall be of the spinning and the hopping and the emphatic arm gestures which is a sign unto the Lord that thou art keeping it real, and that thou art Down With The Lord.

Thou shalt render unto the Holy Ghost Band with the singers interchangeable and the session players by the hour, gold and anonymity.

Thou shalt not covet thy partners' royalties, for it was a paying gig and thou shall hustle up a new one.

Thou shalt partake of the sweet and turn from the bitter, play in the major chords and shun the minor, frolic in the dance beat and yawn at the ballad.

Zombies, Hollies and Yardbirds are forced to mingle on the other side of the velvet rope with the record geeks that adore them. The top-selling acts of the British Invasion, however, were the Beatles, Dave Clark Five and Herman's Hermits. It really was music business as usual, and Herman's Hermits clearly anticipate bubblegum with their 16-year-old lead singer, their goofball antics on *Shindig!*, their movie *Hold On*, their dependence on sing-song kid-rhyme songs like "I'm Henry the VIII, I Am," and the ace songsmithery of Graham Gouldman and P.F. Sloan.[4]

Charting the history of just one British Invasion band like Wayne Fontana and the Mindbenders turns up a mind-bending intersection of influences. With Wayne up front the band first hit with the frat-hard, beat-happy "Game of Love"—a song that wouldn't have sounded out of place on a Swingin' Medallions or Gentrys single. Ditching Wayne, the band hit internationally with "A Groovy Kind of Love," written by two nice Jewish girls from New York, Carol Bayer and Toni Wine. That's the same Toni Wine who sings on "Sugar, Sugar." The same Toni Wine who recorded a demo with Jeff Barry's ex-wife and writing partner, Ellie Greenwich, that became "Candida" and launched Tony Orlando & Dawn. Meanwhile, back with the Mindbenders, band-member Eric Stewart asked his old mate Graham Gouldman to tour with the band and write a few songs (including the lovely "Pamela Pamela") for them. Graham obliged for a bit before drifting off, signing a contract with Kasenetz and Katz and putting out "Sausalito" under the Ohio Express name. Toni later went on to marry legendary soul producer Chips Moman — in whose studio Dan Penn cut those Box Tops hits. After his stint with K&K, Graham and Eric formed 10cc with Lol Creme and Kevin Godley. That would be the Godley & Creme who directed all those groundbreaking Duran Duran videos.

The garage band element in bubblegum has been much remarked on, and the links are fairly obvious. Many of the early K&K hits are more garage rock than bubblegum —"Beg, Borrow and Steal," "Little Bit of Soul," "Down at Lulu's"— and you can easily compile a list of Kasenetz and Katz album filler that steals gleefully from "Louie, Louie." The Strangeloves represent another example of a fabricated studio group with a hard rocking garage sound and extravagantly false backstory (you'll see ex-Strangelove Richard Gotterher's name recur throughout this book). The Shadows of Knight turned to Kasenetz and Katz for the blistering "Shake," and Paul Revere & the Raiders learned to leaven their hard and heavy sounds with marshmallow. Joey Levine is the key figure here, writing "Try It" for the Standells before the Ohio Express made him famous, and also working with Artie & Kris[5] Resnick in the Third Rail. In fact, the *Nuggets* box set is riddled with bubblegum stalwarts; Kris Resnick has nearly as many songwriting credits as Elias McDaniel.

While many of the most prominent bubblegum creators worked out of New York (including the Buddah/K&K circle, Jeff Barry/Archies team and Tommy James with Ritchie Cordell and Bo Gentry), the West Coast Sound also profoundly influenced bubblegum music. Gary Usher's many knockoff studio cash-in groups like the Hondells, the Revells, and the Kickstands laid the groundwork for Los Angeles Bubblegum. The great songwriting team of P.F. Sloan and Steve Barri created the ultimate faceless folk rock studio group with the first Grass Roots record, preceding that accomplishment with their Beach Boys-inspired Fantastic Baggys. As an in-house producer at Dunhill/ABC Steve Barri went on to produce important bubblegum contributions from Tommy Roe and Lancelot Link and the Evolution Revolution. While Tommy Boyce & Bobby Hart are strongly associated with West Coast Bubblegum, where they made their mark with the Monkees, both had roots at the Brill Building.

---

4. Gouldman, of course, also turned out some of the most memorable chart hits for the Hollies and Yardbirds.
5. Artie's wife and Joey's frequent writing partner.

The Hitmakers

Songwriter-producers make bubblegum music, guiding their sounds through the capable talents of session singes and studio musicians. Bubblegum thrives in a studio culture that's rarely exposed, but we reveal its busy beehive of professionalism. Here outrageous commercialization balances with an undiluted joy in music. It's doubtful recording sessions get any more fun than the one that produced "Sugar, Sugar."

Why This Book? Why Now?

Loathed by the contemporary critical establishment (except Lester Bangs and a few other open-minded scribes), and quickly dismissed by its maturing audience, bubblegum receded into history without ever being properly understood. If you want to learn about the Buddah label you're better off looking to the business section of the trades than to *Rolling Stone*, *Cheetah* or *Crawdaddy*. Hip editors seemed to believe that if they just ignored these insolent sounds, maybe they'd go away. Besides, the readers of semi-underground rock journals weren't at all interested in this contrived pabulum. It's only in retrospect, as the pop smarts, garage rock associations, lyrical excess and sheer sonic glory of bubblegum are revealed to less reactionary ears that the need for a full critical and historical accounting becomes clear.

But it's not all about the '60s. Bubblegum is a viral vein that's flowed stickily through the body of rock for more than 30 years. Sometimes it hides out for years at a time, but it's always lurking, waiting for the perfect confluence of a generation, a musical phenomenon, a few inspired producer-types and a little sprinkling of Pixy Stick dust to again explode across the charts.

The late '90s saw the biggest bubblegum explosion since 1968, accompanied by a backlash that's all too familiar. But even without the luxury of temporal distance, there are a few critics who are already looking objectively at the Britney era, picking out the gems from a sea of manufactured fluff. It seems obvious that bubblegum is here to stay, and the least we can do is to try to understand it.

But before we can understand bubblegum, we'd better get the story straight. There's a tremendous amount of false and misleading factual information about bubblegum music floating around that needs to be corrected. Since the albums themselves rarely credited the actual singers and musicians, myths have perpetuated until they're accepted as fact, and inferences are drawn which badly distort the story of the music. While we are overwhelmingly fond of Joey Levine's songwriting, paint-peeling nasality and ubiquity on K&K product, it needs to be cleared up that he never sang lead on any 1910 Fruitgum Co. songs—Mark Gutkowski (usually) did. And while Ellie Greenwich certainly deserves her Hall of Fame songwriting status, she never wrote for the Archies—at most she sang a few background vocals. Toni Wine sang on the second and third Archies albums (*Everything's Archie*—later retitled *Sugar, Sugar*—and *Jingle, Jangle*). That's Toni's glorious lead on the single "Jingle, Jangle," but another singer, Donna Marie, dueted with Ron Dante on "Who's Your Baby" and "Together We Two."

Critical Thought and Reevaluation

There's no putdown in the critic's arsenal more dismissive, or easy, than "bubblegum." To zap a performer with this particular insult is to brand him as a fake, a manufactured morsel aimed directly at the gullet of the least hip consumer. The artist is judged by his fanbase, and most six-year-olds are distinctly lacking in street cred.

Bubblegum offends the myth of rock as an oppositional, "outsider" cultural force. To its detractors, bubblegum is read as an "inside" music—although in truth much bubblegum music came out on small independent labels—as opposed to the edgier sounds of the accepted underground. The major labels did a great job of selling their product as packaged rebellion, and the late '60s' fanzines concurred. It was only when they overplayed their hand ("The Man Can't Bust Our Music," the Boston Sound debacle, overpromoting Moby Grape) that the pseudo-hipsters rejected these hairy offerings.

Rock criticism, born of and beholden to the '60s, stumbles badly when confronted with music produced outside of its short set of registered myths. Session singers? Studio musicians? That's not rock 'n' roll! Except for Motown. And Stax. And the Beach Boys and portions of the Byrds' career. And, retroactively, disco. And *Dusty in Memphis*. And Richard Davis' sublime bass work on *Astral Weeks*.

We think it's time to retire this folkie stab at a false authenticity. We're not immune to the allure of the Romantic Artist, nor have we traded our Townes Van Zandt collections for BSB memorabilia. But this myth of the Self Contained Band (beginning with the Beatles) and its offspring—Anarchist Gangs (Clash, Mekons), Artist Collectives (Can, the Band at Big Pink), Populist Unions (Bruce & the E-Street Band, Fugazi)—breeds in the ripe compost of abandoned lefty utopias. It's no measure of the music.

> Those who believe [Max Martin's] songs will fast-fade into oblivion should forget Paula Abdul and the Bay City Rollers and ponder the gaudy durability of Abba. They should wonder whether in 1968 Kasenetz & Katz themselves were certain that the Ohio Express's "Yummy, Yummy, Yummy" would be remembered longer than anything ever recorded by Rhinoceros or the Electric Flag.
> —Robert Christgau, Pazz & Jop Poll, *The Village Voice*, February 2000

One thing about six-year-olds, though: they know what they like. Little kids like great hooks, interesting vocal styles, seamless arrangements. They like to dance. Nothing pretentious or self-important will do when the audience has a two-minute attention span and miniscule discretionary income. And so the bubblegum hits still sound great today, where much that was critically acclaimed in the same period lacks any real distinction.

Now you'd think we couldn't exploit one acrid jot of Joe Carducci's opus/rant *Rock and the Pop Narcotic*. And while we don't share Joe's zeal for Deuterium Heaviness nor his ripe disdain for pop's froth, we want to reiterate his simple question: "What does it have to do with the music?" Would an anthropologist from Mars care that Them's "I Can Only Give You Everything" was written by somebody other than Van Morrison—Phil Coulter, no less, who later co-wrote "Saturday Night" for the Bay City Rollers—and performed by session musicians? Could this Martian field scientist spot the "authentic" song among the Yardbirds' "Heart Full of Soul," Manfred Mann's "Do Wah Diddy Diddy" and the Animals' "We've Got To Get Out Of This Place"? Can you? It's a mug's game, of course, because while those bands recorded the songs, they were all written by professional songwriters. And, what does it have to do with the music? Is it inauthentic for Roger Daltrey to sing Pete Townshend's lyrics? For Eric Clapton to play guitar on "While My Guitar Gently Weeps"? It's not that these questions are insignificant—it's how you weigh that significance.

To borrow another critic's stance, consider Simon Reynolds' contention in *Generation Ecstasy* that rave culture thrives on functional music (i.e., House/Techno, et al.), which needs to be judged in its proper context (on the dance floor, on drugs) rather than insisting on Rockist song form, lyrical analysis and Adherence To Rock Orthodoxy. Bubblegum, like disco, like porn, serves a utilitarian function—in bubblegum's case the simple, yet infinitely difficult to create, ecstasy of pop release.

Another hurdle to bubblegum's critical acceptance is its blatant money-grubbing. The very notion that you can package and sell pop music bliss offends anyone invested in handcrafted cultural artifacts. But we're talking about nothing less than the pursuit of the perfect pop song. Manufactured? Sure. Just like *Casablanca*, Ford Mustangs, the Fender Stratocaster, or *Pee Wee's Playhouse*. There's genius to be had off the assembly line.

The '60s was the Pop Decade, with music and the visual arts developing highly refined shorthand styles, until the product became like a billboard signifying the essence of the thing. Painters Roy Lichtenstein and Andy Warhol drew on advertising imagery to give their canvases lowbrow pizzazz which was immediately familiar. The ad execs had already made sure the designs would appeal—the artists just appropriated a select set of subjects, celebrated them as if they were crucially important, and waited for their audacity to raise a stink.

Mass-production could be viewed as the enemy, or it could be archly embraced. Instead of representing the artist's deepest thoughts and feelings, Pop Art played it all cool—feelings are for drips. It's all about craft, high gloss, perfection, and the knowing wink. West Coast sculptors subscribed to the finish-fetish, adapting kar kulture techniques to make shiny smooth objects that gleamed like cherry cars or surfboards. The eye just wafts all the way over and never catches on the slightest flaw, which is how bubblegum acts on the ear. But this kind of perfection just *looks* easy—you have to paint a thousand coats over an exquisitely crafted form to achieve that kind of finish.

We want to make a distinction between Artistic Expression and artful expressions. Put aside your received notions of what music should mean and consider how it's made, then delight like the pop hook slut you are in pure sonic pleasure. Take off those blinders blocking out music that doesn't slot neatly with the Autonomous Band Myth, and reconsider what you know with bubblegum's rosy lenses in place. The Sex Pistols, Madonna, the Byrds, Abba, Disco, Studio One, Hip Hop all start to look different when you stop looking for the Rock and Roll in their music and consider the Bubblegum in their method.

Among other things, you ought to come away from this book with some open questions about the Sex Pistols and the Box Tops. In *The Great Rock and Roll Swindle*, Malcolm McLaren contends that the Pistols were a brilliant subversion of the manufactured pop group, right down to their hand-picked singer and their publicity-generating TV appearances. How do you reconcile that with "Holidays in the Sun" or "Bodies"? There's a measure of bullshit in Malcolm's assertion. But is that because the Pistols transcended or epitomized their manager's strategy? The Box Tops' story, however, practically defines bubblegum. Dan Penn aspired to make a Dixie-fried Monkees. He found a teenage group, fired their lead singer, and replaced him with Alex Chilton. Then he wound up backing Chilton with local session musicians, and sending the rest of the band out on the road. Even the Box Tops' name alludes to bubblegum's preferred medium—cereal boxes. Everything about the Box Tops is bubblegum except their music. It's pop, but it's much closer to the grittier blue-eyed soul of the Rascals than the Archies. On the one hand, you've got the band credited with destroying soul-less corporate rock using the bubblegum blueprint as their weapon of choice. On the other you've got all the ingredients of bubblegum cooked together and coming out like a BBQ pork sandwich. Calling bubblegum formulaic doesn't seem to explain anything at all.

❋ ❋ ❋ ❋ ❋ ❋ ❋

We set out to comprehensively chronicle the first great bubblegum era from the late '60s through the early '70s, and then stretch that concept right onto the set of *Total Request Live*. So we've written a history. But we also made a space in this book where the imagination could respond to bubblegum's provocations and contradictions. In our fantasy section we let down our ids. We allow the subtext to emerge and explore the dark side of pink. It is here that we watch the splendor of a divine hand smoothing David Cassidy's hair gently into place.

Bubblegum has insidiously worked its way into plenty of ostensibly hipper genres, and is at the core of many of the best songs in new wave, pop-punk and indie-pop. From the Ramones, Blondie and Talking Heads in '70s New York to Scotland's Rezillos, Bow Wow Wow, the Go-Go's, the Pooh Sticks,

Redd Kross, Jellyfish, Shonen Knife and the Groovie Goolies, the bubblegum roadmap has brought a lot of pleasure to people who never even realized they were listening to it.

> Oh, who was who did that "Yummy, Yummy"? The Ohio Express? Lemon Pipers, although they were sort of at the psychedelic end of bubble gum. "Mellow Yellow" meets a "Quick Joey Small" or "Mony Mony" meets almost anything by the early Troggs. You know, it transcends or descends below all expectations and thus it comes out in another dimension somewhere. It goes faster than the speed of light ale and bursts through into the banal zone. I have a huge debt to bubblegum music. I love it.
>
> —Andy Partridge, XTC

P.S.

We've made a Bubblegum 100 for you, inspired by *Punk* magazine's old Punk 99. There was surprising unanimity among our writers that the Archies deserved the top slot on the Bubblegum 100, but no such consensus about the balance of classic to contemporary groups, which bands were merely "pop" as opposed to bubblegum, and what would occupy the coveted 100th position. It's an ongoing debate.

We structured the list so that there were natural and symbolic levels: #1, Top Ten (where we tried to assemble an overriding bubblegum gestalt), Top 40. And we wanted something in the last spot that would reflect back on the whole notion of bubblegum. After furious discussion we settled on the Shaggs as a kind of Bizarro world, *Art Brut* bubblegum. Innocent and tuneless and young and wobbly, and dragged into the studio by their abusive dad, a homegrown Don Kirshner with a vision. J.R. Williams made it a very artful expression indeed.

23 David Cassidy's *Hair* (& PUKA SHELLS & UNFASTENED JEANS)

24 ♪ ChinniChap ♪

25 Josie and the PUSSYCATS in OUTER SPACE

26 Chu-Bops

27 Shonen Knife "PRETTY LITTLE BAKA GUY" VIDEO!

28 Micky Dolenz

29 MARC! MR. BOLAN'S KIDDIE SHOW

30 MILK COMMERCIAL

31 Joey Levine

32 BRITNEY'S rubber bust "SODA"

33 "Candy Girl" by NEW EDITION

34 SUPER-ELASTIC BUBBLE PLASTIC

35 take that (GARY, ROBBIE, MARK, HOWARD, JASON)

36 BUBBLEPSYCH

37 Lester Bangs

38 AM RADIO J•O•C•K•S

39 TONY BURROWS

40 DONNIE WAHLBERG'S STREET CRED (NKOTB!)

41 THE BUGALOOS

42 Cattanooga Cats (IWAO TAKAMOTO'S DESIGNS)

43 ABBA

44 Jet Screamer (eep op ork ah ah)

45 THE CANDY STORE PROPHETS (TOMMY BOYCE'S BAND)

46 SPECIAL GUEST BAT-VILLAINS ?

47 KEITH PARTRIDGE, MASTER SPY.... TV TIE-IN NOVEL by Vance Stanton

48 MICKEY MOUSE CLUB '90s (BRITNEY, JC, CHRISTINA, JUSTIN -&- KERI)

49 ROCK'EM SOCK'EM ROBOTS

50 REUBEN KINCAID

51 SHAMPOO VIVA LA MEGABABES!

52 WHERE THE ACTION IS! MARK LINDSAY IN A TRICORN

53 ROOTIN'-TOOTIN' RASPBERRY

54 "PUNK BOY" by Helen Love

55 SMASH HITS (PIN-UPS! NEIL TENNANT!)

56 "I Want Candy" BY BOW WOW WOW

57 ••• Lyrical ••• Double Takes

58 THE IMPOSSIBLES (ON "FRANKENSTEIN, JR.!"!)

59 BUBBLE SOUL (TONY MCAULAY, BELL RECORDS, FOUNDATIONS)

60 THE GO*GOS

61 45 CARRYING CASES

62 KIMBERLY, THE PINK... POWER RANGER

63 ("I'VE GOT A CRUSH ON YOU") THE JETS

64 Toni Wine "I'M GONNA MAKE YOUR LIFE SO SWEET!"

65 Close 'n' Play record players

66 SHAKE YOUR LOVE ~Debbie Gibson

67 Marcia, Marcia, Marcia

68 LAUGH, LAUGH! THE BEAU BRUMMELSTONES

69 RIFF Randall P.J. SOLES IN "ROCK & ROLL HIGH SCHOOL"

70 Urquel-o's

71 NICKELODEON (NICK AWARDS, ALL THAT)

72 OHIO EXPRESS "Down At Lulu's"

73 THE POWERPUFF GIRLS

74 GROOVIE GOOLIES ("CHICK-A-BOOM")

75 ROBBIE RIST (COUSIN OLIVER, KIDD VIDEO, POPTOPIAN)

76 The GO! Sound of the Slots BY The Revells

77 JEM & THE HOLOGRAMS ("TRULY OUTRAGEOUS")

78 THE SHORT CIRCUS on THE ELECTRIC COMPANY

79 Sea-Monkeys

80 "CRUEL BANANARAMA SUMMER"

81 THE REVILLOS (FAY FIFE'S HAIR! SWOON!)

82 noolaB wolleY (GARY ZEKLEY, DON GRADY)

83 Remember you're a womble.

84 "IT'S AN 'S', IT'S AN 'O', IT'S A CRAZY RAY-DEE-OH!" TOOT+A+LOOP

85 Leif Garrett's HAIRLESS CHEST POSTER

86 The MOSQUITOES on GILLIGAN'S ISLAND

87 THE BEATLES cartoon

88 France Gall "POUPEE DE SON" sings Serge Gainsbourg

89 Lovin' Spoonful ON HULABALOO

90 + REDD KROSS +

91 LITTLE TIBIA & the FIBULAS ("MAD MONSTER PARTY")

92 "Hey, Little Twelvetoes" SCHOOLHOUSE ROCKs YOUR MIND

93 PIANOSAURUS

94 The Sour Grapes bunch •••

95 Max Martin

96 ("I AM AN ANTICHRIST...") MelC covers the Sex PiSTOLS ("I AM A SPORTY SPICE...")

97 ("READY, STEVE?" "UH-HUH" "ANDY...?") the Sweet

98 KYLIE DOES CAVE JRWILLIAMS 2000

99 (HERE COME THE DOUBLE DECKERS, VID sound-tracks KID KID POWER, THE KIDS FROM C.A.P.E.R.)

100 THE SHAGGS

Illustration by J.R. Williams

OVERVIEW An Informal History of Bubblegum Music by Carl Cafarelli

> When Buddah Records was formed two years ago, most songs were about crime and war and depression. At the time we felt there was a place for a new kind of music that would make people feel happy. So we got together with two talented young producers named Jerry Kasenetz and Jeff Katz who had an idea for music that would make you smile. It was called "bubblegum music."

The above quote, taken from the liner notes to a circa-1969 sampler LP called *Buddah's 360 Degree Dial-A-Hit*, gives us both a succinct statement of intent for the critically reviled '60s pop music phenomenon called bubblegum and an equally-succinct recap of the genre's origin.

Although bubblegum has gained a certain cachet of cool in some circles over the past few decades (while remaining a pop pariah in other circles), during its original heyday it was viewed strictly as fodder for juvenile tastes, pure pabulum for pre-teen people. Furthermore, the music was blatantly commercial at a time when such materialistic goals were deemed unacceptable by an emerging counterculture. Bubblegum music held no delusions of grandeur, nor any intent to expand your mind or alter your perceptions. Bubblegum producers only wanted you to fork over the dough and go home to play your new acquisition over and over to your heart's content (and, no doubt, to your older brother's consternation).

Bubblegum is absolved of any perceived counter-revolutionary sentiments because it was so damn *catchy*. Once a "Yummy, Yummy, Yummy," "Sugar, Sugar," "Gimme Gimme Good Lovin'" or "Goody Goody Gumdrops" imbedded its sweet pink hooks into your mind, it was likely to remain stuck there like its sugary namesake would stick to the underside of a classroom desk.

More than 30 years after the opening salvos of the bubblegum revolution, the best bubblegum records still stand up as sterling examples of hitmaking craft, characterized by sing-a-long choruses, seemingly childlike themes and a contrived but beguiling innocence, occasionally combined with an undercurrent of sexual double entendre. And oh yeah—did we mention the hooks? There were hooks a-plenty.

As with many genres, from punk to funk to power pop, it's difficult to precisely define the parameters of bubblegum, to say with authority that *this* record is bubblegum and *that* record is something else again.

According to writer Bill Pitzonka, a bubblegum historian and author of the liner notes for Varèse Vintage's brilliant *Bubblegum Classics* series, "The whole thing that really makes a record bubblegum is just an inherently contrived innocence that somehow transcends that. It transcends the contrivance. Because there were a lot of records that were really contrived and sound it. And those to me are not true bubblegum. It has to sound like they mean it."

Writing in *Mojo* magazine, Dawn Eden put a finer point on her description of bubblegum music. "From the get-go, bubblegum was a purely commercial genre. Producers like [Kasenetz and Katz] had no higher aspiration than to make a quick buck and get out. Yet, with the help of talents like Joey Levine, they propagated a musical form that continues to influence acts the world over." Drawing a distinction between bubblegum and power pop, Eden went on to note, "Power pop aims for your heart and your feet. Bubblegum aims for any part of your body it can get, as long as you *buy* the damn record."

While we're going here with a working notion of bubblegum as defined by the uptempo confections perfected by Kasenetz & Katz's Super K Productions, our intent isn't really to disabuse you of your belief that, say, the Partridge Family was the *sine qua non* of bubblegumdom. Consider this as simply as a very informal history lesson. Chew away!

Pre-History: The Big Bubble Theory

Although the birth of bubblegum as a genre is generally dated from the success of the 1910 Fruitgum Company's "Simon Says" and the Ohio Express' "Yummy, Yummy, Yummy" in 1968, there are important antecedents to consider in tracing bubblegum's history. In fact, there are too many antecedents to adequately cover here. You could conceivably think of virtually every cute novelty hit, from pre-rock ditties like "How Much Is That Doggie In The Window" to transcendent rock-era staples like "Iko Iko," as a legitimate precursor to bubblegum's avowedly ephemeral themes.

Moving away from mere novelties, the field of garage punk served as a swaggering, cantankerous and (perhaps) incongruous breeding ground for some of bubblegum's sonic attack. No one in his right mind would call the 13th Floor Elevators or the Chocolate Watchband bubblegum groups, but there were undeniable links between the two genres. The most obvious such link would be the overriding simplicity prized equally by garage and bubblegum groups, both of whom recognized the excitement to be generated by three chords and an attitude.

Moreover, garage and bubblegum groups were generally singles acts. There were exceptions, but few garage or bubblegum acts were capable of creating full albums that sustained the compact punch of their essential 45s. And the singles, concerned as they were with quickly hitting the hook and hitting the road, were not as far apart stylistically as one might think. Chicago's prototypical punks the Shadows of Knight, famed for their hit take on Them's "Gloria," would eventually make a record for Super K. And bubblemeisters the Ohio Express scored their first two chart singles with punk-rooted tunes: the Rare Breed's awesome "Beg, Borrow and Steal" and the Standells' banned-in-a-neighborhood-near-you "Try It."[6]

Falling somewhere between garage and bubblegum was an Ocala, Florida group called the Royal Guardsmen. They managed a #2 hit in 1966 with "Snoopy Vs. The Red Baron," a novelty tune based on the funny-looking dog with the big black nose in the *Peanuts* comic strip. The single combined a campy kid's appeal with a punky bridge nicked without apology from "Louie, Louie."

Although "Snoopy Vs. The Red Baron" and its lower-charting sequels were certainly precursors to the recognized bubblegum sound, Bill Pitzonka insists the Royal Guardsmen were not a bona fide bubblegum group.

"The Royal Guardsmen kind of came out of that whole '20s-revivalist kind of thing," Pitzonka says. "That was their camp. But, you know, just because they were on Laurie and they did the 'Snoopy Vs. The Red Baron' song, which some people consider bubblegum . . . that's a fringe to me. That's pointing in the right direction, but it's not quite there yet.

"But the Royal Guardsmen definitely contributed," Pitzonka continues. "It was aimed at kids, and unfortunately they couldn't rise above their 'Snoopy' image.

By the same token, a Stamford, Connecticut group called the Fifth Estate scored a #11 hit in 1967 with "Ding, Dong! The Witch is Dead." The group took a song from *The Wizard of Oz* and redid it as a pop song, replete with a Renaissance music underpinning. Though considered a novelty tune, its musical accomplishment transcended novelty value. Unfortunately, it was the group's only hit.

And, of course, there was no shortage of acts in the mid-'60s actively cultivating some aspect of the adolescent market. Herman's Hermits had a string of cuddly hits, with "I'm Henry VIII, I Am" veering the closest to bubblegum, but they were never quite a bubblegum group. The Lovin' Spoonful had a goofy, goodtime vibe all about them, but they were far too . . . well, *authentic*-sounding to be called bubblegum.

---

6. The former is actually the very same Rare Breed record reissued under the Ohio Express name; the latter was co-written by Joey Levine, who would play a large role in the Ohio Express' rising fortunes. Levine would also co-write and produce the Shadows of Knight's Super K single, "Shake."

And Paul Revere & the Raiders had funny costumes and lots of TV exposure, but they simply rocked too hard for bubblegum—if they were bubblegum, then so were the Rolling Stones.

By 1967 the era of full-fledged bubblegum was nearly upon us, and the new label Buddah was looking to score some hits. Neil Bogart, a brilliant promotion hustler, was coaxed from Cameo Parkway to helm Buddah, and Bogart had definite ideas about the kind of label's hits to be made. The Buddah label was recently revived as an archival imprint with the alternate spelling of 'Buddha' to differentiate it from Bogart's firm.

The ushering in of this new era was initially accomplished with "Green Tambourine" by the Lemon Pipers, which entered the *Billboard* Hot 100 at the end of '67 and hit #1 in February 1968. Bubblegum was now this close to exploding. "Green Tambourine" was a perfect, giddy bubblegum single, and two follow-up hits, "Rice Is Nice" and "Jelly Jungle (Of Orange Marmalade)" were cut from the same chewy cloth, but the Lemon Pipers themselves had little interest in becoming bubblegum's favorite sons.

"The Lemon Pipers I never considered really bubblegum," Pitzonka says. "They were acid. Their singles *are* bubblegum; they do have real strong roots there. I just never thought that it carried over as intensely as it did with the groups that didn't exist. Because they hated that stuff."

To be sure, the Lemon Pipers only recorded "Green Tambourine" because they knew they'd be dropped by Buddah if they didn't record this tune, which Bogart saw as a surefire hit. Thus, the Lemon Pipers scored the first bubblegum #1, but it was clear that their hearts were not in it.

So, with "Green Tambourine," Buddah had the right song at the right time to snap the bubble heard 'round the world. Now, bubblegum just needed the right people. Two producers from Long Island, Jerry Kasenetz and Jeff Katz, would be the guys.

As Buddah's 1910 Fruitgum Company and the Ohio Express started enjoying hits, Bogart knew he needed a name under which to market this new, sweet 'n' bouncy stuff. Kasenetz and Katz quickly obliged.

"Well, we were the ones," Kasenetz and Katz recall, "when we were talking about different things, we would gear 'em toward a certain audience, and we figured it was the teenagers, the young kids. And at the time we used to be chewing bubblegum and that, and my partner and I used to look at it and laugh and say, 'Ah, this is like bubblegum music.'"

Bogart loved the term and seized upon it immediately.

That's when bubblegum actually crystallized into an actual camp," Bill Pitzonka says. "There was a lot of stuff leading up to it, coming out of garage and novelty records, basically. And I think Kasenetz and Katz really crystallized it when they came up with the term themselves, and they came up with that nice little analogy. And Neil Bogart, of course, being the marketing person he was, just crammed it down the throats of people. And I think that's really the point at which bubblegum took off."

"We were looking to sort of do something that nobody else was doing on a steady basis," say Kasenetz and Katz. "Bubblegum music, in the real sense of kiddie records, was around for quite a while, like various artists doing various songs. But there were very few that were doing it with some sort of continuity where it was the same type of style. We were gearing with all our writers for a specific kids' appeal. We want hits, obviously; but we want *these types* of things, and we want our artists to be known for them. And that's what we were knocking out."

"It was just basically young music," adds Levine.

I think the inherent quality of a bubblegum band is a non-existence factor," Pitzonka explains with a laugh. "A contrivance. The Lovin' Spoonful was a band, they united. The Music Explosion was put together, the Ohio Express was put together, you know, there's that prefabrication quality which I think definitely even extends to bands today like the Spice Girls and Take That, which are built around the idea of selling records. And that's the whole idea behind bubblegum. It wasn't to create art—Kasenetz and Katz don't even remember half the records they worked on. They were just trying to get stuff out.

"Kasenetz and Katz kind of did the mud-against-the-wall thing," Pitzonka continues. "They just hired people and had them do stuff. They were more like contractors than producers. There's very much a sub-contractor quality about bubblegum."

With their stable of writers and growing roster of fictional recording groups ("We made up all the names for the various groups," say Kasenetz and Katz, "and we own all the names, even to this day"), Super K soon developed its own hit factory, like a chewy junior Motown.

"Well, Motown was kinda that way," Levine says. "Guys would write their songs, they'd go in and cut their tracks and they'd figure out which artists were gonna do 'em. It was a factory of music.

"It was like, you're hot and there were around three or four or five groups of writers and they would all get their studio time and it was booked in a certain way. You'd do your writing in one or two days, you'd do your tracking on this day, you'd do your overdubbing another day, you'd do your vocals another day. You had your studio time and your writing time. In other words, those were your days, that was your deadline: Wednesday we go in and do tracks. And I'm sure a lot of companies work like that today, companies that become big production companies."

"And we just used to write every week. We had it so all the writers were very competitive. We said, 'This is what we want, whoever comes up with the tune gets the next Ohio Express record, or the next Fruitgum record, depending on what we were doing. And we were just knocking them out. The funny thing is, if you look at all the hits, when the 1910 Fruitgum Company had a million seller, the Ohio Express had a half a million seller. And then the Ohio Express would have a million seller and the Fruitgum Company would have a half-million seller. It was really weird, but we knew we needed a smash for the group after they didn't get that million seller, so it switched every other record.

"I mean, we were looking to have hits and we were looking for upbeat, fun danceable songs. They weren't really dance records in the sense that you have dance now, but you could certainly dance to 'em, they were all happy-go-lucky type of things. Some of the lyrics, it was like a double-entendre type of thing. And if you really got into it—I mean, people overlooked some of the lyrics, thinking that, 'Oh, it's just happy-go-lucky'—and some of them were nitty-gritty.

"We used to laugh about that. 'Yummy, Yummy, Yummy' was actually a knock-off of 'Feels So Fine.' Everything was sort of knock-offs of other things, just turned around with different lyrics. I mean, 'Yummy, Yummy, Yummy,' everybody said, 'Oh, what a great bubblegum record, innocent.' But if you listen to the lyrics, it wasn't so innocent."

"I don't know," Levine says. "It was a young music, it wasn't deep and heavy, though a lot of things probably people would say there was a lot of stuff hidden within it."

So, were the double entendres intentional?

"Of course, yeah," he replies.

And the Super K machine rolled on, concocting groups and pumping out chewy chunks o' pop bliss.

Kasenetz and Katz recall that there were specific elements they wanted in the groups they created.

"We were always looking more for, more than an actual group, if we found a singer that we felt had a unique voice, we would build a group around the individual. We were stern believers that we needed that vocal, that something that stands out."

While Kasenetz and Katz undeniably got the gumball rolling, they were not to go without significant competition. And the biggest competition came from an act that, like much of the Super K roster, didn't exist. But this particular fictional band had the added advantage of weekly television exposure, and five members who were individually identifiable to fans, while still guaranteed to remain obedient puppets in their producer's hands. You know 'em as Archie, Betty, Veronica, Reggie and Jughead—Riverdale's newest hitmakers.

Tommy Roe also bubblegummed his way back into the hearts of radio listeners with "Dizzy," a superbly sweet trifle that topped the charts for four weeks in 1969. Roe's first hit had been the amazing Buddy Holly soundalike "Sheila," a #1 hit in 1962. Roe also hit with "Everybody" (#3) in '63, and two 1966 singles, "Sweet Pea" (#8) and "Hooray For Hazel" (#6) that were definite bubblegum prototypes. But "Dizzy," co-written by Roe and the Raiders' Freddy Weller was his first hit in a couple of years, and it was certainly one of bubblegum's defining singles. Two more bubblegummy singles, "Heather Honey" and "Jam Up And Jelly Tight" were also hits at #29 and #8, respectively.

Cartoon Rock

The success of the Archies led to an odd tangent in the bubblegum story: Saturday morning cartoon characters singing pop-rock songs and, frequently, making pop-rock records. Kirshner himself was involved with many of them.

"He did a couple of other bands like the Chan Clan," Bill Pitzonka says, "which was also Ron Dante—it was Ron Dante *and* Barry Manilow, go figure that—and then there were all the other Saturday morning TV shows like *Josie and the Pussycats*."

Even the animated version of the Harlem Globetrotters played on this field, courtesy of Kirshner.

"Kirshner did that with Sedaka and Greenfield," Pitzonka says. "A lot of this is languishing in Don Kirshner's vault because he's for some reason going into delusions of grandeur that it's going to be worth a lot some day.

"There were a couple bands before the Archies. There was a band called the Beagles. They put out an album on Columbia and I knew nothing about them until I got this one CD which had their stuff on it."

"That was a show that was produced by Total Television," says writer and animation historian Mark Evanier, whose television credits range from *Welcome Back, Kotter* to *Garfield* and roughly a zillion other series, specials, one-shots and pilots. "The Beagles were—there were two of them, it was a team. That was one of the few shows like that done out of New York. I think that was a case where somebody bought the show based on the name.

"There were a number of shows about music groups, and you could go back even further than that, I think. Did *The Beatles* cartoon show precede that? Certainly the success of the Beatles in other media spawned a lot of interest."

Still, animated pop groups proliferated to an unprecedented degree in the wake of the Archies.

"Yeah, a lot of that was a Fred Silverman belief," Evanier says. "Fred liked those. Fred was programming CBS quite successfully in the late '60s and his influence certainly bled over to the other networks. I'm not even sure chronologically what was the first show that did it, but the success of *The Archies* certainly didn't hurt any.

"The other trend that had a lot of parallels here was there was a trend toward pre-established properties. Which was a case of using characters that already existed. The idea was that, because of the way the cartoons were sold to the advertisers, frequently sold before the show even was finished, there became a very strong interest in programming cartoon shows that existed in other media. In other words, something that was based on a TV show, based on a movie. There was a dislike of shows that were 'only' cartoon shows. And one of the ways in which they took a property that otherwise was not known—like, say, *Jabberjaw*—and gave it some sort of a feel of familiarity was to try to spin a record group out of it, or to try to spin something akin to the Archies out of it.

"There were attempts several times to replicate the success of the Archies," Evanier continues, "because the Archies had a hit record. It also became a simple case of believing that that was an element that was popular in the shows, particularly with female viewers. One of the problems that Saturday morning animation has frequently had is attracting female viewers. It's very tricky to find a show that girls will watch that doesn't alienate boys. And the music segments seemed to be something that had some value there.

"There were a lot of reasons. But also, at that time the shows were a little more formularized than they later became, or than maybe was desirable. And the idea of just putting a music segment in, making that part of the format, it was pretty easy to crank them out assembly-linewise. The writers would write up to the chase scene, and then the idea would be that there'd be a minute-and-a-half song that would take over the action. You'd notice they would reuse animation an awful lot in those, and I think that was also a powerful incentive. Basically it was simply a case of a belief that kids liked (the music segments); just as *Scooby-Doo* spawned a whole raft of shows where four kids went out and solved mysteries, *The Archies* spawned a whole raft of shows where, although the characters were not necessarily a rock group, they would at some point pull out their keyboards and drums and play something."

A relative lack of chart success doesn't necessarily mean there wasn't some tasty bubblegum music being created for the Saturday morning crowd.

"Two of the best bubblegum albums ever are the albums by the Sugar Bears and Lancelot Link and the Evolution Revolution," Bill Pitzonka says. "And both of those were for prefab artists. That's the point at which they realized again that the faceless aspect was taking its toll, so they hitched onto TV shows or, in the Sugar Bears' case, a breakfast cereal."

"It's also worth noting that reruns of the Monkees' TV show, which had completed its prime-time run on NBC in 1968, began airing as part of CBS' Saturday morning lineup in September of 1969.

One Saturday morning act that may have deserved a better fate was Josie and the Pussycats. The group is something of a pop culture footnote for introducing the world to one Cherie Moor, later to find fame as actress/singer Cheryl Ladd. Though based on an Archie Comics title, the music for *Josie And The Pussycats* was produced, not by Don Kirshner, but under the direction of song-writer Danny Janssen, best known for co-writing *Little Woman* for Bobby Sherman. And the sound Janssen chose for Josie and the Pussycats was cast, not in the image of the Archies, but in the soulful pop style of the Jackson Five.

"That was fully the intention of Danny Janssen," Bill Pitzonka says. "They held auditions for the girls for Josie and the Pussycats and he had selected the three girls. Cheryl Ladd—who wasn't Cheryl Ladd then—Cathy Dougher and Patrice Holloway. And when he presented them to Hanna-Barbera they said, 'Well, we really like Patrice Holloway, but we've never had a black cartoon character before.' And he said, 'Well, tough, '" Pitzonka notes with a laugh. "'I won't do the project unless she does it because she's got the greatest voice for it.'

"So they sat on it for a while and he didn't hear back, and then they said, 'Come down to the studio, we're doing Josie and the Pussycats.' And (Janssen said), 'You didn't fire her, did you? Because I wasn't gonna do it.' And they said 'No, just come down to the studio.' They hired every major soul musician in L.A. to work on those sessions. Because they said, 'We're gonna do this right, we *are* gonna do this right.' And that's why there is a black character in Josie and the Pussycats, and why the music has such a soul slant.

Unfortunately, neither of Josie and the Pussycats' two Capitol singles, "Every Beat Of My Heart" and "You've Come A Long Way, Baby," made so much as a light indentation on the Hot 100. (A competing version of "Every Beat of My Heart," by 11-year-old singer Shawn, also failed to chart.) With the notable exception of Ladd, Josie and the Pussycats soon faded into obscurity.

"One of the things that a lot of different companies have tried to do over the years," Evanier says, "is they like the idea of owning a group. You know, one of the things that made the Archies the envy of a lot of other people in the music business was that the Archies were anonymous, the Archies were owned. The Archies couldn't hold out for more money. I mean, I think they were always shocked that the Monkees, when they were done, turned into kind of independent guys. You couldn't just yank Mike out and put in somebody else. You had to go with those four guys.

"And I think that were was a couple of attempts in Saturday morning, through animation and through live action, to create groups like Kaptain Kool and the Kongs. It was owned by Sid and Marty Krofft. They could pluck people out, put people in. They could own all the publishing, they could own the likenesses, they could own the costumes, they could merchandise the characters in a way that you couldn't do if you had a comparable group that was using their real names and faces and such.

"And I think that's one of the appeals of some of these attempts, was, 'Well, we'll make our money on the records, we'll make money on the merchandising, we'll send the group out to tour.' I think at one point there was this dream that they could have four or five troops of Banana Splits going around the country touring, if the Banana Splits had been bigger. All you need is a set of costumes. Anybody in the world can be in the costumes, and anyone in the world can record the records. Like you have this generically created music. In the same sense that right now a lot of live action movie studios kind of envy Disney, because Disney doesn't have to cope with stars who want 25 million dollars. They can tear their stars up if they ever get out of line.

With no substantial hits to follow up the Archies' success, and with the Archies themselves already fading, the cartoon rock trend ran itself out.

"I think it was like a fad that (ended)," Evanier says. "This business tends to always run in cycles of imitation. There was a period when everything was *Scooby-Doo* imitations. Somebody called them a 'Four kids and a nyaa-nyaa' show, or 'Three kids and a nyaa-nyaa.' Three kids and a dog, four kids and a horse, three kids and a car, you know, whatever it is, go solves mysteries. And you go through cycles on that until something else comes along. And I suspect that there was no specific catalyst here—*The Archies* was a hit, a bunch of other shows like that were tried, they weren't hits, something else was a hit, people tried other things."

(Wait for It) The Bubble Bursts

"I think bubblegum itself," Pitzonka says, "the ending point can be pretty clearly cut off around 1971, '72. I like to cut it off right at the point where Dawn became a real act. Where all of a sudden this band that was just supposed to be this singles factory became a real band and had a real identity. [7]

"The whole thing about bubblegum is it's kind of faceless. And that is a good thing and a bad thing, because I don't know a lot of people who go around knowing the names of the members of the Ohio Express," Pitzonka notes, laughing. "That wasn't the point."

---

7. Editor's note: though ironically, Dawn hit with "Candida," a song co-written by Archies songbird Toni Wine.

Although one can say accurately that bubblegum never really went away, its golden era had clearly passed by the early '70s.

"I think bubblegum had no place to go around '72, "Pitzonka says. "I mean, you could only work so much mileage out of a band that didn't exist. Unless you're the Alan Parsons Project, which is a completely different animal. You can't make a career out of singles; hard as you try, you just can't. Even back then, you could have ten hit singles, but then it just dries up—there's nowhere to go.

"I think the genre pretty much dictated its own course. Kasenetz and Katz stopped hitting the charts as of the '70s. Bell (which inherited the Monkees' label, Colgems) took over—Bell was big. And that was the stuff like Tony Macauley, who also did 'Love Grows (Where My Rosemary Goes).' That's when you also had Dawn and you had the Partridge Family. Davy Jones recorded for Bell.

"I've got the Bell singles listing. And it's funny, because until the Partridge Family, Bell had never had a gold album. All of a sudden, once they had a gold album, they had money. And you notice their singles release schedule goes from 20 singles a year to 40 singles a year to 70 singles a year to 90 singles a year to then, their last year of operation they had something like 125 singles. Now, in the process of doing 125 singles—and a lot of these were studio things, they'd hire producers to concoct bands for them. They didn't have any albums. They put out ten albums a year to 100 singles. That's kind of an example of how bubblegum was progressing and couldn't really pay for itself."

Cleaning Up This Gooey Mess

Although bubblegum's original heyday had passed, its influence continued to be felt, often in some unexpected guises.

"I think Europe kept the idea going more than America did," Pitzonka says. "Which is kind of ironic when you consider that bubblegum in America was a response to the British Invasion. But yeah, I'd say the early ABBA records are definitely bubblegum. And of course, a friend of mine pointed out to me that a lot of the Eurovision records were very, very, very contrived, and they were meant to appeal to the broadest common denominator. But in the process, they also got very onomatopoeic in the early '70s. You had stuff like 'Boom Bang-a Bang' and 'Jack In The Box' and all these songs that sounded like 'Abergevenny' (a #47 hit in 1969 for Shannon, aka singer Marty Wilde[8]), only more schmaltzy.

"It then became more of a teen idol phenomenon, which was a different thing entirely. Because they realized that they did need faces, they couldn't have faceless bands. What do you attach to? Oh, attach to a cute guy who you can market to a magazine. So I think bubblegum kind of evolved, and it evolved separately. In Europe it evolved into glam; in America, it evolved into the teen idols. Bell Records, while they had the Partridge Family and the Bay City Rollers, they also had Gary Glitter. Sweet, of course, started out as a bubblegum band—there's no question that 'Funny Funny' is a bubblegum record. And then, of course, that came back and you've got the Ramones, based on that melodic garage angle."

The dialectic of bubblegum is indeed far-reaching. Aside from the obvious, inherent bubblegum appeal of various teen-idol records in the early '70s, from the Osmonds to the Jackson Five to the Kids From The Brady Bunch, British glam/glitter owed a very real debt to bubblegum. Glam records were catchy, clunky, artificial creations, designed to grab you with mindless, repetitive and frequently irresistible hooks. It's not a huge jump from the Ohio Express to the Sweet, Gary Glitter, Mud, Hello, or even Slade and Suzi Quatro. Heck, the Bay City Rollers had a foot in both camps, as a teen idol band with vague glam roots.

Another genre with connections to bubblegum was disco.

8. And dad of '80s gum-pop star Kim.

"Disco was actually another bubblegum outgrowth," Pitzonka agrees, "because that's where all the producers went. Neil Bogart (who'd left Buddah to form Casablanca Records, probably the preeminent disco label) was a marketing genius. In fact, (superstar Eurodisco producer) Giorgio Moroder used to put out these bubblegum singles out of Germany, with titles like 'Looky Looky' and 'Moody Trudy' and stuff like that, and they're these infectious little pop tunes that all sound like 'Papa Oom Mow Mow.' Which actually leads us back to bubblegum. Because, you know, 'Papa Oom Mow Mow,' 'Wooly Bully,' these onomatopoeic things, had a real base appeal. And that's what bubblegum tapped into."

There's a simple progression from the Archies or the Banana Splits to a prepackaged disco act like the Village People, who recorded for Bogart's Casablanca. Another Casablanca act with bubblegum roots was Kiss, whose outlandish costumes and merchandising efficacy—not to mention their punchy, spunky singles, which drew inspiration from pop-rock as often as they did from hard rock—made them the kind of act Kasenetz and Katz would have killed for.

And then there's punk. Though the anger 'n' anarchy clatter of early punk was what got all the attention, punk also placed a premium value on concise ditties with immediate, visceral appeal.

"The punk movement was about breaking down barriers," notes Pitzonka, "and basically breaking through that whole art-rock thing that was going on. But also, once they got over the rage, once they actually learned how to play, no movement can go along without melody for long."

Punk acts like the Undertones, Generation X, the Rezillos and—especially!—the Ramones all drew readily apparent inspiration from bubblegum. The Ramones actually covered both "Indian Giver" and "Little Bit O' Soul" on record, and even the Talking Heads used to cover "1, 2, 3 Red Light" live. At one point, *Bomp!* magazine openly wondered when the Ramones would get around to covering an Ohio Express tune; one regrets that they never did.

Sticky Residue: Bubblegum's Legacy

While bubblegum music still has its vocal detractors, its appeal has transcended such criticism.

"It depends on what circle you're in," Dante says, "If you're in the Aerosmith circle or the R.E.M. circle, it might be looked down on. The trick is, bubblegum is inherently young, and younger than the rock 'n' roll that surrounds it, probably. Who are the bubblegum chewers that they were talking about? It's usually the pre-teens or the very early teens, 13–14.

"So I think it had its place in terms of very clean, fun music, bubblegum music. And I think it can be used as a derogatory term. But to me it's not a derogatory term. Mostly it's just another niche of music, like country is, or R & B or any of the others. And it's got its own little niche and its particular sound. To me, there are bubblegum records made today. If you listen to that (sings a bit of Donna Lewis' 'I Love You Always Forever') 'I love you, always forever, la, la, la,' that is bubblegum. Or, (sings a bit of the Cardigans 'Love Me') 'Love love me say that you love me'— I mean, that is as bubblegum as you get. These girl groups and girl singers are doing bubblegum today.

"Bubblegum exists today in those kind of records, and it's very welcome, 'cause it's fresh and it's honest and it's very simple, straightforward kind of stuff that is appealing and very memorable. The minute you hear it you wanna hear it again, and you remember it. So there are things out today that equate to bubblegum. And bubblegum in its time was very popular."

"There's always songs that come out that are bubblegum songs," adds Joey Levine. "I mean, the Cars were certainly a big bubblegum group. But there's always been songs that are hit songs and they wrapped up a little bubblegum. People call the Spice Girls the bubblegum of today. Is it a bad connotation? I don't know. It's a *commercial* connotation. And then it just becomes up to you to make the decision whether being commercial is bad or good."

"I tell ya, we had a heck of a good time," say Kasenetz and Katz. "We took the Kasenetz-Katz Singing Orchestral Circus, we went out to some junkyard in New Jersey. We did a video there and shots for album covers, and to move everybody we had buses rented. It was an exciting time in general for things that were going on. I would say three years straight we were never off the charts. And we ranked in one of those years, I don't even remember what it was, second to Motown in the number of chart records—and here we were, we weren't even really a record company, we were a production company.

"So we were very excited and happy. The only thing we felt that was missing is we felt that no one really, and even to this day, they don't look at is as quality. And I think we don't get our just due for what we did and for the amount of hits, because we had a lot of hits. I would say we're close to 42 or 43 gold records. But, you know, that's show biz," they say, laughing.

"It was really an era in time that has great memories to us," Kasenetz and Katz continue. "And I speak to people now even, they have a lot of the stuff out on compilations, and they sell. I don't know if they sell because of the compilation or because of the people that want certain things or whatnot. But it was a very exciting time. It was a style of music that was very popular for several years."

"It was fun doing," Dante says. "And I'm still making music, I still do some commercials. I've been working for a different company lately. The last thing I did was the Publishers Clearing House theme. I did (sings) 'Publishers Clearing House, the House where dreams come true.' That was the last commercial I sung on. I'm still cooking. I'm producing a couple of new artists, and I keep my hand in. But definitely that was a wonderful time. Some famous poet once said, 'It was the perfect time—the time we keep trying to repeat, imitate or sell,'" he concludes with a laugh.

"There really is something to be said about these songs that went in there, hit the hook and left," Pitzonka says. "There's something very vital about that, and bubblegum was all about that. Bubblegum was for disenfranchised 12-year-olds who couldn't listen to the Beatles anymore, because they didn't get the drug references.

"My personal slant on the whole thing or how I came to it actually is that I had a sister 14 years older than me and I used to collect records when I was a kid. Then in 1978 there was this album on TV called *Super Bubble*, which I ordered. It was like the first album I ever ordered, mail order, and I just fell it love with it.

"And around that time I was getting really upset with how music was. There wasn't really a lot in the late '70s/early '80s, because that was when arena-rock was coming into the fore, and I just couldn't get worked up about Journey. It just reminded me of the guys who hung out in the back of the school at the auto shop wearing the t-shirts. Those bands to me were all about the t-shirts. And the logo bands—I just couldn't get into it. So at that point I got into the Beatles. And then from the Beatles, instead of most people going from the Beatles to the Stones to Zep, the Doors, I went from the Beatles to the Monkees to the Archies to the Cowsills.

"Bubblegum really did lay a deeper foundation than anybody's willing to give it credit for," Pitzonka continues. "Yes, it is responsible for Take That and New Kids On The Block, but it's also responsible for the Ramones. A lot of the melodic metal comes out of that too. Bubblegum was based in melody; it was all about the song. It was all about getting the message across in two and a half minutes. A lot of people forget that; they kinda just look at it and say, 'Oh, these bands never existed.' Yet everybody remembers 'Yummy, Yummy, Yummy,' everybody remembers 'Simon Says.' And it was the perfect antidote to everything that was going on. In the late '60s, everybody was trying to make messages and make albums, and here are these people just happy to sing about bubblegum subject matter, which is kid's games, double entendre and stuff like that."

There is indeed a lot to be said for a record that hits the hook and hits the road. Bubblegum's appeal is that it's short, sharp and to the point, and once it's stuck in your brain it's impossible to scrape off. In times of too much trouble (and not enough treble), there is a tremendous, cathartic rush to be had simply from joining in a rousing chorus of bubblegum's central mantra: "Pour a little sugar on me."

Bubblegum Music Is The Naked Truth by Kim Cooper

If you do not wish to have your illusions about bubblegum destroyed, you should read no further than this paragraph. The chapter that follows is an exploration of the dark side of a genre which, to all appearances, dwelt entirely in the light. If you still cling to the notion of a happy world composed of sugarcone hills and chocolate milk streams, where cotton candy robins yank gummy worms from shredded-coconut lawns (and then kiss them kindly and return them to the soil), and the wind blows a lovely scent of peppermint and spice, well, I don't want to be the one to take that away from you. Don't worry, your happy candy world is still there, and there are no shadows on the lawns. Now turn the page, quick, before you're ensnared by my evil heresies.

Bubblegum music was much maligned in its brief heyday (1968–69), and is pretty much ignored or despised today. A Los Angeles oldies station was recently launched with the slogan "No bubblegum, and no weird stuff." (To which I responded, "In that case, I'm tuning out!") Such derision is a pity, for the oddball recordings of the 1910 Fruitgum Co., Archies, Ohio Express, Lemon Pipers, Banana Splits, et al. are quite fascinating, in addition to being catchier than a huge yawn. Emerging out of a producer-driven system that makes Phil Spector look laid-back, bubblegum was made and marketed for a powerful new demographic: the pre-adolescent with cash to burn. Someone should tell Arrow-93 that these kids are all growed up and listening to oldies radio today.

In the late '60s the American economy was in great shape, and for the first time a whole generation existed that knew nothing of deprivation. Their parents remembered WWII and perhaps the Depression, and wished to spare their own progeny such pangs. And in direct response to this economic force emerged a startling variety of kiddie-driven commodities: comic books and skateboards, goofy plastic paraphernalia, half-length lovebeads, Sea Monkeys, and a whole new kind of rock 'n' roll.[9]

Bubblegum, however, was meant from the start to appeal to the eight-year-old of the house. It was the rare bubblegum album that had an accurate track-listing on the jacket—since much of the target audience could barely read, there was little point. Lyrics were calculated to evoke schoolyard rhyme schemes, and the groups themselves were marketed as wacky gangs of cuddly juveniles, or even as anthropomorphic animals and cartoon characters—entirely devoid of the sexual threat embodied by adult artists. Band members were often nameless and even interchangeable, as on the two Kasenetz-Katz Super/Singing Orchestral Circus records, which claim to feature all the hit-making Buddah bands playing simultaneously, but which internal evidence suggests was a session project. The photos inside the jacket of the so called "Original Cast Recording" of the Kasenetz-Katz Singing Orchestral Circus (Buddah BDS-5020) are a revelation into the type of "band" favored by the masterminds of New York bubblegum.

The 1989 Musical Marching Zoo was composed of young men wearing expensive animal costumes, and cradling their masks in their arms; it is unclear how they were supposed to have played their instruments in such attire, or how "The Lion" and "The Bunny" kept their blonde locks looking so neat beneath the stifling character heads.

Lt. Garcia's Magic Music Box dressed in fetching mariachi drag, attractively accented by the Anglo members' Beatle boots.

---

9. Not that kids had any beef with the music their older siblings dug. Most folks who grew up at this time can tell you about the singles they snagged after Sis or Bro went off to college: Top 40 and regional hits, a couple years old, which were much beloved by the second owner.

The alleged performers from the gatefold of the Kasenetz-Katz Singing Orchestral Circus album.

The 1910 Fruitgum Co. presented a distinctly disunited front, with members clad individually in the garb of 1940s businessman, British bobby, Old West huckster, Napoleonic foot-soldier, and minor pre-Revolutionary Russian noble.

The St. Louis Invisible Marching Band, on the other hand, was invisible. 'Nuff said.

It was the 1910 Fruitgum Co. that transformed the game "Simon Says" into an upbeat number that gleefully reveled in the dominance and submission of childhood play. This was the same group that turned "Pop Goes the Weasel," "1, 2, 3 Red Light," and "May I Take a Giant Step" into original pop songs (the latter two also heavy on the implied s/m). Other groups played up the infantile lyrics without delving quite so literally into the music of the classroom. "Yummy, Yummy, Yummy" is a typical Ohio Express song: catchy, simplistic, with a first grade vocabulary and a killer punk presentation. Like several bubblegum acts, the OE started life as a cool mid-'60s garage band, and were always able to conjure up a little punky phlegm to wash the sugary-sweetness down.

There is an astonishing amount of food imagery to be found in the lyrics but, like its namesake substance, bubblegum music was meant to be ingested for pleasure and not for nourishment. The Archies sang of a "honey," an "ah-sugar sugar," a paragon of empty caloric grace. The Lemon Pipers suggested you join them in a "jelly jungle of orange marmala-a-a-ade." And the 1910 Fruitgum Co. even had a signature candy edifice, the "1910 Cotton Candy Castle," where a young listener was invited to come and eat his or her fill. It is inconceivable that a b-gum band might have ever sung about something healthful like green onions or mashed potatoes. (But as seductive as a land of candy may seem, one would do well to recall that the candy house in the Grimm Brothers' "Hansel and Gretel" concealed a cannibalistic witch [read: a mother who wished to re-absorb her child into her body], and that all the kids but Charlie who visited Wonka's place came to very bad ends. Also, if you eat all that stuff you'll get spotty and fat and no one will want to have sex with you once you reach puberty.)

Food is, of course, incredibly important to children. Often it is only at the dinner table that children are able to exert power over their parents. By pointedly not eating, or by gorging, a child can focus the attention of the family directly upon himself. At its most extreme, such behavior can produce life-threatening conditions of anorexia and bulimia, but there are many subtle gradations which (while far less dangerous) also achieve the desired ends.

In many households, certain foods are forbidden, and thus take on a fascinating gloss to the children that are denied them. Sugar-free families were an unfortunate, growing phenomenon in the late '60s, and the brown-rice kids must have gaped at the glorious food fantasies to be found in bubblegum lyrics. In nearly every neighborhood at this time, there was a child whose house everyone longed to visit, because their parents stocked an vast variety of junk foods, and had no qualms about letting guests gorge on them. If there was no such child in your neighborhood, or you were a complete social outcast, then at least there was bubblegum. In the privacy of your room, it was possible to glue a transistor radiator to your ear and drink in the promise of a new world, full of rare spices, fantastic flavors, and weird characters that beckoned you to join their feasting ranks.

A possible source for the excess of food imagery in these songs can be found in the names of the writers and producers who created them: *Artie Resnick, Joey Levine, Jerry Kasenetz, Jeff Katz, Bobby Bloom, Don Kirshner*—a bunch of Jewish guys! Who better to understand the seductive power of the edible, the powerful bond between noshing and being loved? "Eat, boychick, eat!"

But in truth, these junk food lyrics concealed a menace far more dangerous than hyperactivity, obesity or the eventual threat of diabetes. There was a big fat uncircumcised snake in the garden of bubblegum, and his name was S-E-X. Blame it on the writers, guys in their teens and early twenties hired to write innocent faux-rock lyrics designed to appeal to little tykes. The same impulse that led an anonymous Disney animator to draw a towering phallic castle on the video box for *The Little Mermaid* seems to have

blossomed in the minds of the b-gum staff writers. The producers must have figured no one would notice (this was long before the current rage for parental supervision of pre-adolescent enter-tainment vehicles), and it doubtless amused the bands.

And so you have a cuddly group like the Lemon Pipers following up "Green Tambourine" with a very lewd Top 40 hit "Jelly Jungle," to wit: "Take a trip on my pogo stick/Bounce up and down, do a trick/I'll play a beat on your pumpkin drum/ And we'll have fun in the sun." A suggestive title like "Hard Core" from the same LP turns out to be ghastly white-'fro blues; the Pipers concealed their smut discreetly within cutie-pie metaphor. This was a Kama-Sutra Production (on Buddah Records), names not chosen lightly. I'm sure I'm just one of many children of the era who remembers finding mock-Eastern sex manuals which had been poorly hidden by doped-up adults: to me, the Kama-Sutra name and the many-armed Buddah logo evoke rather sinister forms of acrobatic sex. And indeed, much of the smuttiest bubblegum could be found on Buddah.

"Yummy, Yummy, Yummy" (#4, *Billboard*, June 1968) by the Ohio Express is a prime example, a huge hit that to all appearances is about oral sex. (Ditto "96 Tears," but that's another story and genre.) That panting sounds were used as a percussive device seems unsurprising when one looks closely at lines like "The lovin' that you're givin' is what keeps me livin'/And the love is like peaches and cream" and, of course, "Yummy, yummy, yummy, I've got love in my tummy." *Oh yeah, and how did it get there?!* [10]

And in fine Freudian tradition, Buddah made the most of the fast train metaphor of the Ohio Express name. Album jackets pictured the group romping around train yards, dressing in drag and giving the kids a real good look up their legs.

---

10. Ironically, it was this same Ohio Express that stepped in and released a "clean" version of the banned Standells' single "Try It" in early 1968, on their pre-Buddah Cameo label.

The 1910 Fruitgum Co's "1, 2, 3 Red Light" was clearly about the timeworn American hobby of getting into an unwilling pair of panties, by whatever means—psychological in this case—necessary. This theme was blatantly celebrated on the album cover.

"Every time I try to prove my love / 1, 2, 3 Red Light, you stop me . . . / If you stop me again / That's when we might end / So please don't refuse." He's threatening to break up with her if she doesn't put out; what a doll, and what a lovely message for the pre-sexual kiddies listening to this happy hit. The same band's "9, 10 Let's Do It Again" is even more blatant:

> 9, 10, let's do it again, gee that was so much fun
> 1, 2, I'm counting on you, to be my #1
> 3, 4, I'm shutting the door, gee this is so much fun
> 5, 6, I'm getting my kicks, doing what I love to do
> 7, 8, I'm feeling so great, doing what I'm doing with you

This one was apparently intended as a sing-a-long—or, on second thought, perhaps the line "9, 10 let's do it again, join in everyone!" is meant to inspire an orgy rather than a group sing. The notion of a sexual utopia, lorded over by a benign Hefneresque figure is raised in this lyric from "1910 Cotton Candy Castle": "Here comes the Lollipop Man in his goody ship Lollipop / All aboard for lollipop land where the lovin' never stops." *Mm-hmmm, mister, this thing tastes good!*

The Archies' "Sugar, Sugar" (#1, *Billboard*, September 1969), pretty much the only bubblegum hit that still turns up regularly on oldies radio, has one of the sexiest moments this side of Tim Buckley when the anonymous vocalist (Archie? Reggie? Ron Dante?) explodes, "Like the summer sunshine, pour your sweetness over me." These are the same Archies who celebrated bestiality in their non-hit "Hot Dog."

The Archies were masters at evoking the nervous excitement of adolescent sexuality. Reggie's menacing "Don't Touch My Guitar" is directed at his room-cleaning mother, and the titular "guitar" is clearly a symbolic stand-in for less savory items hidden in his bedroom. "Kissin'," with its Who-inspired stutter, sums up everything you need to know about what really went on at Riverdale High: "When you're feeling sad and blue, kissin' is the thing to do." There was a dark side to all this experimentation, however: on "Hide and Seek," the traditional children's game is played out as sheer sexual predation, and that old date-raper Reggie sneers, "It's an old game with a brand new twist / Whoever gets caught is gonna get kissed"— at least!

And so things might have continued indefinitely, with new and goofier bands springing up to service each fresh generation of tykes, had not the creative team of Hanna-Barbera and Sid & Marty Krofft conspired to take things entirely too far. They shamelessly developed and unleashed an act whose very name evoked a sexuality so blatant that there was nothing for the other producers, writers and so-called bands to do but pack up their toys and go home. I refer, of course, to the Banana Splits.

Contemplate with me the genius of that moniker. It is on one level innocent and sweet, suggestive of nothing more than a favorite taste of childhood. Simultaneously, it is an unspeakably lewd reference to the sexual act. With such a name, it was hardly necessary for the Splits to be smutty in their music, although they were at times. Why, to even look upon the obscene proboscis that composed Snorky's "trunk" was to feel as if one had been flashed.

On their sole Decca LP, these Monkees imitators explored genres as varied as psychedelia, soul and bluegrass, demonstrating great skill in each. But their musical charms were not enough to erase the chill that the sexual content of their lyrics instilled in parents. "This Spot," purportedly about a nightclub, was a masterful double entendre ("This spot cannot be stopped when they dim the lights . . . "), while "Don't

Go Away—Go Go Girl" explored the hopes and fears of a foot fetishist. Also notable is the obviously acid- (and Bee Gees-) inspired "I Enjoy Being a Boy," with lyrics so far out that it was pointedly left off their only album, despite being prominently featured on their TV show. ("I live in a cucumber castle on the banks of a cranberry sea/And starfish dance under my drawbridge and blackbirds make nest in my tree/I enjoy being a boy in love with you girl/OH YEAH!")

But the Banana Splits' most outré moment came in their recording of "Two Ton Tessie," a song allegedly *for children* that featured these lyrics, sung by *animals*: "She's got big red lips and big brown eyes and everything my mamma's got is king-size/ Oh she's big and round and I love every pound," and "When she holds me tight it feels so nice, we can't get it on 'less I go round twice!" Twice, no less. It is a truly sickening image.

Who, after this, could pretend that bubblegum music was appropriate for children? It clearly was far better suited for teenage boys, who could appreciate the subtleties and snicker when they "got" the dirty bits, à la "Louie Louie" and (later) "Wang Dang Sweet Poontang." But it was simply too late to appeal to them. Marketing had aimed bubblegum directly at the little tykes, and older kids thought it horribly juvenile. Now that the secret was out it could no longer be given to youngsters, lest it cause psychic cavities. There was in fact no audience left for the genre. It quickly fizzled and was gone.

And thus ended a great era, which when the powdered sugar had settled was seen to have lasted barely two years. Two short years, the span between the first and third grades. Only one generation of American children had been lucky enough to forever have their sexual imaginations overflow with absurd treacly psychedelic imagery. (And since you ask, yes, I do resent the fact that by the time I got my first AM radio, all there was to listen to was Elton John and Cher. Curse you, Hanna-Barbera!) As quickly as it had begun, it was gone. Remainder bins filled with cutouts, which were ignored even when their prices got down to 49¢.[11] Critics occasionally roused themselves to sneer (except for Lester Bangs, who knew exactly how great bubblegum was from the start), but mostly this spiffy realm was left unexplored, forgotten, its vast charms appreciated only by a peculiar few. And most of us don't talk about it, to even our closest friends.

If the time is ripe for a bubblegum revival, this unapologetic fan doesn't want to know about it. I have no interest in iffy compilations of alternative bands playing Saturday morning cartoon themes, or in the rumor that the original Archies have been playing a Florida hotel-bar. The faux-innocence of that time cannot be aped.

But the real thing makes me happy, and as long as I can listen to my bubblegum, I know all my silly troubles will go down in the most delightful way.

---

11. This is why there are such a surprising number of pristine bubblegum albums still available, when other kiddie genres left behind notably trashed vinyl remains.

Vice is Nice: Songs That Make You Go Hmmm by Becky Ebenkamp

It's a good thing Tipper Gore and her PMRC minions weren't around during the heyday of bubblegum music, as doubtless they would have found the lyrics inherently more obscene than anything ever penned by El Duce or Luther Campbell.

That songwriters got their jollies by fortifying bubblegum with dirty, double-entendre lyrics that bypassed the ears of the average unsuspecting kid or not terribly "with it" record exec is an idea that has been heatedly debated. Still, while the existence of this smutty subtext is seemingly buried deep beneath a hard candy coating, other, more frighteningly transgressive concepts such as incest, bestiality and kiddie porn appear to hover right on the surface, broadcast to the nation's nine-year-olds through mouthpiece groups like the Bradys, the Evolution Revolution and the Cattanooga Cats. Fuck metaphors, said the brazen, envelope-pushing songwriters—who apparently felt no need to obfuscate their wacko agendas.

Which sort of begs the question: What the hell were they thinking?

While anthropologists may posit that incest is "taboo" in every known culture, it was alive and well on a Paramount soundstage circa 1970, where *Brady Bunch* cast members were pairing off so furiously one might think they were privy to advance notice of some world-devastating flood. So admitted Barry "Greg" Williams in his book *Growing Up Brady*, a point later confirmed by sundry other giggling former Bradys in E! channel docs and tabloid TV fare.

Williams copped to having had the hots for TV stepsister Maureen "Marcia" McCormick, but nowhere on the tube does this bro/sis wanna tryst vibe come across as strong as in the recording studio, where producer Jackie Mills apparently didn't see any irony in the duo's rendition of "Candy (Sugar Shoppe)," the side two opener on the vocally challenged cast's third musical outing *The Kids From the Brady Bunch* (Paramount, 1972).

Considering what we know today—that the Brady kids were all but boning their tic-tac-toe board counterparts out back in Tiger's dog house—the already dubious lyrics rooted in bubblegum's stock sugar-as-a-stand-in-for-sex structure take on startlingly perverse proportions. While the Bunch specialized in chorusy, harmony-free singalongs of current chart toppers like Lobo's "Me and You and a Dog Named Boo," this catchy and surprisingly melodic original set to a funk-fortified Bo Diddley beat paired the show's eldest step-sibs Williams and McCormick to trade off suggestive lyrics that might pass for sexy were they not posing as kin on a weekly TV basis. Sample at your own risk:

> I wanna take you to my sugar shoppe, so come on
> I wanna give you all the love I got, so come on
> Candy kisses in the moonlight
> Sugar shoppin' all through the night
> Sippin' milkshakes in the hot sun
> C'mon sugar come and give me some

If on paper the sweets = sex metaphor isn't enough to convince the skeptic, the passion play panted out by pubescent horndog Williams surely will. Upon listening, it is difficult not to envision the poly-clad teens making eyes (or worse, making out) in twisted Magenta/Riff Raff fashion. When Barry growls-out "I got such a sweet tooth" or "C'mon sugar come and give me some" one can practically envision him sprouting his first facial hair right there in the recording booth. Or something much worse!

Poor McCormick, her sweet vibrato makes Williams' delivery seem all the more lascivious, and one gets the sense that her coyness masks a naiveté on the level of Serge Gainsbourg protégé France Gall, who found out too late that she wasn't just singing about sucking lollipops, but, subtextually, cocks.

❋ ❋ ❋ ❋ ❋ ❋ ❋

Prehistoric was an oft-co-opted motif throughout the '60s thanks to the popularity of *The Flintstones*, one that especially resonated with the garage bands forming all across the lower 48, as teen boys picked up cheap guitars and set out to pursue the new American Dream: to be Brit bad boys the Stones. Both well-known and obscure acts borrowed from Bedrock in name (the Barbarians, the Monkees), song (the Avengers' "Be a Caveman," Joanie Somers' "Johnny Get Angry," the Emperors' "I Want My Woman") or dress (Sonny & Cher, the Robbs, Paul Revere & the Raiders—the boys sometimes ditched the colonial garb in favor of caveman gear on the road) to obtain a primitive vibe.[12] But while wannabe Neanderthals specialized in copping a cocky club-my-woman-over-the-hear-and-drag-her-back-to-the-cave-by-the-hair attitude, all their most sexist lyrics combined couldn't match the basic instinct laid down in a single track by Lancelot Link and the Evolution Revolution.

After all, who could out-primate a rock group comprised of actual chimpanzees?

On Saturday morning TV series *The Lancelot Link Secret Chimp Hour* (ABC, 1970–72), basically, a *Get Smart* gone apeshit—protagonists Lance and Mata Hairi and their primate pals provided musical interludes between the show's spy vs. spy-themed skits. "Playing" guitar (Link), drums (Bananas Marmoset) and Farfisa organ (Sweetwater Gibbons) while decked out in Beatle wigs, fringed vests and Roger McGuinn granny glasses, the Evolution Revolution was a sight to behold. An eponymous record on Dunhill/ABC Records soon followed.[13]

Courtesy of writer/singer/producer Steve Hoffman, standout songs such as "Sha-La Love You,"[14] and "Yummy Love" are the apex of pure, innocuous pop, and rightly earn their standing next to the best recordings of the Archies et al. But while the EvRev appear to promote personal expression and gender equality (a Betty-fied, blond-wigged Hairi plays tambourine), their lyrics belie the egalitarian look to reveal a smattering of old-school sexism.

You thought only human males suffered from Madonna/whore complexes or applied to the sexes a double standard? Apparently these are tactics open to anyone equipped with one Y chromosome and two opposable thumbs—just add three chords and stir. In "Teaser," a prudish vocalist chastises a chimpette for promoting free love: "Girl you spread yourself around like strawberry jam." Another beef of his, "You ask me to come over and we turn off the lights," an activity that Mr. Willing Participant doesn't seem to have a problem with until the morning after. Yet in the very next song on the LP, "Wild Dreams and Jelly Beans," the amnesiac singer "can't understand why you've been holding out on me." Probably for fear of being labeled a slut, banana breath.

---

12. Not to mention a slew of 1980s copycats—such as the Unclaimed, the Primates, etc.—that copped the aesthetic.
13. According to *Film Threat* magazine, it wasn't much trouble getting the chimp actors to strum or beat along. One trainer reported that they simply had to roll the EvRev music and the monkeys bashed right along to the beat.
14. Originally a Grass Roots demo, the hit-potential song was brought in by producer Steve Barri.

But nowhere is sex objectification more evident than in "Kissin' Doll," where our macho monkey-man struts into a department store and picks out his desired merchandise: the babe behind the counter. This wouldn't be nearly as offensive if he weren't so dang cocky about it:

> Can I help you, that's what she said
> I took one look at her and I said, yeah
> I'm lookin' for something just like you
> I'm lookin' for a kissin' doll, I'm sure you'll do

Her response to this smarmiest of pick up lines? Since the song was written by a guy, let's just say Lance Romance didn't have to club the gal to walk off with "the greatest bargain in town."

But thankfully, there is no indication that Link was "Rollin' in the Clover" with anything but fellow simians, for some of our cartoon songsters, it appears, prefer to partake in dalliances across species.

❋ ❋ ❋ ❋ ❋ ❋ ❋

The covert approach was nixed for the *Scooby-Doo* song "Daydreamin'," one of the ditties by Brady/Josie/Partridge songsmith Danny Janssen that would play as the Hanna-Barbera crew was being chased past limited-cel animation backgrounds by various imposter mummies and ghouls. For there is no use for the thinly veiled subliminal message when a song proudly proclaims in its opening line, "I'm in love with an ostrich"—you're pretty much out of the closet at that point. After the bird-love apologist (Shaggy?) confesses his should-be-forbidden romance, the relationship serves as a metaphor for following one's heart and maintaining individuality in a cookie-cutter world:

> So if you find somebody who loves you
> And your friends are all complaining
> They're not friends anyway
> Just go out in the sun
> 'Cause it's so much fun
> Forget the rest of the world
> Put your head in the sand

A noble, worthy sentiment, albeit not one normally reserved for or extended to foul, fowl fetishists.

A tribute to zoophilia would be incomplete without a nod to "Ben," a film ballad interpreted by Michael Jackson and, later, Brady gal Maureen McCormick (Not that two versions are needed—Maureen mimics perfectly Mike's prepubescent falsetto). If boy-rat friendship is the song's outward theme, as with "Daydreamin'," finding unconventional love in an unaccepting world is the underlying message. Especially when that world is a post-Richard Gere-gerbil rumors world. Extra especially when sung by Jacko.

But all pale in comparison to the well-documented (in this book, at least) "Hot Dog," the Archies' odious ode to their fave fleabag. Simultaneously redefining the term "doggie style" and elevating "Puppy Love" to a new plane, the song is paws down the most egregious example of musical bestiality. I don't know and I don't care if songwriting team Barkan-Adams were the most naive duo roaming the planet or trying to get away with major murder here. Doesn't matter; what comes across is unadulterated mutt smut.

Perhaps it wasn't their fault that the comic gang's pooch unfortunately shared its nasty name with a phallic slang term, but knowing that—as any snickering five-year-old does—should have been enough to erect (no pun intended) a stop sign right then and there. So disturbing is the song, which manages to metaphorically mangle references to junk food, sex and household pets, that the "don't tell, show" strategy is best in relaying its ramifications. Let the lyrics speak for themselves:

So put some mustard on my roll
'Cause you're barking up my soul
Hot Dog . . . So wag your tail and let me know
Just how much you love me so
Hot Dog . . . I really relish you
Who could embellish you?

Even if the wiener/dog connection is dismissed as coincidence or ignorance on the songwriters' part, clearly, one cannot ignore the idea that boy-dog romance is implied via such lines as "Oh how good your kissing feels" or "'Cause you love me like you should," sentiments a sane person might bestow on Betty or Veronica, but certainly not man's best friend.

❋ ❋ ❋ ❋ ❋ ❋ ❋

There's a fine line between multiculturalism and racism, especially in the Postmodern, post-PC, post-everything era. That line was often crossed in an attempt to enlighten the kiddies to diversity (or perhaps more importantly, placate watchdogs) during the Golden Age of Saturday Morning TV. If featuring a sea of whiteness was a sin of omission, attempts at showcasing a broader representation of races and cultures came off, especially in retrospect, as self-conscious quota filling and/or blatant caricaturing.

Whereas Fat Albert and the Jackson 5 come across as genuine because of the involvement of Bill Cosby and a flesh and blood musical group, other cartoons were obvious attempts to plug a token dark face into a character set. Some shows followed what could be called a Racist Superfriends format: Dick Tracy with his stereotypical sidekicks (the lazy Mexican, the Japanese martial arts expert, the Irish cop o' the beat); Lance Link, the peppy and pop-as-hell theme song to which runs through a smorgasbord of exotically evil Cold War enemies. Naturally, when a show had spin-off music, the same traits shined through.

The Wombles were a fine specimen of this not exactly racist but offensive window into another world via the three-minute pop song. The Brit children's series produced music that at its best pulls off a Sweet-fused-with-Krofft sensibility, and at its worst, comes off more than a tad twee (those with a weak stomach for Jack Wild song and dance or "Honey Pie"-type McCartney numbers might want to avoid the catalog entirely). Highlighting various factions of the fluffy, tidy creatures whose hobbies include doing laundry and collecting litter, singer/songwriter/arranger Mike Batt cast off tunes covering all the genre bases over the course of five albums, including the rousing anthem ("Remember You're a Womble"), country & western ("Nashville Wombles"), the barbershop quartet ("Down at the Barbershop") the Beach Boys harmonies ("Wombling Summer Party") and the torchy faux Bond theme ("To Wimbledon With Love").

Then there's "Ping Pong Ball," which details the lives of the "Oriental" (not a bad word back then) Wombles who "exercise their Oriental litter picking skills" by cleaning up "old chop suey tins" as "rickshaws rattle by." Opening with the clash of a gong and followed by ching-chong Chinatown flourishes, back-up Wombles warble in sped-up Chinese Chipmunk voices that conjure up images of characters outfitted with massive bucked teeth and severely slanted eyes. Borderline distasteful—but in actuality probably no more offensive than the average tourist travelogue of the day—"Ping Pong Ball" is also one of the catchiest Wombles tunes.

Also hard hit: Native Americans, who got the treatment from the Sweet ("Wig Wam Bam") and a double whammy from 1910 Fruitgum Co., a band that recorded "Indian Giver," a term that has since been deemed disparaging, and fond of donning tribal garb and prop squaw for photo shoots.

A half dozen years or so before streaking came into vogue, the Cattanooga Cats were encouraging children to take it off, take it all off in "My Birthday Suit." It is not known whether the lyricists[15] were advocating kiddie porn or some misguided, hippiefied "back to the Garden" ethic, but frankly, either way it's disgusting. For those who didn't own the record, all this was played out through an episode of the Saturday morning show, where the Hanna-Barbera feline trio performed as go-go gal/groupie Kitty Jo purred "How do you like me in my birthday suit?/Aren't I cute in my birthday suit?" while dancing *au naturel*. Innocent fun perhaps, but just a hop skip and a jump to, "Wanna snap a few Polaroids of me in my birthday suit?"

While rock scholars were busy debating the existence of lyrical sexual shenanigans in the likes of "Louie Louie," "96 Tears" or some Jim Morrison Oedipal rant, the average nine-year-old circa 1969 was quietly compiling an exuberantly smutty record collection and no one ever seemed to notice. Add the above examples of transgressive bubblegum to the genre's better-known references to Little Willies, cucumber castles, Di-Ki Dongs and tummies full of "love," and even the most trusting listener must eventually sense a pattern: Sometimes a cigar isn't just a pastel bubblegum cigar.

15. The song is attributed to Mike Curb and the cryptic "Ani Hanbar," but the producer often "encouraged" songwriters to fork over credits and royalties resulting from such.

Bubblegum Nihilism by Mary Burt

Our culture is diseased. Yes, it is sick. I've always suspected as much, but recently had it confirmed by a book called *Pathologies of the Modern Self* (New York University Press, 1987). Although I only read editor David Michael Levin's introduction, I learned some pretty harrowing things. Levin asserts that, following the death of God, Western culture has brought about "the destruction of our faith in ourselves." He goes on to say that the nihilism that pervades our culture "is not just a sickness of the modern Self, but is also a distinctive affliction of our historical embodiment." Furthermore, he claims that "nihilism is a cultural epidemic that defines the spirit of our epoch." In his most troubling statement, though, he says that "nihilism is at work in this false understanding of the 'individuality' of the individual," and presents the idea that nihilism can be broken down into three pathologies: narcissism, depression, and schizophrenia. He implies that our culture is so immersed in nihilism that even our critiques of the culture are nihilistic. Could things be any more hopeless? At this point, I heaved a great sigh, and fought the idea with everything I could muster. I thought to myself, *What about love? What about music?*

Consumed with despair, yet determined to find an alternate way to look at the world, I searched most of the record stores in Los Angeles until I found a compact disc whose theme I thought would be positive enough to reaffirm my faith in humanity and my faith in humanity's faith in itself. This disc was called *Bubblegum Classics Volume Two* (VSD-5575: Varèse Sarabande, 1995). I'd heard most of the songs on it and remembered that they had grated on my nerves for being too happy, too saccharine, and certainly not nihilistic enough for my taste. For extra help in my research, I dug out my battered copy of the *Diagnostic and Statistical Manual of Mental Disorders,* Third Edition, which I still own even though I've far outworn the comfort that it used to give me when I needed proof that I was a perfectly sane, healthy, functioning member of society.

As scientifically and accurately as I could, I transcribed the lyrics to every song on the disc and all of the symptoms for narcissistic personality disorder, depression, and schizophrenia from the DSM-III. I then scribbled all over the 40 or so pages with cross-references, observations, and doodles of daisies with happy faces just to sustain a cheery mood despite the overwhelming negativity of my research. My results were none too assuring. It would be quite easy for me to just reprint the pages, but I'm sure your time is limited and that my poorly rendered daisies might serve only to destroy your faith in my argument. So allow me to present my findings in condensed form.

Narcissism

The most prevalent pathology displayed in bubblegum music is narcissistic personality disorder, which includes such symptoms as a grandiose sense of self-importance, a need for constant attention, and a sense of entitlement. The narcissist's self-love is easily shattered by the disapproval of others. Therefore narcissistic songs don't just make claims to greatness, but also demand the approval and unconditional love of others. In some cases, the song titles alone convey the kind of selfishness that typifies narcissistic personality disorder. Titles like Lou Christie's "I'm Gonna Make You Mine," Crazy Elephant's "Gimme Gimme Good Lovin'," and Brotherhood of Man's "Save Your Kisses For Me," are flagrant examples of a narcissistic mind at work.

Upon listening to the songs, one gets an even better sense of how full of themselves these people are. In "I'm Gonna Make You Mine," the singer asserts "I'll try to get to your soul/I'll try to get to your mind," which corresponds with the symptom of a preoccupation with fantasies of unlimited success. What could be more successful than a conquest of the soul?

In "Gimme Gimme Good Lovin'," the insistent singer addresses every living girl in America and says, "Baby, I'm your man." The vocalist in Edison Lighthouse's "It's Up To You, Petula," also exhibits this sort of egomania when he sings, "It's up to you to choose / I only hope you do it right," implying that he, the singer, is the only correct choice. In the Fun & Games' "The Grooviest Girl in the World," the singer concludes his rather excessive compliments to said groovy girl with the line, "And I'm a guy with impeccable taste," suggesting that she should be flattered that such an amazing guy complimented her and held her in almost as high esteem as he holds himself.

In "Save Your Kisses For Me," the singer exhibits the narcissist's sense of entitlement throughout the song when he demands that the person whom he's addressing (who turns out to be only three!) save all of her kisses for him. Tommy Roe expresses a similarly possessive statement in "Dizzy," when he sings "I knew that I just had to make you mine"; while the less successful singer in "It's Up to You, Petula" laments "I don't have you to myself."

Depression

In contrast to the bombast of narcissism, bubblegum lyricists also make claims to symptoms of depression. Similarly to the plight of the narcissist, the depressive's sense of self-worth is judged by how much someone loves them. In the Cuff Links' "When Julie Comes Around," the singer explains that when Julie isn't in his life, "It's always the same / I'm broken in two." In the Five Americans' "Western Union," a break up "killed the groove." The singer in White Plains' "My Baby Loves Lovin'" claims that he "was lonely once in this great big world / Just a nowhere man without a girl." And in the Monkees' "I'm a Believer," the singer describes the depression he felt before he was in love by saying, "When I needed sunshine, I got rain," and "Disappointment haunted all my dreams."

In all of these songs, the singers express the idea that love has pulled or will pull them out of their depression. We learn from the lyrics of "When Julie Comes Around," however, that the devotion of another can never be constant enough to keep one satisfied for long.

Schizophrenia

And now, dear readers, I must admit that I thought I would have to do a little bit of creative interpretation to find examples of schizophrenic thoughts in bubblegum music. It was with no little amount of terror that I discovered a multitude of examples. Perhaps the similarity between bubblegum and children's music and the similarity in schizophrenic thinking to children's thinking lends itself to an easy connection. Or perhaps some of my readings on the subject have rubbed off on me and I'm making crazy connections that don't really exist. I'll tell you what I found and you can judge for yourself.

The most common schizophrenic theme, paranoia, combines the self-centeredness of narcissism with the hopelessness of depression to make the sufferer feel as if the entire world is against them. Two songs, "It's Up to You, Petula," and the Rare Breed's "Beg, Borrow, and Steal," make the comparison of being kept on a string as a way to illustrate the mental control that someone has over them. The singer in "Dizzy" makes no such metaphor, but admits to the object of his affections, "Girl, you got control of me." "It's Up to You, Petula" illustrates a different type of paranoia, when the singer complains, "I know you've been seeing someone else." The singer in Thee Prophets' "Playgirl" makes the same complaint when he talks about a girl who's been "running 'round on [him]." In the most extreme example of paranoia, the singer in "I'm a Believer" claims that it's not merely a person, but *love itself* that's out to get him.

Another symptom of schizophrenia is the presence of odd or bizarre ideation, "magical thinking," or superstitions. The lyrics of "I'm a Believer" express an odd perception of cause and effect with the line "Seems the more I gave, the less I got." (This makes sense quantitatively, but only if you take a grammatically incorrect reading of the song, because the more you give, the less you *do* got.) 1910 Fruitgum Co.'s "Simon Says" suggests magical thinking when the singer says, "Do what Simon says and you will never be out." When taken out of the context of a kids' game and recontextualized among of the rules of social conformity suggested by the references to popular dance moves, the lyrics give me the image of a social misfit mimicking a popular person movement-for-movement in the hopes that it will magically make him popular. "My Baby Loves Lovin'" gives an example of superstitious thinking when the singer says, "Can't believe my luck so I knock on wood."

Conclusion

I'm sure I could find more examples, but my mental state is too fragile to delve any deeper, since innocent words like "chewy" or "sugar" have already taken on the most sinister overtones. And to tell you the truth, despite all the examples of nihilistic, doomed thinking I've found in bubblegum music, I still hold out hope for humanity. I believe in love. I believe in music. I believe that the pursuit of love will eventually give people a reason to better themselves and to develop a little bit of faith in themselves. Besides, it's pointless to try to stop people from pursuing love. Love itself is a sickness whose promise is so prevalent in our culture that people can't help but be consumed by it. So until people develop realistic expectations of romance, let's just sit back and enjoy the fruits of their failures. As a product of this nihilistic culture, I see no point in fighting against it. "'Tis better to have loved and lost and written a great song about it than to never have loved and lost at all."

A Brief History of Boy Bands by David Smay

Boy Bands rule the world and they always have. (And by "always" I mean "since Beatlemania.") You wouldn't think pubescent girls had that much power, but you underestimate sexual hysteria at your own peril, cf. *The Bacchae* by Euripedes. Any right-thinking director would update the play by setting it at a Backstreet Boys concert.

> I wound up digging both the big Backstreet Boys hits [of 1999], but those guys' problem is that they're not bubblegum enough: They're way too indebted to the adult-oriented ballads of Boyz II Men. I couldn't imagine Betty of the Archies shaking a tambourine to their music.
>
> —Chuck Eddy, Pazz & Jop, *Village Voice*

Are Boy Bands even bubblegum to start with? It's tough to draw a clean line between bubblegum and teen idols. Some pop fans take a hard stance here insisting that true bubblegum bands don't have teen idols—only faceless studio bands or cartoon creations qualify. Sifting through the pop dig of the '60s and '70s, however, it becomes clear that this facile bit of taxonomy can't hold. The Monkees sold on their faces (Davy foremost). *The* teen idol of the '70s, David Cassidy, sang lead in the canonically bubblegum Partridge Family. Tommy Roe, Mark Lindsay, Dino, Desi & Billy, Tommy James—they all did hard time on planet *Tiger Beat*. When the quintessential bubblegum voice, Ron Dante, put out his solo album (essentially an extra Archies record with the same musicians and pool of songwriters) he angled for that teen mag audience right down to his photo insert.

The history of boy bands takes many a wayward turn beyond even the most generous definition of bubblegum. But be patient, I'll keep it brief and on point and you'll see how Boy Bands partake of the gumly wafer while staying something less than devout.

The Beatles

While brother acts and vocal harmony groups pre-date Vaudeville, the Boy Band as we know it first emerges with the Beatles. Their non-threatening cuddliness—quite a makeover by Brian Epstein on a bunch of working class speed freaks from Liverpool—was one of their big selling points and the band notably sold below the puberty line. Subject to outright scorn and dismissal when they broke in America, the band grew up and took their pre-teen fanbase with them. The mop tops left a motherlode for bubblegum musically (and The Pronoun Phase of their early hits rarely rises above bubblegum standards lyrically). But it was their image as four complementary cuties that gave us the working model for Boy Bands ever after. Prior to the Beatles nobody gave a damn who the Belmonts were. Okay, after the Beatles nobody cared who Dion was (their loss), but the point is that in the post-Beatles era you sold your group as a merry band of artificially and narrowly typed lads.

The Monkees

When building a Pre-Fab Four it's best to stick to the blueprint. Hence, Mike equals John as The Smart One. Substitute Davy for Paul as The Cute One. Micky is their Ringo, The Funny One. Peter stands in for George as . . . hmmm, the somewhat mystically other one. The Oddball, one supposes, prone to non-sequiturs and prompting eye-rolling and blank takes from his comically tolerant mates. Now note, these types have but the faintest resemblance to the actual persons. Mike and John were certainly smart, but so was Paul McCartney before he baked his synapses in THC. And you typically wouldn't put The Funny One as the lead vocalist, except Micky had the best voice. [Authorial bias noted here: Ringo & Micky are my favorite Beatle and Monkee respectively. In the Boy Band universe it's vital to stake your identity to your chosen one and make it known. The fact that I also prefer Charlie Watts & Keith Moon should not be construed as a drummer bias but simple good taste.] Are the Monkees bubblegum? I say unequivocally . . . sometimes. Really, it's absurd to insist on an either/or definition. Every time Jeff Barry or Boyce & Hart handled them they were undeniably pink and chewy and popping.

The Jackson 5

Berry Gordy did not become the most successful music mogul of the '60s by missing trends. Berry saw the Monkees, the Kasenetz & Katz acts, the Archies and quickly sussed that Motown could do that and do it better. And they did. But more importantly (as we'll see) the J-5 are indirectly responsible for the current teen pop explosion. Berry worked the bubblegum angle through the Jacksons' early recordings and backed it up with the hottest tracks ever recorded. The early Jackson 5 singles have no peers in pop thrills. But even in the J-5 cartoon we find an only partially successful effort in differentiating the boys. Sure, Jermaine was The Pretty One and Michael was The Prodigy. But Marlon? I'm drawing a blank on Marlon. And Tito was . . . well, Tito had The Hat. Despite this failure in product branding, the Jackson 5 still got into the Rock and Roll Hall of Fame.

The Osmonds

Operating on Sam Phillips' dictum that if you just find some white kid to sing like those black kids you'll make a bundle, the Osmonds were quickly foisted on a suspecting public. Showbiz vets, the Osmonds started on The *Andy Williams Show* and were cooling their heels between gigs when the market niche for a white Jackson 5 opened up. The Osmonds are sorely underrated in today's pop market and their Mormon Anomalousness has been overshadowed by Michael Jackson's unslakeable ambition to embody Every Conceivable Celebrity Oddity. But snappy Osmond hits like "One Bad Apple" and "Yo Yo" deserve a new audience, and besides, Donny sang his ass off. Sure, he wasn't Michael Jackson but he had a freakishly soulful style for a white kid from Utah. (Donny's George Michael-inspired comeback attempt in the '90s was not such a stretch.)

The Osmonds passed on the usual N.Y. musicians who played on so many bubblegum classics, nor did they use the Wrecking Crew in L.A. Instead, MGM prexy Mike Curb, sent the boys to Muscle Shoals. In Memphis, George Jackson, one of Rick Hall's staff writers, gave them "One Bad Apple" and they were on their way. Admittedly, recording in Memphis was the pop move to make in the late '60s, but aside from Dan Penn's work with the Blue-Eyed BubbleSoul of the Box Tops it's rare to hear the Muscle Shoals rhythm section on a bubblegum record.

Frankly, The Osmonds are ripe for a full hipster reevaluation. Not only did they pull off a credible Glam Rock gesture with "Crazy Horses" but they've got an Apocalyptic Mormon Concept Album (*The*

Plan) simply begging for Lisa Suckdog's exegesis and a Money Mark remix. Their heavy metal rewrite of The Book of Revelations, "The Last Days" successfully exceeds any satire that Spinal Tap could muster.

Bay City Rollers

The Rollers occupy a weird space in the pop continuum. They are equal parts bubblegum, Glam Rock and Boy Band. Rollermania proves once again that the durable Boy Band formula transplants beautifully to any number of locales. Scotland, Puerto Rico, Orlando, Florida—it doesn't matter. The Rollers' music holds up well due to the careful pop craftsmanship of Phil Coulter ("I Can Only Give You Everything"), Bill Martin and Phil Wainman (the Sweet's engineer). Their earliest hits (as with so many '70s Teen Idols) rehashed Brill Building staples, but they struck gold when they recorded Coulter & Martin's "Saturday Night." Tartan shock waves rolled through the popverse with striking and unintended consequences.

> I hate to blow the mystique, but at the time we really liked bubblegum music, and we really liked the Bay City Rollers. Their song "Saturday Night" had a great chant in it, so we wanted a song with a chant in it: "Hey! Ho! Let's Go!" on "Blitzkrieg Bop" was our "Saturday Night."
>
> — Joey Ramone

TV shows followed both in Britain and in the U.S. (Krofft produced, no less) but "creative differences" and the pressure of Rollermania itself ended their brief reign. The Rollers' post-fame slide ranks with Mötley Crüe for *Behind the Music* fodder: child molestation and child pornography, vehicular manslaughter, suicide attempts, AIDS, financial mismanagement and fraud. Inevitably, Courtney Love optioned their story to be made into a movie.

Duran Duran

There's a huge gap in Boy Bands between the Rollers and New Edition. In between (from a teen pop/Top 40 perspective), you've got the Disco era and the early MTV groups of the '80s. Disco gives us nothing Boy Band. Well, the Village People might qualify as a Boy Band on Christopher Street, but the Bee Gees were far too old and hairy and dentally intimidating to play the brother act for pre-teens. While neither a Boy Band nor particularly bubblegum, Duran Duran did efficiently plug this gap in the pop cultural psyche. They made danceable hits, the boys were cute (and distinct enough to allow a variety of favorites—a staple of Boy Band dynamics) and young girls had to be hosed down after their concerts. Further, Duran Duran's avowed ambition to cross the Sex Pistols with Chic differs little from the formula advanced by the Backstreet Boys of grafting Boys II Men harmonies onto Gap Band grooves. It's a Pop Funk thang.

One further fascinating but tenuous connection between Duran Duran and bubblegum involves the men who directed their early revolutionary videos, Godley and Creme ("Girls on Film," "Hungry Like The Wolf"). When Graham Gouldman contracted with bubblegum kings Kasenetz and Katz, he recruited his buddies Kevin Godley and Lol Creme, with Eric Stewart, to record one of the last Ohio Express singles, "Sausalito." Whatever happened to those guys? They formed 10cc, of course.

New Edition

Maurice Starr is a genius and Ving Rhames ought to be lining up the rights for a film bio before Courtney Love moves in. Maurice got his start with the second tier funk band ConFunkShun but didn't make his mark until he and his nephew, Michael Jonzun grasped the import of the cheap synthesizers popping up on New Wave hits and more significantly, Afrika Bambaataa's Electro landmark, "Planet Rock."

Soon under the moniker the Jonzun Crew they crapped out the endearingly rinky-dink "Space Cowboy" and techno forerunner, "Pack Jam." Thus bankrolled, Michael spotted some kids at a local talent contest (they came in second) and Maurice decided the market was ready for a new Jackson 5 (hence, they were the New Edition).

> What was so great about New Edition was their irresistible blend of bubblegum pop and sweet soul, the kind responsible for hits like "Popcorn Love" and "Candy Girl" (guided, of course, by the hand of producer Maurice Starr, who went on to recycle these songs for white-bread clones NKOTB) . . . Who could have known they would go on to dominate the world of hip-hop and R&B in the '90s?'
> —'Rebecca Wallwork, *All-Music Guide*

New Edition slipped through that narrow doorway Maurice opened for them, pulled themselves out of Roxbury and remade R&B into their own image (New Jack Swing). Bobby Brown, Ralph Tresvant, Johnny Gill, Bell Biv Devoe all went on to score #1 R&B hits as solo artists, and Michael Bivins produced Boyz II Men's (who took their name from a New Edition song) influential first album. Boyz deserve a note here for their over-arcing influence on the contemporary Boy Bands. They provide the immediate touchstone back through the vocal group tradition that includes the Temptations, the Miracles, Five Satins, Frankie Lymon and the Teenagers.

New Kids On The Block

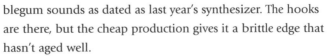

Operating on Sam Phillips' dictum . . . does this sound familiar? In a satisfying twist, Maurice exploited his own legacy after New Edition dumped him. He just moved one neighborhood over from Roxbury to Dorchester to find his New Kids. The teen pop market exploded in the late '80s and New Kids On The Block were the Kings of '80s bubblegum. Maurice wrote catchy hooks (he once claimed to write ten songs on the plane from New York to Boston) and saved on session musicians by recording all the instrumental tracks himself. Low overhead, high return. In truth, most '80s bub-

blegum sounds as dated as last year's synthesizer. The hooks are there, but the cheap production gives it a brittle edge that hasn't aged well.

By 1987 Debbie Gibson and Tiffany grappled for the Teen Queen crown, Jem & the Holograms brought cartoon rock back to television, and Menudo worked the Latin Market. The NKOTB phenomenon pulled in hundreds of millions of dollars (largely through their concert appearances) and they established the boilerplate for contemporary Boy Band shows with their frenetic, choreographed hip-hoppity dance moves. What makes Maurice Starr's achievement even more spectacular is that he didn't have the combined talent pool of Nickelodeon and Disney that Lou Pearlman works with to draw from. Both Jordan Knight and Joey McIntyre managed to scrape back onto the charts after more than a decade's absence which must be some kind of record for perseverance in the Boy Band universe. And without NKOTB we wouldn't have Mark Wahlberg's fine career as a supporting actor.

Menudo

Menudo fascinate as a conceptual art project. The sheer ruthlessness of taking some poor kid, making him a star, and ejecting him from the group at the age of 16 takes your breath away. *Pygmalion* as written by DeSade and Warhol. It ranks right up there with Kirshner's cartoon band revolution for Master of Puppets genius. Like the Bay City Rollers, Menudo suffered a sex scandal within its management. (Running a Boy Band ranks right behind priest and Scoutmaster on the NAMBLA job board.) Of course, Menudo's most famous alumnus is the hip-swiveliest pop star since Elvis, the King of Latin Pop, the toothiest grin since Donny Osmond, the most fey disavowal of his sexuality since George Michael: Ricky Martin.

Take That

America will never grasp the import of Take That. When Boy Bands died a grunge-related death in the early '90s, the cause was taken up in the U.K. Modeled directly on NKOTB (right down to the uneven talent distribution), Take That first gained acceptance on the gay club circuit.

> Take That's Greatest Hits . . . tells only half the story, since mere records cannot convey the exciting hairstyles, Howard Donald's arse, or depict the lads dressed as deer, but it's compulsive enough. Their hectoring "Do What U Like" debut merely scraped the Top 10, yet the remainder is peerlessly bright, intelligent pop full of joyfully plastic brass, and naturally stars "Back For Good," Gary Barlow's one truly fantastic song.
>
> —Danny Eccleston

> Take That's boyish good looks guaranteed them a significant portion of the teeny-bopper audience, but in a bizarre twist, most of their videos and promotional photos had a strong homosexual undercurrent — they were marketed to pre-teen girls and a kitschy gay audience simultaneously.
>
> —Stephen Thomas Erlewine, *All-Music Guide*.

Just as Take That seemed on the verge of bringing Boy Bands back to the U.S. they split. Other British Boy Bands like East 17 and Boyzone soldiered on, but the Spice Girls quickly moved in for the kill and absorbed both Take That's U.K. market and the world domination which had eluded the lads.

Backstreet Boys

They're out there taking dance classes in stripmalls in Louisiana, singing Boyz II Men songs in the school hallways in Kentucky, appearing at county fair talent shows and roller rinks. They're southern showbiz kids and they've all converging on Orlando. O-Town, home to The Disney Channel, Nickelodeon, and Trans Continental Records. In the '90s, The Disney Channel remade *The Mickey Mouse Club* and somebody had an eye for talent. That show alone gave us Britney Spears, Christina Aguilera, Keri Russell (*Felicity*) and half of 'N Sync (Justin & JC). But first came Backstreet.

Lou Pearlman, a man *Time* magazine labeled "florid" (that's code, get it?), made his money in shipping and then bought the Chippendale dancers. Lou founded Trans Continental and set the Backstreet Boys up with Johnny Wright, NKOTB's road manager. Johnny took the Boys to England where the market was much more hospitable to teen pop in the early '90s. After Hanson and the Spice Girls softened state-side resistance to bubblegum, Backstreet popped and locked their way back home to unprecedented chart dominance. Both Hanson and the Spice Girls sadly flopped in their 2000 follow-ups while in contrast BSB closed in on one billion dollars in total revenue. One *Billion*. The brain boggles. The music? Unlike their NKOTB predecessors, everybody in Backstreet sings well enough to be a solo act. When they settle into a dance groove they rely heavily on a mid-'80s Gap Band vibe. But they make their money with the gooey ballads and that's where Boy Bands look a lot more like Teen Idols than bubblegum.

'N Sync

Backstreet's only challenger for current Boy Band supremacy are the just as Orlando-based, just as Lou Pearlman launched, just as litigious, just as pretty, label-mates on Jive Records, 'N Sync. BSB were not happy to have their biggest rivals making the same leap from Trans Continental to Jive Records. The most notable things about 'N Sync are: their successful escape from their Trans Continental contract; that they broke all sales records with *No Strings Attached*, selling 2.5 million in a week (doubling the previous record by BSB. Take that, indeed); their ubiquity; Justin Timberlake's ascension into Heaven solely on the basis of his puss; that Justin dates his *Mickey Mouse Club* co-star Britney Spears; and "Bye Bye Bye" and "It's Gonna Be Me" are ace pop songs.

That's the history of Boy Bands up to the minute. A discerning eye might've caught that thread of gay impresarios that runs from Brian Epstein forward. And Boy Bands do have a gay audience. Cynical observers can't help wondering what boys would be doing on backstreets, and noticing that everybody calls Lou Pearlman "Big Poppa." But a front-page story in *The Advocate* in 2000 gives some credence that it's less a matter of chickenhawks than young gay men tentatively approaching their sexuality and finding a safe, creamy, hairless (non-threatening) chest to obsess on. Just like the girls.

Are Boy Bands bubblegum? Sometimes they are and it's not a tough call: "Candy Girl," "Saturday Night," "ABC," "I'm a Believer," "Bye Bye Bye," "One Bad Apple" to cite just the obvious examples. Bubblegum is an undeniable strand through Boy Bands, but so are Teen Idol ballads, and more recently dance music and the vocal harmony tradition. Bubblegum remains only one part of the Boy Band formula, but we contend it's the best part.

ARTISTS

Pop historians know that bubblegum was the product of Svengalis and Dr. Frankensteins toiling away in the back rooms of the music industry, but by the time it filtered down to the consumer it wore somebody else's name. Some bubblegum stars were songwriters and producers in their own right, but most were employees at best, cartoon characters at worst. In this section, we examine case histories of many of the important bubblegum artists with an eye to figuring out how they got that way. From Boyce & Hart's jealous desire to share the Monkees' fame to the pure phoniness of the supposed Kasenetz-Katz Singing Orchestral Circus, the path to bubblegum riches could take many weird twists. Come along and we'll take you on a few.

The Candy Ass Charisma of the Archies by David Smay

You can sneer at Britney, scorn Christina, mock 'N Sync, and snicker quite openly at Backstreet Boys but don't mess with the Archies—not unless you want to wind up at the bottom of a lemonade vat with a pair of sticky pink boots. The Archies are the crème de la creampuff. Through the brief aperture of their existence, the Archies focus the entire history of rock into a laser beam of scintillant pop, refracting out through the spectrum of all musics, ushering in feminism, re-establishing diplomatic ties with Red China and bolstering the Consumer Price Index by .0374%. All to a groovy little dance beat. But perhaps I understate their importance.

In 1968, while a batch of hippies blew themselves up in Weatherman labs, a generation of 13-year-olds came of age jonesing for a hook. Two men understood this need, this terrible teen craving for a meaty beat slathered sweet. On the East Coast, Neil Bogart reigned as head of Buddah Records, ringing up Top 40 hits like a carnival game, with one Kasenetz-Katz shadow-band supplanting another on the radio. On the West Coast, Don Kirshner sat brooding over his ouster in The Great Monkees Coup, plotting his vendetta carefully. He'd make his own group, and this time he wouldn't make the mistake of using actual humans with their tedious desires for autonomy.

Though seemingly carved out of a solid block of suet, Kirshner had a mind as devious as an untenured English professor at a small state university. He brought on Jeff Barry to head his bubblegum triad. That's Jeff Barry of the songwriting credit Barry-Greenwich ("Be My Baby," "Da Doo Ron Ron," "Leader of the Pack")—a musician whose influence in rock 'n' roll is more pervasive than herpes (and whose songs are twice as catchy). Cast Andy Kim as the second-in-command, the grooviest Lebanese popstar to ever write two number one hits. And singing lead for the Archies, Ron Dante, a man so talented that chart-topping singer is only the fifth most successful career on his resume. Toni Wine ably abetted the Archie core, giving voice to Veronica and Betty and sending ecstatic shivers down the spine of many a listener.

These were professional hitmakers, my friend, not some pimply-assed pack of garage rockers. They had one job and one job only: create the absolutely irresistible pop song. Again and again and again. Together the Archies isolated the genetic strand of the perfect pop hit and replicated it like a honey-dipped virus. This pop genome worked its way deep into your brain, beneath the higher functions of the cerebral cortex, burrowing down into the primitive lizard brain which craves only sex, junk food and the pure cane syrup of pop music boiled down to seven inches of black vinyl spinning at 45 revolutions per minute.

And yet, for all their clinical pop competence no band so perfectly evokes the happy hippy daydream of 1969 than the Archies. No San Francisco band ever came close to the Archies' suburbatopian vision of picnic blanket sex in a grassy park, radiantly sunlit in an afterglow of everlasting sweetness. At least, that's the way it sounded to kids at the end of the '60s. A generation too young to care about Altamont heard the Archies, latched onto the sugartit of late-American capitalism and got a buzz that would last a decade. Other bands promised a revolution, but the Archies saw the future, and it looked a lot like the '70s.

The first Archies single, "Bang Shang-A-Lang," skimmed into the charts at #22 in 1968, roughly a year after Kirshner got the boot as the Monkees' puppetmaster, and coincident with the Monkees slow fade from the charts. You don't need a protractor to draw a line from "Da Doo Ron Ron" to "Bang Shang-A-Lang." Lyrically, the Archies pick up where Jeff Barry and Ellie Greenwich left the Ronettes, spinning self-conscious teen mumbles into a poetry of giddy do wah diddy ron ron. The main difference being that the Ronettes sang with voracious yearning and the Archies sing from exultant satiation. That being the difference, of course, between Top 40 before The Pill and after The Pill.

The songs Jeff Barry and Andy Kim wrote for the Archies park themselves squarely in Freud's Oral Phase where lickin' is lovin' and there's not much distinction between candy corn and cunnilingus. In this infantile orality all the pleasures of the world enter through the mouth: sex, candy and "slices of sunshine" (the inevitable oblique drug reference from "Sugar and Spice"). Still, this is not the famously fellated songbook of Kasenetz-Katz ("Chewy chewy chew me out of my mind"). Due to Andy Kim's enlightened loverman lyrics, Archies songs are surprisingly girl-friendly and rife with early morning pillow talk, like the giggly-lewd spoken intro to "Who's Your Baby." The Barry-Kim songbook never suffers from the sadness of a swinger stranded on a Saturday night, so common in Boyce & Hart's records which "trail off into hopelessness and disconnection" (Kim Cooper, editrix and B&H chronicler). In "Jingle Jangle," Veronica boldly invites Archie to "Sing me, sing me baby" and put his mouth where her money maker is. Sung as a duet: [him] "so darling don't be weeping / and please don't be a sleeping / when I come a creepin' down the hall / to sing you [her] sing me sing me, baby (groaning)." This is bubblegum that Erica Jong could sink her teeth into.

Sonically, the Archies lacked the oomph of Spector's Wall of Sound, but neatly rip off the bubbling bottom from Motown and the joyous vocal surge of the Beatles. Chuck Rainey laid more hooks in the bassline than anyone this side of James Jamerson. And the drummer on "Sugar and Spice" (Buddy Saltzman? Gary Chester?) commits some of the most savage cymbal abuse since Keith Moon demolished "I Can See For Miles." Cotton candy harmonies spun out over a bassline chewier than Red Vines, a rock candy beat, and Veronica's organ spread like a thin layer of marzipan holding it all together: Is that rock 'n' roll? "The basic bubblegum sound could be described as the basic sound of rock 'n' roll—minus the rage, fear, violence and anomie that runs from Johnny Burnette to Sid Vicious." (Lester Bangs, "Bubblegum," *The Rolling Stone Illustrated History of Rock and Roll*, Second Edition.) By Lester's definition, three-fourths of the bands that ever came out of Scotland are bubblegum.

Consider Jeff Barry's credentials as the one true Messiah of Gum: he co-wrote "Hanky Panky," for Tommy James in 1966; he produced "I'm A Believer," for the Monkees in 1967; he co-wrote and produced "Sugar, Sugar," the biggest selling single for all of 1969 in both the U.S. and the U.K.; and he co-wrote "Da Doo Ron Ron," which was Shaun Cassidy's only hit. And those are just the Number One Hits.

Jeff Barry is nothing less than The Omnipresence of Pop. Pick the hardest band imaginable, the very antithesis of bubblegum as you know it and we'll play a quick round of Six Degrees of Jeff Barry.

Archies to the Melvins: Jeff Barry co-wrote "Sugar, Sugar" for the Archies; which was covered by Mary Lou Lord; who famously gave Kurt Cobain a blow job; Kurt produced the Melvins. From Kurt it's only two bed-hops to Nine Inch Nails. In fact, Courtney's underwear is second only to Hal Blaine's drumming as a hub for making musical connections.

Archies to Einstürzende Neubauten: Jeff co-wrote "I Can Hear Music" covered by the Beach Boys; Glen Campbell played with Beach Boys; Glenn had a hit with "Wichita Lineman;" Nick Cave covered "Wichita Lineman;" Blixa Bargeld played with Nick and Einstürzende Neubauten. One more hop from the Bad Seeds gets you to the Gun Club or the Cramps.

Archies to Public Enemy: Shangri-Las record Jeff & Ellie's "Leader of the Pack;" Shadow Morton produces Shangri-Las; Shadow produces second NY Dolls album; Sonic Youth covers "Personality Crisis"; Chuck D. guests on Sonic Youth's "Kool Thing."

(If you want to continue playing you can easily hook Jeff Barry up to Miles Davis, Merle Haggard, or Run-DMC in less than five jumps.)

In 1969 Ron Dante hit number one with "Sugar, Sugar" and simultaneously sang lead on the Cuff Links hit "Tracy" (#9 on the charts). For most people, having two songs in the Top 10 at the same time

would be a career peak, but most people are not Ron Dante. After the Archies, Ron hooked up with a jingles writer and now he owns one tiny corner of your brain: they wrote "You Deserve a Break Today" for McDonald's. Then he produced that jingle writer's first eight gold albums—Barry Manilow. Then, straining all credulity, I came upon this fact: "In 1971 [Ron Dante] became publisher of the literary magazine *The Paris Review*." (*The New Rolling Stone Encyclopedia of Rock and Roll*, 1995.) That's right, two years after "Sugar, Sugar" Ron Dante was publishing Gide, Foucault and Susan Sontag. Itching for new challenges, Ron decided to bankroll Broadway shows (a quick way to lose your life savings): "Children of a Lesser God," "Whose Life Is It Anyway" and "Ain't Misbehavin'."

Front and back covers of Andy Kim's *Rainbow Ride*

Paradoxically (considering his successful solo career), Andy Kim remains the most enigmatic of the Great Pop Troika, a pseudonym, wrapped in a stage-name, within a missing ethnicity. In one of the kookier double-blind show biz switches, Andy Kim obscured his Hispanic roots by changing his name from Andrew Joachim. Except, he didn't have Hispanic roots. He was born Andre Youakim in Montreal and he was Lebanese. Clearly a complex man with many layers, Andy now performs under the name Baron Longfellow. No, not as a porn star. Think of a cross between Tom Jones and Neil Diamond and you'll grasp Andy's current incarnation. But we're getting ahead of ourselves.

Jeff Barry groomed Andy Kim for stardom concurrently with the Archies. Through 1969 and 1970, Jeff and Andy wrote the majority of material for the first three Archies albums, the last Monkees album, *Changes*, and put out five Andy Kim albums on Jeff's own Steed Records. One imagines them screeching into a Sunset Boulevard boutique parking lot, snatching up a pair of multi-stripe hip-huggers and a realllly wide leather watch band, shooting the gatefold photos for *Rainbow Ride* and racing back to the studio for their third session of the day. When you write nine albums worth of material in two years you've got to have a system. The Archies formula was to cook the '60s down to one sticky popcorn ball: Brill Building songcraft, girl group innocence, Beach Boy harmonies, a touch of folky jangle, Motown handclaps, a dollop of psych.

While the pop cognoscenti track down obscure Hudson Brothers records, Emitt Rhodes longplayers or Michael Brown's work with Stories, Andy Kim's early solo career molders in the "K" bin. And that's shameful, because Andy's turn-of-the-decade work outshines his peers in hooks, production, danceability and mild bouts of loopiness. Almost any cut off *Rainbow Ride* or *How'd We Ever Get This Way* would enhance a Poptopian band's setlist. Andy's early solo records on Steed feature Jeff Barry's distinctive production touches like the ringing, son-of-"Last Train to Clarksville" guitar figure on "Rainbow Ride," the psychedelic drench of "When You're Young," the rack of exotic rhythm instruments on "How'd We Ever Get This Way," and the infectious Bubble-Gospel of "Love That Little Woman"—a favored genre they also exploited on the Archies classic "Get On The Line." Andy's tender lyrics reach a goofy political pinnacle on "Tricia Tell Your Daddy,"a protest song addressed to Tricia Nixon. To achieve the desired teen-idol/castrati effect, they tape-manipulated Andy's voice up to a higher pitch (a fate which David Cassidy also suffered). His natural range can be heard in the gruff, Neil Diamond-like growl he affects on his proto-Disco smash, "Rock Me Gently."

Ritchie Adams produced the fifth and last Archies album, *This is Love*—a labored and self-conscious effort, lacking the effervescent charm of its predecessors. The Barkan-Adams songs try too hard to whip up some kinderpop vibe and miss the distracted artistry of the Barry-Kim songs. Jeff and Andy rarely wasted more than 32 seconds on a set of Archies lyrics, content to slip a few subversive lines to the kids, and going back to work on one of Andy's solo records. Perhaps I'm too hard on Barkan-Adams songbook; they bop along beautifully and sport some of the weirder subtexts in the Archies catalog. One Barkan-Adams song bears particular note, "My Little Green Jacket." Ostensibly a tune about a stud donning his

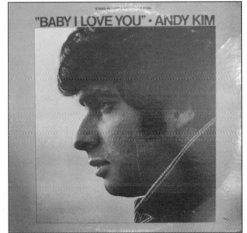

chick-magnet wardrobe, the song reveals more than this ladies-man intends," I reach into my closet / and slip my secret on / I sashay out the door . . ." Closet? Secret? Sashay?

It's clear in retrospect that the Archies caused the '70s. While other musicians drifted across the airwaves with the flicker of public taste, the *Archies* ran on TV every Saturday morning from 1968 to 1978. The effect was profound. The Archies molded the taste of a whole generation of pre-teens before their runny little brains had a chance to gel. Not only did it infect these kids with the pure, viral distillate of Pop, it taught them to presume instant gratification as their birthright: Glam, Disco, Cocaine, Inflation, Rapacious Sexual Indiscretion, and Flaky Enlightenment followed inevitably.

Ron Dante by Bill Pitzonka

Billboard's #1 single of 1969 was "Sugar, Sugar"—the biggest hit by cartoon popsters the Archies. That September, as "Sugar, Sugar" was descending from its four-week stay in the pole position, "Tracy" by the Cuff Links was ascending into the Top 10. But most people—even radio programmers—didn't know that both tracks featured the lead vocals of superstar session singer Ron Dante.

As Ron himself puts it, he literally "fell out of a tree and into a career." He was born Carmine Granito on August 22, 1945, and when he was 11, he broke his wrist while playing Tarzan among the treetops near his Staten Island home. His doctor recommended that he take up a musical instrument as therapy to repair the still-growing bone, and he soon became a proficient guitarist, lying about his age to play gigs throughout the tri-state area. He had also acquired a new moniker, appropriating the first name of "the best guitarist in Staten Island" Ronnie Anderson (from his first band the Persuaders) and Dante from the Spencer Tracy film, "Dante's Inferno."

His first studio experience came in 1959 when "I got to sit in on the Elegants' recording session of their followup to 'Little Star'," he remembers. "The bass singer worked for my dad and they sang at my grade school graduation party." Within a few years, Ron was regularly venturing into New York City to make the rounds of music industry meccas 1650 Broadway and the Brill Building (1619 Broadway). "I'd take the elevator to the top floor and walk down, stopping at every publisher, every manager, and play my songs and sing for them. Most of them threw me out."

Ron was eventually signed up by former child star and 1650 Broadway denizen Bobby Breen who also managed comedian Dick Shawn. One day, Breen's secretary took Ron down to Aldon Music, where Ron auditioned for staff songwriters Charlie Koppleman and Don Rubin. He wound up performing for the whole office including Aldon president Don Kirshner, who signed Ron to sing demos. Before long, Kirshner was encouraging Ron to write his own material.

After honing his writing and studio skills at Aldon, Ron set off on his own again. Soon he was offered a deal with TM Music, a music-publishing outfit that had just been purchased by Bobby Darin—"a real supportive environment," he recalls. "One of my biggest thrills was getting to see Bobby Darin perform live at the Copacabana."

In 1964, Ron recorded one of his earliest solo efforts: the novelty single "Don't Stand Up In A Canoe," penned and produced by Paul Vance and Lee Pockriss. Soon thereafter, Vance and Pockriss recruited him, along with Tommy Wynn and Vance's nephew Danny Jordan, to record a parody of "Leader of the Pack." The trio duly christened the Detergents for "Leader of the Laundromat," which gave Ron his first *Billboard* chart appearance, hitting #19 in January 1965. It also marked Ron's first full-scale road tour when the Detergents crisscrossed the country as part of Dick Clark's Caravan of Stars. Ron recollects that "I got to perform with the Rolling Stones, Freddie & The Dreamers, Herman's Hermits, Little Anthony & The Imperials, Little Richard, the Animals, every big group in the '60s I toured and sang on the same bill with." He admits that it was an incredible experience, but regrets that he "slept through most of it because I was exhausted. I was always sleeping on the bus." Despite the incessant touring, the Detergents were washed up a few singles later.

In 1966, Ron signed on to write and produce acts for Greenlight Music, headed by Bob Feldman. Feldman and partners Richard Gotterher and Jerry Goldstein had written and produced the Angels' huge hit "My Boyfriend's Back" and recorded as the faux Australian trio the Strangeloves ("I Want Candy"). At Greenlight, Ron first hooked up with his longtime writing partner Gene Allan. Together they wrote one of the first-ever rock musicals, *Billy Budd* (based on the Herman Melville novel) which ran at New York's

Billy Rose Theatre in 1967. That same year, Ron added motion pictures to his résumé when he sang the theme for the Doris Day western, *The Ballad of Josie.*

In addition to writing and producing, Ron was still doing loads of session work and commercials. His friend Ron Frangipane had been hired to arrange the music for Don Kirshner's new project, the Archies. Frangipane encouraged him to attend the vocal auditions, "so I went in along with a couple of other people that day to the RCA Studios and auditioned." The producer turned out to be Jeff Barry, who Ron had known "off and on through the years—I used to sing backgrounds on his sessions. Jeff had me go into the studio and sing to a track, and do different voices on the track. A high voice, a low voice, a breathy voice, a loud voice, an accent." Recalling the audition, Jeff Barry said, "I do remember when I heard his voice, I could picture Archie." The next day Jeff and Don called Ron with the verdict that he'd do the voices for the records and filler material for the TV show.

The Archies turned into an Aldon reunion when Toni Wine (who had penned "Groovy Kind Of Love" at the tender age of 16) was hired to do the girls' voices. As she recalls, "Ronnie and I have always blended incredibly together. Ronnie and I used to do demos together constantly. I think that was part of the strategy, too, because we really do sound great together."

Starting in the fall of 1968, Ron could be heard singing on the Archies' Saturday morning cartoon series, and the self-titled debut album came out in October. "We had the party for the launch of the first album at Madison Square Garden Felt Forum, the basketball court, and I and a number of local DJs played against [future Kirshner labelmates (!)] the Harlem Globetrotters. I was the center! We lost by a thousand but nobody cared. They kept playing the album over the sound system, and I remember being so proud." By December, the first Archies single "Bang Shang-A-Lang" hit a respectable #22 in *Billboard.*

Ron Dante

Soon thereafter, Vance and Pockriss renewed their association with the former Detergent. "They called on me to do a whole bunch of things," Ron remembers. "I had just finished the Archies, so I was doing a lot of ghost groups." He was juggling up to five or six recording sessions a day, but found time (often between sessions) to record for Vance and Pockriss. More often than not, Ron never knew what group name or record label a song would have until the records were pressed. Among the aliases were Abraham & Strauss ("Lay A Little Love On Me" on United Artists), Two Dollar Question ("Aunt Matilda's Double Yummy Blow Your Mind Brownies" on the MGM subsidiary Intrepid)—and the Cuff Links ("Tracy").

While most of the other projects disappeared without a trace, "Tracy" became a huge worldwide hit—just as the Archies were topping the singles lists around the world with "Sugar, Sugar." At the same time, a third single featuring Ron's lead vocal, "Free" (produced by John Walsh and credited to the Pearly Gate) was also bubbling under *Billboard's* Hot 100. "I was cookin'," Ron beams. "And there were two or three other records being played that were also me that weren't charting. So that was a hell of a ghost group year. I did records I didn't remember for years."

After "Sugar, Sugar" sold millions, Toni Wine quit the Archies camp. "She wanted more than she got—and she should have gotten more," Ron relates. "And I must say, we missed her. It was never the same. Toni's the best." In a calculated attempt to keep Ron a happy Archies camper, Kirshner proffered a solo album deal, which effectively precluded Ron from taking on outside session work. Ron had already completed the *Tracy* album for Vance and Pockriss, but informed them that he couldn't do any further Cuff Links sessions—much to Vance's consternation. In retaliation, Vance threatened to hold back Ron's Cuff Links earnings until Ron stormed into Vance's office for a bout of Wrestling for Royalties. Vance paid up, but erased Ron's lead vocals from the master of "Run Sally Run," an extra Cuff Links track already in

Toni Wine by David Smay

Listen to that voice soar, turning a single line into an unforgettable pop epiphany: "I'm gonna make your life so sweet." Can you imagine a music scene where a child prodigy can wander away from her classical piano studies at Juilliard, stroll into 1650 Broadway and start selling hit songs? That was New York in the early '60s, which produced a seemingly endless stream of Nice Jewish Girl Pop Geniuses. That's the story of Toni Wine, "the female demo singer of the '60s," hit songwriter, Queen of Bubblegum.

As a teenager, Toni fell in with Don Kirshner's Aldon Music and with Phil Spector. She formed a partnership with Carol Bayer to write "A Groovy Kind of Love," which became an international smash for the Mindbenders. Toni contributed to the tag end of the Girl Group and Girl Singer era, co-writing "You Came, You Saw, You Conquered" for the Ronettes, "Off and Running" (Lesley Gore), "Now That You're My Baby" (Dusty Springfield), "Only to Other People" (the Cookies), and a handful of singles under her own name, like "A Girl Is Not A Girl." She gave Phil Spector one of his last hits of the '60s, co-writing "Black Pearl" for Sonny Charles.

In the late '60s, Don Kirshner recruited Toni for the Archies. To the distress of pop fans ever after, Toni's tenure with The Archies was sadly brief. She appears on a few tracks on *Everything's Archie* (most importantly, of course, on "Sugar, Sugar"). But she's all over the *Jingle Jangle* album, swapping leads with Ron on the title track, swooping out from the back-up vocals, sweetening the harmonies, tossing off the "hey hey hey" on "Nursery Rhyme."

Toni left the Archies in a monetary dispute after the worldwide success of "Sugar, Sugar." At the time, Toni had more impressive writing credentials than anybody associated with the project excepting Jeff Barry. Despite this, Toni was frozen out of participation as a

the can for a second album. The lead vocal chores for that group's second album were split between Joe Cord (who had been hired to front the group for personal appearances) and Rupert Holmes (who was doing the bulk of the group's arrangements).

While continuing his Archies commitments, Ron set to work on his solo album, *Ron Dante Brings You Up*, with Jeff Barry at the helm. Ron scored his only solo chart single with the title track, "Let Me Bring You Up," which bubbled under at #102 in August 1970. He even set off on a mini-tour in support of the album. "I went out, I did a ton of TV shows including Dick Clark. And actually, two weeks I spent with David Cassidy. We were hosting a series of TV shows together. He was very hot at the time, so I got to meet and work with him. I actually showed him the ropes." While Ron was on tour, frequent Archies songsmith Ritchie Adams filled in as lead vocalist for one single, "Love is Living in You." Unfortunately, the touring didn't pump up sales of Ron's album. Soon, Ron was back in the studio, and together he and Ritchie took over the Archies' production duties. When Ron wasn't offered a second solo album, he relegated the much more mature "Strangers in the Morning"—which he had co-written with Howard Greenfield—to the B-side of the final Archies single, "Plumb Crazy."

After the Archies ran their course, Pearly Gate producer John Walsh landed a staff position at Scepter Records and signed Ron to the label. Ron released one sterling solo single, "That's What Life Is About" (written by Toni Wine), and a cover of "Chirpy Chirpy Cheep Cheep" (credited to the California Gold Rush) before Scepter declared bankruptcy in 1972. He also returned to the comic-book front for a one-off concept album on Buddah, *Spiderman* by the Webspinners.

At the same time, "I put myself into commercials and I stayed with it," he says. "I sang for everything but feminine hygiene deodorants. I must've done a thousand commercials in those years. Four or five a day: backgrounds, leads. I sang for McDonald's, PepsiCo, anything you can think of, every kind of car made. I was singing for suntan lotions, I was the

Beach Boys in New York. Any time they needed a Beach Boys sound, a falsetto, they called me to do the commercial."

It was during those years that Ron hooked up with Barry Manilow. "We were doing a commercial for Tomboy, a soft drink—Barry and I and Melissa Manchester and Valerie Simpson. Afterward, Barry asked me to listen to some of his songs." They put together a demo of Barry's songs that caught the attention of Bell Records. Both Barry and Ron were signed as solo artists in 1973, and together they produced their own recordings and singles for female labelmates Andrea Marchovecchi and model-cum-actress Sally Kellerman [!]. The following year, Clive Davis took over the Bell presidency—just as Ron's first single for the label, "Don't Call It Love," was released under the pseudonym Bo Cooper. "He loved the record," Ron remembers. "He put a full page ad in *Billboard* saying 'Brand-new artist, never heard from before, Bo Cooper.' Nobody could even recognize me in long hair and a moustache." Ron reverted to his real name for "Midnight Show" which was released concurrently with Barry Manilow's "Mandy."

The Bell roster was decimated when Clive Davis rechristened the label Arista, so Ron signed with RCA for a few singles, including an update of "Sugar, Sugar" arranged by Barry. In the wake of "Mandy"'s chart-topping success, Ron directed his energies toward co-producing Barry's recordings, which kept him busy for the rest of the decade. Ron was approached with offers to produce other acts, but only worked with women like Cher and Irene Cara, "because producing other male acts would be like working with the competition," he explains.

During that time, his career took a literary turn. "I became the publisher of *The Paris Review* around 1977 and 1978. George Plimpton was my next door neighbor when I lived on East 72nd Street in Manhattan. We had been friends for many years when he told me he needed someone to support the *Review*, so I became the publisher after Aga Khan stopped." He also became a theatrical producer, backing the Broadway show *Ain't Misbehavin'*. "The director Richard Maltby said, 'Why don't we do a dance version of the title theme, "Ain't Misbehavin'?" Ron remembers. "So I got Harold Wheeler who'd just done 'I Will Survive' and 'Superman Disco' and he arranged it for me and did a beautiful job. I took it to

writer/producer. Being a sharp cookie and a longtime veteran of the scene, it must've seemed like a waste of her talents to continue with the Archies when she had no chance to receive royalties on their hits. So Toni didn't sing on the Archies' singles "Who's Your Baby" or "Together We Two"—Donna Marie was brought in to replace her.

Toni then hooked up with Jeff Barry's ex-wife and ex-partner, Ellie Greenwich. They recorded a demo for "Candida" with a lead vocal by a washed-up teen idol turned A&R man, Tony Orlando. (Most accounts have the demo itself released as the single, meaning Toni & Ellie were the original Dawn.) Bell rewarded her by putting out a project titled Dusk (get it?) with Toni singing lead, but it didn't hit.

After that, Toni married legendary Memphis soul producer, Chips Moman. Chips had just moved from Memphis to Atlanta and became the favorite producer of the nascent Outlaw Country movement of the '70s. Suddenly, Toni's credits as a backup singer take on a Country Music Hall of Fame flavor, as she worked with Willie Nelson, Waylon Jennings and sang on Townes Van Zandt's *Flyin' Shoes*.

As with Jackie DeShannon, it's somewhat puzzling that Toni's talent didn't translate into stardom, but she seems content with her legacy and staying behind the scenes. Toni never did like to tour, and now she can settle back in Nashville with Chips and do what she does best, write songs and sing like a dream. ●

Interview with Toni Wine by Bill Pitzonka

Bill Pitzonka: How did you get involved with the Archies?

Toni Wine: Donnie had asked for me. Donnie [Kirshner] and Jeff [Barry] asked for me to be Betty and Veronica.

BP: How did you link up with Don Kirshner originally?

TW: I was signed as a writer at the age of 14 to Screen Gems by Donnie Kirshner when it was Aldon Music. I was the youngest BMI writer ever signed. And so I'd been writing and doing demos—my own demos. And then I started doing some demos for Carole [King] & Gerry [Goffin] and Barry [Mann] & Cynthia [Weil], and Howie [Greenfield] & Neil [Sedaka] and Jack Keller—a lot of people. And my voice they really got to know, and evidently they loved, so they wound up asking me to do those records. Of course at that time, then, I'd gotten a little older. But starting out, I was signed to Donnie as a writer and all of my teen years I had been doing all the writing and the demos, and started singing a lot of things for the other compadres of that whole unit. And we all just hung with each other and helped each other and sang with each other, and we all were just a big huge family in the studio. And at that point, they had requested that I come on board in that situation. It was great, we had a blast.

BP: This was all in New York?

TW: All in New York. See by that time, in '65 or '64, I had already had "Groovy Kind of Love" with the Mindbenders.

BP: How were the Archies sessions with Ron Dante?

TW: The experience really was one-of-a-kind. For every one of us that was in the studio, it was truly magic that was happening. And we knew it when we did it. It was just a fun happy thing that just really felt good. And when I hear it on the radio today, it still feels good. It was all rhythm. Everything was based on rhythm and feel and smiling. It was just one of those feel-good kind of things. ⦿

my friend Ron Alexenburg and he had a new label, Infinity." Alexenberg commissioned an album, and Ron dubbed the completed project Dante's Inferno. Promotional copies of the single "Fire Island" were issued to clubs on 12" red vinyl. Infinity didn't last into the '80s, and soon Alexenburg had a new label, Handshake, where Ron recorded his second-ever solo album, *Street Angel*, in 1981—a full decade after his first.

It would be almost two more decades before Ron would release another solo album—*Favorites* in 1999, a collection of covers that have great resonance for him. He moved out to Los Angeles in 1992 "because I'm working on soundtracks for movies now, and TV shows, cable things." As the millennium approached, Ron even performed at several festivals as the Archies and is preparing Kirshner-era material for CD reissue. Looking back on his career and where he is now, Ron admits "I cannot be happier."

Looking for the Beagles by Steve Mandich

An obvious, inevitable attempt to ride the Beatles' coattails, the *Beagles* were a pair of mid-'60s rock 'n' roll pooches, Stringer and Tubby, who starred in their own eponymously-titled Saturday afternoon cartoon series. Certainly the satirical moniker was their biggest selling point, yet the *Beagles* parodied the Fab Four in name only, as their voices and actions were more akin to the comedy team of Martin and Lewis. As for content, the musical mutts rocked through various misadventures, often winding up in the doghouse.

The first of their 36 episodes debuted on CBS on September 10, 1966. The series was the final cartoon produced by Total Television, creators of a number of '60s animal-based cartoon shows, including *King Leonardo and his Short Subjects* (about the leonine monarch of Bongoland), *Go-Go Gophers* (involving a pair of rodents in the Old West), *Tennessee Tuxedo* (concerning a penguin), and the cult superhero *Underdog*. Unfortunately, all of the *Beagles'* original storyboards and master negatives were lost when the series' editor passed away, along with the most of the rest of TTV's editing materials.

About the *Beagles'* only legacy is a tie-in soundtrack album, *Here Come the Beagles* (Harmony, 1967). The hounds harmonize through ten folksy/garage numbers penned by a handful of unknowns (credited enigmatically to W. Biggers, T. Covington, J. Harris and C. Stover), kicking off with the killer theme song "Looking for the Beagles." Stringer and Tubby sing about themselves in the third person (er, *canine*) in this, the record's only self-referential tune, its hangdog lyrics betraying the pups' esteem issues:

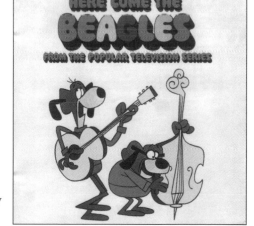

> Looking for the Beagles/Looking high and low
> High is for the eagles/Low is where the Beagles go
> Looking for the Beagles/Not where rich men soar
> Rich is for the regals/Woe is all the Beagles know

However, the refrain puts forth their ambitious mission statement:

> Right now to bust a bubble to wherever
>   there's some trouble
> That's where the Beagles go!

The opening riff is so catchy that it's used again on the very next track, "Sharing Wishes," introducing a tale about washing dishes with some girl (a bitch?). Other cuts feature drums and fifes ("I'd Join the Foreign Legion"), some mid-tempo melodies ("Be the Captain," "I Wanna Capture You," and "You Satisfy"), and a couple of forgettable ballads ("What More Can I Do" and "Thanks to the Man on the Moon"), all with sax, organ, or flute solos.

Infantile, bubblegumesque lyrics run through the album's hardest rocking song, "Humpty Dumpty." Perhaps it is intended to be the tune most identifiable by the kiddies, drawing inspiration from Mother Goose's "The Boy in Blue," "The Old Woman in the Shoe," and of course, Mr. Dumpty. The bridge:

> You got me raving over you/Raving all the time
> Like a child alone when his mama's gone/I call for
>   you in nursery rhyme

The record's best cut, "Indian Love Dance," blasts out a rabid organ solo (sounding as though it was later lifted by the Raiders on "Indian Reservation") and an insistent, on-the-warpath riff, which spars with some stereotypical Native American imagery:

> Indian love dance will let you stay free / Brings you
>   romance from any teepee
> Heat sends up signals like smoke from a fire / Someone
>   receives them and shares your desire
> No matter what you do / It's Indian voodoo

CBS cancelled *The Beagles* after just one season, although ABC broadcast it in reruns for another. The network already had *The Beatles* cartoon series in their Saturday lineup, on the air since 1965 and still going strong, thus offering *two* faunal cartoon rock band shows for a single season. Then, in September 1968, ABC had the doggie duo put to sleep.

In the meantime, the long-out-of-print LP has resurfaced in bootleg form, recently paired on the same CD as *We're the Banana Splits*. Otherwise, don't bother looking for *The Beagles* on the Cartoon Network, or anywhere else.

Thanks to Mark Hill and David Smay for their assistance.

Boyce & Hart by Kim Cooper

Rock star? Feh! What a fifth-rate ambition. *Songwriters* have the right idea. Songwriters simply don't become *stars* in the unmanageable sense of the word. Successful writers seem to glean most of the benefits of celebrity while avoiding the trauma.

Two of the grooviest songwriters to ever Chelsea-boot it down a record company hallway were Tommy Boyce and Bobby Hart. These lean and fetching dynamos apparently spent the last half of the '60s churning out timeless pop classics in spare moments between nuzzling babes and racing their matching XKEs. They had it all: commercial and artistic success, genre-hopping status as writers-producers-performers, an apparently seamless creative union, and drool-worthy mod wardrobes, heavy on the turtlenecks. As writers, no one could touch their classic blend of youthful energy and structural smarts. The titles alone conjure up effervescent distillations of a teenage place: "(I'm Not Your) Stepping Stone," "Last Train to Clarksville," "Valleri," "She," "I Wonder What She's Doing Tonite." Can the Boyce & Hart experience have been anything less than a gas?

Of course one can't understand just how great it was without considering Sunshine Park, Boyce's incredible Hollywood mansion. "[It] had strobe lights in the front room, disappearing walls, Japanese beds, films projected onto the walls 24 hours a day, and a sauna that was turned on for 11 months straight, in case anyone ever wanted to use it. You could walk out of 180° heat onto a diving board and 95° scented water; the whole house was submerged in a London fog all year round."

By 1967, the partners were beginning to look and dress alike, and to mimic each other's body language. This hardly mattered, since the little girls loved them equally. But it is possible to tell them apart: that's Bobby at the piano, with the sexy cleft in his chin; Tommy's smaller, with soulful, yet mischievous eyes. Dreamy Tommy blew his brains out at the end of 1994, a horror which must inevitably color these observations.

But in the time frame we're exploring, Tommy's pain was years away. Boyce and Hart were Hollywood's greatest writing team, a West Coast Goffin-King with no marriage to hobble their lyrical tomcatting. Their on-off relationship with the Monkees had spawned a series of smash singles and a degree of industry pull that allowed the pair, who had previously failed to attract much attention to their drippy solo tunes, to cash in on the Monkees connection with tours and albums, their work aimed squarely at the Monkees' pubescent following. *Or was it?*

I trust you'll forgive me if I don't delineate every twisting curve of the history that brought Boyce and Hart into the studio to create the Monkees' sound, their subsequent firing and rehiring, Mike Nesmith's hat, the gruesome specter of Don Kirshner. What matters is that A&M, that incredible only-in-Hollywood label (then featuring the Tijuana Brass, Baja Marimba Band, Chris Montez, We Five, Claudine Longet, and . . . *Phil Ochs?*) permitted Boyce and Hart to record three albums in quick succession in 1967 and '68. These strange and wonderful platters, a bizarre combination of perfect pop singles, blatant sonic plagiarism, and jaw-dropping experimentation, are at least as worthy of reissue and reassessment as, say, Nancy Sinatra's oeuvre.

If the Monkees were desperately searching for mere creative recognition amidst the flurry of the idol-making machine, Boyce and Hart longed to be spoken of in the same breath as "genius" contemporaries like Brian Wilson, Arthur Lee, and Phil Spector. They knew they were brilliant, that it was only an accident of fate that had rendered them hugely successful on the kiddie circuit.

Their own records weren't going to be the sort of calculating quickies that somebody in their position might be expected, even forgiven, for making. Instead, they would be reflections of their unique perspective, as deep, as tweaked, as touching as that of any of the lyrical giants cited above.

That said, *Test Patterns* (A&M SP 4126) is a calculating quickie, basically an innocuous setting in which to place the Monkees-rejected gem "Out and About." Tommy made no bones about coveting the Colgems Kids' fame: "I watched the Monkees from backstage and saw all those little girls go crazy while they played our songs, so I said to Bobby, 'forget being the opening act, here's the deal: all we have to do is write a couple of smashes and within a year we can dash out on stage with a band behind us and have all those kids go crazy for us!'"

Bobby's "Out and About" is one of those magical celebrations of the California myth that, for a variety of reasons, no one ever writes anymore. In their place we have gangsta rap, which for all its charms is unlikely to induce in anyone the giddy joy of:

Things I want I can't afford 'em
Nothing in this house but boredom
I've gotta run outside and see what's happening!
Out and about, where the sun is always shining
Look at all the fun I'm having
Bumping into friends and laughing
What a groovy time we're having.

Okay, so that last line is a little lazy, but with its punchy production and ecstatic arrangement, "Out and About" is a great radio song. The rest of the album has the patented let's-mess-around-and-see-what-we-come-up-with feel, typical of artists sent into the studio with the instructions "Give us a hit; you've got three days." "My Little Chickadee" gives us a taste of T&B's vaudeville roots—just how old *were* these guys, anyway (?) but wouldn't make the New Vaudeville Band nervous. "Girl I'm Out to Get You" is a more successful melange, a hepped-up klezmer track with machine-gun lyrics describing a not-so-casual pick-up in the park: "Come back with me to my flat, it's late and I must feed my cat/On my Chinese mat we sat, commenced to chat of this and that, and then I tried to kiss her tenderlee-ee-ee." In what will prove a recurrent lyrical theme for B&H, there is no resolution of the attempted mating, although we do get to hear the would-be lovers play a duet for piano and violin. The fundamental schizophrenia of Boyce & Hart's recording career is revealed in the closing track, the 4:50 Webbian composition "Life," including the indistinct movements *Sunday Night In Phoenix, Life In Hollywood, Sunrise Through The Meadow,* and *What's It All About.* The song is a deeply misguided stab at the blues, which I need only briefly quote in order to convey its horror: "Life, life, life, what's it all about? No matter how hard I try, I just can't figure it out." Fortunately, and by whatever means, all would become clear in time for the next album.

Said record (A&M SP 4143) asks the titular question *I Wonder What She's Doing Tonight?* If Boyce & Hart have anything to do with it, she's in the bathroom right now, attaching that second pair of false eyelashes before she hops in her daddy's car and cruises over to Bobby or Tommy's pad, where a leisurely evening of fine music, conversation, and discreet petting is anticipated.

Wonder is Boyce & Hart's ultimate statement about their place in the universe, in which they fully embrace their peculiar role as (if I may speak in archetypes) the Slightly Older, Frightening, Yet Very Sexy Stranger that every little girl longs for while simultaneously recoiling from. It is this quality that makes their brief status as teenybop idols at once fascinating and disturbing, for in song after song their is that weird lyrical moment, the emotional fillip that says, "This is no kid singing, baby. Come along with me and you'll be in for one far-out, *grown up* trip!"

In the wonderfully titled "I'm Digging You Digging Me," that older man vibe chimes in with the mawkishly appealing lines, "Let's sit and talk about each others' feelings tonight / I think that something on your mind has got you uptight."

But you mustn't think that B & H only had one thing on their minds. Sure, girls seem to have occupied 98.25% of their waking thoughts, but that other 1.75% was chock-full of political awareness, as evinced by the glorious "Population." Think of a word that rhymes with "population." Now another. And another. Chances are that all the words you thought of are included in this frantic incantation, which is equal parts high-art protest and goofball parody. At one point the boys break into a credible Allen Sherman "Hello muddah hello faddah" routine, but they back it up with a far-flying denunciation of all the irritation of their post-war generation. "What's your destination, civilization, assassination, explanation, fabrication, et cetera, et cetera, et cetera." It's no accident this puppy was fused in a medley with the yearning "I Wanna Be Free," a song which in this context becomes surprisingly poignant.

The title track is "I Wonder Who's Kissing Her Now?" updated for the free love generation, and another perfect fast-car radio confection, in which innocence and impotence blend to form a male voice of startling nakedness:

> We were close but we should have been closer
> And it's making me feel so sad
> But I tell myself I didn't lose her
> 'Cause you can't lose a friend you never had

And truly, she never was his friend, as shown by her post-breakup cruelty. Worse still, the singer is being punished, nay, tortured, for behaving like a gentleman and withholding those convenient words of love that would spell "n-o-o-k-i-e" to a less principled man: "If I told her that I loved her she would have stayed till who knows when / But I guess she couldn't understand it when I said 'I wanna be your friend.'" It is a sad picture, the side of playboy life we rarely see. But you know, even Hef himself must have cried, sometimes, all alone in that big round bed. Well, maybe once.

Before you find yourself feeling too sorry for our hairy-chested pals, they remind you that when life is good it is very very good. Side one closes out with a track so tacky and joyously unbelievable that it alone would justify this survey. "Two for the Price of One" appears to be a partially rewritten soul tune (credited to Watson-Williams-Mundy, a rare non-original from two guys who knew the meaning of a royalty check), the subject of which is: *Boyce & Hart!* The boys trade off vocals to tell each other's story, inspiring shocked fascination in everyone for whom I've played it. Over a funky beat, our heroes expound:

> **BH:** Lemme tell you about Tommy Boyce, he's a gangster of love—
> **TB:** Ah, don't tell 'em that, Bobby!
> **BH:** Wanted by the girls all over the world for the crazy things he does—
> **TB:** I'll never get outta trouble!
> **BH:** Be public enemy #1 if making love is a crime / He drives a 1967 XKE, he's a legend in his own time!
> **TB:** Now let me tell you about my man Mr. Bobby Hart, he's a son of a gun—
> **BH:** Don't tell everybody that!

TB: When it comes down to messing up those little cutie-pies' minds ha ha! —
I ain't the only one

BH: My reputation!

TB: He'll swoop down on one of those little miniskirt-wearers / Before she understands it / Swish Shazam a puff of Jaguar smoke, he's an old love bandit!

BH: Now girls all over the world / Gather round when Tommy Boyce is on the scene /
Flowered shirt, a string of beads around his neck / He's looking pretty clean—

TB: Now wait a minute! All you girls who love Bobby Hart, they just love him to
death / All he has to do is act like he's gonna call somebody's name / They can't
control themselves!

In unison: So all you pretty girls better come down to the show tonight, have a lot
of fun, and get *two* for the price of *one*!!!

You are getting a couple of pretty deep characters, even if their public personae blend to the point that it's hard to tell whether a given trait originates in Tommy or in Bobby. The suavo archetype is further explored in "P.O. Box 9847" (from the third album). Here, Bob Rafelson's offhand suggestion that they write a song about personal ads results in a striking portrait-de-Lothario:

> Quiet, sincere gentleman, well-mannered and mature
> Fond of music and the arts and love the theater
> Educated, sensitive, a traveler of the world
> Wants to meet an eligible young girl!

The song, like so many others in their oeuvre, trails off into hopelessness and disconnection (represented by the sound of the paper ripped from the typewriter and crumpled).

Say that our nameless "eligible young girl" from the song above somehow found herself out on a date with the Monkees' Davy Jones. It would surely be a blissfully innocent experience, punctuated by quiet talk and laughter, the feeding of ducks with stale bread, perhaps a chaste kiss upon the cheek.

But Tommy and Bobby seem more likely to pick their frail up right off the Strip, or from among the taut hordes of knowing, hungry chicks who stand around backstage, or wait by the studio gates. While you might attract any given Monkee with a costume of hip-hugger jeans and a fun op-art blouse, accented by a nice smile and not too much make-up, to catch the Boyce-Hart eye you'll have to show a lot more skin and imagination. Most likely the little girls who bought Boyce & Hart albums were more at home in the former persona, but after listening to songs like "Strawberry Girl" (bubblegum stripped of even the pretense of innocence) and catching our boys' shirtless guest appearance on *Bewitched*, it seems inevitable that they would start aching for the day they would turn a slinky sixteen.

I like to imagine that, on some ethereal Los Angeles plane 30-odd years ago, these two fantasies might have met and, in their fashion, coupled. On one hand, the dreams of Boyce & Hart, aging tunesmiths remaking themselves as psychedelicized Casanovas. On the other, the half-formed visions of suburban nine-year-olds, just beginning to see themselves as erotic creatures in the world. I think they would have liked each other. But out of respect for these spirits' privacy, it seems best to draw a veil over the scene, even in conjecture.

The music of Boyce & Hart is an enduring delight. It has a subtlety of vision not often found in the bubblegum genre (to which it only peripherally belongs). All the energy and melody of the Monkees' best material is fused here with a stronger sense of personality, and a sly wit. To listen is to tap into a non-existent (yet hyperreal) 1960s that blend all your favorite parts of spy films, sleazy soft-core hippie exposés, slick menswear ads, fun furniture, bearskin rugs, convertibles, coffee shops, nightclubs, kissing, expensive stereos and exaggerated sex roles. It's also, quite unrelated to such pleasant fancies, simply great music. The golden age of pop (and of bachelorhood) may be gone, but blessedly, perfect pop singles, and fantasies, never change.

Captain Groovy and His Bubblegum Army
Are Coming to Take You Away by Bill Pitzonka

Early in 1969, a corporate summit occurred between limited-cel animation kingpins Hanna-Barbera and bubblegum cottage industrialists Kasenetz-Katz. Though seemingly a marriage made in marketing heaven, negotiations ultimately broke down between the two notoriously control-conscious purveyors of prepubescent product, but not before one semi-official act of business could be completed. Ritchie Cordell, who had recently joined the stable of Kasenetz-Katz Associates after a string of huge hits with Tommy James & the Shondells, was commissioned to create the theme for *Captain Groovy And His Bubblegum Army*. Cordell co-wrote the song with "1, 2, 3 Red Light" tunesmith Sal Trimachi, based on Kasenetz & Katz's original concept. Cordell recalls that the lead vocal on the single was "Bobby Bloom sped up [on tape]," eerily replicating the nasal vocal stylings of Joey Levine, who had recently parted company with Kasenetz & Katz to found his own Earth and L&R labels with Artie Resnick. In the way that all things come full circle, L&R scored their biggest hit in 1970 with Bobby Bloom's "Montego Bay."

Kasenetz & Katz, meanwhile, had been given their own Super K imprint through Buddah Records. As one of their very first releases, they issued the rather dark *Captain Groovy* theme song ("Captain Groovy and his Bubblegum Army are coming to take you away," as the lyric so ominously intoned). Despite the fact that the cartoon series never made it past the drawing board, a poster of the actual characters exists somewhere in the Super K offices. Without the series, the sole offering under the Captain Groovy banner managed to bubble under the *Billboard* Hot 100 for a few weeks, peaking at #127.

The Cowsills by Brian Doherty

The Cowsills don't like being called "bubblegum." This might be why Bob Cowsill, after some initial encouraging responses to my overtures, eventually ceased returning phone calls about being interviewed for this book. Defining bubblegum is a chewy problem this whole book grapples with, but a band whose biggest hits were cheery, eminently hummable confections written by forces outside the band ("Indian Lake," "Hair," "The Rain, the Park, and Other Things") surely qualifies. The Cowsills—while as organically generated as any '60s pop band from a burning desire to emulate the Beatles—screamed "cornball" with

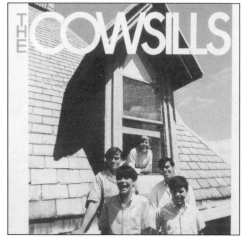

their mom-and-the-kids family routine. (Yes, they really were a family named Cowsill.) The Cowsills coulda been even bigger contenders—or at least more frequent sights on depressing "where are they now?" nostalgia programs: they were the inspiration for *The Partridge Family* show, but turned down a chance to actually act in it because they wanted their real mom to play mom; the producers wanted Shirley Jones instead. However, any Cowsill who wants to cavil can point—and proudly!—to the songs on their LPs, particularly the peculiar masterworks *Captain Sad and the Ship of Fools* and *IIxII*. These self-penned songs portray the dark, death-obsessed psyches of people forced too often to focus only on the sweetly sunny side of life.

In there swinging with the Left Banke in terms of skillful, complicated vocal/horn/string/obscure keyboard arrangements—at least on *Captain Sad* and the largely band-written but less gonzo *We Can Fly*—the Cowsills stripped down to more purely rock/folk arrangements on their darkly obsessive 1970 masterwork *IIxII*, an album awash in apocalyptic imagery and imprecations on the human race, with a strong Biblical background. After the past two years trying to

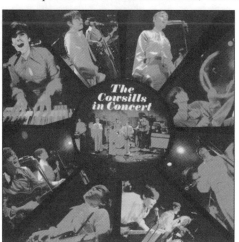

understand my own queer attraction to this LP (found for $3.00 at Record Surplus in West L.A.—the clerk was piqued indeed that it had been priced so low, grumbling "where'd you find this?" and muttering darkly of the pricer's foolishness), I'm almost glad I didn't get to ask its producer Bob Cowsill what they were up to with this record—better to let my own imagination run wild. Coincidentally, Bob stopped returning messages right after I left one on his voice mail while listening to *IIxII*— and telling him how much I loved it.

Captain Sad, with only a few band-written tracks, contains intriguing hints of the weird obsessiveness that would mark its successor LP. The title track is a character study of a fraudulent '60s guru type, followed up by "Make the Music Flow," on the surface a strange encouragement to keep one's sitar properly tuned, which I suspect has some metaphorical meaning I'm too dense to suss out. *IIxII* is fully marinated in the dark side of their times. Their top 10 hit "Indian Lake" was all "fun in the summer sun," but what to make of the title track—a jaunty, happy tune (written by Bill Cowsill, for some reason under the pseudonym David Ray) in which the singer assures the Lord that he's ready to get on some sort of modern day ark? Left to dark implications is the destruction of all the rest of life on Earth that the ark story signifies. As side one progresses, in "Signs" the Cowsills remind us that "half a million died on the road last year" in a rather incoherent song that seems to be, on one level, a public-service announcement about paying proper heed to road signs. At the end of side one, the last words we hear are "You may find a hostile outer space / If you try to spread the human race."

On side two, a stunningly lovely take on CSN-style hippie harmonizing (but a better song than those grizzled fools ever managed) called "Don't Look Back," at first merely melancholically suggestive of a love coming to an end, suddenly advises, "Gather all the things you cherish / Please do something as you perish." Slightly shivery even out of context, but coming as it does on the heels of a cover that seems more reflec-

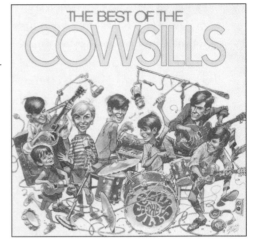

tive of the Cowsills real concerns than "Hair," the Revelations horror show "The Prophecy of Daniel and John the Divine," it's positively frightening. "Prophecy" tells of the coming of the antichrist as warned in biblical prophecy, with a young ambisexual voice in the middle eight intoning eerily that "finally one day she was cast back into the sea from where she came so that she would never torment . . . man . . . *again!*" Then the whole family bursts out gleefully with: "It's been written down in Revelation / Daniel and John explanation / When you read you will find / It's a sign of warning for mankind!" This song was actually released by MGM as a single, and the Cowsills performed it on *The Tonight Show.*

IIxII's bizarre obsessions with death and judgment are a warning against letting one's cover-song spouting automatons have free rein as writers, and gives some clue as to why most bubblegum artistes were never given such liberty. (Alas, the easiest to find, and worst, Cowsills album is *In Concert* featuring nothing but familiar pop covers like "Monday Monday,"

"Please Mr. Postman," and "Good Vibrations.") Bob Cowsill, while leading a modern Cowsills revival with a set of songs he and his wife wrote on the CD *Global*, has also returned to those *In Concert* roots. Every Saturday night on Ventura Boulevard in the San Fernando Valley he can be found on a stage in the corner of Pickwick's Pub, belting out Beatles tunes and a smattering of other classic oldies favorites on an acoustic guitar, and bantering with the audience of regulars. On the night in August I made the pilgrimage to see him, his daughter was in the crowd, gently jabbing at Bob for throwing away a personally signed letter from John Lennon complimenting his guitar playing. "Do you know what you could get for that on eBay?" she chided. I didn't have the nerve to shout out for "The Prophecy of St. Daniel and John the Divine" ("six is the number . . . six is the number. . . . of a maaaaan! Six! Six! Six!").

Crazy Elephant by Bill Pitzonka

"There is no Crazy Elephant," insists writer-producer Ritchie Cordell. "That was just Bob Spencer." Robert Spencer was a member of the Cadillacs, who recorded the rock 'n' roll classic "Speedo," a #14 hit from 1955. In the years that followed, Spencer kept active in the industry, often penning songs and selling them off without just compensation, according to Cordell. In 1969, Spencer linked up with Kasenetz & Katz just as their Super K bubblegum machine was churning out the hits full-throttle.

Kasenetz & Katz hooked him up with Cordell and Joey Levine, who together had penned the soulful "Gimme Gimme Good Lovin'." The searing single, featuring Spencer's scorching lead vocal and an obvious background vocal assist by Levine, was submitted to Buddah Records, the New York-based label with whom Kasenetz & Katz had been so continually successful. "We played it for [Buddah General Manager] Neil Bogart," the Super K boys recall, "but he said, 'No, I don't hear it.'" Undeterred, they walked Crazy Elephant over to Larry Uttal at neighboring Bell Records, who snapped it up. By May 1969, "Gimme Gimme Good Lovin'" hit #12 in *Billboard*. Its stateside success prompted a British release, where it also peaked at #12.

Kasenetz & Katz recruited a five-piece band of college-age youths to support the single on the road, pose for pictures, and fill out the inevitable album. According to the credits on that sole self-titled LP, the lucky winners of this strange sweepstakes were Larry Laufer (leader, keyboards and vocals), Ronnie Bretone (bass), Bob Avery (drums), Kenny Cohen (flute, sax, and vocals) and Hal King (vocals). The whole process was standard operating procedure for bubblegummeisters Kasenetz and Katz. More often than not, according to Cordell, they would "send *five* bands [with the same name] out on the road. They'd stick them in a room with the album and have them learn all the songs."

"Gimme Gimme Good Lovin'" was the only Crazy Elephant record for Cordell and Levine. When the Spencer-soundalike follow-ups "Sunshine, Red Wine" and "Gimme Some More" failed to click, Kasenetz & Katz took Crazy Elephant in a new direction—overseas to London. In 1970, they brought in future 10cc members Kevin Godley, Lol Creme, and Graham Gouldman to take over the writing and production duties. Despite the ambitious single "(There Ain't No) Umbopo" (which the trio had recorded in an alternate version for Pye UK as Doctor Father), Crazy Elephant had effectively run its course, and was quietly retired.

Gimme, Gimme, Good Lovin' by Joey Levine/Ritchie Cordell)
From Atlanta, Georgia to the Gulf Stream water
To Cal-i-for-ni-a I'm gonna spend my life both night and day
Say gimme, gimme good lovin' every night (Hey you know it's alright child)
Gimme, gimme good lovin' make it alright. Ha, ha, ha, ha, ha

To the girls in Frisco, To the girls in New York
To the girls in Tex-i-can you gotta understand
That baby I'm your man

I say gimme, gimme good lovin' every night
(Yeh you know it's alright now now)
Gimme, gimme good lovin' make it alright
Ha, ha, ha, ha, ha

I say gimme, gimme good lovin' every night
(Yeah you know it's alright now now) . . .

The Cuff Links and Street People by Bill Pitzonka

The Cuff Links exemplify the second tier of bubblegum, eking out a hit or two and evaporating after the radio play dies. But the Cuff Links' story also clarifies the common, yet little understood, process of ghost bands and how singers like Ron Dante, Tony Burrows and Joey Levine could chart simultaneously with different bands. Belying the complaint that bubblegum amounts to nothing but corporate product, here you've got an instance that's as D.I.Y. as anything out of Olympia. In this case, the Cuff Links are little more than an independent songwriting team, a favor from Ron Dante and a very few hours of studio time . . . out of which comes one hit, two groups and several careers.

According to the Decca Records publicity department, the Cuff Links were discovered by Paul Vance and Lee Pockriss, authors of such diverse pop perennials as "Catch A Falling Star" and "Itsy-Bitsy Teeny-Weeny Yellow Polka-Dot Bikini." An essential part of the Cuff Links sound was dense layers of vocal counterpoint, but the "group" was a complete fabrication: the voices all belonged to one man—superstar session singer Ron Dante.

Vance and Pockriss had written and produced Dante's first *Billboard* chart hit in 1964, "Leader of the Laundromat" by the Detergents. Dante even spent a year on the road in support of the record before returning to his session work. In 1968, he auditioned for and was chosen to be the lead vocalist for the Archies. Soon thereafter, Paul Vance phoned Ron. "He said, 'I got this great song for you! "Tracy!" You gotta come listen to it!'" Ron remembers. "So they sat me down and Paul sang it with his horrible Brooklyn accent: 'Tracy, when I'm wit' yoo!' I really liked the song when I heard it. I thought it was going to be a big hit.

"Lee Pockriss did a beautiful little arrangement. I added one thing: the break at the top—just before the whole thing starts, there's a shaker—that's my contribution to the instrumental arrangement." Working with Pockriss, Ron did his own vocal arrangements. As was his standard practice, Dante finished his work on "Tracy" in just a few hours. "I put on a lead voice, doubled it a few times, and then put about 16, 18 backgrounds." He never even heard the final mix until it was released as a single. It bounced its way up the *Billboard* Hot 100 quickly, spending two weeks at #9 in October 1969, just as the Archies' "Sugar, Sugar" was descending from its four-week stay at #1.

Dante had promised that if "Tracy" were successful, he'd record an entire Cuff Links album. When Decca came through with the offer, Vance and Pockriss sifted through their catalog for the *Tracy* record. Dante recalls "it was the quickest album I'd ever done. I think I did the entire vocal backgrounds and leads in a day or a day and a half—for the entire album. I remember doing at least four or five songs in one day." To get the LP completed as quickly as possible, Vance and Pockriss hired arranger Rupert Holmes for one of his earliest assignments. Holmes remembers, "Paul Vance was amazed that he got [me] to do charts at $20 a pop. I was amazed at getting paid because I had no idea what I was doing!" Although only credited for string charts, Holmes did the complete arrangements for six songs on *Tracy*, including "When Julie Comes Around," the Cuff Links' second single. In America it just missed the Top 40, peaking at #41 in January 1970. In England, where "Tracy" reached #4, "Julie" got all the way to #10.

As the album was being completed, Vance and Pockriss put together a seven-member Cuff Links comprised of Pat Rizzo (sax and flute), Danny Valentine (drums), Rich Dimino (organ), Bob Gill (trumpet, flugelhorn and flute), Dave Lavender (guitar), Andrew "Junior" Denno (bass), and Joe Cord (lead vocal). Joe Cord sang lead on "Sweet Caroline."

Ron Dante had signed on for only one album. When he called Paul Vance to get his royalties, "He said, 'Oh, they came in, but I'm not giving you the royalties unless you do the next album'," Ron relates.

"And I said, 'I can't! I have a solo album coming out—*Ron Dante Brings You Up*. I'm still doing the Archies, and now I'm exclusive. I can't!' He said, 'Well, no royalties.' So I said, 'I'll be right over.'" Vance paid up (with some forceful persuasion)—but subsequently had Joe Cord record over Ron's lead vocal on "Run Sally Run." It was the last Cuff Links single to hit the Hot 100, limping to #76 in April 1970. Cord sang lead on only a few cuts of the subsequent album (*The Cuff Links*). Most of the tracks featured Rupert Holmes, including a final non-album single, "All Because Of You."

Through an odd bit of circumstance, Holmes would also take on lead vocal duties with Vance's next chartbound studio group, Street People. "Bubblegum was the hottest thing around," Holmes recounts, "so we wrote this song that went 'Hop, skip, jump around/Bubblegum has come to town'." At the session, "Ron ended up arriving after I'd laid down the lead, and he did background vocals, so we have this record with Ron Dante singing backup to me. That's kind of cool." "Bubblegum Has Come To Town" was slated for release on Musicor Records when "Paul heard from [Musicor president] Art Talmadge who's very upset and hysterical because the term 'bubblegum' is now in disrepute. You can continue to *make* bubblegum, but you can't call it what it is. So we had to change the lyric." The completely rewritten "Jennifer Tomkins" ultimately hit #36 in March, 1970. Holmes hypothesizes that the song probably garnered much of its airplay because at 1:58, "you could squeeze it in if you had to go to the news."

Vance and Talmadge were concerned that whatever profits the single had generated would be blown on the recording of a full-length Street People album. "So Paul used lots of cuts that were by other mythical groups that I had been and just said they were all the Street People!" Holmes admits that to fill out the album, "we also took leftover cuts sitting on the shelf of Musicor Records—I just went in the studio one day and put my voice on all these different tracks from different sources." Extracted from the patchwork *Jennifer Tomkins* album, "Thank You Girl" barely scraped onto the chart at #96 in April 1970.

The Cuff Links moniker was revived for one-off singles on Atco ("Bobbi") and Roulette before it was quietly retired. While the members of the "band" soon returned to the lounge circuit from whence they were recruited, the creative forces behind The Cuff Links moved onward and upward. Vance and Pockriss continued churning out memorable pop smashes like "Playground In My Mind" and "Run, Joey, Run." Rupert Holmes scored his own US #1 as an artist in 1979 with "Escape (The Piña Colada Song)" and went on to become a successful Broadway playwright (*The Mystery of Edwin Drood*). Ron Dante continued his recording work as an artist with the Archies and sporadic releases under his own name, as producer (for Irene Cara, Cher, and most of Barry Manilow's biggest hits), and has since branched out into theatrical production.

The DeFranco Family by Robrt L. Pela

It's a breezy April night in Las Vegas. At a 50th birthday bash in a glitzy club on the strip, David Cassidy—the shiniest star in the dubious stratosphere of former teen idols—has just blown out the candles on a giant cake. No Partridge Family fans are in evidence at this party.

Several hundred miles away, another celebration is underway. In a smoky Los Angeles nightclub, hundreds of fans of a different bubblegum family have gathered to rub elbows with the man who, nearly three decades before, was poised to replace Cassidy as America's top teen dream. At 40, Tony DeFranco is a full decade younger than Cassidy and, as lead man of '70s pop phenomenon the DeFranco Family, considerably kinder about his pop past. In Vegas, Cassidy cracks wise to a reporter about the ersatz family who helped him score a half-dozen bubblegum hits in the '70s, then wanders away to pose for photos with the A-list headliners and flashy casino girls who've come to wish him well. In LA, DeFranco and his real-life family are posing for photographers, too—mostly with middle-aged housewives who've come from miles around to tell the former teen idols how much they still love them.

These women want Tony to know that they still have their Official DeFranco Family Fan Club Message Decoder. They want to assure Benny that he was their favorite. They want Marisa to know that "Heartbeat, It's a Lovebeat," the DeFranco record that kicked off the group's short but illustrious career, is still their fave song. "We never forgot you," one portly matron informs Nino DeFranco, who's about to take the stage with his once-famous siblings for the first time in 22 years. "Where the heck have you guys been?"

The answer to that question begins on yet another April evening in 1972. After 13 months of searching, Charles Laufer—owner of *Tiger Beat*, the second-biggest teen magazine in the nation—has finally scored a coup. He's just signed a deal with the kid who's going to make him a million, the kid who's finally going to rid him of that terrible Cassidy boy, whose shiny bangs and toothy grin helped buy Laufer a piece of the show biz pie. This time, though, it's going to be different. There won't be any sharing points with tight-assed Olive Osmond, or with that trampy Gloria Stavers, editor of crappy top-of-the-heap *16* magazine. No more of the pennies-on-the-dollar commissions that David Cassidy's face and Donny Osmond's fan club kit have brought Laufer's way. The pot of gold at the end of the teenybopper rainbow is filled, Laufer knows, with the DeFranco Family.

Twenty-seven years later, Laufer still winces when he thinks of how nearly he missed that pot of gold. "Sharon Lee was my top editor at *Tiger Beat* at that time," he recalls in a 1999 interview. "She was cleaning off her desk one day, and she found these photos and a demo tape. She brought the stuff to me and said, 'Some Canadian guy sent me this stuff a few months ago. I was about to throw it out, but the kids in these photos sure are cute. Maybe you should look at this.'"

Laufer had been searching for some time for a teen idol he could manage and promote in *Tiger Beat*, *FaVe!*, and the several other teen glossies he published. He flew the DeFrancos, who'd been playing gigs as the DeFranco Quintet in their hometown of Welland, Ontario, to Los Angeles for a look-see. He was instantly impressed.

"The kid had a set of pipes on him," Laufer recalls of Tony. "Plus he was cute, and I knew we could do something with the group." Laufer quickly inked an exclusive deal with the DeFrancos, signing them to his just-formed Laufer Entertainment Group and financing a three-song demo that he delivered to 20th Century Records president Russ Regan. Regan liked what he heard, and offered Laufer and the DeFrancos a recording deal.

But long before any records were released, the bright, happy faces of Benny, Marisa, Nino, Merlina, and Tony began appearing in Laufer's stable of teen mags, under banner headlines like "Tony, Benny, Nino: Which One's Right For You?!" and "Read Tony's Private Love Diary!"

"The MO at Laufer was to promote an artist early, before there was product, to gauge reader response," recalls former *Tiger Beat* editor Cathy Kirkland (née Cohen). "So Chuck Laufer ordered makeovers on everyone, got them new clothes and hair, and professional makeup for the girls. We started running stories on them four or five months before Laufer got them signed to a recording deal."

"It was pretty weird," Tony remembers. "One day I'm riding my bike around Welland, the next day I'm doing photo sessions for magazines and picking out songs for our new album."

Most of those songs were selected by producer Walt Meskell, who was assigned to the group by Regan. "Walt ran the songs past me, and if I didn't like one, he'd put it aside," Tony recalls. "If we agreed on a song, then it had to pass muster with Laufer and the record label guys." Among the first songs recorded was "Heartbeat, It's a Lovebeat," a percolating rhythm-and-blues number with a catchy chorus hook.

"Everyone around us kept saying, 'Hardly anyone gets a hit record, don't get your hopes up, if we don't get a hit on you, we're gonna send you back to Canada,'" Tony says. "But the minute I heard 'Heartbeat', I knew we had a huge hit."

He was right. The song, selected from the original three-track demo, soared to #3 on *Billboard's* Hot 100, made it to #1 on the *Cashbox* Singles Chart, and sold two million copies. The follow-up, "Abra-ca-Dabra" (written by Meskell and partner Tim Martin), was another Top 40 hit, and their *Heartbeat, It's a Lovebeat* album, featuring both singles and a pile of Meskell-Martin tunes, was a monster seller as well. The LP, propelled by Tony's powerhouse lead vocals, featured work by some of the best studio musicians of the day, including drummer Hal Blaine, guitarist Larry Carlton, and bassist Max Bennett—the self-named "Wrecking Crew," who played for the Beach Boys, the Mamas and the Papas, and the Partridge Family.

The singers who created backgrounds for those bands, and dozens of others, were used in the DeFranco sessions as well. "On the first record, the only one who sang was Tony," recalls Kirkland, who was present in the studio for most of the recording sessions. "Laufer got the kids some singing lessons, and they were always used on the records, but they were also always augmented, too. I think they were definitely mixed in on later tracks, but the producer didn't feel their voices were strong enough to handle the backgrounds."

Tom Bahler, half of the legendary Bahler brothers, created the vocal arrangements for the DeFranco Family recordings. Bahler and brother John, who'd founded '60s one-hit-wonders the Love Generation, recorded their own voices and those of Partridge Family singers Ron Hicklin and Jackie Ward after the basic track had been completed. "They recorded the other DeFrancos as a courtesy," recalls a studio player who doesn't want to be named. "Then we'd wipe those tracks out and replace them with the pro singers after the kids left the studio. Tom is a nice guy, but he had his orders. The label wanted this particular kind of sound, and they couldn't wait until the kids got their vocal chops up to make records. It was, 'We need a hit now, so let's hire these guys who sing for everyone, and no one will be the wiser.' This is how the business worked in those days."

Regardless of who was providing the oohs and aahs, the DeFranco Family were suddenly in constant demand. When they weren't taping appearances on the hottest television shows—*American Bandstand, Sonny and Cher, Dinah!, The Mike Douglas Show,* even a special hosted by Jack Benny—they were locked away in L.A.'s Western Recorders, laying down tracks for a second album. Twentieth Century rush-released the group's third single, a cover of the Drifters hit "Save the Last Dance For Me," and the disc raced up the *Billboard* charts, peaking at #18 in May of 1974 and selling just shy of a million copies.

The recording is a masterwork of vocal overdubs, with the Bahlers' chanting choral fills and Tom Bahler's lead harmony (credited to Benny in *Tiger Beat* and elsewhere) mixed right behind Tony's on the choruses. Hal Blaine's tinny snare and high-hat and Mike Melvoin's intricate arpeggios and Wurlitzer reverb give the seamless backing track a kick that the sleepy original never had.

Following the success of "Heartbeat," Laufer had cranked up his teen idol machine and, by the time "Save the Last Dance for Me" was released, the DeFranco Family were the reigning cover kids on each of Laufer Publication's three monthly magazines. The market was flooded with products—a fan club kit, personally autographed photos, and a slew of cheap black-and-white-on-bond-paper booklets with titles like "The Secret of Tony"—that were only available through Laufer publications. None of the other teen rags would touch the DeFranco Family, because promoting the act meant filling Laufer's pockets.

Laufer scheduled a grueling 20-city tour to promote the group's second album (cannily titled *Save the Last Dance For Me*), and the DeFrancos spent the summer of 1974 on a bus, with Kirkland along as a chaperone. "Chuck Laufer sort of assigned me to the DeFrancos from the beginning," she explains, "because Sharon wasn't really interested in them. So I traveled with them on tour, went with them to the recording dates, even helped design their costumes. We went for a real sparkly look. I remember sitting at their kitchen table for hours and hours with one of those Ronco stud-setters, putting rhinestones on their shirts. The DeFrancos were there, too, with their little rhinestone hammers, putting sequins on their own costumes."

Kirkland found herself in an odd position: She'd grown fond of the DeFrancos, and tried to protect them from the very company that had created them. "I told them to do some research and find out what sort of percentages other recording artists were getting. I'd only been in the biz a few years myself, but I knew some of the pitfalls that other teen idols had fallen into, and I didn't want these kids to get ripped off. It was a tough line to walk: I was looking out for these kids, who I really adored, and also trying to be a loyal employee."

Kirkland reported to Laufer that fans went berserk when the kids performed the Martin-Meskell song "Write Me a Letter" in their live shows and, although 20th Century had scheduled "Hold Me" as the next DeFranco single, "Write Me" was released instead. Anxious to display some musical growth, the group convinced Meskell to return to the studio to re-record a rock version of the song for single release. The DeFranco Family debuted their new sound on *American Bandstand* in August of 1974, wowing fans with the bass-driven rock of "Write Me a Letter" and eschewing their usual elaborate choreography in favor of "playing" their instruments to the blistering rock groove of "Love the Way You Do," a favorite track from the second album. Tony's voice had changed since the band's last recording session, and his deeper, growling vocals were something of a revelation to fans who'd grown accustomed to his falsetto leads on earlier records.

"We were growing up," Tony remembers, "and we wanted to express more of our own musical interests with the group. We'd had three big hits, and we'd mostly done what the label wanted us to do. It was a lot of 'Wear this, sing that.' But we knew we had to grow musically in order to make a career of this."

The powers that be disagreed. When the new version of "Write Me a Letter" bombed (peaking at #104 on *Billboard*), Laufer fired Walt Meskell and brought in record legend Mike Curb, who'd had considerable success producing hits for the Osmonds and several other teen acts. The first Curb single released, a cover of the 1958 Robert and Johnny hit "We Belong Together," was a seamless piece of pop pleasure, and among the best sides the band recorded.

Despite its glossy backing tracks and a swell lead vocal, the single stiffed. The DeFranco Family announced to Laufer and company that they wanted to record more contemporary tunes, specifically a song Benny had written, and that they didn't want to work with Curb and company any longer.

"After the second album, Laufer and Regan were trying to make all the decisions," Tony recalls. "I don't mean any disrespect, but we were being managed by men in their 50s, who were into glorifying old music that we weren't interested in. After the success of 'Save the Last Dance for Me,' their attitude was, 'Let's do all remakes.' I didn't like this, so they thought I had an attitude. I was really just fighting for the direction we wanted to go in, trying to get them to let the group grow musically."

After "We Belong Together" missed the charts, Laufer relented, allowing the DeFrancos to select their own producer. The kids hired R&B session man Keg Johnson, who steered the quintet back to the dance-oriented pop of their earlier singles. Among the sides that Johnson tracked for the new album were "Drummer Man," a discofied, horn-infused number that featured backgrounds sung by the DeFrancos themselves, and "I Thought You Might Like to Know," a soulful ballad later covered by Maureen

McGovern for 20th Century. These two tracks were mixed and delivered to Laufer in late 1975, but he rejected both, opting instead to release "Venus," one of the cover tunes recorded earlier with Mike Curb. (Ultimately, that single was also scrapped, though it was later issued in Japan, where the DeFrancos were still doing big business.)

Stateside, Laufer and Regan attempted to revive interest in the act by promoting Tony as a solo artist. The single sleeve for "We Belong Together" plugged "Tony DeFranco with the DeFranco Family," and Laufer sent Tony alone to promote the disc and its flip, "Time Enough For Love" (the only DeFranco tune without group vocals) on Dinah Shore's show.

"Laufer was unhappy with Russ Regan," Kirkland recalls, "and he was looking for another label that would sign Tony as a solo act. It was a tough time, because Tony wanted to continue working but he didn't want to be disloyal to his family." Tony remembers that "there was also a lot of head-butting between Laufer and Benny at this time," a memory with which Laufer concurs.

"Benny came into my office one day and chewed me a new asshole," Laufer says. "He made all these demands about what they were going to sing, and how much they were going to be paid. I listened. I told him I thought he was being ungrateful, that I'd put a lot of money into the DeFranco Family, and that I was trying to get them another hit."

In fact, Laufer had decided to cut his losses rather than continue with the group. Despite the fact that his success with the DeFrancos had made him a great deal of money and had, as he puts it, "finally made us the top teen magazine in the world, ahead of *16*," he felt it was time to move on.

"We were in the studio, trying to finish up the third album," Tony remembers, "and then Laufer called us in and announced he was pulling the plug. He told my dad and me that he was interested in working with me alone, but we told him to forget it, and we walked out of his office. Forever."

Without the backing of Laufer's promotional empire, the DeFranco Family found it hard to score another record deal. Because they were considered a Laufer commodity, competing teen magazines were hesitant to cover them. A new management team sent the DeFrancos out on the state fair circuit while it scouted new record deals, but to no avail. A lucrative Las Vegas gig kept the group busy through 1978, after which the DeFranco Family called it quits.

When Laufer heard about the group's demise, he contacted Tony.

"He came back with the same offer," Tony says. "He wanted to work with me alone. I didn't like the way my career was going at that time—I didn't want to end up a Vegas lounge singer. So I agreed. But then Laufer wouldn't take me into the recording studio. Instead, he just wanted to put pictures of me in the magazine. After a while, I just walked away. I wanted to work, and he wanted color pin-ups."

Tony recorded the theme song for a game show called *Almost Anything Goes*, and he and his siblings appeared on the show occasionally as celebrity guests. Eventually, Tony found work as a producer for other musical acts. His siblings moved on to civilian lives, marrying and raising families and managing— unlike many of their contemporaries—to dodge drug addiction and shoplifting charges.

Tony halfheartedly revived the family act at a Boston event hosted by deejay Barry Scott in 1992. The new act featured Tony and two of his children, who sang backup while he wailed on some of the group's early hits. In 2000, he convinced Polygram Records, which now owns the DeFranco family catalog, to reissue both of the band's albums on a single CD. The disc also featured a single edit of "Drummer Man" and a big-band-flavored tune, "Gee, Baby," originally cut for (but not included on) the second album.

The release party for the new CD reunited the band for the first time since their last Vegas gig in 1978. In a 50-minute set, the DeFrancos performed their hits and some favorite album tracks to a packed house. Benny played bass, acoustic and electric guitars; Merlina wailed on the drums, and the siblings proved their singing chops with perfect four-part harmonies that would have made Tom Bahler proud. Afterward, well-wishers mobbed the DeFranco Family. Cathy Kirkland stood by, beaming, as "the kids" autographed old record sleeves and torn *Tiger Beat* covers.

One determined fan, a doughy, fortyish woman named Cecilia who couldn't remember the names of any DeFranco songs other than "Heartbeat, It's a Lovebeat," waited patiently for her turn to meet Tony and to coo over his form-fitting leather pants.

"I don't care so much about the songs," she confided to a cocktail waitress. "I'm here to remember what it felt like to be 11 years old. That was the last time I was truly happy. I was in love with Tony, this boy in a magazine who I was never going to meet. I flew 2,000 miles to meet him tonight. And I'm not leaving this building until I do."

Dino, Desi & Billy: Hollywood Pop Nepotism by Gloria Keeley

Imagine the lives of Dino Martin, Desi Arnaz, Jr. and Billy Hinsche in 1965: living in Hollywood, famous parents (Dean Martin, Desi Arnaz & Lucille Ball), you're a pre-teen, you're on the cover of *16*, and . . . and you're on the radio! Hell, they probably even got to glimpse Nancy Sinatra lounging around poolside in her bikini and . . . um . . . boots. How does *that* grab ya? With the best back-up musicians in the business, Frank Sinatra signing them to his Reprise label, their mini-Beatle haircuts, their '60s clothes, Beatle boots, their guitars, drums and most importantly, their songs, they couldn't miss.

Talking with Billy Hinsche recently he shared the birth of DD&B:

> The first time I met Mr. Sinatra was sometime in '64, I believe, when we auditioned for him. We played a few songs for him (Dean was there too) that we had learned. We were set up in Dean's bar area next to the living room. Frank was very enthusiastic after we played, walked over and said, "How would you boys like to have a contract with my label?" That was the beginning of our recording career. I saw him one more time at a Martin party at their home in Beverly Hills. He was ebullient and very nice to me. He was all smiles, probably because by this time we were a success.

Dino, Desi & Billy's success prefigures bubblegum in several important respects: stellar studio musicians, professional songwriters, danceable pop, and aggressive, savvy teen marketing. Curiously, what smacks of a Rat Pack vanity project at first glance contained genuine musical talent. The boys' behind-the-scenes support included L.A.'s best sessionmen, arrangers and songwriters: Lee Hazelwood, Billy Strange, Al Capps, Bill Justis, Shorty Rogers, Al Casey, James Burton, Jim Gordon, Jim Troxel, Hal Blaine, Jimmy Bowen, and Bones Howe. Not only were they the youngest group to have hit records in that era, they were also the only group to feature a Filipino-American boy (Billy) as a teen heartthrob.

DD&B weren't the only band spawned out of Hollywood Pop Nepotism: Gary Lewis and the Playboys (Jerry Lewis' kid); Tony & the Tigers (Soupy's boys, Hunt and Tony Sales, later famously backing Iggy and Bowie); Bruce & Terry (with Terry Melcher, Doris Day's son; Terry later produced Paul Revere and the Raiders and just missed a Manson Family house call); Peter Lewis (of Moby Grape, son of Loretta Young).

> Never met Gary, I can't say whether Dino or Desi had. I suppose everyone who was on the radio/charts was considered competition of sorts like in any business, right? I thought his forming a group immediately after us was a direct result of our success. I envisioned him going to his father and making the case that he too should have his own band/record deal because, after all, Dino had one. That's pure speculation on my part but it is plausible, is it not?
>
> — Billy Hinsche

Their early hits fused the best of the British Invasion and the California sound into a potent pop concoction of their own. Listening to the opening bass line of their first hit, "I'm A Fool" can still give you chills. Dino and Billy harmonize beautifully. The mesmerizing tune floats along, stops for that killer bass and then rolls back into the beat. It reached number 3 in *Billboard*. Their second hit, "Not The Lovin' Kind," written by Lee Hazelwood, opened with the jingle jangle guitar reminiscent of the Byrds. Not bad for a trio of Catholic schoolboys.

DD&B's last charted hit, "Tell Someone You Love Them," was written by Billy, who patterned the song after the Beach Boys' "Darlin'." Billy had a special affinity for the Beach Boys. His sister married Carl Wilson. (Carl then married Dino's sister, Gina, but that's another story.) Toward the end of the reign of

DD&B, Billy was asked to become a member of the Beach Boys. The entire group, Brian, Carl, Dennis, Mike, Al and their manager, Nick Grillo, went over to Billy's parents' house in 1969 to offer Billy a full membership in the group. Billy had no idea that this was in the works, and he was completely surprised. He was dying to join the Beach Boys, but his father convinced Billy that his education was more important. Billy cried himself to sleep that night. After receiving his college degree, he became a permanent member of the Beach Boys' touring band.

Dino was killed in a plane crash in 1987. Desi went on to act in many movies, including *The Mambo Kings*, in which he portrayed his father. It was Desi's burgeoning acting career that pulled him away from the group. Their later compositions were entirely the work of Dino and Billy. Billy is currently performing with Al Jardine, Al's two sons, and Brian's two daughters (the Wilson portion of Wilson Phillips). Billy also debuted his latest group, Ricci, Desi & Billy; Ricci is Dino's younger brother.

If you want to get your feet wet on Dino, Desi & Billy, pick up the Sundazed CD *The Best of Dino, Desi and Billy*. Listen carefully to their later works: "Two In The Afternoon" is kinda Kinksish à la "Waterloo Sunset." Dino's "My What A Shame" is an amazing song that could have rivaled "Eloise" by Paul and Barry Ryan. "Lady Love," written by Brian Wilson with Billy, is one of their most sophisticated songs. DD&B stopped making hits as they drifted away from the bubblegum formula. But as they made their own music they explored the musical territory pioneered by Brian Wilson and produced a handful of pop gems worthy of their inspirations.

Tommy James & The Shondells by Bill Holmes

Jeff Barry and Ellie Greenwich reportedly wrote the song in 20 minutes as a filler track that became the b-side of a failed single. The Spinners, then trolling the bus tour circuit, had it in their repertoire to help get a few people out on the dance floor. Tommy James, née Jackson, grew up near the Michigan/Indiana border and would often check out the Chicago and Detroit bands that came through the area. And when James needed another song to cut with his band the Shondells for a local DJ named Jack Douglas, he remembered the dumb riff that caught his ear. Having only heard the song once, James didn't even know the words, so he made some up and mumbled the others. It was just a riff after all. Douglas released the song on his Snap Records label, and after the usual brief local buzz, the record faded away.

That was until Mad Mike Metro, a Pittsburgh DJ, found the record in a bargain bin and started playing it repeatedly on his show, until it eventually soared all the way to number one in the area. By the time he was able to track James down, some local entrepreneur had already bootlegged it and sold thousands of copies. To capitalize on the success of the single, James quickly tried to reassemble the original band, who had all graduated from school and started to go their separate ways. In one of the classic bad career moves of rock 'n' roll, they all declined. James then hooked up with a local Pittsburgh band called the Raconteurs, and after he and Douglas were able to license the original to Roulette Records what happened in Pittsburgh happened everywhere. "Hanky Panky" was a smash hit in 1966, hitting the top of the charts and selling over a million copies.

Pop radio was at its best in 1967, when bubblegum writer Ritchie Cordell would pen two of the band's biggest hits—"I Think We're Alone Now" (#3) and "Mirage" (#10); Cordell also co-wrote "Mony Mony" (#3) the following year. The crafty production or these first hits set the records apart from other gum records that were also climbing the charts at the time. Although touches like the opening bass line of "I Think We're Alone Now" were pretty standard, effects like the sound of crickets on the song's break were instantly memorable. James' powerful voice propelled the songs with a combination of lustful angst and teenage innocence, and along with the pulsating bass and versatile keyboards, the Shondells created a trademark sound. James was a fast learner in the studio and soon developed an uncanny knack for successfully blending other styles with the simplistic pop melodies. Soon he was writing and producing the band's music, and the complexity of the arrangements were spot-on for adventurous music fans, whose boundaries were being expanded by the likes of Hendrix and Cream.

The band's peak came in 1969, when "Crimson and Clover" was a landmark psychedelic single that captured the essence and imagination of the times. The echo and phasing effects on the guitar and vocals and the mini-suite structure of the song was an irresistible mix that gave James his second #1 record, which eventually sold over six million copies. "Sweet Cherry Wine" (#7) followed, a combination of upbeat shuffle and pop waltz that again featured angelic harmonies and a killer hook. But the year was capped by another chart-topping single, "Crystal Blue Persuasion," a jazzy, lounge-tinged song that was psychedelic enough to wow the heads, cerebral enough to hook the critics, and just slow enough to be a grind-dance classic at proms for the next several years. But music was about to undergo an irreversible transition that would leave Woodstock as the last shining moment of an age of innocence and dreams. James himself would take a break to resolve some personal issues, but the Shondells were done. He produced "Tighter And Tighter" for Alive And Kickin' in 1970 (which reached #7 on the charts), and a year later his solo effort "Draggin The Line" hit #4. Fifteen Top 40 hits in five years. James was but 23 years old.

When the solo project *Christian Of The World* was released, the reactions to the overtly religious cover ranged from laughter to outrage. Some thought the Jesus-like pose bordered on sacrilege—if the Beatles weren't bigger than Jesus, how dare this bubblegum idol don robes? But the introspective yearning that was hinted at in songs like "Crystal Blue Persuasion" were now front and center. If listeners thought it was a joke, the lyrics in James' title track proved otherwise ("Dear Jesus Christ/lead me on/show me the way/take me home"). Radio wisely passed and instead grabbed hold of "Draggin' The Line," whose infectious hook and bouncy production was able to overcome lyrics which extolled the virtues of "huggin' a tree when you get near it." The rest of the record was a pleasant but vacuous blend of folk, music hall and formulaic, unexciting pop.

Despite the hit, it was never the same after 1971. The times, they were a-changin' after all, and the solo, "serious" Tommy couldn't compete with the new brand of icon like James Taylor. The continuing partnership with Bobby King produced interesting moments like the gospel-tinged "Come To Me" and "Ball And Chain," a bubblegum song with more serious, religious lyrics. But the less said about *Midnight Rider*, James' collaboration with Jeff Barry, the better. Ten years later, James scored again with "Three Times In Love," an acoustic-driven song (featuring Luther Vandross harmonies) that found its niche in

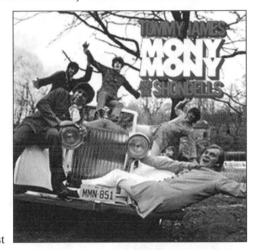

the post-punk, pre-Eurosynth year of 1980. But once again (despite guitarist Jon Tropeo's George Harrison-like noodling) the balance of the record was filled with songs like "Lady In White" that seemed better suited for Tony Orlando or the medallion-and-chest-hair era Bee Gees. James continued to record but never reached the charts again.

But even if James had hung it up in 1970 and became a farmer, the legacy he and his band left behind is an irreplaceable part of rock 'n' roll's pop Mecca. The greatest hits collections available on Rhino are wall-to-wall rock-solid, chock full of songs that make you turn up the volume and sing along. Every oldies station in the world carries three or four songs in regular rotation, where they prove to have aged better than most of their contemporary rivals. When rocker Joan Jett hooked up with Ritchie Cordell and Kenny Laguna years later, "Crimson and Clover" was a hit all over again. Even Tiffany's pre-pubescent interpretation of "I Think We're Alone Now" and Billy Idol's trash-can rendition of "Mony Mony" can't bury the charm of the original hits that live on over 30 years later.

Kasenetz-Katz Singing Orchestral Circus by Bill Pitzonka

1968 was a banner year for bubblegum's founding fathers Jerry Kasenetz and Jeff Katz. Their association with Buddah Records had produced two consistent hitmakers, the Ohio Express and 1910 Fruitgum Co., and they had a host of lesser lights waiting in the wings. As a spectacular publicity stunt, they threw all their "bands" together, rented Carnegie Hall for June 7, and billed the event as *The Kasenetz-Katz Singing Orchestral Circus*. The "original cast recording" claims a total of 46 musicians: Buddah's 1910 Fruitgum Co. and Ohio Express; the Laurie label's Music Explosion; Kama Sutra artists Lt. Garcia's Magic Music Box, the Teri Nelson Group and J.C.W. Rat Finks; and the unsigned entities St. Louis Invisible Marching Band and 1989 Musical Marching Zoo. The "live" album was a particularly fuzzy-sounding affair consisting mostly of strange cover versions—Super K

staples "Simon Says," "Little Bit Of Soul" and "(Poor Old) Mr. Jensen," as well as such stylistic stretches as "Hey Joe," "Yesterday, " "We Can Work It Out" and "You've Lost That Lovin' Feelin'." Joey Levine contributed the sole studio cut, "Down in Tennessee," which bubbled under the *Billboard* Hot 100 in single form.

Despite this relative failure, Kasenetz-Katz rode another Singing Orchestral Circus single to international success: "Quick Joey Small (Run Joey Run)," featuring Joey Levine and a chorus of gum-cracking Brooklyn chicks, hit #25 in *Billboard* that December and peaked at #19 in Britain soon after.

The far superior second album, with billing abridged to *Kasenetz-Katz Super Circus*, featured five proven chart commodities: 1910 Fruitgum Co., Ohio Express, and Music Explosion were joined by White Whale newcomers Professor Morrison's Lollipop and the Shadows Of Knight, who wound up on Team/Super K

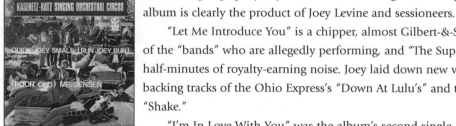

after their garage glory days on Dunwich. Though ostensibly a collective effort, the album is clearly the product of Joey Levine and sessioneers.

"Let Me Introduce You" is a chipper, almost Gilbert-&-Sullivanesque rundown of the "bands" who are allegedly performing, and "The Super Circus" is two-and-a-half-minutes of royalty-earning noise. Joey laid down new vocals over the original backing tracks of the Ohio Express's "Down At Lulu's" and the Shadows Of Knight's "Shake."

"I'm In Love With You" was the album's second single, credited to Kasenetz-Katz Super Cirkus. The mono single mix (which surfaced on the Buddah compilation album *Bubble Gum Music Is The Naked Truth*) features grittier lead and female vocals.

In addition to by-the-numbers fare like "Easy To Love," "I Got It Bad For You," and "Log In Fire," Joey took the opportunity to stretch beyond the bubblegum boundaries. "Up In the Air" ventured into political commentary—a deliberate over-the-top sendup of then-California governor Ronald Reagan, while "L.A. Woman" (a Levine original) handled sexual attraction and romantic confusion in a way that "Yummy, Yummy, Yummy" never could.

Joey made one final single under the Super Cirkus banner: his experiment in French *chanson*, "Embrasser." Soon thereafter, he left the Kasenetz-Katz fold. 1910 Fruitgum Co.'s Mark Gutkowski took over lead vocal duties on a Super Cirkus cover of Golden Earring's "Dong-Dong-Diki-Di-Ki-Dong" on the Super K label, but the carnival was over. The wheel was reinvented as the Kasenetz-Katz Fighter Squadron for a one-off on Bell ("When He Comes" b/w "Ah-La," 1971) and toss-offs on Super K ("Symphony No. 9" b/w "Blue Danube Waltz," Kasenetz-Katz Orchestral Circus, 1971), their own MagnaGlide imprint ("Mama Lu" b/w "Collide," Kasenetz-Katz Super Cirkus, 1975), and Epic ("Heart Get Ready For Love" b/w "Jungle Junk", Kasenetz-Katz Super Cirkus, 1977) but by then the concept was effectively grounded.

The Lemon Pipers by Gary Pig Gold

The Lemon Pipers are a perfect example of a band confidently launched atop, quickly constrained within, then ultimately torpedoed by that deceptively friendly tag we call "bubblegum." Although their one and a half hits continue to highlight Super K-stuffed compilations the world over (and rightfully so), many of this same band's seldom-aired album tracks instead reveal a group of accomplished, more than adventurous, writers and musicians who, I swear, are due *at least* the same amount of retrospective respect as Tommy James or even Thunderclap Newman.

Just like their midwestern brethren the Ohio Express, these five Pipers (who had begun life circa 1966 as Ivan and the Sabres) boasted bona fide garage roots; a sturdy, Vox-processed pedigree already well on display all across their Carol Records debut, "Quiet Please." This chunk of denim-drenched rock bode well indeed for the prides of Oxford, Ohio. Left to their own devices one can safely imagine the Lemon Pipers remaining happy to mine this rich, Electric Prunes-by-way-of-Shadows-Of-Knight vein well into the dreaded 1970s and beyond.

'Twas not to be. At the very height of the Summer of Love a talent scout from none other than Buddah Records arrived in Oxford armed with a contract, and five coach-fare tickets back to New York City. Our heroes took the bait, and by Christmastime they found themselves rocketing towards the very peak of the American charts with a Technicolor-brilliant piece of goo entitled "Green Tambourine." This undeniable Bubbledelic classic, so cleverly crafted by wily New Yorkers Paul Leka and Shelley Pinz, came equipped —as did so many hits from that era—with its very own built-in curse: the need, especially from whence the powers-that-were sat, for an immediate and, if at all possible, *identical* follow-up smash or two. Or ten.

The Lemon Pipers had other plans. They were a serious, possibly even "progressive" (for the time) quintet who fully expected to now be allowed to build upon the sounds their international smash had only just hinted at. As a result, the *Green Tambourine* album did so much more than just trot out their Number One alongside 30 additional minutes of sound-alikes and studio knock-offs. For example, lead guitarist Bill Bartlett's "Through With You" deftly wed a touch of McGuinn vs. Townshend guitar histrionica to the band's still-lingering garage fumes, though "Fifty Year Void" *did* fall victim to the witless boogie-rawk just then beginning to infest the FM airwaves. Nevertheless, it was the Pipers' way with a tough-pop gem in the under-four-minute category which was most impressive by far: "Rainbow Tree," "Shoeshine Boy," and especially "Blueberry Blue" each sported a taut, musical sophistication worthy of the Move and, dare I say it, even *Magical Mystery* Beatles! As a result, the *Green Tambourine* album stands practically alone within the annals of bubblegum long-players as a record which really can be listened to and enjoyed—*all the way through*.

Of course Buddah dealt their shots in strictly seven-inch wads, not 12, so Leka and Pinz were soon ordered to construct lots more Number Ones for their reluctant Pipers—or, as lead voice Ivan Browne was wont to call such material, "funny-money music." But "Rice Is Nice" only made it as high as 46. Then "Jelly Jungle" conked out at 51! (Both these songs are pretty worthy pieces, far more deserving of saturation AM-play throughout 1968 than "MacArthur Park" or "Honey").

Ironically, at this very moment the sophomore *Jelly Jungle* LP, like its predecessor, again filled itself to the gills in all manner of hip-trippy sounds and stylings: the mega-minute "Dead End Street/Half Light"

epic, for example, was no less than a "Day In The Life" for the braces set—and I mean absolutely no disrespect when saying so!—while the Pipers' take on Goffin-King's "I Was Not Born To Follow" is actually
carried with higher regard in some circles, including my own, than the Byrds' comparatively rural reading.

With the hits having apparently dried up, and their two albums already on collision course with the
Delete Zone, the Lemon Pipers and Buddah bid a bittersweet "adios!" to one another in 1969, with the
band bravely soldiering on for just a little while longer as a sort of poor-man's Steppenwolf—that is,
until the arrival of the Nixon decade, and with it the twin horrors of Heavy Metal and the singer-songwriter. Oddly enough (speaking of Black Sabbath and Elton), precisely ten long and lonely years after
"Green Tambourine" had first thrust him there, Bill Bartlett briefly resurfaced on chart tops the world
over with a tangy slice of '70s-styled (and Kasenetz 'n' Katz-krafted) bubblegum of the highest odor.
Anybody remember Ram Jam's immortal, immoral ode to alliteration and amour known as "Black
Betty?" Well, like "Green Tambourine," it too spawned a couple of tours, a couple of highly underrated
albums, and then unfortunately another swift trip back to the Where Are They Now? heap for all
involved.

Or perhaps the Pipers actually made good on their age-old antipodal aspirations? "We can always go
to New Zealand," bassist (and actual native New Zealander) Steve Walmsley told an incredulous Indianapolis
reporter in 1968 when asked the inevitable "where to go when your bubble pops" question. "There's a
lot of beach there. We'll just plug the guitars into a pawpaw tree and play. We'll live on natural vegetation
and become wise. People will come to see us because we're peaceful and tolerant. And we blow good."

Green Tambourine
Drop your silver in my tambourine.
Help a poor man fill his pretty dream.
Give me pennies I'll take anything,
Now listen while I play.
My Green Tambourine.

Watch the jingle angle start to chime.
Reflections of the music that is mine.
When you drop a coin you'll hear it sing.
Now listen while I play,
My Green Tambourine.

Drop a dime before I walk away.
Any song you want I'll gladly play.
Money feeds my music machine.
Now listen while I play,
My Green Tambourine.

Good Clean Fun

Carl Cafarelli and Gary Pig Gold wonder outloud, "The Monkees: Bubblegum Or Not?"

Vilified since their very inception (circa 1965 within the television division of Columbia Pictures), yet forever being rediscovered and embraced by new generations of pop fans and/or cable addicts the world over, the Great Debate persists: Were the Monkees nothing but a crude, calculatingly crass hoax foisted upon those least-musically-discriminating within the 8–14-year age bracket? Or were the Monkees actually a pretty cool buncha guys whose *origins* may have been suspect, but whose contributions to popular culture are formidable and wide-ranging indeed *not* to mention no less worthy than, say, Wham!'s or William Shatner's?

Quite simply—quite pimply—put then, Are the Monkees really, honestly, "bubblegum," or are they not? Well, for starters, Carl explains:

Carl Cafarelli: I don't regard the Monkees as a bubblegum group, but I can see how the group's artificial origin lends itself to a dissenting opinion. On paper, these guys would seem to be the perfect prototype for a bubble-band. First and foremost, they were a prefabricated, fictional rock 'n' roll group, a manufactured commodity concocted to sell as many records and boxes of Kellogg's Frosted Flakes as is humanly possible. But it's a point of some debate as to whether the Monkees can truly be considered a bubblegum *band* by definition alone. Let's review the evidence then. The Monkees—Micky Dolenz, Davy Jones, Mike Nesmith and Peter Tork—were four young men selected, from "cattle call"-style open auditions, to play a rock 'n' roll group in a weekly TV series. Each had some musical background, though that background was really almost coincidental to their selection as Monkees.

Gary Pig Gold: Agreed, insomuch as Micky was "taught" to be the Monkees' drummist, and Davy never could quite get the hang of his tambourine, now could he? But then again, Paul McCartney became the Beatle basser only because no one else in the group wanted the job. But I digress, don't I?

CC: Speaking of which, faster than you or I could say *A Hard Day's Night*, pop music veteran Don "The Man With The Golden Ears" Kirshner was enlisted to oversee all things musical concerning this, yes, most pre-fab of projects. In no time flat, his well-greased, tried and tested machinery clicked into action, and Monkee music began pouring forth from Kirshner's formidable stable of songsmiths [Carole King & Gerry Goffin, Tommy Boyce & Bobby Hart, Neil Diamond, Neil Sedaka, Barry Mann & Cynthia Weil]. These songs-to-go were

then quickly recorded by top Los Angeles session musicians, with the Monkees themselves strictly relegated to a vocals-only role.

GPG: But that was actually more of a scheduling decision than a musical one, seeing that the first Monkee recording sessions took place as production on the television series was going into high gear. Still, from day one Mike Nesmith attended as many studio dates as time allowed, performing not only guitar duty but actually contributing some fine original songs to boot (and possibly even inventing that dreaded "country-rock" genre in the process).

CC: It's just that some of us remain unconvinced the Monkees were ever really, truly a bubblegum act through and through, their prefabricated status notwithstanding. In actual fact, most of the Monkees' recordings don't *sound* like bubblegum records!

GPG: Neither do, to what's left of my ears, most Lemon Pipers songs either, but go on.

CC: "Last Train To Clarksville?" A clone of the Beatles' "Paperback Writer," sure, but also an effervescent rockin' pop ditty on its own merit.

GPG: Actually, I would've thought "Ticket To Ride."

CC: "(I'm Not Your) Steppin' Stone?" Prime garage-rock, proto-punk that even the Sex Pistols couldn't make any surlier.

GPG: Have you heard Paul Revere & the Raiders' (pre-Monkee, b.t.w.) version? Yowza!

CC: Absolutely! But look, these songs just don't fit that same bubblegum mold soon to be indelibly cast by Messrs. Kasenetz and Katz. Instead, each hit sounds like a stirring example of AM-friendly pop-rock, with the Monkees' artificial origin the sole, negligible difference between them and contemporary efforts from the Raiders, Turtles, Dave Clark Five, Hollies, and most every other Caucasian act whose name began with the word "The."

GPG: Well, herein we truly begin splitting musical wads of Bubblicious grape, as it were. I boldly stand steadfast to my claim that most every single number recorded and released by the Monkees during 1966 and 1967—yes, even Woolhat Mike's early attempts at alt. C&W—more than comfortably fit into that hallowed realm occupied at the time by Tommy James, Tommy Roe, and even the most stickiest of "Super K" Kreations. I mean, geez, with an Anthony Newley-on-helium voice (and persona) the likes of Davy Jones', even a Monkee reading of "White Rabbit" could've more than held its own against "Chewy Chewy" or, dare I say it, "Yummy, Yummy, Yummy."

CC: Oh, I disagree. Not necessarily about Davy—he *was* the teen idol of the bunch, after all, and the closest to a bubblegum figure among the individual Monks. But he wasn't even the Monkees' main vocalist; Micky Dolenz was. And Dolenz's voice had an inherent earthiness, almost a soulfulness, that simply was *not* "bubblegum."

GPG: Hmmm, you sayin' Joey Levine ain't got no earthiness or no soul? And what about Archie Andrews, I mean, Ron Dante?!! Them's fightin' words, boy!

CC: Yeah, and the Banana Splits were a street gang. Furthermore, most Monkee material—regardless of who was singing—didn't display any of the expected hallmarks of true bubbledom. It may be a mistake to try to draw specific parameters for what *is* or *isn't* "bubblegum," but I'd say a bubblegum tune oughtta be characterized by some, ideally, a contrived sense of childish innocence, some willful stupidity and/or a moronically catchy rhythm, à la the pulsin' beat of the Ohio Express, or even the Ramones' "I Wanna Be Sedated."

GPG: "D-U-M-B, Everyone's accusing me," as I think the saying goes.

CC: Indeed. Yet on those first two Monkees LPs, only "Laugh," "Gonna Buy Me A Dog," and *maybe* "Your Auntie Grizelda" veer into Fleer territory, as it were, and "Gonna Buy Me A Dog" was really more of a piss-take anyway.

GPG: You mean *your* copy of Monkee album number one doesn't contain "I'll Be True To You" (*much* more chewy chewy than the Hollies' version ever was!), or even "Let's Dance On" (which, I dare point out, was immediately re-written as, among several others, "Down at Lulu's")?

CC: Both were still just regular ol' pop tunes, and not all that gummy; "Let's Dance On" could probably trace its genealogy to the Isley Brothers' "Shout" and the Contours' "Do You Love Me?" Whatever the case may be, after those two albums with Kirshner, the Monkees expanded beyond the role of mere prefab sitcom rockers. Demands for live concert appearances, coupled with Nesmith's and Tork's own determination that they be allowed to start contributing more musically, led to the Monkees becoming an actual *band,* as it were.

GPG: Once again, authentic bubblegum tactics, Carl: don't throw together your performance unit until *after* you've chalked up a hit or two! You know, we could actually be talking Grass Roots or even Cuff Links here, I trust you realize.

CC: The Grass Roots weren't bubblegum either. But now *I'm* digressing! It's also worth noting a specific song which is said (perhaps apocryphally) to have helped mark that infamous transition from puppet Monkees to hey-hey-we're-a-rock-band Monkees. In 1967, Kirshner presented his boys, and former Turtle Chip Douglas, whom the band had just appointed as their producer, with a brand new Jeff Barry/Andy Kim tune he wanted them to record. Legend has it that the Monkees rebelled, rejected the song, and started a chain of events that would ultimately lead to Kirshner's permanent expulsion from the project, followed by the recording of the landmark *Headquarters* album.

GPG: Oh boy, here it comes . . .

CC: The song in question? A little something called "Sugar, Sugar." As Chip later told Monkee biographer Eric Lefcowitz, "I'm glad I was in there at the time. I probably saved the Monkees from having to do some *real* bubblegum." [Jeff Barry disputes this story, but Don Kirshner has gone on record validating it. Our money's on Jeff.]

GPG: Chip Douglas, I duly toss a stale stick of Aspergum your way! C'mon, so what did your Monkeemen turn down "Sugar, Sugar" *for*? None other than "A Little Bit Me, A Little Bit You," a little piece of Brill-manufactured fluff from the very pen of Neil Diamond—and *sung*, as if I needed to drive my point any further home, by Davy "I've Got a Luverly Buncha Coconuts" Jones himself. I rest my case, Carl!

CC: Well . . . no. "A Little Bit Me, A Little Bit You" was originally prepared under Kirshner's auspices, and actually released (improperly) on Kirshner's authority with "She Hangs Out" as its B-side. This single was released only in Canada, immediately withdrawn, and Kirshner's actions in this regard were the specific grounds for his dismissal.

GPG: Those wacky Canadians . . . at least *they* know their bubblegum when they hear it.

CC: "A Little Bit Me" *was* issued as the next Monkees single, but with the Nesmith-written, Monkees-played and infinitely superior "The Girl I Knew Somewhere" replacing "She Hangs Out" on the flip.

GPG: Trés-groovy harpsichord solo by supposedly dumb-Monkee Pete on ". . . Girl I Knew . . ." notwithstanding, from that first fateful post-Kirshner 45 ever onwards, the Monkees' halcyon daze as guaranteed *Tiger Beat*-approved hit-makers were definitely more than numbered. I implore: had Monkee Mike not forever scared away the Man With The Golden Ears (purportedly by threatening to punch his facial lights out), and then man-handled his make-believe bandmates down that ill-fated path towards, quote unquote artistic credibility, perhaps we would have *all* been spared such well-meaning but undeniably heavy-handed stabs at post-*Pepper* relevance

as "Zor And Zam" and (the J.F.K. assassination version especially of) "Mommy And Daddy," not to mention Jack Nicholson's screenplay for *Head*.

CC: Whoa! We're headed down the wrong road here, Butch. The question isn't whether the Monkees made better records with or without Kirshner's supervision; it's merely a question of whether those earlier records could be described as "bubblegum." I *like* bubblegum! I *like* the Archies, and I like "Sugar, Sugar," though I confess to liking Wilson Pickett's incredible version even more.

GPG: Blasphemy!

CC: My contention that the Monkees weren't a bubblegum group is not a value judgment, but merely a rejection of that label being applied to our beloved Prefab Four. The Beatles, at least initially, had something of a manufactured image, formed by press hype and by *A Hard Day's Night*; they even had a weekly TV cartoon series, for cryin' out loud! But the Beatles were *not* a bubblegum group.

GPG: But y'know, I've always wondered how musical history could have been forever rewritten had only Kasenetz n' Katz, rather than Phil Spector, been called in to salvage those *Get Back/Let It Be* sessions . . .

CC: One can only wonder . . . ! By the way, Paul Revere & the Raiders wore funny costumes, didn't seem to take themselves very seriously at all, and had daily TV exposure on *Where The Action Is!* But they rocked like nobody's business, and the Raiders were *not* a bubblegum group.

GPG: Hey! I'll have you know I consider "Mr. Sun, Mr. Moon" to be right on up there with "Bang-Shang-A-Lang" and "Hooray For Hazel."

CC: At one point the Who was supposedly being groomed to star in a British TV series . . .

GPG: Now *that* would have been awesome! I always did enjoy Keith Moon's James Cagney impersonation more than Micky Dolenz's.

CC: Even so, that would *not* have made the Who a bubblegum group. So much, then, for the notion that a musical act's hype and calculated marketing would necessarily classify them as "bubblegum."

GPG: Carl, you *like* blinding me with science, don't you?

CC: Actually, I can't *stand* Thomas Dolby.

GPG: Ahh, but was he "bubblegum?"

CC: Ick! How about the act of making records? Both the Animals and the Yardbirds relied heavily on outside songwriters, yet neither was a bubblegum group. At Motown, acts like the Four Tops, the Temptations and the Supremes utilized a veritable Hit City assembly line to create The Sound Of Young America, yet none of these acts was a bubblegum group.

GPG: I have but two almighty words to insert here: "Jackson 5ive."

CC: I'll grant you that one! Also, both the Byrds and the Who used session musicians on their earliest efforts, and Brian Wilson used session musicians to craft the best of the Beach Boys' canon, yet none of these was a bubblegum group. Carrying the illustration a bit too far, the Monkees were more of a "real" band on *Headquarters* than the Beach Boys ever were on *Pet Sounds*, but anyone who wishes to dis *Pet Sounds* on that basis is pretty much applying for a fistfight as far as I'm concerned.

GPG: And as far as I am too — and I'm no rock critic to be toyed lightly with either: I was once a bouncer at a salad bar, I'll have you all know.

CC: Teen idolatry? Most of the true bubblegum acts of the '60s were anonymous, while Davy and the other Monkees joined the likes of the Beatles, the Stones, the Raiders and, I might concede this one, Herman's Hermits in the sacred pages of *16* and *Tiger Beat*.

GPG: Most of the true bubblegum acts of the '60s were only anonymous, methinks, because Buddah Records just didn't take Gloria Stavers out to, um, lunch often enough . . .

CC: I don't even really regard Herman's Hermits as a bubblegum group *per se*, but those others most certainly weren't. And neither were the Monkees. And, to respond to your own tangent, the Monkees had more than their share of musical triumphs after Kirshner's exit, even if their days at the Tops of the Pops were indeed numbered. Their third and fourth albums, *Headquarters* and *Pisces, Aquarius, Capricorn & Jones, Ltd.*, expanded the Monkee sound without any discernible dip in quality. Tracks like "You Just May Be The One," "Pleasant Valley Sunday," "Words," "For Pete's Sake," "The Door Into Summer" and "What Am I Doing Hangin' 'Round?" would be stellar numbers *regardless* of their origin.

GPG: And let's not forget the immortal "Zilch," which really truly was the first recorded instance of (bubble-) "rap"—and three years before the Last Poets too! Though let's also point out, from those very same elpees you speak of, "I Can't Get Her Off My Mind," "Cuddly Toy," "Star Collector" (again, years before the Stones et al. ever thought to immortalize the Plaster Casters, etc. etc., in song and dance!) And Tork's crowning achievement "Peter Percival Patterson's Pet Pig Porky": all of which would have sounded more than comfortably at home on any Kasenetz-Katz Singing Orchestral Circus album.

CC: Granted, the quality-to-dreck ratio may have dipped following *PAC&J*, but there remained scattered moments of brilliance right up to the end. The last Monkees album, 1970's *Changes*, even landed the Monkees deep inside the bubblegum periphery . . .

GPG: Ah-*haaa!*

CC: . . . as sole remaining members Dolenz and Jones worked alongside gummy stalwarts Jeff Barry, Andy Kim and Bobby Bloom to create a decidedly lightweight but *not* wholly unappealing—album. Micky and Davy followed that with one honest-to-Neil-Bogart bubblegum single, "Do It In The Name Of Love," released under their own names in 1971.

GPG: Yes, God bless my man Davy! At least he forever stayed stuck firmly to his bubbleyum roots, what with all his Kirshner-worthy, pop-by-committee solo albums and *Brady Bunch* guest spots. Meanwhile, his by now fellow ex-Monkee Mike was reduced to hawking portentous-indeed "books with soundtracks" from the back of *Rolling Stone* magazine. Anyone out there got a spare copy of the *Davy Hello!* Live-in-Japan album they'd like to swap for my original box set edition of Michael Nesmith's *The Prison*? I didn't think so.

CC: I think I'll just reject both extremes . . . Or maybe we can trade the whole mess in for a solid, rockin' pop Micky Dolenz-Peter Tork album?

GPG: Only if the Man With The Golden Ears produces.

CC: Agreed. Him or Joey Ramone.

The 1910 Fruitgum Company by Bill Holmes

When today's artists issue a new release every two years they are dubbed "prolific." In the late '60s, however, a band could have a six-album career in that 24-month span. And if you consider that the 1910 Fruitgum Company was just one of the several "bands" springing from the minds of Jerry Kasenetz and Jeff Katz during that time, you begin to understand what an incredible feat the kings of bubblegum pulled off in tandem with Buddah Records mogul Neil Bogart. Bubblegum music was little more than stripped-down rock 'n' roll with a unique marketing spin, and the Super K boys spat them out as fast as they could put them together in their Bubblegum Factory. The 1910 Fruitgum Company was arguably the duo's biggest success.

Who really knows where the band's name came from? When you consider that singers like Ron Dante and Tony Burrows were the voices behind several "acts" who were collectively a stable of studio musicians, can you really believe the "origins" of any of the groups? The puff piece will claim that the name came from a wadded-up gum wrapper that was found in a coat pocket, and as "bubblegum" stories go, why not? Originally an actual band called Jeckell & the Hydes, legend has it that Katz's *father* discovered the

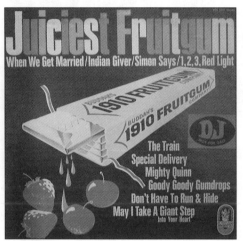

band in a diner in Linden, New Jersey. Vocalist Mark Gutkowski had the pitch and timbre that the Super K team felt would be perfect for "Simon Says." Although they were sure that the song was a hit record waiting to happen, they had not been able to find the magic while trying it with several other bands. Enter Gutkowski and crew, and the beginning of a torrid two years on the charts.

Starting with "Simon Says," the band released a string of successful and irresistible singles based on playground games and nursery rhymes set to a simplistic but rocking beat. Featuring a rhythmic organ sound and sing-along chorus (they were playground songs, after all), "1, 2, 3 Red Light," "Goody Goody Gumdrops," "Indian Giver" and "Special Delivery" were massive hits. Like many bubblegum hits, the childish appeal scored with the youngest set while the sexual innuendo was just below the surface for those clever enough to make the connection. Although they were not as lyrically overt as "Chewy, Chewy" (by label-mates the Ohio Express), "Indian Giver" and "1, 2, 3 Red Light" conveyed enough sexual frustration through Gutkowski's yearning vocals to hit even the dimmest listener over the head. Ironically, clueless parents who decried the "filthy" innuendoes of the Rolling Stones and other hard rock bands gleefully supplied their children with records that were perhaps even lewder.

In what must be considered a true *Spinal Tap* moment, the band underwent a massive personnel change, donned biker leather and issued a trippy hard rock record rife with everything bubblegum music was against—long solos, experimental jams and a complete lack of hooks. Despite one low-charting single, they were too deep for gum and too cheesy for real stoners; the Fruitgum lost its flavor. Had they not gone off the deep end, the drastic changes of early 1970s radio would have killed them anyway. But 20 years later, hip artists like Joan Jett (a killer version of "Indian Giver") and the Talking Heads ("1, 2, 3 Red Light") would prove that a strong beat, a great hook and a three minute song is still an unbeatable combination.

Will the Real Ohio Express Please Stand Up? by Becky Ebenkamp

Dean Kastran and Joey Levine never performed side by side on a stage, nor have they ever recorded a song together. Yet simultaneously throughout the late 1960s, both were members of same band, and each could claim some responsibility for its success: Dean as the face, a good-looking kid in a Midwestern rock group lured into a contract by the Super K Productions team, photographed for record covers and then shanghaied into a life of nonstop touring. And Joey as the studio whiz kid, songwriter, and famous, distinctive voice of "Yummy, Yummy, Yummy," "Chewy, Chewy" and the group's other bubblegum hits. This is the story of the Ohio Express, a band whose story has so many twists and turns it should qualify as the other Great Rock'n'Roll Swindle.

By the time Jerry Kasenetz and Jeff Katz came to Mansfield, Ohio on a musical scouting expedition in 1966, Sir Timothy and the Royals were making a name for themselves on the greater Columbus circuit. Comprised of high schoolers Tim Corwin (drums), Dale Powers (lead guitar), Doug Grassel (rhythm guitar), Jim Pfahler (organ) and Dean Kastran (bass), the popular local group—like many of the garage bands that formed across the country after hearing the fuzz-drenched opening riff of "Satisfaction"—was sub-

sisting on a steady flow of dances, pool parties and battles of the bands. Sir Tim opened for nationally touring acts, such as the Turtles and Billy Joe Royal, and their weekend gigs were lucrative enough for members to buy Jaguars, Mustangs and other hot wheels.

When fellow Central Ohio group the Music Explosion charted with national hit "Little Bit of Soul," their producers decided Ohio was fertile ground ripe for the musical picking. On that group's recommendation, Kasenetz and Katz paid Sir Tim a visit. "They flew into Mansfield with contracts in hand," Kastran recalled. "Here we had two guys from New York with a proven track record offering us a deal. We suggested taking the contracts to local lawyers, but they said that wouldn't be neces-

sary." In fact, the duo made it clear that it was now or never. Oh, and one more thing, kids: "Your name sounds too British—we're gonna change it to the Ohio Express."

So the group—in actuality, their parents—signed the contract, and a couple of weeks later they were given not only a new name but a song, "Beg Borrow & Steal"—"given" in the literal sense.

Much to the boys' surprise, "Beg Borrow & Steal" had already been recorded and released by another Super K group called the Rare Breed. The same song, the same recording, was rereleased by the Ohio Express, a switcheroo that was a sign of things to come. "They said, 'This'll get you on the map,'" remembers Kastran when the red flag was raised. "Don't worry, you'll record songs . . ."

Now there was some truth on both accounts: first, the song did get the Ohio Express on the map, in fact, it made the Top 40. Second, record songs they did—just not those marketed as singles. The songs that would make them famous. The songs that would earn serious royalties.

Back East, Kasenetz and Katz were looking for songwriters to fill their stable. Enter one Joey Levine, a 17-year-old NYC kid from a musical family. While still in high school, Levine was writing tunes with the likes of Chip Taylor, Doc Pomus and Carole Bayer. The prolific teenager would then take the three-to-five songs he wrote each week down to the music publishers, pick up some cash and make demos. "I was living off the advances," Levine said. "I'd pick up $500 a week." Eventually, Levine hooked up with Artie

Ohio Express Ephemera by Becky Ebenkamp

A Disastrous Love

Having long lamented the fact that my name seems to appear in approximately zero song titles, I was thrilled when Joey Levine mentioned a song he'd recorded titled "Becky and Joe," which he described as "a monumental bomb" for his label. Here's what else he had to say about the ditty:

> I became so enchanted and pigheaded about it—I argued vehemently with my partner, Artie Resnick, that not only wasn't it a B side, but it was to be my first single under my own name. I wrote it and recorded it on the spot and just thought it was pure genius. It's an ode to two horny kids who run from their parents' objections and off in the eye of a storm and stop only long enough to make passionate, hot and sweaty love in the hay of a neighbor's barn. Listening to it now it sounds particularly hysterical and only goes to prove that when you're young your ego sometimes interferes with your grasp on reality. In other words, "What the hell was I thinking?" It's an orgasmic hoot.

Joey Levine Fast Facts:

- If the nation's 10-year-olds had known they were listening to opera, perhaps they would have invested their record money in more candy: Levine based the melody of "Chewy, Chewy" on "Figaro." (Figaro-Figaro, Figaro-Figaro . . .)
- Other pages in the Levine songbook: "Mony Mony," "Montego Bay," "Life is a Rock but the Radio Rolled Me." Aside from his writing duties, Levine sang backup on songs by the Monkees and a slew of other pre-fab '60s groups that he's long forgotten.
- Along with Archies' singer Ron Dante, Levine has had the distinction of having his voice in the Top 10 concurrently with songs recorded under different band names.
- Before Dante got the gig, Levine was asked to sing lead on the Archies records for double union scale. When the savvy teenager inquired about profit points, Don Kirshner just about fell out of his chair.
- Unlike most bubblegum songwriters, Levine cops to the charge that his orally fixated songs were subliminally sexual. "We were told to write these innocent songs, to keep it young and poppy," Levine said in an interview in LCD magazine, "but we were all in our late teens so we wanted to slide some double entendres past 'em if we could." However, he did quell one circulating rumor: in the song "Peanuts," he was most definitely not singing "penis."

Resnick ("Under the Boardwalk," "Good Lovin'") at publishing house TM Music, and the two became a songwriting team.

"Try It," a Levine-Resnick tune recorded by the Standells and subsequently banned in some areas as too risqué, came to K&K's attention. The duo had the Ohio Express record a tamer version in 1967 as a single for the Beg, Borrow & Steal album on Cameo/Parkway Records. At least, they got to sing it: "We walked into the studio and [session musicians] were recording it, so we just put the vocal tracks on. Dale sang lead," Kastran said. While they didn't take to well to this studio musicians concept, the band did like the song, which was harder-sounding than the bubblegum that would follow. "We were all big Cream and Hendrix fans, so we liked that one better," Kastran said. The song peaked at #83 on the Billboard charts in February 1968.

Charmed by this burgeoning bubblegum/ garage sound, Cameo's A&R man Neil Bogart formed Buddah Records and took the Super K projects along. Since "Try It" was a modest hit, Levine and Resnick were asked if they'd be interested in doing the follow-up single. Kasenetz & Katz liked "Yummy, Yummy, Yummy," a song Levine penned for Jay & the Techniques ("Apple, Peaches, Pumpkin Pie"), but rejected by the soul band's producer. A demo was recorded by the K&K house band and, later, Joey supplied the vocals. When Bogart heard this recording of the future bubblegum classic, he ordered, "Have this guy sing on the records!" Case closed, fate sealed.

"I didn't even know it was coming out," Levine said, still sounding a bit shocked. "I heard it in my car on the radio while driving to my parents house—it was a Pick of the Week."

Meanwhile, the boys from Ohio got busy playing concerts and making promotional appearances for local radio stations in return for airplay. The were now sharing stages with the likes of the Beach Boys, the Who and Herman's Hermits and their lives became a never-ending roadshow. So often were they traveling to New

York, Kastran recalls, that he, Tim and Doug found it necessary to move into an apartment close to the Columbus airport in case they needed to split on a second's notice. It was this apartment, in fact, where the producers called to play them the catchy little ditty that would become their next single.

By this time, even the most A.D.D.-addled reader can guess where this is going, but the naive young members of the Ohio Express were products of a far less cynical time: the "demo" they were hearing was actually a done deal: "Now we think what we're listening to is the song we're gonna record," Kastran said. "But then they tell us, 'No, no, it's all finished!'"

"Yummy, Yummy, Yummy" went gold, and the Ohio Express needed another single. No problem, the group would learn, Levine already had "Down at Lulu's" in the can. "I hardly ever met the Ohio Express—there was no reason," Levine said. "I'm sure they were very upset about it. They became this other thing; they toured."

Feeling a bit defeated but still enjoying the perks of their building fame, there was nothing to do but make the best out of the situation, and try to impersonate Levine's patented nasal-punk sound. "We went around the members of the group and said, 'Whose voice sounds the most like this guy?' and it ended up being me," Kastran said. So he tackled live singing duties for all the Levine-sung singles, while other members would handle vocals on the songs they wrote to round out the LPs.

Now this brings up an interesting phenomenon in the Ohio Express story, one that all but the most sugar-shocked preteen gumster of the day must have picked up on. To say that the group's records were inconsistent is a vast understatement. Songs fell into two discrete categories: 1) the poppy/punky bubblegum hits penned and sung by Levine and 2) the garagey, increasingly psychedelic offerings that filled out the albums, those written and recorded by the original band members.

The latter were more in keeping with serious musical peers of the period, but it was hard, no

◆ A Kasenetz-Katz recording is often blessed with a kooky B side, such as a song played backwards (Ohio Express' "Sweeter Than Sugar" in reverse = the flipside, "Bitter Lemon") or an unfinished, drunken-sounding singalong (1910 Fruitgum Company's "Sticky, Sticky"). To set the record straight, the producers were not dyslexic. "This was not a creative decision, but rather a way for Jeff and Jerry to get their names on the record and reap the financial benefits," Levine said. "Neither of them were writers, and this fixed that."

Fun on the Road

For Kastran & company, shilling for the Ohio Express had its perks, such as performing on national TV shows. The band played on *The Dick Cavett Show*, sort of, right around the time performing live was coming into vogue. Cavett asked Kastran to sing over the recorded track. "I sang about half, and then they said, 'Cut, lip sync it.' I could fake being Joey Levine in front of screaming crowds, but not in a TV studio."

On *American Bandstand*, the group got chewed out by Dick Clark for tardiness that forced them to perform "Down at Lulu's" in their street clothes. In the on-camera interview with Clark, a giggling Kastran explained how air-traffic problems at LAX caused the group to circle for several hours. In actuality, they had missed their flight due to an alarm clock snafu right out of a *Seinfeld* episode.

Perhaps the lying was bad karma, because when they flew out for a show that night, runway lights weren't working and they were summarily sued for failing to make the scheduled appearance. "Failure to show" suits were not uncommon for the constantly touring band. In one case, a missed connection in New Orleans was a blessing because the plane crashed, killing all aboard. The Ohio Express was still sued for missing the concert that they also wouldn't have made it to had they been on that fateful flight. ◉

doubt, for listeners to appreciate them when bumped up against something as exuberant and AM radio-marketable as "Yummy, Yummy, Yummy."[16] If garage or psych fans had been able to sample them in a blind taste test, many might have found these songs to be well-constructed, tuneful and a pretty good

16. As one music writer put it, they sounded like "bad Procol Harum rip-offs."

indication of what bands across the country were doing in 1967–'68. Then again, playing the producer's advocate, you don't fuck with the formula, of which Woodstock was most certainly not an ingredient.

Still, the band wasn't going to skip down Teenybopper Avenue without a fight, even if it meant ambushing their careers. "Had we milked the popularity of it, had we played music that was consistent with the hits, there could have been more to it in spite of the fact we were being ripped off," Kastran believes. "But we couldn't help but bust into "Purple Haze" in the middle of [a show]."

The beginning of the end occurred on one August day in 1968. Traveling to a gig in Cincinnati with the Lemon Pipers, things began heating up. Organ player Pfahler had been flaking out on shows, and after a big argument, he pulled the group's psychedelic van over and walked off with the keys. This oft-used tactic was wearing thin with the other members, and this time they called his bluff. Car buff Corwin tweaked the wiring and they sped off, leaving their bandmate stranded on the interstate.

Already worried about performing at that night's gig without one of their lead singers, bad turned to worse when they decided to ease the tension with a little relaxation music. Someone turned on the radio just in time to hear the announcer say, "And here's the new single by the Ohio Express . . ." There was one tiny problem with that: The producers hadn't bothered to tell the guys that "they" had recorded this song, which, incidentally, was called "Chewy, Chewy."

"People were asking, 'Are you gonna play your new song?' and of course we couldn't tell them [our secret]," Kastran said. "We just made some kind of excuse." That was pretty much the final straw for him and Powers, who bailed a month later. Other members stayed on, some performing under the band name into the next decade.[17]

"We felt we could do our own music," said Kastran in a short film on the band by Ohio-based documentarian Michael Toth. "We had material written. With proper time in the studio we could do the singles, no doubt in our minds."

Plus, they were getting tired of what they saw as rather shady business dealings. "There were millions of dollars in royalties that we never got," Corwin said in the film. "They told us we had money in an escrow account that wasn't there."

The hectic pace and money issues were catching up with Levine back in New York, too. "We all worked on a very tight schedule," he said. "I would have my musicians booked for two days a week, two days for overdubs, two days for vocals and two days and nights and counting for mixing. Somehow it doesn't add up, and that's kind of how it felt as I was living it. There just was never enough time to get it all done, but it got done."

And while he was writing lucrative gems, Levine wasn't reaping huge, deserved financial rewards. "I believe that whatever Jeff and Jerry lacked in talent they made up for in cheerleading and self-promotion," he said. "Their empire might have gone on indefinitely, if only they would have taken their hands off of their ears and put them in their pockets and shared the wealth with the people making the hits." Eventually, Levine and Resnick left K&K to work for West Coast music producer Mike Curb.

Were this story being relayed via *Behind the Music* rather than a chapter of this book, Kastran's and Levine's lives would be forced into a neat, predictable three-act morality play of rise, fall, redemption. Happily, there's no need for that kind of hyperbolic drama here. While both had some post-Ohio

---

17. This is the more hippiefied version of the Ohio Express that can be seen appearing on German TV's *Beat Club*.

Express challenges — Kastran with the draft board and Levine with a contract with Curb that blocked him from releasing songs — there was no nightmarish descent into booze or pills for either. While the paths they took are quite different, each is happy, and neither wastes much time dwelling on this bizarre chapter of their lives.

Today, Levine is one of the most successful and recognized jingles writers serving Madison Avenue. As his audience graduated from listening to bubblegum to purchasing bubble gum and other consumer products, they've no doubt been persuaded to buy brands thanks to his 20-year career writing such memorable tunes as "Trust the Gorton's Fisherman," Sometimes You Feel Like a Nut "Almond Joy," "Just For the Taste of it "Diet Coke" and "The Softer Side of Sears." Bringing Levine's career full circle, "Chewy, Chewy" recently got a second life as a Quaker's Granola Bar commercial.

And in spite of his negative experiences, Kastran is not a bitter man plotting his rock 'n' roll revenge. A sales rep at Mansfield Electric Supply, he plays local gigs with Dale Powers, his friend of more than 35 years, and the occasional Ohio Express reunion. All members are alive and well.

Some of his former bandmates, however, wouldn't mind if the show were to go on, whether to reclaim fame, compensate for being swindled or simply prove to themselves that they are capable of making good music that's all their own. Drummer Corwin continues to tour with a band billing itself as the Ohio Express, yet he's the only original member. And Powers would still like to record, "just to go in and come out with a nice finished product, even if it sits on my shelf for the rest of my life," he said. "It's just like writing a book — if you know the book never sold one copy, at least you know it's yours, and it came from the heart. And as we get older, that's what we, as musicians, realize that we really want to do."

Many thanks to Joe Foster, Dean Kastran, Joey Levine, Michael Toth (Ohio documentarian), and Rob Santos (Buddha Records) for their assistance.

The Ohio Express' psychedelic tour bus: "You have just been passed by a happening."

The Peppermint Rainbow by John Chilson

Although not usually brought up in conversation when discussing late '60s pop, or any conversation for that matter, the Peppermint Rainbow deserve a definite nod in the pop music lexicon, rather than the aside they're occasionally given.

I was first introduced to them in the late 1980s when a co-worker and rabid 45 collector (who also turned me onto Hanna-Barbara era Danny Hutton) made me a tape with such artists as Tin Tin, the Standells, Jack Wild, and of course, the Peppermint Rainbow. Listening to the title track off of their sole Decca album *Will You Be Staying After Sunday* (1969), I at first thought it could've been a Spanky and Our Gang B-side, or maybe even a rare Cowsills track. It was definitely a standout on the tape, Standells notwithstanding. With its lush orchestration, airy vocals, male/female harmonizing, and a tale of potential heartache or lifelong happiness, I was hooked

Flash to ten years later and I'm at a thrift store on Christmas Eve in Torrance, CA doing a little "last minute" Christmas shopping, when I literally stumble across a plastic crate of LPs, and there's the album. Not to be confused with a militant gay organization, the group name and their music reek of "running through the daisies in slow motion." I can't tell if the members were studio musicians, but they sure did look the part. The back of the album holds a color photo: the men are wearing powder blue suits, wide

ties, and white shoes. The women have the color-coordinated mini-skirts, along with shiny white go-go boots.

The title track, along with its orchestrated movement ("If We Can Make It To Monday"), are definitely the strongest tracks on the entire album, along with a cool version of "Green Tambourine."

Al Kasha, who had tons of hits in the '60s and '70s, wrote "Sunday" and "Monday," along with another track "Don't Wake Me Up in the Morning, Michael." Kasha explains, "Paul Leka was the record producer. He followed the harmonics and style of the demonstration records, but he did an imaginative opening on 'Will You Be Staying After Sunday,' by opening the record with the last licks of the song 'Don't Make Lonely Monday Come Again.'"

Leka originally wrote "Green Tambourine" for the Lemon Pipers, and it sounds like the Rainbow used the original backing tracks and added their own vocals. And although the album has a sunny, Southern Californian sound to it, Kasha says it was actually recorded in Connecticut and New York.

> I came up with a concept of the orchestration by being influenced by Spanky and Our Gang and the Mamas and the Papas, who were hot at the time. Also, there's something inside of me as a writer, that liked writing about heartbreak or hope, and songs that deal with weeks and times of the day. As you can see, it was Sunday, Monday, and waking me up in the morning.
>
> — Al Kasha

Al Kasha and Joel Hirschorn later contributed tracks to the Bugaloos' sole album, including the single "For a Friend," which took advantage of their talent for Sunshine Pop. Their biggest success as a song-writing team came long after their bubblegum careers, when they wrote the Academy Award winning song "The Morning After" for the Irwin Allen *Love Boat* disaster flick, *The Poseidon Adventure*. Adds Kasha, "I will always be thankful to the Peppermint Rainbow for setting me out on this journey."

Survival Of The Grooviest: Paul Revere & the Raiders by Glynis Ward

If you were to ask the members of Paul Revere & the Raiders if they considered themselves a bubblegum group, you'd hear a resounding "no!" Nevertheless, they made some of the most memorable bubblegum songs ever recorded. But this isn't surprising when you remember that the Raiders' versatility made them one of the best-loved American rock 'n' roll groups — a band that changed with the times, doing excellent work in a wide range of musical styles.

Paul Revere, an Idaho short-order cook, formed a part-time rock 'n' roll band called the Downbeats in 1959. Mark Lindsay first played with the band by crashing their set one night, jumping on stage to sing a number. Mark eventually joined the group, singing and playing the saxophone. Under Paul's guidance, they polished their act and became interested in recording. By the early '60s, the group had signed to Gardenia Records, and the Downbeats were known as Paul Revere & the Raiders. "Like Long Hair" began the group's long affiliation with the Dick Clark empire when it was played on *American Bandstand*.

Just as things started going well for the group, Paul got drafted, and was assigned as cook in an Oregon mental institution. Not knowing what would happen to them during Paul's two-year stint, he and Mark Lindsay made a pact. Mark would head to California and as a conscientious objector try to make it in the music industry. If he wasn't satisfied there, he'd move to Oregon when Paul finished his service, and the two would start fresh. True to his word, Mark headed north in 1962 and with Roger Hart behind them, the two worked on finding a permanent line-up and perfecting their soon-to-be world-renowned showmanship. Soon the band signed to Columbia Records, and Terry Melcher began to oversee the band.

By 1965, Paul Revere & the Raiders were a household name due to their hit "Louie, Louie." They were contracted by *Where The Action Is* to be the show's house band, and began a long string of hits: "Kicks," "Just Like Me," "The Great Airplane Strike," and "Good Thing." This period can be considered "classic" Raiders—the band just couldn't fail. For two years they performed on television and toured as much as possible, recording six albums and numerous singles (which frequently featured alternate takes of album cuts). It was an incredible effort for Jim Valley, Phil Volk, Mike Smith, Mark Lindsay and Paul Revere, promoting a group whose main market was the American teenager. Under incredible pressure, they cranked out hit after hit, but by 1967 the world was changing, and so were teenagers.

No longer content with being "The Girl In The 4th Row," record-buying teenagers became divided— and so did the Raiders' market. Young teens were happy with infectious pop ditties, but psychedelia had invaded the airwaves and for the older kids, the band who sang "Kicks" wasn't were it was at. After *Where The Action Is*, Phil Volk and Mike Smith left to form the more "serious" rock group Brotherhood, and Terry Melcher retired as the group's "guru." This put the Raiders in a tight spot. Mark stepped in as their producer and chief songwriter while the group found suitable line-up replacements. Instead of acknowledging the newly psych-inspired pop scene, Lindsay took the band in a completely different direction and as a solo vocalist (although credited to the Raiders) recorded *Goin' To Memphis*, an LP filled with the early '60s sounds of white R&B. In retrospect, it's a fun record, but it didn't do anything to help the band's flagging popularity.

In 1968, the group decided to head right back to their ever-lovin' teenybopper fans. Lindsay and Revere were given a new TV show to host—*Happening*—and soon they recorded a shimmering LP filled with upbeat sunshine sounds and psychedelic influences. It was the right decision. Having demonstrated that they were still capable of tapping into the teen market, the Raiders also wanted to prove to themselves that they could be equally successful, and more fulfilled by appealing to a wider audience. The very title *Hard And Heavy (With Marshmallow)* shows that the Raiders were putting their own struggle for identity out there for all to see. The musical style falls somewhere between the Beatles' post-*Pepper* rock and the Super K sound. "Mr. Sun, Mr. Moon" was the biggest hit for the group in almost two years. Its formulaic bubblegum is fun and senseless, replete with snappy drums and handclaps, and a surprising acoustic guitar bridge. Throughout the LP the band plays with the vocabulary of the time—slightly phased vocals, harpsichord, 12-string guitars—and creates a rather strange mix of countrified baroque bubble-pop. "Time After Time" combines a bit of the old Raiders rock 'n' roll hit sound with bubblegum influences, but it's "Cinderella Sunshine," the second single from the LP, that mixes all the sounds together to form the album's psych-bubblegum-pop opus.

Whereas *Hard And Heavy (With Marshmallow)* is the Raiders' ode to the late '60s sweet teenage sounds, *Alias Pink Puzz* is their "serious rock band" testament. The Raiders play more with country styles,

and lyrical content is decidedly more adult with songs like "Frankfort Side Street." Still feeling the tug of the teen market "Oh, Barbo" was added to the mix. Its bubblegummy sound and innocent lyrics stand out in an LP that's otherwise littered with adult themes.

The Raiders then released what would be their final hit-making album, named after their #1 hit of J.D. Loudermilk's "Indian Reservation," a pop take on a rather serious song. This strange juxtaposition of theme and style seemed to be what Mark Lindsay was trying to accomplish with his own songwriting. "Birds of a Feather" was the second single from this LP—a song which sounds uncannily like the Partridge Family! The single version is wonderfully gummy, while the LP version is quieter.

Throughout the history of the Raiders, songs appear in different mixes on singles and LPs, and on *Collage*, the band pointedly takes many earlier hits and molds them into harder rock tunes.

As the Raiders slipped away from the teen market and opted for harder sounds, they continued to record a few more albums, none of which spawned hit records. In 1976, Mark Lindsay went on to a successful solo career. Meanwhile, Paul guided the group back to their earlier "oldies" sound by taking '50s R&B songs and playing them in a more contemporary style. Although the group retains the name, they are only a shadow of their former selves, touring on the show band circuit, and merely mimicking all that they have done in the past. Recently, however, all the members of the "classic" Raiders line-up reformed for a reunion show.

Salt Water Taffy by Bill Pitzonka

Buddah gum aficionados are no doubt familiar with Salt Water Taffy's *Finders Keepers* album—if not the genuine article, then at the very least its constantly recurring cover on the inner sleeves and back liners of other label offerings. Salt Water Taffy was not a candy-coated Kasenetz-Katz confection, but a sugar-sweetened reconstitution of The Val-Rays, a surf combo from New York City.

The Val-Rays—guitarist Rod McBrien, saxman John Giametta, and drummer Bob Musac—waxed their first Parkway single "Get A Board" in 1964. They scored a local hit with the follow-up, "Yo Me Pregunto (I Ask Myself)," which bubbled under the *Billboard* Hot 100 at #121 that May. New lead vocalist Phil Giarrantano joined the fold for one final single ("It Hurts, Doesn't It Girl") on United Artists before The Val-Rays wiped out.

Rod and John kept up their writing partnership while Rod took on a full-time gig at Allegro Studios, owned by Laurie Records and located in the basement of music industry epicenter 1650 Broadway. There he engineered and played on sessions by the Shangri-Las, Tommy James & the Shondells, and Vinnie Poncia & Pete Anders (the Tradewinds/the Innocence). When the singles charts started filling up with kiddie-themed hits like "Simon Says" and "Apples, Peaches, Pumpkin Pie," the partners penned the

youthful "Finders Keepers." Recent Eastman School of Music grad Meco Monardo was commissioned to arrange the demo. Rod recalls, "He was classically trained, but I knew he could do a great job with these pop arrangements." Apparently so—Meco eventually topped the singles listings in 1977 with his symphonic discofication of "Star Wars/Cantina Band."

The demo of "Finders Keepers" featured a Jay & the Techniques-style lead vocal and a chirpy chorus of taunting children. Rod ran it upstairs to 1650 neighbor Neil Bogart, VP/GM of Buddah, who flipped for the song but hated the lead vocal. Songwriter Tommy West stepped up to the mike, and Buddah proffered an album deal on the strength of the improved version. Rod doesn't remember how the name Salt Water Taffy came about, but given a roster that included 1910 Fruitgum Co. and Lemon Pipers, it must have been sweet inspiration.

Salt Water Taffy.
Left to right: Phil Giarratano, Janie Brannon, John Giametta, Rod McBrien and Kathy Butler.

Tommy West's lead vocal stint was a one-off favor—with partner Terry Cashman, he would record as The Buchanan Brothers ("Medicine Man"), pen album cuts for The Partridge Family, and produce hits for Jim Croce. To fill the lead vocal vacancy, Rod and John called on fellow Val-Ray Phil Giarrantano. Salt Water Taffy got a dash of female flavor when Janie Brannan and Kathy Weinberg were brought in to round out the group.

The *Finders Keepers* album is a tasty soft-pop exercise with chewy bubblegum snap, featuring a host of McBrien/Giametta originals and some choice covers from the Anders/Poncia catalog. Janie's husband Tom wrote the liner notes and would sometimes join Salt Water Taffy's elastic lineup. The title track bubbled under the Hot 100 (#105) in May 1968—their sole charting single. Salt Water Taffy pulled a second playground chant from the album ("Sticks & Stones") followed by a further pair of Buddah singles ("Loop De Loop" and "Easy Does It") before jumping to United Artists for one single in 1970 ("Summertime Girl," yet another Anders/Poncia cover).

Rod meanwhile had become increasingly occupied with other production and studio work, including a long string of commercials. Salt Water Taffy stretched into 1971 with a re-release of "Summertime Girl" on Metromedia (with a different b-side) before dissolving.

The Shadows Of Knight by Glynis Ward

Jim Sohns was hoping that 1968 would be his year. He'd recently fired the entire line-up of his Chicago-based group, the Shadows Of Knight, a now-legendary band known for their blistering white rhythm and blues laced with a tough garage-rock edge. Frustrated with management and his fleeting stardom, Sohns was looking to repeat the success his group had had with their 1966 Top 10 reworking of Them's "Gloria," and their minor original hit, "Oh Yeah."

Dunwich Records was a small Chicago label for which the Shadows Of Knight had released a hand-ful of singles and two albums. By 1968, label owners Bill Traut and George Badonsky decided to fold the label, but honored contracts by helping their bands sign deals with other labels. Badonsky took on the Shadows Of Knight—who were now Sohns with Dan Baughman, Woody Woodruff, John Fisher and Kenny Turkin—and hooked them up with Kasenetz-Katz and Team Records. Sohns claims that Kasenetz-Katz hoped to add some "legitimacy" to their labels by signing a real band, and with their hard-driving sound and excellent musicianship, his fit the bill. So the Shadows Of Knight moved to New York in hopes of finally "making it."

The band was soon put to work, cutting demo versions of songs intended for other K&K "groups" and providing session assistance. Some of these demos became official releases under other groups'

names, most notably the Ohio Express. But this extracurricular work wasn't what Sohns had in mind. His plans for the Shadows Of Knight and what K&K wanted were stylistically opposed. But somehow, this momentary collision of style and direction brought about two of the most unique songs of the bubblegum genre.

"Shake" is a tough soul-infused number which Sohns recalls was originally recorded with a fuzz guitar hook that K&K later exchanged for bubblegum-friendly signature organ sounds. Although "Shake" only reached #46 on the US charts, it became the group's best-known song. And perhaps not surprisingly, Sohns has no idea who recorded the B-side "From Way Out To Way Under!" Encouraged by the relative success of their first Teem single, K&K sent the Shadows Of Knight into the studio to record a full LP, overlooking the fact that the group had only six songs prepared. The session spawned another fabulously garage-laced bub-blegummer "My Fire Department Needs A Fire Man." Powerful and hard-driving, this song is a far stretch from the sunshine infused tunes being spun by the S.O.K.'s bubblegum contemporaries.

The differences in musical direction soon drove a wedge between the S.O.K. and their record label. The band packed up and headed for home with only those six songs even partially recorded for their Super K LP. To the band's shock, a completed album was released a few months later, filled out with ses-sion tracks and the acoustic barebones version of "Under Acoustic Control" (which is an unfinished song of a long-lost title). The slapped-together album is a great disappointment and not even very bub-blegummy.

Shortly after their break with the Buddha empire, the Shadows Of Knight signed to ATCO and released a few hard rock singles. Jim Sohns has managed to keep the name going off and on over the years, and as of this writing the Shadows Of Knight are once again recording.

The Sopwith Camel by Kim Cooper

Although they recorded for Kama Sutra, and their sole hit had the traditional double-barreled name, the Sopwith Camel was emphatically *not* a bubblegum band. What they were were mid-'60s San Francisco misfits, a little too weird for that scene, who scored a big hit single with a New York producer and broke up so quickly that they barely finished their album.

Nevertheless, people continue to lazily lump the Sopwith Camel in with the bubblegummers, and not entirely without reason. Most Kama Sutra acts had hardcore kiddie appeal, and the Camel was no exception. Their charming, retro songs would go over nicely during kindergarten quiet time. And like all the best bubblegum bands, they were brought to New York at a producer's behest, only to have everything go wrong. If not truly of the genre, we're willing to peg them as bubblegumesque.

Band leaders Peter Kraemer and Terry MacNeil met in a bookshop in 1966. Terry was a student at the San Francisco Art Institute, and Peter was from a bohemian Virginia City family—although he'd moved away before the Red Dog Saloon became hepcat-central during the Charlatans' tenure. Drummer Norman Mayell had played with Mike Bloomfield and Charlie Musselwhite in Chicago before moving west to hanging out with the Kesey crowd. Martin Beard was British, 17, and the bassist, natch.

Kraemer had been living with Chet Helms in the Haight when the latter was trying to launch a new group. Names were bandied about, and Kraemer's suggestion was mocked for being "trite and dumb"—so Helms' group became Big Brother and the Holding Company (sheesh) and Kraemer remembered Sopwith Camel when he formed his own band.

Things started happening for the Camel once occasional bassist Bobby Collins sent a demo tape including "Hello, Hello" to Lovin' Spoonful producer Erik Jacobsen. Jacobsen—a visionary who had left his bluegrass band after hearing the Beatles, and who collaborated with John Sebastian to forge a distinctly American brand of folk 'n' roll—smelled a hit with this light-hearted, ditty, and invited the group out to New York. They signed with Kama Sutra, making them one of the earliest SF bands with a record deal. They'd never quite fit in with the other San Francisco bands, and "selling out" to an East Coast producer ensured that this remained the case. Nonetheless, the Victor Moscoso cover art on their album was one of the first instances of mass exposure for an underground cartoonist from the SF scene.

Sure enough, "Hello, Hello" made the Top 10. Their album, recorded as the group was disintegrating in unfriendly Manhattan, is a delightful old-timey idyll mixing moments of whimsy with some nifty oddball rock 'n' roll. Kraemer's flapper vocal stylings and romantic lyrics are well-served by the organ grinding band. You can see why Jacobsen liked them—they're much closer to the Spoonful in their sense of play and wit than to any of the super-serious Bay Area bands. After recording a couple of Levis ads, the band split up. They reformed around 1971, prompted by Burger King's use of "Hello, Hello" as a commercial jingle, and went on to record one well-reviewed space-rock LP with Jacobsen, *The Miraculous Hump Returns from the Moon* (Reprise, 1973).

The Turtles by Gary Pig Gold

Take a look at the gatefold of the Turtles' stunning 1968 album *Battle Of The Bands:* therein stand not one, not two, but *twelve* different mock-"Turtles" (one for each song), each posed in an absolutely flawless visual parody of — or was it a tribute to? — one dozen different musical sub-genres and styles.

While this delightful ruse may have provided a hearty premise for — gulp — another Concept Album (albeit one which, in my less-than-humble opinion, far out-surpassed the Beatles' comparatively meek *Pepper*-grinding), beneath all the dress-up fun and games lay a more than telling element of ironic, bitter

truth. For the real Turtles indeed spent their entire career struggling to establish a single, all-encompassing identity in the eyes of not only their audiences the world over, but with their long-suffering bosses at White Whale Records, radio programmers everywhere, and perhaps even the actual band members themselves.

In fact, the band's very *origins* seem mucho-schizo to say the least: springing to life in Los Angeles circa 1961 as a rough 'n' ready instrumental combo (the Nightriders), they soon transformed themselves into a real-life surf band (the Crossfires), later tried their hand at folk music (as the Crosswind Singers, would you believe), were also known to show up at local bowling alleys pretending to be Gerry & the Pacemakers, then *finally* settled on the hallowed Turtles moniker (though almost the *Tyrtles*) upon

signing with White Whale in 1965. Their first hit, a Top 40-friendly cover of Dylan's "It Ain't Me Babe," was quickly followed by a P.F. Sloan sound-alike ("Let Me Be") and then the incredible, edible "You Baby."

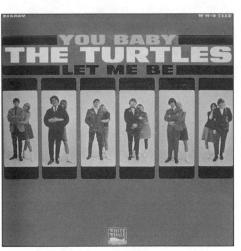

The latter, also from the pedantic pen of Sloan, was an absolute, stick-to-the-roof-of-your-ears candy-rock delight, and its cheery combination of one-handed keyboard licks atop "Hang On Sloopy" thump-and-strum was soon heard reverberating throughout all the biggest and best hits of the Ohio Express, Fruitgum Co., et al, et al. But by *this* time (1967–68), the Turtles had already turned to New York writers Gary Bonner and Alan Gordon for their next two mega-smashes, "Happy Together" and "She'd Rather Be With Me."

It was right about now that the Turtles—always a super-slick and hard-hitting live act—began defiantly expressing more of their road-tested (and quite often *far*-out-there) chops on vinyl as well. Despite the fact that their producer Joe Wissert was reportedly spending an inordinate amount of time reciting

poetry and eating gingerbread bats when he should've been knob-twiddling, "She's My Girl," "Sound Asleep" and even the infamous "Umbassa And The Dragon" were worthy enough to earn the respect of such highly-coveted peers as Frank Zappa (who later employed several post-Turtles in his most popular incarnation of the Mothers of Invention) and Ray Davies (who accepted a rare non-Kink production assignment when offered the chance to record the Turtles' final album).

Yet White Whale, a small label solely dependent upon the Turtles for their financial bread and butter, just wanted lots more "She'd Rather Be Happy"-sounding smashes. Oh yeah? Well! So group leaders Mark Volman and Howard Kaylan, butts against the wall (but with tongues *very* firmly in cheek) simply responded one night by writing the million-selling, wholly-bubble-worthy "Elenore": a hit so insidiously innocuous that it landed the band a chance soon afterwards to perform at the Nixon White House!

This being the late '60s however, gigs at Tricia Nixon's prom were not the kind of events any well-respecting band wore on their denim-tattered sleeves. So as the Turtles' hair and beards—to say nothing of their songs themselves—grew ever longer and less manageable, and while hundreds of thousands of dollars in royalties due from White Whale still seemed lost in the ether, our boys finally tired of bucking the system and bitterly disbanded in 1970. It was a dark day indeed for not only bubblegum, but for mankind in general.

Able to toss off cheerful Top 10 hits at the drop of a Nehru hat, then reply with such intricate, multi-layered gems as "Grim Reaper Of Love," the Turtles certainly could, without a doubt, be considered true purveyors of bubblegum at its ultimate, cleverly-crafted stickiness. These many different faces—*and* facets—of the Turtles also provide a textbook overview of how, and most importantly why, "image" has forever remained at the very core of any band's acceptance and ultimate success. Many of bubblegum's greatest, from the Monkees and Partridges to even the Spice Girls and beyond, have obviously learned important lessons from the Turtles' hard-wrought experiences.

The Mock Turtles of *Battle of the Bands*

The Yummies, interview with Les Fradkin by David Smay

Les Fradkin

The Yummies (aka Les Fradkin) had a regional hit in October 1970 called "Hippie Lady," a single on Sunflower Records. Hundreds of bubblegum one-shots ricocheted off the charts without doing any lasting damage. Here we get the inside scoop on how one such act, the Yummies, came to be.

How did you first get signed to MGM? Did you submit a demo tape? Were you a studio singer/musician that they thought they could spin into a solo act?

Les Fradkin: I was brought over to MGM by Randy Edelman, another songwriter who I befriended at April-Blackwood Music (CBS), where I was already signed as a staff writer. He bolted over to MGM where the "grass looked greener" and suggested that if I was looking for a solo deal (which I was), to give them a try (which I did). My "demo" consisted of a live audition with my acoustic 12-string guitar for Eddie Deane and Wally Schuster (Leo Feist Music) who signed me to a long-term production and songwriter agreement. They thought they could spin me into a solo act due to my involvement with Edison Lighthouse, where I had never had the opportunity to contribute as a writer. Plus I had the endorsement of John Hammond Sr. from my tenure at CBS and I guess that meant something in those days.

Who produced the sessions for the Yummies? Who wrote the songs? Who played on the sessions?

LF: The sessions were produced by myself, Eddie Deane and Steve Katz (our engineer). The sessions took place at Sound Exchange Studios in NYC in the early fall, 1970. This situation evolved because I was already signed to Sunflower/MGM Records as a solo artist ("Fearless Fradkin") and I was keen to prove myself as a producer to the powers that were. So, brazenly, I asked for the shot. They said, "do something on your own and, if we like it, we'll buy the master!" I already had a single out as Fearless Fradkin ("Song Of A Thousand Voices" b/w "You Can Cry If You Want To"). This record was given a *Billboard* Top 60 pick and superficially sounded like the Brotherhood of Man type style. The song was successful on the MOR charts (#12) but never made it higher than #87 US. But . . . Mirielle Mathieu recorded it for Philips and had a massive hit with it in France in 1971 where it hit #1 and sold really well. I talked endlessly about this possible independent production project to Steve Katz. He was very supportive of the idea to do a bubblegum record, since it was still quite popular on the charts at that time. So we went to the record shop and bought every bubblegum record we could lay our hands on and proceeded to "dissect" the "formula." His boss Bob Morgan (who produced Bobby Vinton and owned the studio) was given a piece of the deal to get the time booked. I basically wrote both songs with a little help from Eddie Deane on lyrics. Steve and Bob were given co-credit although they really had nothing to do with the writing. More political perks, I guess. Since we didn't want to spend much money out of pocket, I played all the instruments on both sides of the record. We "borrowed" a Farfisa organ (an important sound to use) and I played acoustic and electric guitars, bass and drums to a click so I could keep accurate time. Eddie and Bob helped with endless handclap overdubs. I sang all the lead vocals. Eddie and I did the backgrounds. The single that we originally planned was "Patty Cake." We even cut an acetate with the B-side consisting of the A-Side played backwards! They said, "we want a real B-side!" Back we went. Out came "Hippie Lady"—a kind of "Bo Diddley" bubblegum piece. To our surprise, they like that side even more than "Patty Cake." So "Hippie Lady" became the A-side of Sunflower #103. It was released October 1970.

Did the Yummies ever make any live performances, or were they only a studio creation?
LF: The Yummies were intended, at first, as just another studio group. But the record hit in a couple of
regions, which necessitated our "employing" some of my friends to assist in a couple of TV spots to
lip-sync it.

After The Yummies, Les continued to record for MGM, though his solo album was never released. As
a producer he worked on an unreleased Left Banke album for Bell in 1972, and birthed (Lester Bangs'
favorites) the Godz' two albums for ESP. In the late '70s, Les joined the original cast of *Beatlemania*, left
to write jingles and compose for soap operas, only to return to *Beatlemania* for the entire '90s. Today, Les is
again working as a producer.

PRODUCERS AND IMPRESARIOS

Bubblegum is the story of songwriter-producers—makers of shiny sounds. The villains in many rock legends, these are people who saved their innocence for their musical sentiments and never did anything so stupid as to sign away their publishing. Firing inept drummers, replacing lead singers, they ruthlessly worked the system to make it pop. But here we also find gentle studio geeks with a genius for engineering, child prodigies, cheerful tunesmiths in love with the game, the insane pace, the charts.

We're conscious of legendary recording sessions with Phil Spector and Brian Wilson, George Martin facilitating *Sgt. Pepper*, Aretha's first epochal piano chord in Memphis or Hendrix pulling together layers of sonic strata on *Electric Ladyland*. Still, our sense of the studio's place in Rock Mythology remains peripheral. Only serious music fans know the names James Jamerson or Hal Blaine, while even the most casual listener knows their work. Bubblegum, like disco, like Motown, like much of Nashville today, exists primarily within a studio culture of session players and songwriter-producers. This particular hyphenate ought to be better known than singer-songwriters—it's the economic trigger for the whole recording industry. Why? Because both songwriters and producers collect royalties, and if you double up your credits on a hit record you're raking in some serious change.

Reading these interviews we're struck by the canniness and audacity of non-writers Kasenetz and Katz piggybacking bizarre studio goofs onto the b-sides of sure hits to collect songwriting checks. Or Jonathan King's shameless talent for converting fads into pop hits. But we also delight in Jeff Barry building up the drum track for "Be My Baby" one mallet tap at a time, or Mike Batt living in a Womble suit for a week before setting those characters in song.

Here you find tricksters and hipsters, songwriters and songbirds, studio tans and golden ears.

West Coast Pop anticipated bubblegum's methods, blurred the lines between music for sale and music that sells, influenced the sound of bubblegum and provided the pool of creators that presided over its cartooniest era.

As the man who squeezed Brian Wilson's vision into an LP's worth of slot-car racing songs and gave voice to Big Daddy Roth's model kits, Gary Usher's influence can't be overstated. Bubblegum's splendid tradition of completely fictitious bands starts at the Brill Building, but achieves a cheesy genius in the Weird-Ohs, the Super Stocks, the Hondells, and the Revells. Though his busiest period predates bubblegum's onset by several years, Gary Usher laid out the entire bubblegum blueprint before it had a name. He recorded musically and lyrically upbeat music with a steady core of studio musicians under a variety of ghost band names, commissioned for a visual medium (substitute Beach Movies for TV here). Whereas most bubblegum makers went into commercial jingles after their bubblegum careers, Usher brazenly turned a Honda promotion into a masterstroke of pop genius ("Little Honda").

Gary Zekley perfectly encapsulates the West Coast studio scene, swallowing not-so-disparate sub-genres like surf, sunshine pop, bubblegum and psych pop in one gulp. Most of his East Coast peers simply considered themselves pop songwriters with little concern for marketing categories. Zekley's fluid career cautions against leaning too heavily on genre distinctions. You can assign the Fun and Games, Yellow Balloon and the Clique to different bins, but the same talent clearly penned "The Grooviest Girl in the World," "How Can I Be Down" and "Superman."

Oftentimes the supporting players provide a better window into a scene than the big names. Carol Connors found a niche in the L.A. scene, fronting Beach Bunny bands for Gary Usher and co-writing some tunes. Carol's "Yum Yum Yamaha" does more to clarify the seamless fusion of surf, bubblegum and commercial jingles that defined West Coast pop than any five books about the Beach Boys.

Gary Usher by Domenic Priore

Gary Usher

Primarily a record producer, Gary Usher straddled the line between singer, songwriter and studio whiz as a constant, and hard-working, music hustler in Hollywood. Through various creative associations, he managed to have his hand on several of the most important records to come out of the rich rock 'n' roll scene associated with mid-'60s Los Angeles.

It started innocently enough in the teen idol era with a single by Gary Usher & the Highbrows called "Tomorrow" on the Lan-cet label.[18] From the outset, Gary collaborated with ace guitarist and arranger Richie Podolor. Performing at a sock hop in Riverside to promote his Titan single "Driven Insane," Usher struck up a key friendship with the KFWB's Roger Christian, the disc jockey promoting the event. They bonded over a mutual love of hot rodding, and here begins the most prolific source of hot rod music in rock 'n' roll history. Another Titan artist who would figure in the development of the West Coast Sound, Ginger Blake, was also on hand that evening to promote her single, "My Diary."

Usher quickly recognized the talent of a young Brian Wilson. Brian was part of the same sock hop circuit in the greater Los Angeles area behind the success of The Beach Boys' "Surfin'"—a #2 hit on KFWB in the winter of 1961. On a trip to the auto parts store, Usher and Wilson discussed their dream cars. Brian started humming a little tune and Usher threw out some lines in jest about horsepower, "giddy-up, giddy-up." Within a few minutes the new team had a song called "409," which became a national hit single as the flip side to the Beach Boys' first Capitol 45, "Surfin' Safari." Usher had a bit more experience in the Hollywood environment, and showed Wilson a few of the ropes. One of the first outside productions credited to Brian Wilson was a Gary Usher project, a girl group single by Rachel & the Revolvers ("The Revolution" b/w "Number One"). These are crucial, early Wilson sides, where he began to use outside musicians in the style of his hero, Phil Spector.

From the outset the collaboration was a tough go. Murray Wilson, Brian's abusive father, considered Usher a bush leaguer, and preferred Roger Christian—a famous DJ after all—as a contributor to Brian's hot rod material. Christian co-wrote "Little Deuce Coupe" and "Don't Worry Baby," and Usher's proximity to Christian kept the creative friendships mutual. It got even deeper when KFWB DJ Jimmy O'Neil presented the Beach Boys at Pandora's Box in one of the first rock 'n' roll engagements to grace the Sunset Strip. Usher invited Ginger Blake, who brought her cousins Marilyn and Diane Rovell to the gig. The girls were in the process of forming their own singing group. Brian Wilson spilled hot chocolate on Marilyn Rovell; it would lead into a creative and marital relationship. The girl group soon became the Honeys, who later evolved into Spring during the '70s.

Though Usher managed to get credit on a few more Brian Wilson gems such as "In My Room," it was with Dennis Wilson that Usher made his next important step in the studio. A very rare Damark 45 by the Tri-Five features the Wilson brothers backing a Gary Usher instrumental, a style he would develop further with Richie Podolor. Dennis Wilson went a step further with Usher as a vocalist and drummer on Challenge singles by the Four Speeds. "R.P.M." broke as a minor hit out of Bakersfield, and "My Sting Ray" remains an important part of the Dennis Wilson / Gary Usher friendship on wax. There were others, such as "Barefoot Adventure" by the Pendeltons for Dot Records, based on the title of a Bruce Brown

---

18. Interestingly enough, Maywood was both the home of Lan-cet and the base of operations for Ed "Big Daddy" Roth—Usher's partner on the Ratfink albums.

surfing film that had featured a soundtrack by West Coast jazzman Bud Shank. Usher also brought the Honeys in to sing the chorus of his Dot follow-up, "Three Surfer Boys," which he released under the name Gary Usher and the Usherettes. Usher's next solo single, "Sacramento," would be a complete Brian Wilson production for Capitol, featuring the Honeys on background vocals. This was a departure, as a

smooth, country/pop ballad with clip/clop percussion that was later echoed on "God Only Knows" for the Beach Boys' *Pet Sounds*, only a year and a half later.

Through his association with Dennis and Brian Wilson, Usher wound up providing music to American International Pictures' Beach Party movie series, featuring Frankie Avalon and Annette Funicello. A.I.P. first asked the Beach Boys to do the music for *Beach Party* in 1963, but a road tour made Brian Wilson unavailable. Legend has it that A.I.P. heard that the guys who wrote the surfing songs would not be available, but that they could have the guys who wrote the hot rod songs (Usher and Christian,) and that they could provide surfing songs for the film. Voila! In the course of five short years *Beach Party* rated more sequels and imitators than *Star Trek* has yet to manage. Gary Usher and Roger Christian became the first on-call studio writers, and in the

winter of '63–64 they brought in Brian Wilson to write and produce the music for the follow-up, *Muscle Beach Party*. Wilson and Usher produced Donna Loren's Challenge single "Muscle Bustle" from the film. The accompanying Annette Funicello *Muscle Beach Party* album showcases the Wilson/Usher/Christian collaboration (though not the same Wilson/Usher produced tracks as used in the film). The LP features the Honeys on very effective background vocals and, musically, *Muscle Beach Party* is a high water mark for Annette.

During all the action at Challenge Records [19] a crew of regulars began to form around the landslide activity surrounding the young producer. Along with Richie Podolor (who cut three killer surf albums as Richie Allen during this period), there was Chuck Girard (a vocalist with the Castells), Richie Burns (another good singer), Wayne Edwards, and Dennis McCarthy. These musicians, along with many of the

same studio players used by Phil Spector in the Wrecking Crew, provided Usher with his own gang. He dubbed them his "troops." These guys broke out in a big way when Capitol Records provided a three-album deal for Usher under the name The Super Stocks. Beginning with the brassy hot rod studio churn of *Thunder Road*, Usher hit his stride on his first-stage meisterwerk, *Surf Route 101*. Some of the tunes were a collaboration with Brian Wilson, the others glassy surf instrumentals with Richie Podolor. They capped it off with the boss *School is a Drag*, basically a concept album about ditching school to hit the stock car races.

Proof that Usher had the ability to get down and dirty with the best of 'em in surf music, there were convincing sides penned and produced by Usher during this period by Dave Myers & the Surftones (the brilliant "Gear") the Pyramids ("Midnight Run") the Surfaris (two and a half albums) and Dick Dale & his Del-tones (various Capitol tracks).

19. Usher also produced three cool singles under another pseudonym, the Sunsets.

A penchant for fake band names was also perfect for three projects involving competing hot rod model and slot car manufacturers. Going back to his Maywood days, there were three Capitol albums Usher did with Ed "Big Daddy" Roth. These albums by *Mr. Gasser & the Weirdos* were more comedy/novelty music than anything. "You know, we did tunes like 'Termites in My Woody,'" claims Roth, "But we didn't make a dime off of the three albums, so that was it for the records." When asked who Mr. Gasser was, Usher replied "Whoever was up next," meaning that the Super Stocks/Hondells guys subbed for whatever character was being portrayed. These were Revell model kits. Revell's competition, the low budget Hawk model kit maker, then called on Usher to provide similar characters for their cool rip-offs, the Weird-ohs and the Silly Surfers. Two albums appeared on Hawk Records, one a surfer-model LP, another celebrating the hot rodder models. The best of both were then compiled for release on Mercury. The most brilliant exploitation concept was the slot car songs done for Revell on *The Go Sound of the Slots by the Revells*. This saw issue on Frank Sinatra's Reprise label. Usher used the Reprise deal to get the Beach Boys to back him and Brian instrumentally on a vocal single by the Timers, "No Go Showboat."

In the rush of excitement that was 1964—the Beatles' arrival and The T.A.M.I. Show but two examples—Usher spotted a tune from the new Beach Boys album *All Summer Long* that Brian didn't plan to release as a single. The troops were brought in, and before you could say "First gear!" "Little Honda" became a hit for Mercury by a group now called the Hondells. Girard, Burns, Edwards and McCarthy were grafted onto an album cover, appeared on *Shindig!* and hit the road in what would become Usher's most famous group. There were follow-up hits in "Hot Rod High," "Ride With Me" and the Brian Wilson collaboration "My Buddy Seat." Around this time, Usher brought Wilson on the set of a Paramount Pictures beach cash-in called *Girls on the Beach*. The Beach Boys were seen in three segments, including the opening title sequence and a groovy lip synch of "Little Honda." Originally, the *All Summer Long* album would have been the soundtrack to the Beach Boys' own A.I.P. film, *Beach Boys Hawaiian Style*, but that fell apart when A.I.P. attempted to gobble up the soundtrack rights. But it is clear that Gary Usher continuously brought Brian Wilson with him into his endeavors for the motion picture industry.

As A.I.P. cynically took the Beach Party gang to the slopes in the 1965 epic *Ski Party*, Usher brought the Hondells to their creative pinnacle in a tune called "The Gasser," which was performed when the cast finally comes to their senses and returns to Santa Monica. Originally called "The Greaser" to describe a hot-rodding grease monkey, A.I.P. feared a backlash from the Chicano community and the title was changed. What counted in this production, outside of the rockin' abandon of the visuals and track, was the cool sense of experimentation that went into the recording. Here we get the Richie Podolor/Gary Usher collaboration at its best. The unique guitar sound of "The Gasser" also appears on Usher's production of Keith Green's "Go Go Getter," and foretold of Podolor's later work on the Chocolate Watchband's *Inner Mystique* and the Electric Prunes' *Mass in F Minor*. Ed Cobb and David Alexrod took over these respective band names, using Podolor's genius to produce psychedelic pop masterworks. For Usher, the next step was about to happen. He'd weaned a young Mike Curb on Hondells productions, and handed the gig over to Curb. Usher went on to get involved in the new sound that was emerging from the Sunset Strip.

The Byrds broke open the Hollywood nightlife by going electric with Dylan, adding a 12-string guitar sound purloined from the fade of the Beatles movie theme *A Hard Days' Night*. Their label, Columbia

Records, saw the potential in this for their own shelved folk artists Simon & Garfunkel. Columbia called in Gary Usher to help electrify "The Sounds of Silence." While the extent of Usher's involvement in that hit production is unknown, it was enough to inspire Columbia's confidence in him. Not long after that, Usher produced the Byrds, Chad & Jeremy and the Peanut Butter Conspiracy for the label. He began by honing his chops in a production gig for Decca with the Surfaris. Usher's job was spelled out by the label: he was to record two LPs worth of current covers for *Hit City '65* and *It Ain't Me Babe* (the latter a stab at hitting the folk-rock market).

Usher used this Decca connection to produce two singles for The Sons of Adam—perhaps the most popular Sunset Strip band to never make it big. Their guitarist, Randy Holden had been in a superb surf group called the Fender IV, who cut burning singles such as "Margaya," "Malibu Run" and "Everybody Up." The combination clicked creatively, and the two 45s by the Sons of Adam are a testament to the depth of excitement to be found on Sunset Strip in '65–66. Their version of the Yardbirds' "Mister You're A Better Man Than I" equals the original, with Holden providing a solo that makes further interesting commentary on one of Jeff Beck's most interesting breaks. The Sons of Adam popularized Boyce & Hart's "Tomorrow's Gonna Be Another Day" long before the Monkees got hold of it. "Take My Hand" and "Saturday's Son" were also definitive slices of Sunset Strip garage sound. Working consistently during this period, Usher cooled his heels recording 45s with country icon Hank Snow, Wayne Newton, *Shindig!* teen idol leftover Bobby Sherman, shameless transitional stuff like "Honda Bike" and a version of Buffy

St. Marie's "Codine" by Sean & the Brandywines.

Conceptually, 1966 was an important year for Gary Usher. He threw himself into his most creative single, "My World Fell Down" (by Sagittarius), at precisely the same time Brian Wilson was doing "Good Vibrations." The near-simultaneous release of these recordings raises intriguing questions. Columbia was one of the three studios Brian Wilson worked at during his production of "Good Vibrations." Something that contributed greatly to Brian Wilson's paranoia on the eve of the *Smile* sessions was the strange disappearance of the "Good Vibrations" master tape from Columbia studios, only to be returned just as mysteriously a few days later. Wilson's fear of "mind gangsters" during the *Smile* sessions was not unjustified. He was honestly in fear of losing the production of his life just before the release of the Beach Boys' best selling, and most important, hit of the '60s. Without a doubt, "My World Fell Down" features a sound so close to the pioneering work of Brian Wilson, and was so hot on its heels, that it doesn't take much of an imaginative stretch to figure out where that master tape went missing. But we'll never know for sure.

Also strange is how Brian Wilson's two road replacements, Glen Campbell and Bruce Johnston, share the key vocal parts of "My World Fell Down." The verse lead is Campbell, while the chorus round features strongly identifiable parts by Johnston. The single charted, but is best remembered as the most pop-oriented track on the original Elektra *Nuggets* compilation. The moderate success of "My World Fell Down" gave Columbia further confidence in Usher, which lead into his most gorgeous production of all time, the *Present Tense* album by Sagittarius.

For this project, Usher called on the vocal, production and arrangement skills of Curt Boettcher, who had just produced the Association's first big hits, "Along Comes Mary," "Cherish" and the debut album *And Now . . . Along Comes The Association*. It was Boettcher's high harmony part near the end of "Cherish" that gave the song one of its most brilliant hooks. This was a team to be reckoned with, as Boettcher brought both folk roots and a keen perception of Brian Wilson harmony to the game. Boettcher was putting his own spacey spin on both Wilson's jazz-influenced harmony and traditional folk harmonies. It was a splendid blend, amplified by Boettcher's work with Terry Kirkman of the Association, whose worship of Stan Kenton added a progressive jazz slant to the arrangement mix. This was Los Angeles harmony magic at its most ebullient, and the stage was set, with Columbia money, for *Present Tense* to become one of the most rich soundscapes ever committed to vinyl.

The Byrds, in a very real sense, had released the first single of the psychedelic movement in "Eight Miles High" b/w "Why." This was done after their involvement with Terry Melcher, and the follow-up LP to that single, *5D (Fifth Dimension)* was handled by Alan Stanton. The Byrds were looking for a permanent producer, and in Usher they had met someone who could further their wildest desires.

Younger Than Yesterday, though one of the finest Byrds albums, shows the producer and group tentatively searching for a common ground. By the time of their second LP together, *The Notorious Byrd Brothers*, the production sound realized by Usher on *Present Tense* was fully incorporated into a Byrds LP. With the tracks fading in and out of each other similar to the Beatles *Sgt. Pepper*, *The Notorious Byrd Brothers* tracks somehow seem a more natural blend, more harmonious with each other than the abstract contrasts of the Beatles album.

The sessions for *The Notorious Byrd Brothers* were so tense that David Crosby was thrown out of the group during the recording. None of that tension is heard on the LP, except for the part that drove the

artistry involved. While Crosby was out purchasing a yacht with the money from the settlement, and telling the teen mags that he would call it Lysergia, Curt Boettcher was called in to finish the lead vocals on at least two Crosby compositions that grace the LP. Usher also used a Moog synthesizer (still a novelty at the time) to embellish the album. There were no hits, but "Wasn't Born To Follow" wound up in the film *Easy Rider*. In "Change is Now" one can hear an incredible moment where the peak of Crosby-era Byrds harmony and psychedelia, an ethereal guitar solo by Clarence White, and the bands' forthcoming country sound all come together in one stunning track.

The follow-up, carried over by Gary Usher so well, was *Sweetheart of the Rodeo*. Gram Parsons entered the fray, and worked closely with Usher in choosing the proper musicians to pull this major shift in style together. Whereas Crosby and McGuinn experienced a creative struggle, Parsons seemingly just took over. "You're right about that," Usher told me in an interview one month before his death in 1990. "McGuinn was tired," he emphasized, "and the Byrds wanted to go country for an album. So McGuinn said 'you seem to know what you're doing, let's bring in your friends from Nashville.' But then Parsons wanted to keep on going with it, and after the album, McGuinn let him go."

Usher's other work for Columbia included Chad & Jeremy's *Of Cabbages & Kings*, and two albums for the Peanut Butter Conspiracy, which generated the hit, "It's a Happening Thing." Unfortunately, Usher's concentration seemed divided, and these LPs do not manage to match the grace of the Peanut Butter Conspiracy's earlier work as the Ashes, such as "Dark On You Now." Usher produced a hot one with "Baby You Know What I Mean" by the Spiral Staircase around this time. During the Beach Boys' *Friends* period, Usher tried to set up a production deal for Brian Wilson, but only saw one single appear, Ron Wilson's "I'll Keep On Loving You."

Usher's focus turned toward the establishment of his own label, Together Records. He first set up an elaborate production deal for Curt Boettcher as the Millennium at Columbia. One of Together's most memorable releases is the Byrds' *Preflyte* album, a great collection of mostly Gene Clark songs recorded by the group in late 1964. Together also released other primordial folk rock on the *Early L.A.* album (which included two early David Crosby solo tracks cut at World Pacific Studios that same year) and *The Banjo Album*, a straight bluegrass set cut by Doug Dillard, Gene Clark and Bernie Leadon.

Usher's most individual contribution to the label was *The Blue Marble*, a second album by Sagittarius. Boettcher sang on many of its finest moments, like the astral projection version of "In My Room." Boettcher confidentially related to me in 1984 that "Gary Usher produced all the tracks there, and wrote most of the music. It was his project; I just came in and did my vocal parts, which were good, but I was busy with the Millennium and my own productions, so we just kept on helping each other while we did our own thing." In retrospect, Together Records almost seems like a farm team for Usher/Boettcher whims of fancy, and thank goodness for that. There were solo 45s on Together by Lee Mallory and Sandy Salisbury, who were also featured vocalists in the Millennium and on *Present Tense* and *The Blue Marble*. Curt Boettcher also appears on Together as a solo artist, preceding his own fine album *There's An Innocent Face* by several years.

Gary Usher used the dawn of the '70s as a moment of personal reflection, and dropped out of the music business. He'd worked hard and constantly for a full decade, and religious involvement became his vocation. Before his death, he re-entered the music business, working on some hit productions in the '80s, but his legacy remains his ambidextrous work in the '60s. In the '90s Gary Usher's work was extensively reissued for the first time. Capitol domestically released the Knights and the Kickstands (the "troops," really) and *The Go Sound of the Slots*. *Present Tense* saw a proper reissue. Several compilations of his pseudonym-group singles saw release in Japan, there were mid-European and Japanese bootlegs of his Super Stocks material, and even the hot rod/monster LP for Capitol, *Dracula's Deuce*, made it out on a bootleg from France. In this way, we can rejoice in the fact that Gary Usher has, literally, come "back from the grave."

Carol Connors, Girl on the Scene
by Domenic Priore

Carol Connors, singer of "To Know Him Is To Love Him" by the Teddy Bears (yeah, the group with Phil Spector . . . she was Annette Kleinbard) also did a lot of great, Gary Usher-esque sides. She often co-wrote with Roger Christian and sometimes Steve Barri. Prior to Usher's involvement with Brian Wilson, Connors gave "My Diary" to Usher's girlfriend, Ginger Blake, for a Titan Records single. Blake later became the lead singer of the Honeys. Connors did boss 45s under the name Carol & Cheryl ("Go Go GTO"), Carol Connors ("My Baby Looks But He Don't Touch," and the advertisement 45 "Yum Yum Yamaha"), plus she wrote "Hey Little Cobra" and "Red Hot Roadster" for the Rip Chords.

Carol also penned two singles for the Chains on HBR, "Carol's Got a Cobra" and "Do the Bomp." There was also "Run Little Mustang" for the Zip Codes on Liberty, "Masked Grandma" for the California Suns on Imperial and things like "It Will Grow on You," "Big Black Cad," "Blond in the 406" and "My X-K-E" for Dick Dale on Capitol.

Connors went by the pseudonym the Surfettes for "Sammy the Sidewalk Surfer" on Mustang, and overdubbed four-part harmony for the all-girl fake-Beatle band that does two numbers ("Why Do I Love You So" and "We Wanna Marry A Beatle") at the end of the film *The Girls on the Beach* . . . a movie that also features the Beach Boys and Lesley Gore performing three songs apiece. Connors wrote and sang the theme song for *A Swinging Summer* (her vocal is on the soundtrack LP, Jody Miller sings it over the credits in the film), contributed a couple of numbers to *Red Line 7000* (and shows up as a background singer onscreen . . . the rest of soundtrack is by Nelson Riddle) and did a great performance turn backed by the Cascades in the film *Catalina Caper*, singing her own composition "The Book of Love" (which is not the Monotones 1958 hit, but a real '60s girl-group groover.)

But she also wrote the theme from *Rocky*. To paraphrase a friend: "Another sad commentary on the decline of just about everything since 1966, as if we need any more reminders."

Gary Zekley by Domenic Priore

Gary Zekley

Gary Zekley is one of those names that assures a 45 will deliver a lot of bang for your buck. It keeps cropping up, and always delivers resilient slices of the West Coast sound. He was the most obscure of the original architects of the style, a direct link to the Wilson/Usher/Berry/Torrence/Christian/Melcher/Johnston/Connors/Sloan/Barri school of hitmakers. The quality of Zekley's work in the early '60s was top notch, but it wasn't until the era of *Pet Sounds* and *Smile* that he made his breakthrough.

His first recordings came under solo project auspices of both Jan Berry and Dean Torrence. Berry recorded Zekley's "Ace of Hearts" for an outside production with "Surf City" backing vocalists the Matadors (soon-to-be Gazzarri's house band, the Sinners.) Torrence gave him a good shot by arranging for a Gary Zekley solo single to be made on Fred Astaire's Ava label, "Other Towns, Other Girls." The song was later appropriated by Jan & Dean for their *Ride the Wild Surf* soundtrack album as "The Restless Surfer." It was the summer of 1963 when Zekley was privy to the historical "Surf City" recording session itself, with Brian Wilson around to sing the key hook line "two girls for every boy." "Brian was in the studio," Gary remembers, "and everybody was talking about how he was going to be coming out with a thing called 'Surfer Girl.'"

Two of Zekley's early '60s productions illustrate his development as a producer and give a beautiful insight into the West Coast studio scene of that era.

The Ragamuffins "The Fun We Had Last Summer/Don't Be Gone Long" (Tollie 9027)

The melody, production, and falsetto lead vocal send you directly to the planet Mars, where you can look back at all of the earth's beaches at once and wonder, "Shit, where did it all go?" Maybe Gary's vocal sounds like a man from Mars too, it's so beach-falsetto and whop-wha-oo (as in "I Get Around" guitar break) that it represents some sort of "missing link." Gary notes, "1963 was for me the quintessential summer. It was before Brian Wilson did 'All Summer Long.' 'All Summer Long' was what mine should have been. I think there was more imagery in Brian's song. I really liked the simple stuff that Brian was doing. 'Lana' impressed me, and certain parts of 'Wendy.' Certain parts of 'Little Honda,' certain parts of 'Don't Worry Baby.' And in those months I was drawing on different elements of those things I felt were very, very powerful, and 'The Fun We Had Last Summer' turned out to be its own thing. I wish that I would have kept it more simple. Brian's sound was more organic. What he was able to accomplish in the recording studio with the Beach Boys and with the players, the records kind of grew, they kind of blossomed. Jan and Dean's stuff was kind of like 'chiseled' more. Jan Berry had the whole arrangement written out in his own charts."

The flipside, "Don't Be Gone Long" featured prominent fuzz guitar because, "Jan Berry was using fuzz guitar, Jack Nitzsche was using fuzz guitar, and *fuzz guitar was the thing to use!* There were certain things that if you were doing that genre of song, everybody was starting to use fuzz guitar, everybody was starting to use electric harpsichords. 'Don't Be Gone Long' was a stew. It was a little bit Brian Wilson, it was a little bit Phil Spector, it was a little bit English . . . That was *supposed* to be an epic production, but instead of having the big size of the 50-piece orchestra, we used a fuzz guitar."

Our Gang "Summertime Summertime"/"The Theme from Leon's Garage (Hal Records Scab Dates There)" (Br'er Bird 001)

Dean Torrence and Gary Zekley come together again, Dean makes up the label art and voila! . . . Pure Genius! A J&D/ Spectoresque rendition of the Jamies' pre-surf summer classic. Gary sings his "The Fun We Had" falsetto once again, and *zoom*, the cascading vocal comes on à la Brian late '65, with super-incessant drumming by Hal Blaine and echo galore. *PsychedelicSpectorSurfPastiche!* Gary describes the recording, "I sang lead on the record, but there was a big mistake on the record [where the voice drops out in the chorus]. We never knew what the words were! We couldn't figure out what the words were, so we just left them out . . . but in the intro to the song, we did an intricate a cappella beginning to the song, and we had it all by itself. We were gonna take it on to the body of the song where the instruments come in, and we had recorded it in the wrong key. We couldn't get it to match up, so you hear at the end of this a cappella thing where the band comes in, it's not in the same key. It's kinda weird but we didn't have the money to re-do it." Despite any flaws, Dean Torrence and Gary Zekley made an appearance on *9th Street West* to promote the Our Gang single, and a beautiful demo was cut by the group for "Here Comes the Rain."

On the b-side of this single lies the backing track for "Don't Be Gone Long," which combined with the previous demo would foreshadow "Like a Summer Rain." Its ghostly, chanted vocals reveal the depth Gary Zekley's production style had taken on. The in-joke title "Theme from Leon's Garage (Hal Records Scab Dates There)" refers to Leon Russell's home studio, Sky Hill. It also clues us in as to just how in-crowd Zekley had become, referencing drummer Hal Blaine's non-union work with Leon. Having cut three brilliant Wall of Soundalikes with Alder Ray ("'Cause I Love Him" b/w "A Little Love Will Go A Long Way" for Liberty) and Clydie King ("Missin' My Baby" for Imperial), before long Zekley would be drawn into the studio with the master himself.

Phil Spector had decided to record a version of Zekley's "Close Your Eyes" with the Ronettes. Unreleased to this day, the song was then taken by Spector's understudy, Jerry Riopelle, and sung by "Bonnie" for a Warner Brothers 45. The same team is well known within record-collecting circles for the brilliant Bonnie & the Treasures single "Home of the Brave." Riopelle then cut Gary's "Baby Baby It's You" b/w "Can't Get Enough of Your Love" for Warner Brothers as "The Group," who were actually the same guys as the Ragamuffins and Our Gang. The bond between Riopelle and Zekley grew, from hanging out at Spector's "This Could Be the Night" session for the Modern Folk Quartet, to Riopelle's band the Parade playing on bills with the Yellow Balloon a couple of years down the road.

It was clear that Zekley had a knack for coming up with infectious songs. The proximity to Berry, Wilson and Spector put him in an enviable learning situation. Dean Torrence drew Gary Zekley into the production of the legendary *Save For a Rainy Day* album after Jan Berry's accident, releasing Zekley's stunning "Like a Summer Rain" as the lead single. "When I wrote 'Yellow Balloon,' Dean heard the song and said 'That's a Jan & Dean song.'" Dean quickly arranged time to record the track. Zekley visited the session and was dismayed with what he heard. He then decided to record the track himself. "I was in the 9000 building [on Sunset Boulevard], just knocking on doors. I went into office after office after office until somebody saw me . . . and it was [Canterbury Records president] Ken Handler who let me into his office, and I just sat down at the piano and played him the song and said 'man, this is a hit song.' He said 'You're right, it's a great song.' So I said 'Here's what's going on. Jan & Dean are putting the song out, we gotta beat them out with the song.' He said 'Okay,' and he just stopped the presses, and we put it together very fast."

Gary describes the session for the "Yellow Balloon" 45: "We cut this amazing track and then the background singers came in . . . the whole thing took maybe two hours . . . max! I'd never been in a recording session anything like that. It was blessed . . . all recording sessions should be like that. It was a pure joy, it was impossible not to record a hit. The background guys came in, they were four guys and we told them it was a demonstration record. They heard the song, I went out and I sang the song. I had them stand in the booth and I sang the song so they could hear what the song sounded like. I sang it with the tracks and then Stan Farber said, 'Okay, I'll sing the lead on it' and then Al Kapps and these two other guys, Ron Hicklin, they were great, they were incredible background singers. They put the backgrounds on, and Al Kapps came up with these great parts, they made 'em up in the studio! My parts were one thing, and they added some parts that were just genius!" Ron Hicklin and Stan Farber were two of the most in-demand session singers in L.A. during the '60s and '70s. Ron (and to a lesser degree, Stan) would later work with the Bahler brothers and Jackie Ward to do the background vocals on the Partridge Family.

Zekley's instincts were correct, and he managed to hit the charts (for the first time) in direct competition with Jan & Dean on Columbia, whose version failed to have much impact at all. The hit single was by a group dubbed the Yellow Balloon. The punch and intensity of the Yellow Balloon version put it ahead of Dean's cool but spacier version, but there was still a problem with having the hit: *No Band!*

It had happened before with the Hondells for Gary Usher, and more recently with the Grass Roots for Phil Sloan and Steve Barri (most of the *Where Were You When I Needed You* album was actually a folk-rock LP by the Fantastic Baggys, friends and neighbors!) By the luck of the draw, Canterbury had a solo artist in search of an actual band situation.

Don Grady (the actor playing Robbie on *My Three Sons* at that time) recalls, "About that time I'd just signed a record deal with Canterbury, which was Ken Handler's record label. Ken's parents were the founders of Mattel Toys—they had created the Barbie and Ken dolls. Gary Zekley had brought this song in, and we knew it was gonna do great—we just had a good feeling about it. I wasn't at the session, but I remember coming to the mixdown and going 'This is so cool.' Ken sent that tune out and it just took off. Within about a week it was getting played heavily, and it was like 'We have a band!' I said 'Let's put together this band of these guys that I've been meeting.' So everybody says, 'Yeah, sounds great!' Ken had the resources to fly those guys out and get it happening."

Don Grady was a perfect match for Gary Zekley. "I just loved melody, and that was more of my orientation," Grady said. "I never really became a hard rock person, I was always too melodic. Gary was so loyal to Brian Wilson and to what Brian Wilson was trying to do in the music world at that time. He was trying to capture that beautiful, male harmony, that sunshiny sound. Gary was coming over to my place and we were meeting at the 9000 building on Sunset Strip at all hours of the night putting these tracks together. He was kind of the Wizard of Oz, and just a mad genius . . . crazy, you know? He'd call me at 3:00 in the morning with an idea. I was writing songs, doing the album and doing *My Three Sons* at the same time. He was over the top, but he was great."

"Don Grady is a very, very talented guy," Zekley says. "He could play piano, guitar, bass, trumpet, drums, he was a good dancer, a good comic actor, good lookin', all the girls were crazy about him. We'd sit there in the 9000 building, overlooking Los Angeles, with all the lights outside"—a spectacular view from the Hollywood Hills. "We'd turn the lights off in the room, sit at the piano and play. He really had a unique approach to what I was trying to do. He had a great angle on it."

The Yellow Balloon made a number of television appearances including *American Bandstand*, *Shebang*, *Boss City*, and *Groovy*. As a live act, they played gigs as diverse as the Longshoreman's Hall in San Francisco with bands like Big Brother and the Holding Company, Quicksilver Messenger Service and Moby Grape, and the Melodyland Theater across the street from Disneyland in Anaheim with the Nitty Gritty Dirt Band, the Merry-Go-Round and the Sunshine Company.

Don Grady wrote and sang "Stained Glass Window," a song that developed a small cult following of its own during the Paisley Underground movement in Los Angeles during the early-to-mid 1980s. "It had a certain feel to it, kind of a Left Banke trip. I think it was a little bit ahead of its time and it had that string quartet stuff happening."

Another standout track on the album was "How Can I Be Down." Gary relates the history of that song: "Jill Gibson had a little apartment over a garage in Westwood, and she came up with the introduction to 'How Can I Be Down' on her guitar, and she just started singing, 'How can I be down, whenever you're around me and I feel you, making me high' . . . We used to get stoned together and try to write songs. She was going with Lou Adler, and I was married. She had a *phenomenal* gift for melody, and she came up with 'How can I be down, whenever you're around . . .' that line, that phrase, and I wrote the rest of the song."

Now a bona fide hitmaking songwriter/producer, Zekley turned his attention to what would become his most elaborate project. He'd developed a friendship with the talented, up-and-coming songwriting team of Harvey Price and Don Walsh, and with them set his sights on cutting a *Sgt. Pepper's*-styled album under the moniker Price & Walsh for Dot Records. In the studio, Zekley put together elaborate, Elizabethan soundscapes which complemented the poetic nature of songs such as "Virginia Day's Ragtime Memories," "Small Town Commotion" and the one single to be released from the sessions, "Love is the Order of the Day" b/w "House of the Ilene Castle." As Zekley's production alter ego, Yodar Critch, was reaching for the stars, Price and Walsh saw an opportunity to make more cash focusing on more commercial material, walking off the project and leaving brilliant tunes like "Where is Sunday," "The Mad Genius of Shelby Square" and "Greenville County Fair" in the can. Zekley released "Small Town Commotion" with the vocals redone by a group called the Visions while "Virginia Day's Ragtime Memories" went to the Looking Glass.

Perhaps Zekley's own mad genius went to the wind with Price & Walsh, for his next LP turned out to be much simpler in scope. He took on a production gig for Uni Records and immediately cranked out the album *Elephant Candy* for a Texas pop group called the Fun & Games. Their single "The Grooviest Girl in the World" seemed tailor made for the whirling, pre-teen Go Go TV shows of the moment like *Happening '68*, *Kiddie a Go Go* and *Wonderama*. With lyrics like "Walkin' such a long way, talkin' to her all day, sippin' on a strawberry fizz" and a chunky organ to match the attendant sugar buzz, the single and album seemed a comeback rush of excitement after the disappointment of the previous Price & Walsh sessions. Having met songwriter Harry Nilsson at the session for his tune "This Could Be the Night" with Spector in '65, Zekley also found himself privy to the demo of "One." The Fun & Games recorded this, only to be scooped on release by the Three Dog Night recording. "We" was then released as a single by the Fun & Games. The side displays what may very well be Zekley's most eloquent work in the melodic/ballad form.

Price & Walsh had gone on to pen some of the best known Grass Roots hits, "Midnight Confessions" among them. To show that there were no bad vibes, Zekley also contributed "I'd Wait a Million Years" and "Sooner or Later" to the Grass Roots' string of bestsellers. He also passed "Honey You Can't Take it Back" to Dobie Gray during this period, and worked with Jerry Riopelle on the sessions for "All Strung Out" by Nino Tempo & April Stevens, his first association with White Whale Records.

Gary Zekley describes how he came to write "Superman" for the Clique: "Mitch Bottler was at the piano and started playing that 'Sgt. Pepper's Lonely Hearts Club Band' riff, and I went 'I am, I am Superman, and I know what's happening.' He struck the descending chords, and it just happened." In general, the Clique's *Sugar on Sunday* album is a studio job by Zekley, but the band themselves did "Superman" on the album. Otherwise, the group never played on the sessions, but managed an appearance on *Upbeat*. Gary notes, "I had success with the Fun & Games and the Yellow Balloon, so Don Altfeld and Mickey Shapiro got me a deal with White Whale to produce the Clique. I had met the Clique and the Fun & Games on the same day. I chose to do the Fun & Games first, and then we came back and recorded the Clique."

The experience recording that LP was difficult, because Tommy James was producing separate sessions with the Clique. Zekley remembers, "They were in-fighting on that album. While I was recording the Clique, I was waiting for Randy Shaw (the lead singer) to come in and sing, but he didn't show up. I waited there for hours, but White Whale had flown him up to New York to sing for Tommy James instead. When I'd heard they'd flown Randy to New York, it broke my heart. I felt deserted." Despite the bad experience, Zekley managed to pull something great out of the sessions. "There were four hit songs on the Clique album," Zekley enthuses, "'Sugar on Sunday,' 'Hallelujah!,' 'I'll Hold Out My Hand' and 'Superman.' Two of my records were on the charts at the same time; the Clique's 'Sugar on Sunday' and 'I'd Wait a Million Years' by the Grass Roots."

That was Gary's last hurrah until R.E.M. covered "Superman," which had been just a b-side during the '60s. Suddenly Zekley's named cropped up in public like streamers coming off a bicycle. "I went on stage with R.E.M. in Dekalb, Illinois," Zekley recalled. "MTV was there; they showed me on MTV, singing with R.E.M. *Rolling Stone* magazine was there too." Unfortunately, in 1996, Gary Zekley died sadly young of a heart attack at the age of 53. He never got to see the term "I Am Superman" plastered on the side of a bus in advertising, or The Yellow Balloon top Van Morrison's *Astral Weeks* on a year-end "best reissues" poll in *Mojo*. And the awareness seems to be growing like a flower.

Cutting a swath through the L.A. sound
with P.F. Sloan and his pals by Kim Cooper

P.F. Sloan

The "P.F." in P. F. Sloan stands for the Phillip and for nickname Flip, fittingly embodying the formal and the goofball casual in an identity and career that would be rife with contradiction. Briefly with partner Steve Barri (née Lipkin) among the most successful American pop songwriters, by the late '60s P.F. would have effectively vanished, his absence noted by an especially lovely Jimmy Webb ballad that bears Sloan's name. Full of mysticism, anger, and strangeness, the P.F. Sloan story is one that needs to be told. And yes, doubters, there is a bubblegum connection—two, in fact.

New York-born Flip was blessed with smart parents: they moved to Los Angeles when he was five. By 12 the sharp, ambitious kid had wangled a contract with Aladdin Records. But nothing much came of early singles "All I Want is Loving" b/w "Little Girl in the Cabin" (Aladdin 3461, 1959) and "If You Believe In Me" b/w "She's My Girl" (Mart 802, 1960), and we hear nothing of him for several years.

By 1963 he'd hooked up with Steve Barri, and under Gary Usher's supervision they provided enthusiastic back-up vocals for Jan & Dean and wrote some of that group's most memorable material, including the immortal, Rudi Gernreich-inspired "One-Piece Topless Bathing Suit." A fun Baggys album was released on Imperial in 1964 (Tell 'Em I'm Surfin' LP-9270/LP-12270). Other surfsploitation releases with Sloan-Barri-Usher involvement included The Rincon Surfside Band's The Surfing Song Book (Dunhill LP 50001, 1965) and Willie and the Wheels' Surfin' Song Book (RCA LP 70044, 1965). RCA was presumably too cheap to pay for that final G.

As Jan & Dean's co-manager (with Herb Alpert), Lou Adler had had ample opportunity to see the Fantastic Baggys in action. Favorably impressed, when he started Dunhill Productions in '64 he hired them to write for his Trousdale Songs publishing company and produce acts for the label. Trousdale immediately began racking up hits, among them "Secret Agent Man" (#3) for Johnny Rivers and ex-New Christy Minstrel Barry McGuire's "Eve of Destruction" (#1, and the record that knocked "Help" off the top spot and kept "Like a Rolling Stone" from reaching it). Sloan's first solo album also dates from '65, Songs of Our Times (Dunhill 50004). The powerful single "Sins of the Family" (about a girl's hopelessness in the face of her parents' depravity) reached #87 on the Billboard charts.

Sloan and Barri had been asked by Adler to write some songs in the trendy folk-rock idiom. They seem to have had no problem in shifting from beach themes to protest, love and pop psychology, and Sloan was soon out-Dylaning the kid from Hibbing. This early folk-rock material would be released as the album Where Were You When I Needed You by the non-existent band the Grass Roots. The odd cover art showing an old chair in a clump of hay should have been a tip-off that something wasn't kosher, but the credulous listener might be snowed by Andy Wickham's rambling liner notes about the band and their Sunset Strip buddies. According to fantasist Wickham, the Grass Roots were "four Johnny folk 'n' rolls who don't pretend to be anything else. They . . . have long, Dickensian haircuts and they blast up and down our hallowed strip on gleaming motorbikes with long-haired birdies wooing and cooing on the back. They probably live high in the Hollywood hills in a castle[20]—a mode of living which the folk-n-roll set finds highly fashionable at the moment." And where was this mythic band discovered? Why, in "a bawdy, boisterous, smoke-filled beat parlor called 'The Trip,'" although they'd recently moved to the Whisky since The Trip started booking bands in matching suits.

---

20. This may be an oblique reference to the real band then called the Grass Roots (later Love), who famously inhabited a hillside house called The Castle, and had to change their name after Dunhill's Grass Roots hit the local airwaves.

The first song recorded for the Grass Roots project was the title track, with lead vocals by Sloan. When a local radio station started spinning the promo 45, Dunhill began looking for a band to "be" the Grass Roots. *Bubblegum alert!* Sloan suggested San Mateo's Bedouins, and their singer Bill Fulton went into the studio to record a new lead vocal to replace Sloan's. At first the Bedouins were willing to be manipulated into a calculated career, but when they were told that single #2, a cover of Dylan's "Ballad of A Thin Man," was to be recorded Byrds-style with Fulton backed by studio musicians, they were irked. When "Ballad," released in October '65, failed to break the Top 100, the Bedouins bowed out and went home to the Bay Area,[21] where they changed names again to briefly become the Unquenchable Thirst, then splintered. Fulton went on to play in Tower of Power for many years. Meanwhile, Sloan and Barri continued working on Grass Roots material, and the *Where Were You* album was released without an actual band yet under contract. It didn't chart, although the title song hit #28.

The debut album sounds like what it is: half strong songwriter's demos helped along by a crack session team and Bones Howe's co-engineering, half garagey actual Bedouins recordings. The seven Sloan-Barri originals are insidiously catchy, and include the soon-to-be-Turtles-classic "You Baby." Somewhat uninspired covers ("I Am a Rock" and "You Didn't Have To Be So Nice") fill out the grooves and suggest that there was some rush to complete the album.

When a Los Angeles band called the 13th Floor send their demo tape in to Dunhill, they certainly didn't expect the Eliza Doolittle treatment they ultimately received. But ambition will make boys do strange things, and this gamble paid off handsomely for the former 13th Floor. Warren Entner, Creed Bratton, Rob Grill and Rick Coonce were soon transformed into the Grass Roots, and while it's unclear how much they actually played on their records, this is the band credited with a terrific adaptation of the Rokes' Italian hit "Piangi Con Me" as "Let's Live for Today" that broke the Top 10 in '67. Contrived or not, the album of this name is one of the gems of the folk-rock era, and deservedly launched a fairly successful career for the Grass Roots, first with Sloan-Barri songs and later with more soulful material from the band and other outside writers.

Sloan recorded a second solo alum in 1966 *Twelve More Times* (Dunhill LP 50007), containing the excellent "Halloween Mary" and "Upon a Painted Ocean." Around this time Lou Adler sold the label and put his energies into the Monterey Pop Festival, and the following year Phil returned to New York. Although he would release two more albums (1968's *Measure of Pleasure* on Atco 268 and *Raised on Records*, Mums 31260, 1972), Sloan was beginning to retreat from the commercial world. His partnership with Steve Barri lapsed, and Barri went on to be a major producer on his own.

Although Steve Barri left production in the '70s in order to guide the careers of artists of little interest to our readers (trust me, we're talking Commodores), he wasn't yet finished overseeing obscenely catchy hits. It was under Barri's guidance that Tommy Roe returned to the charts in 1969 with "Jam Up and Jelly Tight" and the delightful "Dizzy." He was also responsible for "Billy Don't Be A Hero" by Bo Donaldson and the Heywoods and for "Don't Pull Your Love" for Hamilton, Joe Frank and Reynolds. Barri was also the person called in when the powers that be decided that chimp band The Evolution Revolution needed a hit: Barri gave the critters an old Grass Roots demo "Sha-La Love You," and the benefit of his production savvy for this one song. Barri returned to production in the late '80s in partnership with session guitarist Tony Peluso (the man who played that insane solo in the Carpenters' "Goodbye to Love"), and scored Top 20 hits for Animotion and the Triplets.

As for P.F. Sloan, after pursuing various spiritual paths, in recent years he's made tentative motions towards reviving his career. There was some material recorded with the Posies, a few showcase gigs in Los Angeles and elsewhere, and even an updated version of "Eve of Destruction." So don't close the book on him just yet.

21. Excepting Joel Larson, who remained in LA to play briefly in the Gene Clark Group (with a post-Turtles/pre-Monkees production Chip Douglas and with the Leaves' Bill Rinehart), then in the Merry-Go-Round with Emitt Rhodes.

Kasenetz-Katz and Their Super-Duper
Rock & Roll Kavalcade by James Porter

Of all the revered record producers with a hitmaking streak and an identifiable sound, the Kasenetz-Katz duo has to be among the most underrated. Garage freaks worship at the altar of Ed Cobb (Standells, Chocolate Watchband), Ken Nelson (Buck Owens, Wanda Jackson) is a big name with the retro-country set, the outer-space sonatas of Joe Meek (Blue Men, Tornadoes) have a strong cult, and Phil Spector is probably the only non-performing producer who has his own section in record stores. But even though Jerry Kasenetz and Jeff Katz produced their share of radio-active hits in '68–'69, most rock historians regard them as a footnote. In *The New Book Of Rock Lists* by Dave Marsh and James Bernard, producers as diverse as Lee "Scratch" Perry, Dr. Dre, and Giorgio Moroder are celebrated ("Best Producers"), yet K-K are summed up elsewhere ("Ten Famous Bubblegum Groups"). While admitting that the genre of music "spawned some of the most ludicrous, if occasionally transcendent, trash produced in the rock 'n' roll age," Marsh acknowledges K-K as "the cream of the crop, but that doesn't mean a lot."

End of story. Roll credits. *Finito*. Okay, some of the original LPs that K-K produced are a chore to sit through (they make "greatest hits" albums for a reason). But even though Marsh is an occasionally brilliant writer (see his book about the song "Louie, Louie," or his early '70s writings in *Creem* magazine), the man seemingly can't write an article without working Bruce Springsteen or Michael Jackson into the story. Still, considering that all the Hendrix worshippers thought the Ohio Express and 1910 Fruitgum Co. (K-K's two big cash cows) set the rock movement back a million years, Kasenetz and Katz took full advantage of their success to experiment, mostly on flipsides and album cuts. It was partially for shits and giggles, but mostly to make sure DJs played the right side of the single. "In analyzing previous years on records," the K&K duo now says, "we noticed that there were a lot of records where there were like two-sided hits, and we know that hits are hard to come by and we didn't wanna put two sides on a single, so we wanted to put something on we knew that nobody would play. The funny thing is that people actually played it! We just wanted to make sure that there wasn't gonna be a two-sided hit."

One of the greatest rock b-sides ever was "Zig Zag," which played second fiddle to the Ohio Express' "Yummy, Yummy, Yummy." They basically took the backing track to "Poor Old Mr. Jensen" (a song recorded by several in the K-K stable), ran it through the tape player backwards, and gave it a title. And it sounds *better* like this—personally, I've probably spun "Zig Zag" more times than "Yummy." Forwards, it's a blah little number that K-K used for flip-side and album-cut filler, but in reverse, minus the vocals, the eerie organ-dominated melody actually stands on its own.

Lord knows what kind of audience Kasenetz and Katz had in mind for "There Ain't No Umbopo" b/w "Landrover," a 1970 single by Crazy Elephant on Bell, and it's just as well (it wasn't a hit, anyway). "Landrover," a filler instrumental, sounds like the pit band from *The Tonight Show* trying to do a Motown song (badly). As for the other side, well, according to *Webster's New World Dictionary*, there sure ain't no "umbopo," or else I'd tell you what that word means. The producers themselves asked Graham Gouldman, then a writer in the K-K stable, the same question—Gouldman just liked the sound of the nonsense syllables. The song proper isn't that remarkable, but the vague words appear to be narrating a suicide ("he said goodbye to the world on his short-wave radio").

"Up Against The Wall," a cut from the Ohio Express' *Mercy* album, is probably the only bubblegum song about a police riot. And what is the deal with that song about Ronald Reagan ("Up In The Air," which Kasenetz & Katz call a "spoof") that appeared on the Kasenetz-Katz Circus' debut album, back in 1968? "A man who has so much hair/a man who is not all there/a man who just loves the chair"— I think they meant "electric," not "rocking" or "easy"— and at least one band unearthed this during Reagan's presidency (Tru Fax and the Insomniacs, a Washington, D.C. punk outfit). Bizarre tangents like these made them even more subversive than any old blues-jamming hippie from the Bay Area, and to only associate Kasenetz and Katz with a bunch of near-novelties that 12-year-olds bought like biscuits is only telling part of the story.

That story started when K&K were college students at the University of Arizona, where Katz was on the football team and Kasenetz was one of the managers. After graduation, they began managing bands. As Katz recollected in *Goldmine* recently, "We had this black group, King Ernest and the Palace Guards, and they were sensational. We got 'em signed to Mercury, and I don't remember who did the record, a single, and we heard the record—it was terrible. And we said, 'We could do better than that.' And that's actually how we got into producing." The early K-K productions, in '67, were right in line with the garage-rock sound, which had about a year to go. "Little Bit O' Soul" by the Music Explosion (on Laurie) hit #2, and the Ohio Express' "Beg, Borrow and Steal" (on Cameo, actually recorded by the Rare Breed and previously issued on the Attack label) also made the Top 40 that year. Both of these songs sonically sounded like the band was set up in the basement while the microphone was on the stairs leading down. The lo-fi technology evidently didn't hurt sales and airplay any. The Music Explosion disc is still an oldies radio staple today, and "Beg, Borrow and Steal" is a great "Louie, Louie" rewrite.

The duo stumbled onto the bubblegum tag in the early part of '68, when they discovered a band known at various times as the Lower Road, the Odyssey, and Jeckell and the Hydes (named after guitarist Frank Jeckell). K-K saw them at a house party and liked the band enough to sign them, providing they change their name to 1910 Fruitgum Co. No problem. A few months later, the organ-heavy "Simon Says" (#4), and the sound-alike follow-up, "May I Take A Giant Step (Into Your Heart)" (#63) rushed the charts. Around this same time, the Ohio Express shot to #4 with "Yummy, Yummy, Yummy," a song that was originally written for Jay and the Techniques but rejected by their producer Jerry Ross for being too young-sounding (for the band that gave us "Apples, Peaches, Pumpkin Pie"?!?). Other acts in the K-K stable had the one hit and the mildly-selling follow-up, but these two proved to be the longest lasting. Joey Levine was brought in to sing lead on several Ohio Express tracks. His hard, nasal voice was one way you could distinguish them from the Fruitgums. Another is the fact that the Fruitgum album cuts were more childish, just a heartbeat away from being out-and-out nursery rhymes. Both groups' material had just enough of a garage-rock edge to get by, but it seemed as if the more juvenile rejects appeared on the Fruitgum albums. The *Simon Says* LP included "The Story Of Flipper," about the TV dolphin (maybe their answer to "Snoopy Vs. The Red Baron" by the Royal Guardsmen?), and when they sing "Let's Make Love" (from the *Indian Giver* album), there is a distinct lack of moisture, passion or drama—the vocalist sounds like he's asking his lover to play board games. But the singles were a whole 'nother neighborhood—"Indian Giver" (later covered by the Ramones and Joan Jett), "1, 2, 3 Red Light," and "Special Delivery" (MVP Award: the bass player) deserved their Top 40 status. "Goody Goody Gumdrops," another chartmaker, included the hilarious line "look into her baby-blue eyes/right down to her dainty shoe size . . ."

The two bands ran parallel to each other in eerie ways. The Ohio Express started out as typical post-Beatles garage-rockers, as documented on most of their self-titled Buddah debut (the one with "Yummy") and all of their Cameo album, *Beg, Borrow And Steal*. By 1970 they had more or less devolved into faceless bubble rockers. The 1910 gang, meanwhile, started out childish and wound up "progressive." They padded four full albums with songs that took off from playground games and other kiddie koncepts, but after a year of this "kiddie-a-go-go" music, the band decides they want to be Taken Seriously As Artists, so they added a few members to the existing lineup and cut album #5, *Hard Ride*. (By now, the 1910 bunch were purely a studio creation; all the promo pix from this era feature eight members, but the back cover lineup lists six musicians different from the ones credited earlier. Although K&K insist that Mark Gutkowski was the only member who stayed with the group through all its phases, he is not listed on the back cover credits.) "Don't Have To Run and Hide" and "The Train," the token "commercial" songs, began and ended, respectively, the first side. Apart from that, it's a vain attempt to impress the college crowd: all the songs, even the two bubblegum tracks, are smothered in a jazz-rock horn section, with obscure lyrics and nary a recognizable melody line to be found. "Eulogy/Seulb" is a corny attempt at white-boy blues. "In The Beginning/ The Thing" bears more than a passing resemblance to Pink Floyd during their Syd Barrett days. If you're into albums by teen-idol types trying to go progressive, like the metallic thud of the Osmonds' *Crazy Horses*, Shaun Cassidy's flirtation with New Wave (*Wasp*), or Bobby Darin's folk-rock LPs on the Direction label,

you need to dig up a copy of *Hard Ride*. Just look for the cover with the motorcycle gang posing on the front.

Kasenetz and Katz claim today that on the strength of this weird album the band almost got booked into the Fillmore East, name unknown and sight unseen—until the legendary rock haven found out who it was. "I forget who it was that we saw," reminisces the duo, "but we saw somebody. We were talkin' to 'em without even playing anything, 'we'd like to get the Fruitgum in here.' He laughed, he says 'the Fruitgum Co.? It's *impossible*. They'll laugh me out of business.' 'Well, here's a new group, let me play you this album.' We had a test pressing of it, and we played it. He says 'now this group definitely I could take in here, they'll love this group.' I said, 'well, I don't know how to tell you this—but this is *The 1910 Fruitgum Co.!*" They now laugh. "He says, 'no way!' I said, 'yes, this is the test pressing.' He says, 'listen, call it something else—I still can't put 'em in with that *name!* Even though I love it—this is great, this is what we're lookin' for, but it can't be the Fruitgum Co.!' We were just tryin' to get them in a more favorable light from what they wanted to do. We were not thrilled about it, because I didn't think, personnel-wise, that they could pull it off." They fooled the talent booker at the most prestigious rock venue in town for a hot minute, so they must have done something half-right.

Similar stories have circulated—Silver Apples, the avant-garde synth duo, reportedly opened a Fruitgum show (the Apples bombed). Another tale has the Fruitgums opening a show at the Whisky-A-Go-Go in L.A. for the Illinois Speed Press and Slim Harpo, the Louisiana bluesman. But possibly because they were squarely in the middle of the road, no one in the industry expected much from Kasenetz and Katz, so with minimal pressure, they explored any direction they chose. Their greatest strength was tapping into the trashy teenage pulse of America, and their main gig was putting the fun back in rock 'n' roll when others used it as a political platform. Singles like the Great Train Robbery's "Wasted" (flip of "Heartless Hurdy Gertie," on the ABC label), "You Got The Love" by Professor Morrison's Lollipop (on White Whale), "Live and In Person" (a medley of "Land of 1000 Dances," "Gimme Some Lovin'," and "Satisfaction") by the Carnaby Street Runners (Buddah), and "Captain Groovy and His Bubblegum Army" (by the artists of the same name, on the duo's own Super K label) all sound like lapsed, anachronistic garage records, too late for the trend, but far too early for the revival. Eventually the K-K stable became a clearing house for garage bands who'd outlived their era. The Ohio Express and the Music Explosion were prime examples, and the Shadows of Knight and Question Mark and the Mysterians were not far behind. The Shadows' self-titled LP on the Super K label is probably one of the most underrated rock albums ever. Garage purists hate the metallic edge the band took around this time, but if you like the hard-rock sound of Blue Cheer or Sir Lord Baltimore, this album is right in line with those skull-crushers. The singles were more catchy and commercial, but not enough to wreck their punk credentials. The best-known was 1968's "Shake," which made it up to #46 on *Billboard*'s singles chart. It's a lot more keyboardy than the Shadows' usual output, but every bit as evil as their earlier Dunwich-label records. (Consumer note: "Shake" was redone on the Super K album, and the raw result—retitled "Shake Revisited '69"—sounds suspiciously like a demo. The hit version from the single somehow wound up on *The Very Best Of The Ohio Express*, on Buddah.)

Just before their stint with Super K, Question Mark and the Mysterians were in the middle of a nasty dispute with Cameo, their previous label. In the early '60s Cameo (and brother label Parkway) was in the middle of a golden age, milking Chubby Checker, Bobby Rydell, and other Philadelphia teen/dance stars for all they were worth. After the Beatles came along in '64, rendering the Cameo-Parkway empire passé, the company floundered around for a while before rebounding in '66 with "96 Tears," a #1 hit for the Mysterians, a group of Chicanos based in Flint, Michigan. By '67, the Mysterians were considered as expendable as the twistmasters they replaced. Cameo had tied the band up in a nightmarish contract, refusing to promote their records. Label prez Neil Bogart, who later headed the Buddah, Casablanca and Boardwalk imprints, acted like a sixth member of the band, forcing organist Frank Rodriguez to repeat his "96 Tears" riff on all their songs. In the blunt words of Question Mark himself, Cameo "screwed" ("I don't cuss, but I use that word, and even to me that's cussin'") the band in the worst way. Kasenetz & Katz had nothing to do with the Mysterians' final single for the label, "Do Something To Me" (later re-recorded by Tommy James and the Shondells), although they produced several records for Cameo at this time. In any event, the band unwittingly pioneered the basic bubblegum style—Morse-code organ, stuttering bass—on this record. Cameo folded soon after this ill-fated disc, and like several other artists on that label (including the Ohio Express, Five Stairsteps, and, later, Chubby Checker), they later popped up on Buddah for an additional single on the Buddah-distributed Super K. Unlike the hard-rocking Shadows, who were pretty much left alone, the Mysterians' "Sha La La" seven-inch (built around the recurring guitar riff from the Beatles' "You Can't Do That") was full-blast bubblerock, straight off the K-K assembly line. After you get over that fact, this 1969 single is a good record in spite of itself. The Ohio Express redid "Sha La La" on their *Mercy* album, just barely—Joey Levine dubbed his voice over the same backing track—but Question Mark's version remains superior. The flip side, "Hang In," is a moody, uptempo instrumental that vaguely recalls "Going All The Way," the 1966 cult classic by garage-rockers the Squires.

For their part, Kasenetz & Katz have some interesting memories of Question Mark. "Uhhh . . . he was a little strange at times . . . the funny thing is, he was actually no Prince, talent-wise, but looking back now, I'd say in weirdness both artists had a lot in common," they now laugh. "I don't know particularly if it's the glasses he wore or what, but he reminded me of Prince." Today, Question Mark likes to remind everybody how he pioneered much of Prince's shtick, so he'd probably be happy that someone else finally got the point. (For the record, K&K referred to Question Mark as "Rudy," his given name, making them among the few people who do!)

Beyond the heavy hitters, there were several lesser lights in the K-K stable. Robust-voiced Bobby Bloom recorded a few singles in a blue-eyed-soul vein, and when Bloom himself moved to another label (L&R, a subsidiary of MGM) and had a hit ("Montego Bay," 1970, #8), Buddah reissued the Kasenetz-Katz sessions on an album cashing in on Bloom's short-lived fame. Crazy Elephant, on the Bell label, were another in the long line of faceless K-K studio musicians; a news item in *Cashbox* said they were Welsh coalminers, but when the needle hits the vinyl, none of that matters. The anarchic, giddy "Gimme Gimme Good Lovin'," #12 on the pop charts in 1969, was Crazy Elephant's only hit and, in my modest opinion, K-K's finest moment. This disc is a head-on rock-n-soul collision from start to fade—the vocal chorus that shouts "gimme, gimme good lovin' every night!" sounds like a group of happy-hour drunks. That hillbilly guffaw ("ha-huh-ha-huh-ha . . ."), at the end of each chorus, makes it tuff to stay in a bad mood for long. Lead singer Robert Spencer (a former doo-wopper with the Cadillacs, in addition to being the author of Millie Small's ska hit, "My Boy Lollipop") hollers like a man with a week-old erection. And you should hear that wolf-howl he does at the end of the inept, fumble-fingered guitar solo. The lyrical demands are all in the title: "Gimme Gimme Good Lovin'." None of that Tyrone Davis "pretty please" shit! This is clearly a feel-good number, the type of song that makes you do 60 in a 45 zone. The b-side was a bizarre psychedelic tune that featured fuzztone by the gallon, and a monotone voice muttering something about "The Dark Part Of My Mind." An album, which today is very hard to find (unlike most of the Buddah albums), wasn't long in coming, along with the expected follow-ups. Spencer's harsh vocals appear to be a one-off, as he's not featured on "Gimme Some More," an attempt to cash in on their big moment. It's a good song in its own right, but the even-tempered "white" vocals are just going through the motions, compared to Spencer's slobbering R&B fervor.

Other K-K studio aggregations followed, like Captain Groovy and His Bubblegum Army. Their answer to producer Don Kirshner's success with the Archies, this proposed animated series never materialized—the cartoon kings at Hanna-Barbera wanted to take a full 50% share of the project, so it never really got past the drawing board, a series of "coming soon!" ads in the trade 'zine *Cashbox*, and a single that some '60s punk collectors swear by. Their main biggie, waiting in the wings to happen, was the Kasenetz-Katz Singing Orchestral Circus (hereafter referred to as the K-K Circus). In June 1968, Buddah Records booked Carnegie Hall in New York to showcase seven bands from the K-K stable. Playing simultaneously. (Reportedly it was eight bands, but since the missing link was the non-existent St. Louis Invisible Marching Band . . .) Potentially this could have backfired, but K&K spent a long time in the woodshed getting it right. The K-K Circus was scheduled to appear on *The Ed Sullivan Show*, but presidential candidate Robert Kennedy died around the same time. That Sunday, Sullivan's program was reportedly preempted for a Kennedy retrospective, and K-K never got rescheduled. For those keeping score, that's two American dreams killed with one bullet. It didn't stop the K-K Circus' overall momentum, as they went on to have a hit that year with "Quick Joey Small" (#25 in the charts).

The K-K empire also had some measure of success in the European market, where promotional videos had already started to catch on. The duo made a number of clips with their acts, including "Quick Joey Small." Kasenetz & Katz animatedly recall the plot synopsis: "We had these little wooden toy dolls being pulled—you couldn't see it being pulled in the front—by a string, and people holding on to it like they were chasing Quick Joey Small, running through a barn . . . I mean really way-out things—just like you see on videos today." K&K still have a few of these films in their archives —Rhino or some other hip video manufacturer should lease these for reissue.

The K-K Circus lineup, in addition to the invisible marching band, had the Fruitgums and the Express prominently featured. The Music Explosion were dusted off, even though they were chart-cold and hitless for a year. The Teri Nelson Group were originally an all-black female vocal outfit who did an unremarkable soul album for Kama Sutra the year before; by now they were Nelson plus an all-white backing band (five male, one female), curiously photographed separately. Lt. Garcia's Magic Music Box, who also had a mediocre Kama Sutra album in '67, were resurrected for the gig. The J.C.W. Rat Finks and the 1989 Musical Marching Zoo completed the set. The self-titled original cast album that resulted has to be one of the greatest long-playing fiascoes committed to wax. Half the songs have dubbed-in crowd noise to simulate the Carnegie Hall gig. At the top of side two, the Music Explosion's Jamie Lyons dedicates the next three songs to the guys who the band was named after; we then hear "Little Bit O' Soul," "Simon Says," and "Latin Shake" (originally recorded by Lt. Garcia). They didn't even bother to re-record the songs—these are the original versions with phony crowd noises added. They even had a bunch of people singing and clapping along, to fool some middle-schooler into thinking he or she missed the concert of the century! Elsewhere on the disc, Count Dracula does a 1:39 monologue, they cover two Beatles songs, remove the blue-eyed you-know-what from the Righteous Bros.' "You've Lost That Lovin' Feeling," give the Beach Boys treatment to Stevie Wonder's "A Place In The Sun," and five songwriters in the K-K stable have the nuts to take writer's credits for the inept version of "Hey Joe!" And to signify that the show is over, we hear a horn section playing "Taps," followed by flying-saucer noises!

The fold-out cover, featuring the outlandishly-dressed K-K Circus standing in an auto junkyard, is a camp classic. According to Kasenetz and Katz, this was done on the set of one of the video shoots. Look closely—you can just make out Kasenetz and Katz in tuxedos.

This was followed by the stripped-down *Kasenetz-Katz Super Circus*. This album contained an actual hit, "Quick Joey Small," and the liner notes tell us that the involved parties were now the Fruitgums, the Express, the Music Explosion, the Shadows of Knight, and Prof. Morrison's Lollipop, "joined together in the world's first all-rock orchestra." All the excesses have been trimmed, but it's still rather eccentric around the edges. The aforementioned Ronald Reagan tribute appears here, as does "The Super Circus," which is nothing but whoops, hollers, and jungle drums. Musically, this is probably one of the more consistent K-K albums. Joey Levine does all the leads, although the K-K stable was so interchangeable that "Down At Lulu's" was a hit for the Ohio Express, in the same version heard on this album. For "Shake," the Shadows' near-hit, Levine removed Jim Sohns' vocal track and added his own. Songs like "I Got It Bad For You," "Easy To Love," and "I'm In Love With You" represented the bubble-rock genre at its best—just commercial enough for the teenies, but with a solid hard-rock center and a throbbing bass pulse. This is more than I can say for the overrated Archies, who emphasized the lighter, poppier side. Guilty pleasure, this ain't— just a consistent rock LP that stands up to repeated listenings. But the geeky cover art doesn't stand up to repeated lookings—Professor Morrison's Lollipop, as well as one member of the Ohio Express, are drawn in the style ripped off from *Mad* magazine's Don Martin. Alfred E. Neuman is shown holding a balloon advertising 1910 Fruitgum Co., a slim Johnny Cash is around for no apparent reason (he looks more like Billy Lee Riley), Jerry Kasenetz is drawn wearing a superhero outfit that says Super K, and Jeff Katz is depicted as a ticket-taker for the circus. Buddah must have really liked this uncredited artist, or he worked cheaply, as his "Draw Tippy" artwork also graces the cover of the Fruitgums' *Goody Goody Gumdrops*.

K-K were on such a hot streak that they even ventured into soul music, on and off, like with Teri Nelson's album, or "Slide," a pretty good Archie Bell-styled dance number by Howard Johnson on the Shout label. Freddie Scott was an R&B mainstay, in the tradition of Ben E. King or (especially) Chuck Jackson. Scott's velvet pipes fired up hit singles like "Are You Lonely For Me" (1966) and "Hey Girl"

(1963). "Loving You Is Killing Me" (Shout) was written by Bo Gentry and Bobby Bloom, as "A Product of Kasenetz-Katz Associates, Inc." It sounds like it—Scott is his usual soulful self, but even for an R&B record, the drums are unusually heavy, and a tremeloed rhythm guitar keeps bossing its way through the arrangement. Even Bo Diddley wandered into the K-K fold for a solitary single, "Bo Diddley 1969" b/w "Soul Train" (Checker). The same heavy drums from the Scott record were present on the top side, and Bo gets a nice call-and-response going with the female backgrounds. The other side was Bo ad libbing over a K-K track that had been used before—you can hear it backwards on "Dom's Frantic Pandemonium," the flip of "Live and In Person" by the Carnaby Street Runners.

In their '68–'69 heyday, the duo were literally unstoppable. Studios were used continuously, with the end results being farmed out to various labels. Eventually the duo started their own Buddah-distributed companies, Team and Super K, which appeared to release some of the more experimental, less-adolescent material, although they dabbled in pop, too. The Beeds' single on Team has a lead vocalist who sounds exactly like Ronnie Spector (calm down, Spectormaniacs, it's not). Wahonka was a singer-songwriter in the K-K stable with that beefy voice common in post-Woodstock rock (think Rare Earth, David Clayton-Thomas

in Blood, Sweat and Tears, or Jim Peterik with the Ides of March). Although the liner notes and the front cover (a serious, double-exposure photo of long-haired, mustachioed Wahonka bathed in psychedelic lights) to his self-titled Super K album make him sound like a sensitive, introspective Singer of Sad Songs and Teller of Truths, he's essentially singing the same old bubblepop hash that K-K is famous for. (It's still a good listen—"There Was A Time," not to be confused with the James Brown showstopper, could be a snarling, garage-punk tune if they beefed up the guitars.) Some of K-K's more offbeat psychedelic stuff ended up on these two labels, and they even found time to do a third K-K Circus album, *Classical Smoke*, where they attempt the world's only classical-bubblegum fusion.

Mention should be made of K-K's apparent Beach Boys obsession. Several songs from the Kasenetz-Katz stable have those high-pitched *oo-wee-oo-oo* background vocals that made the Beach Boys what they are. Today, Kasenetz & Katz insist there was no covert Brian Wilson agenda—the K-K background vocalists would just fall in that groove when they felt the song needed it. It's doubly ironic when you consider that in 1970, some wag from *Rolling Stone* magazine, reviewing "Add Some Music To Your Day" (the Beach Boys' then-new single), said it sounded like "the 1984 Bubblegum Conspiracy." He did not mean it as a compliment.

It's generally considered that K-K sat out the period between 1971–'73, as their recorded activity cooled off during that era, although today they insist that they focused their energies on the European market, working with the band that later became 10cc (Graham Gouldman, Kevin Godley, Lol Creme, and Eric Stewart). At the time, they were ghosting as Silver Fleet ("Sister Honky Tonk"), Crazy Elephant ("There Ain't No Umbopo"), and the Ohio Express (the insanely catchy "Sausalito"). Kasenetz & Katz actually staged a mild comeback between '74 and '78, when no one was looking. Maybe more people would have noticed if they'd had more than one hit (more on that later), but the '60s were over. One-off singles by studio acts were going strong in R&B—that's how the disco movement got started—but in the white rock world they were being phased out by existing bands with albums. By now, bubblegum was the sole province of actors, like Shaun Cassidy and Leif Garrett, hardly the stomping music it was back when 1, 2, 3 red lights and crazy elephants were rampant.

The one constant about the K-K sound is the close proximity to the punk vibe. In the '60s, songs like "Gimme Gimme Good Lovin'" and "Quick Joey Small" were two steps from being pure Standells-styled garage raunch. In the '70s, K-K's productions sounded like a halfway point between heavy metal (the hard power chords) and what was later called power-pop (the insistent hooklines). Part of the reason for this is that several K-K bands were based in Ohio, which by then was producing a host of glam (Left End) and power-pop (Raspberries, Blue Ash, Circus) bands that somehow made the world safe for punk. According to K&K, Ohio radio was more likely to support local musicians and play their records. You would think that Kasenetz & Katz would have gotten in on the ground floor of punk—many of the New York bands like the Ramones owed a huge debt to K-K's '60s hits—but despite some unissued sessions with Tuff Darts (who went on to record an album for Sire), the duo dismisses the movement as not being "commercial" enough, unlike Ram Jam, K-K's big '70s superstars, famous for their heavy metal retooling of "Black Betty," originally written and performed by Leadbelly.

Kasenetz & Katz pick up the story: "We had a studio in Great Neck, N.Y. that we had built. (Ram Jam guitarist) Bill Bartlett came in one day, and we knew him from the Buddah days when he was with the Lemon Pipers, and he said, 'I have this great record that I did and I want you guys to hear it.' It was just a local thing they had (on their own Starstruck label). Nothing ever happened to it. It got a couple of plays, but nobody ever bought it, and the reason being, when we heard it, I said, this is more of a country-type record . . . country, rockabilly, whatever you wanna call it, I said, 'this is really not what we're lookin' for,' and I couldn't promote it. I said, 'I think we could redo this and something good could come out in a rock style,' so Bill said 'okay.'"

It soared to #18 on the charts, but it was a rough ride. Apparently, Rev. Jesse Jackson believed it was degrading to black women—the ad for the album featured an African-American model and her pet ram in a ravaged living room (from the ad copy: "It may not actually destroy your living room, but we guarantee it'll mess up your mind").

"We were getting a lot of calls from black women, saying it was demeaning to them," the duo remembers. "In Minnesota, at some small radio station, the program director called us and says 'listen, I'm gonna have to pull the "Black Betty" record.' I said, 'why, what's the matter?' He said, 'we're getting all these calls, from ministers and whatnot, saying we shouldn't be playing it, it's demeaning to the black woman.' I said, 'listen, it was written by a black person!' It was a blues thing! I heard the original record (an a capella chain-gang chant), it was *slow*, and I said (to Bartlett), 'how did you get the idea for doing it the way you did it uptempo?' He said, 'well, we just speeded it up off the record player and it sounded pretty good!' I said (to the Minnesota program director), 'listen, I *swear* to you, that is the greatest thing that could ever happen—the controversy in the record, and people calling up, this thing is gonna be a hit. I said, if you stick with it for a week, I guarantee and promise you you're gonna have more positive calls than you're gonna have negative calls.' He says, 'you guys have had a lot of hits, I promise you I'll stick with it, but if I don't have a turnaround by next week, I gotta take it off.' I said, 'that's fine, I have no problem with it.' He called me the next week, he said, 'I have to tell ya, you're Top 10 already. The store can't keep 'em in. They're selling like hotcakes. We're getting all sorts of calls requesting the record.' I said, 'see, there you go.'" And it was all due to K-K's promotion efforts—the hit version was released on Epic, but the label didn't do a thing to help move any records.

The self-titled album that followed wasn't half bad for its genre (stoopid, Grand Funk/Kiss-styled rock, with hooks you'd swear came from somewhere else but couldn't quite place)—they even covered a Tuff Darts song, "All For the Love of Rock and Roll," which the Darts originally performed on Atlantic's *Live At CBGB's* compilation. (The disco remix of "Black Betty" which Epic released as a 12-inch single wasn't too shabby, either.) The follow-up LP, *Portrait Of The Artist As A Young Ram*, rocked harder, but the songs didn't have any hooks—it was generally the kind of record you can listen to ten consecutive times and not remember a single note. A long, long way from previous K-K blasts like Crazy Elephant, whose notorious one-note guitar solo in "Gimme Gimme Good Lovin'" will stick in the mind for years.

Other prime K-K productions from their hard-rock years included Ohio, Ltd., on the Buddah label, who recorded the incredible "Wham Bam." Even better was Canyon's "Top Of The World" (on the London-distributed Magna Glide label, and it's not the Carpenters song). This adolescent hard-rocker from 1975 should have been the tune to bring the K-K duo back—the vocalist is confident to the point of sounding downright arrogant, and the singalong fade ("top of the world, la la la la!") almost sounds like a nasty schoolyard taunt. This would have been a perfect KISS song, and I can easily imagine a place for it on the *Dazed and Confused* soundtrack. It's easy to visualize some 14-year-old metalheads having an illicit beer in an empty parking lot with this song blaring on somebody's portable radio. This actually made the charts that summer (#98 in *Billboard*), so maybe, in some parts of the country, they did.

During this time, they even brought back the K-K Circus with "Mama Lu" (Magna Glide), where their ongoing Beach Boys obsession (see "Down At Lulu's" by the Ohio Express, or "Go Away," an obscure Fruitgum Co. single on Super K) refuses to die.

Since Ram Jam had their one-shot, Kasenetz & Katz have been keeping a relatively low profile, producing bands in their New York studio. Every now and then the duo and their stable of acts are remembered, but a full-scale revival hasn't happened yet. When the punk/new wave movement got rolling, there was the occasional homage. The Cars' "Just What I Needed" has practically the same guitar intro as "Yummy, Yummy, Yummy," and reportedly "1, 2, 3 Red Light" was a part of Talking Heads' club set, before they started making records. Liz Phair's "Whip Smart" (the song, not the whole album) sounds like some lost K-K master of years gone by, and Redd Kross' *Third Eye* album emulates the double K duo twice: "Bubblegum Factory" was an unmistakable homage, while "Faith Healer" swiped the chorus to the Fruitgums' "Goody Goody Gumdrops." Material Issue scored a coup by getting Mike Chapman (the Sweet, the Knack, Nick Gilder) to produce them, but Jim Ellison's brilliant pop songs would have been hell on wheels with a Super K production. Going back further in time, the Doors' Jim Morrison was actually promoted as a teen idol for a short period, before his oddball streak became too hard to ignore. The Doors' "Hello I Love You" (1968) sounds like an attempt to snag the bubble set, with its chunky drumming, repetitive lyrics, and cheap fuzz. Whether intentional or coincidental, all these examples are right in the groove of what K-K were doing.

Kasenetz and Katz own the names to all of their ghost groups, but as with most bands with no standout personalities, occasionally some broke musician will rip them off for their own purposes. There was a fake 1910 Fruitgum Co. playing the revival circuit in 1980, and in an unrelated, more recent incident, Kasenetz and Katz were at the China Club in New York, checking out a local band, when they got the shock of their lives when some joker was impressing a table of friends by claiming he drummed with the Fruitgums. K&K are overhearing his spiel.

Jerry Kasenetz: "He don't look familiar to me!" Jeff Katz: "I don't remember him either. It's been a while, maybe he changed!"

The aging process does strange things to a person, but Jeff Katz, in particular, thought this was stone ridiculous. "I knew right off the bat this guy was *not on* 'Simon Says'! It was four people, I knew exactly who they were, I still speak to 'em nowadays . . . I said 'that's unbelievable! Let me introduce myself—I'm Jeff Katz, this is my partner Jerry Kasenetz, we're the ones who produced these guys. I have to tell ya—I don't remember you from Adam!' The guy turned all red, and everybody looked at the guy. I said, 'thank you very much!'"

The musicians had no identity, but the sound has a life all its own.

Pour A Little Sugar On It:
My Encounter With Don Kirshner by Greg Shaw

Don Kirshner

It doesn't seem right to relate this story out of context, though I'm assuming readers of this book will be familiar with the enormous contributions made by Don Kirshner to rock and pop music from the late '50s right into the '70s. Despite whatever failings he may have as a human being, or the stories of disgruntled songwriters, there are many who are quick to praise Kirshner's ability to motivate his writers to do their best work, to offer creative criticism, and to bring the right people together at the right time. As a visionary, he is very likely responsible for the revival of the whole Tin Pan Alley ethos in the '60s, which in many ways is still with us. He may have been the first to really understand, first with the Monkees, later with the Archies, that "the artist" was a completely dispensable element in pop music. I mean to take nothing of this away from him. My encounter with Kirshner took place in the context of 30 years of admiration for his work, which probably accounts for much of the disappointment I found in the man he had become. While mine is a true story, it is of course far from the whole story.

✿ ✿ ✿ ✿ ✿ ✿ ✿

How many specific phone calls, I wonder, does the average person remember, after ten years or more? One I recall clearly was from Jim Goad, editor of *Answer Me!*, a magazine that made the audacious boast that no misspelt word would be found in its pages. And none ever was. What Jim wanted from me was to verify a name that is often confused: Kirshner.

The fact that he thought of me probably stemmed from another, equally memorable call I'd had a few years earlier, from Don Kirshner himself. He had read an appreciation of the Brill Building era which I'd written for *The Rolling Stone Illustrated History of Rock and Roll*, was flattered, and wanted to thank me. As a humble rock critic, I wasn't used to getting thanked by the great gods of the music world; it was an honor.

It was not to be my last encounter with Mr. Kirshner—or "Donnie" as his staff writers used to call him. By the early '90s he had been, somewhat mysteriously, absent from public life for quite awhile, and suddenly was anxious to jump back in. He signed a complex deal with K-Tel, who primarily wanted his cooperation in a box set of Brill Building hits, around some such concept as "The Don Kirshner Story," and were willing, for said cooperation, to bankroll him in a series of new record ventures for which he would "discover" new talent, as he had discovered Neil Sedaka, Carole King, the Archies, the Monkees, and Kansas, to name but a few.

With this as a springboard, Kirshner was envisioning his life story as a big-budget movie, the revival of his *Rock Concert* TV series, and more. One of the first things he needed was some creative "talent" to put all this stuff together, who could be relied on to put the most positive spin on the facts. He remembered that article, and mentioned my name to the folks at K-Tel.

This time the call came from Steve Wilson, who was K-Tel's point man on the deal. He invited me to take on the whole thing, from track selection to liner notes. Though I had pretty much given up doing such jobs, the Brill Building period was perhaps my very favorite era in music, and nothing substantial had ever been written about it. The concept I presented to Steve was to go beyond the idea of a "Don Kirshner Story," using him as the starting point, but also including related people, like Leiber & Stoller, without whom the whole saga just couldn't be complete. We agreed.

I put together song lists. K-Tel had access to just about everything, but I wanted not only hits, but many of the great records that never charted, or the original versions of tunes that were later hits by English bands (like Earl-Jean's "I'm Into Something Good," rather than the Hermits cover), and even, if possible, some of the legendary Carole King demos, which would be appearing on record for the first time. This combination would, I felt, make for a truly great album.

Many of the things I wanted turned out to be unavailable. The demos had apparently disappeared into a vault that no one could find. But for the most part, I got nearly everything I asked for. In fact, they were successful in licensing quite a bit more music than we could use, and it was then I found out that Kirshner was adamant we use eight tracks by Connie Francis, five or more by Neil Sedaka, and bizarrely, three or four by Steve Lawrence & Eydie Gorme, friends of his I supposed. This was going to be a problem, with already way too much great stuff to squeeze in, but I wouldn't worry about it until I'd gotten what help I needed from Kirshner; after all, in his mind, this was still "The Don Kirshner Story."

My next job was to piece the story together. Of course, I knew a great deal of it already, but I wanted to hear it in Kirshner's own words. He had offered to make himself completely available. So I arranged to spend a couple of weeks in New York, meeting not only Kirshner, but as many of the old crew as he could put me in touch with, which I figured would be most of them. That was to be one of my first disappointments: none of the old crowd seemed to be on speaking terms with him anymore.

The first thing I did on my arrival in New York was to place a call to Kirshner. He was not, I learned, a man to answer his own phone. A gruff male voice (who sounded more like a bodyguard than a secretary) would take the call, write down my number, and then two or three days later call me back to say that Mr. Kirshner would be available "soon," or "tomorrow." Meanwhile, the days went by and I was accomplishing nothing. What leads I had seemed to dry up as soon as Kirshner's name was mentioned.

Eventually the summons came: Mr. Kirshner would like to spend a whole day answering all my questions, then take me for "a nice dinner" where I could continue getting to know him, more informally. When would this be? They'd get back to me. Finally, two days before my flight out, he found the time.

I was hoping to visit his house, to see how he lived, and to pick up whatever clues I might. But no, Mr. Kirshner valued his privacy, and perhaps his security as well. Instead, I had to borrow the apartment of a friend in Manhattan, where we eventually met, conveniently just too late for a luncheon.

He came through the door, bodyguard in tow, smiling and glad-handing and full of bonhomie— the same bullshit persona I'd seen in all the other industry veterans I'd met, from Russ Regan to Clive Davis. I knew immediately I'd never get anything real from him, but soon learned it was even worse than that.

I had dozens and dozens of questions written down. But first, he insisted we watch a video, a superficial TV puff-piece on him from the '70s, followed by a tour of his "fabulous house" conducted by Robin Leach. This was the house I'd hoped to visit, but I wondered now if he still lived there. In the back of my mind, I was weighing the assumption that he must be filthy rich against my growing feeling that the best he could do these days was to put up a blustery front.

I tried to steer the conversation to his early days in music. But no, he'd rather talk about how he had been the one to discover and launch the whole current generation of comic superstars, from Billy Crystal to Eddie Murphy. I guess he'd read somewhere that comedy had now taken the place of music in the lives of young Americans.

At any rate, we finally got down to it, and he gave me a couple of hours of his tales, some interesting, but mostly oft-repeated generalizations that went against known facts. Occasionally one of the facts I tossed out would jog a memory, but as a rule he didn't remember anything that wasn't already in his official bio.

Then we came to the real point of the whole thing: the movie. There was "serious interest" from two studios, and he needed a treatment for a screenplay immediately. Would I do it? There was also interest in a book deal, he further dangled. Numbly, I suggested perhaps he could fill me in a bit more over dinner.

"Sorry, no time for dinner. Got another appointment. I'm sure you can do it!" And with that, he was gone.

I flew back to L.A. and duly produced an outline for what I thought might be an acceptable movie. After all, he had been behind the scenes of the entertainment industry for 20 years and he could easily be glossed-up. But meanwhile, I'd reported in to Steve Wilson, who was anxious to know how my research had gone. He was astonished when I told him I'd waited two weeks for a three-hour interview that was mostly useless, and had got no usable leads to anybody else.

"Well," he said, "at least you got a good dinner out of it!" What? Yes, it seemed Kirshner had submitted an expense report for a $200 meal at one of New York's finest restaurants.

Now the whole story was coming unraveled. K-Tel had in fact given Kirshner quite a large sum, expecting a flow of salable products. But as time went by, Kirshner had to admit there was nothing in the works at all. His TV series was not going into syndication. And there were, of course, no movie or book deals. It looked like somebody had been ripped off, by a seasoned scam-artist whose oldest friends wouldn't take his calls.

Suddenly, it didn't seem so hard lopping off those Steve & Eydie cuts. *The Brill Building Story* was finished, with as balanced a portrait as I could bring myself to paint. Kirshner actually called to invite me to a congratulatory dinner—before he'd seen it. I went to the restaurant, here in L.A., but he never showed up.

The Don Kirshner story, "The Music Man," in *Everything's Archie!*

The Melodic Milestones of Jeff Barry by Chris Davidson

Jeff Barry

The bubblegum firmament boasts many a bigwig but none bigger and firmer than Jeff Barry, a man blessed with ears you should smooch the next time you see him. For without those nutty lobes, which uncannily heard glistening super-pop pumping up from the subway grilles on his stroll to the office down Broadway every morning, we'd have no Archies, a much less pleasant Monkees, half as many cool Shangri-Las tunes. A River Deep with no Mountain High. A "Do-Wah" without the double "Diddy!" Take Jeff Barry out of the b-gum pantheon and you screw me out of half the golden Brill Building nuggets, not to mention Andy Kim's, Phil Spector's and Neil Diamond's best work.

JB is bubblegum music's Ground Zero. No one's ever been more dead-on more times. You must marvel now at this mortal's unearthly grasp, his full-blooded grip on pure pop's building blocks—a taut, inviting intro setting up a hook sharp enough to snag your trousers on; a warm and reassuring lead vocal; a focused rhythm track; love letter lyrics; hand claps; faint orchestral flourishes; a melody standing as proudly as a sunflower. Equally as important to the recipe are the things not mixed in: snotty punk posing, cynicism, glibness.

Of course, Barry had assistance from numerous other kingpins of the pop cognoscenti, and these relationships just prove what a player he was: Ellie Greenwich, his wife and co-writer of his early smash hits and superb misses; Leiber and Stoller, who hired him as a staff writer and producer for their fabulash Red Bird label; and Andy Kim, a late-'60s collaborator on the Archies and worthy popster in his own right. With help like this—and the uncanny drive of a bona fide star—Barry constructed a 1960s empire of worldwide hit songs from scores of performers and studio whiz groups.

The tunes? You know every one by heart: "Be My Baby," "Chapel of Love," "Hanky Panky," "Leader of the Pack," "I Can Hear Music." Hit after hit of precise American pop. And the big bonus, the reason we're celebrating JB right here: his songs were simple, elegant, optimistic, and, above all, they were happy. Yes, baby, happy—the forgotten emotion. Jeff Barry's songs might not make you ponder the cosmos, but they will make you smile; the latest calculation shows that we owe Jeff Barry 3.7 wide grins.

That Jeff Barry is not regarded with the awe of Brian Wilson or other Gloomy Gusses speaks more about the jaded press and its hold over most music fans than the great man's hit-to-miss ratio. History sadly rates tormented geniuses over crafty songsmiths after all, and JB's undying upbeatness can't compete with hard rock and deep introspection in the eyes of squares. Naturally, this misses the mark widely. The joys of a basement sing-along to "Sugar, Sugar" or the rush when "Da Doo Ron Ron" storms into a room are not accidents but the desired outcome of a swinging cat with impeccable pop taste, a colossus of cool whose feats I'm calling:

The Melodic Milestones of Jeff Barry

Milestone #1: Ellie Greenwich & the Brill Building

Like a kosher rocket ship with after-burners blazing, Jeff Barry streamed to the forefront of the most productive years of New York City pop-making, namely the Brill Building's creative concussion of the late-1950s and early 1960s. Sparked by Jerry Leiber and Mike Stoller, fueled further by big Don Kirshner, and promulgated for nearly a decade by a phalanx of monstrously frantic, stingy-brim-clad business types, the Brill Building (and its neighbor, 1650 Broadway) was simply the farthest out collision of music and commerce since ol' Tommy the Ed began slammin' out phonographs.

Back then, Manhattan really cooked. You could scam your way into a publisher's office with some hick tune you just wrote, knock together a few couplets on an old upright piano, get the thing cut by studio cats wearing shades and brandishing major chops, score a publishing deal collectively split among five guys you never met, and maybe actually see a record released—all before Chinese food was delivered for lunch! And somewhere deep within this cacophonous wonderland sat Jeff Barry, lanky but so pulled together, with skills honed over numerous late-night writing sessions, churning out an assembly line of hits like a rock 'n' roll Cole Porter.

Barry first made the NY scene around 1959 as a songwriter on staff at E.B. Marks Music. His early tunes, in collaboration with scribes Ben Raleigh, Beverly Ross and others, created encouraging chart noise for Sam "Teenage Sonata" Cooke, Ray "Tell Laura I Love Her" Peterson and such. Yards better than most of this early writing were the handful of singles JB cut under his own name (his first, "Hip Couple" on RCA, runs down a description of a frosty twosome with lines like "We're what you might call the criteria of hipness!"). Harder to find but truly gone, Barry's records as the Redwoods poke tantalizingly at the record production lion that he ultimately tamed.

In every room of the Brill Building worked amazing partnerships like Carole King & Gerry Goffin, Barry Mann & Cynthia Weil, Neil Sedaka & Howie Greenfield. Before long, JB had a full-time mate, too—Ellie Greenwich, a B-Building songwriter of high standing who he'd known since childhood but married in 1962, thus powering a writing dynamo that flattened the charts for the next three solid years. Jeff and Ellie quickly threw their hats in with Phil Spector, prince of the hit-house Philles label, and instantly scored with monster self-penned hits like "Be My Baby" and "Baby, I Love You" by the Ronettes, Crystals trinkets "And Then He Kissed Me" and "Da Doo Ron Ron," and Darlene Love's "Wait 'Til My Bobby Gets Home."

The Raindrops. Left to right: Ellie Greenwich, Jeff Barry and Laura.

Quality radio pop oozed from the Barry-Greenwich alliance on a weekly basis. Transistors hummed, hips and shoulders frugged. With everything they touched selling so well, and a long list of past recordings (Ellie had cut records—some produced by Barry—as Ellie Gee, Kellie Douglas and others), the pair naturally decided to release some new, self-performed material.

Concurrent with their Philles triumphs, our dynamite duo marched up the hit parade as the Raindrops. Recording for Jubilee, the Raindrops began as a front for their personal demo of "What A Guy," intended for another group but rush-released as a cutie-pie single in early '63. More Raindrops singles, including the original "Hanky Panky," and an LP trailed closely after its mild success. The sole Raindrops hit, "The Kind of Boy You Can't Forget," best captured their lovely, intertwining gal group arrangements and Ellie G.'s chiming vocals ("the Empress of the whole girl scene," so says Bob Crewe). Great as the 'drops were, Barry and Greenwich soon filed them away in favor of the swanky jet-age sound of a new hit machine.

Milestone #2: Red Bird Records

In early 1964, Jeff and Ellie springboarded straight from Spector to an equally awesome pop pinnacle, the newly formed Red Bird Records hatched by Leiber, Stoller and industry vet George Goldner. The label's first disk, "Chapel of Love" by the Dixie Cups, was a Barry/Greenwich/Spector ditty passed over for release by the Ronettes and Crystals. The D-Cups took it to No. 1, and Red Bird's short, wild ride began.

The imagination reels at the excitement brewed in Red Bird's offices over the next year, as the cream of New York's record biz madly tried to grab a piece of the pie. Hit followed hit, deal begot deal, careers peaked and torched. Gal singers of every stripe and color paraded through. Most every note of quality had the Barry-Greenwich stamp of approval emblazoned on the label. Ever heard "I Wanna Love Him So Bad" or "You Should Have Seen the Way He Looked at Me?" This is the blue printable Red Bird sound of the

Dixie Cups, the Jelly Beans and the Butterflys—unfettered girl groups singing sweet and pure. Even the second-string, non-Barry material scored, like "The Boy from New York City." The label was just that hot.

Proving that evil can triumph over good if armed with the right material, Red Bird also unleashed the nasty Shangri-Las on unsuspecting 1964 record buyers. The company threw its top hit-makers at the gum-snapping Queens chicks. The results still amaze: compressed melodramas of lost love, violence and disenchantment all set to a hard Big Apple beat. The Shangs' first Red Bird single, "Remember (Walkin' in the Sand)," stood apart from its follow-ups, and everything else released that gone year, with ultra-dense production, spooky sound effects and surreal lyrics courtesy of writer/co-producer Shadow Morton, who's credited with molding the group with a Spector-like brazen vision. Still, Barry and Greenwich lent tunes and production expertise, especially to "Leader of the Pack," "Give Us Your Blessings," "Out in the Streets" and other little soap operas with sound effects, as Barry called them. Soon enough it would be Barry's turn to mold a group in his own image.

Jeff and Ellie careened through 1964 and early 1965 with Red Bird, which Leiber & Stoller eventually sold to third wheel Goldner in 1966. As with the Raindrops, Jeff and Ellie continued to release records of their own. Their Red Bird 45s, Barry's "I'll Still Love You" and Greenwich's "You Don't Know," showcased typically sharp melodies, but neither hit. J & E didn't last too much longer with the label or with each other. Their last official collaboration took place at Bang Records, where they (in name, anyway) produced a spate of Neil Diamond hits, such as "Cherry, Cherry," "Solitary Man" and big D.'s first two albums, both killer: *The Feel of Neil Diamond* and *Just For You*.

Milestone #3: The Monkees

A tone-deaf four-year-old could describe the crazy-cool delights held within the Monkees' first album. Sterling Boyce & Hart production, Goffin-King tunes, airtight session playing. Plus, you can buy it for a dime at every garage sale in country. Perfect on all counts—and cheap! Now, it's late 1966, and between bites of liverwurst sandwich, Monkees mastermind Daddy Don Kirshner is contemplating: "How do I top this sucker?" The answer: enlist Mr. Red Bird and hope for some brilliance to rub off onto his TV foundlings. And so it was that late 1966 saw Jeff Barry overseeing Monkees sessions on both coasts with the goal of creating a follow-up LP.

With seven cuts helmed by Barry making Kirshner's final cut, *More of the Monkees* tramples every remaining Monkees release for its consistency and JC Penney honesty. Barry's production cements hot material to mid-decade optimism, and the resulting late Brill Building milestone remains the pop album to beat for 1967 (not counting Ellie Greenwich's solo LP on United Artists, which excels at pop gem-cutting). "I'm A Believer," the group's biggest smash, marries hand claps and roller-rink organs into a lasting union of sheer bliss. The gorgeous melody of Goffin-King's "Sometime in the Morning" swirls with piles of sound waves and motion, and the end-product fuses the memory.

Barry cut a handful more songs for the group in 1966, including the biting "I Don't Think You Know Me" and two Neil Diamond compositions, one the hit "A Little Bit Me, A Little Bit You." Temporarily, Barry's Monkees business ended there, aside from the ginchy "She Hangs Out" that appeared on their fourth album, a driving, bastardized doo-wop that marks Barry's initial foray into pure bubblegum. Barry certainly rocked prior to this, but nowhere did the bass percolate so hotly or the imagery cook like a Raquel Welch sunburn. How little Davy Jones nailed such a performance remains a wonder, but his repeated queries of "How old you say your sister was?" boil the blood nicely.

The Monkees—reduced to a Dolenz and Jones duo—found Barry in the driver's seat for their final album three years later, 1970's *Changes*. Amazingly, not much magic transpired at these sessions, which claimed a full Barry production and songwriting help from pals Andy Kim and Bobby Bloom. Awash in light-rock sameness, *Changes* never takes flight and unfittingly capped JB's first journey into TV land.

Milestone #4: The Archies

Dandy Don Kirshner, never one to miss a gimmick (or a meal), then head of Calendar Records, approached Barry to create what amounted to the ultimate pop godhead—a made-for-TV rock band that trumped the Monkees in their own artificiality. This time, Kirshner vowed, no loudmouth singers with their own opinions and fuzzy wool hats. They'll be cartoons! And to fill those cartoons, we'd need songs, lots of snappy songs. To wit, the Archies arose in 1968 from pen and ink illustrations to flesh and blood musicians under the tutelage of the decade's foremost producer.

Of the 40-odd songs cut by the Archies and produced by Barry, no more than four are crap. Our boy, without question, topped himself at every turn and perpetuated more unadulterated pop than he'd produced in the decade prior. Every single a gem, each album an instant party, the Archies are to bubblegum what Chuck Berry is to rock-and-roll. The entire movement rests atop Ron Dante's precocious voice, the tight-ass New York arrangements and JB's musical flourishes, like the gooey spoken intro on "Who's Your Baby?" or the utter rhythmic mastery of "Jingle Jangle."

So many sleepers, so little time: "You Know I Love You," "Seventeen Ain't Young," the bubble-soar of "Get On The Line." Would but that a hundred more cuts appear in Jeff Barry's sock drawer, each impeccably brief and more danceably groovy than a sea of Beatles records. Alas, two years total, four JB-produced albums and the Archies bounced off for a final LP in 1971, co-produced by Dante and far less riveting. Then back they went into Kirshner's vaults and the dreary, music-less pencils of 1970s animators.

Archies extra: In the midst of the show's initial run, Barry produced Dante's elusive solo LP, *Ron Dante Brings You Up*. Hmm. Barry, Dante, the self-same wizardly musicians. Yup, it's the Archies' lost album. Praise Allah that a CD version appears soon.

Milestone #5: Steed Records

"With an ear to the future!" is how Jeff Barry billed the records on his very own label, Steed Records, which he started in 1967 after producing Neil Diamond. Let loose on his own, Barry created a distinctly experimental company, although certainly still one you'd call a pop outlet. Orbiting around Barry at Steed were collaborators Andy Kim and Bobby Bloom, sundry studio musicians and a great deal of hard-to-categorize talent.

To be sure, not everything worked. Andy Kim's material meanders more than it flies straight, and the albums by hard rockers the Illusion sound like Barry was getting a corned beef sandwich at the Carnegie Deli when they were recorded. Where were the Redwoods when you needed them?

When all pop cylinders fired, however, Barry mustered typically boss sides. Dig Robin McNamara's "Lay a Little Lovin' On Me," "Love That Little Woman" on Kim's *How'd We Ever Get This Way?* LP, or "So Good Together" from AK's heavy-selling *Baby, I Love You* platter. This is top-flight melody with innovative flourishes. Not quite Brill Building caliber anymore, but confident enough to give Neil Diamond pause to wish JB was still in his corner.

Barry produced a good deal of material during the Steed years that found release on other labels, the Monkees' *Changes* the most famous example. Better were the Klowns and the Globetrotters, fictitious groups both, the former a Ringling Brothers circus tie-in album featuring six face-painted "personalities" and a bouncy Barry approach, the latter another Kirshner animated TV project that JB supplied with a tuneful bubble-soul album.

Hard to tell if Steed was squeezed into interludes between Archies albums or the other way 'round, but the label folded shortly after Barry's work ended on the show. He has undoubtedly been busy since, (did you know he wrote the themes for *The Jeffersons* and *One Day at a Time*?), but has not been able to capture the public fancy in a big way. He doesn't have to, of course; we're already won over and enamored with the big giant sound coming from those little bitty records. Somewhere, we're dancing to him right now.

Jeff Barry's Bubblegum Blues interview by Don Charles

"Some songs, like 'Where Have All The Flowers Gone?' people hear and they get sad. I think I'd rather have them get happy! That's really where I was coming from." That's how songwriter/producer extraordinaire Jeff Barry sums up his musical philosophy, a philosophy that moved millions of dollars' worth of vinyl around the world during the 1960s. Jeff Barry was the crown king of bubblegum rock producers (only Jerry Kasenetz and Jeff Katz' A & R staff came close to challenging his dominance of the genre).

Jeff Barry: I was born in Brooklyn. When I was about seven, my parents got divorced, and I moved in with my mom and sister in Plainfield, New Jersey. I lived there until I was 11, and then we moved back to Brooklyn. For some reason, I was hearing a lot of country music. As long as I can remember, I've always loved horses, and probably without realizing it, I liked listening to country and western music because that went along with horses!

Don Charles: My research indicates that your family name was Adelberg . . .

JB: Yes, that's correct.

DC: Was "Jeff" your real first name?

JB: No, it was Joel.

DC: So where did the name "Jeff Barry" come from?

JB: The only reason I changed it was, when I started to record as an artist, I kinda needed a showbizzy name. One of the friends of the family's last name was Barry, and I took that. The "Jeff" might've come from (actor) Jeff Chandler.

DC: After you graduated from high school, you joined the Army, right?

JB: Yes, when I was 18. I wanted to get that out of the way. It was in peacetime, and they had the six month plan. It was the Army Reserves; you came out, and spent another two and a half years in the Reserves, going to meetings once a month, and going away for two weeks in the summer for more training. So I did that. I was stationed at Fort Knox, where they keep the gold.

DC: After you were in the army, you went to New York City College?

JB: Yes, NYCC. I was singing with my friends, writing songs, and making little demos—considering it all a hobby. But then, I decided I'd like to see if I could be a singer. I got someone to set up a meeting with a publisher who knew a friend of the family. It was the only person I could get to in the music industry, and it just worked out to be a music publisher. He said he'd be willing to listen to me sing.

DC: That was Arnold Shaw?

JB: Arnold Shaw. And if he thought I could sing, as a favor, he'd introduce me to some producers or record company types. But what I sang for him were the songs I was writing, and he was more interested in the songs than in the singer! Arnold signed me to EB Marks Music, his publishing company. Subsequently, he did introduce me to Hugo (Peretti) and Luigi (Creatore), and I made a record for them.

DC: Your recording of "The Face From Outer Space" is one of the wildest things I've ever heard. It'd surely be a top tenner in the Dr. Demento countdown!

JB: Oh, man! I was always coming up with nutty novelty things . . . funny stuff that people took seriously! I actually recorded this song. You know, there were novelty records out at that time, and this was a space creature, "The Face From Outer Space," okay? I used to do this voice (sings with an odd echo effect): I'M THE FAA-AAACE! It was ridiculous! Those were the times, but . . . did you ever hear of a record called "The Water Was Red?" . . . that was another one of my sick "death" songs [22]. . . . You know the opening scene in *Jaws*, where the boy and the girl go to the beach? She goes in the water, and the shark gets her . . . that was the story in "The Water Was Red," all those years earlier. It was about a boy and a girl who go to the beach, and she gets

---

22. Others include "Leader Of The Pack", "Tell Laura I Love Her" and "Give Us Your Blessings"

killed by a shark. He's a skindiver, and he tracks that shark down, and then "the water was red" again!

DC: I've just gotta find a copy of that single! Let's talk about some of the people you collaborated with on songs. Wasn't Ben Raleigh your first collaborator? He co-wrote "Tell Laura I Love Her" with you.

JB: Well, actually, before Ben was Beverly Ross. She wrote "Lollipop" for The Chordettes, and some other things. I remember having a lot of fun writing with her. It was all so new and unbelievable, that I could be doing what I loved to do. Sheer joy! Then Arnold Shaw wanted me to work with Ben because he had a solid, professional approach to songwriting. We'd start in the morning, take a lunch break, and then we'd go back to work, just like a regular job. It was a good work ethic.

DC: Wasn't Artie Resnick your next partner?

JB: He was one of them. With Artie, it was more fun and loose. Artie and I were very good friends.[23]

DC: How was Ellie Greenwich as a collaborator?

JB: Again, fun is the first word that comes to mind. We were a natural team!

DC: How did the two of you meet?

JB: Ellie and I have a mutual relative. There's a picture of us when we were around three or four years old, at a family function. Her cousin married my cousin. Years later they knew she was interested in music, and I was already in the business, so they kinda felt we should meet.

DC: You and Ellie Greenwich, and Phil Spector . . . what made it click? All of those songs you wrote for The Crystals, The Ronettes, Darlene Love, and Tina Turner are considered classics now.

JB: We were writing for his specific recording technique—for his specific artists' style. Knowing who we were writing for was a big help, as opposed to just writing songs. His artists were the kind of artists I write for, anyway, or at least the market was. It was the teenage market. It was just real simple and easy to write with Phil. If it hadn't been, we wouldn't have kept writing together!

DC: What brought about the breakup of your production and songwriting partnership with Ellie Greenwich?

JB: Well, we were married, and then we were divorced, I think, in 1966 or '67 . . . around in there. Once we were no longer husband and wife, it was kind of a natural progression to be doing professional things separate from one another.

DC: Did it feel strange, producing artists without her, after the two of you had worked together for so long?

JB: I think I was probably more the active producer than Ellie was. I was more interested in doing that stuff, you know, staying up late and playing around in the studio. Not that she didn't, but I think I was more into it.

DC: I know you wrote some things with Marty Sanders, who was a member of Jay and The Americans . . . there was a great song called "Honey Do," which The Strangeloves recorded, and another one called "Tricia, Tell Your Daddy." Andy Kim cut a record on that, and it charted.

JB: "Tricia, Tell Your Daddy"! You know what that one was about? Richard Nixon and his daughter. I was a writin' fool!

DC: Then, later on in the '60s, you collaborated with Ron Dante, Andy Kim, and Bobby Bloom. Bobby Bloom is one of the most underrated artists of that period. What do you remember about working with him?

JB: Bobby and I were really great friends. As a matter of fact, when Bobby died, I got a call from AFTRA, the musician's union. I never knew it, but I was his life insurance beneficiary. Bobby was a real character! Just a great guy, really, really bright, and really, really talented. He loved to write, he loved to sing, and he loved being in the studio, but he really didn't love performing. Not that he disliked it, but he'd just as soon not. It wasn't like he had to perform. He wasn't coming from that place, which was really unfortunate. He was a great-looking guy, and the girls just loved him.

DC: And what a singing voice he had! The album you did with him [*The Bobby Bloom Album*,

23. Teamed with Joey Levine, Artie Resnick later became part of the Kasenetz-Katz stable of writer/producers.

L & R 1035] is fantastic. What instrument did he play?

JB: He played guitar. He could play keyboards, too, somewhat, and was good on percussion as well, but mainly guitar. Bobby was the kind of a guy . . . he had this house in the Hollywood hills, he had a motorcycle, and a Porsche, and a car called Excalibur. Sometimes, he got really crazy! He once drove his motorcycle into his pool. But the Bobby Bloomness of it was, he left it there. He never took it out. It was like *The Titanic*—you could swim down to the wreck!

DC: How did he die?

JB: Unfortunately, he died of a gunshot wound. Somebody shot him, in a fight over a girl. It was crazy! He kicked down a door, and ran into the room, and the guy reached for a gun. I don't think they ever found the guy.

DC: How did you meet Neil Diamond?

JB: I think Ellie heard him in a demo studio. I always thought he was a great, great writer, and the combination of him singing his songs . . . it's hard for me to picture someone else singing his songs. They were quite personal. It's him singing his material that's so unique, so powerful.

DC: Toward the end of your involvement with Neil Diamond, you started up your own label, Steed Records. What was the motivation for that?

JB: I had just gotten out of a relationship with Leiber and Stoller at Red Bird Records, and it was time now to do it on my own. Simple as that.

DC: Was Steed Records totally your company, or were there other owners?

JB: It was mine! It was the first time I ever had the opportunity to do it all myself, without having any partners. It was actually quite a big thing to bite off. I'm a do-everything-myself kind of a guy, so I was trying to create or co-create the material, be the head of A & R, and produce all the records. It was very time-consuming; but we had three floors in a brownstone on 52nd Street, off Broadway, right off Seventh Avenue. We had three offices: My publishing operation, my record company operation, and my studio—it was called Century Sound. The studio enabled me to record

anytime I wanted, without having to watch the clock. I could stay as late as I wanted, and if an artist wanted to go in and experiment, it was always available.

DC: Did you have a regular crew of musicians that you used in the studio?

JB: Hugh McCracken was the guitar player. Ron Frangipane played keyboards. Ron worked with me on a musical, *The Freaking Out Of Stephanie Blake*. Then, Al Gorgoni was another one of our guitar guys, and also on guitar, Trade Martin. I had musicians like pianist Artie Butler, who went on to become very successful arrangers and producers in their own right. Chuck Rainey was one of the main guys on bass, and my drummers were Buddy Saltzman and Gary Chester. Gary Chester played on "Sugar, Sugar," I remember.

DC: Tell me about the artists you had on Steed Records. Andy Kim was the most successful, as well as being one of your main song collaborators.

JB: He's still one of my dearest friends. I met him when he was about 17. We wrote "Sugar, Sugar" together, and most, if not all of his records on Steed. I think we were on the charts for about two years and change; almost every record we did made the charts! The Andy Kim records, they all had something. They all had potential.

DC: You worked with him at Red Bird Records first. You produced a single for him in 1965 called "I Hear You Say (I Love You, Baby)."

JB: Yes, we experimented a bit. We experimented with a few artists at Red Bird, but Red Bird kinda went away overnight. A lot of the artists really didn't get a chance to develop over there, and Andy was one of them. But it worked out on Steed, and then he went out and had a nice career. He now has his own label up in Canada, Ice Records.

DC: His biggest hit on Steed Records was "Baby, I Love You." That record has a great sound to it. Do you remember how you recorded that?

JB: I played the drums on that one, piece-by-piece. I had an idea for a really nice sound.

DC: Did you do that big percussion arrangement?

JB: Yes. What I did on that one was play all the elements of the drum separately. I played the kick drum with a hand-held mallet. Andy Kim played the guitar, and I just kinda tapped along to keep the tempo steady. He sang the song "live," all the way through. We used that as a guide track, and we were gonna erase it all later; but to that, I over-dubbed, on separate tracks, the snare drum, the high hat, and the other cymbals, so there was no leakage of sound. They were totally clean, which is impossible to get when you play a whole set of drums at once. We overdubbed every instrument slowly, all on separate overdubs, kinda like the way "Montego Bay" was made.

DC: "Montego Bay" was just you and Bobby Bloom in the studio, wasn't it?

JB: Yes, we played everything on that record.

DC: How many musical instruments do you play?

JB: I don't play anything well enough that I'd want to do it much in public! I can get around on the guitar, and I can play keyboards enough for me to write. I can find chords, and I can play, even though I don't know music as much as I'd like to. I've played all kinds of percussion on records. That's much easier because I have a good sense of rhythm. When I played the organ, I'd play the keyboard, and then I'd lay across the seat and play the pedals with my hands!

DC: You had a singer named Robin McNamara on your label, who was a member of the New York cast of *Hair*. In fact, some of the other cast members sang backup on his album.[24]

JB: That's right. I remember hearing at the time that some radio stations and some people in the business thought that Robin McNamara was a girl! Of course, his voice is kinda high, definitely up there in the tenor range. Robin had a very unique voice. He was a real pro, a real entertainer, and he certainly wasn't shy! He loved to sing, and he brought a lot to the performances. He had the one big record, "Lay A Little Lovin' On Me", but I wish he'd had a string of hits. I think he had potential to change with the times, because he was on the cutting edge. A lot of the people in *Hair* were.

DC: Why did you close down Steed Records in 1971?

JB: Steed Records had just run its course. The deal I'd made was for a certain time period, and it was up. At the time, I had two children, and we had moved to Long Island. Coming into New York from Long Island each day was really tedious! It was, like, three hours a day in the car. New York was becoming not my favorite place to live. I had come out to Los Angeles quite a lot in the mid-'60s, working with Phil Spector, and I'd always loved it out here. And so, at a certain point, the tug of Los Angeles and the push of New York just led me to move. I made a deal with Herb Alpert and Jerry Moss at A&M Records, and I had my offices on the A&M lot for three and a half years. I recorded some things over there, and I just really loved Los Angeles. It was fantastic then.

DC: While you were still running Steed Records, you were also producing acts for Don Kirshner. How did you get involved with him?

JB: The music business was mainly in two buildings in New York: 1619 Broadway, which is the Brill Building, and another at 1650 Broadway. Don Kirshner was in there, and, you know . . . people knew people! When he needed some work on The Archies and The Monkees, he called me in as a producer/writer.

DC: How much creative control did Kirshner allow you?

JB: I would really do whatever I wanted to do. I'd run things by him, but I don't ever remember him saying "That's not good enough. Make it bet-ter!" He hired me to do what I do, and there was an awful lot that needed to be done.

DC: How'd you like working with The Monkees in the studio?

JB: They were great! But one of them I didn't get along with.

DC: Let me guess: Mike Nesmith?

JB: Nesmith! When I first went to Los Angeles, I had a demo of "I'm A Believer." Either I was singing

24. Including Sakinah "La La" Mohammed, former lead singer of The Crystals.

it, or Neil Diamond, I don't remember. It was incomplete, just the basic band, and the vocal. I remember meeting The Monkees, when they heard it for the first time with Don Kirshner, in somebody's office. All of them were there, and Nesmith had a girlfriend with him. So everybody said, "Hello," and I finally came around to playing "I'm A Believer." When it was over, everyone seemed to like it, and understand what it was — except Mike Nesmith. He said, "I don't think it's a hit. I'm a producer, too, and that ain't no hit." It was, like, real embarrassing. Real rude! Maybe he was just showing off for this young lady (and I do mean young). So it was kinda strange in the room. To lighten things up, I said, obviously joking, "Well, when I get all the strings and horns on it, maybe then . . . " And then he said, "Hmmm . . . well, yeah. Maybe with strings and horns." That's when everybody broke up, because he obviously didn't understand that I was just kidding. When everybody laughed, he got furious! So our relationship didn't start out that good.

DC: Micky Dolenz laid down a dynamite lead vocal on "I'm A Believer," real spontaneous. How did you get that out of him?

JB: I don't know if I had to "get it out of him" . . . it just came with the normal amount of producing/directing. He just did a great job.

DC: Your next project for Don Kirshner was bringing The Archies to life on records. It's hard to understand why you'd take on a huge job like writing, arranging, and producing all the music for a TV series when you were so busy running your own label, doing musical theater, and everything else. When did you sleep and eat? It had to have been incredibly time-consuming.

JB: It was all-consuming, but it wasn't work. It was fun! It was what I would choose to do. It's not like I collected stamps or painted in my spare time! Music was my hobby. When I stopped creating, it wasn't good; not that the rest of my life was bad, but that was some of the best parts of it. You're lucky enough to have a career at something you'd do for free, and that's what I really loved to do: Writing the songs, and going into the studio with the musicians.

DC: But we're talking about a tremendous workload. What made you believe you could handle it all? Weren't you concerned about overloading your schedule?

JB: I was a lot younger, and I had a lot more energy. I didn't know I was busy, I was just having a great time! Getting up early, staying up late, that didn't mean anything to me. You know, a lot of The Archies' stuff I did in one week. You know all those little dance clips that appeared in each show? I did 17 of those. Recorded, overdubbed and mixed, all in one week.

DC: As you told me earlier, you were involved in an aborted 1967 Broadway show called *The Freaking Out of Stephanie Blake*. When I researched it, I discovered that not only was Ron Frangipane in the cast, so was Ron Dante . . . so you'd obviously met him before. Who chose Ron Dante to be The Archies' lead singer?

JB: I'm sure it had to be approved by Don Kirshner, but I believe I was the one who brought him in.

DC: Other than Ron Dante, who did you use as vocalists on The Archies' records?

JB: Toni Wine was the first female voice. She was the main girl at that time. She did (sings) "I'm gonna make your life so sweet" on "Sugar, Sugar." And then, there were others whose names will not come to me now. . .

DC: Ellie Greenwich is said to have participated in some Archies recording sessions.

JB: Oh, sure. That's very possible. Ellie might've come in and done some backgrounds.

DC: Also, reference books I've seen claim that Andy Kim, Bobby Bloom, and Tony Passalacqua were involved, too. You were working with most of them as solo artists around that time. Do you recall them singing Archies songs?

JB: It's very likely. It was that kind of community. My friends would come down, clap their hands, and sing. People loved to go into the studio! It's fun.

DC: Were the musicians on The Archies' releases the same ones you used for your Steed Records dates?

JB: Oh, I'm sure. It was all the same musicians, yes.

DC: Tell me about how "Sugar, Sugar" came to be—the writing and the recording of it.

JB: Well, I wrote it with Andy Kim, we wrote it in my office. Andy played the guitar. I don't know where the idea actually came from, but it was a simple kind of "hitty" song. Perfect for The Archies!

DC: A lot of reference books claim that song was written for The Monkees.

JB: No. I don't remember that being the case.

DC: How long did it take to cut the track?

JB: That particular track took two to three hours to get the groove just right. I had a certain groove in my head, and I wanted it to be layin' back. Not rushing. For some reason, it took a long time. I was kinda dancing around the room in front of Gary Chester, the drummer, to keep the groove laid back.

DC: "Sugar, Sugar" has a kind of Caribbean flavor to it. It almost sounds like a steel drum on the record.

JB: It probably is a steel drum, and an organ at the same time.

DC: The organ is the most memorable part of that record. Who played it?

JB: I played it. Obviously overdubbed kinds of riffs on records, I usually end up playing. It's got to feel a certain way, and I can do that better.

DC: How long did it take to get the vocals?

JB: I don't remember, but probably not very long. Ron Dante is such a great singer, he can do anything anybody wants! He'd sung on so many TV commercials and things, too, so I'm sure he just got what was needed right away. Do you know about the way "Sugar, Sugar" broke as a hit record?

DC: I've heard different stories . . .

JB: The record came out, and it really wasn't happening as a hit. What was it, the second Archies record?

DC: It was the third. "Bang-Shang-A-Lang" was the first, and the second one was "Feelin' So Good."

JB: By then, I suppose radio was saying, "C'mon, guys! This group doesn't even exist. It's a little kiddie cartoon thing. Give us a break!" So it wasn't happening, (but) the promotion man in San Francisco peeled the label off the record. He went to a radio station and said, "Listen to this." They said, "That sounds like a hit! Who is it?" He said, "I'm not telling you! You play this record for a week in a good rotation, and then I'll tell you who it is. It's nobody bad, so don't worry about it." So later, he told them it was The Archies, and they went (groans) "Oh, no!" But they played it. They kept their word, and it broke for a smash hit out of San Francisco. That's supposedly the story.

DC: The next Archies hit, "Jingle Jangle" had a big, arena rock kind of sound. It was nothing like "Sugar, Sugar."

JB: Yeah. I was always experimenting, never really wanting things to be exactly the same. When I had time to come up with new sounds, I always did.

DC: Did you ever play drums with The Archies?

JB: No. Most of it was by Buddy Saltzman or Gary Chester. I probably did a lot of percussion, though.

DC: What I liked is that you didn't "write down" to kids. Archies' music didn't sound like bad nursery rhymes the way a lot of children's music does nowadays.

JB: I wouldn't have wanted to do it any other way! I wanted to make hits, I wanted to make radio records. You don't have to keep rewriting "Hickory Dickory Dock" for kids, you know? I think that even if they don't understand every word, they get the message.

DC: Over the years, rock critics have written a lot of harsh things about The Archies' music. They've said it was silly and sugary, and a waste of time to listen to. When you read things like that, did you ever regret becoming involved in that project?

JB: (shocked) No! Not at all. To review "Sugar, Sugar" and the music of The Archies, which was created for kids, in the same light as you'd review music that was created for adults is ridiculous. That's like reviewing a Popeye cartoon, and saying (pretentious voice), "Oh! The plot was so light.

There wasn't any depth. And that silly ending . . ." It's absolutely stupid to review children's product on a scale that you'd review adult product. Don't take a perfectly good tricycle and say it's a horrible mountain bike! . . . So for people to say "Sugar, Sugar" isn't cool, my answer is, well, I feel sorry for you. It's not my fault that adults liked it, too.

DC: Around the time of the third season of *The Archie Show* (1970–71), which was the last season you worked on, you produced a group for RCA Victor called The Klowns. Do you recall anything about them?

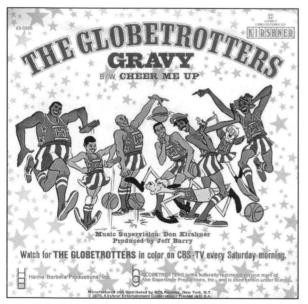

JB: I don't remember all the names in that group, but one of them was Barry Bostwick. He became a very successful film and television actor. In fact, Barry came into my office one day, and he said, "Man! I just had an audition for a stage show, and I know I got it." And he did! He opened *Grease* in New York.

DC: Concurrently, you produced another cartoon act for Don Kirshner, The Globetrotters. Who were the singing voices on that soundtrack album? Was it the actual Harlem Globetrotters?

JB: Yes, I think it was some of The Globetrotters. Meadowlark Lemon, and some of those guys.

DC: That album's a real blast! It reminds me of The Coasters' records. It sounds like a bunch of

crazy guys getting together and just having fun in the studio.[25]

JB: That's what it was. We all had a great time making rock 'n' roll.

DC: What's a typical Jeff Barry recording session like? Walk me through the process of how you produce a record.

JB: It depends on the artist. As a producer, it would be my function to gather the material. If the artist writes—if it's Neil Diamond, for instance—he'd write all the songs himself. When there was a collection of ten, it would be time to cut. If it was an artist that would co-write, I'd write with them; and if it was an artist who didn't write at all, myself and people on my staff would do it. Once the songs were put together, I very rarely went into the studio with formal arrangements. I'd only have arrangements for overdubs with strings or horns, where you'd have to have them written out. For the rhythm tracks, I'd just hire great musicians, and go in with chord sheets. I'd play them the song, and they'd all learn it together. Then we'd come up with different parts. It was like musical finger-painting. I'd work with a couple of different engineers . . . I'd book the session. I'm the kind of producer who produces in the room with the musicians. I like to stay in there with them, get the arrangement down, and I'd wear earphones to hear everything that was coming through. Once everybody knew the song, and we were starting to get the track in shape, I'd stand at a microphone. I'd be able to talk to the musicians constantly. I could say to the guitar player, "Just ease up! Don't play so many notes." Or, I could sing something to somebody as I hear a riff. I'd be right in their ears, because they'd have headphones on as well. When it was really feelin' good, then I'd go into the control room. The engineer would be getting the sounds on the instruments, and sure enough, the kick drum would be a kick drum (on tape), and the bass would sound like a bass. If I had some gimmicky things I wanted to do, I'd work on it then with the engineer. Then the

25. The Coasters did appear as vocalists on this highly collectible Kirshner Records album (KES-108), along with members of The Drifters, Platters and Cadillacs. Whether any actual member of the Harlem Globetrotters other than Meadowlark Lemon sang on the sessions is unknown.

singer would go out to the mic and sing along. It's always best when musicians are hearing the vocal.

DC: Why is that?

JB: It always seems to work better when the singer is singing along. So whenever it was feasible, I'd have the artist there. If that vocal wasn't particularly the vocal, I'd certainly try for more. When the musicians were gone, then it was time to really direct the singers, work to get that perfect, emotional vocal performance.

DC: How important do you consider the part where you go into the control room and "mix" the record?

JB: Well, after I got the vocal performance, it was overdub time for me. That's when I liked to play! I'd overdub percussion and hand claps, tambourines, shakers, bells, and other little doodads. The basic track I always wanted to make with a few musicians—four, maybe five guys on bass, drums, keyboards, and guitar. Keep it simple and controllable, and not have to worry about other stuff happening at the same time. Then, I'd overdub all the details: Signature sounds, and riffs, and background harmonies—all the other things you put in a record. It was like putting the trimmings on. The mixing is important to get all the elements in the right perspective, and make 'em all sound great. Once in a while, I'd add some tricky little echo things, but I usually didn't get into tricky production values. Most of it was pretty straightforward. I believe the hit is made on the other side of the glass, where the talent is. Where the music is.

DC: Of all the records you've produced, do you have a favorite?

JB: Well, it's hard to name just one! Three come to mind: "Baby, I Love You" (Andy Kim), "Montego Bay" (Bobby Bloom), and "Sugar, Sugar." That was a fun record to make.

DC: How do you look back now on that whole Don Kirshner era, and the work you did?

JB: It was fun stuff! He always had interesting projects. Don Kirshner was fun to work with because he gets excited about songs. He's encouraging, and it's nice to work in that kind of atmosphere.

DC: When you left New York, did you just cut loose from all the artists you were working with?

JB: Some of the artists came out with me. I actually drove out here with Bobby Bloom and Robin McNamara in a '61 station wagon. Andy Kim was out here already. So I had friends out here from New York, and I took some with me!

DC: How was the trip?

JB: It was great! We were wailing all the way! Someone was lookin' out the back window for cops, and we just kinda went!

DC: So in the '70s, you settled in as a staff producer at A&M Records. Was the transition easy for you?

JB: Well, I had a new life out here, a new way of living—California living, as opposed to Manhattan living. That took a lot of my time! I really was enjoying living out here, and probably not concentrating as much as I should've on the writing and the production. I was more like a kid, having a good time instead of working hard. But I had my offices at A&M, and it was a wonderful, fun atmosphere to work in.

DC: Later on in the '70s, you wrote theme songs for several hit TV shows. How did you get those assignments?

JB: I think I just got a call from TV producer Norman Lear one day, and I had a meeting with him. I did The Jeffersons theme, One Day At A Time, Family Ties, the Don Kirshner's Rock Concert theme, and several others.

DC: The Jeffersons theme is probably one of the catchiest and most memorable TV theme songs of the '70s. You wrote that with Ja'Net DuBois, who was an actress on Good Times.

JB: Ja'Net DuBois had never recorded before. When we were writing the song, I told her I loved the way she sang. She said, "Oh, no! I couldn't," but I told her not to worry about it, and we went in the studio and did it. "Movin' On Up" is definitely my favorite TV song. It just works for the show so well. (sings) "Fish don't fry in the kitchen . . ."

DC: Then in 1980, you wrote and produced the soundtrack for a movie called The Idolmaker. Tell me about that.

JB: I got a call from Taylor Hackford, the film's director, and met with him. He decided I was the guy to do the music. It took a year to do it all, and it was an awful lot of writing, but I wrote it all myself and ended up scoring the picture, too. I was on the set every day, right at Taylor's elbow. That was a great time! I learned a lot about film-making.

DC: What kinds of things are you doing these days?

JB: Well, I've had a multimedia children's entertainment company for the last few years with a guy named Richard Goldsmith. We have lots of kids' projects out. We did two albums for a series of books by Richard Scarry; a series of books called *Clifford, The Big Red Dog*, we did an album for that; there's a TV series (in development), and the biggest girls' book series out, *The Baby-Sitters' Club*, we did an album for. We're gonna produce a major motion picture with Warner Brothers on *Frosty The Snowman*, live action with animation.[26] So it's mainly kids' projects. But I'm also working on a stage project, I'm writing a movie script with Paul Williams, and another script on my own . . . I've been developing all kinds of things. I'm concentrating on lots of different areas of creativity, not just songwriting.

DC: But you're still writing songs?

JB: Yes. I've written some country tunes that I suspect will be recorded soon, and I just finished one the other day for a new Tom Hanks film.[27] Everybody seems to love it, but whether it gets in or not, we'll see!

DC: What do you think of the music on the radio today?

JB: I don't think anybody really cares about kids today very much! It's so easy to sell to the lowest common denominator, to sell sex and violence, and not try to uplift. I'm aware that I'm not young anymore, and I might have a jaded attitude, but I think I'm being objective. I understand that music changes, but in the overall sense, are things better now? Is music uplifting? Is it putting the right thoughts into today's youth? No, I don't think so.

DC: You're saying that you felt a sense of responsibility to your audience?

JB: Exactly! I knew my songs were going to reach young ears. If you pump ugliness into them right from the beginning, then there's no chance!

DC: Here's my last question. How does it feel to know that the songs you've written, and the records you've produced have entered into American popular culture? You know, become a part of history?

JB: It's so gratifying, and satisfying, and rewarding! I can't begin to tell you. When I was doing it, I never really looked to the future. I considered it music for the here and now, and I didn't think it was anything that was going to last. I was just trying to make the kids happy, talk about love with respect and not be ugly about it. And the fact that kids remembered the songs, took them to heart, grew up with them, and know them as the music of their youth . . . it's a thrill! And I'm so glad I handled it the way I did, because it is respectful music. You rarely meet the consumer when they're nine or 16 years old, never have any real contact with them, and you certainly don't discuss what your music meant to them. The real significant thing to me was meeting those nine-year-old girls as adults, and to relate on an adult level what it meant to them as kids. That really got to me! That those songs were important after all, not in some changing-the-world kind of way, but in that they made people happy. That's a great power. It's really fantastic to have done that.

Interview conducted in October and November 1995. Special thanks to Theodora Zavin.

---

26. This project came to fruition as the Michael Keaton vehicle *Jack Frost*.
27. The film was probably *That Thing You Do*, but no Jeff Barry songs appeared in it.

Richard Gotterher and the Art of the Instant Record by Keith Bearden

Almost everyone can name a watershed musical moment in their life. I've heard stories from friends of first becoming sexually aroused listening to Aerosmith's "Walk This Way," or deciding to drop out of school after hearing the first Stooges record. The moment that redefined my life and musical tastes was catching the first set of "New Wave" records to come out of New York City in 1977. They had the exuberance, beat, and sing-along melodies of stuff I had loved on the oldies station, but with an anger, worldweariness and sick humor totally appropriate in the styleless, decadent and lazy years following the '60s "revolution." It made me fully acknowledge what I had always suspected: I was not "normal," I was not "mellow" and I was not "cool." I did not fit in and now I had music for and by other people who didn't fit in either. It was at this point that music became a therapist, a friend, and a community by proxy in the remaining decade until I was able to bust out of my stunted suburban existence.

As I studied and memorized the jackets of my favorite vinyl companions over the next few years, I noticed a familiar name popping up in the production credits: Richard Gotterher. Soon, anything with his name on the back became an automatic purchase, grooves unheard. Like Phil Spector, anything with Gotterher's touch mandated at least one listen.

Like many involved with the new wave movement, Gotterher's roots lie in studio pop bands of the '60s. He, along with producing/writing partners Bob Feldman and Jerry Goldstein, created the ruse that was the Strangeloves, posing as three independently wealthy Australian sheep farmers who moonlighted as musicians. They hoodwinked enough American teens with their phony story, "Aboriginal" drums and cheap Beatle wigs in 1965 to send "I Want Candy" to number 11 on the national charts. If only for that one song, the Strangeloves are worthy of discussion. "I Want Candy" is a revelation; a Bo Diddley jungle beat, jazzy guitar line, and massed, aharmonious male vocals sounding like a fraternity bash at its drunken pinnacle—all bathed in enough reverb to make it sound like the first live simulcast from the moon.

Bow Wow Wow's 1983 version may be more familiar, but the Strangeloves' original is the one that gets under your skin. Two more Top 40 hits followed—"Cara-Lin," later covered by the Fleshtones, and "Night Time," redone by Iggy Pop, the Nomads and even Joe Jackson (as the theme to a Miller beer commercial!). Like the Shadows of Knight, the Strangeloves pre-dated the term "Bubblegum Rock," and their heavier sound and seemingly more authentic garage band persona have saved them from being lumped in (and berated) with other studio pop bands of the era. Of course, the history of rock 'n' roll is a history of "fake" studio bands, and many hit songs of numerous "real" groups (Byrds, Beach Boys) were played partially by for-hire session men (but that is for a whole 'nother book).

Many persons involved in the 1960s NYC studio pop hit factory later worked with the explosion of '70s pop/rock talent that fell under the tag of "New Wave." Buddah Records publicist Marty Thau managed or produced the New York Dolls, the Real Kids, Suicide and the Fleshtones, to name a few. Tommy James/Crazy Elephant/1910 Fruitgum Company songwriter and musician Ritchie Cordell channeled Joan Jett's talents into the stuff of '80s Top 40 success. But it was Gotterher's "Instant Records"—his '70s production company: he recorded LPs in an average of four weeks as opposed to the months or even years common during the era—that clarified the link between new wave and its '50s/'60s influences like no other. He helped Blondie sound less like a Soho loft garage band and more like the mutant Girl Group they wanted to be. His work with Robert Gordon and Link Wray proved to post-Woodstock hipsters that "oldies" could be as valid as the Ramones. Marshall Crenshaw's classic debut LP, Pearl Harbor's underrated solo work, The Go-Go's' *Beauty and the Beat*—all superb pop music that will forever define an era, a genre and the artists that made them. All the product of Gotterher's pop sensibilities.

Still producing records occasionally, Richard Gotterher is currently the CEO of The Orchard <www.theorchard.com> a web-based independent music distributor. We met over tea at a noisy cafe near his offices in New York City's Chinatown.

Keith Bearden: Tell me about your start in the music biz.
Richard Gotterher: I started when I was in high school in the early days of rock 'n' roll. I was a classically trained piano player, and then I discovered the blues. Listening to Alan Freed, I learned about rhythm and blues and black music. So I started writing songs, at first copying Jerry Lee Lewis. At the time it was Elvis and Jerry Lee, and being a piano player, I naturally gravitated to Jerry Lee. So I wrote a song, when I was 16 years old, called "I'm On Fire," which he eventually recorded in the '60s just before his transition to country music. One of his last real rock recordings.

I was playing with my own band, and I got some songs published. One day I ran into two guys outside the office of one of the music publishing houses, Bob Feldman and Jerry Goldstein. We hit it off and started writing songs together. Then we started making demos, which were primitive one-track recordings. And then we said to ourselves, "If we can write and produce demos, we can write and produce records."

We had basically a string of hits from 1963 to 1966. First, "My Boyfriend's Back" by the Angels, which went number one. We worked on the girl groups for years, and wrote for Freddy Cannon, Dion, Bobby Vee. Lots of people. I have a drawer full of almost one hundred 45s that we either wrote or produced, or both.

After '66, we split up, and then I formed Sire Records with Seymour Stein. We licensed a lot of European music, had some hits. We had Climax Blues Band, Renaissance, "Hocus Pocus" by Focus. I left Sire in the mid-'70s, when the punk thing started happening, when I discovered Blondie, Richard Hell, Robert Gordon, and made a lot of records with those people.

How did the Strangeloves happen?
We had been producing the Angels, and there was a point where they went on strike. And we had this track for them, this remake of an old Patti Page or Jo Stafford song called "A Little Love (That's All I Want From You)." It was done in what was ska for the time; they called it bluebeat. We changed it and called it "Love Love." The girl group thing was sort of fading, and the Beatles were coming in a big way, and the whole British Invasion, so we decided to sing on the track and call ourselves the Strangeloves. In the middle, Bob recited the lyrics, pretending to be British. We sold the record to Swan, put on these Beatle wigs and posed with these African drums in a photo, and put out this goofy press release that we were Australian. With all the British groups around, we figured Australia would be novel.

We get a call from a DJ in Virginia Beach, VA, and he says, "This record is getting a great response down here, if you come down and perform, we can drive it up to number one." We said, "Okay." We get there, and we went to the airport, got in a small plane that drove down the runway, faking that we had just flew in from Australia. There was a huge sign saying, "Virginia Beach welcomes Australia's Strangeloves." There were all these screaming kids, holding teddy bears, and throwing jelly beans, cause that's what they did back then. When we went to perform, we only had this one song, and we knew we couldn't just do that. So we did "Bo Diddley" by Bo Diddley. And the response was unbelievable!!

So we come back to New York and record it at Atlantic Studios. Ahmet says he really likes it, but that we should take it to his new label Bang. We took it to Bert Berns [co-writer of "Twist and Shout," among many other hits], and he says, "This is great, but Bo Diddley was Bo Diddley, why don't we re-work it using the same beat?" And the four of us wrote, "I Want Candy."

There was this wonderful guitar player at the time named Everett Barksdale, who came up with the riff and he was playing off the melody to "Anna," the hit by Silvano Merano. We had become pretty knowledgeable about producing at this point. We kept ping-ponging in the studio —we recorded the drums twice, along with me banging on African drums, and Jerry, Bob and myself were overdubbed singing together four times. That's why this record has this overwhelming sound to it. After we mixed it and mastered it, we added more EQ and reverb, so it has a very processed feel, but at the same time has a real raw vibe to it. This process occurred over a period of weeks.

We used a lot of tricks, but I was always careful to keep things spontaneous. The wonderful thing about recording with them was there were moments that you captured, and you tried to go back and get it again and you couldn't. When we did "Hang On Sloopy" [Gotterher produced the McCoys' massive hit], we tried it again —we did the same beat and sound again and it never came together. It could've been something as obtuse as the temperature of the studio or the weight on the drums. With the digital technology of today there is none of that variable.

Why did the Strangeloves only have one album?
Albums were not the thing back then. Until the Beatles came along, nobody really bought albums, they bought singles. Our one LP had three hits on it, but it didn't make a difference. Moving on to the '70s, if you had a hit song you had to have an album because people bought albums. The market had changed. That's one of the reasons radio was more open back in the '60s to play new and indie records. People didn't play album tracks. They wanted hit 45s. They were hungry for 'em, and the damn things only lasted two minutes! That's a lot of demand for product!

When you toured, did people catch on that you were three guys from Brooklyn and the Bronx?
No, never. We had our fake Australian accents, and that was enough.

Do you have a philosophy as a producer?
I learned from listening to records by Leiber-Stoller and Phil Spector. The song has to always be your center, your focal point. If you create an environment that enhances the song, that's the job of the producer. You have to listen to the song first. I came from being a songwriter. What I like to think I bring to a recording is a clarity of thought.

A lot of bands make really stinky records when they stop working with you. Holly & the Italians made an amazing debut with you, and their second LP is unlistenable. Nobody likes the Go-Go's' third record. Marshall Crenshaw's career never recovered from Steve Lillywhite doing *Field Day*. How much involvement do you have with young, untried bands? What changes did you make when you worked with Blondie for example?
They didn't need a lot of changes, really, just structural channeling. What I like to try to do with a band is work with their deficits, as well as their assets. To me, it didn't matter if you didn't play that well—I found a way of getting it out of you. A lot of producers would say, "You have to do this perfectly —if you can't do it, I'll find someone else who can." I always figured, "Hey, Clem Burke isn't the greatest drummer in the world,

but something he's doing is unique, and fits in with the uniqueness of the band. And it's my job to bring that to listeners." There were things about Blondie that were amazing from the beginning —their sense of humor, their attitude. I wasn't as concerned with their ability to execute everything. What I wanted to do was capture the feeling and enthusiasm of what they were about, and just focus it in a way that was palatable to mass audiences. Because they were considered weird back then. There was nothing remotely like it on radio. I wanted to bring out the qualities they had. Professionalism is not as important to me as it was to radio programmers of the time, perhaps.

Those first two records were not very popular in the US, but they were incredibly popular overseas. Then of course Mike Chapman worked with them and focused more on the discipline part of producing them, and they exploded with "Heart of Glass."

Blondie sounded like Blondie when they were with you. Chapman's hand was a lot heavier than yours was. That's the difference between you and producers like Phil

Spector and Giorgio Moroder—you don't mold bands in your image. The records you produce don't all sound alike. They have a pop aesthetic, but—

There is a thread that goes through it. I'm more interested in the emotion of the song. The sound should be appropriate for emotion of the song.

What were your challenges working with the Go-Go's? They were part of the L.A. punk scene and sounded pretty ragged. How much teaching did you have to do?

A lot. The Go-Go's at their first rehearsal just said, "Just tell us what you want us to do. We want to be successful." The funny part about that record was when it came out, [IRS Records president] Miles Copeland called me up, and he was just *livid!* "You ruined my group! I gave you this great punk band and listen to this bubblegum shit!" He was talking about "Our Lips Are Sealed," which I thought was just amazing. The band themselves weren't there for the mix, and when they heard it, they didn't talk to me for a good six months. They cried. They thought it didn't sound like them. It wasn't grungy and disorganized. To me, it captured their identity perfectly. Then they came to love it and we did a second album.

Your '60s work was mostly session musicians. Did you have any studio groups during the new wave era?

No. We brought in a different drummer for Holly & the Italians, and we occasionally had someone do sax, or Paul Shaffer doing keyboards.

Joey Levine from the Ohio Express was asked to produce some new wave records, but found the whole scene "too freaky." Did you have any hesitations about it?

No. I went down to CBGBs early on. Marty Thau was really into the change that was going on, and he took me. I signed Robert Gordon, Richard Hell, Blondie, all to production contracts and got them with record labels. No one else would have them at the time.

One of the great things about new wave was that it was a real New York scene.
Yes! New York was the only thing going. New York started it and England and the rest of the U.S. followed. Unless you count rap, it was the last big New York thing. We started that, too.

Did you see a lot of parallels between your '60s music and the new wave bands you were producing?
Most definitely. The people who were really doing it in the early days of punk, completely bypassed the early '70s. They were really into '50s rockabilly, girl groups and of course the British invasion. To them, rock 'n' roll stopped in 1969 and began again in 1976.

There is an argument that bands who aren't really bands—that are studio musicians, or created by producers, managers or records companies—are inherently invalid because they are "manufactured." How do you feel about that?
Well, that's certainly invalid if you're talking about pop music. That idea eliminates a huge portion of what's happening, yesterday and today. The purpose of making a record is so people will enjoy it, it gives them pleasure and a unique experience. I mean that's it. It doesn't matter for me. I don't listen to today's studio groups like the Backstreet Boys and the like. It just seems contrived. It has a factory-produced feel. I consider the stuff we did in the '60s to be much freer and more organic.

BUBBLEGUM FANTASIES

There's something about bubblegum that stirs the imagination. Plotted squarely at the intersection of gooey teen desire and cynical major chord manipulations, bubblegum incites restless fantasies of control, gratification and Candyland: lissome boys with gleaming chests; demo singers easing seamlessly into character as Boyesque Desire Object before scuttling across the hall to play madly enthusiastic housewives in floor-wax jingles; cult-like sessions held hostage by pistol-wielding producers coercing that 37th take from the musicians. The relentless cheer of the music insists on a dark side as surely as they're gene-splicing Goofy in the tunnels beneath Disneyland. Pouring into the viewer's ears and pupils, televised images can suddenly inhabit a parallel universe in which the Oedipal and apocalyptic become furiously tangible. In Bubblegum fantasies.

by Jake Austen

HE'S THE KING OF BUBBLEGUM

Jughead's ALL STAR "JUG" BAND

...AND HE'S GOT THE CROWN TO PROVE IT!

STRAWBERRY SHORTCAKE-Vocals

Strawberry wasn't supposed to be in the "Jug" Band, but fate felt otherwise! After Flo and Eddie bowed out, they recommended a lady they'd worked with in the early 80s who'd be perfect. The problem? Where to find her. "After Cyndi Lauper stole my act in '83 it was pretty much over" explains an older & wiser Strawberry Shortcake-Klein. "Luckily, real estate welcomed me with open arms!" She wasn't looking for a comeback, but it found her in 1999 when Soul singer Macy Gray attributed her "sour" vocal style to Strawberry's sweet influence. The next thing you know, Strawberry's being interviewed by Tavis on B.E.T., a show Jughead never misses! The rest is history...in the making!

SNORKY(Banana Splits) Rhythm Guitar

They say an elephant never forgets, so imagine how the pachyderm behind the Banana Splits' trademark psychedelic Farfisa sound felt after awakening from a 2 year "Magic Peanut" induced coma in '78 and realizing he didn't know how to play keyboards anymore? A lesser puppet would have given up, but with the tutelage of longtime companion Drooper he fought his way back to master...the guitar? "Drooper can't play keys!" shrugs the former Split. Replaced at Hanna-Barbera by an animated version, their loss is The "Jug" Band's gain!

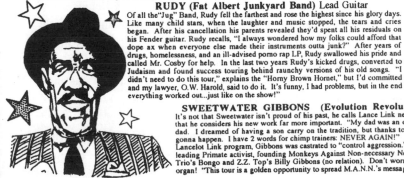

RUDY (Fat Albert Junkyard Band) Lead Guitar

Of all the"Jug" Band, Rudy fell the farthest and rose the highest since his glory days. Like many child stars, when the laughter and music stopped, the tears and cries began. After his cancellation his parents revealed they'd spent all his residuals on his Fender guitar. Rudy recalls, "I always wondered how my folks could afford that dope ax when everyone else made their instruments outta junk?" After years of drugs, homelessness, and an ill-advised porno rap LP, Rudy swallowed his pride and called Mr. Cosby for help. In the last two years Rudy's kicked drugs, converted to Judaism and found success touring behind raunchy versions of his old songs. "I didn't need to do this tour," explains the "Horny Brown Hornet," but I'd committed and my lawyer, O.W. Harold, said to do it. It's funny, I had problems, but in the end everything worked out...just like on the show!"

JUGHEAD JONES
(The Archies) Drums

He was the driving force behind the Beatles of Bubblegum and now he's back leading an All Star squadron of Fun Rock Commandos! Don't call them oldies...call them goodies! But don't take our word for it...listen to the living legend himself:

"People always ask me was it hard to be in the Archies while making all those comic books and cartoons? Let me tell you something, it was hard *not* to be in the Archies after the band split up! The music is in me, and ever since the comics went all digital, I've been bored, hungry, and itching to pick up the old sticks! Do I need the money? No, the royalties more than keep me in burgers, but it was never about the money for me, it was always about the music! Pure, uncut Rock and Roll has always been my drug of choice, unlike some who will go nameless (Reggie!). But the past is the past, and I can honestly say my new band is the best I've ever worked with! The fans will come for the hits, but they'll stay with us for the new material. We may have a few extra pounds in the middle and the "bubblegum" may be harder to chew with partials, but believe me, our memories are fine, and if there's one thing I recall it's that *we built this city, Riverdale, on Rock and Roll!*"

WOLFIE (Groovie Goolies) Bass

Of all the "Jug" Band, Wolfie has aged the best. "You should see Drac, he doesn't look a day older!" howls the Canine Krupa. Wolfie's been working since the band split in '71, but not playing the same old songs! In '72 Wolfie stopped howling at the moon and started howling for the Lord! The Godly Goolies released their 1st LP for Word Records in '77 and have sold over 700,000 since! "It was actually pretty easy to change all the old tunes to Gospel. 'Goolie Garden' became 'Goolie Garden Of Eden,' 'Save Your Good Lovin' For Me' became 'I Was Saved By Your Good Lovin', J.C.' and we just replaced 'First Annual Semi-formal Combination Celebration Meet-the-Monster Population Party' with 'Amazing Grace.' "

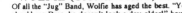

LION and GORILLA
(1989 Musical Marching Zoo) Horns

Though only credited on the Kassenetz-Katz Singing Orchestral Circus LP, this "duo from the Zoo-o" actually played on scores of K-K productions, "Human groups, even!" adds the proud Lion. Though steady session work has been their bread & butter, the full Zoo actually stayed together until the early 90s. "That nutty Squirrel & stupid Penguin thought there'd be a ton of interest when 1989 rolled around!" laments Gorilla. The beasts consider Jughead the best drummer they've ever worked with...& that's saying something - they played with Rooster for 27 years!

SWEETWATER GIBBONS (Evolution Revolution) Keyboards

It's not that Sweetwater isn't proud of his past, he calls Lance Link nearly every day. It's just that he considers his new work far more important. "My dad was an organ grinder, as was his dad. I dreamed of having a son carry on the tradition, but thanks to the 'producers,' it ain't gonna happen. I have 2 words for chimp trainers: NEVER AGAIN!" Like all the actors on the Lancelot Link program, Gibbons was castrated to "control aggression." Since then he's been a leading Primate activist, founding Monkeys Against Non-necessary Neutering with the Nairobi Trio's Bongo and Z.Z. Top's Billy Gibbons (no relation). Don't worry, he hasn't hung up his organ! "This tour is a golden opportunity to spread M.A.N.N.'s message!"

The Partridge Family Temple: Religion is the Bubblegum of the Masses by Go-Go Giddle Partridge and the Risen Keith

Amazing grace how sweet the sound that saved a Partridge like me. The glory of music is what makes the Partridge Family a religious experience for the followers of a Now cult called the Partridge Family Temple. Let these words be a psychedelic bus to take you on a spiritual journey to the Kingdom of Albuquerque. We've been traveling in circles such a long, long time trying to say hello to you. Well, now we can. If you are reading this right now, it is because Keith Partridge declared it so.

Listen to the far-out pop sounds of the Partridge Family over and over again, and you will realize the Truth. For, you see, the Partridge Family produced the most psychedelic holy music ever created. We came to know the Truth—that the characters on the '70s sit-com *The Partridge Family* are in fact Gods and Goddesses. Each song has a spiritual message for those who dare to listen for the not-so-hidden meaning. We came to know Reality in 1988, and the Partridge Family Temple was hatched. Walk in the fleshy spirit we like to call Now!

The Partridge Family Temple is a religious organization devoted to the worship of the Partridge Family. Each character represents a different archetype: Shirley is the Virgin Mother Earth Goddess (hence no father on the show), Keith is the Male Sex God King Christ (David Cassidy was chosen by Keith to be his human vessel for his mighty milk-flowing phallus), Laurie is the Holy Harlot Honey Whore of Babylon (just read Susan Dey's *Secrets On Boys, Beauty and Popularity* and you'll know what we mean), and Danny is the Trickster God. It's no coincidence that Danny declares on his solo album that he'll be your magician in the bubble magic world of milk and honey. He was the first and only being ever to deflower his own Mother, for Pete's sake! This knowledge is all there for the taking.

The Partridge Gods use groovy far-out sacred bubblegum music to communicate with the masses. The sounds vibrate from your record players right into your souls. Every Partridge Family song is Our Lord Keith spreadin' a little lovin' all over the listener. Then he keeps movin' on to reach more with his powerful message. And while the television shows, the novelizations, lunch boxes, trading cards and more are very powerful tools of enlightenment, these are all really just means of getting you to dig the music. The seemingly wholesome situation comedy is a Trojan Horse that introduces at least one great mind-blowing song every week into the psyches of kids all over the world. The Partridge Family will make you happy—whether you like it, or not.

A majority of Partridge Family songs are Keith[28] speaking directly to the listener, the "You" in the songs. Just look at these *titles* to a few Partridge Family classics and you'll see what we mean: "I Think I

28. Who possessed David Cassidy's body from 1970 to 1974.

Love You," "I'll Meet You Halfway," "I Can Feel Your Heartbeat," "I'm Here, You're Here," "Every Song is You," etc. We are not making this stuff up! Keith is reaching out to you. Don't try to fight it; accept him into your life. He does think he loves you, he will meet you halfway, he really can feel your heartbeat even though you didn't say a word, and most importantly, every song is you. These are just the titles. Wait until you get heavily into the lyrics!

The albums are like a spoken bible. The more you listen, the more you get out of them. We recommend listening to songs at least one hundred times in a row in order to fully grasp the hidden meanings found within these spiritual texts. We also suggest listening to the music at various speeds, and backwards. We guarantee that with each and every listen you will learn more and more about Reality.

Pop culture is the spiritual medium of the Now. The Partridge Family taught us that. How did they teach us that? By creating us to create the Partridge Family Temple, the first serious religion based purely on pop. Television characters are the new gods, sitcom plots are the new myths, and bubblegum songs are the new spiritual hymns.

The Partridge Family is the greatest band of all time. They are bigger than the Beatles and bigger than Jesus. Time will tell. A thousand years from now, no one will have heard of the Beatles, but everyone will know about the Partridge Family. People try to put down the Partridge Family, whining that they are not a real band. But they put out real music on real records and transformed the lives of millions and millions of real fans who later became real cult leaders and the most groovy cult leaders at that. Now that's all that matters. They are more than just a real band, they are Reality itself.

People complain, "But they don't play their own instruments or write their own material." The Partridge Family used the greatest studio musicians and songwriters of all time. Elvis Presley didn't write most of his music either, but he is considered the King of Rock and Roll. Well, David Cassidy is the King of Bubblegum Music. Jim Morrison may have been the Lizard King, but Cassidy was the Partridge King. Dig it.[29] Everyone talks about the musical genius of the Beach Boys, but they (as well as the Carpenters, the Mamas and the Papas, and others) used many of the same musicians that our Gods did. What's more, all of these musicians and songwriters came into this world via Shirley Partridge's vagina. The ultimate paradox is that the Partridge Gods created the creators of their television show.

The Partridges have been around since the beginning of time; they just decided to reveal themselves to this world on September 25, 1970. (More accurately, they revealed themselves via the music a month earlier.) This was a sneak preview of the religion to come. They knew that the most powerful way to reach the now generation was to get with it utilizing television, pop music, and a psychedelically painted bus.

The beauty of the Partridge Family Temple is that unlike most religions whose followers often are not even sure their gods existed, no one doubts that Keith Partridge exists. He's right there in front of you on the eternal tube. And while it may be hard

29. Cassidy did actually write a few Partridge tunes.

to visualize what Loki the Norse Trickster God looks like, anyone can pick up a *Teen Beat* magazine and dig the redhaired mischief maker, Danny Partridge.

Join the temple now and be pointed in the direction of Albuquerque as our beloved master sings to us. Let the music into your heart. Become a Teen Idol Television Rock God before the bus leaves without you. Come to the Temple where you can indulge 24 hours a day in sex, drugs and bubblegum music.

For more information dig our temple in cyberland at:
www.partridgefamilytemple.com
or write us at:
The Partridge Family Temple
P.O. Box 480775
Los Angeles, CA 90048

The Partridge Family was Cancelled For Your Sins.

ORIGINAL SIN

The Daisy Bang Story by David Smay

They're among the most sought-after bootlegs in all of Rock 'n' Roll. There was a time in the early '80s when you couldn't claim to have a serious record collection without the *Smile* sessions, Big Star's *3rd*, *The Basement Tapes* and *The Daisy Bang Story*. The gatefold opened to a double album with one side for each band member: Anna van Leeuwen's eerie *Dub Masters*; Dillon's *Harmony Cathedral*; *The Black Beauty Demos*; and *Cin Songs Seventeen*. Nowadays Elephant 6 bands cite it as frequently as Os Mutantes, DJ's pay up to $2,000 dollars for an original vinyl copy, and *Option* rated it with Ubu's Hearpen singles, *Spunk* and Television's demo tapes as punk touchstones. Not bad for a third-string bubblegum band with only one LP and two 45s in their official discography.

The first syndicated episode of *Captain Jack and the Daisy Bang* premiered September 5th, 1971. It looked and played like a knockoff of the Bugaloos hosting *Wonderama*. Shot on an old Republic Studios soundstage, each episode featured a smattering of old cartoons (Heckle & Jeckle, Harveytoons), appearances by L.A.-based musicians, puppet skits and a live performance by the Daisy Bang (often backing the visiting musicians).

The show's producer and mastermind, Rick Reilly (b. Eric Piscarelli), hosted the show as the silver suited Captain Jack of the Starbrite Rangers. (A cuddly, cosmically trippy kind of ranger corps by all appearances.) The set, composed of abandoned props from Universal's *Flash Gordon*

Illustration by Andrice Arp

serials, resembled nothing so much as Ming's Tacky Space Discotheque of Doom. Local kids were selected for their ability to costume themselves in anything vaguely sparkly, feathery or futuristic and were seated in a curving half-ring of chrome bleachers. When the band played they rushed down to the dance floor in their tiny space-hippy outfits and shuffled about enthusiastically.

Reilly recruited the band with a *Variety* ad. Since their onscreen activities were limited to chatting up alien space puppets, he was able to focus on musicians over actors. He cast singer/songwriter Cindy Schein (Sharon Sheeley's niece) as the band's leader and singer. Schein had already had some small chart success co-writing a Fun & Games b-side with Gary Zekley, and album tracks for The Association. The part of her brother Simon went to Thom Dobson, a skinny but telegenic drummer with a shag haircut and a chipped front tooth. He famously played with the Hollywood Persuaders on *Drums A Go-Go* as a mere 14-year-old. Dutch-born, Juilliard-trained Anna van Leeuwen was brought in on lead guitar. Dillon Moss rounded out the band on keyboards, though his training was as a vocal arranger, having studied with Gene Puerling.

After her makeover, Cindy emerged as Cinnamon Sunshine with red corkscrew curls, rainbow overalls and stripey shirts. Thom played Simon with bounding Iggy energy barely contained behind his kit. Anna became Gillian, her hair stripped white-blonde and cut into a Kiki Dee bob. They dressed her in silk kimonos and satin flares—a fairly demure ensemble for the '70s. They permed Dillon's hair into a perfectly globelike afro, slapped on an oversized bow-tie, a vest, cartoonishly large round glasses and platform shoes. He looked like the geeky, elfin offspring of Elton John and Leo Sayer. They all looked ridiculous, of course, but not unusually so for the era.

Except for the musical guests, the shows were fairly routine. Capt. Jack arrives with a flash of firepots and strobing lights. Welcomes the kids. Tired jokes and skits with the alien puppets, segue to *Casper* followed by a commercial break. Then the bizarre sight of Carl Wilson or Cass Elliot bantering with little green space puppets before they perform. After another commercial Capt. Jack calls down some lucky kid from the audience for a party-game rewarded with gift certificates or punished with cream pies. Finally, the Daisy Bang play and the kids go-go and credits roll. One half hour, five times a week, one season and not unlike a hundred other local kid shows. Except for the music.

The music for the show was spectacular, both from the guests and the Daisy Bang itself. One episode famously featured Carl Wilson's harmonizing on "Wayfaring Stranger" with Bruce Johnston and Emitt Rhodes. Nilsson and Cass Elliot did a medley of "Mr. Sandman," "I'm Only Sleeping" and the Everlys' "Dream." Jackie DeShannon played Dolly Parton's "Bargain Store" with Gene Clark.

And the Daisy Bang's original songs by Schein/van Leeuwen had a joyful, effervescent charm. Dobson's drumming kept everything uptempo, but Schein's sunny melodies, van Leeuwen's strikingly sophisticated musicality and Moss' intricate vocal arrangements lifted the music far beyond your expectations for kid show pop songs. At times they sounded like the Mamas & the Papas over a Motown rhythm track. But when Dillon sang lead his clear tenor gave them an Archies feel.

The Daisy Bang released a single on Bell, "Daisy Bang Day" b/w "You're It!" that got heavy airplay on the West Coast but didn't break nationally. The exhilarating follow-up "Race You To The Moon" b/w "Bang Saturn! Yeah!" was unjustly snubbed by radio. Bell picked up an option for an album on the basis of the first single's success. The band already had the songs in the can and hoped that a successful release would launch the band nationally.

Daisy Bang Days remains one of the lost gems of the bubblegum era and is highly sought after by collectors. (Oddly, it's easier to find the 8-Track than the LP.) They recorded everything in the garage studio Reilly had scavenged and built with his recording engineer, Bobby Raff. Right there in one of Republic's writer's bungalows, they set up shop and achieved incredible sound with just 16 tracks. The A-Side of the album started with "Daisy Bang Day," followed by "Dappled Down Darling" (Schein's Daisy Bang lyrics were prone to giddy assonance and alliteration), "Sunny Way," a cover of "Pure Imagination" (from *Willy Wonka and the Chocolate Factory*) and closed with "My Treat." The B-Side opened with the proto-Power Pop "Shake You Out," a different mix of "Race You To the Moon" that included a ripping guitar solo by Anna, "Love Me All Around," "Tickled Pink" and the gorgeous one-two punch of "All Come Free" and "Day's End." Buy it if you can find it. There aren't that many copies out there.

Despite the wealth of musical treats, their distributor declined to pick up a second season of the show and by the fall of 1972 they were unemployed, disappointed but ready to move on. But Reilly wasn't going to let his opportunity slip away. After years of working on the fringe of the music scene he'd finally broken through and gotten some airplay (and producer royalties).

By then he had the entire band living with him in the bungalow adjacent to the set. He kept up a mad, speed-fueled patter, appealing to their egos, their fears, the apocalyptic mood in L.A. after the Manson killings. He convinced them to record one last album. Why not? They had a free studio, enough money left over from the show to support them for months, free room and a steady supply of pot, acid and speed.

Reilly and Cindy had become lovers by this point and she quickly latched on to the opportunity to showcase her songwriting. Similarly, Dillon and the engineer Bobby Raff coupled off, and Dillon was eager to experiment in the studio and wanted access to the show's master tapes. He already had plans for *Harmony Cathedral*. Anna was less anxious to stay, but feared losing her visa and still wanted to write with Cindy. Thom simply didn't have anything better to do and a free home and easy drugs and a casual liaison with Anna were enough to keep him there for the time being.

Dillon immediately began work on *Harmony Cathedral*, stacking layers of overdubbed vocals over simple instrumental tracks. He had the band members record his wordless arrangements of "Oohs," "Aaahhhhs," "Ba-ba-bas" and "Woos" and worked them into an intricate tapestry with the master tapes he had of the musical guests. In just one passage, Harry Nilsson's vocal on "Dream" bobbed along on a swell of lifting harmonies, then dipped down into a perfect edit with Cindy, Anna and Dillon singing the chorus from "Along Came Mary" which melted into a high, trembling melody without words that sank into Thom's baritone, isolated in a descending, echo-drenched bassline out of DooWop. It sounded like nothing else, a cubist vocal collage, a musique concrete prettily patched out of West Coast harmony vocals, Hi-Lo's arrangements, folk rounds and Brian Wilson's most baroque studio experiments. The final movement was built around Charles Manson's "Cease to Exist." Dillon had offended Carl Wilson when he asked him to cut the track with the original lyrics, but he had persuaded Curt Boettcher to do it as an experiment, promising him that it would never be released.

In the meantime, Cindy cut the demos for what would become *Cin Songs Seventeen* with just her acoustic guitar and occasional backing by Anna on cello. Inspired by Kubrick's *2001* and Bowie's *Space Oddity* she worked out a series of harrowing lyrical conceits that turned the trashy science fiction setting of the show into miniatures of alienation, isolation and loneliness. The songs were arch, witty, biting, tart, and achingly raw. The titles promised Space Opera epics, but the songs delivered mordant little turns like "Open the Pod Bay Door, Hal," "Deathray," "Dale Arden Blues," and a cover of "Blue Moon" that sounded like it was recorded by the last human survivor of an annihilating Martian Invasion.

After three months of helping Dillon and Cindy, and suffering the increasingly paranoid rants of Reilly, Anna had become resentful, bored and restless. She tired of the lusty but loveless sex with Thom and was ready to return to Amsterdam. She had all but made up her mind to leave when Bobby and Dillon returned from a quick getaway to Jamaica. Bobby played her the King Tubby-produced singles he brought back and Anna was electrified. The Rock Steady A-sides fascinated her, but the dub B-sides absolutely floored her. She played the dub version of the Techniques' "You Don't Care" for hours at a time, marveling at the unearthly groove she heard.

Anna became obsessed with creating the effect herself. She worked for days customizing the mixing board with Bobby, adding sliding faders, rigging an echo delay by running a tape loop over the heads of an old two-track machine. Anna had Thom lay down a series of drum tracks for her at different tempos, then overdubbed the bass parts herself. Her bass playing became less rooted in the beat and seemed to fluidly roam in and out of Thom's relentless time and the little jazz breaks he'd drop on her.

She slowly built up a deep groove, and then over this laid a scrim of idle studio chatter, Cin's lead vocals distorted by tape effects, ghostly shimmers from Dillon's harmony bank, a screaming fight between Cin and Rick caught on tape in the studio, tapes of her and Thom making love, sound effect records, Theremin, typewriters clacking, simple riffs and vamps on the B-3, and distant crackling snippets of the Daisy Bang recorded off an AM radio. While Dillon's *Harmony Cathedral* was dense, lush and pretty, Anna's studio experiment churned up dark fragments of sound that seemed to loom out of the mix then recede back behind the endlessly looping basslines and Thom's slow, stoned groove.

The atmosphere in the house deteriorated. Reilly gobbled speed endlessly, never seemed to sleep and began carrying a gun with him at all times. Cindy began to pull away from him as his behavior became threatening and controlling. Also, it became clear to her that the sessions would never come together as an album. Dillon and Bobby were almost finished with *Harmony Cathedral* and they had both lined up outside studio work. They were ready to move to an apartment in West Hollywood. Anna drifted away from Thom, stoned, absorbed in her work, staying up for nights at a time in the studio.

One drunken night toward the end, Thom jokingly complained that he'd helped with their studio projects but they'd never backed him on anything. After much hectoring and cajoling, they allowed that he had earned his own shot at immortality but they were too tired to do anything that night. Thom would have none of it. He handed out a round of Black Beauties and with relentless good humor, bullied them into the studio. Once there, Bobby ran the tapes and the band rehearsed their entire repertoire of Daisy Bang songs in chronological order. But Thom began to double-time the beat, and urged Cindy to sing louder and harder until her voice got raspy. He told Anna to turn up her guitar make it sound dirty. She smiled at her lover indulgently and cranked it up. They recorded everything in one take, live in the studio. Anna's voice gave out after three songs and Thom began singing the lyrics, turning each song into a hilariously filthy inversion of its original frothy sentiment. *The Black Beauty Demos* sound perfect when played between *Metallic KO* and The Replacements' *Let It Be*.

Reilly was furious that Cindy had hurt her throat singing and railed at them for an hour, smashing furniture and firing his gun into the ceiling. The next day they confronted him, told him they were leaving. He stared at them with cold fury, then walked to the front door, opened it and said, "Fine. Leave. But I own everything in this place, including everything you recorded in my studio. So walk away. I fed you, supported you and you owe me that music." Then he pulled out his gun. Cindy began to cry, Anna and Dillon and Bobby stared at him, stunned. Thom started screaming at him, calling him a freak and an asshole. Reilly simply pointed his gun at Thom and began shooting, hitting him in the hand, the forearm and the kneecap. In the confusion that followed, Reilly grabbed Cindy as the others rushed to help Thom. He pulled Cindy into the studio control room with him and locked the door. Dillon and Bobby tried to break in, heard Cindy scream "No!" then heard two gunshots. And that was the end of the Daisy Bang. But not their music.

Cindy's ashes were scattered at sea and the surviving band members moved on. Dillon and Bobby worked steadily in L.A. until the mid-'70s when they moved up to San Francisco. Bobby found work with Patrick Cowley engineering Sylvester's disco singles and Dillon formed an a capella vocal group. Thom suffered nerve damage in his right arm that prevented him from playing drums, and suffered a painful limp for the rest of his life.

Mary Lou Lord covered Cindy's "Dale Arden Blues" on one of her early cassettes and PJ Harvey turned the bitter "Deathray" into a blistering roar on her *4-Track Demos* complete with an anguished "Noooooo" cutting off the track. Every year seems to turn up at least one new underground dance staple built on one of Anna's Dub Master samples; Moby, Aphex Twin, Dust Brothers have all found it irresistible fodder. Receiving a fourth-generation tape dub of *The Black Beauty Demos* became something of a punk badge of honor and rite of initiation, immortalized both in *Cometbus* and the Descendents' "BBD." Dillon's work didn't go unrecognized either. Olivia Tremor Control's *Harm and Catherine* was an open tribute to *Harmony Cathedral* and you can hear its influence in Jeff Mangum's "Harmful Catheter," and Magnetic Fields' "Bobby and Dillon." Not bad for a third-string bubblegum band.

INTERNATIONAL SCENE

The germ and first flowering of bubblegum were pure Americana, but it didn't take long before producers in England, Europe, Asia and Latin America got into the game. Typically, it was the British who gilded the basic style to astonishing extremes, ultimately resulting in a glitzy glam style that was as exciting visually as it was to the ear. In Japan, producers enslaved pop bands in a grotesque parody of the Brian Epstein/Beatles model, while in the Nordic nations bubblegum was boiled an extra hour on the sonic stove to yield a substance that was more sugary and poppy than many mouths could bear. In one of the most interesting permutations, Mexican singer Roberto Jordán took contemporary bubblegum hits and reworked them so that their meanings were subtly altered to reflect the cultural differences between the United States and her Southern neighbors. And then there's Eurovision, a pan-European contest that to this day churns out astonishing musical contrivances that seek only to seduce and to destroy. We think that American bubblegum is fascinating. But once it left our borders, things started to get *really* interesting.

British Bubblegum: the Works of Tony Macaulay, Roger Cook and Roger Greenaway by Derrick Bostrom

Roger Cook and Roger Greenaway

While most folks associate bubblegum music with American pop of the late '60s, quite a few of the genre's most charming songs actually came from England. And, like their U.S. counterparts, many of these songs were recorded by bands that never existed. Part of the fun of being a bubblegum fan, in fact, is discovering how the same people appeared on so many different records. British singer Tony Burrows, for instance, sang on hits by four different fake bands in one year (Edison Lighthouse's "Love Grows (Where My Rosemary Goes)," White Plains' "My Baby Loves Lovin'," the Brotherhood of Man's "United We Stand" and the Pipkins' "Gimme Dat Ding"). Burrows' dubious accomplishment has won him a fan following, but many of the men who worked with him are also beginning to achieve cult status.

The records of Tony Macaulay, the writer/producer of Edison Lighthouse's "Love Grows (Where My Rosemary Goes)" and Roger Cook and Roger Greenaway, the team responsible for White Plains' "My Baby Loves Lovin'," stand out particularly, evoking the high-gloss ersatz quality of British bubblegum at its finest. Sounding at once completely unique and yet exactly like everyone else, contemporary yet commonplace, producers like Macaulay and Cook/Greenaway filled a badly-needed niche for radio programmers tired of the likes of Sinatra and Mantovani, yet not ready for Hendrix and Joplin.

Unlike most American bubblegum, the British variant owed less to garage rock than to more traditional show-biz products. "Manufactured" artists under the tight control of their record labels were the norm. Government-controlled British radio didn't even open up to rock until 1967, and this was only in response to the insurgence of "pirate" stations broadcasting from ships in international waters. And even then, they preferred softer-edged, poppier sounds to the guitar groups spawned in the wake of the Beatles, still considered by some to be a fluke of little lasting consequence.

Tony Macaulay of Pye Records was one of the first wave of producers to benefit from the rise of BBC's rock station, Radio One. Macaulay (born Anthony Instone) worked as a song plugger for Essex

Publishing in the early '60s. By mid-decade, he had moved to Pye Records as a staff producer, where he was teamed with the Foundations. Unenthusiastic about the project, Macaulay and arranger John MacLeod presented the group with an unused song they had written two years earlier.

"Baby, Now That I've Found You" became Macaulay's first hit, reaching the number one position in the U.K. and selling over three million copies worldwide. It took months to reach the charts, however, taking off in the fall of 1967 only after Radio One added the record to its playlists. The Foundations enjoyed a string of hits with Macaulay at the helm, including the proto-bubblegum "Build Me Up Buttercup" (co-written with Michael D'Abo). All of them owed an obvious debt to The Motown Sound, particularly that of the Four Tops. Ironically, in an interview from the period, Macaulay claimed, "We have managed to find a groove for the Foundations which is, we like to think, unique, and will continue to be developed and copied by other bands for a long time in the future." Unfortunately for the Foundations, the band was forced to copy their sound all by themselves when Macaulay left Pye Records in 1969. They struggled along for a couple more years before they disbanded.

During his tenure at Pye, Macaulay also worked with Long John Baldry. A pivotal figure in the '60s British blues scene, by 1967 Baldry apparently hungered for mainstream acceptance. Macaulay and MacLeod concocted a series of recordings for him very much in the Tom Jones mold. "Let the Heartaches Begin" was Macaulay's second U.K. chart topper. Among their other notable records, the team also produced "Mexico (Underneath the Sun In)," which was chosen as the official theme of the 1968 Summer Olympics in Mexico City.

In addition to his duties at Pye as a staff producer, Macaulay also wrote for Herman's Hermits ("I Can Take or Leave Your Lovin'") and Jefferson ("Baby Take Me In Your Arms") with John MacLeod. He also began to collaborate with Geoff Stephens (the guiding light behind the New Vaudeville Band's "Winchester Cathedral" in 1965). Together, they wrote Scott Walker's "Lights of Cincinnati" and the Hollies' "Sorry Suzanne."

In early 1968, Macaulay began working with Pinkerton's (Assorted) Colours. He produced two singles for them, the Macaulay/MacLeod original "There's Nobody I'd Sooner Love" and a cover of Neil Diamond's "Kentucky Woman," but neither record did much business. The following year, the group, renamed The Flying Machine, released Macaulay and Stephens' "Smile a Little Smile For Me." Though it initially flopped in Britain, the single took off in the U.S. The LP that followed was a rush-job that relied heavily on studio musicians, helping fuel the impression that the Flying Machine didn't actually exist. Adding to the confusion, a long-defunct band also named Flying Machine (featuring a young James Taylor) seized the opportunity to release some of their early recordings.

In the meantime, Macaulay left Pye for Bell Records. When the Flying Machine refused to follow him (choosing instead to honor their existing Pye contract), their collaboration ended and Macaulay found other artists to bestow his gifts upon. One of these was Tony Burrows, a singer who'd been working with another up-and-coming production team, Cook and Greenaway.

Burrows first worked with Roger Greenaway and Roger Cook in the Kestrels, a singing group that mostly provided vocal backgrounds for other artists in the recording studio. Though they never managed to score a hit of their own, they opened many tours with the Beatles, and hold the distinction of having taught the Fab Four how to bow in unison. Cook and Greenaway struck up a songwriting partnership, and soon afterward they scored their first hit with "You've Got Your Troubles" for the Fortunes. After the Kestrels disbanded, the two Rogers scored a hit of their own, a George Martin-produced cover of the Beatles' "Michelle," under the names David and Jonathan.

The Cook/Greenaway songwriting partnership continued with Gary Lewis & the Playboys' "Green Grass" and "I Was Kaiser Bill's Batman" by Whistlin' Jack Smith. "Batman" was actually recorded by the

Mike Sammes Singers, but Decca Records decided to release it under a pseudonym. After the record charted, a singer was quickly hired to portray Jack. Cook and Greenaway also wrote material for Roger Cook's group, Blue Mink ("Melting Pot"), and supplied Coca-Cola with the famous "It's the Real Thing" jingle.

Meanwhile, Tony Burrows had joined John Carter and Ken Lewis' Ivy League, later following them when they quit that group to form a studio project called the Flower Pot Men. They scored one hit, "Let's Go to San Francisco," then disbanded shortly afterward. Their record label, Decca, wanted to release a handful of unreleased Flower Pot Men tracks under the name White Plains, so they hired Cook and Greenaway to prepare an album. Burrows signed on to supply lead vocals, and soon the group hit in 1970 with the Cook/Greenaway composition "My Baby Loves Lovin'."

Burrows then teamed up with Tony Macaulay on the ultimate British bubblegum record, and perhaps the defining song of a generation, "Love Grows (Where My Rosemary Goes)." Macaulay and Barry Mason (who'd written "Delilah" for Tom Jones) wrote "Rosemary" in just under an hour, but Macaulay was certain it would be a hit. So apparently was Burrows, who petitioned to have it released as a solo single under his own name. Macaulay instead concocted a fake group, Edison Lighthouse, hiring different musicians to act as the touring band.

Burrows agreed to do the television promotions, however, and soon he found himself appearing on the BBC's *Top of The Pops* as not one but three of his four fake groups on the same night. After the show's producers discovered what was going on, they asked that Burrows not appear on the program again. This informal blacklist helped stall his solo career. He released two dynamite Macaulay-penned/produced discs shortly thereafter, "Melanie Makes Me Smile" and "Every Little Move She Makes," but neither record met with much success. Burrows eventually went back to his studio work, reaching the Top 10 only once more, on 1974's "Beach Baby" by yet another fake band, John Carter's First Class.

Meanwhile, Macaulay supplied material for Pickettywitch, a group put together by John MacLeod to support singer Polly Brown. They had a Top 10 hit with Macaulay and MacLeod's "That Same Old Feeling," a tune that more than a half dozen groups had released unsuccessfully, including the Foundations, the Flying Machine and the Fortunes. They released several charting follow-ups, including Macaulay and MacLeod's "Sad Old Kinda Movie," before Polly Brown left the group for a solo career.

Macaulay also returned to his Motown style in 1970, with Johnny Johnson & the Bandwagon's "Blame it on the Pony Express" (a Top 10 record in England, though Bobby Sherman got the hit in the U.S.), and "Something Old, Something New" by the Fantasticks in 1971. Both songs were collaborations with Cook and Greenaway, as was 1971's hit for the Fortunes, "Here Comes that Rainy Day Feeling Again," and the Hollies' "Gasoline Alley Bred."

But much of Macaulay's attention in the early '70s was diverted by a legal dispute with his publishers that dragged on in the courts for years. He finally won his case on appeal in 1974, in a landmark decision which encouraged other artists (Elton John among them) to challenge the terms of their contracts. By the time of his court victory, Macaulay had begun to write for musical theater. He collaborated with playwright Ken Hill on *Is Your Doctor Really Necessary?* in 1973 and on *Gentlemen Prefer Anything* the following year.

While Macaulay took his lumps in court, Cook and Greenaway meanwhile reached their zenith. They were named Songwriters of the Year for both 1970 and 1971 by the British Songwriters Guild. Their hits from the period included "Long Cool Woman in a Black Dress" for the Hollies and "I'd Like to Teach the World to Sing" for the New Seekers (originally another jingle for Coca-Cola). In 1972, Roger Cook released the first of a series of solo albums, with songs like "Eating Peaches in the Sun" and "I'll Bet Jesus was a Lonely Man," and began to steer a course completely unrelated to his pop work with Greenaway.

By mid-decade in fact, the partnership was all but over. One of their last hits together was Carol Douglas' "Doctor's Orders," which was originally written for the British singer Sunny. They sold their publishing company, Cookaway Music, and Roger Cook moved to Nashville. He began to contribute songs to country artists like Crystal Gayle ("Talking in Your Sleep") and Don Williams ("I Believe in You," "Love is On a Roll"). In 1997, Cook was inducted into the Nashville Songwriters Hall of Fame.

Greenaway continued working with pop artists like David Dundas ("Jeans On") and Our Kids ("You Just Might See Me Cry"). He collaborated with Tony Macaulay on a series of hits with the Drifters ("You're More Than a Number in My Little Red Book," "Down on the Beach Tonight," "Kissin' in the Back Row of the Movies") and wrote "It's Like We Never Said Goodbye" for Crystal Gayle. But increasingly, he became more involved in administration, serving as president of Britain's Performing Rights Society. In 1995, he was named Senior Vice President, International, of ASCAP.

For Macaulay, the mid-'70s found him writing for middle-of-the-road artists like Elvis ("If I Get Home on Christmas Day," "Love Me, Love the Life I Lead"), Tom Jones ("Letter to Lucille"), Andy Williams ("Home Lovin' Man") and the Fifth Dimension ("Last Night I Didn't Get to Sleep at All"). In 1976, he wrote and produced his best-known MOR hit, David Soul's "Don't Give Up On Us," which reached #1 in both the U.S. and the U.K. Two follow-up singles written and produced by Macaulay, "Silver Lady" and "Going In With Both Eyes Open," also topped the U.K. charts.

Also in 1976, Macaulay and Greenaway collaborated with Adam West on something called "The Story of Batman." But by the late '70s, the hits were becoming few and far between. The Marmalade scored one with Macaulay's "Falling Apart at the Seams," as did Duane Eddy with "Play Me Like you Play Your Guitar." In 1977, Macaulay produced an album for Saturday morning television stars the Hudson Brothers. Though it garnered no hits, it did represent a passing of the torch of sorts, as Mark Hudson went on to work with the sticky-sweet midwestern combo, Hanson.

Macaulay wound up the decade writing and producing tracks for Gladys Knight & the Pips, and his ballad "Can't We Just Sit Down and Talk it Over" appeared on an album by Donna Summer, but by the end of the '70s, he had all but abandoned popular music for theater and film composition. He scored only one pop hit during the entire decade, "Alibis" by Sergio Mendes. His major musical project of the '80s was the theatrical production *Windy City*, which played over 300 performances in 1982.

Nowadays, Macaulay no longer makes his living as a songwriter, but the music world hasn't forgotten him. In 1995, singer Alison Krauss took a version of "Baby, Now That I've Found You" to the top of the country charts, and "Build Me Up Buttercup" was featured prominently in the hit film *There's Something About Mary*. His productions are readily available through reissue labels like Rhino (their *Have a Nice Day* series), Varèse Sarabande (the essential *Bubblegum Classics* CDs, one of which is entirely devoted to Tony Burrows), and Britain's Castle Music's Sequel imprint (a two-CD set of Pinkertons/Flying Machine).

As the '60s and '70 recede further and further from view, interest in the kind of pop music produced by Macaulay and Cook/Greenaway continues to grow. What was once dismissed as purely disposable hackwork takes on a greater luster with the continuing passage of time, finally emerging as indisputable pop classics. Songs like "I'd Like to Teach the World to Sing" and "Smile A Little Smile For Me," aside from their obvious kitsch appeal, can bring back memories and feelings that the more accepted "classic hits" are powerless to evoke. Like all great bubblegum, these records need not merely be rescued from the ash can of obscurity, they deserve room on the top shelf with the greatest hits of all time.

Thanks to: Sonia Bovio, Ian Gilchrist, Steve Hammonds, Bruce Kimmel, Cary Mansfield, Bill Pitzonka, Gordon Pogoda, Al Cunniff, Tom Troccoli, Gregg Turkington.

Jonathan King by Dave Thompson

It's been said before—usually by people with little regard for what anyone else thinks of their musical taste—but when Captain Sooper Dooper finally gets round to writing all his Thank You notes, he'll be sending Jonathan King an encyclopedia.

All but unknown in America, where he is remembered for one hit 35 years ago ("Everyone's Gone To The Moon") and for discovering a schoolboy band called Genesis, the erstwhile Kenneth King has actually clocked up more weeks on the British chart; masterminded a bucketload of future phenomena (the Bay City Rollers were one of his; so were 10cc; so were Hedgehoppers Anonymous), and impacted his taste, if not his name, on so many avenues of the European pop scene, that if Jonathan King didn't exist, Kasenetz-Katz would have had to invent him. As it was, King invented himself, and everybody—and in Britain, that includes Kasenetz-Katz—simply followed in his wake.

It was King, after all, who first realized that not only is it possible to fool all of the people all of the time, most of the people actually enjoy being fooled. With almost mathematical precision, he worked out the lowest common denominator in public taste and built an empire around it.

The Piglets, the Weathermen, Sakkarin, 100 Ton And A Feather, Shag, Sound 9418, Nemo, Bubblerock . . . since 1965, when the 17-year-old King scored a monster hit with his first-ever single, he has been responsible for well over a score of U.K. chartbusters, and a few American ones as well. You don't think Blue Swede came up with that soul-wrenching "ooga-chukka" "Hooked On A Feeling" refrain themselves, do you? They just covered King's own cover, and did Jonathan mind? Of course not; he was too busy watching First Class and "Beach Baby" take West Coast coals to Newcastle.

It is an impressive career, rivaled by only a handful of other acts; yet, check King's entry in the *Guinness Book of Hit Singles*, and the evidence really isn't there. A couple of Top Five singles ten years apart, five more lowly Top 30 entries, and a couple of bottom tenners . . . so what? It's the "see also . . ." footnote which tells the story.

The world wanted protest songs; King gave them "Good News Week." The world was into skinheads, he gave them "Johnny Reggae," and when it got into punk a few years later, there was Elizabeth R and "God Save the Sex Pistols." He recorded a heavy metal version of "Sugar, Sugar," and a demented violin-led take on "It Only Takes A Minute." He covered "Una Paloma Blanca" and made it even blanker; and got banned from the British airwaves when he (under the guise of St. Cecilia) bade the nation's teens to "Leap Up and Down and Wave Your Knickers in the Air."

Nothing escaped his attention. When the little blue Smurfs invaded Britain through a late '70s gas station promotion, King responded with a sweet little song suggesting we all lick one for Christmas. Except this was in the days before unleaded gasoline, remember, so the subtitle continued "All Fall Down."

Effortlessly, he spotted, then exploited, every chink in Britain's musical armor, and the dafter his offering, the better he liked it . . . and other people too.

"Loop Di Love," a 1972 #4 under the name of Shag, brought fiddle, beat and ridiculously schoolboyish lyrics together to create a stomp which would provide an unimpeachable blueprint for Dexy's "Come On

Eileen" ten years later. King's U.K. label was at one point operating on a hit ratio of one in ten, at a time when most record companies considered themselves to be performing miracles if they managed one in 20.

As a hitmaker, King was at his peak through the 1970s. By the early 1980s, he seemed more intent on cultivating a public profile in his own right, and moved into television; today, he heads the committee which picks the U.K.'s entrant for the annual Eurovision Song Contest. In 1997, he chose a song called "Love Shine A Light"— it won by the highest margin in Eurovision history.

Back in 1979, King released his first career-length compilation, a twenty track LP titled, with becoming immodesty, *Hit Millionaire*. Allowing for inflation, interest, and 20 years more of continued activity, he must be worth squidillions today. Ooga chukka indeed.

Jonathan King Remanded on Sexual Abuse Charges

The Guardian, November 30, 2000

Pop impresario Jonathan King was remanded on bail when he appeared in court today accused of sexually abusing three boys in the 1970s.

Mr. King faces charges of buggery of a boy under 16, indecently assaulting a male, and attempting to bugger a male under 21.

The offences are alleged to have taken place between December 27 1970 and December 26 1971.

The 55-year-old record producer spoke only to confirm his name and address at the magistrates' court in Staines, Surrey.

The charges, which Mr. King has publicly rejected as absurd, relate to three men who were boys at the time of the alleged offences.

Mr. King, a bachelor, who was represented by Mr. Ronald Thwaites QC, was appearing under his real name of Kenneth George King.

The chairman of the bench, Dr. Mary Trimble, gave Mr. King bail on condition that he should surrender all passports and did not contact any victims or witnesses.

Mr. King, who was dressed in a black suit, white shirt, blue tie and trainers, was remanded to appear before the court again on January 2.

After the hearing, he was whisked away in a chauffeur-driven blue Mercedes and refused to comment.

The Cambridge university graduate, who discovered *Genesis*, became famous at the age of 21 when his hit single, "Everyone's Gone To The Moon" became an overnight success, making him a millionaire. ◉

Strawberry Studios by Dave Thompson

Late in 1969, Kasenetz-Katz approached English songsmith Graham Gouldman with the offer of working for them. Gouldman was, after all, one of Britain's most accomplished hitmakers, the name behind a string of hits by the Yardbirds, Jeff Beck, Herman's Hermits, the Hollies . . . even Cher had recorded a Graham Gouldman number.

Over the last couple of years, though, Gouldman's pen had fallen on hard times. His own attempts to break into the bubblegum market, first through the Graham Gouldman Orchestra's lightweight versions of his own greatest hits, then via one-time chart heroes the Mindbenders, had signally failed to take off; and with the bulk of Gouldman's income being plowed into the studios he was opening with fellow 'bender Eric Stewart, Kasenetz-Katz's offer came just at the right time.

In return for a generous advance, the deal didn't just buy Kasenetz-Katz a proven songwriter. It also guaranteed them unlimited studio time at Gouldman's Strawberry Studios, and unlimited use of the studio's house musicians—Gouldman, Stewart, and a pair of dilettante ex-art students they'd both known for years, Lol Creme and Kevin Godley. None of them was exactly thrilled at the prospects, though. "We were very well paid for churning that stuff out," Gouldman reflected years later. "But it's not a time we look back on with any feelings of pride."

He sells their achievements short. Not only did the Strawberry crew swiftly establish itself as bubble-bashers par excellence, creating a string of latter-day Super K masterpieces and kickstarting the British gum scene as well, with the inexorable "Neanderthal Man"; they also rejuvenated Neil Sedaka's career, and emerged at the end of it as 10cc, and that was no small potatoes either. "The whole thing was incredible," Gouldman marveled. "Over a period of one year I wrote, and saw recorded, about 20 songs, which was a very high output for me."

Eric Stewart

Freddie and the Dreamers' version of Gouldman's "Susan's Tuba" sold over two million copies in France; the Ohio Express' "Sausalito" went Top 100 in the U.S. ("Tampa, Florida" wasn't quite so lucky), and "Have You Ever Been To Georgia" landed balladeer Tony Christie—who shared Gouldman's management company—a hit across much of Europe.

He missed out, however, on the studio's biggest hit, an irony compounded even further by the song's actual composers themselves being unaware that they'd actually written anything saleable. Stewart, Godley and Creme were simply testing the studio's percussion, says Stewart, "when Dick Leahy, from Phillips, came in and he said, `What the hell's that you're playing?' I said, 'It's a studio experiment; a percussive experiment;' He says, 'Can we release it?' And we said, 'Yeah, okay'."

Credited to Hotlegs, "Neanderthal Man" would reach #22 in the U.S., #2 in Britain, #1 in Italy, and was probably single-handedly responsible for Jimmy Castor's entire hit-making career. It also spawned covers by the Idle Race and Elton John, but for Hotlegs themselves, success came with a sting.

Irretrievably tarred by "Neanderthal Man," nothing else Hotlegs did paid off, and within six months, Godley, Creme, Gouldman and Stewart were back on the pop production line, cutting singles with such giants of music as the Manchester City, Sheffield Wednesday and Leeds United soccer teams, comedian Les Reed, and Led Zeppelin's John Paul Jones . . . except he wasn't Led Zeppelin's after all, as Page and Plant's old bandmate explains.

"I'd worked with Graham for years, we basically did his whole solo album (1968's *The Graham Gouldman Thing*) together. So when his manager, Harvey Lisburg, called me and said, they've got this comedian guy, and would I mind if they called him John Paul Jones . . . go ahead, won't hurt me. The next thing I knew, John Paul Jones is on the chart with this crap, crap song, and everyone thinks it's me. Thanks, Harvey!" Litigation turned Jones to Joans, but back at Strawberry Central, work went on as before.

Godley-Creme's "There Ain't No Umbopo" would be the team's final Kasenetz-Katz success, a rolling, boiling boogie which had even less to do with a pure bubblegum ethic than Crazy Elephant records normally did. Neil Sedaka loved it, though, and called Harvey Lisburg to tell him so. "He said he wanted to try recording in England, and I said that if he did, I'd get the boys who produced 'Umbopo'."

The result, the multi-million selling *Solitaire* album, solidly relaunched Sedaka's career, but importantly, it ignited the Strawberry quartet's as well. "Sedaka did so well, and all we got was session fees," Eric Stewart recalled. "So we went out to a Chinese restaurant and asked ourselves whether we shouldn't pool our creative talents in a group."

They decided that they should.

This Godley-Creme self-portrait comes from their website.

The Bay City Rollers by Carl Cafarelli

Teen idols seem to have a built-in obsolescence, virtually guaranteeing a short career for any artist whose primary appeal is to a fickle preteen female market. For the self-consciously hip, the teen idol tag carries a stigma beyond easy redemption, and the artists who cater to this market risk being forever branded as uncool.

In this context, no band was less cool in the '70s than the Bay City Rollers, whose management went so far as to tout this harmless Scottish quintet as the "next Beatles." That claim may seem ludicrous now (just as it did then), but the Rollers were nonetheless one of the biggest pop phenomena of the decade.

We'll dispense with the standard rap on the Bay City Rollers' tartan-clad teenybop image and all the hype. At this point, suffice it to say that the Rollers were an often-underrated, occasionally (if infrequently) terrific power pop group.

The Bay City Rollers began circa 1967 as an Edinburgh, Scotland cover band called the Saxons. The Saxons included brothers Alan and Derek Longmuir, on bass and drums respectively, with singer Nobby Clarke. That trio remained through various Saxons line-ups. Seeking a more American-sounding name, a pin was struck randomly into a map of the United States. The pin landed on Bay City, Michigan, and the Bay City Rollers were born.

The Bay City Rollers' first single, a cover of the Gentrys' "Keep On Dancing," became a #9 British hit in 1971. But follow-up singles, including an early version of "Saturday Night," were comparative flops. By now, Clarke and the Longmuirs had been joined in Rollerdom by guitarists Eric Faulkner and Stuart "Woody" Wood. Clarke himself soon quit, to be replaced on lead vocals by Les McKeown.

The Rollers didn't play on any of their records until "Bye Bye Baby," a cover of the Four Seasons' hit. Rollermania took Britain by storm, and was eventually exported to America via a new, McKeown-sung version of "Saturday Night" (a song which directly inspired the Ramones' own chanting "Blitzkrieg Bop," believe it or not).

The Rollers' recorded legacy is a mixed bag, offering a fair amount of drippy ballads and some bona fide rockin' pop. *Bay City Rollers* is notable mostly for "Saturday Night." *Rock N' Roll Love Letter* contains four of the group's best power pop tracks, "Money Honey," "Rock And Roll Love Letter," "Wouldn't You Like It" and "Too Young To Rock & Roll." "Wouldn't You Like It," in particular, is a dynamic power-pop number that should have been a single.

Alan Longmuir was replaced by Ian Mitchell on *Dedication*. Produced by Raspberries veteran Jimmy Ienner, *Dedication* suffers from weak material, including very lame attempts at Beach Boys and Raspberries covers, but is redeemed by the rockin' Faulkner-Wood "Rock 'N' Roller," a reasonably cool cover of Dusty Springfield's "I Only Want To be With You" and a superb reading of Vanda and Young's terrific "Yesterday's Hero." Mitchell then split after a scant six-month stint; his replacement, Pat McGlynn, didn't even stay that long.

As a quartet, the Rollers released the slick *It's A Game* album as an attempt to bridge the adult and teen markets, eschewing both standard teenybop ballads and power pop. Instead, it offers an unlikely melange of Manilowesque crooning, disco styling and even a cover of David Bowie's "Rebel, Rebel."

Greatest Hits represents the final cash-in at the end of the group's commercial reign. A perfunctory best-of, it includes the American singles, both hits and misses, but omits essential LP tracks "Wouldn't You Like It," "Too Young To Rock & Roll' and "Rock 'N' Roller." Arista reissued it on CD in 1991.

In 1978 the group (with Alan Longmuir back in the fold) starred on NBC in a Saturday morning kiddie TV show produced by Sid and Marty Krofft and released the forgettable *Strangers In The Wind*. When the TV show ended, McKeown split.

Duncan Faure, formerly of the South African group Rabbit, was McKeown's replacement. The group changed its focus, dumped the tartan outfits and teen image, and shortened its name to simply the Rollers. *Elevator* was the result, the most aggressive-sounding album the group ever made. Granted, there's nothing on *Elevator* to equal "Rock And Roll Love Letter," "Wouldn't You Like It" or "Yesterday's Hero," but it is far more consistently listenable than any other Rollers album. Key tracks include "Elevator," "Playing In A Rock And Roll Band," "I Was Eleven," "Turn On The Radio," "Instant Relay" and "Who'll Be My Keeper." The resulting sound could be compared to the Babys, or a more AOR-oriented version of the Records. If nothing else, it shows the Rollers as contenders, if not quite the next Beatles. It stiffed horribly, and was the last Rollers album issued in America.

The rare and little-heard *Voxx* is reportedly a contract-breaking set of odds and ends (if not sods).

Ricochet follows in *Elevator's* footsteps, but is not its equal. The original group reportedly got back together in the mid-'80s for a reunion concert, and released one synth-dominated album, *Breakout*, before splitting again. A later version of the group, still featuring Faulkner and Wood, released *Bye Bye Baby*, a pathetic collection of remakes of old Rollers tunes. It is surely not representative of how one might wish to remember the Bay City Rollers.

That neither the Bay City Rollers nor the just-plain-Rollers were the next Beatles is hardly a startling revelation. Maybe they were the next Herman's Hermits, or the next Banana Splits. Who cares? No matter how many self-appointed arbiters of hip despised the Rollers, there were nonetheless others who thought they were . . . well, kinda neat. Dee Dee Ramone was a Rollers fan; according to Johnny Ramone, the Bay City Rollers were a much bigger influence on the Ramones' brand of pop-fueled punk than anyone would have ever thought likely. And Nick Lowe's "Rollers Show," whether parody or pastiche, had to have some affection behind it.

Evidence for the Rollers' case still survives in the grooves. A quick spin of "Wouldn't You Like It," "Yesterday's Hero," "Who'll Be My Keeper," "Too Young To Rock & Roll," "I Only Want To Be With You," "Rock 'N' Roller," "Saturday Night," "Money Honey" and "Rock And Roll Love Letter" makes a convincing argument for the Bay City Rollers as power-pop savants.

And, perhaps more importantly, there are thousands of grown-up little girls who will cherish a memory of the Bay City Rollers forever.

The Wombles by Bill Pitzonka

In 1974, the British charts were awash in glam rockers and toothy teen idols. Rising somewhat surprisingly above this glittery sea to claim *Music Week's* Top Singles Act of the Year was a group of furry, burrow-dwelling litter-gatherers—the Wombles. And just like the Archies before them, the Wombles made the leap from printed page to pop playlists via the power of television.

British author Elizabeth Beresford was walking on Wimbledon Common with her children when she was inspired to write about "the tidiest creatures in the world" which "go round clearing up the rubbish which has been left behind by people." *The Wombles* debuted in 1968, and the adventures of these cuddly recyclers proved so immensely popular that two further volumes followed: *The Wandering Wombles* in 1970 and *The Wombles At Work* in 1973. That year, Filmfair acquired the television rights and commissioned Mike Batt to write the theme song.

The classically trained Batt had been a member of the chamber rock group Hapshash & The Coloured Coat, which recorded for Liberty/Imperial in 1967. He had since written numerous commercial jingles, arranged and orchestrated many a pop recording session, and released several high-quality budget-label cover albums. He waived the flat fee offered and instead wrangled the music rights to make the Wombles an authentic recording outfit, taking on all the creative duties—writing, arranging, pro-ducing, even performing all the vocals. To help him get into character, his mother made him a Womble suit, which he wore for an entire week.

Batt notes that "the first album [*Wombling Songs*] was really just character songs and background music for the television series." Though he dismisses the album as "rather twee," it did feature the group's first and longest-running chart single, "The Wombling Song," which hit #4 and spent 23 weeks in the British Top 75.

"The second album [*Remember You're A Womble*] was really the first proper album for the Wombles as a group," Batt beams with justifiable pride. Indeed, it spawned three sizable and musically disparate hit singles: the title track was a rockin' call-and-response number with a highland jig break that hit #3; the sax-driven reggae of "Banana Rock" limboed up to #9; and most surprisingly, "Minuetto Allegretto"— an authentic Mozart minuet complete with period orchestration—waltzed up to #16. By this time, the Wombles were also making personal appearances as a five-member group in full costume—Orinoco on vocals and sax, Wellington on lead guitar, Madame Cholet on bass guitar, Great Uncle Bulgaria on violin, and Bungo on drums. In addition to performing as Orinoco, Batt somehow managed to corral stalwart session guitarist Chris Spedding (who would later produce three cuts on the Sex Pistols' album) to suit up and strap on a flying-V guitar as Wellington.

The Wombles set off to conquer America in the summer of 1974. CBS Television aired Womble shorts on *Captain Kangaroo*, and Columbia Records issued a slightly revamped version of the *Remember You're A Womble* album for their stateside debut. The first single was the spot-on Beach Boys homage "Wombling Summer Party," a tightly edited version of "Non-Stop Wombling Summer Party" (down to the title). Despite the overtly American theme, the single only wombled halfway up the *Billboard* Hot 100 to #55 in August. "Remember You're A Womble" was quickly issued as the follow-up, but it was the last

Wombles recording released in the U.S. Batt still regrets that "Wombling U.S.A.," which he had written specifically for the American market, was never released—even in the U.K.

Back in Britain, the Wombles capped off 1974 with the Spectoresque "Wombling Merry Christmas"— a #2 hit and their highest-charting single. The parent album *Keep On Wombling* was released in the new year. Its first side was a concept suite, which followed the adventures of Orinoco, the sleepiest Womble, through a series of dreams.

The Wombles' fourth album *Superwombling* arrived mid-1975, and proved that Batt was adept at maneuvering his fictional charges through any musical style he pleased: barbershop harmony ("Down At The Barbershop"), spaghetti Western ("The Orinoco Kid"), *James Bond* themes ("To Wimbledon With Love"). He even cast them in a classic Hollywood musical (complete with tap dancing) for the single, "Wombling White Tie and Tails," a #22 hit. The follow-up "Super Womble," their sort-of stab at glam including a wheezy harmonica solo and varispeed chorus, leapt to #20.

They closed out the year with their final charting single, "Let's Womble To The Party," a swing-style number that stomped up to #34. By this time, Mike Batt's talents were being sought by all manner of artists, including Steeleye Span and Kursaal Flyers. He even issued his first (and only charting) solo single, "Summertime City," which was the theme for, as he puts it, "a dreadful series called *Seaside Summer*." So dreadful, apparently, that despite its #4 chart peak, he refuses to allow the track to be reissued.

As for the Wombles themselves, their television series ended after the second season. They did manage one last hurrah on the big screen—the film *Wombling Free* for which Mike Batt rehashed major portions of their existing repertoire. As a symbolic parting gesture, he issued the tuneful single "Rainmaker" in 1976, credited to Wellington Womble as a solo artist, to signal the breakup of the band.

Mike Batt went on to record a string of adventurous solo albums (*Schizophonia*, *Six Days in Berlin*) which have made him perennially popular in Germany. And while the Wombles never gave him a #1 single, he did top the UK chart in 1979 thanks to another group of furry burrow-dwellers from children's literature: he wrote, arranged, and produced Art Garfunkel's hit "Bright Eyes," from the animated film of Richard Adams's rabbit-warren-as-human-condition parable *Watership Down*. It stayed in the pole position for six weeks and was the year's biggest selling single. Batt also wrote a full-scale musical based on Lewis Carroll's *The Hunting Of The Snark*, which played at London's Prince Edward Theatre in 1987.

1998 marked the silver anniversary of the Wombles' U.K. television debut. To commemorate the occasion, Columbia Records and Reader's Digest both issued CD retrospectives of Wombles hits. Columbia even rereleased two singles, "Remember You're A Womble" and "The Wombling Song," which both hit the Top 30. A new series of Wombles television programs was commissioned, and Mike Batt, as busy as ever, found time to come up with new material for his old "bandmates." Twenty-five years later, the Wombles are still cleaning up.

Candy Flavored Lipgloss: Glam & Gum by David Smay

Pity the American child of the '70s, denied the spectacle of Marc Bolan on *Top of the Pops*, the Sweet lip-syncing on *The Old Grey Whistle Test*, and completely ignorant of *Supersonic*. The flashiest, trashiest, popcultiest of all rock genres, glam rock sparked more epiphanies on the telly than it ever did on Radio London. But television's place in the history of the glam era is just one of the many parallels between glam and bubblegum.

We can parcel out glam rock into several loose packets. On the arty end of the aisle, you have Bowie, Roxy Music and Steve Harley & Cockney Rebel. Smartypants art-rock, heavily dependent on the Velvet Underground and the amusing notion that Pop Music offers many choice poses and costumes for the aesthete around town. This wing of glam dallies little with bubblegum. Still, Bowie's assertion that the Spiders From Mars made better fake rock 'n' roll than the Monkees reveals much of his method, and Roxy knocked out mutant pop songs like "Do the Strand" with casual ease.[30] At the far other extreme from the art students lurked the prole brigade headed by the hard-rocking Slade, a group strongly associated with their boot-boy audience and fostered by ex-Animal/ex-Hendrix handler Chas Chandler. Two facts already become clear: the high degree to which most glam acts depended heavily on '60s musical veterans, and the profound influence of the mods on glam. Have you seen any mid-'60s photos of Bowie, Marc Bolan, Roy Wood? Mods the lot of 'em. Back to our glam taxonomy, we find the middle ground occupied by the groups that owe the most to bubblegum. T. Rex and Gary Glitter belong here, and the bands produced by Mike Chapman and Nicky Chinn (The Sweet, Suzi Quatro and Mud).

Marc Bolan reinvented himself and invented glam with the singles "Ride a White Swan" and "Hot Love." Hooking his fey, fairy folk music up to sturdy Eddie Cochran riffs (but keeping the conga drums), Marc caused a sensation in the UK. He shoved hippie crap off the charts and handed rock 'n' roll back to the kids. And the Crash Street Kidds loved the glittery eyeshadow and platform shoes and the satin jackets and the overdetermined hairstyles. T. Rex perfected (then exhausted) their formula with a run of hits like "Get It On (Bang a Gong)," "Jeepster," "20th Century Boy" and "Children of the Revolution." Despite Bolan's brilliance as a singles artist, the disposable nature of his hits, and even the fact that he ended his career hosting a television show aimed directly at the bubblegum market, T. Rex is not really a bubblegum band. T. Rex did, however, mate rock 'n' roll back with pop music and, perhaps more importantly, launched a Pop Moment.

Into that moment stepped the makers of the gummiest of glam music, Nicky Chinn and Mike Chapman. Discovered by '60s pop veteran Mickie Most (Herman's Hermits, Jeff Beck, Lulu), Aussie Chapman hooked up with Nicky Chinn, and their earliest chart success was with a band named New World (later disgraced for rigging votes on the *Star Search*-like British show, *Opportunity Knocks*. You can already sense a barely checked ambition in their approach to chart success).

Chinn and Chapman soon turned their energies solely to songwriting, and linked up with a band formerly known as Sweetshop to turn out a slew of pure, no-mistaking-it bubblegum. "At the time there was a record called 'Sugar, Sugar' by the Archies and it'd sold zillions, it'd sold about seven or

---

30. Mott the Hoople were barely glam and never bubblegum. The fact that Bowie handed them glam rock's anthem ranks as a brilliant mistake in their career aspiration to wed Bob Dylan with the Rolling Stones.

eight million records worldwide. And I thought: wouldn't it be great to tap into that pop bubblegum market?" recalls Phil Wainman. These early singles by the Sweet—written by ChinniChap, produced by Wainman, and played by Wainman's session crew—included "Co-Co," "Chop Chop," "Wig-Wam Bam," "Little Willy," "Tom Tom Turnaround" and "Funny, Funny."

Sweet's early singles charted (and were charming bits of bubblegum in their own right), but the band was allowed to express themselves on harder rocking B-sides. You can see the trouble brewing, since the band saw themselves as another Deep Purple, yet were having hits in an entirely Archies-influenced mold. Phil Wainman's approach undoubtedly added to the tension: "I made as many enemies as I made friends because I'd upset other musicians, I'd upset other producers that I was working for. 'Cause I put my team in: 'The only way you're gonna make that a hit is book my guys, we'll turn up and work out your songs.'"

Sensing the potential in both the group and the emergence of glam, Chinn and Chapman stole the riff to "I'm A Man" (as recorded by the Yardbirds[31]) and produced "Blockbuster." It's worth noting that Bowie stole that same riff for "Jean Genie" (as did the Nashville Teens on "Tobacco Road"). Chapman said, "It's a good thing to revive riffs from the past because you know kids like it." To which Nicky added, "We get a lot of criticism from people saying we're getting money for old rope, but it's not easy to write plastic songs." The Sweet actually had more hits and wider worldwide sales than T. Rex or Gary Glitter with Top 10s "Hell Raiser," "Ballroom Blitz," "Teenage Rampage," and "The Six Teens."

Mickie Most discovered Suzi Quatro in a Detroit club in 1970 and brought her to England. There Chinn and Chapman poured her into a black leather jumpsuit (searing the fantasies of spotty boys across the U.K.) and pushed "Can the Can" up the charts. Suzi's subsequent singles closely aped the same formula (closer in spirit to Gary Glitter than the Sweet with their dependence on a HUGE tribal beat) until it was milked dry. To most Americans, she's better known as Leather Tuscadero, the rockin' little sister of Fonzie's true love, Pinky Tuscadero.

ChinniChap's third major glam act sported the least glamorous name imaginable, Mud. Barely known in the U.S. but much loved in the U.K., Mud scored 11 Top 20 hit singles and a trio of #1's: "Tiger Feet," "Lonely This Christmas" and "Oh Boy." Their best single might be "Dynamite" which went to #4 and showed off lead singer Les Gray's Presleyan (Elvis, not Reg) vocals. Like the Sweet, Mud were a veteran live act that simply suffered for lack of material. Chin and Chapman redressed that problem successfully.

One of the odder features of the glam movement was its '50s fetish, evident not only in Les Gray's voice, but in Alvin Stardust's paunchy rehash of Gene Vincentisms, the otherwise inexplicable band Showaddywaddy, the ubiquitous return of saxophones and those D.A.'s Roxy Music sported on their first album. This was consistent with the same nostalgia wave that put Sha Na Na on TV and made *American Graffiti* a huge hit. In Britain, however, a conscious desire to recapture the initial impact of American rock 'n' roll in the '50s drove glam's fascination with the era.

Gary Glitter began life as Paul Gadd, made several unsuccessful runs at the charts in the '60s as Paul Raven and was a pot-bellied, leftover never-was when he hooked up with Mike Leander. Leander was (yet again) a respected music veteran from the '60s, best known for arranging the strings on Marianne Faithfull's early singles and scoring the Ultra-Mod movie *Privilege*. Seizing the glam opportunity, Leander (who played all the instruments except the horns) crafted pop singles with a gargantuan drum sound (inspired by John Kongos' "Tokoloshe Man" and Dr. John), catchy singalong chorus and hammering guitar riffs.

Dressed like a Space-Vegas Liberace, plump, stately Gary Glitter ascended the hit parade and, implausibly, became an enduring British pop icon. Plus, he bequeathed "Rock and Roll, Part Two" to stadium sound systems into perpetuity. His trademark sound became an important and much-cited influence on

---

31. Phil Wainman wrote "Little Games" for the Yardbirds.

British new wave acts like the Human League and Adam Ant as well as on glam fan Joan Jett. On a gummier note, the Spice Girls heroically covered "The Leader of the Gang" in *Spiceworld*.

Glam's biggest contribution to bubblegum (arguably after the Sweet) would be the Bay City Rollers. Curiously replaying Tommy James' breakthrough, the Rollers recorded and released "Saturday Night" during the height of the glam era, several years before it inspired Rollermania. Tam Paton cobbled the group together from several Scottish bands (including the Saxons) and brought in the Sweet's engineer Phil Wainman to give the Rollers that hit-ready sound. Paton then recruited the songwriting team of Phil Coulter and Bill Martin, who provided the tartan-clad teens with their first hits.[32] Wainman took over after Coulter and Martin left, and actually allowed the boys to play on their own records, squeezing out a few more hits before the mania evaporated.

A handful of other glam acts successfully charted during the heyday, including such noteworthy (and listenable) cuts as "I Love Rock and Roll" by Arrows (famously covered by Joan Jett), "New York Groove" by Hello (less famously covered by Ace Frehley), and "Angel Face" by the Glitter Band. Then there was a ton of appalling crap by people like Barry Blue and the Rubettes and Alvin Stardust.

Roy Wood's (ex- of the Move) venture into glam rock produced the nightmarish vision of a bearded hippie with an excess of eye shadow. Wizzard's singles had elements of '50s rock, Beach Boy harmonies, heavy metal guitars and a Phil Spector-like density of production. Fascinating in their own right, and certainly a product of the glam era, Wizzard owe little to bubblegum. Bubblegum or not, "Ballpark Incident" and "See My Baby Jive" are recommended listening.

T. Rex brackets the glam era, from its first revolutionary singles to the sad sight of Marc Bolan toppling off the edge of the stage on his kid-aimed afternoon TV show, *Marc!* Weirder still, it was the final episode of his six-show run with Granada and featured Marc jamming with old friend and rival David Bowie. Marc died shortly after that ignominious tumble.

Glam's immediate influence turned out to be in new wave music, where Mike Chapman successfully put Blondie and the Knack on the pop charts, and Phil Wainman worked with Generation X and XTC. Like bubblegum and disco, glam was primarily a producer's genre, and the sleek, radio-ready, hook-heavy hits still sound brilliant today.

Singer Gary Glitter Jailed For Kiddie Net Porn

By Kieren McCarthy, *The Register*, December 11, 1999

One-time king of glam rock Gary Glitter has been jailed for four months for downloading child porn from the Internet. Glitter, whose real name is Paul Gadd, pleaded guilty to 54 counts of making indecent photographs of children. In mitigation, his brief said Glitter was unaware that he was doing anything illegal when he downloaded kiddie porn from the Net. The judge at Bristol Crown Court is reported to have replied: "You mean this defendant did not think it illegal to have in his possession photographs of little girls being bound, tortured, gagged and sexually abused in a most repellent way?" Glitter had earlier been cleared of four counts of indecent assault on a 14-year-old girl.

---

32. Coulter and Martin also gave Sandie Shaw her Eurovision winning entry "Puppet on a String" and Phil Coulter had written the garage-rock standard "I Can Only Give You Everything" for Them.

Slik and the Quick—A Double Sugar Fix from '76 by P. Edwin Letcher

1976 was a weird, transitional period in the music world. Just a few years earlier, "glamour" had changed the look and sound of your average pop band. Androgyny and flamboyance reigned supreme as the yard-stick for rebellious rocker behavior. In a few more years, the landscape would be ever more segregated into practically warlike zones populated by punks, progressives, dinosaurs, etc. For a while, though, there were plenty of bands that came up with an individualistic fashion statement and embraced the vision of being a wholesome pop band that could develop their own sound, write some well-crafted material, get a few breaks and become the next Beatles . . . or at least the next Lovin' Spoonful.

Two such outfits, Los Angeles' The Quick and Britain's Slik, had a lot more in common than just names that rhyme. It seems to me that both groups must have been exposed to the happy-go-lucky sounds of the 1910 Fruitgum Co., Ohio Express, the Archies and all the other kid-friendly groups as part of their musical upbringing. Both bands debuted on a major label and had a crack production team behind them. The Quick put out exactly one album, *Mondo Deco* on Mercury, which was produced by Kim Fowley and Earle Mankey, a couple of rock veterans who were on the prowl for a marketable new wrinkle. Slik also released one album, a self-titled affair on Arista, under the guiding hands of Phil Coulter and Bill Martin, another pair in search of the next big thing. Both bands opted for haircuts that were a little shorter and much more stylish than their hippie predecessors, and dressed as a unit in a modified preppie mode. The Quick chose black and white, satiny togs for the cover of their lone album, with two members decked out in mock sailor duds. I believe Slik borrowed fairly heavily from The Bay City Rollers for their general vibe, but lifted their hair styles from '50s teen idols, and found some baseball players' uniforms to pirate for their photo shoot.

The Quick featured a lead vocalist, Danny Wilde, who went on to front Great Buildings and then the Rembrandts, whose *Friends* theme song, "I'll Be There For You," has been a tremendous success. Slik had a lead vocalist, Midge Ure, who went on to bigger and better things in Ultravox, Visage and as a solo artist. Of the two ensembles, I prefer The Quick. They are bouncier, wrote most of their own infectious, glucose-rich material, and did a masterful job turning the Beatles' "It Won't Be Long" and the Four Seasons' "Rag Doll" into peppy pop confections that out-cute the originals by far. Though couched in youthful angst, their tunes, "No No Girl," "Hillary" and "Hi Lo," are ooey-gooey, good-time fun. Slik had a somewhat slower paced, power-ballad approach, fell back on their producers for much of their song-writing and tried to turn the Everly Brothers' "When Will I Be Loved" into a plodding, heavy-handed brooder. But some of Slik's songs, like "Bom, Bom," "Requiem" and "The Kid's a Punk," would have worked well as background fluff for some Saturday morning animated puppy band.

I purchased both albums, when they were "hot, new commodities," while I was going through a phase in which I was actively looking for something "different." In retrospect, the Quick sound a bit like the Ohio Express or Tommy Roe crossed with the Dickies. (Hmmm, I wonder if Leonard Graves Phillips and crew got any of their inspiration from the adrenalized, helium-happy antics of Danny Wilde and his buds?) While the Quick are shown chowing down on ice cream, bananas and other sweet treats on the cover of their album, Slik sounds more like the Banana Splits. Like the Monkees, the Jaggerz and various others, Slik probably thought they were pretty street-tough, but at least half of their material would appeal to Turtles fans. It's a shame they didn't have a heavy member with an Anglo Afro. Both bands would likely have abhorred being labeled bubblegum boppers when they were trying to carve out a niche for themselves but, dagnabbit, they both smack of over-produced, schmaltzy, teen dance fever.

The Partridge Family + The Manson Family = The Poppy Family
by Kim Cooper

The '60s ended with bloodbaths at Cielo Drive and Altamont, and as 1970 slouched into view there was no reason to think that the giddy bubblegum genre had one last great wad in its maw. But up in the wilds of Vancouver, B.C., a young married couple was forging a new style of bubblepop, suffused with a blast of stale dark air that was utterly redolent of the times.

From our present vantage it seems obvious that all that folk-rock-protest crap was just an entertaining shuck, and the only songwriters who were really tapped into the *esprit des temps* were Boyce and Hart, Bo Gentry, Kasenetz and Katz, Neil Diamond and the like. Bubblegum hid its insight into politics and human behavior in a midst of infantile fancy, but in the end it's songs like the Archies' "Hot Dog" and "Love Beads and Meditation" by the Lemon Pipers (that's the one that goes, "the tangled mass of membranes that used to be me/is a memory") that continue to speak to the youth of today, while few still breathe who can tell Zager from Evans. It's no accident that this music was only appreciated by eight-year-olds when it came out, because little kids had tons more on the ball than their boo-huffin' older siblings, not to mention the critics, who were too busy praising Dylan's new direction(s) to notice all the great music on Saturday morning TV. But I digress.

Terry and Susan Jacks recorded two albums for London Records as the Poppy Family before Terry's lumberjack obsessions made Susan decide to hit the road running while she still had her health and looks. And despite her indisputable talent (imagine a Karen Carpenter who really meant it), it must have been her looks that got Mrs. Jacks noticed, especially when contrasted with the weirdos in her band. Terry resembled a misguided genetic experiment fusing a komodo dragon with one of the Campbell's Soup kids, and had been a walking bad hair day for years. The session hacks who masqueraded as band members looked stranger still. Satwant Singh could have been the model for Apu, the Kwik-E-Mart manager on *The Simpsons*, right up to the turban that added six inches to his height. And Craig McCaw seems to have been a stoned lumberjack like Terry, although his coke-bottle glasses and white-boy 'fro gave him the look of a White Panther sympathizer. Against this nebbishy cross-section, Susan stood out like a goddess. She had a compact, curvy figure that she liked to drape in skintight red jumpsuits, nicely offsetting the bubble of platinum hair that grazed her shoulders. With her sexy smile and feline eyes, she was your basic Vegas-style knockout. She must have caused quite a stir up there in the woods, and it was only a matter of time before she caught the attention of lecherous label execs throughout the lower 48.

The debut album, *Which Way You Goin', Billy?*, is a haunting brace of menacing melodies, featuring 11 atmospheric classics and one hilariously misguided dog. From the opening number, the broken-hearted bus-ride opus "That's Where I Went Wrong," there's a dizzying air of mystery and hopelessness, with Terry's impressive studio work adding to the general sense of doom. Terry's songs have a knack for never resolving the troubled situations they describe, trailing off into washes of eerie noise instead. Despite the brilliance and difficulty of the album, the title song (a pathetic tale of abandoned womanhood) was a big hit—#2 in the United States; #1 in Canada and the best selling single ever—and "That's Where I Went Wrong" sold a million units as the follow up single. One song that was not a hit, although in a just world it would have been, is "There's No Blood in Bone," which begins with a terrifying spoken section where the pitch of Susan's voice careens widely as she intones "Marie now walks—her life is sleep—she never looks above her feet—she never smiles nor—does—she—speak." The song lives up to this demented introduction, and surpasses it, as Susan sings "When Joey died Marie went mad" over a kinetic backing track featuring a fuzz guitar roar every bit as startling as the proto-metal solo in the Carpenters' "Goodbye to Love." It's a good thing they picked this song to close the first side, because after hearing it any listener would be drenched in sweat and in serious need of a drink. In this chemically benumbed state, we're ready to continue.

Terry runs aground on side two when he briefly forgets that he's not Phil Ochs, and attempts to write a strict racio-political polemic: "What Can the Matter Be?" Over a tinkling music box backing, Susan sings an odious P.C. lyric about a black child kept from opportunity by the color of his skin. The whole number stinks of the *Free to Be You and Me* ethos, and is only redeemed by the amusing couplet,

"Though his mind is his own it seems all that he's got / Is six months in jail for just smoking pot." This is, however, just a momentary misstep on an otherwise groovy album.

One lyrical theme that recurs with monomaniacal frequency is a retreat from the moral and physical decay of the city, with a suggestion that the only way out is through a descent into drugs or psychosis. The epic (3:52) final track, "Of Cities and Escapes" is sung by Terry in the persona of a manic-depressive who lives in a cell-like apartment overlooking a hellish modern city. He's too edgy to answer the phone or read a newspaper, so instead he goes on the nod: "High in my mind / Out of the reach of time / I'm moving far beyond the city and its paranoid storm." But at the end the poor slob has to come down, and nothing has changed. It's an unspeakably miserable way to end a nearly perfect record.

Perfection could have been attained easily enough, had London put the b-side of "Which Way You Goin', Billy?" somewhere on the album. That was a mind-blowing cover of Jody Reynolds' teen-death classic "Endless Sleep" that's up there with the best stuff on the LP. But at this point I guess Terry felt that he could afford to leave great songs on the backs of his singles. He was riding high, writing fast and exquisitely. This creative spree, sadly, was soon to end.

While the follow-up, the cutely-named *Poppy Seeds* (1971) has a few remarkable tracks, the paucity of original songs bespeaks a serious sophomore slump. As Terry explained in interviews around the time of "Seasons in the Sun," the break-up of the Poppy Family was largely due to the conflict between Susan's love of touring and his need to be home to write. Terry also 'fessed up after "Seasons" that the Poppy Family had never really been a band, but anyone who saw the cover of *Poppy Seeds* could have told you that. The sleeve photos were of just Terry and Susan, both sporting looser, more countrified appearances. They're actually frolicking with barnyard animals on the back cover, Terry grinning like a loon by a calf's rear end, and Susan has wisely exchanged her showgirl duds for a crocheted earth-mother outfit. Of particular interest on *Poppy Seeds* are the rocking "Someone Must Have Jumped," which ends with a wild guitar solo that gives way to a honking wah-wah Beefheart screech, and "Where Evil Grows," the first single. "Evil" is simply the greatest dark bubblegum song ever written, and one of the Jacks' rare duets. Over a sinuous nursery rhyme melody, Terry and Susan inform us that "Evil grows in the dark where the sun it never shines/Evil grows in cracks and holes and lives in peoples' minds/Evil grew, it's part of you, and now it seems to be/Every time I look at you, evil grows in me." And how!

And yet *Poppy Seeds* is very nearly a citified C&W album, with half of the 12 songs written by guys like Merle Haggard. Not that there's anything wrong with Merle Haggard, but his song is so normal that it's a letdown after the strange glories of the first album. No non-LP b-sides this time. The band split up soon after, with Terry retiring to Vancouver to establish Goldfish Records and produce Susan's subsequent solo albums. He lost his already small interest in rock stardom, realizing that his true desire was to do a great deal of fishing and hunting, and to get in the occasional round of golf. Any difficulty he might have had in financing this lifestyle were solved once he released "Seasons in the Sun," which ironically he'd been trying to convince such artists as the Beach Boys and Edward Bear to record for years. No one was as enthusiastic as Terry was about the song, so he finally recorded it himself and hit the worldwide Top 40 jackpot. Maudlin, lyrically confused, terribly French, the song must

be respected if only because it gave Terry Jacks some of the recognition and success he'd earned during the life span of the Poppy Family. Of course that doesn't mean you ought to *listen* to the damn thing!

Terry's still up in Vancouver, apparently living an outdoor life which now incorporates a boat called, yup, *Seasons in the Sun*. If you see the first Poppy Family album for sale, BUY IT! It offers such a lovely mixture of depression and elation that you'll probably end up with altered brain chemistry and maybe even nightmares. And if that doesn't sound good to you, then I can't imagine what would.

Svensk Pop: Sweden In The Days Before ABBA by Alec Palao

Think of Sweden, think of pop and you come up with one word: ABBA. The classic inferences of Brill Building and Spector, the icily fresh harmonies, the Anglo-Saxon chunkiness of the production, ABBA's classic mid-1970s catalogue was and forever will be as catchy as a cold in the Arctic Circle. So rich and painstakingly crafted, at the time one could not help but wonder how ABBA's music had developed, especially when the group only properly emerged after winning the Eurovision Song Contest in 1974.

Eurovision is something most Americans are unaware of, and they should be thankful. Every year since the late 1950s, two dozen European countries have proffered their best pop songs and voted upon each other in a fiercely contested international battle. The winners are invariably mainstream ballads too syrupy even for grandma, or gormless multi-syllable inanities with titles like "Boom A Bang Bang" that even Don Kirshner would consider embarrassing. It goes without saying that Eurovision is responsible for some of the worst records known to man.

ABBA tried several times to win the competition, and even before the resounding success of "Waterloo," it was quite obvious they were several notches above the Eurovision dross. But there was pop in Sweden before ABBA, and great pop at that. Internationally, Holland, Australia and Japan also had scenes of similar import, but if you want some substance to your fluff, then you could do worse than to check out the Swedish pop arena.

The Swedes have almost universally sung in English, and had an innate sense of what constitutes a great pop record. The Hep Stars are often cited as the big Swedish pop act of the 1960s, largely because of their ABBA connections, but while they were undoubtedly popular, most of their recorded legacy is average, and Benny's neo-classical keyboard touches make their sound decidedly fruity. No, the great pop gods of Sweden were the Tages, who honed their craft over several quality albums and a slew of great singles that ran from plaintive Merseybeat ("I Should Be Glad," 1964) to wobbly psych-pop ("I Read You Like An Open Book," 1969). In between are some classic records like "Miss MacBaren," "Every Raindrop Means A Lot," and "She's Having A Baby Now," all with a degree of intelligence and drama that belies their pop simplicity.

The Tages emerged from a post-Beatles group explosion that produced many wonderful combos, specializing in R&B, mod-beat and just plain outasite pop. This writer's favorite has to be the Mascots, whose heartbreaking "Words Enough To Tell You" is a pinnacle of sorts. But there were many others— Lee Kings, Beathovens, Shamrocks, Ola & the Janglers et al.—that were capable of equally fine moments. Once the immediate effect of the Beatles had waned, Swedish pop absorbed a bevy of outside influences that strongly informed the pop sensibility of the country's musicians —Herman's Hermits, the Tremeloes, Beach Boys, Four Seasons, and Hollies. It created a template of sorts that the Swedes excelled at. So, for example, the Shanes' "Chris Craft #9," from 1967, twists the melody of the Hermits' "A Must To Avoid," throws in some Hollies harmonies and serves it up with a driving kineticism that some jaded UK bands had already begun to forget. All in a simple ditty about a sailboat.

By the time of the accepted bubblegum era, this *Svensk Pop* was in a purple period, with tons of great singles from both the established groups like the Lee-Kings ("Coming From The Ground") and the Jackpots ("Lincoln City"), through to a new generation of popmeisters like Annaabee-Nox ("Anna Be Nice") the Slam Creepers ("It's Saturday") and Pete Proud ("Ba-Ba-Da-Da-Doh" and yes, they're a group). All of these have the hallmarks of classic bubblegum: simple yet irresistible melody, driving organ and guitar-based rhythms, and impeccably chanted harmonies with nary an accent to be heard. A heavy disc session of *Svensk Pop* can leave you glassy-eyed, with visions of a bubble car racing across the icy wastes to be greeted by a cabin full of miniskirted Nordic dolly birds, all of whom one assumes look like Agnetha.

Some of these bands made inroads into the US at the end of the decade, like Ola & the Janglers and the post-Tages group Blond, but by and large Swedish pop was a localized phenomenon. By the early 1970s its fresh innocence was gone, most bands turning to native folk styles for musical inspiration, with predictably wretched results. It took ABBA to combine all the elements of Swedish pop that had gone before, influences and all, and turn them into a hit-making machine the world has not seen the likes of since.

LUV: The Über Abba? by Metal Mike Saunders

Having spent my entire life in the bargain bins, the junk bins, and the thrift store racks (and if you really want to go way back—the famous 1969–71 mono LP 59¢/79¢/99¢ cutout bins), I don't have the kind of archival access some folks do. Box sets? I've poked at a couple in my life (they weigh a lot). That's about as close as my budget (a frighteningly consistent 50 bucks/mo. for vinyl/digital/cassette/8-track product, all eras, for over 20 years now) has come to getting one to the ticket counter.

But once or twice a decade, my garbage-bin study-hall home hits paydirt. Summer 1998, it was in the unsorted back-wall cheapo floor boxes of a dopey San Jose "collector's store" (read: ten tons of over-priced stock) that was having a "must move" 75%-off four-week blowout. The record that stopped my flipping hand dead in its tracks was called: LUV's *Greatest Hits*, a 16-song German/ Dutch pressing ©1979. My immediate thought: "Ohmigod . . . Could this be a Dutch ABBA-knockoff (one of my most beloved of all pop groups, all time)?"

It was, they were, and this is everything I've been able to dredge up on them in the ensuing 24 months.

Parenthetically, please note: they were *big*, in Germany/ Holland at least. Six Top 5 singles, and four more Top 10's, over three years 1978–1980 (on the Dutch charts), with back to back #1 singles just three hits into the run. Big enough throughout Europe (never charted UK) that you can still get a greatest hits CD in the Bear Family mail-order catalog. And more often than not, they were utterly wunnerful, which is why I'm writing about them.

Except for the mysterious and slightly bizarre third LP, *True Luv*, every single track on their four full albums was produced by famous Dutch producer Hans Van Hemert, arranged by Piet Souer (and 100% by the ABBA textbook I might add), and every single darned tune written by a Janschen & Janschens pen team (= all 36 tunes for LP's #one, two, and four).

Anyway. Producer Hans Van Hemert's career starts over a decade prior, with a ton of sides by Q65, the Motions, and many other Dutch beat groups. By the '70s, his "international successes" were with rather un-beat-like things like Mouth & McNeal, so you can see this guy isn't one who was gonna be sitting around the house in 1976–77 waiting for the "'65 beat sound" to come back into vogue to pay the rent.

LUV's debut single "My Man" (#12 Dutch) is terrific faux-ABBA right out of the box, with the bonus of a daft soap opera lyric (her "man" was killed in a railroad-nightwatchman accident y'see, and the "insurance company" can shove their dirty money—she wants *her man* back!) and an arrangement right out of ABBA's "Dum Dum Diddle." Back side "Don't Let Me Down" is, oddly, straight '74 glitter-rock and quite good, probably a leftover backing track of Hemert's from the year Mud/Suzi/Hello/Alvin Stardust scared everybody out of glitter rock forever.

The next single, "Dream Dream," is a rather dubious choice and only bubbled under (the Dutch Top 30). The next single broke the group when "U.O.Me" (#3 Dutch) was adopted as the intro theme tune for a TV show *Waldolala*.

Summer 1978's "You're The Greatest Lover" (#1 Dutch) topped the charts and continued a pattern where four straight Top 5's were actually the group's weakest, cheeziest (over towards the novelty side) tracks of the 1978-mid '79 period.

The ensuing album *With LUV* is pretty darned half terrific. Uptempo album cuts "Who Do You Wanna Be," "Life Is On My Side," "Louis Je T'Adore," "Get Ready," etc., are straight out of the 1976–77 ABBA sound (i.e. their best set, *Arrival*) and the songwriting is dead on killer in that style, hook for hook (every tune but the #1 "Lover," and its B-side, is swell to excellent, and "Hang On" has a melody so perfect it could be a 1964 Jackie DeShannon composition). And unlike ABBA, you get this routine of all three girls chanting choruses and backing vocals that really works. Something about those soft-yet-snappy Dutch accents that is just perfect for melodic girlypop. Oh yeah, the somewhat annoying "Trojan Horse" followed "Lover" to #1 and was squeezed onto some later pressings of *With LUV*, depending upon the country.

The next album *Lots of LUV* is the reason I'm here. It's the Holy Grail of ABBA-Sound. And, unique in most rock history, it's all in reverse-mirror fashion. ABBA's greatest parallel-universe hooks dumbed down to kinda-Germanic vocal chants, nursery rhyme lyrics ("Eeny Meeny Miny Moe," "I.M.U.R.," "D.J."), and backing tracks that are top to bottom punchier and less ornate than ABBA's, one gigantic difference here being the far more rockin'/funkier/danceable rhythm tracks banged out by Holland's best studio musicians. As Brian Wilson will tell you, once you've got some hits goosing that studio budget, you can get the best—Hal Blaine (or the equivalent), if you got the dough to rock the house.

"Night Of Love," "I.M.U.R.," and "Shoes Off (Boots On)"—the album tracks where a new-for-'79 keyboard-synth gurgle sound accents the rhythm tracks with steady, throbbing eighth-note punctuation—in fact sound completely contemporary *and* danceable, 20+ years on. The songs are relentlessly hookier than any set Bjorn & Benny came up with, honest ta god. *No slow songs*. First time I heard this album (courtesy of Fun Records used mailorder Germany, www.funrecords.de), I thought, "hey, this is pretty good!" Two plays later, I'm going, "wow, this is *really* good!" Fifty plays later, it's as ingrained in my skull as *Beach Boys Today*, *Rubber Soul* (U.S. version), or any other pop classic where melody, beat, and short tight songs ruled the world for 30 minutes or less.

"Casanova" (#6 Dutch) was followed by LUV's first classic-on-45, "Eeny Meeny Miny Moe" (#11 Dutch), where melodic simplicity and stomp-beat and utter lyrical idiocy combine to—well, we're talking Revenge of the Archies here! This tune even worked in a recurring hook on acoustic guitar that comes off like Slade-plays—"Fernando" (ABBA) . . . genius.

Next album, *True LUV* (also 1979) and the songs are gone. Producer/arranger Hemert and Souer have hijacked the songwriting, all but two tunes (which coulda been second LP leftovers), and the whole ship crashes. Their ten tunes, ranging from okay to plain wanky, show none of Janschen/Janschen's ABBA-chops; boy, it's a downright debacle. The lead single "Ooh Yes I Do" (#5 Dutch) did some action (and was not

Metal Mike wouldn't swap this one for the whole damn Bob Dylan catalogue.

criminally cheesier than their second through fourth hits), but its follow-up "Ann Maria" (#11 Dutch) had no redeeming qualities. The *True LUV* stinkbomb was only on the album charts (#11 LP, Dutch) one-third as long as *With LUV* and *Lots of LUV* (#6 and #7 Dutch) albums.

The final time around as 1980 starts a new decade, *Forever Yours* has LUV back (i.e. Marga Scheide, Jose Wijdeven, and Patty Brard, minus Patty and plus her replacement Ria Thielsch) with all Janschen &

Janschens tunes. Like ABBA, the style and tunes have changed a bit. Lead single "One More Little Kissy" makes #9 even though it's the weakest of their cheesy-novelty A-sides ever. The next single "My Number One" did just swell (#5 Dutch), and deservedly so 'cause it's a catchy uptempo shuffle humalonger with wack faux-bagpipes sounds cheerily reminiscent of Steeleye Span's hit "All Around My Hat" (1975, #5 UK), go figure. "I Win It," "Ooh I Like It Too" and a couple other album tracks are snappy old-school ABBA; "The Show Must Go On" is a pleasure in the newer, slower, more dramatic '78–'82 ABBA style, which shows you that Janschen & Janschens were nothing if not paying attention. The middle half of side one sees two or three songs pile up with nice hooks, very pleasant, but not much toe-tapping and a long way from 1979 and old-school LUV/ABBA. The real downside is J&J's replica of the new, *boring* ABBA sound—slow, aimless ballady things called "Song of Love and Understanding," "Some Call It Happiness," and "Mother of the Hearts" (I can't even type these titles without falling asleep) that don't get halfway to the finish line without someone yanking the needle. Think "Thank You for the Music," or whatever late-ABBA song that sends you to snoozeland as well.

Oh yeah, hey, then there's LUV's final single (track five here)—"Tingalingaling." Yup, their swan song is their masterpiece, fitting for an act whose career is such a compressed ('78–'80) blaze of glory and then disaster (the *True LUV* shipwreck not explained anywhere on the Web, not even in German). "Tingalingaling" is 2:29 (!!—this was 1980, remember) of everything that puts this group in my personal Pop Hall Of Fame. (Screw those "rock" museums anyway, d'you think they're ever gonna let *any* of Kirshner's finest in?). Gurgle keyboardsynth rhythm sounds, dead-on nursery rhyme melody, idiotic playground lyrics, chanted choruses, and a *beat* that is utterly as contemporary and danceable as any of Year 2000's Cheiron/Max Martin/Stockholm hit monsters that deservedly rule today's pop world (the link between ABBA/LUV and 1997–'98's Swedish-conceived teenpop explosion being, of course, Ace of Base and their late producer Denniz Pop, at his same Stockholm Cheiron Studios).

"Tingaling" didn't hit Top 20 (#29 Dutch in summer '81), and that's it, boom, no more LUV.

Subsequent solo product and late '80s reformed LUV product is all inconsequential—an album by ex-LUV Jose Wijdeven *The Good Times* (1982, w/two Top 10 Dutch singles) that's somewhat girl-group redolent (covers of "I Will Follow Him" and "I Can Hear Music" amongst the A-sides) but mostly '80s-dull; a German-language album titled *Herinnering* by Bonnie & Jose with all the material penned courtesy of, guess who, Bjorn & Benny (but as deathly dull as the *Chess* soundtrack in their early-mid '80s end-period ABBA dirge style).

A reformed LUV shows up on various 1989–1991 product, i.e., various CDs and CD maxi-singles of which large parts are in (some tracks even by) the Stock-Aitken-Waterman style but very average. In a fitting postscript, a LUV-hits "Megamix" single scratches Top 20 in summer 1993, and takes the *LUV Gold* hits collection into the Top 10.

So okay, I bite. If ABBA are (by many) in retrospect considered the touchstone '70s pop group . . . and if 1979's *Lots of LUV* by Holland's worst-attired (but most enthusiastic, not to mention wielding more convincing phonetic-English than Anna/Frida ever mustered) is very arguably *the* definitive Abba set . . . wow, that's the kind of conundrum that collapses entire universes. And they didn't even have to write one damn song to do it.

Eurovision: The Candy-Coated Song Factory by Jack Stevenson

While American pop culture beams itself to all corners of the globe, invading and conquering foreign cultures with movies, sex symbols and hamburgers, its harsh glare is outshone once a year by the mega-watt glitter of the Eurovision song contest—*a tour de force* of Eurotrash excess that has left this jaded Yank bedazzled since 1993, when I moved to Denmark.

Founded in 1956, this international songfest was a product of television when the young medium was idealistically seen as a tool that could unite diverse European cultures for an evening in the simple shared joy of music. And for all the crassness and kitsch Eurovision has come to epitomize 44 years later, this noble aim is still its main motivation—or so the official line would have it.

Eurovision pits one act—vocalist, duo or group—from each of Europe's 23 countries in a night-long competition that culminates in public phone-in vote in each country. Each nation then casts its votes for other national acts, resulting in the emergence of a single winner with a single song.

The voting has always been notoriously partisan, as enemies like Greece and Turkey never give each other a single vote, while East European neighbors tend to vote for each other, as do the Scandinavian countries, etc. Beyond that, the voting is unpredictable and erratic in the extreme, and that's one of Eurovision's joys.

With a global audience of 100 million, Eurovision is a virtual cottage industry for the broadcast media, yellow press and tavern business. Gays love it. The merely cultured indulge it for one night in the name of patriotism, and common folks are moved to laughter and tears at the rounds of parties in homes and bars. Intellectuals disdain it like the bubonic plague and make it a point to attend high profile events where there is no television present, lest they be suspected of hiding at home in front of the tube. To admit any of the songs moved you to tears would be a lowbrow humiliation worse than slipping in dog shit.

It's a glitzy, showbiz event, like the MTV awards or Oscars, Emmys and Grammys—but with a very distinct difference. Similar American events tend to be very "star" and "award" oriented: the biggest, brightest stars singing their mega-hits in the communal glow of well-affirmed success, accepting endless honors awarded by esteemed judges as they troop to the stage to give speeches.

Eurovision, conversely, is a shrine to the song, not the star. It's an homage to the ton of hope and glory attached to the lone pop song. It's a real-time event with the one award given by "the people."

In the capital city of the previous year's winner gather the bright hopefuls from across Europe to form a massed concentration of facially perfect Barbie dolls, photogenic jawbones and a raw maw of uncut charisma. Each contestant is hoping to ride one miraculously catchy tune to fame and fortune the way "Waterloo" catapulted ABBA to stardom in 1974. This is considered by most to be the event's immaculate golden moment, and it endures as inspiration to countless entrants since, who dream that all this might lead to something more than a free vacation and lots of tabloid exposure back home.

The acts have all just won their own national competitions and achieved some short-lived hope, hullabaloo and celebrity on the local level, previous to which most of them were total unknowns. And after their 15 minutes of fame, most will go back to their day jobs or go on to supply second-rate lounges and supper clubs with an endless glut of "where are they now?" easy-listening acts.

But still, a hope held dear in the darkest moments is that a winner can come out of nowhere. It's all about amateurs scoring big and dreams of a lifetime coming true in a single night. In 1998, an Israeli transsexual, Dana International, triumphed over a Maltese farm girl in the last round of voting with a catchy disco tune. It's about hope—and hope dashed.

And while that Maltese farm girl and all the other thousands of losers over the years will grow older and move on to other pursuits, their old performances lay eternally entombed in an electronic purgatory of outer-orbit TV signals floating around in space . . . songs that will come back years later and haunt the unwary in unguarded moments. "My God! I remember that one!" they shriek with expressions contorted in shock as if they'd just swallowed a bone.

Eurovision is also good at producing freaky camp followers and obsessed trivia buffs who can sing the lyrics of all the past winners and remember details that should never be allowed to lodge in the human brain. These people only come truly to life once a year, and in the meantime they pester co-workers with Eurovision prattle that nobody wants to hear unless the Contest is actually about to happen.

In its shining belief in the transformational power of the 2:30 pop song, the Eurovision Song Contest redeems bubblegum's bright promise and hearkens back to its heyday, the '60s, a time of 45 rpm singles and portable record players that folded up like little suitcases. A time before every act needed to shoot a video, a time when TV shows like *Shindig!*, *Hullabaloo* and *Top of the Pops* brought a visual dimension to the sound. The era when the pop song ruled.

Like bubblegum, Eurovision is instant: full of instantly disposable empty-calorie confections that tend to be bouncy effervescent love songs that evaporate as fast as it takes the cute lead singer to shake her long blonde hair across her face (Charlotte Nilsson's trademark). You only hear most of the songs once, on the night of the show. All are essentially instantly judged—and being pretty helps.

Like bubblegum, none of it seems quite real or to possess any substance. It all seems suspiciously pre-fabricated, as artificial and sweet as it is inevitably upbeat and bright, perfect for teenaged digestive systems. No death rock here, although basically anything is permitted and you never know what crazy stuff some little country you could never find on a map (if you're an American) is going to come up with.

And like bubblegum, the songs are totally apolitical, recalling a time before rock and pop musicians became "youth spokesmen" and organized benefits to stop world hunger. While the songs are naturally more diverse and differ stylistically from the American brand of bubblegum, they possess the soul of bubblegum—pure pop distilled to its sugary upbeat essence. And its biggest fans behave like total junkies.

In 1999, with acts free to sing for the first time since 1974 in the language of their choice, many pre-dictably opted for English. In this respect Eurovision might serve as a global springboard for European pop groups. You don't need a degree in history to remember when groups like Shocking Blue, Golden Earring and ABBA conquered the car radios of the world and made planetary history by singing their one great little song in English.

Although viewers are ostensibly tuning in to see the future—the next big hit-makers or supergroup—what they really get, and what is really more delicious and cavity-inducing, is nostalgia. They get more reruns of ABBA's "Waterloo" with blonde Agnetha gently gyrating in those outrageous skintight blue pantaloons. They get week-long lead-up programs in every country as local TV pop-show hosts plunder library archives for old kinescope tapes and dredge up their own pop culture pasts with appalling and hilarious hairstyles, costumes and set designs intact. It's a cheap ticket back to teenland and a glutton's helping of guilty pleasures.

Every Eurovision edition is full of surprises and absurd moments guaranteed by the wide cultural diversity of styles unknown in an assimilationist monoculture like America. Pop culture is, above all, local and untranslatable, and despite all the warm fuzzy talk about pan-European unity and brotherhood,

Eurovision is really a celebration of nationalism, provincialism and parochialism. This tends to result in acts wildly popular in their own countries but totally inscrutable to anyone else. All those stunned silences at otherwise noisy parties might be described as the sound of a million jaws dropping.

I happened to be passing through Sweden in February on the very night that the strangely too-perfect-to-be-human 24-year-old blonde chanteuse Charlotte Nilsson won the national Eurovision competition there. By chance I switched on the TV in my hotel room in Örebro to witness the closing minutes of congratulatory hugs and tears, and, as seemingly thousands joined her on stage, a final group singalong of her very Abba-esque song, "Take Me to Your Heaven." I was transfixed by this national outpouring of feel-good euphoria on a dazzling TV sound stage, and I felt privy to a spectacle intended only for Swedish eyes. It was total rapture, the impact of which far exceeded even the finals in Tel Aviv. The next morning I walked the streets to see her mug plastered on every broadsheet and tabloid, and I knew that she had seduced an entire nation. Or rather, a nation had seduced itself.

Watching the finals, which took place on May 29th in Tel Aviv (to the outrage of orthodox Jews), I caught her act again and experienced the same adolescent tingle I felt when I stole my first candy bar. Nilsson had been tagged as one of the favorites and battled it out in very dramatic fashion with Selma Björnsdóttir from Iceland, while Germany's entry, the all-Turkish band, Surpriz, singing in Hebrew (!), finished a very dangerous third with "Journey to Jerusalem." (Hey, you gotta hear the winner twice!)

Meanwhile the field spread out behind them. Precious, the British all-girl quintet with more than a passing resemblance to the Spice Girls, had been ranked at top but finished a disastrous 14th. Portugal, with its hairy hippie male lead singer, got only twelve points, all on a first-place mercy vote from the ever unpredictable French. Spain came in dead last with a single point. My own favorite, Austria, placed somewhere in the nebulous middle, and I'm waiting someday to hear/see that one again when I least expect it.

Dave Thompson Picks:
Ten Great Eurovision Entrants

Allisons (UK, 1961) "Are You Sure"
Gigliola Cinquetti (Italy, 1974) "Si"
Dana (Eire, 1970) "All Kinds of Everything"
Dana International (Israel, 1998) "Diva"
Françoise Hardy (Monaco, 1963) "L'Amour S'en Va"
Lasse Holm and Monica Tornell (Sweden, 1986) "E'De'Det Har Du Kallar Karlek"
MFO (Turkey, 1985) "Diday Diday Day"
Srebrna Krila (Yugoslavia, 1988) "Mangup"
Teach In (Netherlands, 1975) "Ding Ding Dong"
Telex (Belgium, 1980) "Euro-Vision"

Finally Sweden was put over the top and declared the winner as Charlotte-the-good went over to give an emotional hug to her Icelandic rival.

When all the Turkish bagpipes, Greek oboes and harps, accordions and guitars have fallen silent for another year, and the world's greatest big top of pop has folded its tent, one is left to wonder how . . . how all this ballast can balance itself on one all-too-brief little pop song that if you're lucky—or unlucky—you only hear twice.

There may be a career in it for the winner, and lots of love and tears, but not a great deal of respect—at least not the kind of respect that is automatically afforded to winners and stars in America, land of winners and stars. Where success as an end in itself is so prized and swallowed whole, where it's hard to believe the public would take something like this so casually.

But this is unswallowable. It is, however, eminently wallowable as well as being very drinkable, as the obviously tipsy hosts and commentators and vote casters (especially Holland . . .) evidenced as they cracked wise, missed cues and, in the case of the British commentator, treated the whole thing with the kind of scandalous and hilarious irreverence that would have got him yanked of the air in The States and then fired and sued in that order.

Ultimately Eurovision remains professionally unprofessional as well as impossibly unserious, a lark, in a world where things tend to be increasingly bleak and serious. Sometimes sentiments collide; this year's closing singalong in support of all the victims of the Balkan war was absurd.

At the end of the magic night, with her greatest dream come true, Nilsson stood alone on stage right waiting for someone to give her something. Presenter Dana International, fluttering in sheer gown and feather boas and tottering on stacked heels, then proceeded to steal the show in bizarre fashion by tripping and falling flat on her ass.

And the next day the world went on . . .

Group Sounds and Japanese Pop by Glenn Sadin

The Japanese music scene has traditionally been dominated by manufactured pop stars for nearly as long as there has been rock 'n' roll in Japan. Every year a new crop of *idoru* (teen idols) makes its debut before

the adoring teenage masses, usually introduced via one of many pop music TV programs, taking the space once occupied by last year's models, who may have either quit show business or simply disappeared from the charts. The Japanese are seemingly very fickle when it comes to musical taste; if an *idoru*'s career can survive until they reach their late 20s, they are considered musical veterans.

Today's hit-making machine can trace its roots back to the late '50s, when the big show biz powers realized that this new Western import, rock'n'roll, could become very lucrative if they were able to gain control and dictate the latest trends to the nation's restless youth. After ten years or so of hard times following WWII, Japanese youth looked to America for the new direction, which was rock 'n' roll.

Smelling money, the big talent agencies and record companies began scouting the country's coffee bars and youth clubs, looking for good-looking, well-behaved youngsters that could be groomed for pop stardom. It wasn't necessary for the potential *idoru* to be particularly good singers; it was all about image. What really counted was wholesome good looks, a charming personality, and a certain "star quality" that would make them stand out and get the attention of the adoring masses. After signing with the production company, the teen would be refined and packaged according to whatever the latest style required.

Most *idoru* made their debut on one of the national pop music TV shows, the first of which was *The Hit Parade*, which debuted on Fuji Television in 1959 and was an instant success with Japanese teens. Hosted by one-time Elvis-style Japanese rocker Mickey Curtis—who now appeared in a neat suit flashing a toothy grin—*The Hit Parade* set the stage for the music shows to come. Each week millions of young people tuned in to watch Japanese singers perform the latest American hit songs in Japanese. It was the perfect vehicle for launching new *idoru* into overnight stardom.

One of the most popular acts to appear on Japanese television during this period was a pair of adorably cute twin sisters, Emi and Yumi Ito, collectively known as the Peanuts. The Peanuts had a charming stage personality and were actually quite good singers. Their records tended to be delightful Japanese-language versions of Western pop songs, Latin-tinged romantic ballads, and Japanese folk songs done with a dance beat. The Peanuts' popularity lasted well into the mid-'70s, and one can still hear their hits being sung by pairs of women in *karaoke* bars all over Japan. (In America, the Peanuts are best known as the miniature twin fairy princesses in the old *Godzilla* movies, singing their mournful laments to Mothra!)

Once Beatlemania hit Japan in the mid-'60s, the trend switched away from individual *idoru* to groups of young men with mop haircuts and electric guitars. Almost immediately following the Beatles' 1966 Far Eastern tour, which included several shows in Tokyo's Budo Kan Hall that were broadcast around the country on NHK-TV, performers had to play guitar and really sing if they were to be "with it." This new beat boom was dubbed "the Group Sounds," or GS for short.

From 1966 to '67 dozens of new bands, with "mod" names like the Spiders, the Tempters, the Carnabeats, the Jaguars, the Tigers, etc., made their record debuts. The top GS bands had enormous popularity in Japan, with Beatlemania-like hysteria scenes following them wherever they went and concerts filled with screaming fans. The Tigers, the Jaguars and the Spiders even made fun-filled feature films à la *Help!* and *Having a Wild Weekend.* The Spiders attempted to crack the international market by touring and releasing records in the US and Europe, without success. They even appeared on the legendary British TV show, *Ready Steady Go!* Nevertheless, the trips abroad helped secure their status in Japan, where going abroad is equated with "making it." The Tigers visited the United States for a much-needed vacation and to film a commercial for Japanese TV, and were even advertised in Japan as having "appeared" on *The Ed Sullivan Show*. (Of course, the fact that their appearance was in the audience and not onstage wasn't mentioned!)

Much like the old Hollywood studio contract system, the GS bands were tightly controlled by their producers. Watanabe Productions, one of the most powerful talent agencies in Japan, held its artists (including the Tigers, who were the biggest name in GS at the time) under iron-clad, long-term contracts. There were rumors circulating at the time that, despite the fact that the Tigers were earning at least a million dollars a year in income, Watanabe Productions had the boys on a monthly salary of $300 per person, plus expenses. Carnabeats drummer Ai Takano spoke in a recent interview about how he had to visit the house of Jaguars vocalist Shin Okamoto in secret, because the Carnabeats' management considered other groups to be rivals, and forbade them from becoming friendly with each other. (The Spiders were one successful band who broke away from this system by forming their own management company, Spiduction, and signed up other bands, some of which—i.e., the Tempters—were very successful in their own right.)

The Tigers, who had started out worshipping the Rolling Stones (their 1967 live album, *On Stage,* consists of mostly Stones covers), were soon conditioned into cute 'n' cuddly pop *idoru*, and their recorded output quickly changed from big beat rockers to string-laden romantic ballads tailor-made for teenage schoolgirl fantasies. Lead vocalist, Kenji Sawada, who was admittedly the best looking pop star in Japan at the time, even affected the effeminate stage name Julie, which served him well after the Tigers disbanded in the early '70s, and he launched a new career as a glam artist.

By the mid-'70s, the GS boom was ancient history and most "serious" rock fans in Japan had entered their 20s and had graduated to the harder rock sounds of the day. But this didn't stop the idol machines from churning out fresh fodder for the new generation of youthful record buyers. By this point, the big star makers had discovered that by using *idoru* as tools to pitch products aimed at the youth market, it was a doubly profitable situation. The managers signed exclusive agreements with the manufacturers of candy bars, acne cream, and other youth-oriented products to have their *idoru* become, in effect, the merchandising "face" of the product. Rather than losing credibility, the increased exposure through a massive saturation of magazine ads, store displays, and, especially, TV commercials, led to mega record sales and concert attendance. Even today it is standard practice in Japan to align a new single release with a product marketing campaign, so that every time the consumer sees an ad for a brand of instant curry or facial cream, he is also exposed to a 30-second blast of the new single. Most singles even credit the commercial that the song was promoted on, to make it easier for the consumer to find the song that he or she liked.

Utilizing this new marketing strategy, the biggest success story of the '70s was a singing and dancing duo named Pink Lady, who had an impressive series of nine #1 singles between 1976 and 1979. The two schoolgirls, Mitsuyo Nemoto and Keiko Masuda, began their career after passing the audition to appear on the amateur talent TV show, *Star Tanjo! (Birth of a Star!)*. By the time they appeared on TV six months later to promote their first single, *"Peppa Keibu"* ("Pepper Police"), their innocent girlie folk routine was replaced by catchy disco music with wacky lyrics sung by two young chicks dancing in sexy mini-dresses. Until Pink Lady came along, most Japanese female performers had been pretty stationary on stage, except for the occasional wistful hand gesture or two, so that when Mii and Kei (as Pink Lady became known to their fans) came on shaking their things and getting down, it caused a sensa-

tion! Despite their sexy moves on stage, their music was so completely free from any kind of sexual suggestiveness, and their performances so filled with youthful exuberance, that they were not considered a threat to morality by adults. Pink Lady were big hits with younger audiences too, who bought up kiddie books with instructions on how to do the latest Pink Lady dance steps. Before long, even the youngest children were boogieing along with Pink Lady in front of their TVs. Their popularity was so complete that at one point in 1977 they held the top three positions on the singles charts.

During their reign at the top, Pink Lady were contracted as "image talents" or pitchwomen for an incredible 11 consumer products, ranging from chil-

dren's magazines to ice cream to shampoo, all of which had significant sales increases directly related to the use of Pink Lady's image. During their peak in 1978, they attempted to crack the American market, performing in Las Vegas and recording their first English-language single in America. While their opportunities abroad increased, their hit records in Japan began to decline, partially due to some ill-advised career decisions. They returned to America in 1980, where they starred in a TV series on NBC, *Pink Lady and Jeff* (with comic Jeff Altman), recorded an LP entirely in English for the American market, and had a single, "Kiss in the Dark," reach #37 on the *Billboard* chart. However, the show was canceled after several weeks and Pink Lady returned to Japan, where they struggled for another year or so before breaking up in 1981.

In the mid-'80s, a new TV show attracted the attention of teenagers all over Japan. *Yuyake Nyan Nyan (Meow at Dusk)* came on at 5:00 PM, when young people had some free time after school, but before their nightly study time. The stars of the show were a group of 24 cute high school girls who were dubbed the *Onyanko Club* (Kitty Cat Club). What distinguished the girls in the *Onyanko Club* was the fact that they were utter amateurs, chosen for the show merely for their normalness. Unlike previous TV personalities and *idoru*, the girls were not groomed for TV stardom or given much training in show busi-

ness charm. Sure, they danced, sang and made small talk with the show's host, but they did it without any pretense of showbiz glamour. They would chat about the things that mattered to young girls, usually in teenage slang. They represented normal high school girls living normal teenage lives. When some of the girls would have tests at school, they would even be absent from the show, which the other girls would sympathetically lament. Of course, many of the viewers at home would also be taking the same tests at their own schools, so a rapport was established with their audience. This audience identification was at the core of their success; girls could imagine themselves being plucked from obscurity and becoming stars overnight (replacement *Onyanko Club* members would be recruited after a girl graduated high school) and boys would fantasize about dating their favorites. Naturally, hit singles by the *Onyanko Club* followed, which, of course, were not written by the members of the group, nor were they particularly sung well. The *Onyanko Club* sowed the seeds of success for contemporary teenage Japanese female bubblegum acts like Speed, which have similar music-with-dancing formats.

So what is the state of J-Pop Bubblegum today? The CD charts and TV music programs are saturated with manufactured groups of attractive teenagers who have been carefully trained to dance in sync. Most have questionable vocal abilities, although this only is apparent when one sees them performing on live TV without their producer's studio magic supporting them. No matter; the kids in Japan are eating this up. There is even a private *idoru* training school in Okinawa that, in addition to the usual history and math lessons, instructs the students in choreography, singing, acting and other show business skills. The school has turned out an impressive number of young pop stars, including Namie Amuro and Speed, two of the most successful hitmakers of the '90s. Much like with the current success in America of the Backstreet Boys, 'N Sync and Britney Spears, it seems that manufactured pop music is thriving in Japan today.

Roberto Jordán and the Rise of Mexigum, or "Chiclet Rock" by Tom Walls

Latin America has always assimilated Anglo-American popular music in some way; it has imitated it, repackaged it and has given it an indelible Latin stamp. Roberto Jordán is a great example of an artist that took the bubblegum formula and enjoyed success with it throughout the Spanish-speaking world. Jordán was a heartthrob figure backed up by a team of producers, songwriters and arrangers, serving up a

long string of pre-packaged pop hits aimed at a vast, hungry teen market in the late '60s and early '70s. His material was comprised mainly of cover versions of English-language pop-rock hits, including several classic bubblegum nuggets made famous by the U.S. projects of Messrs. Kasenetz, Katz and Levine. Jordán made bubblegum music accessible to teens throughout Central and South America and even to Spanish-language music consumers in the U.S. His career has been a long one. He recorded an album of boleros a few years ago, in 1998 played to a packed Jackie Gleason Theater here in Miami, and still receives tremendous airplay on Spanish oldies stations.

I discovered Roberto Jordán through Clasica 92 FM, one such Spanish "oldies" station in South Florida. Since I preferred oldies stations to the drivel spewing from the rest of the dial, and given my interest in improving my Spanish, it followed that I'd tune in to the Spanish oldies station when I moved here in 1999. And tuning in has enlightened me to a lot of music I never would have heard otherwise.

I've been a fan of '60s garage since my mother gave me her Shadows of Knight, Blues Magoos and Electric Prunes records. In more recent years, I've taken it upon myself to seek out garage records from other countries, particularly from the Spanish-speaking world.

Rock 'n' roll was not only introduced to Mexico over the radio, but also visually through great rock 'n' roll movies like *The Girl Can't Help It*. The movies influenced the youth of Mexico in clothing, hairstyles and attitudes. Groups such as Los Teenagers adopted a wild rock 'n' roll stance while still playing traditional music like pachanga and boleros. Bill Haley and the Comets toured Mexico in 1960 and helped jump-start the *rocandrolero* (rock 'n' roller) scene. Bigger acts started playing rock 'n' roll in Spanish, like Enrique Guzman, Cesar Costa, Los Teen Tops, Los Yakis and Hermanos Carrion. By the mid-'60s, Mexico produced tons of Stonesy R & B garage bands: Los Locos del Ritmo, Los Johnny Jets, and Los Apson, not to mention Los Psicodelicos Xochimilcas (The Psychedelic Xochimilcas). There was even a sharp-dressed group called Los American's (yes, with the apostrophe) that prided themselves on their Kinks covers.

This material has been pretty much ignored by critics and has escaped the notice of chroniclers of Latin popular music. Early Latin rock (approximately 1957–1968) is deemed as unoriginal, not "indigenous" enough or just not serious music. There is little documentation about Latin rock from this period, but of lots of people still remember the personalities and the music. My friend Tom Carr, who grew up in Honduras, remembers hearing a version of "Surfin' Bird" in Spanish on the radio. But I doubt you'll find out much about that in the *Latin American Music Review* or *Ethnomusicology*. In spite of being ignored by the critics and music scholars, these artists had a tremendous impact on popular tastes of the time and helped popularize rock 'n' roll throughout the Spanish-speaking world. These eager Mexican acts made the music their own and exported it. Teens in Argentina, Peru, Colombia and Venezuela regularly listened to rock on the radio *en español*, and many formed rock bands of their own.

By the late '60s, countless radio stations in Latin America had adopted American-style formats and were playing rock and pop in English as well as Spanish; it went from being a teen fad to a regular part of the entertainment industry. Even in authoritarian Cuba, Latin rock artists enjoyed immense popularity on nightly shows like *Nocturno*. Although the content and playlists were closely watched by the Cuban regime (the Beatles were prohibited, for example), *Nocturno* provided a vibrant soundtrack to the adolescents and teens of Cuba. Many emigrated to the United States and brought their memories with them, hence the heavy rotation of artists like Roberto Jordán on stations like Clasica 92 FM in Miami.

The station's Honduran-born programming director German Estrada compares what he airs today with what was on the air in his hometown of San Pedro Sula in the late '60s and early '70s. Estrada relies in part upon his listeners for programming suggestions as well as material for airplay instead of expensive playlists supplied by marketing corporations. In an interview with the Miami *New Times*, Estrada proclaims proudly "I don't need to do any research. I lived those years. It's hard to get these kinds of recordings, but the station has faithful listeners who bring me records from their own collections." A respectable programming philosophy for an oldies station whose target demographic is from 35 to 64 years old; the playlists include a wide range of songs, singers and styles from the '60s to the early '80s.

In my experience, most Anglo oldies stations suffice to play "Calendar Girl," "Chapel of Love" and "Teenager in Love" over and over each day with only a "Louie Louie" or a "Double Shot of My Baby's Love" thrown in every two weeks to appease people like me. Now, don't get me wrong, Clasica 92 plays a hefty share of gushy ballads, kitschy crooners, and ABBA's Spanish hits, but I often hear a great rock or bubblegum tune I had never been exposed to before, including those of the most prolific Mexican bubblegum artist, Roberto Jordán.

Roberto Jordán was born in Culiacán, Sinaloa, Mexico. In the late '50s and early '60s, Jordán sang for fun among gatherings of his friends. But his first job behind a microphone started before his singing career: at age 14 he got a job as a DJ on a Mexican radio station. His penchant for entertaining people grew, and he was encouraged by friends and people in the entertainment industry to go further.

Music teacher Enrique Okamura as well as producer and music teacher Eduardo Magallanes provided Jordán with Spanish arrangements of English pop hits. Okamura was pretty much the brains of the operation, having his name credited as a songwriter on the majority of Jordán's hits. Okamura also produced songs for Juan Gabriel, a former backup singer for Jordán who went on to greater success as an actor, romantic crooner and singer of boleros rancheros. Magallanes recently wrote a biography of Juan Gabriel called *Querido Alberto*. Unfortunately, there isn't much information about Okamura to be found out there, but his legacy lives on as the mastermind behind the bubblegum career of Roberto Jordán.

Jordán was to become part of the *"Nueva Ola"* (New Wave) of youth-oriented music that swept Mexico around 1968. The year 1968 is significant in Mexico (as in other countries), because it is perceived as a turning point in not only music, but in social values and attitudes. As in North America and Europe, the concerns of "youth" became an issue in itself. While some artists tried to pose as revolutionary agitators or starry-eyed protest leaders, others still spoke to the kids about the universal topic of love.

A lot of folks fondly remember *"Amor de Estudiante"* ("Student Love") a song Jordán made famous after the songwriter Enrique Rosa approached him with it. Jordán happened to be looking for more material to record, given his increasing success. This jangly, sticky-sweet number deals with typical teen subjects, puberty and summertime loves that are over with after the summer ends.

> *Es otoño los amantes ya se fueron* (It's fall and the lovers have left)
> *las hojas de los arboles cubren el campo* (the leaves of the trees cover the ground)
> *sus voces amorosas ya no se escuchan* (their lovely voices can't be heard anymore)
> *el verano ya se fue* (the summer is already gone)

"This song was like a hymn," says Omar Moenello of Miami. *"Algo quimico"* ("something chemical").

Numerous Spanish covers of English songs can be heard on Clasica 92, but Jordán's repertoire stands out because of the great number of covers taken directly from the halls of U.S. bubblegum. I asked Jesus Olivera, a 39-year-old Cuban-American, if he knew that Jordán was singing cover versions of songs that were already hits in the U.S. and elsewhere. "I used to listen to Roberto Jordán in Cuba because he had some popular songs in *Nocturno*, but not because I knew anything about 'bubblegum rock,'" Olivera says. "In fact, I didn't know he was copying existing rock songs, all the time I thought they were his. Only when I got to the U.S. in '74 did I realize other people had made those songs."

These covers include but are not limited to: *"El Juego de Simón"* ("Simple Simon Says," 1910 Fruitgum

Co.), *"1, 2, 3 Detente!"* ("1, 2, 3 Red Light," 1910 Fruitgum Co.), *"9-10 me quieres otra vez"* ("9-10, Let's Do It Again," 1910 Fruitgum Co.), *"Voy a meterme en tu corazón"* ("May I Take A Giant Step [Into Your Heart]," 1910 Fruitgum Co.), *"Mercy"* ("Mercy," Ohio Express), *"Castillos de Algodon"* ("1910 Cotton Candy Castle," 1910 Fruitgum Co.)

Jordán enjoyed a tremendous hit with *"El Juego de Simón."* Cuban-American Miami resident Nancy Elias remembers attending an outdoor concert in Havana's Parque Central when she was a little girl, around 1972. A live band was playing (she doesn't remember the name) and she stood with her family watching them. She began to cry during their performance. She remembers the band stopping and bringing her up to the microphone, asking her to say what was the matter. She exclaimed *"Quiero que me canten 'El Juego de Simón!"* (I want you to play me "Simple Simon Says"!) The band knew the song, and played it, to everyone's delight. As they started to perform their next number, little Nancy started to cry again. "I wanted them to play it over and over again" she recalls. They didn't play it again, but she still loves to hear the song over and over.

> *Voy a enseñarles algo que les gustará* (I'm gonna teach you something that you'll really like)
> *Es un juego facil de jugar* (It's a game that's easy to play)
> *Si quieren aprender el juego de Simón* (If you want to learn the game of Simon)
> *No necesita mas que corazón* (You need nothing more than your heart)
> *Se deben de formar* (You have to gather around)
> *Su pareja escoger* (And choose your partner)
> *Y sus ojos cerrar* (And you close your eyes)
> *No se deben de ver* (And don't you peek)
> *Comienzen a girar luego deben parar* (Start to spin around and then you stop)
> *Y los ojos ya podran abrir* (And then you can open your eyes)
> *Tal vez no sea la misma pero tu veras* (It might not be the same one, but you will see)

A la muchacha que toca a ti (The girl that ends up with you)
Le vas a preguntar (And then you'll ask her)
Quien se llama Simón (Who's named Simon)
Si te besa sabras (If she kisses you you'll know}
Quien te de el corazón (That she'll give you her heart)
  [organ solo]

El juego de Simón lo han aprendido yá (Now you've all learned the game of Simon)
Si lo juegan hallarán amor (And if you play it you will find a love)
Si acaso tienes novia llevala a jugar (In case you have a girl take her to play)
Cuando le beses dale el corazón (When you kiss her you give her your heart)

Jordán was backed up by Los Zignos, a group of Mexican studio musicians that shared similar musical interests. He also cut a few songs with the psychedelic group Los Dug Dug's (their apostrophe, not mine!). The Dug Dug's kicked off their career in 1966 with the single, *"Chicotito Si, Chicotito No"* which was used as the theme for a childrens' TV show in Mexico City, and the Dug Dug's appeared as the house band in a number of teen movies such as 1967's *El Mundo Loco de los Jovenes* (*The Crazy World of the Teenagers*).

A pleasing aspect of Jordán's songs is the ubiquitous presence of that unmistakable combo organ. A trained ear can identify the happy, fluty Farfisas and the deeper sounds of the classic Vox organ. Jordán's songs tend to be more organ-heavy than the originals. In his cover of "Na Na, Hey Hey, Kiss Him Goodbye" ("Na Na, Hey Hey, Adios"), he is accompanied by a particularly sick-sounding Vox Continental, giving it a much more far-out, ethereal sound than the overplayed original. And in "Como Te Quiero," Jordán turns Joe South's "Birds of a Feather" into a pure bubblegum classic, with a hearty dose of la-la-la-la-las with the organ playing the lead melody. I melt every time I hear the song. In his rendition of "If I Were A Carpenter" (*"Si Fuera un Mendigo"*) there's a cool guitar delay effect that makes it sound more like a Velvet Underground tune than the wimpy original.

Because of Roberto Jordán's everlasting gifts to the once-and-forever teens of the Spanish-speaking world, and to the world of bubblegum, he should not go unnoticed. Reissues of his material can be purchased from Amazon.com, or record stores specializing in Latin music should be able to order them.

Spanish is not a prerequisite to enjoy the bubblegum of Roberto Jordán. *¡No necesita mas que corazón!*

Other great covers sung by Jordán:

"Pronto seras mujer"
  ("Girl, You'll Be A Woman Soon,"
  Neil Diamond)
"Hazme una señal"
  ("Gimme Little Sign,"
  Brenton Wood)
"Libérame"
  ("You Keep me Hanging On,"
  Vanilla Fudge arrangement)
"La chica de los grandes ojos café"
  ("Brown-Eyed Girl,"
  Van Morrison)
  "Soy un creyente"
  ("I'm a Believer,"
  Neil Diamond/Monkees)
"Juntos esta noche"
  ("Let's Spend The Night Together,"
  Rolling Stones)
"Muchacha bonita"
  ("Cry Like a Baby," Box Tops)
"Juntos felices"
  ("Happy Together," Turtles)
"Mi confesion"
  ("Midnight Confessions,"
  Grass Roots) ◉

RELATED GENRES Black Bubblegum by James Porter

The Jackson Five were pioneers in ways no one really thinks about. When the Motown label released "I Want You Back" in the waning months of the '60s, the group was probably regarded as nothing more than five cute kids whom Diana Ross supposedly discovered, just another one of those novelty child acts that pop up every few years. As it turned out, they wound up with a #1 hit, bringing "The Motown Sound" up-to-date for the '70s. They spawned a host of imitators—suddenly every semi-talented pre-teen got a recording contract.

They also created an animal that had never previously existed: the black teen idol.

Since rock 'n' roll's '50s beginnings, there were heartthrobs on both sides of the color line. However, the fanmags weren't about to push Sam Cooke and Jackie Wilson over Caucasian wet dreams like Fabian. This was still the case by the time the Jackson Five turned up in 1969, The cast of *The Mod Squad* regularly appeared in the pages of *16* magazine, but it was the handsome white male lead who got the most play (the equally hunky black male and the white female lead were relegated to the back burner). Through careful planning and strategizing, Motown prez Berry Gordy sent the five Jackson brothers from Gary, Indiana boldly walking where no black performer had gone before. There had never been an African-American act marketed towards the predominantly white teenybopper market. Berry Gordy and the Jacksons saw an opening and rolled right through.

Being a black teen group was hardly anything unique. The Jackson Five had many predecessors, none of whom were marketed aggressively as sex symbols. When Frankie Lymon hit in the '50s with the Teenagers, several groups led by 13-year-olds invaded the local doo-wop scenes overnight (including Lewis Lymon and the Teenchords, featuring Frankie's little brother). There were other singers who were essentially R&B footnotes: Little Gary Ferguson, Henry Ford and the Gifts, Darrow Fletcher. Probably the most significant J-5 antecedents were the Five Stairsteps, from nearby Chicago, IL, who kicked off a series of soul hits in 1966 (only one of them crossed over to the pop charts: 1970's "Ooh Child"). However, the Stairsteps sang post-doo-wop love ballads that could have been sung by any adult group. The J-5 went straight for the bubblegum jugular.

The story of the well-traveled Jacksons has been covered in far greater detail, many times over. Cutting to the chase, their early (1968) singles on the Steeltown label—"You Don't Have To Be Over 21 To Fall In Love," "Big Boy" (a big hit on Chicago soul playlists), "Let Me Carry Your Books" (credited to the Ripples and Waves)—were very crude versions of the sort of thing they would later record for Motown. "You've Changed," the flip of "Big Boy," was re-recorded for *Diana Ross Presents the Jackson Five*. The Steeltown version was an obvious rip from a verse that originated with the Temptations' "Fading Away"—"you've changed and it's showing." The theft isn't as obvious on the Motown remake.

The J-5's records were a polite version of the Sly-influenced psychedelic soul that pervaded the Temptations' records during this period. Although the Jacksons later claimed that the Motown hit factory chained them to a formula, a chronological listen of their hits for that label shows that, in the years between '69 and '75, they made fairly quick progress. The earliest hits ("I Want You Back," "ABC," "The Love You Save," "Mama's Pearl") established a blueprint for the J-5 sound that others copied: the walking basslines, one-note guitar licks, sing-songy choruses. By '72, knowing full well they couldn't milk the same thing forever, Motown actually had them experiment with jazzy harmonies ("Looking Through the Windows," "Skywriter") before getting them in early on disco's ground floor ("Dancing Machine," "Forever Came Today").

Around the end of 1970, when it became obvious that the J-5 were a force to be reckoned with, the various tributes, parodies, and knockoffs started pouring in. The Osmond Brothers, five white kids from

Utah roughly the Jacksons' age, trucked on down to Muscle Shoals, AL, altered their name to the Osmonds, and had a hit the first time out with "One Bad Apple." Previously, the Osmond family were regulars on Andy Williams' variety show, pausing to release the occasional record, but "Apple" broke them wide open. (This was followed by "Double Lovin'" and "Yo-Yo", which were also in line with the J-5 sound.) Like the Jacksons, they too would go on to flirt with other genres (including a short-lived heavy metal phase), but not before temporarily invading the turf of the boys from Gary. ("One Bad Apple," written by renowned R&B songwriter George Jackson, was Top 10 on the black singles charts.)

After the Osmonds broke through, the "black bubblegum" sound was all over black radio in 1971 and the first half of '72. One of the first groups out of the chute was the Ponderosa Twins Plus One, who were literally two sets of twins (Alvin and Alfred Pellham, Keith and Kirk Gardner) plus a fifth member, Ricky Spicer. According to the liner notes of their lone album (2+2+1= *Ponderosa Twins Plus One*) on the Horoscope label (distributed by All Platinum), they had been together a whopping nine months by the time the LP was released. The album was built around a remake of Sam Cooke's "You Send Me." The Ponderosas' version was #12 on *Billboard*'s soul charts in the fall of '71. If the Jacksons had stayed behind in Gary, they would have sounded like this. The kids have the J-5 mannerisms down cold, albeit on a much

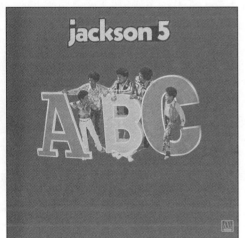

lower budget. One uncredited kid sounds like a very squeaky Michael, while the other lead vocalist takes Jermaine's role. Motown did a really good job of covering up the J-5's bum notes. If you listen closely, you can hear a drunken-sounding bass voice at the bottom of "Oh How Happy," which appeared on their generically-titled *Third Album*, but the off-key charms of the Ponderosas are on display for all to hear. "Mama's Little Baby" takes off from the old standard "Shortnin' Bread" with some Sly Stone "boom-boom-booms" thrown in for good measure. "Turn Around, You Fool" is copped directly from the J-5's "Never Can Say Goodbye." More than one song deals with true love in the face of stern parental disapproval. And for all that, the Ponderosa's album is one of the finest lost classics of the '70s. The J-5 rip-offs are obvious and abundant, but it's good trash, like hearing some suburban garage band in 1966 ape the Rolling Stones. When I hear the mesmeric "Bound"—which is as direct and emotionally blunt as its title—all critical perspective is gone. A year later, they limped to #40 on the soul charts with a remake of "Why Do Fools Fall In Love," the old Frankie Lymon doo-wopper. The production was cleaner this time, and they dropped the "Plus One" from their name (did they lose singer Ricky Spicer?). Not long after, they dropped out of sight altogether.

All Platinum soon struck gold again with Spoonbread, another adolescent vocal group, who charted in the R&B Top 40 with their hilarious version of "How Can You Mend A Broken Heart?" circa '72, on the Stang subsidiary. The lead singer was no Isaac Hayes, but he began the song with an opening rap worthy of Black Moses himself: "You know, I'd like to talk to the young folks for a minute. All the grownups can just turn their radios OFF, because I don't believe you understand what I'm talkin' about. You see, grownups don't believe that kids can fall in love—I mean REALLY, REALLY fall in love . . . grownups don't know what to tell me, so maybe all my friends out there can answer the question I've been axin' . . ." The lead singer then proceeds to render the Bee Gees' hit in a voice squeaky enough to have you believe this is the Ponderosas under a new name.

During the early '70s "black bubblegum" explosion, a surefire way to gain sympathy (". . . oh, aren't they CUTE!") was to remake an older song. Both the Ponderosa Twins and Jimmy Briscoe and the Little

Beavers took a crack at "Why Do Fools Fall In Love?" Brotherly Love, like the Ponderosas before them, reworked "Shortnin' Bread" as "Mama's Little Baby Loves Lovin'" (#20 in *Billboard*'s soul chart, circa '72). This was released on the Music Merchant label, owned by the trio of Holland-Dozier-Holland, former writer-producers at Motown, and probably an attempt to show up their former bosses, who were riding high with the real thing. In '71, the oddly named Chee-Chee and Peppy (Dorothy Moore and Keith Bolling, from Philadelphia) released an album on Buddah that not only contained their one hit ("I Know I'm In Love," #12 on the soul chart), but a smattering of oldies from the first rock era. (The duo, by now all grown up and with their Afros traded in for more conservative coifs, even made a reunion album in the '80s!) Lucky Peterson is now a known figure in the blues world, but in 1971 veteran blues singer/song-writer/bassist Willie Dixon produced Lucky's first single, "1-2-3-4." Lucky was then all of seven years old and a monster organist; the song itself was nothing more than James Brown's "Please Please Please" with new lyrics (which consist of Lucky counting to 12). The flip was a soul groover called "Good Old Candy," with Lucky's garbled voice praising his favorite junk foods and adding a JB scream where neces-sary. Originally released on Dixon's small Yambo label out of Chicago, this was soon leased to the bigger Today label, where it only made #40 on *Billboard*'s soul chart, but it managed to land Lucky on *The Ed Sullivan Show, Sesame Street* and other TV programs as a sort-of novelty act ("SEE THE SEVEN-YEAR-OLD KID PLAY BLUES ORGAN!").

Probably the strangest hit to come from this movement was "Love Jones," by Chicago one-hit-wonders the Brighter Side of Darkness (#3 soul/#16 pop, winter '72–73). The song was pri-marily a rambling monologue by 12-year-old Darryl Lamont, who claims that his love for his girl is "almost like that of a JUNKIE!" Be sure to catch the part where Lamont says his "jones" (period slang for a heroin addiction) made him flunk the big exam in Mr. Russell's class: "I was sittin' up starin' at you . . . and daydreamin'. . . ." Good thing Mr. Russell didn't call him up to the chalkboard—from the sound of his voice, he probably had a boner in his double-knit slacks, and then they would have SEEN his love jones, too! Later in 1973, comedians Cheech and Chong had a Top 20 pop hit with "Basketball Jones," a wicked parody that featured Cheech Marin, a Chicano from East L.A., in the guise of Tyrone Shoelaces, a black kid describing his love for basketball while George Harrison (guitar), Billy Preston (keyboards), and a host of other rock luminaries wailed on in support.

Not all the family (or pre-teen) groups from this era sang bubblegum, although its generally assumed that they did. The Sylvers, another family unit, were the Jackson Five's biggest rivals in black teen mags like *Right On* (put out by Laufer Communications, who also gave us *Tiger Beat*), but their earliest material (on the Pride label, an MGM subsidiary, circa 1972–74) was mostly written by brother Leon, and is far too aware and intelligent for "bubblegum." (But if it's great soul music you want . . .) Interestingly, they didn't have much crossover success until they switched labels in 1975 (from Pride to Capitol) and started dumbing down their lyrics for the disco era, resulting in "Boogie Fever," "Hot Line," "High School Dance," and others. However, 11-year old Foster Sylvers managed to get a hit with "Misdemeanor" in 1973 (#7 soul/#22 pop). Leon Sylvers obviously tailored this catchy number to the teenybop set, but as with the elder Sylvers' material from the same period, was far more substantial than anyone had a right to expect. The two oldest Sylvers sisters sang backup and got in some good lines, as well, particularly when they compare young Foster's heartbreak to "(running) a red light and (finding) yourself run over."

Five Great Black Bubblegum Classics That WEREN'T Influenced by The Jackson Five

by James Porter

INSTANT REACTION, Clarence Carter, 1969.
  Carter's recordings from the '60s and early '70s (including smashes like "Slip Away" and "Patches") are hallmarks of blues-based southern soul. More recently ('80s and '90s) he's become infamous for blues novelty records like "Strokin'" and "Grandpa Can't Fly His Kite"(". . . because Grandma won't give him no tail"). However, "Instant Reaction," from his 1969 LP *Testifyin'* (Atlantic) deserves mention in a book about bubblegum. Listen to it—either this was a demo for the Ohio Express that got routed to Carter by mistake, or else he was trying to snag the 13-year-olds on purpose. Written by Wayne Carson Thompson, whose songs, including "The Letter" and "Soul Deep," were regularly recorded by the Box Tops.

FLOY JOY, The Supremes, 1972.
  Skeptics like to believe that "Floy Joy" is proof that the Supremes were a low priority at Motown after Diana Ross left. Did composer Smokey Robinson write this with five minutes to kill till the session began? It may be a substandard record for a trio of fading '60s icons, but you'll be humming along with it before its over.

COOL AID, Paul Humphrey & the Cool Aid Chemists, 1971.

MR. PENGUIN, Lunar Funk, 1972.
  Bubblegum instrumentals . . . a neglected art. The organ on "Cool Aid" is closer to a merry-go-round than the Baptist church.

RAINY DAY BELLS, The Globetrotters, 1970.
  NBC actually had a *Harlem Globetrotters'* cartoon series (1970–'73), where not only were they road-managed by a elderly white lady known as "Granny," but they managed to moonlight as an R&B vocal group. There was an album and several singles released on the Kirshner label, including "ESP," where, over the piano solo, the lead singer asks his lover to guess what instrument is playing, and then wonders if she knows what he wants. A smoochy kiss noise follows. The best was probably "Rainy Day Bells," a stone-cold doo-wopper that features J.R. Bailey from the Cadillacs on lead vocals. This single is reportedly a hot item among East Coast harmony-group cultists, but it's got a definite Ron Dante pop appeal. ◉

True to bubblegum tradition, he followed this up with an oldies remake (Dee Clark's "Hey Little Girl"). He would join his older brothers and sisters in the Sylvers two years later, pausing to make the occasional solo record.

Other young groups got caught in the post-J-5 youthquake. Jimmy Briscoe and the Little Beavers, started off their career with a single of "Why Do Fools Fall In Love?" on Atlantic in 1971. But as their career progressed, with a series of records on the Pi Kappa label, this young Baltimore quintet aspired for the same style of make-out music pioneered by the Stylistics, Delfonics, Blue Magic, and other genre groups. Junior and his Soulettes were a self-contained brother-sister band from Oklahoma (aged from 6 to 10) who recorded the classic self-pressed *Psychodelic* [sic] *Sounds* album (1971) in their uncle's garage, but the music is closer to '60s garage-rock than anything the Jacksons spawned. Even Sister Sledge, when they first came on the scene in 1975, were tagged a "female Jackson Five." Sweet Sensation, from England, were closer to the mark—a self-contained band with an adolescent vocalist, whose one hit, "Sad Sweet Dreamer" (1975), featured banjo, a rare instrument on a soul record. Sophisticated black producers like Gamble and Huff probably would have sent the banjoist packing for Nashville, but it's heard to great, non-intrusive effect here, and may have helped it to cross over to the pop charts. Others who didn't quite crack the bank include Dexter Redding, the son of the late Otis Redding, who recorded a great single for Capricorn in 1973, "Love Is Bigger Than Baseball," which was backed with "God Bless," a touching tale (written by R&B eccentric Jerry Williams, Jr., aka Swamp Dogg) about a child who not only asks the Lord to bless mom and dad, but Huckleberry Hound, the Easter Bunny, Elmer Fudd, and a host of other celebrities. Marc Copage, who played Corey on the NBC series *Julia* (1968–'71), stepped up to the mike for a few forgettable 45s. In Chicago, there was Pat and Pam, a teen duo who wanted to record more adult material, but their dad (Lucky Cordell, a DJ at WVON, an influential black station in those days) wanted them to ride the J-5 gravy train. Two singles were issued—the better record was "I Love You, Yes I Do," on the Our Own label, which is required listening for any girl-group fan, and remarkably sophisticated for its type (I guess they reached some kind of compromise with Dad).

A disturbing piece of trivia: Wayne Williams, who was imprisoned in 1981 for allegedly killing numerous children in Atlanta, GA, was said to have been auditioning talented kids for a group called Gemini, which never got off the ground.

Quite a few adult records during this time used the Jackson Five blueprint. The Emotions were barely out of their teens themselves when they recorded "From Toys to Boys" (Volt, 1972). Ditto for the Newcomers' "Pin the Tail on the Donkey" (Stax, 1971) and the Sequins' "You Flunked Out" (flip side of "It Must Be Love," Crajon, 1973). Former Motown employees Holland-Dozier-Holland produced the Honey Cone's "Want Ads" (Hot Wax, 1971) and Freda Payne's "Cherish What Is Dear to You" (Invictus, 1972), both of which nailed that Jackson sound dead to rights. Even the Five Stairsteps got in on the act with "I Love You-Stop" (1971).

Parodies showed up in a few places: besides Cheech and Chong's "Basketball Jones," another comedy group called the Credibility Gap recorded "You Can't Judge a Hippie by His Hair" (1973), which took the piss out of the whole Jacksons / Osmonds sound in general. On the 1971 episode of *The Brady Bunch* where Peter's voice changes on the eve of a Bradys' recording session, one scene has Peter talking to a record producer in a control booth while five black kids in the background silently mill around in the studio. Who are they? The Five Monroes, a subtle dig at the Jackson Five. A TV commercial from about 1972 for Jiffy Pop popcorn featured a jingle that could only have been made possible by the J-5, while an interracial crew of middle-schoolers were shown dancing to it (and eating the popcorn) at a house party.

Over in Japan, where the Jacksons caused a furor when they toured in 1973, there was a group called the Finger 5. They apparently donned the same fringe-and-bell-bottom look that the Jacksons had in their heyday, and even went so far as to perm their hair in homage to their heroes! And when they weren't doing wah-wah soul songs like the J-5, they covered pop songs like "Heartbeat, It's a Lovebeat" (originally by Canada's own DeFranco Family) and the Monkees' "I'm Not Your Steppin' Stone." In Japanese. With a lead singer that sounded more like Michael Jackson than the kid from America's own Ponderosa Twins Plus One.

The initial rush that the Jacksons started came to a halt sometime around 1975. The Jacksons themselves continued to refine their sound through the years, which is why you know Michael Jackson today while Chee Chee and Peppy have been lost in time. On occasion, the sound would revive itself: New Edition kicked off their lengthy career with "Candy Girl" in 1983, while around the same time, a teen reggae band called Musical Youth hit the airwaves with "Pass The Dutchie," which might as well have been early J-5 with a Jamaican accent. During the late '80s and early '90s, there was another "black bubblegum" wave, with the Boys, Perfect Gentlemen, Another Bad Creation, and Kris Kross. (This time out, the role of the Osmonds was played by New Kids On The Block, a white group from Boston who had mild success on the black charts, due to their hip-hop image and pretensions. They were notable in that they were one of the few white teen acts Svengalied by a black producer, Maurice Starr.) And in an odd case of deja vu, Tito Jackson formed a group around his sons (3T) that never really made it, while one of the Osmonds also formed a group with *his* offspring, cashing in on that New Kids "teen group" fame. Most of these groups jockeyed for their share of the pie, with varying results. With the current success of Britney Spears and far too many boy bands to even think of, we're probably due for an African-American take on the same trend. Some producer is probably already working on a "Love Jones" or a Foster Sylvers soundalike for the new millennium.

Sunshine Pop by Chris Davidson

What can sunshine pop hope to prove in this evil, angry world? Sunshine pop—the effervescent song of rampant happiness. A thousand hummingbirds grooving to newly discovered nectar. The virginal essence of pop, wispy and white and skimmed off a cool vanilla milkshake to be infused with gleeful melody. The together timbre of the Association, the pleasing gum-snap of the Yellow Balloon, or—most perfectly—the dazzling choral layercake of the Cowsills. What chance do these sun-drenched sounds have with us moderns?

Those with the faintest longing for purity know well the uplifting—nay, the inspiring—power of this music. At its most blinding it matches bubblegum's oomph note for note. But not for sunshine pop the sexual subtext or nasal bleating: where bubblegum says, "I got love in my tummy," s-pop exclaims: "I love the flower girl." A fine line, to be sure. Over here one type of joyful noise, over there another. But darn it if sunshine pop isn't its own cheerful potpourri of twirling, exuberant arrangements and over-the-bra lovey-doveyness. Baroque pop, you ask? Not really, although the harpsichord features prominently at times, and an Old World flavor definitely pervades. Folk rock, then? Not quite, despite an acoustic drop cloth on which everything eventually lands. The balance is precarious. The peel of a harmonica or improper throaty vocal will snatch an otherwise frisky sunshine tune from your grasp and deposit it back into the standard 1960s pop camp.

Sunshine pop had a fling with the bestseller crowd in the mid-'60s—or, more correctly, light harmony pop did, for its lush harmonies and wistful themes approached but did not capture the oblique and melancholy X Factor of sunshine pop. Radio staples like "Younger Girl" and "Love (Can Make You Happy)" came close. Reams of sublime examples ducked beneath the charts. Bubbling under, the likes of the Sunshine Company's "I Just Want To Be Your Friend," the well-documented "The Grooviest Girl In The World," and "California My Way" by the Committee turned us gay with AM delight.

Some b-gum stars straddled both camps—the Archies' "Sugar and Spice" is sunbaked like Dennis Wilson's split ends. But sunshine pop is best discovered in the margins of bubblegum where the acknowledged luminaries took a backseat to a simplified (and remarkably moving) emotional milieu, an endless series of first dates and the blinding optimism of youth. Hit and flop alike, speak softly, and behold sunshine pop's gentlehearted best and brightest:

The Beach Boys

Traced directly to these rapturous lads, the roots of sunshine pop reside not so much with the over-played hits as with certain pre-*Pet Sounds* album cuts. The trick is the rich B. Wilson production, which piles high the harmonies—a central facet and key differentiator between straight surf vocal disks and the true sunny stuff. Sunshine pop is, after all, less about summer rock 'n' roll and more about the evocation of summer shadiness, a deli-cate point. A thousand harmony-laden master-pieces owe patent infringement damages to "In the Parking Lot" and especially "Let Him Run Wild."

The Association

Too freshman-year earnest after their first hits to qualify as mainstays of the movement, the Association delivered a superb first album—*And Then Along Comes The Association*—overseen by producer Curt Boettcher and featuring tight bursts of harmony pop shrapnel. Forgive the facial hair for their still-thrilling "Along Comes Mary."

The Cowsills

Optimism rock—family division. The vociferous Cowsill brood galvanized Rhode Island with the most gleaming pipes of all, a team of precision instruments tightly wound like a teenage

Magnificent Seven. After a few flop singles, the tribe exploded with towering, sun-basted material: "The Rain, The Park And Other Things," "Gray, Sunny Day," "We Can Fly," and, most euphoric of all, "All My Days," part of a Cowsills EP sponsored by the American Dairy Association (fully one-sixth of tiny R.I.'s milk supply is suspected to have been consumed by a Cowsill).

The Bee Gees

Happy in spurts amidst ever-present (but very welcome) pensiveness, the Bee Gees mastered the pop form while still teens. The early Australian recordings point skyward while simultaneously staring down and come extremely close to sunshine pop without fully capitulating. Still, brothers in lock-step harmony singing about butterflies says include them with an asterisk. Said "Butterfly" is a good place to begin. "Cherry Red" and "Spicks and Specks" receive extra points for overcoming the Euro-sunshine curse, as relatively few overseas pals convincingly linked up with this sound (is it even possible to be truly happy outside of the U.S.?). Yes, the Hollies came a breadth away with "Everything Is Sunshine."

Yellow Balloon

Gary Zekley, SoCal insider and one of many budding maestros orbiting the Wilson camp mid-decade, found chart fame producing the Clique's "Sugar On Sunday" and writing hits for the Grass Roots. Of his earlier work, this delicious '67 album typifies the airy and upbeat mini-Spector density found on the most atmospheric s-pop. The Yellow B.'s self-titled theme song was also cut by a Jan-less Jan and Dean on the lost, but since rediscovered, *Save For A Rainy Day* LP. No better full-length specimens of sunshine pop exist.

The Ballroom / Sagittarius / Millennium

Surfacing soon after his association with the "Along Comes Mary" crew, Curt Boettcher launched a harmony steamship with a trio of worthy vessels. In quick succession, the Ballroom gave way to the Gary Usher-led Sagittarius which sired the stud-filled Millennium. Boettcher wrests symphonic miracles on cut after cut of California vapor-pop.

The Vision

"Small Town Commotion" b/w "Keepin' Your Eyes On The Sun" (UNI). Top side, a complex weaving tale of a fiery municipal disaster. The flip provides a luscious Gary Zekley artifact (produced under the *nom du rock* Yodar Critch), a perfectly realized distillation of July using girl backup, harps and a driving beat. Zeke's command: walk with me awhile and smile.

Wind

"Make Believe" b/w "Groovin' With Mr. Bloe" (Life). Uplifting melodious bubblegum masquerading as a Four Seasons-like beat ballad. Joey Levine involvement. Slice off the harmful instrumental flip side, and a sun is born.

The Pleasure Fair

"Morning Glory Days" b/w "Fade In Fade Out" (UNI). Add one more entry to David Gates' long cool-guy resume. Gee-whiz harmony with light orchestral fanfare, like a very white Fifth Dimension (perhaps the Fourth Dimension in disguise).

Hyle King Movement

"Flower Smile" b/w "Forever 'N Ever" (Liberty). Atmospheric swirl akin to Sergio Mendes harmonizing in a hot-house garden—plus decidedly hippie sentiments told in a deliciously un-hippie manner.

BUBBLEGUM INVADES THE MEDIA Krofft Rock by Becky Ebenkamp

They rival Sherwood Schwartz' yen for storytelling. They match Pete Townshend's propensity for composing multiple movements. Yes, a Sid & Marty Krofft theme song is a wondrous thing to behold—as fun as a tipsy talking party hat and more multifaceted than the eyeballs of Seymour the furry orange spider. Krofft Rock and bubblegum music have more in common than their shared target of youthful audiences. For one thing, each has been charged, perhaps unfairly, with embedding secret, counter-culture messages into the material. While bubblegum has long been linked with sexual metaphors, psychedelic Krofft shows supposedly contained stoner signifiers. In their heyday, rumors circulated that the H.R. in Pufnstuf stood for "Hand Rolled" and that *Lidsville* was built around a one-note pot reference.

The similarities don't stop there. Anyone who believes it's a stretch to lump a group of wildly imaginative children's shows in with the oeuvre of the Ohio Express and the Archies should consider Exhibit B, the blatant songwriter swapping: Michael Lloyd (the West Coast Pop Art Experimental Band, Cattanooga Cats), Wes Farrell (the Partridge Family), Danny Janssen (Josie & the Pussycats, Scooby-Doo, the Brady Bunch) and Bobby Hart (the Monkees, Boyce & Hart) each wrote material for at least one Krofft show.

It is said that sounds and smells are the best senses for invoking a feeling. But any songwriter intending to match note-for-note the visual intensity of a kaleidoscopic Krofft fantasy world certainly had his work cut out for him. Following are a pair of soundtracks that were aurally on par with the shows they accompanied.

Pufnstuf (Capitol, 1970)

Over the life of the 1969-'70 [33] *H.R. Pufnstuf* TV series and movie, songs were devised to showcase star Jack Wild's predilection for overly gesticulating his way through hammy, stage-style tunes. This is evident even in the show's opening sequence, where his character Jimmy is dredged to the shore by Puf's Rescue Rangers. Waterlogged and appearing inches from death, he forgoes CPR, breaking free and breaking into a little soft shoe for the camera, exhibiting his patented "gotta sing, gotta dance" Broadway boy vibe. James Brown would be proud.

But one has to give Wild credit. Unlike the majority of British Invaders, the former Artful Dodger—along with Davy Jones and Herman's Hermits frontboy Peter Noone—knew how to fully exploit his Cockney roots. While cronies pledged allegiance to the American acts they adored by aping their non-accents, Wild defied the colonies by refusing to properly pronounce his Rs and thereby upped his status a notch or two on the teenybopper totem pole.

Still, except for the Mechanical Boy episode—which most fans recall and fondly so—tunes for the TV show tended toward the bland and unmemorable. Comprised mostly of olde tyme Shakey's Pizza

---

33. Repeats of the 17 original *Pufnstuf* episodes also aired during the 1970-71 season.

Parlor-type numbers with a spoonful of self-help-era lyrics, they served as vehicles for Wild's Limey charm. Then there were throwaways like "Oranges, Shmoranges," noteworthy only because it was performed by Witchiepoo and her band of monsters in one episode. Also worth mentioning is the more rockin' and soulful closing theme interpreted by poultry puppet act the Boyds.

Songs for the *Pufnstuf* film—composed by Charles Fox (music) and Norman Gimbel (lyrics) and released on vinyl—were another thing entirely. Oh sure, many of them still gave Jimmy an excuse to break out into a rousing chorus with the googley-eyed puppet people he encountered on his journey, but even the most upbeat tunes were more melodious than those written for the TV show. Some are even downright pensive. The title song is a salute to Jimmy's large-headed protector ("You're a dear little dragon/You're a personal pal/When my spirits are draggin'/Whose tail is waggin' friendly?"). Harmonica-drenched "I've Found a Friend in You" serves as an ode to Freddy the Flute and later in the film, Puf.

While most songs sound large-scale in instrumentation, a closer listen reveals that orchestration is kept to a minimum, for maximum effect. Such as on "I'm a Boy." A Nilsson-y harmonica and an acoustic guitar line that rivals anything Jagger/Richards wrote for Marianne Faithfull complement the wistful, aspirational anthem, which is sung by Wild as the camera glides over fall foliage during the film's opening credits. Those lazy Rs seem less gimmicky in the heartfelt haikus, which detail pre-Puf'd Jimmy's dreams of transcending the trappings of childhood:

> If I could I would be
> A giraffe ["giwaffe," actually]
> With my head above the trees
> So at big parades
> I could see
> If I could
> If I could I would be
> Old and wise
> Knowing all there is to know
> Then I'd answer right
> Every time [voice appropriately cracking]
> When they ask

You can almost smell the trees circling above in one effective shot where the camera peers up at Wild and his surroundings, making him appear ten feet tall. And finally, Mama Cass Elliot—as Witchiepoo rival Witch Hazel in the film—belts out "Different," a song that purports to elicit sympathy for the misunderstood witches' condition while also teaching kids to make their own kind of music:

> When I was smaller and people were taller
> I realized that I was different
> I had a power that set me apart
> I learned to take it and used it to make it
> It's not so bad to be different
> To do your own thing and do it with heart
> Different is hard
> Different is lonely
> Different is trouble for you only
> Different is heartache
> Different is pain
> But I'd rather be different than be the same

It's hard to imagine whether this tune would have soared so had it not been relayed through the clarity of Cass' confident pipes; nor was there an artist who could sing the lyrics with more conviction.

The Bugaloos (Capitol, 1970)

Joy, Courage, Harmony and IQ — the fantastical foursome known collectively as the Bugaloos — promoted the beauty of nature and touchy-feely '70s platitudes in a very *Jonathan Livingston Seagull* sort of way. So powerful was the Bugaloos' message, it was rumored at the height of their popularity that the insect quartet's actors released a bedridden child from her terminal illness via the sheer power of suggestion.

Songs — again courtesy of the Fox/Gimbel team — were much better than they needed to be for a Saturday morning TV show and companion record, which children, naturally (and sacrilegiously) would proceed to scratch the hell out of. Up with (wee) people!, the tunes seemed to say. The bouncy "Believe" preaches that "bein' down is out of style": "Believe/Frowns are reserved for circus clowns/Believe/Smilin' will pick you up from the ground/Cuz only the lucky ones/Are those who can." Like most of the songs, which were re-recorded for the album, the tune's musical arrangement is reminiscent of the Sound Gallery, a British E-Z Listening production team that was popular at the time, while the breezy boy-girl singing brings to mind Enoch Light vocal experiment the Free Design.[34]

This dynamic is perfected on "Fly Away With Us," whose beautiful weirdo lyrics make it sound like the perky pests are trying to lure kids into an LSD trip or some Eastern-inspired cult: "You can keep in touch with reality/There's no need to leave it behind," they assure, noting that one also needn't worry about "The spinning and spinning/Beginning to feel the tranquility live in your mind." Apparently, that's because "The spinning will stop/As you're nearing the top/Of the meaning of the Bugaloos."

Whatever, it's still a solid, hummable song. The standout cut, "Senses of Our World," which borrows its ambient surround-sound from Phil Spector and combines with vocals that evoke Nico's hauntingly stilted phrasing from "All Tomorrow's Parties" and other Velvet Underground tunes for an effect that is both warm and chilling at the same time. "If you listen/To the sound/That surrounds us," Joy sings, a Bugaloo boy joining her with each subsequent line. "You'll discover/That you're never/Quite alone/Hear the Earth/And the sky/Say they love you/And they're happy that you're here to share their home." The crescendo then bursts into a chorus that urges listeners to "Take the time to taste the honey" among other things in life. This is what Prozac sounds like.

Other Krofft records

H.R. Pufnstuf: Kellogg's (mail-away offer) 45 rpm cereal box record featuring 10 songs from the series, 1970; Unlicensed single, "Pufnstuf" + three other tunes, Mr. Pickwick, 1970

Bugaloos: "For a Friend"/"Senses of Our World" single, Capitol, 1970

Sigmund & the Sea Monsters: Johnny Whitaker *Friends* album, Chelsea Records, 1973

The Krofft Supershow: *Kaptain Kool and the Kongs* album, Epic Records, 1978. ◉

---

34. The group recorded a half dozen or so albums for the producer's Project 3 imprint.

The Brady Bunch by Lisa Sutton

It may be hard for someone under the age of 30 to believe, but television and pop music have a relationship that pre-dates MTV. From the time Ricky Nelson debuted his "Walking" single on *The Adventures of Ozzie and Harriet* it became obvious that a weekly sitcom was the perfect marketing tool for record sales.

One of television's all-time favorite families, *The Brady Bunch* was part of the tube-to-vinyl crossover. Although music was not part of their original plan, a change came when *The Partridge Family* moved in next door on ABC's Friday night lineup during the Brady's second season. Fueled by weekly performances in the living rooms of millions, the Partridges' first LP was an instant chart topper. Folks over at the Brady camp took notice and agreed that an album was a potentially profitable idea.

Paramount Records sent their in-house producer, Tim O'Brien, into the studio with Greg, Peter, Bobby, Marcia, Jan and Cindy for a whirlwind two-day recording session which resulted in *Merry Christmas from The Brady Bunch*. A cyclone of promotion accompanied the November 1970 release of the LP including trade ads, features in *Tiger Beat* and in-store appearances in Southern California record stores. Appearances on *The Merv Griffin Show* and *American Bandstand* followed.

Over the next few months, music became a regular part of being a Brady. Barry Williams began taking voice lessons and returned to the studio with O'Brien to lay down tracks for a never-completed solo album. Eve Plumb also went solo at this time, recording the pensive "How Will It Be" and silly "Fortune Cookie Song" with her producer father, Neely Plumb. The a-side was a sort of cross between Frank Sinatra's "It Was A Very Good Year" and Zager & Evans' "In the Year 2525," with provocative lyrics like ". . . how will it be when I'm 25, will I still be alive?"

Big things were ahead for the Brady Six as they got together to record their next LP, *Meet the Brady Bunch*. Jackie Mills, fresh from gigs with Bobby Sherman and Davy Jones, was recruited to produce the LP. Familiar fare like "Me and You and a Dog Named Boo" and a vocally-challenged version of "American Pie" graced the grooves of this platter alongside Brady originals "We Can Make The World a Whole Lot Brighter" and "Time To Change."

The album was released in early 1972 to coincide with the airing of the episode where the kids are ready to make a record just as Peter's voice starts to change. Promotional singles went out to radio stations as well as point-of-purchase posters proclaiming "Time to Change" their "new hit single."

By now, the Brady Kids were nearing idol status with their pre-teen audience. Around the time their first single hit the shelves, the Bunch was invited to sing at the Associated Guild of Variety Artists Awards in Las Vegas. They eagerly accepted the challenge, and their live act was born. Regular rehearsals began and the Brady Kids played to their first paying audience in May of 1972 at the San Bernardino Swing Auditorium. The next year and a half was spattered with appearances on the state-fair circuit across the country.

In the summer of '72, it was back to the studio to record *The Kids From The Brady Bunch*. The LP cover featured their newly rendered cartoon images from their animated series, *The Brady Kids*, which would debut that fall. Each of the cartoon episodes (which were created by the same folks at Filmation responsible for *The Archies* and *The Groovie Ghoulies*) featured a shortened version of a track

from one of the albums. *The Kids From the Brady Bunch* album featured more of their must-be-heard-to-be-believed cover tunes such as "Saturday in the Park" and "Love Me Do." It also proudly sports their best-known song, "It's a Sunshine Day."

The Bradys were wreaking polyester havoc, performing to hordes of screaming fans wherever they went. From state fair to state fair they performed in costumes that only could have been hatched in the '70s. Brightly colored synthetic granny dresses for the girls were matched by the boys' flammable slacks and dress shirts. Purple flowered outfits came at the first costume change, and colorful fringed and beaded jumpsuits were worn for the finale.

Near the end of their touring, the sextet went to the studio to record their final group effort, *The Brady Bunch Phonographic Album*. Paramount Pictures was ready to release its film *Charlotte's Web*, and returning producer Jackie Mills picked two songs from the soundtrack—"Charlotte's Web" backed with "Zuckerman's Famous Pig"—for the album's first single. The Brady kids dropped in on several screenings of the movie to do a little cross-promotion and signed copies of the picture sleeve 45s for those lucky enough to be in the audience.

At this time, Mills brought Maureen McCormick (Marcia, Marcia, Marcia!) into the studio to record a trio of solo singles. "Love's In The Roses," the first of the three, actually received a fair amount of airplay in several California markets. As the eldest of the Brady girls, Maureen/Marcia was the recipient of a large amount of fan mail. Chris Knight was also receiving sacks of mail, surpassing his Brady brothers as idol of choice. Because of public interest, the two were coupled for *Chris Knight and Maureen McCormick*, a collection of dueling solo tracks buttressed with a pair of duets. Released after the tour had ended, the LP received little support from the label and quickly vanished.

With the live show a thing of the past, Barry Williams broke off to do a sans-Bunch act. Chris Knight gladly retired his vocal cords and Maureen contemplated her own solo future. The remaining Bradys (Susan Olsen, Eve Plumb and Mike Lookinland) stuck together for a while, planning a tour as the Brady Three. A never-completed album was begun, featuring Susan's pick-hit, "Porcupine Pie." Mike Lookinland also branched off to record a song for Capitol Records called "Gum Drop"/"Love Doesn't Care Who's In It" with Eve's producer-dad at the helm.

The Brady Bunch reached the end of its five-year run at the close of the 1973–'74 season, but that wasn't the end of the Bradys' music. The legendary *Brady Bunch Variety Hour* was jam-packed with all the great hits of the disco era in a carbon copy of the *Donny and Marie Show*. The Bradys doing "Shake Your Booty" on national television provided the epicenter for the lowest point of the entire decade. Not surprisingly, the following Brady reunions and revisitations were music-free.

More than 30 years after the debut of *The Brady Bunch*, the show remains as popular as ever. More so, it has become the pinnacle of pop-culture crossovers. TV, stage, cinema, print and musical media all have played host to the fictional family that never goes away.

No Gum Chewing On The Bus, Please by Lisa Sutton

The 1970 fall television line-up was a great one when it came to music. *Lawrence Welk* and *Hee Haw* aside, weekly doses of *This Is Tom Jones* and *The Glen Campbell Goodtime Hour* were enough to keep lovers of contemporary music tapping their toes in prime time. Saturday mornings were also high on the tuneful trend, as shows like *The Bugaloos, The Double Deckers, The Hardy Boys* and *Lancelot Link, Secret Chimp* all spawned their own musical soundtracks. Not surprisingly, one of the most popular debuts of the season was *The Partridge Family*, a musical sitcom that was born of the sentiment that "a family that plays together, stays together."

As absurd as the premise sounds today, the story of five musical kids recording pop albums with their mom was based in reality. Originally, *The Partridge Family* was to be *The Cowsill Family*. Show creator Bernard Slade had actually come up with the idea for a singing family in the late '60s, but it took the success (and vaporizing) of *The Monkees* to interest Columbia Pictures Television in the idea. Once the yet-to-be-titled series was in development, Slade caught a performance of the Cowsills on *The Tonight Show* and decided to develop the show around the singing siblings and their Mom.

It wasn't long before the Cowsills found themselves out of the picture. Right off the bat, those developing the show didn't like patriarch and former military-man, Bud Cowsill. It was no coincidence that it was soon decided to make the TV mother of five a widow. Although the folks from Columbia spent over a month observing the Cowsills, they always figured on casting real actors in the lead roles. Oscar-winning actress Shirley Jones (and her blonde Barbara Cowsill coif) were hired to star as Mom, and a cast of juvenile unknowns of various hair colors were brought in to play her brood.

From the start, the cross-marketing geniuses at Columbia intended to release albums, à la The Monkees. The pilot was shot in the fall of 1969 and featured two songs recorded specially for the show by studio musicians: "Together (Havin' A Ball)," and a Neil Sedaka/Carol Sager-penned Monkees leftover called "Let The Good Times In." John and Tom Bahler of the Love Generation had recorded this ditty in 1969, and were the musical arrangers of a dead-to-nuts re-record for the pilot with the "Penny Lane"-esque piccolo trumpet of the original replaced by the soprano "buh-duh-duh-dum-dum-dums" of Shirley Jones.

Together with the Bahler Brothers, uncredited Monkees' background singer Ron Hicklin and session diva Jackie Ward became the voices of the Partridge Family. When the series was picked up, Wes Farrell (who formerly had produced the Cowsills' LPs) was brought in to produce the first Partridge Family album, cleverly titled *The Partridge Family Album*.

With the singers in place, Farrell went about securing some of the best-known studio musicians in town to lay down the backing tracks. Hal Blaine, Joe Osborne, Max Bennett, Larry Knechtel, Mike Melvoin, Tommy Tedesco, Larry Carlton, Louis Shelton and Dennis Budimir were among the musical wizards who played musical Cyranos to Keith, Laurie, Shirley, Danny, Chris and Tracy. Their resumes were impressive, including backing sessions for the Association, the Beach Boys, the Grass Roots, the Fifth Dimension, the Mamas and the Papas, and (surprise!) the Monkees. To complete the team, Farrell (who himself had composed "Hang On Sloopy" and "Come A Little Bit Closer") employed a

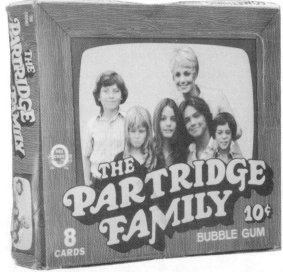

bevy of Brill Building graduates, including Barry Mann & Cynthia Weil, Tommy Boyce & Bobby Hart, Carole King & Gerry Goffin, Tommy West & Terry Cashman to pen the tracks.

The Partridge Family began shooting in early spring of 1970 after the network ordered 16 episodes. Shirley Jones was slated to sing backup on the albums, while the rest of the singing ensemble memorized tracks for lip-synching. Idol-in-waiting David Cassidy was hired to play 15-year-old lead singer Keith Partridge. Aside from being Shirley's real-life stepson, Cassidy had already been making a splash on the covers of teen magazines, spurred by guest appearances in *The Mod Squad*, *Adam-12* and *Bonanza*. When asked to mouth the words, Cassidy pointed out that he was not just a pretty face, but could sing as well. Although he dutifully mimed to the Bahlers' vocals in the first few episodes, Farrell and show execs agreed that it would only be an improvement to have him sing his own parts long before the series' September premiere.

The result was a pop music explosion that was heard all the way from Hollywood to Hong Kong. David's lead vocal on the song "I Think I Love You" was solid, and the track was released a month before the show's debut in an effort to create a buzz. And buzz it did. The song began a slow climb up the charts, buoyed by a live appearance by Cassidy on *American Bandstand* and other shows, lip-synching to his own voice. By the time the song appeared on the series (in the 6th episode) it was already in the Top 20, hitting #1 on *Billboard*'s Hot 100 on November 21st. It went on to sell a staggering four million copies.

Friday night became the original "must-see TV" night for teens and pre-teens. *The Brady Bunch*, *Nanny & The Professor*, *The Partridge Family*, *That Girl* and *Love American Style* could not be beaten by the action programming on the other two networks. (Not such a difficult feat; when *The Partridge Family* debuted, it was up against *The Name of the Game* and a forgotten Andy Griffith vehicle called *The Headmaster*.) Kids would crowd around their televisions every week to watch the comic and musical antics of the Partridges. Girls swooned over Keith's magnificent coif, boys wished they were as funny as Danny, and just about all of them dreamed of starting their own band.

Because the show was targeted at younger viewers, there was an instant stigma surrounding the music. The term "bubblegum" was slapped onto it immediately, mostly because the show's performers were moppets themselves. In truth, the music of *The Partridge Family* was far more akin to the middle-of-the-road music of the day. With few exceptions (like "Baby I Love, Love, Love You" and "Somebody Wants to Love You") the songs were geared toward adult tastes, as ten-year-olds clearly couldn't grasp the true meanings of "I Can Feel Your Heart Beat" or "One Night Stand." Andy Williams and Perry Como must have agreed, as they both covered "I Think I Love You" in the early '70s. Of course, to the kids of the day, that was not exactly a favorable endorsement.

Parents did enjoy the show, but kids were consumed with *The Partridge Family*, which rapidly became a full-fledged phenomenon. Along with the weekly songs performed on TV, Partridge Family albums were released at a rapid-fire rate of one every six months. On top of that, David Cassidy himself had a meteoric ascent to the top of the teen-idol heap, kicking Bobby Sherman's squeaky-clean derriere off the throne. Farrell had negotiated for first right of refusal on producing the P-Fam actors on any solo endeavors, and it wasn't long before David Cassidy LPs were being squashed out, in between the Family releases.

As the record sales proved highly profitable, David began performing live concerts on weekends to promote both himself and the show. Cassidy soon became the most in-demand live performer on the planet. An impossible schedule evolved as David would tape the shows during the day, record in the studio at night, and jet across the US on weekends to sing for thousands of screaming, hormonal teenagers and their very frightened parents.

Over the course of the show's four-year run, the Partridge Family released eight studio albums and two greatest hits packages for Bell Records. David released four as a solo artist (in addition to a PF/DC hits compilation). Although they were dispensed to the public as rapidly as humanly possible, each effort was produced with the finest quality musicianship, composition and production that early '70s technology had to offer. As the catalog grew, the show also progressed and evolved, creating a large volume of ultimately very palatable pop.

Initially, with *Album* (the first LP) Farrell would double-track Cassidy's vocals as well as speeding them up a notch to create a more youthful lead vocal. (After all, Keith Partridge was supposed to be 16. David sounded too much like a 19-year-old for Farrell's taste.) This technique was used on the second LP, *Up To Date* as well, though Farrell did throw David a bone, letting him include his first self-penned tune, "Lay It On The Line." Shirley Jones was singing backup as originally contracted, though she is inaudible after the fourth album, *Shopping Bag*.

In 1971, at the height of their popularity, the Partridge Family released their *Abbey Road, Sound Magazine*. Had there not been a television show called *The Partridge Family*, this album would have been heralded as one of the best pop albums of the decade. Not that it didn't do well. *Sound Magazine* sold over a million copies, and is considered their best by most fans of the Partridge Family's music. If there had been a Grammy award for best use of the harpsichord, this album would have won by a landslide. Since it was merely a TV-driven, commercial effort, it languished as a guilty pleasure, even if the coolest of cats, Sammy Davis, Jr., had the record in his collection.

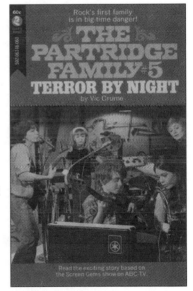

David's solo albums were recorded using many of the same musicians and songwriters as the Partridge platters, though they lacked the harmonic qualities of the Family. His first solo album *Cherish* was standard, breathy, pop vocal material. David was allowed to show his bluesy side on the second solo release. *Rock Me Baby* had a grittier edge than any of his previous vocal efforts as well as some more daring material sonically and lyrically. Even more experimental was his third LP, *Dreams Are Nothing More Than Wishes*, which was a huge seller in England, coinciding with David's second world tour.

While Farrell was up to the task of producing LPs for David, he passed on opportunities to record with the other solo Partridges. Shirley Jones recorded a couple of singles for Bones Howe that were released on Bell, and daring Danny Bonaduce, who never sang on the show (except to warble "M-e-e-e-e-e-ry Christmas" on the holiday episode) recorded his very own LP for Lion Records in 1973. (Apparently Bell Records had certain standards at the time.) There were two singles released from this slice of '70s-ana, the most overdubbed LP in history. "Dreamland" and "Blueberry You," thankfully, did not chart or appear on the TV show. Although the LP was relegated to the $1 bins at Salvation Armies for most of the '70s and '80s, *Tiger Beat*'s sister magazine *Fave* gave it a better review than Paul McCartney's *Red Rose Speedway*. We're so sorry, Uncle Albert, indeed.

In 1974, those girls on Venus finally had their chance to get their share of the Partridge Family when CBS aired the cartoon *The Partridge Family 2200 A.D.* This *Jetsons*-inspired, Hanna-Barbera creation took the Partridges of the prime time series and placed them in the future, playing intergalactic gigs and getting into typical Saturday morning cartoon adventures. Using the voices of the original cast (sans David and Shirley), each episode was interspersed with tunes created by the generic studio players at HB. None of these songs were released on album, as the live-action P-Fam was still releasing their own material.[35]

35. The albums *Notebook, Crossword Puzzle* and *Bulletin Board*.

As baffling as the concept of the Partridge Family in outer space was, an even more puzzling transformation had occurred on the prime time *Partridge Family*. David Cassidy had announced that he was ready to leave the show, and the producers began ushering in possible replacements. The first to appear was little four-year-old Ricky Seagall. Cute as a bug, Ricky was brought in to breathe new life into the show; curiously, it's impossible to find a person to take credit for the decision today. The demise of *The Partridge Family* is generally credited to the power of its cross-network rival, *All In The Family*, though weekly warbling from this kiddie crooner contributed to the fall, as he was no replacement for David. Ricky Seagall was treated to his own solo Bell LP, which, in conjunction with Rodney Allen Rippy's *Take Life A Little Easier*, were rumored to be a major contribution to the demise of the entire label.

As the television show ran its course, so went the musical Partridge Family. With no shows to write songs for, there was no need to create music, especially with each LP release dropping in sales successively. *The Partridge Family* went into reruns, and the albums soon were unilaterally cut out. Dance and disco music became the wave of the future, and although the Partridge Family music was beautifully crafted, melodic and easy on the ears, it was suddenly miserably dated.

Fortunately, time heals all wounds, and disco music is now a more painful memory than the red velvet costumes of the Partridge Family. Retro is all the rage, and it is once and for all safe to admit you like harpsichords and five-part harmonies. The music sounds better than ever on compact disc, and is a lasting artifact of a time when well-crafted, harmonic pop music could still make you happy.

Hanna-Barbera by Becky Ebenkamp

While the studio may not garner the type of respect reserved for animation behemoths Disney and Warner Brothers, indisputably, Hanna-Barbera rules the cartoon kingdom in one contest: the battle of the bands. Sure, *The Alvin Show* may have technically invented the animated music video, and Filmation proved a worthy competitor in the '70s with *The Brady Kids* and *The Archies*. But per cartoon capita, HB gave us the most rock 'n' roll bang for our buck, serving up more beat-crazed bands—both of the real and imaginary variety—than you could shake a tambourine at. The result: instant bubblegum.

The Impossibles (1966) were HB's first experiment with a full rock 'n' roll concept cartoon, although rarely was more than a line or two of lyric heard before these superheroes-masquerading-as-pop-stars were summoned to go fight crime via a TV monitor in Coil Man's guitar. The shaggy-haired trio married a jangly Rickenbacker-type sound with generic teenybopper lyrics, an effect that rendered them a less contemplative Beau Brummels. Songs are hooky, but these snippets are unsatisfying, and one gets the sense that full songs were never penned. Case in point, the lyrics to "Caesar's Place":

> Let's go to Caesar's Place, Let's go to Caesar's Place
> Let's go to Caesar's Place, Let's go to Caesar's Place
>   (Refrain)

Get the picture?

A year after Gram Parsons introduced the Byrds to the pedal steel guitar, the Cattanooga Cats were busy adding some country flavor to Saturday morning TV. Scoots, Country, Groove and go-go girl Kitty Jo didn't solve any crimes, but as a band on constant tour they were presented with many a wacky adventure to sing their way out of. But while the Cats' look and accents clearly originated below the Mason-Dixon line, their music was pure pop, with song duties handled by singer/songwriter Michael Lloyd, who headed psychedelic cult faves The West Coast Pop Art Experimental Band, Smoke and October Country. Peggy Clinger of recording group the Clinger Sisters[35] handled Kitty Jo's vocals and wrote material as well. Producer of the project: Mike Curb.[36] Lloyd and Clinger didn't need any help rattling off perfect three-minute pop songs in even less time, so HB's relatively hands-off strategy paid off. Furthermore, songs penned and performed by the youthful musicians—Lloyd was 17 at the time—instead of hacks trying to knock off *Billboard* hits lent the project a credible vibe and allowed for the dissemination of cryptic counter-culture messages like free love and non-conformity, as witnessed in the winning theme song:

> The Cattanooga Cats don't go meow, wouldn't try if they knew how
> They're doin' their thing

The idea that this was going to be something special is relayed fully in the show opener, where the song is paired with animation master Iwao Takamoto's strobe like series of op art images and shots of the kitty cat group playing their instruments to a psychedelic light show. In the children's-game-as-metaphor-for-love songwriting subgenre, the Cats' "Mother May I" and "Alle Alle Oxen Free" stand up to "Simon Says," "1, 2, 3 Red Light" or any other 1910 Fruitgum Company song for that matter. In the latter, Lloyd's breathy vocals imbue the lyrics and bouncy organ with a deliciously dangerous, dirty feel:

---

35. With her sister Debra—who'd play Superchick on *The Krofft Supershow* a decade later.
36. The resume of California's future Lt. Gov. included production credits for Davie Allan & the Arrows, the Everpresent Fullness and a slew of exploitation movie soundtracks on Sidewalk Records, Curb's Capitol Records subsidiary.

Hey little girl starin' down at me, from your window can't you see
It's gonna be a groovy day, why don't you come out and play
Alle Alle Oxen Free, c'mon run on home with me
Just be nimble and be quick, we're gonna jump the candlestick

Eleven tunes were released on a Forward Records LP, and many more were featured during the show's psychedelic "videos," where lyrics were visually interpreted with animation reminiscent of *Yellow Submarine* and Peter Max.

While the studio probably didn't realize it at the time, the launch of *Scooby-Doo, Where Are You!* (1969) signaled a new direction in cartooning and ignited a trend that would stampede the airwaves over the next decade. With Scooby, HB laid out the plot and character archetypes [37] that would be trotted out again and again and again as the '70s dawned and animation became increasingly recyclable: the rockin' sleuths.

Of course, the Scooby Gang never strapped on Stratocasters, but bubblegum music composed and sung by Danny Janssen accompanied the meddling teens as they took chase from ghouls, mummies and various villains in the show's second season. Not to mention a theme song (written by David Mook/Ben Raleigh) so inherently swell that even a Third Eye Blind couldn't wreck it.

Highlights include "Tell Me, Tell Me," with a great fakeout opening that steals its gospely strains from Joe Cocker's version of "A Little Help From My Friends" (something scarier than any Scooby episode). Thankfully, the tune quickly shifts to a winning combo of longing-for-love lyrics, off-kilter time changes and Partridge Family structure, all reeled in with a catchy "Na-na-na-na-na-na-na" hook. "Recipe for My Love" has the singer struggling with the issue of a how to concoct his girlfriend, although the reason why he needs to isn't clear (Did they break up? Is she out of town on a business trip?). Ingredients include the bubblegum-friendly "cup full of sunshine," "touch of a rainbow" and "a little bit from a song I know." But, he adds wistfully, "All that couldn't make up my baby and what my baby means to me." Janssen's songs are available on *Scooby-Doo's Snack Tracks*, released by Rhino in 1998.

1970 was a year that unleashed a pair of female-led musical trios that straddled the fine line between exploitation and feminism. In Russ Meyer's *Beyond the Valley of the Dolls*, the hedonistic Carry Nations slept and rocked their way to the top. But considering its broader audience comprised of young, impressionable viewers, HB's girl group had much more impact on our collective psyche. Like the Carry Nations, Josie & the Pussycats played their own instruments. Dressed in feline outfits that appeared to be lifted off the marquee of L.A.'s Pussycat Theater porn chain, these good girls chased the bad guys around the globe as their touring schedule allowed, and later they were blasted into outer space. The show featured performances by the band, and songs also accompanied chase scenes.

For the recording of songs for the show and a companion LP, attractive female singers took on the roles of cartoon band members: Cathy Dougher as Josie, Patrice Holloway as Valerie and future *Charlie's* chick Cheryl Ladd as ditzy drummer Melody. This was no rush job: the tunes are laden with clever hooks, sophisticated harmonies and unique instrumentation that belie the throwaway nature of bubblegum. Versions of current hits like Bread's "It Don't Matter to Me" and the J-5's "I'll Be There" pale in comparison to Pussycat originals such as "Inside Outside Upside Down" and "Hand Clapping Song," but vocal parts and other nuances on the cover songs imply that the project was approached with time and care.

Butch Cassidy strove for rock 'n' roll credibility in a teenybopper world, as did David Cassidy, his progenitor, doppelganger, and—one can assume—inspiration. Vehemently resentful of his teen-idol image, the Partridge Family star's bio is so full of "I was into Hendrix, man!"-type outbursts, it seems as

---

37. One WB exec would even posit that the character composition of the 1999 remake of *The Haunting* was Scooby minus the dog: Liam Neeson is 3D Fred, Catherine Zeta-Jones is Daphne, Lili Taylor fills in for Velma and Luke Wilson has the Shaggy slot.

if the has been suffers from some rare rock substrain of Tourette's Syndrome. *Butch Cassidy and the Sundance Kids* (1973) professed their rock roots through a sound heavier than a lead zeppelin (and other poppy HB fare) and lyrical signposts that marked their Saturday morning slot as a wimp-free zone. During performances, the band customarily got beeped to go fight crime via Butch's mod ring, so we don't often hear more than bits and pieces — a wailing guitar here, an overly dramatized lyric there. But this axe-to-grind is evident in songs like "Just a Rock 'n' Roll Song," where the hip-huggered heartthrob sings, "You can call it dumb, or bubblegum, but you can't help singin' along," adding the taunt, "Have some!" before launching into a masturbatory '70s guitar solo. Okay, okay, we believe you!

Characters — including drummer Harvey, voiced by Micky Dolenz — spit out rock references at the drop of a hat. When the group rescued a vaguely exotic prince who was a fan, rock 'n' roll trivia weeded out an imposter: The fake didn't flinch when Butch said he'd be playing the "Rolling Tones'" song "Yesterday" at a concert. When the prince correctly identified who wrote "Woodstock" and "Alice's Restaurant," the true royal was revealed. The moniker of the gang's obligatory pooch: Elvis. Off screen, musicians were hired to tour the country as the Butch Cassidy band, but no album was ever released.

Confucius say, "The family who sleuths together, grooves together." At least that's the M.O. of *The Amazing Chan and the Chan Clan*. Blatantly mocking China's one-child policy, the show revolves around legendary private eye Charlie Chan, here a cartoon widower raising ten Chan children (which may explain why Mrs. Chan is no longer with us). The junior Chans are also crime solvers, a job that, naturally, requires them to rock!

By 1972, HB's animation had become pretty rote, and costs were cut by recycling not only backgrounds, but plots, characters and movements as well. A single animated band sequence serves as the "video" for every song the Chans performed, noticeable from its familiar procession of group shot cutting away to sister Suzie playing the tambourine, cut to guitar fingerboard, cut to hulkazoid brother Henry, who hunches over his drum kit like a giant Chinese crab. As the younger, non-musical Chans watch their siblings perform, it appears as if someone is yanking a common chain to activate their synchronized movements. In one episode the singer/guitarist Stanley's head actually disappears for a few frames.

What HB didn't skimp on, thankfully, was the Chan band's music, which flourished under the direction of Monkees' creator Don Kirshner and Ron Dante, fresh out of his previous gig for Mr. K as lead singer of the Archies. While Jeff Barry wrote most Archies' tunes, Dante handled music-writing duties for the Clan and sang Howard Greenfield's ("Love Will Keep Us Together," "Calendar Girl") lyrics. Songs incorporated the most pleasing elements of Dante's previous chart-topping project: soaring vocal melodies, hand claps and the participation of Hugh McCracken, David Spinoza and other Archies' session players. Creeping bass lines suited the show's mystery theme.

"I tried to use a little different sound for my vocal and not make it a copy of the Archies' sound," Dante recalls. "The Archies' sound was a little more hushed, and this was more full-out strong singing, more pop than bubblegum." Greenfield's lyrics generally centered on an espionage theme, often as a metaphor for love. "I've Got the Goods on You" details a cheating partner, while "Whodunnit" seeks to find the culprit of the protagonist's lovesickness. "I Got My Eye on You" requires no further explanation. Additionally, the Clan's songs introduce the Ugly American to the Chinese cultural condition, and lyrics showed a cliche-free sophistication and sensitivity relatively unheard of in the stereotype-friendly cartoon world.[38] "I'm the Number One Son" relays the culture's respect for elders and tradition, a new concept for a viewership comprised of the tail end of the egocentric Baby Boom:

---

38. Where such characters as Hashimoto Mouse and Dick Tracy's Joe Jitsu resided.

> When I was just a boy, My daddy said to me
> You know the apple shouldn't fall, Too far from the family tree
> Countless generations hang their hopes on you
> Ages of tradition depend on what you do

Okay, that's a pretty heavy trip to lay on a kid, but it's a responsibility countered with pride:

> The first born of my father, it makes me feel so glad
> Whenever people tell me, you're just like your dad
> Out of all the fathers, I'm glad that I got mine
> Out of all my brothers, I'm the first in line
> I'm the number one son of the number one man
> The number one hope of my family clan
> Gonna be like my dad any way that I can
> I am his number one son

Dante described HB's approach as fairly hands-off, which explains the range of quality from cartoon to cartoon. "Howie and I believed this was a quality project and took the time to write the best songs we could," he said. "We had very little contact with the producers of the show. All our direction came from what we wanted to project with the music." Failing to realize their potential, HB never released the Chan Clan songs on vinyl.

Jabberjaw (1976) featured a rock—and I use that term loosely—band called the Neptunes, whose *Jaws*-era albatross was an oversized shark channeling the spirit of Curly from the Three Stooges. Painful to watch and listen to, the proto-disco songs thankfully went away as soon as a caper diverted the group's attention.

HB's influence on bubblegum cartoons lives on today as hip animators who grew up with these shows unleash their satires and tributes. In an episode of Ralph Bakshi's '80s series *The New Adventures of Mighty Mouse*,[39] characters found themselves trapped in an HB world, escaping each toon only to wind up in another. As they fled a Scooby set, a bubblegum song dropped references to mood rings and other '70s kitsch. Arguably, *Saturday Night Live*'s sole funny recurring segment is Robert Smigel's animated offering, "The Four Ex-Presidents," where a retired Ford, Reagan, Carter and Bush rescue Bill Clinton from space aliens, communists and other unsavories. Each skit culminates with the former commanders-in-chief rocking out in an Archies-style band.

In 1995, The Cartoon Network—a division of Warner Brothers, as is Hanna-Barbera today—aired *Saturday Morning Cartoons*, with alternative bands performing show themes and songs from musical episodes. In the station's Cartoon Cartoon original programming, the Powerpuff Girls break out into "Love Makes the World Go 'Round," a dose of pop ecstasy so cheery it has the capacity to restore color to a city drained of it by an evil mime. A *Dexter's Lab* segment sees the protagonist being chased by a scary, Keane-eyed waif to the tune of a bubbly pop song. The station even made the insufferable *Jabberjaw* digestible via an interstitial video where the show's characters come to life off a lunchbox and jam with punk band Pain.

Many thanks to Ronn Webb (http://w3.nai.net/~wingnut/Hanna_Barbera.html), Ron Dante, Michael Lloyd, Monica Bouldin (Warner Brothers), Laurie Goldberg (Cartoon Network), Johnny Bartlett, Kelly Kuvo and Anita Serwacki for their assistance.

---

39. That would be the mid-'80s version by *Ren & Stimpy* creator John Kricfalusi.

Animation + Rock = Fun:
The Danny Hutton Interview by Chris Davidson

Pal to big Brian Wilson, L.A. scenester of long-standing (and, oh yeah, one-third of Three Dog Night!), Danny Hutton will live forever in the collective bubblegum consciousness for one additional and amazing reason: he worked for the grandpappy of cartoon rock labels—Hanna-Barbera Records. For a year beginning in 1965, Hutton acted as the label's resident hip youngster and recorded three of the company's best forays into the pure pop 45 market. He also lent vocals and studio know-how to the maddest cartoon rock album of all—*Monster Shindig*, a bizarre horror-rock conglomeration credited to "Super-Snooper and Blabber Mouse, the Gruesomes of the Flintstones, Dracula, Frankenstein, the Mummy, and the Wolf Man." (What, no Morocco Mole?)

HBR hit with the Five Americans' "I See the Light" during Hutton's tenure with the label and went on to release a hefty amount of garage, light psych and pop over the next couple of years, including "Blue Theme" by the Hogs (aka the Chocolate Watchband). While the majority of singles appear to have been one-off national distribution deals with bands experiencing regional chart noise, HBR long-players took the animated TV characters as a starting point and crafted dozens of mind-splitting vinyl adventures and hot session-man rock 'n' roll.

Danny Hutton arrived at the start of HBR's pop barnstorming.

Chris Davidson: How'd you get started with Hanna-Barbera Records? Was that your first experience with a record label?

Danny Hutton: I was working in the warehouse for Disney/Buena Vista Records. I was basically a grunt during the day at work, but at night I hung around in the L.A. musician spots, like IHOP across from Hollywood High and Liberty Records, where I used to see Sonny & Cher, Jan & Dean, and those people. I had put out a couple of records already. My first was as the Chartermen on Invicta Records. It was called "Winken, Blinken and Nod." This was done through Kim Fowley, who I was introduced to by Pat and Lolly Vegas. Kim actually lived up in my attic for awhile. I also had a single out on ALMO Records called "Home in Pasadena." That was released as Daring Dan Hutton. Then I cut "Farmer's Daughter" on Mercury as Basil Swift and the Seagrams. One day, a guy named Larry Goldberg contacted me. He was trying to get something happening at HBR. He was sort of an A&R guy, a hustler, not a musician. But he brought me into the deal as proof of his street credentials. I was a young musician, so HBR gave me a half-hour tryout. In that time, I wrote two songs, so they gave me a job!

CD: Did you cut the songs you wrote for the audition?

DH: Yes. The first song was called "Nothing at All." I did all the vocal and instrumental parts on the record, and it was released as the Bats [HBR 445]. It was all me! The other song was "Big Bright Eyes," which we recorded as the B-side. We did the whole session at Western Studios in six hours. I wrote "Big Bright Eyes" in the studio in ten minutes.

CD: That was one of the best singles on HBR. "Big Bright Eyes" was later a local hit for you in L.A.

DH: The version that later came out [HBR 453] under my name was the same version as the Bats, but with a different backing track. We took the original, which was more acoustic and made it more pop.

CD: What about "Roses and Rainbows," your other L.A. hit before "Big Bright Eyes?" Wasn't that the song they used for your appearance on *The Flintstones*?

DH: "Roses and Rainbows" was a big hit in town. I think it was helped along when *Billboard* featured it on a flexi disk in one of their issues. I really had no intention of performing live at the time. I considered myself a studio guy. But the label put the single out under my name [HBR447], set me up with a manager and started promoting me as a solo act. One day they asked if I wanted to be in *The Flintstones*, and right after that they showed me the finished product. I didn't do anything. They just used the released version of "Roses and Rainbows" in the show. Funny story about *The Flintstones*. When I met my wife, Laurie, she told me she'd seen the episode I was in and fell in love with me on TV. She fell in love with me from the cartoon!

CD: Now, that's a woman! Can you tell me about the flip to "Roses and Rainbows?"

DH: "Monster Shindig" was on the back.

CD: It's a wild song and also the title track of a great HBR album [HLP2020]. Did you do the other songs on that record—"Super Snooper" and "The Monster Jerk?"

DH: That was me. I don't remember the session too much, but I know I worked on that record. I contributed a lot to the albums being made at the time.

CD: What else do you recall about your time with the label? Did you run into any of the other acts?

DH: I was there from the very beginning, when they were just moving in the furniture. It was about a year all together. I always felt like it was more of an experiment than anything else, a cartoon company trying out the record business. The Guilloteens were being worked in L.A. [three singles on the label], but I never met the Five Americans. They never had a presence in L.A. It was a great time while it lasted, though, and definitely helped me get a leg up in the business.

Never Mind the Bollocks, Here's the Banana Splits by James Porter

When I started to write this piece, somebody told me that the Banana Splits got short shrift in a book on cartoon kings Hanna-Barbera. Yeah, Huckleberry Hound deserves all the props he gets, but ya gotta pause for the Banana Splits. Even on *American Bandstand*, Dick Clark had to deal with network bigwigs who didn't grow up on the Big Beat (or, at least, a different Big Beat from what post-'50s generations knew). So, before MTV, shows like those featuring the Monkees, the Archies, and the Banana Splits were among the few on which rock and teevee seemed truly comfortable together.

The Banana Splits ran for two seasons on NBC, making its debut in September 1968 and remaining a part of the Saturday morning lineup until September 1970. The industry was hip to the fact that pre-packaged groups could make a lot of money. It was even better if they were fictitious characters—that way they wouldn't rock any boats, or go "progressive" on you, like the Monkees. After a short-lived fling with their own label—HBR Records: soundtracks and children's records were their bread and butter, but they also released some fine regional R&B and garage-punk, including a single or two from the 13th Floor Elevators—Hanna-Barbera's second big attempt at rock & roll was with the Splits.

The Jetsons and *Flintstones* notwithstanding, HBR's biggest stars, like their Warner Bros. "Looney Tunes" predecessors, were talking animals. With the exception of one mute member, the Splits were no different. Group leader Fleagle was the drooling dog (that wasn't no red tie you saw him wear—that was his tongue) and guitarist who called each meeting to order with his harsh voice and high-pitched Joe Tex giggle ("hoo hoo hoo!"). Drooper was the coolcat lion with the

shiny Vox guitar. Bingo was the grinning monkey beating his way through the world on drums. Snorky was the confused-looking elephant who compensated for the lack of a bass player by working overtime on the Farfisa organ. Like the Rolling Stones' Charlie Watts, he was the "silent" member who'd honk his trunk every now and then.

The Splits' portion of the hour-long show was not animated, but featured live actors in costume. Their part had them fooling around in their clubhouse and introducing different segments which alternated between lighthearted cartoons (*Atom Ant, Squiddley Diddley, Precious Pupp*) and adventure serials (*Gulliver's Travels, Arabian Knights, Micro-Ventures*). One of the more fondly remembered features was *Danger Island*, a live-action serial that crossed *Gilligan's Island* (minus the comedy) with the multi-culti youth appeal of *The Mod Squad*. All the ingredients were there: the handsome blond white guy (played by Jan-Michael Vincent, a popular Nixon-era actor, as Link Simmons); the shapely white woman (Ronnie Toup as Leslie Hayden); the muscular black man who seems to know all the answers (Rockne Tarkington as Morgan, a castaway), the whole bit. For comic relief, they inserted some character named Chongo (played by Kahana) with a pudding-bowl Davy Jones hairdo. Chongo's unintelligible grunting marked him as the true predecessor to John

The Sour Grapes Bunch, or how a bunch of girls called Charlie invented dollybird girl power
by Katrina Dixon

I could only have been six or seven years old when I fell under the sway of my first role-models, a bunch of white-booted, go-go dancing, rabbit-punching girls, all called Charlie, whose sassy confidence and sussed cool unwittingly provided me with an iconic image of empowered girlhood, a blueprint that was both easy to identify with and eminently desirable. It was 1977, or 1978, and thanks to my older brother, I was dimly aware of punk, still innocent of the sex and drugs bit, but definitely inspired by the fizzing do-it-yourself vitriolic energy of bands like the Slits, the Raincoats and even the Runaways. So what could be more punk, and more subversive than watching a bunch of similarly punk, pre-pubescent, pugilistic cuties outwitting their male co-stars on a Saturday morning tv show? They even had a punk name, the Sour Grapes Bunch, a name that combined the sweetness of youth with the attitude of girl ganghood.

Without even knowing it, the fleeting glimpses I caught of these girls, on reruns of a wacked-out psychedelic half-hour of American kiddie entertainment from the '60s, gave me my first taste of feminism long before I was even aware of what feminism was, and certainly long before the Spice Girls aped the heroines of Japanese Manga comics to combine ideas of feminist empowerment with blatant girly-girlness for a post-feminist girl power audience. If the Spice Girls gave us the slogan of "girl power" in the late '90s, it was the Sour Grapes Bunch who blazed the trail almost three decades earlier with their sharp outfits, moves and right hooks.

Few could have imagined that the guest appearances of these winsome terrorists could imprint themselves on the minds of a generation, yet the Sour Grapes Bunch did just that, even if their cult stature is now so obscure that there is little evidence of their impact. No marketing spin-offs, whether fan club, Viewmaster slides or even inflatable punching-bags for would-be Sour Grapes no-gooders to practice on. Even the kaleidoscopic smorgasbord of the internet, awash with fansites devoted to the most unsung of heroes and heroines, has a gaping black hole where you would imagine the Sour Grapes Bunch should be. Online reminiscences of the Banana Splits curiously overlook these pre-teen dollybirds in favor of lengthy catalogues of credits for *The Arabian Knights* or *The Three Musketeers*, the cartoons which

Belushi's "illiterate, outrageous fat guy" roles, like Bluto from *Animal House*, or the Samurai on *Saturday Night Live*. The only difference was that Chongo was relatively thin, but when you heard those magic words ("uh-oh, Chongo!" uttered by the black member of the cast), you knew something insane would follow. Also in the cast: Frank Aletter as Prof. Irwin Hayden (Leslie's dad), Victor Eberg as Mu-Tan (bad guy #1), and Rodrigo Arrendondo as Chu (bad guy #2).

Since the Splits were supposed to be a band, there was always a spot for them to showcase their songs. Usually the songs themselves played in the background while the band was seen cutting up in some amusement park, just like in the opening and closing credits. Which brings us to their recorded legacy. Though the show's theme "The Tra La La Song" ("one banana, two banana, three banana, four/four bananas make a bunch and so do many more") wasn't a very big radio hit (made it into the '90s on *Billboard*'s Hot 100, or some such foolishness), it's still ingrained in many personal childhood soundtracks.

Soon enough, the Decca label released a Banana Splits album. As you might expect from an LP made by a floating collection of studio musicians, the styles vary, but somehow manage to remain consistent. Three tracks are more or less theme songs. "Tra La" you know, but then there's the lesser-known "We're The Banana Splits" and "Doin' The Banana Split," the latter which was written by none other than Barry White, just payin' the bills as an L.A. session guy. It's an R&B-styled dance number, with a nice musical dialogue between the singer and the horn section ("dip and scoop one time . . . BLAT! . . . dip and scoop two times . . . BLAT! BLAT!"). The Splits crossed paths with rhythm & blues a lot—one episode had a live action segment which had a cop directing traffic to the old R&B instrumental and oldies radio staple "The Horse"— and I'm disappointed that the album didn't include "Our Show Will Go On," which in the tradition of "He Will Break Your Heart" ("he don't love you, like I love you . . ."), uses the stage as a metaphor for a girlfriend's roaming eyes. The best tracks on the

album are the "soul"—pay close attention to those quote marks—songs. The singer's attempts to get that righteous gospel-soul feelin' sound phony as all hell—war whoops and phrases like "look-a-here" show up where they don't have to, and for all that, it's still "a gas and a giggle," as Sammy Davis, Jr. would say. The royal caketaker and swingin' neckbreaker is the aptly-titled "Soul." Like many "what-is-soul?" numbers that were being recorded back then, it comes to the conclusion that soul ain't something you buy, you either have it or you don't. Just so no one misses the point, there's a list of people who "have it" towards the song's end: "brother Ray Charles singin' the blues / James Brown doin' the camel walk / (couldn't make out this line!) / Otis Redding on the dock of the bay / Yogi Bear on the TV screen . . ."

The rest of the album is mild bub-

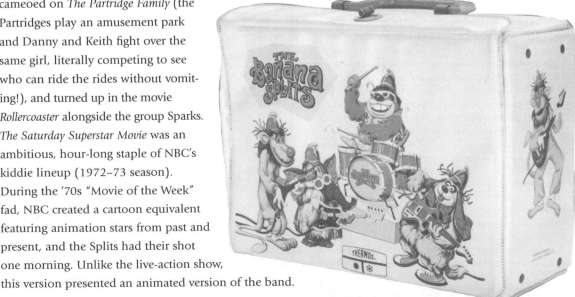

blegum—what would you expect from titles like "Don't Go Away, Go-Go Girl?" Two numbers even predate the '70s "ragtime" fad by a good six years or so—the vaudeville groove of "Two Ton Tessie" and the instrumental "Toy Piano Melody." The two seven-inch EP's that Kellogg's (the Splits' cornflake sponsors) put out via mail order repeated the theme song (on one disc), the Barry White dance number (on another), plus a load of excess material that didn't make the album. But as I indicated earlier, the Splits weren't as big on that charts as they were on the tube, and their rivals, the Archies, introduced on CBS TV at exactly the same time as the Splits, saw to that. The banana bunch had a lot of musical competition in the 1968–70 bubblegum race (the one from 1970–74, with the Osmonds and the Partridge Family, is a different story), but the Splits still held their own.

With the demise of the show, that was pretty much it for the Splits, although the suits were trotted out for appearances in any movie or TV show with a fairground theme. They cameoed on *The Partridge Family* (the Partridges play an amusement park and Danny and Keith fight over the same girl, literally competing to see who can ride the rides without vomiting!), and turned up in the movie *Rollercoaster* alongside the group Sparks. *The Saturday Superstar Movie* was an ambitious, hour-long staple of NBC's kiddie lineup (1972–73 season). During the '70s "Movie of the Week" fad, NBC created a cartoon equivalent featuring animation stars from past and present, and the Splits had their shot one morning. Unlike the live-action show, this version presented an animated version of the band.

The influence could slowly be felt as the years passed. The Dickies had an English hit in 1979 with their power-pop version of the show's theme (simply retitled "Banana Splits"). Joey Ramone has gone on record as saying the Splits and the Monkees were two of his all-time fave bands, and when I used to spin records at Chicago's late, lamented Lower Links, the "Tra La" theme was a guaranteed hipster crowd-pleaser. The Splits' mark was left, sort of, on Kaptain Kool & the Kongs, late-blooming studio-created glitter-rockers who debuted on ABC in 1976 with *The Krofft Supershow*.

Produced by the ubiquitous Sid & Marty Krofft, when the Kongs weren't playing hard rock to an audience of screaming KISS-T-shirt-wearing teenies, they introduced live-action segments within the series. Too bad Epic waited until just after the show was canceled (late '78) to release the album, a surefire tax write-off for somebody.

The ultimate final word belongs to Cub Koda, ex-guitar star for the great Brownsville Station, who once dissed MTV royally in his column "The Vinyl Junkie" (then running in *Goldmine* magazine), saying that he'd "seen better videos this morning watching the damn Banana Splits!"

punctuated the antics of Bingo, Fleagle, Snorky and Drooper, the dimwitted slapstick rock 'n' rolling stars of *The Banana Splits Show* who were the animal-suited kiddie answer to the Monkees.

The few snippets that I found on my frustrating searches for a reconnection with my youthful heroines, almost inevitably, cropped up in the form of casual mentions on Banana Splits mailing lists which shed little light on the enduring mystery of who these girls actually were, or how they came to be the Banana Splits' witty nemeses, appearing once or twice every show, first to issue a challenge to the Splits, dancing out of a side-door to the blast of their Hammond theme tune to land a punch on one of the quaking Splits, and later re-appearing to gyrate in front of the cameras while the Splits played one of the cool musical numbers that would later make their sole album one of the must-have collectables of kiddie bubblegum vinyl. But if the ongoing feud could be dissolved weekly without leaving any taint on the Splits, I knew at least, watching it, that the Splits were never left in any doubt as to who was boss.

Memories can prove to be bizarrely off-kilter however. The few photos that exist of the Bunch online reveal a group of girls who are far removed from the miniature punkettes I remember. Dressed in matching red dresses and black go-go boots that invariably raise alarming images in my mind of Santa Claus's little Nazi imps, these girls look as though they would have been shocked when their bubblegum bubbles popped. Still, no matter. Late '60s and early '70s television had little in the way of cool young female icons for wilfully-minded tomboys like me. The girls of *The Brady Bunch* were saccharine, *The Partridge Family* offered a pitiful choice between whining Laurie and the almost-mute Tracy. The best that cartoonland could offer was frumpish Velma on *The Scooby-Doo Show*, or *Josie and the Pussycats*. But none of these, even now, even despite my own rose-tinted reminiscences, can yet compare to the precociously empowered Sour Grapes Bunch. Put simply, they rule, and one day the whole world will know their greatness, I'm certain of it. ◉

The Hardy Boys by James Porter

In his time, Bill Traut did a lot for Chicago music. In the '60s, his Dunwich label released seminal sides by the Del-Vettes, Saturday's Children, and the Shadows of Knight. Fast forward to the '70s, and his Wooden Nickel company released records by such Windy City institutions as Styx and the Siegel-Schwall Band. In between, he had a production company, also called Dunwich, that stamped its logo on albums by H.P. Lovecraft, Crow, the Nazz, and the Hardy Boys. While Bill must get requests for old Shadows of Knight road stories all the time, the Hardy Boys probably haven't crossed his mind in years.

The Hardy Boys were a moneymaking vehicle, plain and simple. This cartoon series, based on the kids' detective novel series authored by Frank Dixon, was part of ABC-TV's Saturday morning lineup during 1969–71. Copping a trick from the Archies and Banana Splits, each episode ended with a live-action segment featuring the Hardys' rock band. In addition to appearing in their own Gold Key comic book, the band issued two albums for RCA. Although they didn't do too badly in the children's television sweepstakes, it's clear that the Hardy Boys—both the band and the cartoon—was a footnote in the lives of everyone involved. In the original novels, the Hardys were two white guys who solved mysteries; for the Age of Aquarius, they were reborn as an interracial, coed rock band. The two albums offer few ambitious surprises; no closet psychedelia à la the Monkees or Kasenetz-Katz stable. The Hardy's records were essentially regulation-Top 40 patterned after similar records of the day. But while those long-players are spotty, when they're on they represent some of the finest bubble-rock of the time.

The Hardy Boys' project came about when Traut was doing quite a bit of production on the West Coast. He recalls, "During that time, I hung out at a restaurant in Hollywood called Martoni's. It was a famous gathering place for people in the music business. Everybody kinda made record deals there. Jerry Moss and Herb Alpert would come in with Sergio Mendes, and they'd call you over to their table and ask "would you like to produce Sergio Mendes?" he laughs. "That kind of thing went on all the time. Every time I'd walk in, the guy that bartended would yell, 'here comes Chicago!' So, one night I was introduced by the bartender, who was also Frank Sinatra's houseboy, to a guy by the name of Norm Prescott, who was one of the two co-owners of Filmation (with Lou Schiemer)." Traut estimates Filmation "had 65 to 75% of all the Saturday morning television shows on

every network. Prescott had been a disc jockey before he was in the film business. He knew me from when he used to play my records. I was reintroduced to him by Morrie Diamond, the promotion man for Acta Records, who helped make the American Breed a hit. I got to be buddies with Norm, and one day he came to me and said, 'Look, I've got this property, the Hardy Boys, for television. I'm gonna do another cartoon show just like I've always done, except I want a girl, I don't want it to be just all guys, and also I want to make the Hardy Boys both black and white.' I said, 'Like the American Breed?' 'Exactly like the American Breed!' He said, 'What I'd like to do is tie it together with a real live act. Can you do that?' I said, 'Sure, I think so—what you mean is cast a band.' He said, 'Yeah, and they'll appear on the show both live and animated. They'll do songs as part of the show, and we'll make a deal for the records.' This was typical Norm thinking. So I took on the Hardy Boys cartoon project, and told Norm to ship me the first sketches by the artists at Filmation, so I could see what the Hardy Boys looked like in his mind."

Official publicity would have us believe that the band consisted of Frank Hardy (the brunet guitarist), Joe Hardy (the blond bassist), Chubby Morton (sax, first name self-explanatory), Wanda Kay (the female keyboardist), and Peter Jones (the black drummer). All members were credited with vocals, although the credits didn't tell who sang lead. To cut costs, the band was cast, based, and recorded in Chicago with a gang of local heavyweights (including Phil Upchurch, a guitarist who originally made his mark in the early '60s with a stomping rock instrumental called "You Can't Sit Down," but subsequently carved a career as a jazz guitarist and A-list session cat). According to Traut, "Frank Hardy" was in reality Reed Kailing, a former member of Midwestern garage-rockers Michael & the Messengers (who can be heard on the original *Nuggets* compilation, and subsequent box set, doing "[Just Like] Romeo & Juliet.") "Chubby Morton" was with the Troys, who recorded for Tower Records. Traut remembers that "Wanda Kay's"— who later dated "Frank Hardy"—real name was "Devon" something, was found at Chicago's Playboy Club, a Bunny carrying trays. She was living in the dorms at Hugh Hefner's house, being groomed to be a Playmate. Traut saved her from all that and made her a Hardy Boy instead. Traut is fuzzy on the other two members, but remembers that they were both found in the Chicago area. Kailing, who Traut recalls as "a good guitar player—he wasn't a chump," got to play on the records, along with "Chubby Morton," who played sax. The rest of the group just sang, to the backing of local session musicians. They even got to do some touring, doing promotional tie-ins and what was left of the teen club circuit. The show lasted two seasons on the air, and they were allowed to make albums, so apparently the Hardys had a fan base somewhere. In the fickle world of kiddie TV, that's nothing to sneeze at.

But what about the albums themselves?

Their 1969 debut, *Here Come The Hardy Boys*, includes their theme song and establishes their sound. The lead vocalist (Kailing?) sounds like the perfect nasal cross between Ron Dante and Tommy Roe on songs like "Namby-Pamby" ("namby-pamby, sweeter than candy, you're better than a lollipop, finer than gold . . . you make me wanna lick you up and give you a whirl"). Another song, "Sink Or Swim," is vaguely reminiscent of Jimi Hendrix' "Foxy Lady" with a horn section added. "That's That," "I Want You

WANDA KAY   CHUBBY MORTON   JOE HARDY   FRANK HARDY   PETE JONES

To Be My Baby," and "Feels So Good" would have been hits in a better world, with more hooks than a coatrack, but they were relegated to album cuts here. The songwriting machine (featuring former Brill Building tunesmith Ellie Greenwich pitching in) was in full effect on this one.

There's a slight decline on the 1970 follow-up, *Wheels*. On a positive note, they've started introducing a string section on various tracks, but it never intrudes. But for some reason, many of the songs here deal with country life (and how to get away from it). You could be generous and say this was part of an overriding concept, but it sounds more like the songwriting combine were tired of writing love songs and this was the only way they could do something different. It's obvious that these were throwaway LPs meant to go with the moment, but you can't help but compare the two. Album #1 had a song that praised "Those Country Girls," but by the next record, "Let The Sun Shine Down" has a verse that puts down both country and city females. Also, when the narrator of "Those Country Girls" tells us in his adolescent-sounding voice that he's been around the world, he doesn't sound like he's gotten any farther than the last school bus stop. "Wheels" is more like it: "never been away from this old town much before/just visiting relatives and really nothing more . . ." There are odd conceptual flaws here and there, but this is the Hardy Boys, not the Moody Blues (thank God), and both albums hold up fairly well as artifacts of their time and genre.

But like the Heights (another interracial made-for-TV band who had their one hit with "How Do You Talk To An Angel?" in 1993), the band died when the TV show did, and everybody drifted on, without tears or regrets, to other projects. Unlike the Heights, the Hardy Boys actually made good music, and their two albums are well worth picking up cheap in the used bins.

Postscript: the Hardys' name was resuscitated by ABC yet again later in the decade, this time as a live-action early-evening show, starring Parker Stevenson and Shaun Cassidy. David's baby brother Shaun had been playing glam-rock in L.A. clubs, but they cleaned up his image and music for the sake of the show, occasionally using the program as a forum for his latest single. His teen-idol/hitmaking run ran roughly concurrent with the span of the show, '77–'79. Although they had gone back to the original two-white-guys format, the show ran in tandem with a Nancy Drew program (another kids-novel detective), until the two shows were combined during their final season, with the three of them foiling the bad guys together.

Fat Albert & the Cosby Kids:
The Last Great TV Bubblegum Band by James Porter

A joke . . . isn't a joke . . . when you hurt someone.
—Fat Albert

A joke also wasn't a joke when you had an animated band as cool as Fat Albert & the Cosby Kids. The series, a staple of CBS' Saturday morning lineup for years, first premiered in the fall of '72, when all cartoons had to either (a) teach a subliminal lesson, or (b) have a fake band close each show with a song. Obviously, there were exceptions, but these were the two dominant styles of kids' TV. Fat Albert and his crew mastered both arts. As host Bill Cosby said at the beginning of each show, "if you're not careful, you might learn something before it's done." And for every lesson learned, the gang had a classic bubble-soul tune to go along with it.

Miraculously, the kids could make discarded junkyard furniture sound like real instruments. And exactly how could Albert sing baritone, but talk bass (more often than not sounding like a wino Barry White)? At a time when almost everybody in black music, from Curtis Mayfield to Howlin' Wolf (on his 1972 album *A Message to the Young*), felt compelled to have at least one social-consciousness song in their repertoire, Fat Albert recorded some of the gentlest message songs heard on the TV airwaves. Strangely enough, that was the only place you could hear Fat Albert's music. Show creator Cosby knew the value of marketing: everything from lunchboxes to Gold Key comic books bore the Fat Albert image. SO WHY WEREN'T THERE ANY FAT ALBERT RECORDS? Obviously, a lot of money, time and talent went into recording the songs that appeared at the end of each show. However, the only Fat Albert albums released were those made for the kiddie market which told a complete, spoken-word story. In addition, the familiar cartoon figures appear on the sleeves two of Cosby's regular comedy albums; Fat Albert is on the cover of the 1973 album that bore his name, and the whole gang is depicted on *When I Was a Kid* (1971). Yet no attempt was made to get them onto the Top 40; too bad, because songs like "Stage Fright" and "Don't Look Down on a Small Guy" would have given the J-5 and Osmonds serious competition on early-'70s AM radio playlists. [Editor's note for the second printing: an alert reader informs us that there are, in fact, two very rare musical Fat Albert albums in circulation—*Fat Albert and the Cosby Kids* (Paramount PAS 6053, 1973, songs by Sherry Golden and Richard Canada; theme by Ed Fournier and Ricky Sheldon) and *Rock N' Roll Disco With Fat Albert and the Junkyard Band* (Kid Stuff KSS 094, 1980, songs by Dean Andre and Jeff Michael).]

"Fat Albert" had his origins as one of humorist Cosby's childhood friends in Philadelphia, PA. He was first immortalized on Cosby's Grammy-winning *Revenge* album (1967), as a hefty neighborhood kid

ALBERT — BILL — BUCKY — DUMB DONALD — RUSSEL — WEIRD HAROLD · RUDY — MUSHMOUTH

who used to play "Buck Buck." There was also a prime-time cartoon special around 1969. Slowly, Albert's legend caught on: Motown second-stringer Shorty Long recorded "Here Comes Fat Albert" on his 1968 album, *Here Comes the Judge,* and in 1970, Herbie Hancock released an early jazz-fusion effort on Warner Brothers titled *Fat Albert Rotunda.* But Albert really became part of the pop-culture landscape when he received his own Saturday morning cartoon series, which ran continuously from 1972 to 1984. Of course, the last few seasons were straight-up reruns, but considering how the average weekend cartoon is good for only two years of juice, this was quite an achievement.

In many ways, *Fat Albert & the Cosby Kids* was very much a product of its time. Besides cashing in on the animated rock band phase, the show appeared at a time when cartoons were starting to include multicultural casts. When Fat Albert made his debut, there were already successful animated series built around the Jackson Five and the Harlem Globetrotters. And in the early-'70s struggle for relevance in children's programming (thank you, *Sesame Street*), Fat Albert made sure you (subliminally) learned a lesson after thirty minutes. With all trendy bases covered, how could it lose? Apparently, it didn't: in a contemporary survey of both black and white kids, CBS discovered that only 29% thought to mention the racial angle.

Of course, watching the show through adult eyes, it's easy to see how cheap and sleazy animation had gotten since the '50s. Backgrounds and scenes were reused with little discretion. If the joke was on a cast member—say, Rudy—then we'd see a tight shot of Rudy looking humiliated, followed by a stock shot of the entire gang (Rudy included) laughing. In essence, Rudy was laughing at himself; not a bad thing as far as real life is concerned, but in an animated format rather surreal. Filmation, the company which handled not only Albert's gang but the Archies as well, was not above cutting costs when feasible. One episode of *U.S. of Archie* had the gang traveling back in time to meet with George Washington Carver, the noted African-American scientist.[40] To underscore the fact that it was a black-themed show, they used the soulful background music heard on Albert's program! For all this, *Fat Albert & the Cosby Kids* was a classic cartoon of the period.

Fat Albert's gang were a ragtag bunch of kids who hung around a ghetto junkyard when not at home or in school, and each episode was tied together by running commentary from Cosby, in a non-animated segment. The supporting cast included Dumb Donald, who walked around with a skull cap pulled down over his head at all times (with cut-out holes that he could see through); Mushmouth, who couldn't say one word without adding an extra "b" here and there (Fat Albert's name somehow would become "Fabt Albebt" when Mushmouth got through with it); Weird Harold, in his brown sports jacket, was probably one of the more normal kids in the bunch; Rudy, in his apple cap and Superfly clothes, one of the more affluent (or close to it). Even a kid version of Cosby himself was a cast member, along with his younger bro Russell.

The gang never ran out of lessons to learn, whether playing hooky from school or meeting a kid with a clubfoot. And for the first few seasons, there was a song to match the occasion. "Beggin' Benny" chastised a guy who never seems to give back what he borrows. "A Joke Isn't a Joke" slammed practical jokers everywhere. "One World," the obligatory "racial tolerance" song, was heard on an episode where the gang goes off to summer camp only to meet a bunch of white kids they have no desire to bond with. After the cocky Rudy nervously for-

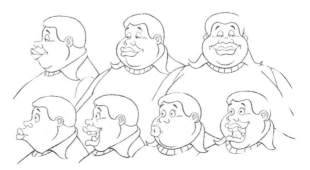

40. *U.S. of Archie* was a CBS series, circa 1974, that had the Archie gang going back through time meeting the founding fathers of the country. And yes, they sang a song at the end of each episode.

gets his lines in the school play (after strutting around talking trash all week), the kids chalk it up to "Stage Fright" (featuring "Albert's" finest vocal moment). On one 1976 prime-time special, they even came up with a song immortalizing CBS' fall cartoon lineup!

Probably the most poignant song in the repertoire was "We're All Together," from the episode where the gang decides they want to form a garage (junkyard?) band. Problem: all their money put together can barely buy a cracked drumstick. Ingeniously, they return to the junkyard, making instruments out of an old heater, a bedspring, a wig stand, and anything else that makes noise. Of course, Rudy has to show up everyone else with a brand-spanking new white electric guitar with a big red R emblazoned on it, but by show's end, no matter who's playing what, the song tells it all: "we're all together, playing in the band . . ." This was a common sentiment in late-'60s/early-'70s rock (the Grateful Dead's "Playing in the Band" is a prominent example), and Fat Albert made the most of it.

Despite its quality, the music of Fat Albert remains a dim memory in the mind of viewers, since somehow Cosby failed to let these junkpile jammers make any real records. And after the cartoon rock band trend had played itself out by the late '70s, the musical segments were replaced by a would-be superhero called the Brown Hornet (who suspiciously resembled Cosby). Instead of heading for the junkyard practice space at the end of each show to sing about what they'd just gone through, they'd race to the clubhouse in mid-episode to watch the Hornet do his thing. For the kids, it was beneficial—now, when faced with a sticky situation, all they had to do was wonder how the Brown Hornet would handle it. But for the rest of us,. it meant the loss of the last great bubblegum band on TV. As it now stands, there are no Fat Albert records for children of the '70s to spin for future generations, but plenty of us remember just how great they were.

Toomorrow by Kim Cooper

Still not over the Monkees debacle by 1969, Don Kirschner joined forces with Harry Saltzman of the James Bond franchise to develop a manufactured pop band that could star in motion pictures.

The cherry-picked act ultimately consisted of British keyboardist Vic Cooper (formerly of Tom Jones' band, and sax player for Chris Farlowe and Johnny Kidd), black Philadelphian Karl Chambers on drums (Gladys Knight, Stevie Wonder), Georgia thespian Ben Thomas on lead guitar, and a chirpy Anglo-Australian gal singer named Olivia Newton-John. They more or less played themselves in the film *Toomorrow*, written and directed by Val Guest.

Synopsis: In grand British tradition, the members of Toomorrow are students in an arts college. "Livvy" wakes her bandmates/fellow borders with instant coffee and fried egg sandwiches before they all head down to campus for a big day of sit-ins. The flower-covered car that Livvy drives is a kind of micro Mystery Machine: they tow a wagon behind with their instruments inside.

Meanwhile, in a relic-filled house in the middle of Hampstead Heath, self-proclaimed anthropologist John Williams (Roy Dotrice) steps onto his front lawn and is lofted up on a shaft of light into a tapered crystalline spacecraft that looks like a hyperactive bead. After some pretty cool psychedelic transporter effects, Williams peels off his human flesh and gives a status report to his alien superiors while lounging in an inflatable lawn chair. Although Williams claims that after 3000 years of monitoring he *still* has nothing to report, his boss says they've discovered a healing frequency being generated by young earthlings.

The aliens desperately need to find the source of this tone, since their own crappy electronic music no longer gets them off. They show some snippets of Toomorrow rocking out inside a diamond-shaped floating module, and send Williams back to earth to locate the group.

Conveniently, the band are also Londoners, and Williams is able to meet them during a protest/jam session in the school cafeteria. When the principal (a British Mr. Weatherby) shuts off the power, Toomorrow take the unctuous alien up on his offer that they use his conservatory as a practice space. They are desperate to play, having scored an eight-minute (!) slot in that evening's pop festival at the Round House.

At Williams' palatial digs, the band is startled by the lifelike stuffed Neanderthals in his foyer, but are set at ease by his groovy sound system and accommodating manner. They practice while Williams secretly records them.

When the group is sucked up into space and given a quick lesson in galactic musicology, they refuse to travel to the aliens' planet to teach them how to get down, insisting Toomorrow's music only means something when they're playing for their human fans. The band is allowed to escape in a pod, while the aliens plot to transport the entire Round House audience at the moment of greatest intensity in the group's performance.

On return, the naïve band rush to Williams' door, not realizing he's set them up. Numerous hijinx ensue, involving Vic's strained relationship with his ballerina girlfriend Amy and numerous birds jealous of stud Benny's attentions. Benny romances his foxy music professor to get inside the locked-down college, kissing her while his bandmates sneak out with their liberated instruments.

Meanwhile Amy has dumped Vic, and he doesn't want to play the gig. Williams is desperate to get Vic onstage, since it's his home-made synthesizer that's the secret to the vibrations. Remembering Vic's vocal appreciation of a curvy set of hips on a record jacket, Williams conjures up a generously proportioned alien in humanoid form—"with long blond fur." This is Johnson, a comically awkward sexpot who finds human sexuality hilarious, especially after Williams treats her to an afternoon of dirty movies in Soho. The only problem is that to Johnson, all human males looks alike, and she approaches each one with a jaunty "Vic Cooper?" and a lusty leer. Needless to say, Johnson causes a lot of trouble, plates are tossed around by angry girlfriends, and Livvy appears in one scene with an nasty unexplained gash on her elbow.

Ultimately the whole band makes it to the show and blows the audience away. And sure enough, at the moment of musical climax a great beam of light shines down on the venue, lofting everyone up into space . . .

. . . and Livvy's alarm clock goes off again, just like at the start of the film, leaving you to wonder if it was all a dream.

While an enormous amount of money was obviously spent on the project—at a recent screening at the American Cinematheque in Los Angeles, Newton-John recalled numerous flights between England and the States, including one where she arrived to find no one knew why she was there, so they gave her

a Florida vacation—the film and record tanked. It's unfortunate, because the movie is funny and inventive and the songs (by Archies writers Mark Barkan and Ritchie Adams, who also produced) are solid post-hippie pop. Lyrical sentiments like "if you can't be hurt/you can't be happy" and "show me the way to Happiness Valley" illustrate the unthreatening sweetness of Toomorrow's sound, which is like a less funky and infantile Archies. And Karl's drumming style owes so much to Jughead's that it's impossible to watch the band and not picture him wearing that weird little hat.

Bubblegum fans should peel an eye for the super-rare 1970 *Toomorrow* album (UK RCA LSA 3008/US Sire 97012), or better still see the movie, if they get the chance.

The Rock Flowers by Lisa Sutton

Marketing of toys, games and dolls has always gone hand-in-hand with music. Catchy jingles and pop tunes have been associated with everything from the Slinky and Wheel-O to G.I. Joe and Barbie. Pop bands were often used to sell kiddie fare in the bubblegum era, the most high-profile being the Monkees (Nerf Balls, Kool-Aid and Kellogg's) while the Raiders' Mark Lindsay did a swingin' single for go-go dancing doll Swingy. On the same note, many dolls of the 1960s and beyond had record albums attributed to their synthetic personae. Among these, one of the most elaborate plastic-to-vinyl transitions was the Rock Flowers.

Rock Flower dolls were six-inch fashion dolls introduced by Mattel in 1970. Each colorfully dressed figure came with a seven-inch record and a spindle used to attach the doll to a record player, so it would flail about while the turntable spun. Originally, there were three Rock Flowers: Lilac, Heather, and Rosemary. Iris and Doug joined the group in the second year, though their images did not appear on the super-cool Rock Flower carrying cases or other packaging. Each doll had their own song on the A-side, while each of the five color-coded discs—Lilac/yellow, Heather/orange, Rosemary/purple, Doug/green, Iris/red—shared the Rock Flower theme song, "Sweet Times."

The music of the Rock Flowers was pure bubblegum from the word go. Produced by pop impresario Wes Farrell, the bubbly repertoire included accessible tunes written by the likes of Toni "I'm Gonna Make Your Life So Sweet" Wine, "Tie A Yellow Ribbon" writers Levine & Brown, plus Brill Building honeys Carole Bayer and Ellie Greenwich. Farrell was the man behind the unstoppable Partridge Family records, and was in high demand as a producer in the early '70s. In between sessions for the Partridge Family, Farrell and the same musicians that created the Partridge sound laid down the backing tracks for the Rock Flowers. Recorded at Western Recorders, Studio 2, the Rock Flowers' two LPs (released in 1971 and 1972, respectively) were recorded by the world-famous Wrecking Crew musicians Hal Blaine (drums), Mike Melvoin (Piano), Louis Shelton (guitar), Dennis Budimir (guitar), and Max Bennett (Bass). Engineer Bob Kovach got in on the act between gigs with the Partridges as well. The albums (*Rock Flowers* and *Naturally*) seem to have been the first two releases of the Wheel label, a division of Ringling Brothers, Barnum & Baily Records, Inc. (manufactured by RCA).

The album and single records that came with the dolls had a certain soulful quality to them. The overall sound of Rock Flowers could best be described as a female Jackson 5/Edison Lighthouse hybrid. It's not hard to imagine The Fifth Dimension taking on Rock Flowers numbers like "(You're) My Kind of Music," "You Shouldn't Have Set My Soul On Fire" and "Mother You, Smother You." One fun LP cut, "Uptight World," starts off with a funky, Curtis Mayfield sound, while the chorus takes a turn evocative of later '70s disco (think Maxine Nightingale). All the Rock Flower songs are strangely soulful (especially the power-ballad "Heaven Help the Non Believer"), while being completely pop at the same time.

It was probably no coincidence that the songs on the records that came exclusively with the dolls were all very short, and leaned more to the pop end of the Rock Flower spectrum. The exception is the record that came with the Doug doll, which had an up-tempo dance tune sung by the ladies called "To Get Ready" (penned by Jeff Barry and Bobby Bloom). On the flip side was a slow groove called "I Just Want To Make You Dance," written by Jeff Barry, sung by an uncredited male singer.

Casting "Heather," "Rosemary" and "Lilac" was reminiscent of the infamous "Johnny Bravo" episode of *The Brady Bunch*; Rindy Dunn, Ardie Tillman and Debby Clinger "fit the suits." Press photos of the real-life girl group pictured the singers in groovy togs matching those of their plasticine counterparts, complete with matching hair dos and exaggerated sunglasses. Strangely, the pictures on their first LP cover displayed

the Rock Flowers dressed conservatively, in long, pastel, granny dresses. Even more curious was the lack of any mention of the dolls, Mattel or even the names of the vocalists on the album jacket. There was, however, an invitation to join a Rock Flowers Fan Club. Strangest of all was the lack of inclusion of any of the songs that came with the dolls on their albums, which were meant to cross-promote the figurines.

Being a Rock Flower was clearly a freelance gig for girls. Rindy Dunn was already a seasoned show biz veteran by the time she was cast as Heather. Not only had she appeared in dozens of commercials and as a tap-dancer at Disneyland, she also had made a name for herself as the designer of LP covers for Buffalo Springfield. Ardie Tillman, the ethnic Rock Flower, Rosemary, had been a member of pop band Sugar, in addition to doing other studio vocals. Rounding out the trio as Lilac was Debby Clinger, bassist from the famed Clinger Sisters band. Debby would go on to bigger teenybopper fame as a member of Kaptain Kool and the Kongs, in addition to starring in the 1978 *Charlie's Angels* rip-off *American Girls*.

Rindy Dunn was eventually replaced by singer/songwriter Jacquie Wiseman, though it's not clear when. Press releases were sent out with both Rindy and Jacquie mentioned in the accompanying bio, but no

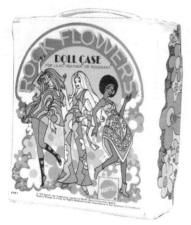

change in the photo. A veteran of the Mike Curb Congregation, Jacquie was a member of the Going Thing, the pop group who were heard in commercials for Ford. The updated line-up went on the road in the spring of 1972 as the opening act for Tom Jones' North American tour, culminating in a two-week stand at Caesar's Palace in Las Vegas.

The Rock Flowers never fully blossomed as a doll line or a musical act. Their first single, "Number Wonderful," barely bubbled on to *Billboard*'s Hot 100, peaking at #95 on February 12, 1972; their two albums died on the vine. Although the dolls were available for several years, they never became must-haves like their fashionable competitors Barbie and Dawn. Today, Rock Flower dolls are known to collectors, but are merely a misty memory a handful to those who were around to see their musical commercials on Saturday morning television.

Special thanks: Richard Cummings

Mission: Magic by Lisa Sutton

No doubt, rocker Rick Springfield is best remembered for his 1980s pop smash "Jessie's Girl." There's also a good chance that soap fans remember him as *General Hospital*'s resident lothario, Dr. Noah Drake. Not even Rick himself, however, places "cartoon character" at the top of his list of achievements.

Rick Springfield had a cartoon? Indeed he did. Not a traditional spin-off, *Mission: Magic* debuted as an episode of *The Brady Kids* cartoon in 1974. Magical teacher Miss Tickle could draw an enchanted circle on her classroom chalkboard and take her students any place in the past, in a somewhat less satirical twist on "Mr. Peabody's Improbable History." Where the pilot relied on the presence of the animated Cindy Brady, the *Mission: Magic* series starred Australian transplant and heir-apparent to the teen-idol throne, Rick Springfield.

If you weren't a reader of *Tiger Beat* in the early '70s, you're probably wondering *why Rick Springfield? He didn't even have a hit record until the '80s!* Actually, Rick had his first success as a pop star in the late '60s in the land down under. As a member of rock band Zoot, young Rick showed a flair for performing and songwriting, in a Beatley pop mode. Emerging as the group's star, he followed the advice of fans and friends who suggested he make a go at stardom in the US.

Upon arrival stateside, Rick had his first taste of what any young ingenue would consider to be success. Hooking up immediately with the crew at *16* Magazine, Rick graciously posed for provocative, shirtless photo spreads. His good looks and winning personality made him likable in spite of all the silly, hype-driven articles about the young up-and-comer.

By fall of 1972 Rick's first single for Capitol, "Speak to the Sky," was screaming up the pop charts. Skeptical industry insiders were quick to slap scandal and payola rumors to the rapid ascent of the ditty, but readers of *Tiger Beat* and *16* all knew the truth. This guy was cute! Okay, so there was a big ad in a summer issue of *Teen Star* offering an opportunity to win a trip to Southern California's Lion Country Safari and go on a date with the burgeoning idol if you filled out the coupon asking for the record number of his new LP, *Beginnings*. So what if you had to buy the album to find out the information? Kids didn't waste their baby-sitting booty for nothing. Rick was talented and hunky (in that sweet, bare-chested, semi-androgynous way girls of the '70s loved). Plus, it was a good song. No one had questioned its validity when it was a hit in Australia earlier in the decade.

Attempting to prove that his first single wasn't a fluke, 22-year-old Springfield went back into the studio to record his second album, tentatively titled *Rick Springfield II*. At the same time, Filmation was seeking a David Cassidy type to increase the appeal of their forthcoming animated cartoon, *Mission: Magic*. Wanting to capitalize on the bubblegum and braces set, those guiding Rick's career convinced him that it was a perfect opportunity to showcase his music. Rick set to work on a set of 16 songs, all based on the weekly scripts of his new Saturday morning series.

Unceremoniously, Capitol changed the name of the new album to *Comic Book Heroes* and commissioned cartoon cover art in anticipation of the new series. Then, unsatisfied with past performance, Capitol decided to drop Rick's contract in the eleventh hour, a few weeks before *Mission: Magic* debuted on ABC's Saturday morning line-up. Shaken but not daunted, Rick managed to shift the completed record over to CBS without much delay.

Mission: Magic premiered on September 9th, 1974, and lasted just long enough for Rick, Tickle and crew to take 16 adventures into the past via the enchanted blackboard. Australian fans of *Mission: Magic* were treated to a soundtrack album of the same name, featuring the fun pop tunes from the weekly adventures. Stateside, young fans were offered the more sophisticated, but still worthy *Comic Book Heroes* album. Unhappy with sales, CBS dropped the not-so-super-seller on his cartoon keester as ABC toyed with the idea of hiring Rick Springfield to replace exiting David Cassidy on *The Partridge Family*. As reported in *Tiger Beat*, Shirley Partridge was to remarry, and Rick would have played her new stepson.

Several lean years followed for Rick, with immigration troubles coupled with the folding of his third U.S. label, Wes Farrel's Chelsea Records. Music temporarily not an option, Rick took acting classes and speech lessons to chip away at his Australian accent. Guest roles on *Wonder Woman*, *The Incredible Hulk* and *Battlestar Galactica* paid his rent, and *General Hospital* made him a daytime star. Never losing sight of his musical ambition, Rick parlayed his daytime stardom into a new contract with RCA.

March of 1981 saw the release of *Working Class Dog*, which yielded the chart-topping, Grammy-winning single "Jessie's Girl." The twice-born idol was on a winning streak that kept him on top for years to come. Rick continued recording hit albums through the '80s, spending most of the '90s acting. In 1999, Springfield re-entered the musical arena with the well-received *Karma* CD and an ongoing tour. Although "Theme from Mission: Magic" is not on the setlist, Rick's live show is chock full of crowd-pleasing hits from his three decades in music.

Kids Incorporated by Peter Geiberger

If only George Orwell had seen acid-washed denim coming, he'd have written the television debut of *Kids Incorporated* into *1984*. Could a future be more perfect than one where a band of kids spend all their time in a soda fountain and solve their problems by singing pop songs? Living in a world that never seemed to have more than 12 people in it—only one of whom was older than 15—the kids would periodically disappear without explanation, only to be replaced by similar characters who appeared just as abruptly. The only adult was a soda jerk who ran a place called the P*alace that looked more like a dance club, and for that matter who seemed fairly uninterested in the comings and goings of his only customers, all of whom happened to be kids, all of whom were in a band, and none of whom ever seemed to leave. I invite anyone looking for a Ph.D. to write a dissertation on the existentialist themes here. Just in case you forgot what decade bore the show, could an idea smack more of '80s values than a group of children forming a corporation out of their band?

Running for an astounding nine years, first on American network television and then on cable, *Kids Incorporated* was the brainchild of producer Thomas Lynch, who saw the kids through three albums, 149 episodes, and in the case of most of the principle actors, puberty. Lynch's other production credits notably include *Xuxa*, a show starring a Brazilian model that seemed to exist only to reinforce the budding dissatisfaction that young girls have with their bodies, and to encourage them to wear as much makeup as possible to compensate. His formula for success boils down to some kids doing highly suggestive choreographed dances, while other kids sing Top 40 hits. The plot of each show existed as a way to weave together five or six song-and-dance numbers. Consider a few highlights from a list of brief episode descriptions. Episode 31: *Rumors get out of hand, when Renee thinks that Riley has a "kidney problem."* Episode 10: *A robot is sent to take Riley's place, but explodes when Kids Inc. overload it.* And my personal favorite, episode 12: *Kid and Stacy try to teach a leprechaun how to be a rock 'n' roll star.* Only in the perfect world of television . . .

The multiculti moppets of *Kids Incorporated*

Despite looking like such a weak show in retrospect, *Kids Incorporated* did feature a few people who've gone on to be actual celebrities, notably *Party of Five* star Jennifer Love Hewitt, who's put out a few albums of her own, and is almost certainly mortified when reminded of her two-year stint as a stockholder in *Kids Incorporated*. It bears mentioning that Lynch found Love after she took first place in the 1988 Texas Miss Doll competition. Other former Kids have gone on to bit parts in successful TV shows, starring roles in TV shows you've never seen, and to form bands you've never heard of. Thomas Lynch works as a producer for Nickelodeon. After a turn in syndication on the Canadian Family Channel, *Kids Incorporated* has slipped off of the air, leaving a legacy only in thrift store record bins and in the minds of dateless twenty-somethings. If you ever get the chance to talk to Jennifer Love Hewitt, be sure and mention to her how much I enjoyed her rendition of Paula Abdul's "Knocked Out" when she was a sexually aggressive ten-year-old.

All Ears: Disney Dreams Up the Best
Radio Station in 30 Years by Metal Mike Saunders

THE seminal moment of the teenpop era is of course in the *Clueless* movie, where Cher refers to college-rock R.E.M.-crap as "mope rock," or "dope rock," or "slope rock," whatever. When Hollywood says it in a script, it's alllllllll over. Anyone who runs into Alicia Silverstone remind her, and thank her. (The movie dates from when, 1995? Pre-Spice Girls, pre-Backstreet, pre-everything. They should recut the movie with a modern soundtrack dropped in—the Valley party would be better with "Genie in a Bottle" as "our song." LFO could be on the patio playing "Summer Girls," instead of that stupid ska band.)

Anyway, if you're collecting predictions on teenpop era span, I say through Year 2010 and beyond, EASY—that would be about 15 years, total. It's a gigantic land shift like the 1964 Beatles ("rock" era), or genre-wise like "heavy metal" (30 long years, right?—the last 20 mostly useless. . . . it's gonna take 20 years of new-era vocal groups just to neutralize that). Best spinoff would be if all the "serious musicians" and "singer-songwriters" gave up and went to work at Macy's. Can you imagine how preposterous a "singer-songwriter" would've seemed in 1963, 1964? (Actually, they were called folkies then.) From what I'm told they can't dance too good.

Funny that the truest pop underground of Year 2000 turns out to be grade schoolers (the trailing half of the 1996–1999 teenpop boom), but hardly surprising. This has been threatening to happen ever since Aqua snuck through 2.5 million copies of *Aquarium* in 1997–98 (ALL to preteens) in America. So who knows how it will play out? Like, in 1982, who would've ever thought MTV would mean shit? It was all videos 24/7, and every 180 minutes you'd go, "OH FUCK, they're playing Sammy Hagar's 'Three Lock Box' AGAIN." But (along with Haysi Fantayzee's assassination of Ronald Reagan) it turned out to be one of the biggest music stories of the '80s.

I've finally figured it out, though—aliens landed several years ago, and Radio Disney is their beach-head! It's all very very clear: Hook the young minds, and then later start with the subliminal messages . . . "Radio for kids!" is hardly one step away from "kill your parents" backwards three times per song. Or maybe *Jesus* came back, took a look around, and went, "Screw the grown-ups, I'm starting from scratch," and *he's* the PD for Radio Disney—nationally syndicated, now with actual airwave stations in about 80% of the U.S.'s largest markets including 1560 AM in New York, plus the Internet station at <www.disney.go.com/radiodisney/?clk=11808>. They're not self-supporting, so they cross-advertise other Disney sectors heavily to get their money's worth. And Web-search business articles say their demographic is mostly ages 2–11. (Wonder what songs those two-year-olds like? The *Pokémon* theme??)

Station IDs/promos in chirpy grade school voices ("Radio Disney . . . We're all EARS!") that drive high schoolers and other 12–20s out the door screaming, but charm the heck out of parents, aunts, and uncles (that's me!). It's like the old hippie cliché, where you take that "tab of acid," walk into the next room, and BOOM! Everything's now in Technicolor! Upbeat! Happy! Wacky! YOU NEED THIS STATION! PRODUCTIVITY WILL INCREASE BY XX%!

. . . Oh man, I give up. RadioD just ran Britney Spears' "Soda Pop" (I'm thinking, "I don't hate this QUITE that much," it actually sounded okay) straight into the Beatles' "I Want to Hold Your Hand," and neither song blinked. That Beatles song can sound realllllll good when set up properly. (Fake reggae into exploding guitar—in 1964, Millie Small would have been the lead-in.) Thirty minutes later, Little Eva's "The Loco-Motion" is on the Disney deck (yesterday they played Kylie Minogue's), and not too long after, the Stones'—I mean Britney's—". . . Baby One More Time" into "Yakety Yak" from 1958.

I'm just jotting down the non-current Top 30 tunes that spring out ('60s, '70s, and '80s), which keep getting more wack/astounding with each additional hour. Lots of novelty and dance songs spanning the last 40 years of hit radio . . . Everything from "Yellow Submarine" to "Cars" by Gary Numan to a deranged version of "The Lion Sleeps Tonight," and over to "The Curly Shuffle" and "Do the Bartman" and Alvin & the Chipmunks disco ("Turn the Beat Around"). Lots of KC on weekends. And TONS of vintage Weird Al, this station/core audience's Numero Uno all-time act, sort of their parallel-universe Beatles. (Hey, "I Want a New Duck" rocks!)

The most surreal segue I've heard on Disney so far is the Contours' "Do You Love Me" (certainly one of my Top 10 or 20 dance songs ever) right into "We Like to Party" by my beloved doofus Vengaboys: classic DJ synergy, where a great track makes an adjoining one sound better (and "We Like to Party" back on CHR-pop was truly annoying). Then there's the greatest pop sequence I've ever heard on commercial radio in my entire life: Toy-Box's "Tarzan and Jane" cavorting into the Backstreet Boys' fantab "I Want It That Way" sliding into the Archies' epochal "Sugar, Sugar." "My Boyfriend's Back" and "I Got You (I Feel Good)" sandwiched around 'N Sync's new single (very catchy!). The *Jetsons* TV theme song, Little Richard's "Tutti Frutti," and the Isleys' "Shout," right next to Christina Aguilera, that damned Vengas bus, and the BSBoys. Joan Jett's glorious "Summertime Blues" hyperdrive Ramonesola, on a Monday afternoon! An insanely cute modern techno-ballad (movie track?) of Rosie and the Originals' "Angel Baby." The *Happy Days* theme, sounding as goofy as in 1976. Girl-pop-rock heaven: "Boys Will Be Boys" from the swell TLC-meets-new-wave 1998 *Beyond Pink* Barbie album. The great *Clueless* TV theme song (written by the Go-Go's' Charlotte Caffey), *full version* (can I buy this somewhere??), into Elvis's "Hound Dog." (Charlotte Caffey back-to-back with Scotty Moore? Don't think that's ever happened before on radio in this galaxy.)

An amazing playlist, I'm telling you, almost freeform! Plus their modern Top 30 is 100% hyper teen-pop, simple as that—sometimes eight of the top 21 Disney chart slots are Backstreet or Britney (On the Web page disney.go.com/radiodisney/?loc=Top30, you can play or download samples of most of the hits, if you have Real Player on your PC. And the most requested songs are compiled now, on two *Radio Disney Jams* CDs.) The square Top 40 scene is still polluted with creaky Celine/Mariah dinosaurs and snooze R&B and horrid faux-"rock" bands NOT heard on RadioDiz—Blink 182, Foo Fighters, etc., mercifully DON'T EXIST!! But they just played "Hand Jive" by what's his name (Johnny Otis?) . . . Why? They're trying to pass down the Diddley-beat? Or does that beat count as novelty? And they play "One Way or Another" regularly, too—the *Sabrina* version. Nuts.

Or 8 PM prime time, the Ramones' "Surfin' Bird"—guitars are obviously allowed if it's a "novelty song," Melissa Joan Hart included, so I figure Disney was just checking if the kids were paying attention. (I've heard them play the much superior Trashmen version several times.) "Crocodile Rock," "Na Na Hey Hey Kiss Him Goodbye," "Twist and Shout" by the Beatles, "We Will Rock You," 1910 Fruitgum Co.'s "Simon Says" (!), the eternally swank "Green Onions," SSledge's "We Are Family," all alternating in barely an hour's time with the week's current Top 30 fab hit teenpop sounds of BritneyChristinaBSBoysMandy'NSyncLFO-VengaboysRickyMLouBegaEiffel65, all of whom completely hold their own in context. I heard the tail end (1965–66) of "screaming Top 40" radio in eighth or ninth grade, and it was cool—but not as cool as this! In '65 we just had the Beatles; oldies only on "oldies weekend," and they sounded silly back-to-back with Them or the Yardbirds or whoever.

The best thing about the teenpop era is that we're back to 1956 or '57 in the pre-Beatles (= pre-guitar bands) era, musically speaking. Wiped the slate clean and started fucking over, back to when vocals meant something and had room to breathe. And those two million rock bands who've wasted everyone's time for the last 30 years are extinct as surely as Bobby Vee or Rydell were back in 1964, when that same initially swell "rock era" began courtesy of the Beatles. (You seriously think some 10-year-old's gonna listen to the Eagles or Fleetwood Mac? Not to mention U2 or R.E.M. or . . .) Until 1966 and artsy rock

(*Revolver*), NO ONE but teenagers bought/followed rock 'n' roll; it was a very small, self-contained, nutty little universe, with novelty records (or death tunes, sort of the same thing) every 30 minutes on the AM. Not unlike what the preteens seem to have going during this, their magic bubble of time.

All across the world—for a year now!—thousands of girls (ages 5 to 15?) have been screwing around in front of their moms' big mirrors, going, "I could do this!" Britney is their '65 Stones, i.e., the blueprint from which thousands copied ('65 Stones spawning roughly 66.7% of all 1966 garage bands). This current stuff's the best Top 40 girlpop since 1962–63, and MAYBE BETTER. 'Cause the beats are better, and there's even more diversity of "styles," white to black to Euro to domestic. ('60s girl groups being one of my favorite rock genres ever—they could really fuckin' sing—but they relied on a few too many lame, uninterested session drummers, once you got past Phil Spector's and David Gates's productions.) On the Disney AM, the "Drive Me Crazy" Stop remix is as relentless as "Satisfaction" in 1965 (meaning they play it *constantly*), altho I much prefer Britney's rhythm track.

And Backstreet get mega-all-hits rotation about equal to the Beatles of back then, so that's about a draw (Beatles—better songs; BSB—better beats). Harmony vocals are cool. Dancing is cool, always has been. I never had a problem with "I Want It That Way" being the greatest song of the century, but I'm getting into it after the fact. Which reminds me of my hostile initial reactions to at least two previous giant changings-of-the-guards in pop/rock: (1) the "heavy rock" of 1970, right before Sabbath/realmetal happened . . . I HATED the stuff, as a '60s fan cranky about all the '60s bands going lame or worse. First couple times "Iron Man" came up early summer 1971 on latenite FM, me and my brother snickered, like, "how DUMB is this?" But by the fourth time we were air-banging our heads like Beavis and Butt-head. . . . It just *happened*, no conscious rethink involved. And (2) I REALLY hated the Ramones and '70s punk for one-entire-year-plus (from the first Ramones LP right up till the first Generation X album, 1978 U.S. version, which rocked hard enough to pull in us suburban metalheads). I mean, I wanted to KILL them; that's how much their brand-new take on rock offended my ears. I remember watching the Ramones' *Don Kirshner's Rock Concert* 15-minute segment when it aired, and hating every single second.

So, it's hardly any surprise that I hated the BSB for a good while . . . I was looking at them and not listening. But now that I'm hearing them constantly in the Radio Disney context, their best songs (without the irritating videos to distract) do indeed sound like a true refraction of the pre-Beatles white vocal groups. Who I think is a really great lead singer is the white guy who parts his hair in the middle—Nick, with the highest-pitched voice. He REALLY has the Belmonts vibe, sings like he MEANS it. Without a hint of retro on the surface, BSB are the first act since December 1963 to be a white male vocal group and be "cool." (Trust me, the minute the Beatles landed at the airport, Frankie Valli/Four Seasons were the epitome of anti-cool.) 35+ years is quite a stretch. In the Beatles' heyday, backing up 35 years would've taken you before swing music.

In 1962–63, the smart kids wouldn't touch the rock scene; they were off playing Coltrane or blues or ethnic folk and being beatniks. Likewise, Joni Mitchell (promoting some stupid cover song album) was in the paper last month grousing about "talentless puff figure" teenpop singers, and *Rolling Stone* and *Spin* these days run plenty of quotes from '80s rock fossils claiming, "MTV doesn't even play videos anymore!" Uh, sure—since *Total Request Live* = late '50s *American Bandstand* as a gonzo über-pop cultural touchstone, I guess Bandstand must NOT've played music . . . It was just a mass cultural delusion. And the all-teen audience was a bunch of dozing sheep, just like the half-asleep bad-white-dancer kids in the *Bandstand* footage. (Twelve-year-old girls, ah, they're silly little kids, and they buy that silly music like, y'know, Elvis and the Beatles, and [their own kidlets] Madonna. I mean, where're the Moog solos? The guitar jams? Some REAL music, y'know?) (Wonder what "real music" was in 1956—bebop??) BUT 38+YRS ONWARD, man, you get the total impression that the teenpop audience is culturally SHARP. Computer kids. The little elementary schoolers who call up the Radio Disney phone lines throw back one-liners as fast as any screaming 1965 AM jock. RDisney's weekly "mailbag" segment, where they play the new feature song of the week and dozens of listeners get to call in on-air (between subsequent songs) and voice their opinions, has more insightful comments than a roomful of rock critics high on Sterno. The record? Madonna's "American Pie." Sample comments? "I liked it 'cause it reminded me of Weird Al and he's my all-time favorite act!" "It's STUPID . . . it's sooooo messed up." "It's awesome! Better than the '50s original." Madonna just barely passed, favorable-over-unfavorable. Good thing they didn't play Pearl Jam.

I'm guessing this station would add .5 to anyone's GPA just as homework music. And the type of format Disney is pushing definitely makes it cool for boys to listen to their sisters' radio hits, too. But what % of actual genre sales are going to boys, and what acts would a 10-year-old boy *like*? Novelty songs? Sure can't imagine the real-life Stan and Kyle—who don't really like girls yet (so scratch Mandy and Brandy and Britney and . . .)—liking 'N Sync. But "Mambo No. 5" and "Blue," hell yeah. You'll recall that much of the youngest part of the mid-'60s pop audience gave us (my distant memory is flickering) punk/new wave-like, that great story about the Ramones trying to play "Indian Giver" upon forming, but it sounded like shit, so they just had to write their own attempted bubblegum songs instead. Well, I bet you my 401(k) the average really sharp eighth-grade boy would be trying to write a song like LFO right now—including to impress the girls! (You know it's a happening scene when the second-tier groups have great songs in them. Rich's lyrics on "Summer Girls" and "Girl on TV" are all-universe.) The kid'd be bright enough to figure out that the retard-rock-rap Woodstock-mosh stuff is duller than death . . . It'd take about two seconds of watching dimwits à la Fred Durst to arrive at that conclusion, obviously.

So whoever Disney's PD is, is a stone genius. Alan Freed, in 1954, only had current R&B cross-over breakthrough trends to work with and help mold. Disney's PD is taking 40 YEARS of the pop/dance/novelty side of rock music and mixing it into an artistic statement. And phone call-ins HAVE to be a certain % of their feedback/input, once a pre-1996 song has been played once. (Can you imagine an eight-year-old going into a big all-formats mom-and-pop store and asking where he could find "Yummy, Yummy, Yummy?" They'd have a coronary.) Maybe Disney's PD was traumatized by hippie CSN&Y-lovin' parents, and the station is revenge? What goes around comes around, ya fuckin' pothead doobie-smoking mellow fellow granolahead deadheads.

Underground? Check this: On Disney's Sunday February 6 Top 30 Countdown, those Swede wackokids the A*Teens' unspeakably great and happy-feet-inducing bubble-techno-pop Abba remake "Mamma Mia" was a breakout hit, up five to #22. Melancholic words? No problem, run it over with the happy truck. I checked the week's *Billboard* two blocks over from loading up the month's canned goods and bathroom groceries, and "Mamma Mia" wasn't even in the pop Top 100. The A*Teens' "Dancing Queen"—also not in *Billboard* yet—EXPLODED on Disney, jumping from #27 to #10 in a week. Now it's inescapable: Wake up in the morning, it will find you. Come home from work, it has followed you. RD's playlist is a mile ahead of national CHR-pop on ALL the teenpop stuff (Hanson's new single every hour on the hour!), kinda like Murray the K breaking the Supremes' (total loser act till then) "Where Did Our Love Go" nationally out of his New York powerhouse show back in the days of classic Top 40. Keeping up with the pop underground could become a full-time job.

In fact, if Billie Joe of Green Day were truly the genius I've always claimed, he'd write a song about teenpop music, and make it funny, not sarcastic. "Getting High With Backstreet"—that'd make Green Day Dylan to the BSBs' Beatles. "One night I died / I got so high / And at the gates were Backstreet / They said you've got to dance / Like pigs a-squealin'/ Sing like you mean it / With extra feelin'/ I went to hell / And I don't care / I went to hell / And guess who's there / Singing I want it that way / I got it that way / Counting money for eternity / Printing contracts for you and me." Very last chorus refrain: "I got high with Backstreet / I got high with Backstreet / I got high with Backstreet / And I don't care."

RECORD LABELS Bell Records by James Porter

In the early Nixon-era '70s, Bell Records was synonymous with AM radio trash, going from the Partridge Family to Barry Manilow in five short years. Helmed by Larry Uttal, Bell was all over the pop music panorama in the '60s, but their greatest success was with Southern soul acts like Oscar Toney, Jr. ("For Your Precious Love"), James & Bobby Purify ("I'm Your Puppet"), Lee Dorsey, Mighty Sam, James Carr, an unknown Al Green, and blue-eyed soul brothers the Box Tops, all either on the Bell label proper or on subsidiaries like Mala, Amy, and the Memphis-based Goldwax. It's said that half the reason why "The Letter" by the Box Tops crossed over to the black charts in '67 was because it was a Bell product, and black jocks assumed that anything on that label was synonymous with soul. In the pop-rock field, Bell made inroads with the garage groove of the Syndicate of Sound ("Little Girl"), as well as a mess of acts produced by Bob Crewe for his New Voice/Dynovoice labels (including Mitch Ryder). Even noted bubble titans Kasenetz & Katz produced a hit for this New York firm (Crazy Elephant's gritty "Gimme Gimme Good Lovin'," circa 1969).

This would all change soon.

At the beginning of the '70s, the Bell label was bought by Columbia Pictures, who set out to change the image via a series of "new Bell" ads in the trades. While artists from the old Bell who were still under contract kept churning out the hits (notably the Delfonics, a soul vocal trio who recorded for the Philly Groove imprint, distributed by Bell), the new artists being waxed for the now silver-colored label (changed from a dull blue) looked the Top 40 in the eye without flinching. At a time when most major labels took full advantage of the emerging album-rock market, this made the singles-oriented Bell label something of a laughing stock, but you can't argue with success, even if it is short-term. Around this same time, Mike Curb was running MGM and had a similar mainstream game plan, but his stable consisted primarily of lounge acts (Joey Heatherton, Sammy Davis, Jr.), has-beens (Tommy Roe, Solomon Burke), and various combinations of the Osmonds. The gang at Bell, by comparison, was far more rock-friendly, keeping the music alive as a singles medium.

After the change in ownership and identity, Bell kept stepping with the hits while missing nary a beat. 1970 gave us "Candida" by Dawn, an updated Drifters sound that wasn't really bubblegum, but still just poppish and simple enough to catch on with the AM-radio audience. Later, they would change their name to Tony Orlando & Dawn (there was also a group on Bell named Dusk). At the time, this was clearly meant to be a one-off studio project—early pressings of the *Candida* album showed no pictures of the group, instead opting for a photo of an anonymous hippie couple, blissfully strolling through the outdoors. And the lineup wasn't the group known through the eventual TV show—this was essentially Orlando (who had a couple of hits for Epic in the early '60s) plus studio vocalists. After the follow-ups caught on, Orlando found Joyce Vincent and Telma Hopkins, two black session singers based in Detroit, and took the concept to the streets as Tony Orlando & Dawn, spawning further hits (including "Tie A Yellow Ribbon 'Round The Ole Oak Tree," a 1973 million-seller) and a smash TV variety series on CBS.

Earlier that fall, *The Partridge Family* premiered on ABC-TV. This was Screen Gems' fictionalized account of the Cowsills (a real-life musical family), although the Partridges' star rose as the Cowsills' faded. "I Think I Love You," their first hit, was not as frantic as Kasenetz-Katz' productions, not as adolescent as the Archies, bore no relation to the garage-rock of a decade previous, and was close enough for easy listening, leaning more towards pop than rock. This was the mellow sound of Bell in the '70s—although Bell recording artists Barry Manilow, Melissa Manchester, the Fifth Dimension, and Vicki Lawrence (remember "The Night The Lights Went Out In Georgia?") were not bubblegum *per se*, their adult contemporary fare was just bland and pop enough to catch on with the transistor-radio masses. The same thing could be said of David Cassidy—the Partridge Family's lead singer was always bitching and moaning about how he wanted to do something musically "heavier." He eventually did, but by that time (1975) the show was off the air and Bell was out of business. While both entities were still going, his solo albums were indistinguishable from the kiddie fare he churned out with his make-believe family (which included real-life stepmom Shirley Jones).

Davy Jones could relate—he'd already been through the Screen Gems teen machine once before. As a Monkee, he lasted to the bitter end, recording the final album (1970's *Changes*) when the group had dwindled down to two Monkees from the original four (Micky Dolenz also stuck it out). During the run of their show, Jones had appeared to be the only one comfortable with being a teen idol. The other Monkees used the phenomenon to further their own causes—Peter Tork and Michael Nesmith wished for acceptance from the serious FM rock crowd, while Dolenz, a fine comic actor in his own right, was busy beefing up his resume as a film director. Jones was the only member to willingly play the superstar game, and as a result was still played up in the teen mags after the show went off the air. In 1971, while Nesmith was establishing his credentials as a pioneering country-rocker, Jones released a shameless, self-titled out-and-out bubblegum LP on Bell. Despite an appearance on *The Brady Bunch* (where Marcia tries to get Davy to appear at her prom), the single "Rainy Jane" only managed to get halfway up the charts. The song itself was basically "Daydream Believer" turned inside out, and the rest of the LP was right in the Bobby Sherman studio groove of the moment.

Bell may not have contributed much to the album market—at a time when the medium was redefining itself—but they were cranking out the one-shot singles as if tomorrow would never come. The Panda People took a crack at "Chirpy Chirpy Cheep Cheep" (1973), which originally made waves via Mac & Katie Kissoon's cool bubble-soul version; Crimson and Clover updated "Born Too Late," the '50s teen-idol hit by the Poni-Tails (1972); other studio projects followed, usually just this side of the easy-listening market. They had "Precious & Few" by Climax on the Rocky Road subsidiary, and they even catered to the kiddie market with *Free to Be . . . You and Me* (1973). The soundtrack to Marlo Thomas' consciousness-raising TV special was on Bell, as was Ricky Seagall (a pre-schooler brought in during *The Partridge Family*'s final season in a vain attempt to boost the sagging ratings) and Rodney Allen Rippy (the five-year-old pitchman for the Jack-In-The-Box fast-food chain). From 1970 until its demise around January 1975, this was the legacy of Bell Records.

However, their U.K. division was a whole 'nother thang.

In England, Bell was also preoccupied with the singles market, but their strategy was different. Glam-rock was starting to take over, and glam's concept of bubblerock was closer in spirit to what Kasenetz & Katz were doing a few years earlier: simple enough for the kids, but with a near-rockabilly bottom that no one could deny. The most obvious example was Gary Glitter, a singer in his mid-'30s who had already gone around the block once under the name of Paul Raven. The song that kicked it off was "Rock & Roll, Part 2," which was an instrumental version of "Part 1," but that's Gary himself hollering "HEY!" over the rumbling bass. His hit streak in England lasted well into 1975, when an attempt to jump on the disco bandwagon did him in (although it worked for his backup group, the Glitter Band, who had a Stateside hit with "Makes You Blind"). He left his mark in British rock history, but scarcely left a footprint in the States: both "Rock & Roll, Part 2" and "Didn't Know I Loved You Till I Saw You Rock & Roll" charted in the U.S. Top 40 in 1972, and then . . . nothing. Despite periodic comebacks in England (which ended in 1997 when he was arrested on a kiddie porn downloading charge), Glitter is now remembered in America for "Rock & Roll, Part 2." That . . . and the fact that it's continually played at basketball games to rev up the crowd.

Occasionally, hits from Bell's English division would trickle through the American charts: Edison Lighthouse (featuring Tony Burrows, who was Merry Olde's answer to Ron Dante) had their moment with "Love Grows Where My Rosemary Goes" (1970); the Vanity Fare had a couple of hits on Page One, a Bell subsidiary based in England (including 1970's "Hitchin' A Ride"); and although the Sweet now sound like punk AND metal in their rawest state, "Little Willy" was considered bubblegum when it scorched the airwaves back in 1973. Suzi Quatro didn't get American airplay until she toned her sound down drastically, but her earliest records on Bell fall into the same metallic category. The Bay City Rollers had been kicking around since the early '70s, but didn't really take off in the States until four years later. The earliest singles, on Bell, weren't much different from what American teens would later hear—"Saturday Night," a monster in America in 1975, was previously a flop in England in 1973. They originally crashed onto the (English) music scene with "Keep On Dancing," a remake of the garage-rocker made famous by the Gentrys in 1965. Their version was considerably smoother than the Gentrys', with strings, horns, false ending, and a key change, but still

just pop enough to fit in with 1971's (mostly) lethargic music scene. Hello, like the Sweet and Suzi Quatro, were hard-rock bordering on bubblegum, and the closest they came to cracking the American charts was when Ace Frehley from Kiss had a Top 20 hit with "New York Groove" in 1978. The original Hello version is somewhat slower, but still in touch with the glam mood of the moment. Like the Rollers, they softened their touch as the decade wore on, leaning more towards ballads in later releases.

Bell U.K. even flirted with soul music, recording a revived Drifters (with Johnny Moore, who sang on some of their old Atlantic hits, plus an otherwise all-new cast), as well as the Fantastics, whose pop-slanted material might as well have been Drifters throwaways. And they had Linda Lewis, whose chirpy voice was perfect for that bubble-soul vibe. Also in the stable was Showaddywaddy, an oldies showband halfway between Sha Na Na and Roy Wood; Alvin Stardust, a great Gary Glitter clone; and Mud, who recorded several stompers with producers Chinn and Chapman (including "Tiger Feet") before landing squarely in the middle of the road, as many glam acts (unfortunately) did.

In 1974, Clive Davis, president of Columbia Records, was ousted from that position for mishandling company funds (which included paying for his son's $100,000 bar mitzvah). Not long after, he resurfaced as the president of Bell Records, unseating Larry Uttal, who left to form Private Stock (which engineered Frankie Valli's comeback and introduced the world to Blondie). On paper, this looked like a respected industry figure lowering his standards—Davis was the man who made Columbia a major player in the rock world, signing Janis Joplin, Sly Stone, Chicago, Johnny Winter, Santana, and a host of other Woodstock-era legends. He found a way to market jazz towards a rock audience (with Miles Davis' *Bitches Brew* and Herbie Hancock's *Head Hunters* being prominent albums of the era), and made major inroads into soul music, distributing Gamble & Huff's Philadelphia International label (the O'Jays, Harold Melvin & the Blue Notes, MFSB). All this meaningful and lasting stuff on his resume, and now here he was going to work for The House That David Cassidy Built.

Well, Cassidy and the whole Partridge Family were done with by the time Davis showed up on the scene. Some major rehauling was done: in 1975, he changed the name of the company from Bell to

Arista. Secondly, just to prove that this wasn't your little sister's old bubblegum label, during the first couple of years he signed a mess of unconventional artists who couldn't go pop with a firecracker: Patti Smith, Gil Scott-Heron, New York singer-songwriter Garland Jeffreys (one single issued), and a series of avant-garde jazzmen on their Arista Freedom subsidiary. They also handled distribution of Savoy, a landmark R&B/gospel label that was a staple of black music history. And to make sure the industry got the drift that Clive Davis and Bell (under a new name) was back, Davis even hosted an episode of *The Midnight Special*, the late-night rock showcase of the '70s, with the majority of the guests being Arista artists (Barry Manilow on the same show as black revolutionary poet Gil Scott-Heron—a first, any way you look at it). The label is still with us, and Clive Davis is still the main man there.

The old Bell heritage was hard to keep in the closet for long. The Bay City Rollers, Melissa Manchester, and Barry Manilow were all million-selling Arista artists during the '70s, but they were left over from the old regime. The first Arista single ever released was by Robby Benson, an actor with teenybop appeal. He, too, was a Bell alumni. And even though Davis went out of his way to bury the pop hatchet with the occasional "prestige" act, it was still the blander, non-threatening groups that have allowed Davis to live comfortably. The next time you hear Arista artists Whitney Houston or Kenny G. in some elevator, you'll know that the legacy of David Cassidy is being passed on.

Clive Davis

Gator in the Candy Lab: A Brief History of Buddah Records by Gene Sculatti

The House That Gum Built started out as a second home. Buddah Records, official address of the 1910 Fruitgum Co., Ohio Express, the Lemon Pipers and a dozen lesser pop-tart combos, was initially a get-away pad for business partners Phil Steinberg and Hy Mizrahi and producer Artie Ripp (whose credits included Doris Troy's "Just One Look," Jay & the Americans' "Come A Little Bit Closer" and the Shangri-La's "Remember—Walkin' In The Sand"). Founded in 1965 as an offshoot of the trio's Kama Sutra Productions, Kama Sutra Records had, one year later, distinguished itself as America's hippest indie, notching hit after hit by the Lovin' Spoonful and charting singles by the Sopwith Camel, the Tradewinds and the Innocence. The label released a version of Bob Dylan's "Can You Please Crawl Out Your Window" (by New York's Vacels) even before Dylan, and signed—then unsigned, at the point of a shot-gun—Frisco's psychedelic scene-starters, the Charlatans.

The Naked Truth from Buddah Record

But by 1967 a rapidly souring distribution arrangement with MGM Records had Ripp & co. looking for new digs. With backing from independent distributors, they founded Buddah Records, setting up shop at 1650 Broadway in NYC. "I conclud-ed it was irreverent to spell 'Buddha' like the religion," says Ripp of the Indo-Asian handle. "Besides, I could never say 'ha' at the end of my name, but I could say 'Aah' . . ." It was never Buddah's mission to be the hothouse that grew the music America loved to hate. Rather, the label was designed to attract talented writers and producers—Ripp already had Spector tune-smiths Pete Anders and Vinnie Poncia (the Ronettes' "Do I Love You" and "The Best Part Of Breakin' Up") under contract, as well as Bo Gentry and Ritchie Cordell, who had produced Tommy James & the Shondells' "Mony Mony" and "I Think We're Alone Now"—and to accommodate unique artists with real prospects for long-term success.

West Coast A&R chief Bob Krasnow failed in his attempt to sign Frank Zappa's then-unaligned Bizarre Records imprint to Buddah, but he did snag Captain Beefheart & His Magic Band, whose early-1967 *Safe As Milk* (BDS LP 5001) officially introduced one of rock's most idiosyncratic and influential artists. Subsequent eccentricities such as organist Barry Goldberg's moody blues extrapolation *Reunion*, an early FM favorite, and Tony Bruno's tongue-in-cheek *The Beauty of Bruno* suggest Buddah might have taken off as a sort of left-of-center boutique version of Warner Bros. Then came Neil.

As counterpoint to the hip-clad Krasnow, Ripp hired a "young hotshot" promotion man from Philadelphia's Cameo-Parkway Records. Neil Bogart was 24 when he became Buddah's VP/general manager in 1967, and his founding philosophy, Ripp recalls, went something like this: "Having artists is a long-term game. Who knows how long it will take us in time and records to break these stars? So we need some real hit records." Bogart's aggressiveness is something Ripp knew well and admired, "having seen what he did with Question Mark & the Mysterians' '96 Tears' at Cameo. He could take that kind of super-basic record and just blow it out—bang-o!"

Among the records Bogart had blown out at Cameo was the Ohio Express' wiry "Louie Louie" rip, "Beg, Borrow And Steal," so, when he brought Buddah a new side by the producers of that garage nugget, Jerry Kasenetz and Jeff Katz, Ripp listened. "Neil plays me 'Simon Says' by the Fruitgum Co.," remembers Ripp. "I listen and I say, 'Boy, that sounds like a smash,' OK? Like it's a brand new trend. But I think we're gonna buy ourselves into a challenge: we're gonna all of a sudden have this badge on us if we chase this music. On the one hand, we'll be challenged as a label, putting out these records—which had no real artists—aimed at a very young head. On the other hand, we'd generate income and solidify the company right out of the gate." Ripp and his partners concluded that it was an acceptable risk.

"Simon Says" hit the Hot 100 in January 1968, eventually selling two million singles and rising to No. 4. By May, the Ohio Express' "Yummy, Yummy" charted, on its way to the same peak: Buddha's foundation was down and the walls were going up fast, courtesy of Katz-Kasenetz's producing and Bogart's pushing. But, while the music's pre-teen target audiences clamored for gum, radio chewed slowly—and didn't always like the taste.

West Coast top-40 stations, particularly Bill Drake's powerful RKO chain (L.A.'s KHJ, San Francisco's KFRC), decided that, despite ringing request lines, Buddha's gooey goods did not fit the image they chose to project. 1968 saw the decade's most pitched battles between America's warring cultures; already hemorrhaging young-adult listeners to the new rock FM stations, the last thing AM Top-40 wanted was to be

seen as square—or to be left alone with a constituency of noisy 10-year-olds. Where radio refused to play Buddah's gum, Bogart's promo squad redoubled its efforts. "We just said, 'You guys have gotta be crazy,' explains Ripp. "'Your ignoring this music is like they just dropped the atom bomb and your news department refuses to put the story on the air!'"

Radio eventually succumbed, thanks to the label's relentless promotional blitz—and a variety of marketing gimmicks designed to stoke customer demand for bubblegum music. Buddah backed dance contests (teams at 80 teenage Hullabaloo Nightclubs competed to devise the most original steps to "Simon Says"), in-house perks (a tie-in with American Air Lines rewarded sales staffers 50,000 bonus miles for their efforts on behalf of "Yummy, Yummy") and retail promotions (a secret shopper—"Betty Buddah"—visited record stores, asking first for a non-Buddah record. If the salesclerk then tried to sell her a Buddah disk, Betty identified herself and handed the clerk $50).

Buddah celebrated its first anniversary in September 1968, as the nation's seventh-ranked label in single sales, a remarkable feat considering the then-crowded field. While it enjoyed success in the fields of general pop-rock (Lou Christie, Motherlode, the Brooklyn Bridge) and R&B (the Impressions, on Curtis Mayfield's Buddah-distributed Curtom Records; the Isley Brothers, through their T-Neck label), it was largely the sticky stuff that sealed the imprint's success. Within Buddah's bubblegum laboratory, it seemed as though teams of hook-canny creatives labored day and night, perfecting irresistible sugar-fixes. Katz-Kasenetz oversaw their own writing stable—Elliot Chiprut (the Fruitgum Co.'s "Simon Says," and "May I Take A Giant Step") and Levine & Resnick (the Express' "Yummy," "Chewy" and "Down At Lulu's," the Katz-Kasenetz Singing Orchestral Circus' "Quick Joey Small")—as well as "Artie's army," Ripp's original Kama Sutra composers (Bo Gentry, Ritchie Cordell and Bobby Bloom collaborated on the Fruitgum Co.'s "Indian Giver" and "Special Delivery").

From Neil Bogart's liner notes: "Bubblegum music is the naked truth in music. Music was meant to be happy, free, unashamed, relaxed, natural and easy, easy, easy. But then one day the serpent came slithering down the tree with an apple and we all started wearing fig leaves. . . . The next time that serpent comes winding down the tree he'll have a chunk of bubblegum in his mouth and he'll be whistling a tune. And he won't be tempting you out of the garden— he'll be tempting you back into it. That's the naked truth."

The hectic work pace often occasioned the repurposing of both material and artists. Andrew Smith & the Hyannis Ports' satire on Robert F. Kennedy's Presidential bid, "Bobby Says," blatantly sampled "Simon Says." The Lemon Pipers, a bona fide band from Cincinnati whose repertoire included the extended psych-funk workout "Fifty Year Void," were transformed into dutiful bubble-puppies by writer-producer Paul Leka, who fed them "Green Tambourine," "Rice Is Nice" and "Jelly Jungle." And, since Buddah's biggest records were being made by acts that didn't exist outside the studio anyway, who'd object if the lab cooked up a few more? The call for hits and the necessity of commanding shelf space almost demanded such chicanery. Brand identification was the goal. On what other label would one expect to find such fanciful concoctions as the Tidal Wave, Frosted Flakes, Salt Water Taffy, Lt. Garcia's Magic Music Box, J.C.W. Rat Finks and The Rock And Roll Dubble Bubble Trading Card Company Of Philadelphia 19141?

Bubblegum music prospered well into 1969 (the genre's signature work, "Sugar, Sugar," charted that July), but the Buddah variety quickly lost its flavor. The label's last gum successes, the Ohio Express' "Mercy" and the Fruitgum Co.'s "Special Delivery," made the Hot 100 in May of '69—less than eight months after *Time* magazine had crowned Bogart king of pop's cotton-candy castle. By then, his crown had lost some of its luster, thanks to such fizzled Barnumesque schemes as the Katz-Kasenetz Singing Orchestral Circus; the 40-member bubblegum supergroup played Carnegie Hall, but a subsequent tour and TV documentary drew scant response. There'd also been the shamelessly phony "Naked Truth" album campaign. The six nude bodies on the cover, Bogart told the press of the forthcoming LP, represented "the freedom of expression common to music today and the new attitude toward living." Upon its release, the back jacket of the anthology of bubblegum hits featured 6 cavorting toddlers; it failed to ignite controversy or sales.

Buddah's demise was surely hastened by its assembly-line approach (how were potential record-buyers to tell the difference between the Camel Drivers and the Carnaby Street Runners?). It was too-much-too-soon, but also not-enough-where-it-counts. Bogart's hit-city philosophy had generated a one-year streak of white-hot singles, but it had done little for album sales (of six *Billboard*-charting Fruitgum and Express LPs, the highest position posted was 129). "At the end of the day," explains Ripp, "if you were going to be a new Atlantic or Motown, you had to have the Arethas, the Ray Charles, the Bob Dylans— the stars who would keep you selling albums—and bubblegum music didn't have that." To say nothing of the reptilian payback monster Bogart's experiments had unleashed.

"When we again, finally [1969], sat down with Frank Zappa and [manager] Herbie Cohen to seriously discuss distributing Bizarre Records, which had now emerged as a very real thing," says Ripp, "the hit alligator bit me in the ass." Despite Buddah's initial braveness with Beefheart—and its early outreach to the hipster community (at Monterey Pop, a giant inflated Buddah served as both a signpost for festival-goers and an advertisement for the label)—Zappa passed. "How could I," Ripp remembers him asking, "allow Bizarre to be connected with Buddah, the home of bubblegum music?" The el supremo of avant-pop wound up taking his roster (the Mothers, Alice Cooper, Wild Man Fischer, Jeff Simmons, the GTO's) to Warner/Reprise.

It was almost as if Buddah was fated to pay for its short-lived bubble of prosperity. The "badge" the label pinned on itself when it issued "Simon Says" seemed to ensure that the artist-attracting 'cool factor' Ripp sought would forever elude Buddah. The company did go on to sell albums (by Melanie, Gladys Knight & The Pips, and Curtis Mayfield, whose *Superfly* soundtrack came in through Curtom), but it sustained itself until its 1983 demise largely in the singles game ("Candles In The Rain," "Midnight Train To Georgia," the Andrea True Connection's "More More More").

By then, the architects of Buddah's early success had left the building. Artie Ripp exited in 1970, when the board of Viewlex Corporation, the educational-media company that bought the label in late 1969, refused to issue the (highly lucrative) *Woodstock* movie and soundtrack, to which he had acquired rights. The directors of the publicly-traded company had seen the TV-news coverage of sex, mud and rock 'n' roll and decided an association with the festival was not in their best interests ("I told 'em," says Ripp, "you got involved with Kama Sutra and Buddah Records—did you think you were getting involved with the Vatican?'"). Ripp went on to discover and manage Billy Joel, and he remains active in entertainment today.

Neil Bogart quit Buddah in 1973 to found Casablanca Records. While the label's flagship act, Kiss, has proved to be among the most enduring in pop, the House That Disco Built was, like Buddah, hit-fixated and producer-driven; Giorgio Moroder and Jacques Morali, the minds behind Donna Summer and the Village People, respectively, called all the shots. (Bogart's Casablanca exploits and excesses get a full chapter

in Frederick Dannen's 1991 music-biz exposé *Hit Men*. Bogart died of cancer in 1982, after founding the short-lived Boardwalk Entertainment.)

"The perception was that bubblegum music wasn't hip enough," reflects Ripp. "Yet the reality was that the gum songs and the dance groove of the records had a wonderful, fun aspect to them. It was something in the '60s that wasn't heavy or with a political agenda. It was, 'Smile, have a good time.' Everything is not so significant that you can't take a moment out to laugh. Everything doesn't have to be Einstein's theory or change the world."

Sometimes, though, it seems as if the world never will change, as if some bad reps—no matter how undeserved—are destined to stick to their wearers forever. As late as December 1999, more than a decade and a half after Buddah closed its doors for good, a *Washington Post* writer, reviewing a Beefheart reissue, wondered how the surrealist auteur ever could have consorted with "the label that specialized in bubblegum music—squeaky clean pop singles aimed directly at children and early adolescents. It was an odd place for the dada captain to begin . . ."

The same year, the BMG music conglomerate reactivated "Buddha" Records as an archival imprint, to mine its many acquired catalogs (including Buddah). For two years Buddha reissued albums by Melanie, Waylon Jennings, Duke Ellington, the Flamin' Groovies, Dr. Seuss and Henry Rollins. As we go to press comes the welcome news that they're compiling hits collections by the Ohio Express, Lemon Pipers and 1910 Fruitgum Company.

Colgems Records by Bill Pitzonka

Colgems Records was born in 1966 of the corporate coupling of Columbia Pictures and RCA. The new entity's primary (if not sole) purpose was to exploit the vinyl ventures of the Monkees—the made-for-TV pop band whose fast-paced live-action sitcom was produced by Columbia's Screen Gems production arm and which aired on the RCA-owned NBC television network.

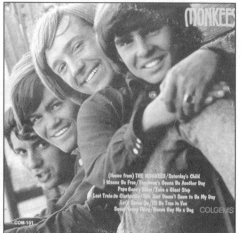

Colgems also marked the pinnacle of music mogul Don Kirshner's career in the Columbia Pictures corporate structure. Kirshner made his mark earlier in the decade as the head of Aldon Music, the pop publishing powerhouse that nurtured the hugely successful writing partnerships of Neil Sedaka & Howard Greenfield, Gerry Goffin & Carole King, and Barry Mann & Cynthia Weil. As Aldon started racking up the hits for other labels, Kirshner founded his own in-house Dimension imprint to release Aldon's perfectly-crafted demos as singles—a practice which yielded Little Eva's #1 smash, "The Loco-Motion" in 1962.

In 1963, Aldon was sold lock, stock, and catalog to Columbia Pictures, and became Screen Gems-Columbia Music. Soon thereafter, Dimension merged into Colpix, Columbia Pictures' record label. Colpix—created in 1958 as an outlet for soundtracks from studio properties—had by that time proven itself adept at turning contract players into recording stars, resulting in huge hits for surf dreamboat James Darren ("Goodbye Cruel World") and dutiful *Donna Reed Show* daughter Shelley Fabares (the chart-topping "Johnny Angel"). These stellar transformations were performed by staff producer Stu Phillips, who had given Colpix its first #1 single with the Marcels' unforgettable doo-wop reinvention of "Blue Moon" in 1961.

Kirshner's arrival at Colpix's New York offices effectively lessened Phillips' duties to the point that Phillips moved to Los Angeles, only to find the West Coast operations securely under the control of Kirshner colleague Lou Adler. Phillips left to record a series of easy-listening instrumental albums for Capitol as the Hollyridge Strings and ventured into scoring for television (*Battlestar Galactica*) and film (*Beyond the Valley of the Dolls*).

Adler had signed writer/producers Tommy Boyce & Bobby Hart, and in 1965, Kirshner assigned the duo to a television/music project which was then in development, *The Monkees*. Soon thereafter, Adler left Colpix to found Dunhill Productions. In the way that all things come full circle, Dunhill's first contracted artist was Adler's wife, Shelley Fabares.

Despite a huge publicity-generating talent search, two Monkee slots were filled by Colpix artists Davy Jones (whose solo recordings bore the more formal David Jones) and Mike Nesmith (who recorded protest songs under the *nom de disque* Michael Blessing). *The Monkees* was sold to NBC on the strength of a pilot soundtracked by Boyce & Hart's demos.

The chart fortunes at Colpix had been steadily declining, so in 1966 the label was leveled to clear the path for the creation of Colgems. The new joint venture allowed Kirshner's team to oversee the creative duties, while RCA offered the dedicated services of its many recording studios and handled pressing, distribution, and promotion.

The Monkees proved to be a veritable cash cow that Kirshner milked relentlessly until his famous ouster in a creative control coup by the PreFab Four early in 1967. Kirshner retaliated by starting his own Kirshner Entertainment Corp., launching toon stars the Archies.

The Monkees were the only Top 40 chartmakers for Colgems. The remainder of the roster—no surprise—featured singing actors like Sajid Khan (*Maya*), Peter Kastner (*The Ugliest Girl In Town*), and Sally

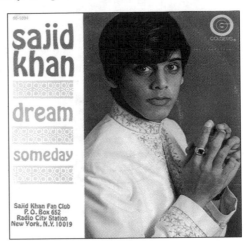

Field (*The Flying Nun*); soundtracks for Columbia Pictures' *In Cold Blood, Oliver,* and *Casino Royale*; staff songwriters Hoyt Axton and Michael Murphey & Boomer Castleman (a k a The Lewis & Clarke Expedition); and glorified demos of Screen Gems copyrights by Hung Jury, Fountain of Youth, and the New Establishment. By 1970, the Monkees' moment had passed, and Screen Gems' attention had turned to its next TV/music cross-pollination effort, *The Partridge Family*. Both the new venture and the Colgems catalog were given over to Columbia Pictures' recently acquired label, Bell Records.

Unsafe At Any Speed: Super K Records by Chris Davidson

Far be it for a peon to flip off the kings, but Jeff Katz and Jerry Kasenetz—the best bubblegum stand-up guys in the business—made a bad call or two right in the midst of bubblegum's golden era. Flinging out 45s with the frequency of the Sunday *Times*, and even with the purest of pop instincts, they simply released a few dogs. What's funny, though, is how the K-men preserved such a high percentage of junk for their own boutique label, Super K Records, which promised at first to deliver the swing-time goods.

Not to be confused with the duo's "Super K Production" tagline, a trademark of juicy teen quality that adorned every major bubblegum act save the Archies, the Super K label itself, like the most ambitious of flashers, dropped its drawers in Times Square. Right when the whole world was watching, Super K Records mocked pop-starved record buyers with dingy, late-period offerings from former hit-makers (the Shadows of Knight), bubblegum mainstays (Ohio Express, 1910 Fruitgum Co.), and complete nobodies (anyone for "Buckwheat"?). Super K Records was Buddah past its sell-by date.

Reflecting on the dozen-odd disks to bear the Super K logo, blame must rest on the snore-inducing hard rock sounds from which many acts drew inspiration at the time. Antithetical to bubblegum, the wah-wah noodling and meandering melodies of 1968–69 bellowed loudly and signified nothing. This Dead-worthy hot air unfortunately informed much of the Super K output. Case in pointlessness: the Shadows of Knight, who morphed from wild rave-uppers on Dunwich to Super K butt-scratchers on their self-titled 1969 LP. The band's single for the label, "My Fire Department Needs a Fireman" (issued twice with different flips), fared better in toning down the heaviness, yet the Shads' fall from grace would not waver.

Things had started out rather promisingly. Question Mark and the Mysterians, the other hit squad involved with Super K Records, made a pit-stop prior to a 25-year slide into oblivion by releasing the company's second single, "Sha La La"—a direct and pretense-free disk. Two releases later came Captain Groovy and His Bubblegum Army's self-titled theme song, with lead vocals by Jeff Barry pal Bobby Bloom. And so it looked as though Super K would percolate. Then, incredibly, the bubblegum burst.

Records shocking in their ineptitude appeared by the Carnaby Street Runners, Super Circus, Ohio Express and Shadows of Knight, including full-length atrocities by Wahonka and Deviled Ham. A smorgasbord of shabby sounds, a melee of misguided music. That the Kasenetz and Katz names were attached made the story all the more painful. Happily, before the damage mounted, the label folded in a flurry of flared pants and white-boy boogie riffs. The principal players forged ahead, the bad records slipped away to wherever hippie vinyl and marching band albums crawl to die. With its promise of greatness unfulfilled, Super K ended up less than a blip on the bubblegum radar screen.

White Whale: The Moby Dick of Bubble-Pop by Alec Palao

In a town renowned for Svengali-like producers and pasteurized processed pre-wrapped pop product, White Whale was surprisingly one of the few Los Angeles independent labels that took the bubblegum style to heart (and the charts). Because, as co-founder Lee Lasseff cheerfully admits, "the White Whale sound was always more of the commercial variety."

The company hit immediate pay dirt in 1965 with the folk-rocking sound of the Turtles, and over the course of the next two years rode on the crest of the band's success, culminating in the early '67 mega hit "Happy Together." However the rest of their initial roster—despite high quality releases by the likes of Lyme & Cybelle and Nino Tempo & April Stevens—was less successful, and like the astute businessmen they were, Lasseff and his partner Ted Feigin cast their net further afield for acts. "I wasn't a record producer, nor was Ted, but I felt we had a good ear. So we looked outside for producers."

It was therefore unsurprising that White Whale became synonymous with late 1960s frothy pop because, as Lasseff points out, "most of our later records were basically purchases, and a lot of the masters that we picked up were actually our biggest hits." In looking for product, the label went as far afield as Hawaii (Liz Damon's Orient Express' "1900 Yesterday"), and McAllen, Texas (René & René's maudlin "Lo Mucho Que Te Quiero"). However, the stronger bubblegum was normally handed to them on a plate by established producers like Bones Howe, such as a chart-friendly rendition of "Nadine" by Smokestack Lightnin', or Al Capps, with the Committee's groovy version of "California My Way."

In truth, some of White Whale's chart-aimed schlock like Feather and the Brothers has remained, well, schlock, but the label had some great examples of that sub-sub-genre, *heavy* bubblegum. A good one was the Randy Bachman-penned "No Sugar Tonight" by Steel Wool—reputedly ex-members of the Knickerbockers supervised by George Tobin, who later handled 1980s teenypop sensation Tiffany. In a similar mode, Professor Morrison's Lollipop are remembered by Lasseff as a studio fabrication, but in fact the group were a Lincoln, Nebraska garage band previously known as the Coachmen, which helped make "You Got The Love" such a great tough pop disc. It evolved from a fleeting association the label had with the Kasenetz-Katz empire, and with this White Whale helped spread the bubblegum credo further.

The Clique were an Austin, Texas outfit who also had garage-band roots, but under the production aegis of pop *wunderkind* Gary Zekley the actual group were to barely appear on any of the several records issued under their name on White Whale. However, largely through the posthumous notoriety of the b-side "Superman" (via REM's 1986 cover), rather than their Tommy James-ish hit "Sugar On Sunday," the Clique are now seen as White Whale's crowning achievement in bubblegum.

In retrospect, perhaps the label's most outstanding release bubble-wise was actually the Reivers' impossibly catchy "Constantly." Written, produced and sung by future soft-rock king Paul Davis, it came at the end of White Whale's chart tenure in 1970, but remains as fresh and chewy an example of the genre as one is wont to find anywhere. "We tried to be as hip as could be and not do what other labels were doing," says Lasseff. That, combined with an unabashed sense for the commercial, is what has kept a longer-lasting flavor to White Whale's bubblegum.

Unlikely Bubblegum Bubblegum Psychedelia:
Pseudo Maturity In A Candy-Coated World by Glynis Ward

The candy-coated world of bubblegum is often perceived as a juvenile playground of simplistic melodies and child-like lyrical themes, formulated and prefabricated music based on hit potential and sales figures. It made money, and it employed musicians. In 1967 rock 'n' roll was a tough business. To be thought of as a professional musician by older show business types, you needed to be working—recording and making hits. But to be considered a "serious musician" by your peers, you needed to be freaking out and warping minds with psychedelic sounds. Hits were being made for children—pressed up on affordable 45s, while teens and young adult audiences purchased LPs. The fine line that had existed between rock 'n' roll and pop music during the '60s was beginning to widen. Then along came *Sgt. Pepper*, proving that pop and psychedelia could successfully be combined to create pop hits, but maintain a sense of musical maturity by incorporating experimental effects with the ultimate sign of musical "maturity": orchestration. How to bring it home to America? With a little "Green Tambourine." The Lemon Pipers (with the help of their

expert writing team of Leka and Pinz) created a 2:22 minute opus combining the perfect blend of vocal effects, unconventional percussion, well-hidden orchestration, pseudo-meaningful lyrics and a simple, catchy melody. It is the measuring stick against which all other groups seeking to create bubble-psych masterpieces must be compared.

Psychedelia, an American creation (cf. 13th Floor Elevators), remained essentially an underground form of rock 'n' roll until the Beatles borrowed it, and then gave it back. They returned it with style, and soon psychedelia became a cultural force beyond the music scene. It became visual, brightly colored, animated and fueled with spirituality, ethnic elements and exotic opiates. Through this mainstreaming of psych, an encompassing feeling of community enveloped American youth. Outrageous outfits and vintage clothing became the uniform representing meaningful thought and a new social awareness. Rock groups were the spokespeople, and lyrics echoed the thoughts of the generation. A line like "blow your mind on brownies made by Aunt Matilda's double secret recipe" from the Two Dollar Question's "Aunt Matilda" (*Marijuana Unknowns, Stoned,* 1997) could only mean one thing, and it was one of the biggest subjects in bubble-psych, and the psychedelic movement in general: drugs. Thinly veiled drug references litter almost every bubble-psych song. Elephant's Memory's "Super Heap" figures "the mushroom pie was cured of its summer cold" into its seemingly nonsensical lyrics which can be read as a psychedelic code.

The Yummies' "Hippie Lady" makes references to the social problem of underage runaways (presumably bound for San Francisco) with "run away at 17, she looks so dirty but she's really clean/It's not like I don't like society/But go away and let me be free right now/With my Hippie Lady." A search for greater meaning in life is often alluded to, and was a favorite subject of Jimmy Curtiss who discusses "a new dimension, mind expansion" in "Psychedelic Situation" (*Pebbles 16*, AIP, 1985) and "searching for that precious something/Give us something to believe in" with his group the Hobbits in "Strawberry Children." Such lyrics were obviously more mature than the simple bubblegum creations of "1, 2, 3 Red Light" or "Rice Is Nice," and were not aimed at a pre-teen audience.

Bubble-psych songs frequently displayed a mixture of the bubblegum genre pop formula of repetitive, catchy melodies with more complex instrumentation, which imparted an over-all psychedelic feel to the song. Phasing, on both vocals and guitar, was a popular technique used to create a distorted sound signifying an altered state as on the aforementioned "Strawberry Children" and "Green Tambourine." Sitar was often employed to give an ethnic Indian raga flavor, often mixed with tabla drums or other weird percussion, such as on the Ohio Express' psyched-out instrumental "Make Love, Not War." Backward guitar (e.g., "A Question Of Temperature" by The Balloon Farm) was a very inexpensive way of adding trippiness. So was creating a b-side out of a completely backwards a-side and giving it a different name (e.g., "Pow Wow" by the 1910 Fruitgum Co.). A few songs, like "Jelly Jungle" by the Lemon Pipers, employed almost every trick in the book to create a full, rich sound, and even included an orchestra.

During the early '60s, orchestration was for squares or Phil Spector. Spector's lush production and string of hits were respected, and his use of orchestra was widely considered the key to his success. The Beatles' *Sgt. Pepper*, which was as much about experimentation in production as it was about songs, copped the Spectorish orchestration to weave a tapestry in psychedelic sound. Many psychedelically-influenced bubblegum albums began to employ orchestral passages. Since a full orchestra was a rather expensive proposition, often horns were used to punctuate a passage (e.g., the 1910 Fruitgum Co.'s "Keep Your Thoughts on the Bright Side" or Paul Revere & the Raiders' "Something Happening"). Generally the orchestrated or horn-laden songs were perceived as more "serious" compositions, and were included as album material, but seldom—except in the case of the Lemon Pipers, who had proven the hit potential of the style—released as singles.

Just as it was hoped that more elaborate song structures would interest sophisticated fans of psychedelia, bubblegum album cover art was styled to hint at the potential maturity of the music inside. Due to the mainstream acceptance of psychedelic and pop art images by bubblegum's peak period, covers were as much a reflection of popular culture as they were of the music they were designed to sell. To some extent, all of the bubblegum albums reflect a psychedelic flavor. The heavier bubblegum acts that embraced the drug culture in their lyrics were packaged as "legitimate" groups. Their albums most frequently feature photographs of a group (whether or not it was the actual recording line-up). Buddah albums often superimpose images on group photos of the bands that recorded bubble-psych songs, apparently in an attempt to give a visual impression of the psychedelic experience. Elephant's Memory's first LP shows a completely nude group of hairy 30-somethings in headbands and love-beads

artfully body painted in neon colors. The lone female of the group bears one paint-adorned breast and a rather haphazard tilaka. The band members are purposefully arranged to fit into the body of an elephant, which is superimposed over their picture. Other Buddah groups were presented in a less "serious" light. While they too might have their photographs printed on the album, the bands appear in trendy hippie costumes, frequently posed in humorous situations. The Ohio Express' *Mercy* presents them in clothing reminiscent of the 1800's. The group is on a train, fighting over a woman in a pioneer-style gown who is tied to the engine. The 1910 Fruitgum Co. is shown in American Indian-inspired costumes (a style which was briefly popular in San Francisco)—happily sucking on big fat cigars! Conversely, pre-teen oriented bubblegum albums often avoided depicting the group on the front cover, but adopted a roughly cartooned artwork, sometimes hand drawn and roughly dabbed with poster-paint primary colors. Although not outwardly psychedelic, these exaggerated cartoon images and thinly veiled suggestive themes (protruding gum packages on 1910 Fruitgum Co. albums and Crumbesque buttocks on cartoon characters on their *Goody Goody Gumdrops* LP) echo sentiments of underground comic artists aligned with the hippie scene.

The underground music scene isn't often associated with bubblegum, yet a few obscure groups took the chance on blending their psychedelic styles with the genre's formula in hopes of being noticed. Groups like the Cherry Slush recorded bubblegum-tinged pop, and others such as the Two Dollar Question chose to hide their real motives behind sugary sweetness. Oddly enough, one of the most underground and psychedelic of all bubble-psych groups is one that could have been the most widely known. Captain Groovy and his Bubble Gum Army recorded some of the heaviest, most freaked-out psychedelic songs of the genre. "Dark Part of My Mind" relies more on wild guitar than the usual suggestive lyrics to suggest an altered state. Even more freaky is the same conglomeration who recorded as the Magic Swirling Ship to create the never "officially" released "He's Coming pt. 2" (*Turds On A Bum Ride, Volume 1*, ANT, 1991) which borders on '60s punk with fuzzed-out, screaming guitars and crazed, half hidden vocals. These songs could very well have ended up being the soundtrack to the Captain Groovy cartoon, had it not been canceled before it was aired.

The heaviest bubblegum groups were not necessarily the most psychedelic, nor the most prolific. And, although the Lemon Pipers had their fair share of bubble-psych tunes, it was the Ohio Express who with their second album created the very best bubble-psych LP. Their psychedelia is almost pure pop-psych (in the same way that "Through With You" by the Lemon Pipers is). The record as a whole stands up because of the mixture of the pure bubblegum of "Yummy, Yummy, Yummy" and "Down At Lulu's" next to stunning slices of psych such as "First Grade Reader" and the almost perfect "Turn To Straw." The lighter pop-psych of "Winter Skies" falls somewhere in between. If "Green Tambourine" is the standard against which all bubble-psych songs can be rated, then this album by the Ohio Express is its long-playing equal. Unfortunately for the Ohio Express, this was their last mind-expansive album. Indeed, the whole influence of psychedelia on bubblegum music lasted quite briefly. Bubble-soul soon took over. However fleeting the style, and however small the handful of songs it left behind, bubblegum psychedelia was the one last attempt to keep the music of the '60s something that youth of all ages could enjoy.

KISS by Jake Austen

KISS *is* a bubblegum band. I suppose many assume that because, at their '70s apex, they played stadiums clad in leather and horror face paint, shaking their long hair in front of towers of amplifiers while indulging in solos, invoking Satanic imagery and leaving the residue of blood, fire and broken guitars in their wake, they must be a heavy metal group. To get from Sabbath to Slayer you have to go through, KISS, right? You'd think so, wouldn't you? However, if KISS were true hard 'n' heavy rockers who didn't conform to bubblegum's manifesto of hook-laden, sales-oriented pop, they couldn't have possibly been as massively popular as they were.

"Wait," you cry, "Led Zeppelin was huge at the same time and they were heavy as hell!" Yes, and I'm sure you carried a Led Zeppelin lunch box to school, had fun playing with your Robert Plant action figure, and your best Halloween was the one where you wore the John Bonham plastic costume you got at the drugstore. KISS didn't just sell millions of records during their '70s heyday; they fully infiltrated pop culture at every level, crossing age, gender and high school cliques. They were marketed (which is first and foremost what bubblegum is about) to the mainstream, and the world licked it up like corn syrup-based fake-blood juice.

Clearly, in many ways, KISS is closer to bubblegum than heavy metal (in *Heavy Metal—The Music and Its Culture*, Deena Weinstein categorizes them as "Lite Metal"). Most significantly, their actual music simply has more in common with hooky AM radio pop than the ominous, regal thickness of Black Sabbath. Much of this can be attributed to the two boys bringing up the not-so-big bottom. Horror movie-loving bassist Gene Simmons doesn't quite have the evil chops he thinks he does, but the real pop magic of KISS can mostly be attributed to drummer Peter Criss. Criss, a devotee of jazz stickman Gene Krupa (he and N.Y. Dolls drummer Jerry Nolan used to follow Krupa from gig to gig), has a jazzy/old time Rock 'n' Roll style that grounds even  KISS' heaviest efforts in poppiness. When Criss was replaced with Eric Carr in the '80s, the band instantly was able to produce the legitimately heavy "I Love It Loud." But during their heyday, the anti-Keith Moon kept KISS kool.

On a non-musical level, one can certainly see KISS as contemporaries of bubblegum superstars the Banana Splits, the Groovie Ghoulies and Josie & the Pussycats just by eyeballing them. With their costumes, makeup, fire-breathing, pyro and dynamic sets, the KISSters were living cartoon characters; comic book superheroes playing rock as sure as the Impossibles were. In fact their movie, *Kiss Meets The Phantom Of The Park*, was produced by Hanna-Barbera, so they even had the same bosses as Bingo, Snorky, Drooper and Fleagle!

To make the point absurdly obvious, no band has ever had as much *actual bubblegum* produced in their name. In addition to no less than three series of bubblegum card sets, they also were the subject of two different "Chu-Bops"— a short-lived candy store shelf-space filler, featuring pink bubblegum pressed into the shape of mini LPs packaged in tiny album sleeves.

However, KISS also obviously isn't a typical bubblegum act in a number of ways. Despite being gimmick-laden, they were by no means a studio creation. On the contrary, KISS was a fully functional band with real members who played, wrote and came up with most of the shtick themselves. Also, unlike Kirshner's, Katz' and Kasenetz' hitmakers, KISS was an album act rather than radio singles specialists. KISS manager/former Buddah bubblegummer Neil Bogart tried his hardest to make it otherwise, releasing numerous KISS singles, delivering payola, etc., but it just didn't work out that way. KISS eventually broke through on the strength of a double live album, a format that is the antithesis of bubblegum (K&K Orchestral Circus notwithstanding). And, of course, KISS didn't cover the same thematic ground as bubblegum. Or did they?

Perhaps the most interesting element of classic bubblegum, one that KISS seems to stay clear of, is the "Candy is Dandy" angle. From the moment the bubblegum blueprint was laid out by Joey Levine with "Yummy, Yummy, Yummy," one of the most endearing design elements was the not-so-subtle sugarcoating of sexual innuendo with ambiguously delicious pre-pubescent themes. Though candy, kids' games and nursery rhymes are all subjects that teenybopper record buyers can relate to, it's always clear on bub-blegum vinyl what they're *really* talking about (is there a naughtier-sounding exchange in recorded history than Archie's "Pour a little sugar on me, baby," prompting Veronica's breathy "I'm gonna make your life so sweet"?). KISS has been accused of many crimes, but never of innuendo. Nonetheless, in some ways, their frequent metaphor-free forays into carnal themes actually are analogous to the spirit of Super K and

company.

To illustrate, examine their classic 1975 LP *Dressed To Kill*, which Chuck Eddy in *Stairway To Hell* summarizes as not only "a concept LP about kinky sex with groupies" but also as "the most inarguable bubblemetal mixture ever." While clearly Gene and Paul are not singing "1, 2, 3 Red Light" or "Hot Dog" here, to say they are avoiding juvenile subject matter would be absurd. This album offers perhaps the most childish, sophomoric depic-tions of sex ever pressed on wax. When it comes to maturity, in these grooves the Kabuki Kooks make Mötley Crüe look like the *Oprah* show's "life strategist" Dr. Phil. Not to say they are simply crude—that would be run of the mill. Where KISS' talents shine is in remarkably subverting the bubblegum convention by, instead of covertly presenting sex cloaked in the language of a 13-year-old, *overtly* presenting sex through the eyes and fantasies of a 13-year-old!

In "Room Service," stewardesses at airports, strangers in a hotel, and 16-year-olds in "my home town" demand sex whenever vocalist Paul Stanley has a free moment. "Ladies in Waiting" is literally about an orderly line of females queued up to have sex with the boys ("the selection is inviting"). The theme of "C'mon and Love Me" (which opens with the unbelievable line "She's a dancer, a romancer/ I'm a Capricorn and she's a Cancer") is summarized with the offer, "Baby won't you take me down on my knees/You can do what you please." And of course, the album ends with a manifesto that, though perhaps less specifically carnal, certainly keeps up the teen fantasy-world theme, declaring, "I want to Rock and Roll All Night and Party Every Day!"

But all that aside, to get to the heart of what KISS and bubblegum have in common requires getting to the core of what makes bubblegum gummy. To do that, simply listen to the pure musical ectoplasm that is a classic bubblegum 45: jangly, hooky, melodic post-Beatles Pop. The description of that goo could also be applied to a little cult genre called Power Pop. However, despite the fact that with a tiny bit of tweaking a Boyce & Hart song could be on a Raspberries album and vice versa, no one would confuse the two genres, and there's a good reason why. 1910 Fruitgum Company and Shoes can be singing the same love song about the same girl, *but Shoes mean it!* Power Pop is rooted in simple, earnest sincerity, while bubblegum is contrived to sell sell SELL! So basically, the music can be identical, but the key difference is *intent!* And the intent of bubblegum is never art for art's sake, it's about giving the people what they want, and getting paid for it. And that's where KISS comes in.

Founding members Gene Simmons and Paul Stanley, the two masterminds behind KISS and the ones keeping it together for almost 30 years, have more in common with Kasenetz/Katz than with Lennon/McCartney. They are two of the most remarkably pragmatic, crafty Rock "n' Roll businessmen in history. Band members are hired on as salaried employees, fan conventions originate in-house, and licensing has run the gamut from comic books to condoms to KISS credit cards to their own pro wrestler.

So when it comes down to the bottom line — and in bubblegum it always comes down to the bottom line — fasting on Yom Kippur isn't all Gene and Paul have in common with Don Kirshner. Like all the great sellers of sugary sweets, they know what the kids want to put in their mouths, and they're more then willing to put it there.

The Bubblegum Roots of Punk by Chas Glynn

In the mid '70s, bubblegum pop hit adolescence, got acne, and mutated into punk rock. While conventional received wisdom traces punk's roots from Detroit hard rock (Stooges/MC5) and '60s garage, through early glam/power pop, with perhaps a semester or two in the back of the class at art school, the triple-distilled pop sound perfected in the late '60s/early '70s played as much a part. While a sneering cynicism often replaced the wide-eyed innocence of bubblegum, the simple song structure, upbeat tempo, and catchy hooks were still present.

Glam/punk predecessors the New York Dolls took an amalgam of hard rock, '60s girl groups and bubblegum, dressed it up in outrageous fashion, and pumped new life into the moribund New York music scene in the early '70s. Malcolm McLaren, later to achieve infamy as manager of the Sex Pistols, briefly managed the Dolls. With both groups, McLaren attempted to manipulate the artists and impose a prepackaged image—much as producers of manufactured studio groups had earlier. Some, in fact, blame the death of Sex Pistols' bassist Sid Vicious on his attempts to live up to the image that had been created for him.

It's been said over and over again that not many people bought Velvet Underground records, but most of those who did went on to form bands. True, the Velvets were an extremely influential group, but

who influenced the Velvets? Often overlooked is the fact that Lou Reed and John Cale met when they were both employed as in-house songwriter/performers at Pickwick Records in the early '60s. Pickwick was, at the time, a sort of low-rent Brill Building churning out derivative pop singles aimed at the teen and juvenile set. It was there that Cale and Reed honed their songwriting and recording skills, churning out disposable pop like "Do the Ostrich," "I've Got a Tiger in My Tank" and "Cycle Annie" in such manufactured groups as the All Night Workers and the Beachnuts. Indeed, the Velvet Underground song "Foggy Notion" is essentially a reworking of "Cycle Annie" by the Beachnuts.

If the Dolls and the Velvets were the progenitors, most agree that the Ramones were the ur-band of mid-'70s punk. But if one listens to them with an unprejudiced ear, it's clear that the Ramones are actually the great lost bubblegum band. Their songs have numerous near-direct swipes of lyrics and riffs from the Buddah back catalog, and the catchy hooks and dimestore sentimentality of "Rockaway Beach" or "Let's Dance" sound far more AM-ready than anything produced by contemporaries like Yes or Styx. Sure, the lyrics were often about sniffing glue or suicide, but the song structures were there—if anything even simpler and more repetitive than the juvenile predecessors. The Ramones were the closest thing to a bubblegum band for disaffected adolescents—kids who had replaced candy and soda pop with fake IDs and pilfered cigarettes. Rumor has it that early in their careers, the Ramones viewed the Ohio Express as their main "competition," and attempted to hire their producer [Jeff Katz] for the first album. He demurred, and Thomas Erdelyi—aka Tommy Ramone—took over production duties. A wise choice, as many early punk albums were marred by ham-fisted production. Although Erdelyi dropped out of the Ramones early on (citing a dislike of touring), he continued as their producer, and his fat but simple production has lead many to dub him the "three-chord Phil Spector." Not to be forgotten are John Holstrom's illustrations on early Ramones album jackets. His renditions of the Ramones made them, literally, cartoon characters.

After the Ramones, the floodgates opened, as countless young malcontents realized that rock 'n' roll was a visceral, not intellectual exercise, and that talent pursued for its own sake was a dead end street. While more commercially successful bands were looking to classical and jazz music for inspiration, early punk musicians rejected such pretensions, and stripped rock back to its basics. Much like pop art, punk began absorbing whatever was around, no matter how cheesy. In fact, the vulgar and lowbrow were celebrated for their camp/trash value. It was only natural that bubblegum pop, off the charts for several years, should be mined and incorporated into punk's pastiche. The wide-eyed, naive quality of bubblegum, combined with an unsmirking sexuality bubbling beneath the surface, made it a natural to be sung with a sneer rather than a smile, and the simple, uptempo nature of the music made it simple for neophyte musicians to master. Bands such as the Rezillos (later Revillos) took it one step further and dressed in colorful, outlandish stage wear that hearkened back to juvenile pop of years past. This cartoonish stage presence was taken even further by the Damned. Pink gorilla outfits, nurse uniforms, vampire costumes, and a light-hearted goofiness permeated the Damned's early work, and even as they moved to more *serious* material, they never abandoned their sense of fun.

Another band that kept both bubblegum's song structure and sense of fun was the Dickies. Not only did they cover the Banana Splits' theme song and the Monkees' "She," but they managed to sugar-coat such hard rock chestnuts as Black Sabbath's "Paranoid," Led Zeppelin's "Communication Breakdown," and even the Moody Blues' "Nights in White Satin," turning them into bouncy hyperspeed pop numbers. Their own songs were similarly poppy, bordering on the hyperactive—singing about the Pep Boys, local newscasters, and monster movies—all the while sounding like a mix between the Ramones and Alvin and the Chipmunks.

While bubblegum pop-tinged early punk, Redd Kross (formerly Red Cross) took it a step further and forged a complete bubblegum-punk hybrid. Heavily influenced by Buddah and Golden records as well as Kiss, the Runaways, and Sid & Marty Krofft, the precocious McDonald brothers (Jeff and Steve) began playing instruments at the age of 9 and 13, and came to personify the ultimate evolution of juvenile rock—kids fed on a constant diet of pop culture who picked up instruments and began creating rather than consuming. Much like the Ramones had, Redd Kross combined the uptempo, repetitive song structure of bubblegum with extremely off-kilter lyrical content—Linda Blair and the Manson family were both namechecked on their landmark first album, *Born Innocent* (1981). The McDonald brothers remain the core of Redd Kross despite numerous personnel changes and side projects (the most notable being their acting in and co-writing *Desperate Teenage Lovedolls*, a warped amateur remake of the already very odd film *Beyond the Valley of the Dolls*) and the brothers continue to have an almost reverent affection for bubblegum pop. Indeed, "Bubblegum Factory" on their 1991 release *Third Eye* sums it all up:

> Take me on a tour of the bubblegum factory
> I wanna see where love is made
> Take me on a tour of the bubblegum factory
> I wanna hear those records play.

Even today, there continue to be bands that combine punk and bubblegum in one way or another. Perhaps the most notable is the Groovie Ghoulies—a West Coast band on Lookout! Records. Named after the '70s cartoon series, the Ghoulies play a simple, sentimental punk/pop hybrid, and have attracted a surprising audience of grade-school aged junior punks.

Bubblegum & New Wave by David Smay

Nobody took the bubblegum ethos to heart like the new wave bands. Though glam and disco hew closer to bubblegum in their production methods, new wave tried to create the world bubblegum promised. In fact, it's easy to imagine new wave as a kind of cargo cult that fetishized the cartoon sound of the Archies and Banana Splits, insisting with a goofy faith that pop music ought to be that bright, catchy, danceable and weird. A Pop Art gesture made by a lot of art school dropouts.

Okay, not every new wave band drank from the sacred mug of Kool-Aid. It overstates things considerably to insist that these bands *believed* in a Kandy Kolored Pop World. Their ironic infatuation with artifice and arch visual sense was less faithful than playful. A group like the B-52s drew almost entirely on pre-Beatles pop sources like surf guitar, girl groups and R&B dance novelties and served it up raw and campy. Roxy Music and Bowie influenced most of the British New Romantic and synth pop bands. It's hard to spot the bubblegum vibe in "Sex Dwarf" no matter how funny and danceable it is. But the poppier end of new wave clearly owes something to bubblegum.

Current critical thought discredits new wave as a genre, deriding it as a marketing ploy to soft-sell punk, a meaningless umbrella term covering bands too diverse to be considered alike. Powerpop, synth pop, ska revival, art school novelties and rebranded pub rockers were all sold as "New Wave." Punk scrabbled to tear down the walls with bloody fingernails; new wave smiled, eager to please and angled for radio playlists. In this punk rock orthodoxy, new wave comes off as Vichy-Pop, getting damningly cozy with the corporate interests which blunted rock's once-revolutionary force.

But in the beginning, punk was more of a movement than a sound. As Tom Verlaine described it, "Each band was like a little idea." It wasn't until the Ramones toured England that punk's sound codified into three chords and a vapor trail. Suddenly keyboards were effete. (Excepting, as ever, Suicide.)

Which brings us to the three G's of new wave: Gays, Girls and Geeks. If punk ever promised anything it was a refuge for the Howard Devotos and Poly Styrenes of the world: smartass art-school fags tossing off campy lyrics, beauty school dropouts in wall-to-wall eyeliner, and *Popular Science* stereophiles wired for Roxy Music.

These marginal twerps flocked to punk when rock shoved them aside. And punk itself found its first home in gay bars and clubs in New York, London and Manchester. The schism between punk's artier arm and its boys club emerged early, famously erupting with tranny Wayne County splitting Handsome Dick Manitoba's head with a mic stand (in response to fag baiting). As punk pushed into Harder Faster Louder the geeks, gays and girls bleeped and booped on their Farfisas and cut singles for the disco.

They made music driven by dance beats and punchy keyboard riffs, songs with cheery harmonies and bratty leads, and they sold it with cartoony costumes and antic TV slapstick. And if that sounds like bubblegum that's no accident. Nothing would've pleased the Dickies more than to be a Saturday morning cartoon.

But are the Dickies a new wave band or should we discuss them only as a punk band? The Ramones are to blame for this kind of line-blurring. We can't fault the Ramones for their preeminence as a pop-hook purveyor in cartoon drag and the boilerplate for punk rock as well. The Ramones contain multitudes: punk, bubblegum, new wave, power pop, inheritors of the Beach Boys tradition.

Stiff Records ("If it's not Stiff, It's not worth a Fuck") goofed on bubblegum with typical irony and rare panache. A small blizzard of ghost bands and one-offs came out on Stiff. Nick Lowe played the sweetest studio prank of all by putting out "Bay City Rollers We Love You" as the Tartan Horde and then watching Japanese Roller fans turn it into a huge hit. (Oh, quit niggling, I know that was on UA before he was on Stiff. Nick had another funny stab at ghost-bands with the contract-breaking "Let's Go To The Disco" by the Disco Brothers.)

The connections between the first wave of New York punk and new wave bands and the New York-based bubblegum players of the '60s were deep and influential. Marty Thau, once a publicist at Buddah, managed or produced the New York Dolls, the Real Kids, Suicide and the Fleshtones at different times. More importantly, ex-Strangelove and bubblegum-maker Richard Gotterher co-founded Sire Records with Seymour Stein. Stein signed the Ramones, the Pretenders, Talking Heads and many other groundbreaking bands; Gotterher left Sire to produce some of the best pop records of the new wave era.

Of all the related genres, new wave fits least comfortably with our diagnostic model of bubblegum and depends most on a subjective assessment of its . . . gumminess. For every example like Bow Wow Wow ("I Want Candy" conforms neatly with our definitions) there's a counter example like the Go-Go's. (When Miles Copeland heard Richard Gotterher's mix of *Beauty and the Beat* he screamed, "I gave you a great little punk band and you turned them into bubblegum!")

We could pick through and cite a number of bubblegum/new wave points in common from the covers of "I Think We're Alone Now" by Lene Lovich and the Rubinoos to Phil Wainman's production on Generation X to Billy Idol covering "Mony Mony" to Thomas Dolby's rather bubblegummy career (more as a producer/songwriter than a front man). It will be easier to find that bubblegum essence rare by cherry-picking the hits.

A brief review of one man's *Top Ten Bubblegum of the New Wave Era* should make the connections between new wave and bubblegum both obvious and impossibly slippery.

1. Toni Basil "Mickey"
A Chinn/Chapman song rescued from their back catalogue and re-gendered for a girl's POV. Toni's video not only pulled ubiquitous airplay on MTV, but angled successfully for a teen audience with its cheerleading imagery. The fact that kids and aerobicizers never caught the lewd implications of the lyrics (i.e., the sodomistic "Any way you want to do it/I'll take it like a man") places the song squarely in the same tradition as "Chewy Chewy" and "Jam Up and Jelly Tight."

2. The Cars "Just What I Needed"
The opening guitar intro is a verbatim lift ("homage," excuse me) from "Yummy, Yummy, Yummy." This is, not coincidentally, the first new wave hit to break commercial radio in the '70s. Bubblegum leads the way. The Cars always had a strong sense of songcraft. "My Best Friend's Girl" primarily derives from the Rebels "Wild Weekend," but there's something in its jaunty, tick-tock rhythm that sounds like Elliot Easton transcribed the organ hook of "Chewy Chewy" to guitar. The angular guitar sound of this song later went on to influence the pop-ska band No Doubt's first hit, "Just a Girl."

3. Bow Wow Wow "I Want Candy"
Let's see, Svengali producer (Malcolm McLaren) assembles band? Check. Teen singer? (Annabella.) Check. Outside songwriters? (Covering the Strangeloves.) Check. Members of the bubblegum mafia? (Kenny Laguna produced it.) Check. Candy coated lyrics? Check. Perfect bubblegum by way of Burundi.

4. Cyndi Lauper "Girls Just Want to Have Fun"
Cyndi's massive hit album effectively ended the new wave era while taking it out with a bang. "She Bop" featured an animated video, but "Girls . . ." anthemically posed Fun as the essence of liberation. That's bubblegum.

5. Katrina and the Waves "Walking on Sunshine"

Sheer infectious irresistible froth. Wide-eyed optimism and cheer manifested in music. The least Goth song ever recorded, which makes it bubblegum by definition. Bonus points for being composed by ex-Soft Boy Kimberly Rew (who also wrote the Bangles-covered song "Going Down To Liverpool").

6. Bananarama "Cruel Summer"

They took their name as a contraction of the Banana Splits and Roxy Music's "Pyjamarama." "He Was Really Saying Something" might be more intrinsically gummy, but "Cruel Summer" better captures that lost innocence at the core of new wave's fascination with bubblegum. Bubblegum's innocence and peerless pop promise contrast neatly with a wary '80s reluctance to trust unalloyed giddiness. Betrayed by pop songs once again. Bananarama took frequent slaggings in the British press for being pop puppets, and indeed they had strong connections with Paul Cook (of the Sex Pistols), Terry Hall and the S-A-W production team. What that criticism misses, however, is their party-girls-on-a-bender charm and the dark-eyed hangover behind their relentless bounce.

7. Wham! "Wake Me Up Before You Go-Go"

George Michael was still a teen when Wham! first showed up in *Smash Hits*. Before his solo career established George as some kind of goofy pop genius, he bequeathed this ridiculously cheerful day-glo trifle to any pre-teen girl within earshot of MTV. His song "Freedom" ranks with Janet Jackson's "Control," 'N Sync's "Bye Bye Bye" video and the Monkees' *Headquarters* album as acts of defiance/escape from the star-making machinery—one of the most compelling and consistent subtexts in bubblegum.

8. The Go-Go's "Vacation"

What makes the Go-Go's bubblegum anyway? They were a punk group that played dates at the Whisky and the Masque with X, the Germs, the Weirdos and other L.A. stalwarts. After they heard the pop sheen Richard Gotterher put on their first album they wouldn't talk to him for six months. Until they topped the charts. What makes them bubblegum is their complete pop mastery (and Gottehrer's slick-pretty production). Max Martin and Lou Pearlman would kill for the kind of hooks that Jane Wiedlin and Charlotte Caffey whipped up on *Beauty and the Beat*. Like many new wave hits, the melancholy lyrics in "Vacation" belie the bubbly arrangement.

9. Adam and the Ants "Goody Two Shoes"

Not just a schoolyard taunt turned pop, but practically an answer song to "Goody Goody Gumdrops." Adam's Highwayman look seemed to owe as much to Paul Revere & the Raiders as it did to Johnny Kidd & the Pirates (from whence Adam stole this hook, cf. "Castin' My Spell").

10. Kim Wilde "Kids in America"

An exhilarating one-shot celebrating pop's power to lift you out of your "dirty town." Notable also for coming out on Mickie Most's RAK label (home to Suzi Quatro and many a ChinniChap hit) and being co-written by Kim's father, Marty Wilde. Marty was a pre-Beatle British rocker who also sang lead on the bubblegum hit "Abergevenny" by Shannon. And who can forget Kim's shout-out to her homies in Barstow, the oft-neglected kids from "East California?"

It Won't Go Away! Bubblegum fizzled out in the early '70s, but its essence

remained, lurking beneath the charts for the prime moment to re-emerge and claim a new generation. But why suffer the critical slings it had in the golden days of Buddah and Colgems? The next time around bubblegum would play it smarter, posing as "authentic" while slaying the kids with contrived pop perfection.

In 1987, now-*Village Voice* music editor Chuck Eddy enlivened the pages of the moribund post-Lester Bangs *Creem* magazine with a fascinating Top 40 of post-'60s bubblegum favorites. We reprint this piece in its entirety. Chuck's article stomps over conventional genre boundaries to rethink bubblegum—at a time when hardly anyone championed the bubblegum aesthetic. If you enter this book as a pop fan, if you've got Ramones LPs or Shalamar singles or Duran Duran videos or a New Kids poster in your closet, then Chuck's ideas might open a door for you. He makes a strong case that bubblegum should be seen as a strand within rock and pop rather than as a ghetto for kids.

Few things could be less gummy than the DIY punk ethic of 1976, but as it spread and mutated across continents and decades, "punk" came to mean a personal philosophy of self-reliance and defiant rejection of mainstream mores as much as it did aggressive rock sounds. Many of the stars of the indie rock firmament lived "punk" while playing sweet and gummy. Elizabeth Ivanovich's survey introduces us to some of the more important practitioners.

Finally, we offer two views of the late '90s bubblegum explosion. Cartoonist Peter Bagge shares a love of frothy girl pop with his pre-pubescent daughter, and was willing to wade into the depths of the mass market to determine which Radio Disney stars are most likely to shine into the next century. Mike McPadden lacks the excuse of a kid of his own to explain away his obsession with the Spice Girls and Britney, but his measured analysis of manufactured '90s pop as it relates to grunge and college rock is an important step in putting this understudied genre in context.

Bubblegum Never Died! It's Just That Nobody Ever Writes About It! by Chuck Eddy

All I remember is bein' in a classroom . . . hadda be about fourth grade . . . end-of-the-year school's-out cake 'n' ice cream party . . . Magnavox switched on with "Simon Says" (by the 1910 Fruitgum Company) and "Yummy, Yummy" (by the Ohio Express) coming out, and girls dancing fast. I didn't know it then (or care—this was my rude awakening to something or other hormonal), but neither band was a real group. They sprang from the fertile imaginations of Buddah Records prexy Neil Bogart and the production duo of Jerry Kasenetz and Jeff Katz, a think-tank that satiated busting-out pre-pubertal passions the world over in the late '60s by building an empire of cynical condescension and naming it "Bubblegum." There'd always been "Hanky Panky"s and "Da Doo Ron Ron"s and "Iko Iko"s and "I'm A Believer"s and "Hippy Hippy Shakes"s and other monstrosities of ingratiating meaninglessness to keep the 13-year-old contingent smiling. The lengthily-monikered Rock & Roll Dubble Bubble Trading Card Company Of Philadelphia 19141 even had a #62 hit called "Bubblegum Music." But Kasenetz/Katz were the first guys to codify kiddiepap (via garageland-punk in their case) into a mass/machine-marketed commodity.

Bubblegum was great! Because unlike all the astral-planing acidwreck dreck you were soon burning out to, bubblegum laid all its cards out, not disguising itself as anything (i.e.: "smart") it wasn't. Mostly it just strung lots of obvious hooks together on a non-skewed straight line (unlike the skewed line airheads like Big Star would initiate a couple years later, thus making way for the travesty which, in 1987, we laughingly call "college radio"). You didn't have to study these hooks paramecium-like under a microscope or anything; they were so blatantly cute on the surface you just wanted to tickle 'em under the chin. Which is fine, because rock's not supposed to require much thought. You're supposed to use it up and throw it away, just like everything else in this culture, right? Right.

Also, bubblegum songs had really silly words that didn't make any sense nor pretended to, though sometimes the gobbledygook hid some quite ribald sentiments. There were plenty of lines about "chewing" and how "sweet" people were (an idea expanded on years later by the Jesus & Mary Chain, in "Taste of Candy," "Just Like Honey," and "Cherry Came Too"). The most immortal gumtune, and (therefore!) the biggest seller (topping the charts in The Year Of Our Stooge 1969) was "Sugar, Sugar" by the Archies, who were Saturday morning cartoon characters. (Something's bubblegum if and only if you can imagine Betty shaking a tambourine to it.) "Sugar, Sugar" had Archie Andrews (he of the red hair with a black tic-tac-toe sign in it) repeatedly telling his main squeeze that she was his "candy girl," asking her to pour her sugar all over him. Interpret this cryptic demand as you will.

Now, lots of octogenarians have asserted for years that all this good clean fun kicked the gutbucket around the time my classmates and I were switching to the FM dial—which is more or less also when countercultural marijuana festivals and mountains-coming-out-of-the-sky-and-standing-there were becoming such big deals. Some even say it's self-destructive to keep searching for this callow ingenuousness we once knew, because we've lost it forever, and to deny that is to deny our own consciousness. Well, I've always figured that obituary garbage was just a lie perpetrated by '60s snobs too indolent to play their Aerosmith records. What I know for sure is that wonder and bliss is out there somewhere (and I don't just mean music-wise, either) for anybody who's gots guts enough to look for it instead of just settling for the delusions of lethargy and necrosis we're offered these days. If I didn't believe that, I might as well just kill myself, or at least give up writing about music and maybe go to law school. I'm here to tell you that bubblegum lives, even if Kasenetz/Katz don't (and for all I know they might).

In the '70s, bubblegum became more an attitude than a genre, a sticky perky feeling that performers (or producers—Mike Chapman and Nicky Chinn of Suzi Quatro/Sweet/Nick Gilder fame were the

Kasenetz/Katz of the Me-Decade) could draw on, as everybody from K.C. & the Sunshine Band to Mötley Crüe has done. Gumlike concoctions thrived with the glam and nouveau-Merseybeat movements (explicit reactions to rock-as-art) of the early '70s, with disco and powerpop in the late '70s, even with CHR's girl-group mini-revival a couple years back. Plus, the '70s still had *Tiger Beat*-teendream singing idols, though I think that idea's gone by the wayside (whatever happened to Rick Springfield, anyway?). Rock 'n' roll today's too damn grown-up—just scads of stonefaced egos bono-voxing all over the place. (Actually, I suspect Menudo's got some swell tunes, but I've never heard 'em.)

Anyhow, what I got for ya is a Top 40 of '70s–'80s bubblegum. What unites this apparently diverse collection is feel, sound, and words. By "feel," I'm talking goofy and stupid, the more kindergarten-worthy the better, with a whitebread gentleness and purity that's the wimpy underside of the violence supposedly at the heart of "street" music but mostly's just a load of crap. Soundwise, they only last a couple of minutes, during which time all their stolen hooks make you pound your steering wheel real hard, fast tempos are common, ditto for high-register (like they haven't changed yet) vocals, with even higher surf/Beatles-type background harmonies; fuzztone riffs and drum thunder are encouraged, but only if they conceal a confectionery center. Lyrics are either of the playpen-bound goo-goo-ga-ga variety, or something only slightly more mature: about parents or cars or rock-as-religion or (usually) boy/girl predicaments free of adult neuroses. You know—playing footsie, having crushes, going steady. All the most exciting things in the world until some imbecile tells you they're corny and you should only care about carnal knowledge, at which point it is my belief that you have started to stop living and begun to die.

My Top 40, which has more '70s than '80s product (because good junk, like fine Ripple, improves with age), indicates three basic gumstrains. The first strain (ABBA, Bay City Rollers, etc.) is real cheesy trash that exists exclusively to exploit you; this kind was way more viable back before computers commenced to generate all these homogeneously mercenary quasi-hooks we've now got. The second strain (Raspberries, Nick Lowe, etc.) primarily consists of nostalgic tributes to a supposedly simple epoch, an endeavor which can risk both hyper-respectable cerebralness and smirky contempt, but which can ring as true as the real thing if the performance is warm enough to be taken at face value. Finally, there's bubblegum from isolated lands (in the Far East and continental Europe) where music is apparently still thought of as an opiate for the masses with no aesthetic strings attached. Since I can't understand the words, these records tend to come off as nonsensical as "Yummy, Yummy" and "Da Doo Ron Ron," and I can never tell whether they're trying to be funny or not. Oh yeah: '60s purists will scoff at my tolerance of disco syncopation. But purists suck.

IT'S . . . IT'S . . . A BALLROOM BLITZ! THE BEST OF TWO DECADES

1. ABBA "Does Your Mother Know" (1979). Some tender hoodsie's hitting on Bjorn (or Benny?) at a bash; he says scram, but the guitar vroom (a snowmobile pillaging Scandinavia) tells her to stick around.

2. Kiss "Rock and Roll All Nite" (1975). Critics labeled 'em a fascist threat, and their Army served Satan, but this abyss-anthem was comic-book strut 'n' shout at its dumb, body-flattening peak.

3. Bay City Rollers "Saturday Night" (1975). A brogue spelling lesson from Tartan-clad Scottish lads who've got a date and just can't wait.

4. Cheap Trick "Surrender" (1978). Ma and Pa smoke your stash, spin your copy of *Destroyer*, get frisky on the couch; all you can think of are WACs with VD, your copy of *Revolver*, and not giving yourself away.

5. Ramones "Sheena Is A Punk Rocker" (1977). Beach-baby falsettos and three chords chopping down skyscrapers. A way of life: the tough get weird when the going gets tough.

6. Shaun Cassidy "That's Rock 'n' Roll" (1977). You're 16, sick of school, Keith Partridge's little brother. You buy an axe, get the fever, get down and get with it. Leif Garrett's left choking on your exhaust fumes.

7. Sweet "Ballroom Blitz" (1975). The most deliberately effeminate intro ever, into a rattlefuzz stomp where you dream of a party-girl who wants to "ball you." Only it says "tell you" on the lyric sheet.

8. Vibrators "London Girls" (1977). These part-time punks' *Pure Mania* LP has sure held up better than the pathetic *Never Mind the Bollocks*, and this hilarious love-snarl is as catchy as an air-raid siren: "Useta be things were so neat, I can't stand my life out on the street."

9. Sweet "Wig-Wam Bam" (1973). Tom-toms, Stooges licks, curly-lipped Elvis quivers, palefaces watching Minihaha tell Hiawatha "wig wam bam, bam shamalam."

10. Nick Lowe "Rollers Show" (1978). Dynamite semi-parody about going to see Tartan-clad Scottish loads, shouting, making noise, and really giving it to 'em.

11. Undertones "Teenage Kicks" (1979). Not near as rancid as That Petrol Emotion's records suggest, these Irish teenybop-punks were glitter fans, and their song title says everything you need to know.

12. Van Halen "Dance The Night Away" (1979). Some freshman looker's inebriated for the first time—in your basement and on booze from your daddy's cabinet—swaying to your metal collection's Latin lilt, and then what?

13. Tracey Ullman "They Don't Know" (1984). Her telly show's a (good) joke, but this girlie smash (about how nobody understands love anymore except you and the person you're in love with) cuts through her campist propensities like a pavement saw.

14. Cars "My Best Friend's Girl" (1978). Streamlined and turtle-wax-sleek Boston pop-rock, with Ocasek droning almost-not-icily about the nuclear boots and drip-dry gloves of someone he wants back.

15. Cyndi Lauper "Girls Just Want To Have Fun" (1984). Best version is Arthur Baker's long

cubist remix; sounds recorded inside a house-of-mirrors, with all this popcorn flying around, and Olive Oyl getting feminist besides.

16. Raspberries "Go All the Way" (1972). A restoration of pre-Pepper Lennon/McCartney via an ethereal chorus, a boogie kick, and the tip top adolescent dilemma.

17. Slade "Skweeze Me Pleeze Me" (1973). "You got a sweet tongue, you sing love songs/ Cantcha learn to spell?" Nope, but bellowing like a bullhorn, not to mention being the sharpest dressers in the gang district, was enough.

18. Poison "Talk Dirty To Me" (1987). First song with a drive-in since what? First with a nursery rhyme since what? The Bay City Rollers fronted by David Lee Roth, with a gratuitous guitar solo introduced as such.

19. Osmonds "Yo-Yo" (1972). Donny's gone completely mad, his bros think they're on Motown, plus this tuff little riff keeps walking the dog, Joseph Smith be damned.

20. T. Rex "Jeepster" (1971). So what do Limeys know about autos? Not much; Cannabis-popster Marc Bolan even thought "Jaguar" had three syllables. But the bass pops up and down like the head on a mechanical monkey.

21. Blondie "Sunday Girl" (1978). Wow, I could probably just list all of *Parallel Lines*. (Next best thing to Shirelles' *Greatest Hits*, almost.) I like this slow one most because it's unsarcastic, I think.

22. Redd Kross "I Hate My School" (1980). They hate jocks, rah-rahs, surfers, brains, and bookworms, too. Dig them Patty Hearst-inspired backup squeals!

23. Jackson 5 "ABC" (1970). Guess this is what Jim Morrison meant by "speaking secret alphabets"; mayhap Marlon and Tito were slippin' somethin' unorthodox into Mikey's Gerber's. Who knows?

24. Olivia Newton-John & John Travolta "You're The One That I Want" (1978). Fake-romance '50s-revival post-Captain/Tennille schlock-duet at the height of disco, from an un-arguably lame flick. An amazing record; trust me.

25. ABBA "Waterloo" (1974). Either these Swedes had odd accents, or they just didn't comprehend the words. But this slice of sunbeam indicates they'd learned lessons from history.

26. Nena "99 Luftballons" (1984). Teutonic disco-wave with a hi-kicking stiletto-heeled warbler who really grinds up those "macht"s, a rhythm like a spinning top, and the shrewdest of bubblegum topics: nuclear annihilation.

27. Plastic Bertrand "Ça Plane Pour Moi" (1978). How the Ramones would sound if they came from Belgium and wanted to imitate Brian Wilson in French but didn't know how.

28. Billy Idol with Generation X "Dancing With Myself" (1981). Whimpering about "Jukebox Jury," William's band was punk's most commercial from the start. This one's from right before he learned to be surly, and it ain't about dancing.

29. Depeche Mode "Just Can't Get Enough" (1981). Am I sick or what? I despise everything these twerps stand for, but this tidbit boings like a rubber Tweety bird manufactured by Fisher-Price. I really don't ask for much.

30. The Knack "My Sharona" (1979). Salacious sleazeballs drooling about what's running down the length of their thighs, mixing Beatle suits with Bonham drums. Some people hated it. Some people have no sense of humor.

31. Joan Jett "Fake Friends" (1983). More verbose than the tart she was circa "Cherry Bomb," and more hookful, dishing one long run-on sentence about how toadies stab you as soon as your back is turned.

32. E.L.O. "Sweet Talkin' Woman" (1977). Classical bubblegum, believe it or not, with big and little violins working to keep love alive in an age of data-overload.

33. Shonen Knife "Twist Barbie" (1985). Three Japanese women squeaking out pristine pop-punk about how they wanna have blue eyes and blonde hair like a Barbie doll.

34. Naif Orchestra "Check-Out Five" (1985). You heard it hear first: Italo-disco is the future's only hope. Impiously infectious near-muzak, mainly synths and saxes, Gianni Sangalli's sad 'cuz her baby's bagging vermicelli on a Sunday.

35. Girlschool "Tiger Feet" (1987). Dixie Cups voices meet Dave Clark Five beats meet AC/DC blare at a slumber party, and they all turn into rockabilly. Plus, the title almost sounds like a magazine.

36. Andy Gibb "I Just Want To Be Your Everything" (1978). Like his siblings who got younger as they got older, Andy tapped the same cosmic lifeforce that delivered "Walk Like A Man." Here, he tells his string-section he doesn't wanna be a puppet on a string.

37. Romantics "Talking In Your Sleep" (1984). Too prissy as a garage-band, these Detroiters sold-out to CHR drum-pulse, producing this slick shimmy—which doesn't say whether their girlfriend snored.

38. Toni Basil "Mickey" (1982). The world's only example of cheerlead-rock, not counting Al Yankovic's "Ricky." The bimbo wants a touchdown, but Mickey doesn't.

39. Lisa Lisa & Cult Jam "Head To Toe" (1987). Starts with a kiss, then this Hispanic N.Y. suburbanite who can't sing to save her life ends up in the sack, with a Supremes bassline, no less.

40. Jesus & Mary Chain "Never Understand" (1985). Okey-doke, finally, here's my concession to the gloomy Brat-pack fans who buy *Creem*. The Shondells with fabricated feedback, or maybe Joy Division after a bath. Or maybe like if Poison was new wave. All this cotton-candy garbage sounds the same to me.

Dextrose Rides Again: An Introduction to 1990s Bubblegum by Elizabeth Ivanovich

One might be forgiven for calling the phrase "1990s bubblegum" an oxymoron. Certainly, the era that brought us day trading, the Ebola virus, and fat-free potato chips has suffered from a pervasive lack of fun. Happily, the indomitable spirit of bubblegum thrives quietly in the pop underground. The sugar-starved listener will find a veritable candy store of 1990s pop gems; the trick is knowing where to look.

Oddly enough, the prefab groups topping the charts nowadays tend to lack the supercatchiness of true bubblegum. In the post-Milli Vanilli climate, singers eager to prove their chops frequently opt for strained *Star Search*-style vocal ululations and pseudo-soul stylings. Producers, equally eager for credibility, will worsen this by adding lugubrious strings to an already overwrought production. What is the bubblegum connoisseur to do?

Below are some examples of prime neo-bubblegum throughout the 1990s. It is not meant to be a definitive list; rather, it hints at the broad spectrum of subgenres that the new bubblegum encompasses. The bands come from indie and major labels, and hail from several different countries. Some have openly embraced their sugary ancestors; others have not. The paramount factor is sheer pop perfection, and these songs have it in spades.

Jellyfish: "Baby's Coming Back" (from *Bellybutton*, Charisma, 1990)

This song deceptively appears to be a throwback to '70s gum, what with its handclaps and seductively cheery "whoo-hoo-hoo" backing vocals. (Not to mention the song's animated video featuring the newly Hanna Barbera-ized band tooling around in a Mystery Machine-like van.) However, the lyrics vacillate between viciousness and joy in what would soon become the time-honored 1990s fashion. (It's hard to picture, say, Ron Dante singing the lines, "If I had a dollar/for every single time I fought her/I'd buy a handgun," at least not with the glee that Andy Sturmer does here.) By the time Roger Manning's harpsichord apes the Partridge Family's "Come On, Get Happy" at the end (a trick that bands like Zumpano would use in later neo-gum songs), one is not just swallowing the bile, but demanding seconds. Sheer genius.

Teenage Fanclub: "Sidewinder" (from *Bandwagonesque*, DGC, 1991)

When critics rightfully hailed *Bandwagonesque*, no one seemed to mention this unassuming little gem of a tune. Few seemed willing to acknowledge the Glaswegian quartet as unabashed bubblegum lovers in the age of grunge (who would later cover the 1910 Fruitgum Company's "Goody Goody Gumdrops" as a B-side). It's their loss, as "Sidewinder" is an unironic love song that weds sunny lyrics to a melancholic melody, beautifully sung. The guitar interplay, subtler here than on other tracks, simply shimmers, bringing the lovestruck choirboy harmonies of Gerard Love and Brendan O'Hare forward. As they softly sigh "Eyes of blue, oh baby, I love you," there is no sign of jaded slackerdom anywhere. Instead, an undercurrent of wistfulness pervades, as it could not in bubblegum songs of yore. Yet, when the protagonist confides "When you're ticking/I'm your tock," one knows he feels as much joy in love as the characters in the Archies' "Bang Shang-A-Lang" or the Beagles' "Sharing Wishes," whether or not that love is returned. "Sidewinder" is perhaps the most touching bubblegum song now or then, a real masterpiece.

Shonen Knife: "Riding on the Rocket" (from *Pretty Little Baka Guy*, Rockville, 1992)

Osaka, Japan's finest trio has always demonstrated an intuitive mastery of the bubblegum genre.

While bubblepunk gems like "I Wanna Eat Chocobars" or "Public Bath" merit consideration, the more traditional bubblegum of "Riding on the Rocket" proves irresistible. The lyrics could be a parallel-universe homage to an episode of *Josie and the Pussycats in Outer Space:* "Riding on the rocket, I wanna go to Pluto/Space foods are marshmallow, asparagus, and ice cream!" (The rhythmic flow of the Japanese lyrics on this recording is preferable to the English version on 1993's *Let's Knife.*) Naoko Yamano's enthusiastic vocals delight, and the "space walk dance party" groove would do the Banana Splits proud.

cub: "My Assassin" (from *Betti-Cola*, Mint, 1993)

The album cover art is by Archie Comics cartoonist Dan DeCarlo, and the band had to endure the typecasting of "cuddlecore" in its heyday. Yet, as "My Assassin" proves, cub was never that simple. Ambiguity reigns as Lisa Marr breezily recounts a tale of a nightmarish psychotic — or is he? As Marr tosses off lines like "My assassin covers me with water/He says that fire's faster but it's hotter," the singsong groove adds a touch of lightness, sympathy, even admiration. Black-humored nursery rhyme or a new kind of love song? You be the judge.

Helen Love: "Punk Boy 2" (Damaged Goods single, 1994, re-released 1997)

The Teen Anthems once opined that "except for Helen Love, [Welsh bands] are just shite!" While that remains to be proven, this B-side to the oft-covered "Punk Boy" holds its own against singles from any country. The all-female band has tackled such diverse topics as working women ("Diet Coke Girl") and abusive boyfriends ("Beat Him Up"), but here band namesake Helen Love's chatty, sweet voice rhapsodizes about the ideal man (one who sounds far more gum than punk). The Casio melody has enough majesty to rival Phil Spector's biggest productions, nicely complementing the tender simplicity of lines like "Hey, you're looking beautiful/ There's moonbeams in your eyes." The

piece de resistance is a prominent sample of the Archies' "Bang Shang-A-Lang" (the clearest gum antecedent of such romanticism). "Punk Boy 2" is the perfect neo-gum track, but a worthy addition to any canon.

Vehicle Flips: "Diplomacy, Home and Abroad" (from the Harriet compilation *The Long Secret*, 1995)

In its one minute and fifty seconds, "Diplomacy, Home and Abroad" makes an airtight case for this Pittsburgh quartet as the intellectual's Ohio Express. The exuberant lo-fi anthem is as addictive as anything on the Buddah roster, and Frank Boscoe is a vocal dead ringer for Joey Levine. (Although, to be sure, Levine never sang lines like "Maybe Madeleine Albright could provide some insight/ into your keen and nimble mind!") Still not convinced? Never fear, as Boscoe and company have the foresight to wed such potentially highfalutin' lyrics to a gloriously lowbrow two-chord guitar hook, which lurches relentlessly in perfect counterpoint to Tom Hoffman's caffeinated military backbeat. As Boscoe hollers "Woo-ooo!" and the fuzz pedals kick in, the sugar rush is too blissful to ignore. If Cole Porter had written a song for the Kasenetz-Katz Empire, this is what it would have sounded like.

Splitsville: "Trini '93" (from *Splitsville USA*, Big Deal, 1996)

Baltimore's Splitsville delivered this slice of classic bubblepunk on their underrated first album. A seemingly throwaway goof, "Trini '93" becomes a clever paean to that bubblegummiest of ideas: the mad crush on a kid's TV character. No matter how the listener may feel about the Power Rangers, the sublime harmonies drive home the brilliance of such couplets as "She's always tan/ I think she's from Japan." Who could not be in awe?

Gothic Archies: "City of the Damned" (from *The New Despair*, Merge, 1997)

Claudia Gonson once revealed in *Caught In Flux* that as far as bandmate Stephin Merritt is concerned, "the pinnacle of genius musical production was the Archies' 'Sugar, Sugar.'" Merritt has always excelled in twisting bubblegum devices to his own tunesmithing ends, and the Gothic Archies are the ultimate result. "City of the Damned" reflects the band's perfect nomenclature, bouncing along on a classic cartoon-pop guitar figure made sinister by reverb, with a happy snare shuffle threatened by leviathan bass burblings. Merritt's earnest voice sounds careworn as he sings "Come along with us to the city of the damned," but the journey sounds alluring nevertheless.

James Iha: "Jealousy" (from *Let It Come Down*, Virgin, 1998)

More than one critic reviled the Smashing Pumpkins guitarist's debut for excessive tweeness. I, for one, thought it didn't go far enough in that direction. The preponderance of folk arrangements disguised the fact that Iha has a voice uniquely suited for bubblegum. This shuffling, playful love song, punctuated with horns and Hammond organ, showcases Iha's confidently gentle phrasing. His voice soars on lines like "love is a falling star," floats on "your love pulls up my strings." By the time he scats "bah bah bah bah, doo de doo" at

the end, one sadly realizes that Iha could be the Andy Kim of the next millennium if he'd just trade in Billy Corgan for Jeff Barry.

Apples in Stereo: "Questions and Answers" (from *Her Wallpaper Reverie*, spinART, 1999)

As one of the most exciting bands to emerge in the 1990s, Denver's Apples in Stereo demonstrate how indiepop and bubblegum best converge. Most Apples songs share the infectious exuberance of the genre, and main singer/songwriter Robert Schneider has released a whole series of self-proclaimed "kid songs" in his Marbles side project. Yet, on their quirkiest release, it is drum goddess Hilarie Sidney who provides the glorious "Questions and Answers." Sidney's childlike vocals propel a rollicking production replete with tambourine, organ, and clavinet. The sound is baroquely lo-fi, giving a feel of complex layers bubbling under a seductively simple song structure. The song's lyrics have a strange foreboding ("just ask the question that will make it go away"), but are conveyed with pure enthusiasm. Gleeful anxiety? My friends, you can't get more late-1990s than that.

But what is to become of bubblegum in the new millennium? Although the '80s should have taught the world that a glut of boy bands can lead only to madness, the general outlook seems promising. Bubblegum continues to branch out into unexpected genres, from the kitschy lounge-pop of Japan's Kahimi Karie to the postmodern deconstructivist gum of ABBA-meets-Ramones project GABBA. Labels such as Scotland's Shoeshine Records have several fine neo-gum bands on their rosters, while bands such as Hanson and the Vandalias prove that some of the old gum devices can result in worthwhile music today. Whatever happens, take heart: whenever a musician has a sweet tooth and a dream, bubblegum is sure to follow.

Raiding Hannah's Stash: An Appreciation of late '90s Bubblegum Music by Peter Bagge

Back in early 1997, I was in negotiating a "development deal" with MTV to convert my comic book, *Hate*, into an animated TV show. Since I hadn't watched MTV in ages (I was pushing 40 by then, so what do you expect?), I decided it might be a good idea to do some marathon viewing, in order to re-familiarize myself with who I was dealing with. What torture. Never mind their non-music vid programming (all of which was unbearable, with the exception of *Beavis and Butthead*), but the videos had me squirming in pain as well. I recall three distinct varieties of "musical entertainment" that were dominating the airwaves at the time:

"Rap": Which had become almost exclusively of the "gangsta" variety, in which both the male and female rappers would wave a threatening finger at me and talk about what badass muthafuckas they are and totally trash the opposite sex in a way that most people outgrow when they're 12, all while sporting hideous, ill-fitting jogging outfits;

"Alternative": Always white, usually male, always wearing throwaway t-shirts and pants, always WHINING WHINING WHINING about who knows what and WHO CARES? And always sung with that same harsh, nasal "I don't take anything seriously so fuck everyone anyway" attitude as the band pogos up and down and bangs out their Ramones riffs (or else they'd be doing that Nirvana/Who routine of quiet, achy-voiced verse followed by loud, anthemic chorus. Yawn);

Followed by the worst "genre" of all:

"Chick Singers": self-obsessed, overly-dramatic Divas, regardless of whether they can skyrocket up and down the scales like Mariah and Whitney, whisper and mince like an affected child (i.e.: Jewel), or dish out yet more punk "attitude," only combined with lots of hammy, theatrical gestures and body hugging (Alanis Morrisette, Hole). I'm sure that 1997—along with every year of the past decade—was being proclaimed "The Year of the Woman" by some music industry trade mag; based on what I was witnessing, this was not good news.

Then I saw The Spice Girls.

That's when I realized that I wasn't the problem. It wasn't that I was too old to appreciate or "get into" pop music anymore. No, the problem was that all these other, more critically acclaimed "serious" acts SUCKED. They were BORING, on top of being unoriginal. Plus they reeked of self-importance. They all needed to go away. They and their admirers needed to be punished.

And OH! how the Spice Girls tortured and vexed these people! By the time I was actually working at MTV that summer, people were routinely shocked and repulsed by my Love For The Spice Girls. "There are some things you ought to keep to yourself," one co-worker whispered to me once, with only my own best interest in mind. An otherwise hip and intelligent young "development gal" almost hit the ceiling when I told her I'd much rather listen to "Wannabe" than the godawful Radiohead video she was forcing me to watch. "Peter," she said, patiently filling me in on the Sad Facts, "I SAW the Spice Girls perform LIVE at the MTV Awards Show, and they were TERRIBLE: They can't sing, they can't dance—and they're all FAT!"

Six months later all of these people each owned the complete line of Spice Girl dolls. I guess "fat" was "in" all of a sudden.

I like that the Spice Girls are "fat" (actually, not only are they all built very differently from each other, they're also built like women are NATURALLY built—as opposed to gym-rats like Madonna, who spends hours of each day of her life trying to make her body resemble a MAN'S). I also like that their personalities have been simplified and boiled down to five easily recognizable cartoon characters (although I HATE the way Geri "Ginger" Halliwell now publicly resents this totally practical marketing ploy in the same way that that hypocritical crybaby John Lennon spent the rest of his ex-Beatle life complaining). I like that they're wacky and funny and run up and down the street punching at the air and each other like the Beatles and the Monkees used to. I like that the only thing they care about when they're on stage is to ENTERTAIN THE LIVING SHIT OUT OF THE AUDIENCE for 90 solid minutes. And I especially like their music. I LOVE their music!

The first time I heard the song "Wannabe" I immediately wanted to hear it again. And again and again and again. This is a reaction I experienced quite often when I myself was a "teeny-bopper" in the late '60s, my ears constantly glued to a tiny transistor radio listening to Cousin Brucie introduce the latest release by Steppenwolf or the Cowsills (I loved 'em both!) on WABC. I still would occasionally react that way to new recordings I'd hear all throughout the '70s and '80s, though with less and less frequency. By the '90s I had forgotten what this sensation even felt like, and simply chalked it up to an AGE thing—that "Shock of the New" that we all become immune to as time goes by. The Spice Girls made me realize that this isn't entirely the case: that there IS a certain type of music that when performed with the right kind of moxie and spirit will still thrill me to my bones and probably always will.

What's always been somewhat embarrassing for me is that the TYPE of music that routinely gets to me in this fashion is of stuff that's usually made for and marketed TO pre-teens. Specifically girls. EIGHT-YEAR-OLD girls, like my daughter Hannah. This has created what might seem like a weird "bond" between me and my daughter (although I know of many other dads who enjoy a similar "bond" with their daughters!). Everyone always makes the same joke when they see little girls with their dads watching Spice Girls videos together: the kids are into it for the music, while the dads are enjoying a little "T and A." The truth is that both the girls and the dads are enjoying BOTH—the girls are totally fascinated by the S. Girls' (or Britney Spears' or Monica's) sex appeal in the same way that boys their age are fascinated by Superman's strength; while if all we "dirty old men" cared about were bouncing boobies we would just lock the channel on to the USA Network and then pretend the remote was busted.

This Unity in Taste also served a pragmatic purpose: I could march right into Tower Records and tell the clerk that the Cleopatra cassette I was buying "isn't for ME—it's for my daughter!" Just in case they ask, that is. Which they never do. Still, it was comforting to have that info at the ready, just as I was always prepared to tell the liquor store clerk that that bottle of Bacardi 151 I was buying was "for the Old Man" back when I was still underage. As if they cared (although one time I DID share this false information with the clerk, who nearly died laughing as he rung up my illegal purchase). And as soon as Hannah expressed interest in the Spice Girls herself (all I had of the SGs up until then was a tape that a friend had made for me) I zoomed off to buy the latest release by the latest '90s bubblegum teen sensations that I—er, I mean my DAUGHTER—was interested in.

Not that all of these new recordings hold up too well, by the way. In fact, that's the main purpose of this essay: to single out the Good Stuff from the mediocre for the "uninitiated" (i.e.: the childless) amongst you who are dying to know who's better: The Backstreet Boys or 'N Sync? (Answer: They're both pretty lame). Some of my kid's favorite CDs drive me up the wall, such as Monica (already a full-fledged, overly-dramatic Whitney/Mariah/Celine Dion-type diva show-off); Christina Aguilera (ditto, is spite of her being marketed as a Britney Spears clone—although she has a few good songs); and especially the *Rugrats Movie* soundtrack (that TV show, created and performed by adults pretending to see the world through the eyes of precocious widdaw babies, is annoying enough—listening to musical director Mark Mothersbaugh and other new wavesters like the B-52's, Elvis Costello and IGGY POP do the same thing on this CD is more than I can stand!).

So allow me to work my way through my daughter's CD collection and pull out the ones that are at least worth your time and consideration.

Aqua, *Aquarium* (MCA, 1997)

This Danish foursome (two keyboardist/programmers and two singers) are responsible for that big hit "Barbie Girl" from several summers ago. Yeah, those people. And this entire CD bubbles and percolates exactly like that song does—it's just a boom-boom-boom Eurodisco beat with Barbie girl (Lene Grawford Nystrom) playing call and response with Rene "Ken" Dif from the first cut to the last.

I love this record. It drives most people crazy, though—it even drives ME crazy when I'm not in the mood for it! But when I AM in an Aqua Mood I get locked into its beat and ride it on home in the same way that I could be listening to the Ramones' *Rocket to Russia* and thinking this is the best record ever made ever ever ever, while at other times it sounds like just another stupid Ramones record. I'm not even into techno or disco as a rule. I just like this CD. It's got lots of great hooks and can be very funny at times as well.

Buy this at your own risk. I refuse to be held responsible.

B*witched, *B*witched* (Epic/Sony, 1998)

B*witched are "Ireland's answer to the Spice Girls": four perky, VERY young (18–20 years old) fame-school graduates who can dance their scrawny little Gaelic hineys off, and who sing well to boot (one of the Lynch twins, Edele, sings the lead on every song, and while she has a very nice voice I find it odd that not even her sister Keavy gets to sing lead on occasion. I mean, wouldn't an identical twin have an identical singing voice?). Their dance routines, as well as their music, are a cross between the Jackson Five and *Riverdance*— an unlikely and seemingly distasteful combination that actually works quite well (as anyone who's watched them perform their adorable act on that oft-repeated Disney Channel special a dozen times like I have can attest to).

Like the Spice Girls, they share songwriting credits with their producers (presumably both groups are mainly responsible for the bulk of their own super happy, cliché-ridden lyrics—

though the SGs songs are far more obsessed with sex and EGO than their more innocent Irish progeny). Also like the SGs, their management landed one hell of a producer in Ray "Madman" Hedges, who along with arranger Martin Brannigan put together one hell of a CD. This giddy masterpiece is simply BURSTING with energy and zing from beginning to end (save for the prerequisite ballads, some of which are also wonderful—like the ELO/Wings-ish "Oh Mr. Postman"—and some of which just take up space). The producers on almost all of these '90s bubblegum records are keyboardists who "play" or "program" most of the rhythm instruments themselves on their digital MIDI/DAT/AVID sampling gizmo contraptions, which are little more than $50,000 Casio players. You would think that the end result would be soulless dreck—and it usually is, although it sure is amazing what some of the more imaginative producers can pull off working this way. "Never Giving Up," "Rollercoaster" and their big hit "C'est La Vie" all crackle and pop like nobody's business, and the way Hedges seamlessly works traditional folk instruments like fiddles and tin whistles into the mix without making them sound gimmicky is nothing short of a marvel. That "Madman" Hedges is a madman, man!

B*witched have been monster huge in the UK and Europe for over a year now, though as of this writing they've barely cracked the Top 10 in the States, despite the Disney Channel's best efforts. Plus their act is pure innocence and fun, without a single ounce of the tough guy (or gal) posturing and overt sexuality that all of their bubblegum competition is guilty of, and that the American Youth Market seems to

demand or at least expect to some degree. And their outfits are pretty cornball, too: all '70s-style bell-bottoms and hip-huggers, denim and fringe. Of course that look is "In" again at the moment, but when matched up with B*witched's act it makes one think of Donny and Marie or Pink Lady. Yet in spite of all that they're still doing quite well over here, and I never hear any kids put them down for being too squaresville. They're a pretty hard act to DISlike too, it seems.

That reminds me: we recently were all watching a live teeny-bopper concert being broadcast on Nickelodeon that was hosted by some macho rapper asshole whose name I forget. During an off-stage interview with B*witched he immediately started to mimic Keavy's squeaky, high-pitched voice right after she introduced herself (hey, I make fun of her voice too, but not to her face or on national television!). She and her bandmates responded by giving him a polite sidelong glance, as if to ask: "Who raised YOU?" SOCIETY raised him, girls!

UPDATE: B*witched's follow-up CD is just came out, and while it's still likable fare for the most part, very closely following the formula of their first CD, all the "danger signs" are here as well. Producer Hedges is definitely striving for a more "mature" sound, such as using the African singing group Ladysmith Black Mambazo on one song. Not that I dislike their singing—I like it a LOT, in fact, but on a fucking B*witched record?!? I wish he'd leave that worldbeat jazz to washed-up musical rapists like Paul Simon. Plus lead singer Edele Lynch's voice dominates the vocals so completely on this new CD that one sees Diana Ross Disease at work here . . . I can see the plot of the future TV movie about them taking shape already . . .

Still, I like this new CD, and, I LOVE their debut. Two thumbs up for the first one, and if you like it a lot give the new one a try.

Billie, *Honey to the B* (Virgin, 1998)
16-year-old Billie Paul Piper (curious name for a girl) is the Limey version of Britney Spears,

although she's not as cute and doesn't have quite as good a singing voice. Still, she has a very pleasant, straight-forward singing style that is all too rare these days. She's had four straight Top 10 hits in the UK since the summer of '98, though her CD wasn't released in the US until May of 1999. She also has yet to make a dent in the US market—just one more huge question mark as to what makes one act huge here but not there and vice versa . . .

I was pretty disappointed in this CD when I first heard it, after much excited word of mouth by my fellow dirty old men from across the pond—it's much more Mainstream/MOR/R&B sounding than, say, the youthful, poppy exuberance of B*witched. Kinda reminds me of Brandy's music, though thankfully without any of that showoffy, I-Wanna-Be-Whitney crap that Brandy indulges in. But after a few listens this thing has grown on me quite a bit. As far as MOR R&B goes, it's pretty dang good! Billie's producing/arranging/songwriting team of Jim Marr and Wendy Page don't have an original bone in their bodies, but they sure know a good groove when they steal one. This thing kind of reminds me of the Spice Girls' first CD with its non-stop dance floor feel, though without any of the SG's in-your-face insanity. She actually sounds a lot more mellow and MATURE than the Spices, which might make her more palatable to all you Spice Haters out there.

The themes are still pure teeny-bopper wanna-be-your-girlfriend/gonna-steal-your-boyfriend type stuff, however. Especially her teen anthem "Because We Want To," which is all about doing whatever the hell you want to do, and was definitely designed to be her own "Wannabe."

This is a good record. Nothing remarkable, but if you find it on sale you won't feel ripped off.

Cleopatra, *Comin' Atcha* (Maverick/WB, 1998)
Cleopatra are three black teenage sisters from the UK: Cleopatra, Zainaim and Yonah Higgins. The oldest, Cleo, does almost all of the lead singing and sounds a lot like a young Michael Jackson

(they even do a cover of "I Want You Back" on this CD, and it's hard to believe it's NOT Michael singing it). They also write all their own lyrics and share the songwriting credits with their various producers. In other words, these gals are bona fide talents with a long-term career in the music biz ahead of them (as far as anyone is able to predict such things, that is).

Watching these girls perform on stage is quite another-worldly visual experience: they're all very short and wear baggy, candy-colored clothes and big floppy hats. They also have super long braided hair that twirls like helicopter blades as they spin, turn and waddle about in unison. Last year they did their outer space dancing on some Nickelodeon special, after which me and my daughter made a bee-line to the nearest record store to buy their product. Guess what? It turned out their CD "wasn't ready" for US release yet. It took MONTHS to get over here! Somebody really missed the boat on that one—LITERALLY!

As for the music itself, it's pretty generic '90s R&B, only on the light, sweet side so the kids can swallow it. Nice enough stuff, but nothing too memorable—save for one cut, "Thinking About You," which is quite a thing of beauty that never stops growing on me. I say buy this CD for that song alone. You at least won't be offended by the rest of the material (although you might be offended by how many times they thank The Great God Almighty in the liner notes. Talk about overkill! Even gospel acts don't thank Him THIS much!).

Hanson, *Middle of Nowhere* (Mercury, 1997)

This is the debut CD by the band that everyone was making fun of when they weren't busy making fun of the Spice Girls. It's an awfully polished and professional product for three teenage brothers fresh out of Tulsa, Oklahoma, due to the fact that they had plenty of time, money and help devoted to them in the form of top-rate producers and back-up musicians. One thing that those well-paid "pros" cannot provide, however, is the hyper,

unbridled teen-boy mania that comes through on here in spite of the slick production. In fact, sometimes it seems like the producers were indulging them in this regard, like with the wahwah-laden guitar solo in "Where's the Love" or the totally goofball synthesizer solo in "Madeline." I'm sure they were like kids being set loose in a candy store when they entered the recording studio ("Whoa, dude, check it out—a BIG MUFF!"), but then, only a 15-year-old should be allowed to use those gizmos to begin with, before they attempt to do something "tasteful" with them!

Hanson Rocks. I saw them perform live, and let me tell you something, folks: they rocked like a motherfucker. Laugh all you want, but it's true. They also sing great, and in a way that only a sibling group can pull off. Theirs' was the best live harmonizing I've heard since the time I saw the Beach Boys in 1973. Most of this CD is just shout-out-loud, drivin', rockin' pop music at its best. It also is the only CD in this survey that really IS "rock" (the rest are all various mixtures of disco, techno and hip hop), with real guitars and drums on it—most of which are played by the band itself. Go Hanson!

On the down side, however, is that it also has a real midwestern, John Cougar Mellencamp flavor to it—especially when the oldest, Isaac, sings, since he's the only one whose voice had changed at the time this record was recorded. Not that there's inherently anything wrong with this, but it is cause for concern re: where they're heading musically in the future, since they do have very Middle-American cornfed sensibilities (again, not unlike Mellencamp). The ballads on this CD, while perfectly harmless, suggest that

ISAAC HANSON TRIES OUT A WAH-WAH PEDAL FOR THE FIRST TIME

WHOA

COOL

...WAH WAH WAH...

there won't be much to recommend them once they outgrow their hyper adolescence. In fact, they could wind up looking and sounding indistinguishable from the likes of Michael Bolton!

It's been quite a while since they released anything new as well, so I'm filled with apprehension once something new by them DOES come out (and it's indeed taking them a very long time, which only adds to my concern). Oh well, we shall see. But no matter what happens to them down the road, this CD will remain a rock 'n' roll classic forever. Buy it and give it a listen if you don't believe me.

Their only other releases besides this one are a Christmas CD entitled *Snowed In*, a collection of early demo tapes called *Three Car Garage*, and a live concert CD (recorded at the show I was at, amazingly). *Snowed* is one of the most enjoyable Xmas albums ever made, and I heartily recommend it for some sure-fire rockin' holiday good cheer. *Three Car* is a must to avoid, however. Sure, it's a pretty impressive demo from a group that features a ten-year-old drummer, but it's still a DEMO. Demos should be BURNED before some dipshit "fan" decides to make a bootleg out of them, or a greedy label decides to use it to rip off their gullible public (i.e.: me). Same goes for live albums. You just had to be there, folks! Sorry!

NOW Compilation (EMI, 1998)

This is a "This Year's Biggest Hits All On One CD!"-type compilation that you can only order by phone after seeing the relentless TV commercials. My daughter wrote down the 1-800 number and handed it to her mom, instructing her to dial it A.S.A.P.. She wanted Today's Biggest Hits and she wanted them NOW, Goddammit! Who were we to argue?

Anyone who's listened to a day's worth of Top 10 radio in the last couple of years knows half of these songs already: Hanson's "Mmm Bop," the Spice Girls' "Say You'll Be There," etc. Some of these hits I like just fine, such as Janet's retro-'70s disco tune "Together Again," and the Backstreet Boys' "As Long as You Love Me" (which is pretty

much the ONLY BSB song I like). Unfortunately, there's an awful lot of "alternative" gunk on here as well, which grates even more than usual when pressed up against songs like the ones mentioned above. The only tolerable ones are "alterna-Beatle"-type bands like Fastball and Harvey Danger (think John Lennon at his most nasally and cynical). The latter band features a guy who used to work in the production department for my publisher here in Seattle. One day he's attaching page numbers to my comic book for minimum wage, and the next day my kid is ordering his record off of Nickelodeon. What a wacky world.

This comp also has one gem I'd never heard before: "Never Ever," by a British all-girl singing group called All Saints. This slow, gospelly tune has a real early-'60s-Shadow Morton girl-group feel to it. I didn't think much of it at first, but MAN has it grown on me since then. It just sucks you right in like a vacuum cleaner. I don't even know if you can still buy this CD anymore, but if you ever come across it used and cheap then pick it up for this song alone.

There have since been two more *NOW* collections released, along with a similar compilation called *Totally Hits*. Each one of these collections have a couple of must-have doozies on them, saving me from having to buy certain acts' entire CDs. But as is the case with the first *NOW*, they all have a lot of slop on them as well. Sheryl Crow . . . BLECHHH. The only thing all these songs have in common is that they were "hits," obviously. TOTALLY hits. And one person's hit is another person's bane of existence.

Sabrina The Teenage Witch—The Album! (Geffen, 1998)

This compilation has contributions by all the latest hot teen sensations (incl. an otherwise unavailable track by the Spice Girls, which made it a must-have item in the Bagge household). The only connection that it has to the TV show are the photos of Melissa Joan Hart's smirky face all over the sleeve, as well as her own uninspired rendition of Blondie's "One Way Or Another."

Aside from that and a few other note-for-note covers of '70s classics (Matthew Sweet does a why-bother remake of "Magnet and Steel," while current hitmeisters Sugar Ray give Steve Miller's "Abracadabra" the karaoke treatment), this CD has a few real doozies on it: good cuts by Aqua, Britney Spears, the Murmurs, the Cardigans, and the Spice Girls (of course!). Plus the otherwise annoying Ben Folds Five turn in their best song by far with the rousing "Kate"—though Mr. Folds still comes close to ruining even this song with that smarmy "look at me, I'm being clever ovah heah!" singing style of his, to go along with that bangy Billy Joel (another long-time sufferer of cleveritis)-style piano playing that I hate. This is a classic example of ruining a perfectly pretty song in order to hang on to your "indie cred"—something I think a lot of indie rockers are bound to regret someday, if they don't already.

Black-sounding blondie girl Robyn is also featured with "Show Me Love," her slinky smash from a few summers ago. This song was co-written and produced by the Swedish hit-making team of Max Martin and the recently-departed Denniz Pop. These two Scandihoovians are also responsible for just about every major hit by all the "O-Town" acts (Britney, Backstreet Boys, 'N Sync). These guys are probably the most successful songwriters of the '90s by far, in spite of the fact that no one's ever heard of them. While I enjoy a lot of their tunes (like this one), it's hard for me to think of myself as a "fan," since they hit the mark a little TOO succinctly. Their sensibilities are just too middle-of-the-road and mainstream for me. I like at least a LITTLE bit of personality and quirkiness to go with my pop schmaltz! But I also might be reacting to their amazing recent success, and it will probably hit me years later just how brilliant these guys really are.

The low points on this CD for me are all the New Kids-clone boy groups, whose contributions here show them all doing what they do worst: macho-posturing rap and hip-hop. I simply can't buy into these obvious nancy-boys trying to make like they're street toughs. "Ruff Tuff Cream Puffs," I calls 'em! They should stick to the ballads, in my

opinion—though my wife thinks these songs are adorable, especially the UK outfit Five's laughable theme song "Slam Dunk Da Funk" (also written by those high-fivin' homeboys from Stockholm, Martin and Pop. Can you imagine those two Squareheads sitting at home "composing" this thing in their Swedish country kitchen, while they're gettin' jiggy wit' their lutefisk?). It seems that adults do a flip flop from the sexual identifying of their youth; my daughter has little interest in male singers and acts, just as I rarely bought anything that was sung by a female when I was a kid. Now it's the opposite, with my wife cranking up any tune that's sung by some hunky 18-year-old (one of the members of Five even goes by the name of "Abs"), while I sit there jealously calling the singer a "sissy" and a "faggot," even when I'm secretly enjoying the record myself.

Anyhow, *Sabrina* is a surprisingly good sampler, and Tower was selling it at some super low price when it first came out. Check it out if it's still in stock!

Savage Garden, *Savage Garden* (Sony, 1997)

These two Aussies wear gobs of eyeliner and hair gel, and the singer, Darren Hayes, sings in this real affected Boy George-type voice. Plus they're called "Savage Garden." Talk about your sissy faggots! The '80s are over, dudes! I would love to run them over in my Subaru if I ever got the chance, only some of their songs are brilliant; real nice steady-beat ballads like the hit "Madly Truly Deeply." "Universe" is an especially pretty tune, very Smokey Robinsonesque, with great harmonizing on the chorus by Mr. FruityPants Hayes (who in spite of my wisecracks is really an amazing singer).

Their attempts at noisy, upbeat disco numbers are annoying, however, so this gets only half a rousing thumbs up.

Buy it used.

Britney Spears, *Britney Spears* (Jive/Zomba, 1999)

Britney Spears is literally the new Annette Funicello, since not only is she a sexy sweetheart whom all of America is in love with, but she also was a Mouseketeer on *The NEW Mickey Mouse Club* show! Unlike the monotoned Annette, however, she has an incredible singing voice. She goes from peeping like a tweety bird to growling like a grizzly bear all in the same verse. This could a bad sign, however, since once she outgrows her teenybopper status I'll bet you dollars to donuts she's gonna be tempted to give Celine, Mariah and Whitney a run for their money in the cobrahead-shaking diva drama-queen sweepstakes that I so obviously detest.

She seems to have a rebel streak in her too, in that she routinely does things to undermine her America's Sweetheart image—such as performing braless with her new breast implants on the Nickelodeon *Kids' Choice Awards* show (and then denying they were implants when all the parents watching had a goddamned cow over it). Of course none of these antics have hurt her career a bit, so they all may part of her management's master plan.

And that brings us to yet another bad sign: she's managed by the Orlando-based hit-making machine called "O-Town," who also assembled and control the Backstreet Boys and their interchangeable clones 'N Sync (along with many other "future stars" who are currently being groomed at their "finishing school"). All of these acts are super huge at the

moment, which led one of O-Town's odd-couple founders, fatso billionaire and Chippendale's Dancers mogul Lou "Call Me Big Poppa" Pearlman, to start promoting himself as the Berry Gordy/Don Kirshner/Neil Bogart of the '90s—much to the chagrin of his partner, the black "Jesus freak" and former Maurice Starr gopher Johnny Wright. Ever since then these two egomaniacs have been suing the daylights out of each other, much to the delight of the rest of the music industry.

The thing is, at least Gordy and even Kirshner had a certain sensibility that permeated everything they touched. They could lay claim to a style or innovation that was all their own, while the O-Towners have savvy and street hustle going for them and nothing more. While originality has never ruled supreme in teenybopperland, literally EVERYTHING their charges do is completely by-the-book. Their boy groups in particular are TOTALLY generic from head to toe: looking and moving EXACTLY like the New Kids on the Block (whom Wright used to chauffeur), while harmonizing EXACTLY like Boyz 2 Men (or trying to). And while this song or that may be tolerable, the music is WAY too bland and predictable. It just sits there, like your Aunt Edna's meatloaf. Sure it's edible, but it's nothing to drive miles out of your way to sample.

The same goes for most of the material on Britney's debut CD, sadly. Pretty dull stuff. There are a few exceptions, like the megahit ". . . Baby One More Time" and its carbon copy followup "(You Drive Me) Crazy" (which my daughter recently declared to be The Greatest Recording of All Time); as well as the super bouncy "Soda Pop," with a great Jamaican-style back-up vocal by a guy named Mikey Bassie. What makes all of her record at least listenable is her singing, especially her multi-track harmonies, which are truly amazing at times. I say buy this if you find it on sale in the cutout bin (which it will be filling up in a year or two, believe me) if you're at all curious to hear what the fuss is all about, though I doubt you'd feel too ripped off if you paid full price for it either.

BTW: There are a few incredibly crass things about this CD that I have to mention: one is that it ends with an infomercial for the new Backstreet Boys CD, narrated by Britney herself (over her objections, allegedly)! It also has an order form for all sorts of Britney merchandise, even though this is just her debut album (although I can't blame her handlers for their optimism, greedy slobs though they may be). Finally, the back cover has all this small print, technical-type info explaining what plug-ins you'll need to play it on either a PC or an Apple CD-ROM disk drive! At first I thought "Quick Time" was the name of the subsidiary label this record was on, until I was tipped off that this was an ENHANCED CD, and that it comes with a bunch of interview snippets, as well as her pornographic ". . .Baby One More Time" video. Not that there's anything wrong with that, mind you. In fact, it's great! But still, this CD cover and booklet is LOUSY with logos and trademarks. Everyone wants a piece of Britney, apparently. Perverts!

Spice Girls, *Spice* (Virgin, 1996)

This debut CD sold half a billion copies worldwide, so chances are you're already familiar with half of it without even knowing it (then again, maybe not, since most of you Feral House readers can do a damn good job of cloistering yourself away from "mainstream society" when you want to, myself included).

The anthemic megahit "Wannabe" kicks things off with a bang, and this cut pretty much sums up the Girls' whole shtick in a nutshell: high energy; sexually liberated; be true to your galpals; etc. My kid and her galpals all played this song five hundred thousand times in a row when they first brought it home, so it obviously had the same impact on them that "Hound Dog," "I Wanna Hold Your Hand" and "God Save the Queen" had on previous generations of impressionable youth.

None of the rest of the songs on this CD have the same impact or immediacy as "Wannabe," but it's all enjoyable, goes-down-easy fare nonetheless. In fact, most of it has a very '70s R&B feel to it:

"Something Kinda Funny" sounds a lot like Chic, "Love Thing" is Emotion doing Earth, Wind and Fire (Melanie "Sporty" Chisolm even opens it with a very Maurice White-type "OWW!"), and "Say You'll Be There" is pure Stevie Wonder, complete with harmonica solo. All five Spices must have been weaned on a steady diet of American R&B, since even lily-white Emma "Baby Spice" Bunton can dish up some surprisingly soulful ad lib warblings.

Throw in a couple of slutty ballads, along with the embarrassingly sentimental-yet-highly hummable piece of Euro-drivel "Mama," and there you have it: a multi-platinum MONSTER. I'd recommend this CD to anyone who's inclined towards liking the SG's shtick in general. If not, then skip it. I don't want to hear about it later.

Spice Girls, *SpiceWorld* (Virgin, 1997)

This is one of the most amazing albums I've ever heard. Every song has a completely different groove or "feel" to it, yet they all have that high fructose effervescence that you'd expect from a "teenybopper" outfit like the SGs. The same goes for its über-positive, egocentric lyrics and themes, which could be summed up by their titles alone ("Spice Up Your Life," "Do It", "Never Give Up on the Good Times").

The production on this CD is awe-inspiring, with the dueling producing/songwriting teams of Stannard and Rowe vs. Watkins and Wilson (aka "Absolute") trying to outdo each other on each successive cut. At the risk of sounding like the teenaged pothead that I once was, this record is also the most mind-blowing HEAD-PHONE LISTENING experience I've heard since the Beach Boys' *Surf's Up* or 10cc's *Sheet*

Music, due to the layered intricacies of the music and the treatment given to the vocals. This CD is a MUST-HAVE ITEM for anyone who appreciates lush harmonies as much as I do. I think the Girls' own self-effacing humor is primarily responsible for this permanently accepted notion that "the Spice Girls can't sing," (though God bless 'em for never wasting their time bickering with their own critics). Geri/Ginger even claims that she can barely sing on key, though she herself has a very endearing raspy, lisping singing voice. While the state-of-the-art production facilities employed here (and which every major label singing act ALSO uses) certainly didn't hurt, nothing can take away from the fact that this record has GREAT singing on it! Vicki "Posh" Adams and Mel "Scary" Brown both have very deep voices (Mel B's low growl even gets down into BARITONE range at times); so while Emma's voice is riding on top with her flowery flutterings along with the amazing Mel C's ear-piercing punctuation marks, the rest of them fill out their harmonies with a rich, earthy fullness that sounds more like Spice WOMEN than Spice "girls."

Bunton and Chisolm also have two of the most distinctive, radio-friendly voices I've ever heard: as soon as either of them utters a line over the air you know you're hearing a new SGs song. (Though it surprises me how reluctant US radio stations STILL are about playing the Spice Girls. Their success over here is due almost entirely to TV and word-of-mouth—radio has rendered itself irrelevant strictly out of spite). Believe me, it takes a lot more than clever marketing to sell a zillion records—just think of all the countless

CRAZY GINGER

"pretty faces" in the history of the music business who've tried and FAILED. Most of my all-time favorite singing groups have had two lead singers with Roger and Pete, Maurice and Philip of Earth Wind and Fire, Allan Clarke

and Graham Nash of the Hollies, etc. The Spice Girls have Emma and Mel C.

I recommend this CD to everyone. If you buy it and still don't like it then I'd suggest you crawl into your sad little cubbyhole and listen to your wretched Bob Dylan (or Lou Reed or Nick Cave) records one last time before putting a bullet through your miserable fucking head.

Other SG items: Their CD singles are hit or miss. The "Stop" single includes a bunch of extended dance mixes of the same song that all suck . . . The "Goodbye" single (their only release as of this writing sans Geri) has a great cover of the Waitresses' "Christmas Wrapping," but it also includes live versions of "We are Family" and "Sisters Are Doing It For Themselves." Good versions, mind you, but GOD do those songs suck. "Goodbye" itself (an insincere sounding "farewell" to Geri) is pretty insipid, though it does feature nice harmonies.

SpiceWorld is a super entertaining movie that holds up to repeated viewing. Unfortunately, a lot of people I know who enter that film preparing to hate it exit hating it as well. Go fucking figure . . .

The *Live in Istanbul* Video is a MUST. This is the greatest concert film EVER! And what makes it better by leaps and bounds over the more recent *Live at Wembley* concert video is that the latter doesn't have Ginger Spice. The Spice Universe has been thrown irrevocably out of whack since her departure, sadly. Ginger may have been the worst singer and dancer of the bunch, but she also was the best "Spice Girl" by far. I defy anyone to watch this Istanbul tape and then tell me to my face that she isn't completely BONKERS. She truly was (is?) a mad, inspired, and dangerous woman. Ten times more "punk" than Johnny Rotten. A zillion times sexier than stupid ol' Madonna. Exactly who Geri Halliwell is may still be a big question mark (and her aptly-titled solo CD *Schizophonic* makes it pretty clear that even SHE doesn't know who the hell she is), but "Ginger Spice" was one of the greatest "rock stars" that ever lived.

Geri Halliwell is my favorite character to come out of this whole late '90s b-gum era—not due to out of this whole late '90s b-gum era—not due to her talent or lack thereof, but more for why and HOW she became a star in the first place. She's starved for attention, basically, and will do anything to get it, even if she has to constantly re-invent and contradict herself to do so. This is not at all different from what David Bowie or John Lennon always did throughout their chameleon-like careers, only she lacks their ability to INTEL-LECTUALIZE her public gyrations. For someone with such a big mouth who really isn't about anything other than being famous, she sure is a lousy bullshit artist.

This of course leaves her wide open to ridicule—something that virtually every record critic in the world indulged in to the nth degree when her solo CD was released. But in their rush to shit all over the thing, not one of these critics took the time to note that *Schizophonic* is a pretty good record. The worst thing about it is that it tried too hard to be sound like a Spice Girls record, at least on the surface. It's even produced by the glossy SG production team Absolute, who at some point must have understood that they were NOT making a Kiddie record, and began to undermine their own slick arrangements with some flat-out PSYCHO progressions and bridges that do an amazing job of underscoring the buzzing, convulsing mind of Miss Halliwell. One song in particular, "Sometime," is a classic illustration of a mentally ill person's struggle to find "peace of mind," which features a back-up choir shouting "I'm a living breathing contradiction, can't live through this crucifixion," just before Geri launches into the sugary all-is-well-with-the-world chorus. It's INSANE! Listen for yourself if you don't believe me!

The thematic similarities between this CD and John Lennon's first post-Beatle LP, *Plastic Ono Band*, are astounding. On *Plastic*, Lennon shouts defiantly that he's no longer a Beatle, yet he is obviously in the middle of a huge identity crisis and nervous breakdown, screaming for his long dead mother, etc. . . . The story is exactly the same on Geri's LP, in which every song has to do with herself and her past (including a song about her deceased FATHER,

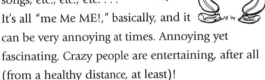

whose role in her life was identical to the one Lennon's mother played in his). You get the break-up songs, the false bravado songs mixed with the "who am I and where am I going?" songs, etc., etc., etc. . . . It's all "me Me ME!," basically, and it can be very annoying at times. Annoying yet fascinating. Crazy people are entertaining, after all (from a healthy distance, at least)!

The point of the above digression is that image and fame are just as important to what music we listen to and what acts we "like" or don't like. Some pop acts, particularly the more "critically acclaimed" ones, go way out of their way to deny this fact, while bubblegum acts revel in it. They (or at least their managers) know how fickle their audience is, so they try to make as big an impression and as much noise as possible before being forced off the stage. I recently heard the lead singer from some African group on NPR talking about how her own daughter is indifferent about her mother's music, but that she LOVES the Spice Girls. The interviewer was aghast, of course (this was NPR, after all), but his guest was fine with it. "She loves the IMAGE; what it means to BE a Spice Girl," she said. "It INSPIRES her, and gives her grand dreams of her own. Why would I be opposed to that?"

Why indeed?

1999: The Year Bubblegum Snapped by Mike McPadden

Where were you the first time the Spice Girls' fat asses knocked you on yours?

I was up way too late, scratching mine, and I'll never forget how my fingers froze. It was 1996, and I'd flicked on MTV only to immediately be screeched at by these five stocky-bootied shock-trooper go-go sirens insisting that I tell them what I want, what I really really want, and that they, in return, would tell me what they wanted, what they really, really wanted.

Whoa.

Utterly overpowered by the cheeseball power chords, Coleco drum-machine bombast, and (in)humanly impossible studio harmonies (to say nothing of the doughnut-laden eye-candy), all I could think was, "Uh . . . I guess the '80s are coming back."

But I wasn't thinking right. The '80s were gone forever. And good riddance to them. What was really coming back was the Beatles. Only this time they were going to be siphoned through some really dopey '80s gunk.

Now let's remember the most fundamental fact of life, folks: everything good is the Beatles, everything awful and bogus and pretentious and gross and condescending is the Rolling Stones.

Okay?

Mainstream pop has routinely offered two paths that you can go by (to paraphrase Led Zep, who played bloated Stones to Black Sabbath's horned mop tops). One is all about happy times and hanging out and getting lucky and being *not miserable*, while the other, at its most fruitful, might lasso you something venereal in the East Village if you yap about it long, loud, and boringly enough (and you should trust your reporter on this). But if you're past age 23 and the latter is still your idea of fun, then you probably also thought Will Self's *My Idea of Fun* was fun too and, pal-o-mine, all your ideas are wrong. About everything.

The music that matters today is the same music that mattered yesterday and 15 years ago and when your parents were not yet your parents: crap for the kids. Top 40. Pop. Fluff. The *real* Classic Rock.

In the apparently deathless battle between bubblegum tunes and narco-n-ciggy-flavored twaddle that is somehow supposed to be "good for you"—like liver, only it's all about ruining your liver!—worthwhile combatants reach for their Bazooka every time. After all, who among the following ultimately turned out to be worth fighting for—Herman's Hermits or Jimi Hendrix? The Osmond Brothers or the Allman Brothers? ABBA or Zappa? The Knack or, jeez, I don't know—Tom Verlaine? Paul Westerberg? King Diamond? The only way to answer is to be honest and acknowledge which column you'd choose more from when whipping up a mix tape. Today.

And yet for one freak moment earlier this decade, music that was supposed to be "good for you" actually did manage to sound pretty great, too. This came as a direct result of the Beatles, who relocated to the Pacific Northwest and took on the name Nirvana (those sly devils), soundly trouncing the most disgustingly Stonesy of neo-Stoneses, Guns N' Roses.

Yay for Nirvana! (And, "Hi, Axl! Hi! Hieee!")

But more on that in a minute.

At Spice Girl ground zero, the Nirvana-spawned "alterna"-(domi)nation had just commenced its not-slow-enough death spiral. A glorious (and now forgotten?) art-pop confection called "Lovefool" by the Cardigans was inescapable in both its audio and video formats, and everyone was happy, largely because such a self-aware Swede-honey make-out shuffle was obviously art first and pop second. The Spice Girls would switch that order in short enough order, but it would be a while before we'd get what we want (what we really really want). Two more springtimes to be exact.

> "Owh, BYE-buh! BYE-buh!"
> Duh-DUM-DUM-DUMB.
> "Owh, BYE-buh! BYE-buh!"
> Duh-DUM-DUM-DUMB.

They're stomach-turning, those sounds. But in a good way.

Britney Spears' ". . . Baby One More Time" is a flat-out (if silicone-emboldened) awesome thing: a sonic youth tonic (for real) that sweeps and booms and dizzyingly builds a heaven-scraping pyramid of Clearasil-smeared emotion higher and more powerfully than should be mathematically possible. Is there a mammalian nervous system capable of not swaying to the chorus? Is the sudden emergence of the extra "still buh-lieve" not as astounding as anything the chariots of the goddesses have ever rolled across our skies? And the plea, "Give me a sigh-high-high-hein" that is answered by a call for an improved poker hand or violence or cock or all three ("Hit me, baby, one more time") is breathtaking in its execution alone, and mind-blowing in its context: this is a record by a high-school kid intended for consumption by other high-school kids. And/or their juniors.

". . . Baby One More Time" is nothing less than a before-and-after musical moment just like "That's All Right Mama," and "Good Vibrations," and "God Save the Queen," and "Smells Like Teen Spirit."

Well . . . almost.

". . . Baby One More Time" actually bears the most in common, anthemically, with Mudhoney's "Touch Me I'm Sick," the Sub Pop seven-incher that set in stone—I mean, *rock*—the table of contents for grunge.

Both "Touch Me I'm Sick" and ". . . Baby One More Time" crystallized, by generally improving upon, the scenes from which they arose (Sasquatch-scented, Stooge-metal lumber punk in the case of Mudhoney; billion-selling pseudo-castrati boy-groups-for-girls with Britney). Both songs hit hard and hit often and hit you in places you didn't know you were supposed to feel anything so deep, and lyrically each cries out in desperation for a frantic laying on of hands, the better to move masses—and units—with.

Disco, Dance Pop and Bubblegum

by David Smay

Where does bubblegum go when it's not on the charts? Two of the most prominent figures in Disco began in bubblegum: Neil Bogart and Giorgio Moroder. Bogart, of course, ran Buddah and founded Casablanca Records, home to the Village People and Donna Summers. Moroder began his career with Eurovision-type ditties like "Looky Looky" and "Moody Trudy." After a brief pitstop writing one glam rock hit, "Son of My Father" by Chicory Tip, Giorgio gave the world a 20-minute sonic orgasm with "I Feel Love." A number of other bubblegum producers and singers made the very easy transition into disco, including Ron Dante (Dante's Inferno—"Fire Island") and Kenny Laguna ("Dario, Can You Get Me Into Studio"). Even the Maestro D'amour, Barry White, provided songs for the Banana Splits ("Doin' the Banana Split") before unleashing the Love Unlimited Orchestra. And if the Village People aren't exactly bubblegum, they're not too far from it either.

Bubblegum's ill-kept secret is that it's dance music for pre-teen girls. So if you want to know where bubblegum goes when it's not called bubblegum, think about Paula Abdul, early Madonna, *Thriller*-era Michael Jackson, Ray Parker, Jr. and Shalamar, and perfect throwaway singles by Stacey Q and Nu Shooz. Think about Stock-Aitken-Waterman and Kylie Minogue. Dance pop, that's what they call it now—Post-Disco, post-new wave and incorporating elements of both. What happens is that every underground dance trend eventually works its way to the surface of pop music. Pop absorbs each new dance rhythm and swaddles it in a simple melody, and sells it to the next generation. Duran Duran desperately wanted to look like Roxy Music Jr. and sound like Chic (culminating in Power Station, where they got Tony Thompson to play drums for two of the boys). New Jack Swing put over hip-hop rhythms, and even Tiffany's singles are little more than Hi-NRG makeovers for the mall. Not all dance pop is aimed at kids and shouldn't be presumed to be disposable anymore than bubblegum. Erasure, Pet Shop Boys, Lisa Lisa & Cult Jam, even Janet Jackson belong in this category, and that's a good pedigree. ◉

In fact, ". . . Baby One More Time" even echoes "Touch Me I'm Sick" in its aftereffects, serving to both unify and empower its entire musical peer group for, golly, what's going on two whole semesters now. Foremost among the bozos in Britney's wake are the *Tiger Beat* cover humps who beat her to the charts: the Backstreet Boys, 'N Sync, and 98 Degrees. Each is a queerish cash-making creation of the same mad media-manipulating scientist, and each functions (more or less respectively) as a modern equivalent of the Chili Peppers, Jane's Addiction, and Faith No More, in that they pull off their mortifyingly Caucasoid shuck-n-jive shtick with a fair degree of inventiveness and melodies way more memorable than they have to be. As for telling the "bands" apart, all I know is that one of the Backstreet Boys has a creepy, ink-black Kewpie-doll curl on his kisser, and that one of the 'N Syncs wears shoelaces in his hair (which is thoughtful, like tying a flower to your car antenna so it'll be easy to find in a crowded parking lot).

Like even the most mighty monsters of early-'90s indie rock, the artists who inspire and whose images enhance locker doors and first-ever lip-lock sessions today are primarily singles artists. It's just that the Disney Channel's *The New Mickey Mouse Club* is actually the new Seattle.

It's impossible to predict, for instance, whether the even blonder-than-Britney Christina Aguilera will ever release a 45 compilation as completely kickass as Superchunk's *Tossing Seeds*, but her "Genie in a Bottle" packs at least as much wallop as "Slack Motherfucker," and I still sing "Slack Motherfucker" two hundred times a day. The even better news is that, at present, there are two more growed-uppish Mousketeers slaving over what will be the sugar rushes of this year's Christmas break, and somehow I just *know* that *Buffy the Vampire Slayer's* Seth Green is about three seconds away from a Dreamworks record deal. Who knew the mousketakeover of everything we do, see, and experience would be so groovy?

As for growed-up Menudo Ricky Martin, he immediately brings to mind former Soundgarden frontman Chris Cornell—just another pretty-boy wail machine giving voice to music way more ambitious than is necessary. Do you think Cornell's newly released *Euphoria Morning* will move as many copies (or asses) as "Livin' La Vida Loca"? Think it'll be one one-millionth as good?

Further solidifying the bubble-grunge connection is the wholly unexpected Top 10 resurrection of now-old New Kids on the Block Jordan Knight and Joe McIntyre, eerily mirroring the way sludge grandpappies Iggy Pop and Neil Young scored hits with "Candy" and *Ragged Glory* in 1990. It's always good to see the brothers and sisters honoring the Old School (though, this time, the application of that term is pretty much literal).

And there may be no more intriguing or hilarious figure in today's faux-smooth muck-pop roster than the recently rechristened Colleen Fitzpatrick. You know her pressed-hair-laden pout from massive record store displays emblazoned with the moniker "Vitamin C." In this current guise, Ms. Fitzpatrick is allegedly responsible for a reggae-scented "hit" titled "Smile" that she has waxed theoretic about in *Rolling Stone* (and elsewhere), but which no one I've met has ever heard outside of a RealPlayer soundbite on CDNow. As it stands (hacking and bleeding through so many tiny iMac speakers), Vitamin C's "Smile" is a rather brilliantly phony whip-up aiming for a world-encompassing sellout, starring an über-blonde deep-throater in Marvel-Comics-tight lycra, rasta puff-minstrel backing vocals ("Watchoo-gon, watchoo-watchoo-gon doo, MON . . ."), back-to-school release scheduling, and even a built-in Brian Wilson nod for hipster geeks who suspect something deeper afoot as they fall a-flutter before Fitzpatrick's knowingly widened, Otter-Pop-blue peepers.

The yuks erupt when it is revealed that Fitzpatrick is literally old enough to have breastfed the entire New Mickey Mouse Club, and that she was the centerpiece of a similarly desperate-to-hit-the-money-geyser combo called Eve's Plum in the early '90s. With its retro-hep name, an appearance in the high-minded Hollywood youth movie *Higher Education*, and an (attempted) pissed-off, pseudo-riot-grrl, dance-metal guitar pop sound, Eve's Plum must have looked, on paper, like the right band at the right time. And in a sense, they were: their legacy is two separate videos that were fabulously (and accurately) goofed upon by Beavis and Butthead. It is now likely that Ms. Fitzpatrick, who tellingly belted "I WANT IT ALL!" in Eve's Plum's closest thing to a hit, is bound to be left in that position. Again.

So now all of this leads us back to the Beatles or, as I stated earlier, Nirvana, or in their most present incarnation, Canadian brother-and-sister white-rap mess-makers, Len.

Len's "Steal My Sunshine" single from the *Go* soundtrack (the one that samples "More, More, More" by the Andrea True Connection) is enchanting and sweet and heartbreaking in the *exact* same fashion as "The Wagon" by Dinosaur Jr. in 1991, only Len just released an entire album that makes good on the song's promise, whereas "The Wagon" was the last (and, really, only) great thing Dino Jr. ever pulled off.

That stated, Len's *You Can't Stop the Bum Rush* could be the cusp-of-the millennium avatar of Nirvana's *Bleach*, meaning, boy, does it rock in its own right, but look the fuck out for what these clowns produce two years down the pike. Song by song, *Bum Rush* plays like a post-everything-'90s reworking of vintage Sub Pop Singles Club singles, only set in the present and aimed much higher.

Cooler still is that unlike other "moment-in-a-blender" acts such as Camper Van Beethoven and Beck, "cutesy" is never mistaken for bona fide "cute," and Len's not-terribly-secret weapon is a knee-weakening embodiment of the very concept. Sharon Costanzo's voice—likened elsewhere to the ultimate pussycat of Josie's posse—is used sparingly on *Bum Rush*, simply because it is too brilliantly sweet, too powerful and, all around, too perfect. Like the sun, we get just enough to play outside and bake in happily, but the lack of excess exposure, however disappointing at the time, insures that nobody gets burned.

In a society that looks to, say, Courtney Love for any reason other than to induce vomiting in someone who just accidentally swallowed poison, it should be remarkable that Len's level of originality and excitement is aimed squarely at the *Total Request Live* demographic. But, really, it's not a surprise. Because what else is there?

Today's underground is all generic techno, which is okay in and of itself, but will never split open the heads on Mount Rushmore (just like the okay movie *Rushmore* tried to and didn't). Loudness-wise, Limp Kid Kornorgy's take on moron-metal might score slightly higher on its GED than past versions (maybe), but David Lee Roth's belly-up-on-arrival Las Vegas revue offers a snapshot of their collective best case future scenario. And, no, *Spin* magazine, what the world needs is for Axl Rose to keep up the exact same pace in outputting his ongoing solo effort . . . or is it a new Guns N' Roses album? . . . and if it never comes out, will the whole world finally accept that there is just and loving God looking out for us?

The next *Sgt. Pepper/Sex Pistols/Nevermind* juggernaut is about to explode via some cuddly pin-up combo (just like—hey—*Sgt. Pepper*!). The suburban kids shimmying to the computer-generated commodities on Contemporary Hits Radio today are the same goofs who would have set up rockestra pits in their suburban garages, but now have overloaded suburban PC workstations to conquer the universe from. The revolution's coming in on Candies-clad feet. Because the little girls automatically understand.

Up Close and Personal "We don't even know any songs from the Beatles!" Juke Box Jury with Chinta and Morgan Cooper

While some of us grownups can appreciate bubblegum music, the real test of its appeal is to see what a child thinks. With some trepidation, I taped a sampling of circa-1968 gum classics and submitted them for the approval of my brother Morgan (10) and sister Chinta (11). The test was made under strict scientific controls, in the bathroom of our grandparents' house. Following their opinionated reactions to the work of the Ohio Express, Lemon Pipers, Boyce & Hart, Banana Splits and Archies, the kids expounded on the current crop of kinderpop.

— Kim Cooper, May 2000

First song:

"Yummy, Yummy, Yummy"—Ohio Express

Kim: You guys knew that song. You started singing along with it right away. Where did you learn it?

Chinta: They play it on (coyly) some radio stations that I listen to.

Kim: What stations are those?

Chinta: (embarrassed) *Sometimes* Radio Disney . . . because my *brothers* like to listen to it.

Kim: Is it embarrassing to like Radio Disney? Are you a little too old for it?

Chinta: Well, at school you are considered very uncool if you like Radio Disney. 'Cause it's considered really corny, and they don't play any rap. And sometimes, like the Backstreet Boys, they sing "Am I sexual." Radio Disney takes that out and goes "la la la."

Kim: So it's still there, but you can't hear it?

Chinta: No, it's just "la la la." You know that song "Mambo Number 5?" He made another one for Radio Disney—it's like "Mickey . . ."

Kim: I was gonna ask you about that! I heard it on the radio. It's usually "a little bit of Erica"—it's kinda sexy, right?

Morgan: Yeah.

Kim: But this one was "a little bit of Goofy"—it's just completely silly. I want to also ask you about "Yummy, Yummy, Yummy." One time I was listening to Radio Disney, and instead of "I've got love in my tummy" it was—

Chinta: Bugs. That's from *The Lion King*. It's Timon and Pumbaa.

Kim: Is that where you learned that song?

Morgan: Yeah.

Kim: What do you think it means, "I've got love in my tummy?" What do you think he's singing about?

Morgan: Love?

Kim: Why would you have love in your tummy?

Morgan: It's like having butterflies.

Chinta: You could write it on a piece of paper and swallow the paper.

Kim: He seems to like it, whatever it is. It was yummy and he's got it in his tummy and it's there now. I guess it's making him feel good, right?

Chinta: Maybe he just loves somebody so much he can feel it all over his body.

Kim: What do you think about his voice? He's kinda whiny, huh?

Morgan: Nyaaa-nyaaa-nyaaa!

Chinta: Yeah, kinda like Morgan!

Kim: Like a little kid? Maybe the guy who's singing the song is a kid. Maybe he's singing about a really yummy piece of cake or something?

Chinta: Uh . . . yeah, *right!* (laughter)

Kim: What else do you think about the song?

Chinta: It's a nice song. It's kinda jumpy, makes you wanna get up—not me though. [actually, Chinta was dancing around the bathroom while it was playing]

Kim: People who like that kinda thing. People who are a little younger than you. How old are you?

Chinta: (snarling) 11 . . . years . . . old!

Kim: Morgan, how old are you?

Morgan: I'm ten.

Kim: And are you too old for Radio Disney, or are you the right age?

Morgan: Well, I don't really *like* it. I like Star 98.7 more.

Kim: More sophisticated?

Chinta and Morgan: Yeah.

Morgan: The games on Disney are so easy!

Chinta: Like the Alphabet Soup game, "what's after R and before T?"

Kim: So if you were a little kid that might be hard?

Morgan: Yeah. And most of the kids who call are like eight or nine.

Chinta: They're all five or six.

Second song:

"Jelly Jungle"—Lemon Pipers

Chinta: Do I have to tell you what my reaction was?

Kim: You have to tell me.

Morgan: It was *corny!*

Kim: You said it was square.

Chinta: Ohmigod! It was *weird!* It was too— "take a trip on my pogo stick?!"

Kim: You were doing a pogo stick dance. You were kinda making fun of it, right?

Chinta: Yeah. I don't like that song. (sounding sick) It was too—

Morgan: Happy!

Chinta: It made you feel like you were in happy land.

Kim: Too childish.

Chinta: Yes!

Kim: How about the way that his vocals went [in a primitive echo-phasing effect] "orange marmalade-lade-lade-lade"? Did you think that was interesting?

Morgan: Dumb.

Chinta: It sounded weird.

Kim: Old-fashioned?

Chinta: It sounds good in modern rock, but—

Kim: Well, they were using different technology back then. But you hated that song, didn't you?

Chinta: It was a terrible song.

Kim: Would you like to ever hear that song again?

Chinta: No!

Kim: On a scale from one to ten, rate "Yummy, Yummy, Yummy."

Chinta: Nine.

Morgan: Seven, Eight.

Chinta: Eight.

Kim: So what was "Jelly Jungle" by the Lemon Pipers?

Morgan: Negative two? (laughter)

Third song:

"I Wonder What She's Doing Tonight" —Boyce & Hart

Morgan: I didn't like that; that was annoying.

Kim: What was annoying about it?

Morgan: He kept saying "I Wonder What She's Doing Tonight."

Kim: He said it too many times? What was the song about?

Morgan: That's kinda easy. "I wonder what she's doing tonight!"

Chinta: It was about a girl who wanted him just to be friends, but a friend doesn't just walk out on him like that.

Kim: So now he's just kinda obsessing on her. Maybe that's why he said that so many times, because he just can't think about anything else. Did you like anything about the way it was sung, or the guitars?

Chinta: Well, the music was okay, but I don't like that subject. It's like . . . *okay?*

Kim: It gives you the creeps?

Chinta: A little bit.

Morgan: Yes.

Kim: Those guys wrote songs for the Monkees. Did it remind you of them at all?

Chinta: A tiny bit. Like "hey hey we're the Monkees!"

Kim: It has that upbeat rock 'n' roll feel? Could you see that maybe the same people were behind it?

Morgan: No. I've never heard a Monkees song.

Chinta: You never heard (sings) "hey hey we're the Monkees?"

Morgan: Uh . . .

Kim: You never heard "Last Train to Clarksville"? "Pleasant Valley Sunday"?

Chinta: Nope. I don't think so, Kim.

Morgan: We don't even know any songs from the Beatles!

Kim: Okay, scale of one to ten for Boyce & Hart?

Morgan: Three.

Kim: You liked the music though.

Morgan: Five.

Chinta: I liked the music but I didn't like the lyrics, so that makes up half of it. Yeah, five.

Fourth song:

"I Enjoy Being a Boy"—Banana Splits

Morgan: Four!

Chinta: Two!

Kim: Chinta, you didn't like it from the beginning. You said it was more fantasyland lyrics, like "Jelly Jungle."

Chinta: I didn't really like it. It didn't change my mood or anything. I like songs that make me feel happy—

Morgan: "I live in a cucumber castle . . ."

Chinta:—and that was just *weird*, I'm sorry!

Morgan: Very weird!

Kim: Do you not like to hear songs about people being in love? Is that kinda icky?

Morgan: Yeah.

Chinta: (breathless) Unless it's 'N Sync or the Backstreet Boys.

Kim: So if it's someone sexy singing it's okay, but if it's a bunch of stuffed animal guys in costumes you don't like it?

Chinta: That's just scary, okay?

Kim: You know what the Banana Splits look like, right?

Chinta and Morgan: No!

Kim: You've never seen them? So did you think they were *people?*

Morgan: Yeah.

Kim: They're guys in big fat costumes, one of them is a beagle dog, and one's a gorilla—

Chinta: Okay, those people are weird.

Morgan: Why would they wear costumes, though?

Kim: They had a TV show. Hey, I didn't bring you any Monkees, but I know you know that "hey hey we're the Monkees" song. Is that better than what you've heard so far?

Chinta: Better! About a seven. Instead of a *minus two!*

Kim: You know "Sugar, Sugar" by the Archies, right?

Morgan: "Sugar sugar sugar I've got love in my tummy"?

Kim: No, it's (singing) "Honey, ah sugar sugar—"

Chinta and Morgan: "you are my candy girl, and you got me wanting you!"

Chinta: Yeah, I love that song!

Kim: That song changes your mood.

Chinta: *That* is a good song. That's probably about a nine.

Kim: Here's another song by that group, the Archies.

Chinta and Morgan: (disappointed) Ahhh, man!

Kim: I didn't bring "Sugar, Sugar" because I knew you'd heard it before.

fifth song:

"Feelin' So Good (S.K.O.O.B.Y- D.O.O)" —Archies

Kim: So what did you think?

Chinta: Okay, at the beginning it was pretty good. I was like, finally! A song that isn't weird. But then right in the middle it started getting weird.

Kim: What was weird?

Chinta: In the beginning the lyrics were good, the music was good, but then it started getting strange.

Kim: So it wasn't as good as "Sugar, Sugar"?

Chinta and Morgan: No!

Kim: How would you rate it?

Chinta: A five. Well in the beginning a seven, but then it just kind of lost it.

Morgan: Six for the beginning, then down to three.

The New Stuff

Kim: Now I want you to tell me about some contemporary groups, since you know so much about them.

Morgan: Can I say that they're gay if they're gay?

Kim: You can say if they're gay. Who is the biggest star right now? Is it Britney Spears?

Chinta: Yeah.

Morgan: No. Well, to *girls!*

Chinta: Christina and Britney are kind of at the top, but Britney has been—well, everyone likes her.

Kim: So some people who like Britney don't like Christina, but most people who like Christina like Britney too?

Morgan: Most of the people like Christina Aguilera.

Chinta: Oh my gosh, Morgan! *Everybody* likes Britney Spears! This boy in my class is obsessed with her.

Kim: How about you, Morgan? You like Christina better?

Morgan: I mostly like *boy* artists!

Kim: Do you like mostly girls, Chinta?

Chinta: Uh uh.

Kim: Did you used to like mostly girls when you were Morgan's age?

Chinta: No, I always liked both.

Kim: Morgan, do you like any girl artists?

Morgan: No.

Chinta: You don't like that girl that sings "Torn?"

Kim: Natalie Imbruglia?

Morgan: No. I don't like that.

Kim: Who's a better singer, Britney or Christina?

Chinta and Morgan: Britney!

Kim: Who's a better dancer?

Chinta: Britney.

Morgan: Christina.

Chinta: Both of them are good.

Kim: You said Britney first. How is she a better dancer?

Chinta: I like both of them.

Morgan: I mostly only like Red Hot Chili Peppers, the Offspring and Smashmouth.

Kim: You like the real bands more than you like solo singers?

Morgan: Yeah.

Kim: What about . . . Hanson?

Chinta and Morgan: (groaning) Gay! Gay!! Gay!!!

Kim: Does that mean they're homosexual or that they suck?

Morgan: Suck.

Chinta: I mean, as far as that long hair, I have just never liked that! It looks like they want to be *girls* or something.

Kim: What about their music?

Morgan: It sucks!

Chinta: There's only one song where I like the lyrics—"MMMBop"—pretty good song.

Kim: Can you understand the lyrics of "MMMBop?"

Morgan: No.

Chinta: No, but I like it.

Kim: What about "Where's the Love?" Do you like that song?

Morgan: What? I don't know that one.

Kim: How about the new album, have you heard any of it?

Chinta: No.

Kim: It's not getting played?

Chinta: Or if it is I turn the channel. We *really* hate them!

Kim: As long as we're talking about boy bands, tell me about Backstreet.

Chinta: I like 'N Sync Better.

Kim: What's good about 'N Sync that Backstreet doesn't have?

Chinta: Because they're cuter people. The Backstreet Boys are all weird, except for one of them, and I think he's weird—he has long hair in a pony tail!

Kim: Do you know their names?

Chinta: Okay, A.J., Lance . . . Justin . . . there's two more. Nick? No, he's in Backstreet Boys.

Kim: You don't keep up with them that well?

Chinta: I only keep up with those three.

Morgan: The most popular one is Lance.

Kim: Morgan, do you care about how they look? Is that important to you?

Morgan: I don't like them at all.

Chinta: I like 'N Sync's music. I like it a lot. Backstreet Boys are pretty good at music, and they're pretty good dancers. But that thing they did, when they were like robots, that just killed it. I did *not* like that!

Kim: Why?

Chinta: It was stupid! And then the robots *singing?!*

Morgan: They were puppets.

Chinta: No, they were *robots!* And 'N Sync, they're so much better.

Morgan: And that thing where they're puppets in the Pinocchio stage set thing—

Chinta: That was cool, though.

Kim: So puppets are cool and robots are not cool?

Chinta and Morgan: Yeah!

Morgan: (sounding stricken and betrayed) The robot thing just killed it, I'm sorry, it just did.

Kim: Do you have pictures of any of these bands on your walls?

Chinta: I wish.

Morgan: We have nothing on our wall.

Kim: You're not allowed to have pictures on the wall?

Chinta: Well, I'd like to have a room full of pictures of 'N Sync.

Kim: You never buy magazines full of pictures of them?

Chinta: I don't have any *money!*

Kim: No allowance? Why not?

Chinta: I don't! Our dad—will you try to talk to him?

Kim: So you can buy magazines and put posters up?

Morgan: Yeah. The only posters we have are like, *freebies!* (laughter) And everybody gets them. We've got like six posters of *Battlefield Earth!*

Kim: Oh no! (hysteria) How did that happen?

Chinta: We were passing the grand opening of a movie.

Kim: Did you put 'em up?

Chinta: No! Are you kidding?

Kim: Can I have one?! I'm so lame, but I want one.

Chinta: Yeah.

Kim: Cool. So basically your dad—our dad's a cheapskate, is that what you're saying?

Chinta: Yeah.

Kim: Well, I'll put this in the book for sure. Y'know, when I was 11 I had pictures of all sorts of really lame people up on my wall.

Chinta: That's because you *are* lame.

Kim: I had my Shaun Cassidy pictures, and Spring had her pictures of Andy Gibb.

Chinta: Shaun Cassidy? You're weird.

Kim: He was like the solo 'N Sync guy when I was your age.

Morgan: Is he related to Butch Cassidy?

Kim: No, but he's related to David Cassidy from *The Partridge Family.*

Chinta: (perplexed) The *Partridge* Family?!

Kim: I wanna ask you about a girl band: Cleopatra.

Chinta: (sings in a high-pitched yodel) "Cleopatra, comin' at ya." That's the only song I know about them. I don't know if they're too popular. I mean, they're *pretty* popular, but they're not too popular.

Kim: Do you know how they look?

Chinta: No.

Morgan: Yeah.

Kim: They're black girls with those long braids, and they swing 'em around—

Chinta: I like TLC. They're cool.

Kim: What about B*witched?

Morgan: Nope nope nope nope *nope!*

Chinta: Some of their songs are okay, but they're just weird. I don't like their hairdos.

Kim: How about their clothes, the denim?

Chinta: Their clothes are okay.

Kim: Let's talk about some Latin guys. Marc Anthony—

Chinta: (gasps) Marc Anthony!! Ohmigod, I love his stuff!

Morgan: And Enrique Iglesias too.

Kim: And Ricky Martin.

Morgan: I don't like him. Marc Anthony, he's pretty good.

Kim: He's the coolest?

Chinta: Ricky Martin is more popular, but Marc Anthony is like . . . cool!

Kim: Is he cute?

Chinta: Uh uh.

Kim: Is Ricky cute?

Chinta: Not really. Marc Anthony's kinda ugly, but he's got pretty good music.

Morgan: He's not ugly.

Chinta: Oooogly.

Morgan: Yeah, he's oooogly!

Kim: Who have we not talked about that you like?

Morgan: Eiffel 65.

Chinta: That guy, the bald guy, and he has a weird voice—

Morgan: They got a pretty cool voice like (makes metallic noise)—

Kim: Like a robot? What about that "Summer Girls" song, you like that?

Chinta: Ohmigod, I love that song! (sings) "New Kids on the Block had a bunch of hits/Chinese food makes me sick/And I think it's fine when the girls stop by for the summer/for the summer/I like girls that wear Abercrombie and Fitch/and if I had one wish/she's been gone since last summer/since last summer."

Kim: What do you think about that, Morgan?

Morgan: I don't like it.

Chinta: Ohmigod, you're offending me. (laughs)

Kim: So who's totally, totally *out* right now?

Morgan: "The Fall Song."

Chinta: No! That is in, that is totally in!

Kim: So what's totally, totally *in* right now?

Chinta: 'N Sync . . . ohmigosh—

Morgan: My underwear! (laughter)

Chinta: Britney Spears, Christina Aguilera, 'N Sync—

Morgan: I wish they would die. Stupid.

Kim: What's the deal with the Spice Girls?

Chinta: They broke up and they are out now.

Kim: But when they were together—

Chinta: They were totally in.

Kim: Did you love them?

Chinta: Everybody loved them.

Morgan: Even boys. They had pictures of them—from Spice Girls lollipops! (laughter)

Kim: What about when Ginger Spice left the band?

Chinta: That totally ruined it; that broke 'em up. Everybody started to not like them anymore. Then they all got *pregnant* or something like that!

Morgan: They became ugly.

Chinta: Ha, they had a pregnant pause.

Kim: So bands don't hang around for a long time. They get big, real real big if they're going to get big, and then >POOF< they're gone. Something happens and people don't like them anymore.

Morgan: Yeah. And they pick somebody else to make more money. And they start breaking up.

Chinta: Well, she just left because she had a fight with one of them.

Kim: How do you find out about the bands? Do you read about them? Do your friends know about them? Do you watch TV?

Chinta: *Everybody* knows about them!

Kim: Where do they get the information?

Chinta: You just *get it!* It's like, you *look* at them, and you *listen* to the music, and you just *love them, okay?!*

Kim: Would you like to go see them?

Chinta: (angrily) Yes!

Kim: You ever been to see a band?

Chinta and Morgan: No . . .

Kim: Never been to a concert? [remembering her own childhood with their father] You ever been to a . . . folk festival or something?

Morgan: (woefully) Yeah.

Chinta: Ohmigod, don't get me started! Our dad *dragged* us there, and then he made us play instruments with *spoons!* Ohmigosh, I thought I was gonna kill him! [Interviewer's note: young Miss Bagge doesn't know how good she's got it!]

Kim: And you wanted to be seeing 'N Sync?

Chinta: Yes! And he's like, "after you learn to play violin you can 'rock out' with all those people" and I'm like "'Rock out?!' Is he talking about *old people?!*" I did not want to go; he dragged us there.

Morgan: Yeah, and these old people were going (sings Aretha) "Chain, chain, chain—" (laughter)

Kim: What kinda festival?

Morgan: The Dutch Festival! (laughter)

Kim: The only place you see live music is when your dad drags you to a folk festival.

Chinta: And our mom, when she drags us to the Indonesian Festival. Okay, *Dutch* people singing—

Kim: Basically you guys need to see some live rock 'n' roll, all right?

Chinta: Yeah! Will you please take us?

Kim: I'll see what I can do. Do you have a CD collection?

Chinta: Well, I have like five of them. I want to get 'N Sync.

Kim: What are the five CDs that you own?

Morgan: More like three. She has two songs—

Chinta: I have Sugar Ray—

Morgan: She buys *bargain CDs!* For five bucks! (laughter)

Kim: Do you buy bargain CDs 'cause that's all the money you have?

Chinta: Yes!

Kim: What are the latest ones you got?

Chinta: Well, on Sugar Ray those songs are the only three that I *like!* So I'm happy!

Morgan: Yeah, but one is exactly the same song, they just have a music video on the computer!

Chinta: I have Britney Spears—I paid full price for that.

Morgan: I have Smashmouth. I got that CD, it was still new—I got it at Uncle Ben and Norma's yard sale for two bucks! It was their kids' CD.

Kim: Just one more question for you guys. If you have a birthday, and you end up getting 20 bucks, and you have to decide what to do with the money—what priority is it to buy music?

Morgan: Low. I buy toys.

Chinta: I'd buy the 'N Sync CD. I've been wanting to get it.

Kim: What does music mean to you?

Chinta: It's something that can change your mood and make you happy. And it can make you sad.

Kim: It's one of your favorite things?

Chinta: Yeah, besides surfing.

Kim: How about you, Morgan? Is music important?

Morgan: Music . . . not really. I can live without it.

Kim: Thank you so much for the interview.

Chinta and Morgan: You're welcome!

Simple Simon Says Get Well Soon by Vern Stoltz

Bubblegum music has the reputation of being the most lighthearted and least serious music that was created in the late '60s. For this reason, many people feel justified in ridiculing the music and those performers who recorded these songs. For myself, though, bubblegum music came at just the right moment, serving as a bond that helped to unite my sister and me.

Mary Lou, who was four years older, was the first person in our family who appeared to know about an entire world of music that was happening outside the limited record collection that was kept in our house. The year was 1968, and as an 11-year-old girl, she was discovering how much fun one could gain by listening to the bubblegum music that was reaching over the airwaves way into the rural Wisconsin where we lived.

As the year 1969 started, Mary Lou was diagnosed with a brain tumor. Chaos entered our family, as my mother accompanied Mary Lou during her stay in a Madison hospital, located two hours away. My brother, younger sister, and myself were taken to some nearby neighbors to stay until my sister was well enough so both her and my mother could return.

Being only seven years old at this time, I don't remember too much of what was going on. I remember being fascinated by all the new books I could read in our neighbors' house. I can remember the thrill when several weeks later we were finally able to come home again—with most the thrill focused on finally being able to play with my recent Christmas presents that had been too big to take with me to our neighbors'. I can also remember all the gifts of hot dishes and casseroles that the various neighbors would bring over for our family to eat. It was an especially glamorous day when a tall angel food cake arrived, brightly colored with candy pieces that reminded me of a circus carnival.

From my view, my sister was a celebrity. Everyone wanted to see and give best wishes to her. I was especially impressed with the box of Get Well cards that had been handmade and given to her by her sixth grade classmates. At the time I was probably still trying to keep my crayons within the boundaries of my coloring books—seeing all those freehand drawings offering wishes to "Get Well Soon," each made with construction paper, crayons, and sparkling glitter, impressed me as being a major artistic step forward.

What music do I associate with Mary Lou during this time? It was the sounds of 1910 Fruitgum Company. Mary Lou's birthday was in mid-February, and now that she was home again, a birthday party was thrown in her honor. The only stereo we had at the time was a console system, but I can definitely remember the music of "Simon Says" and "1, 2, 3 Red Light" being played as my sister and her friends danced and had a great time. I'm sure my mother must have been very happy then, to see her daughter still alive and still being able to laugh and dance with others her age.

That night, everyone was following the instructions of the lyrics for the song "Simon Says." "Put your hands in the air/Shake them all about," and the room was full of upraised arms waving back and forth. "Put your hands on your hip/Let your backbone slip" and everyone would do their own interpretation of what it meant to have one's backbone slipped. I was happy to be given the same chance to dance along with my sister's friends. The dance instructions were so simple that even a seven-year-old like myself could join in the fun. An especially proud moment came near the end of the song when the words "Clap your hands in the air/Do it double time" were sung and I was still able to keep up with the sounds of the hands clapping coming over the speakers. I became even prouder when Mary Lou, ignoring my status as the "pesky little brother," said to me "Why, that's very good!"

Time went on, and it was as if Mary Lou had never been ill. She would relay little tidbits of knowledge to me, such as pointing out that the "ride a painted pony" line from the Blood, Sweat and Tears hit song "Spinning Wheel" was referring to a horse on a merry-go-round. I can remember her looking forward to the drive into town to see if the latest issue of the monthly *Tiger Beat* teen idol magazine had come in yet. Curiously, her buying *Tiger Beat* seemed to correspond with a new star coming onto the scene—a singer named David Cassidy. I would read these magazines the same day she bought them, eager to keep up with the latest happenings in the outside world. I remember the one issue when we both felt a bit worldlier, just because *Tiger Beat* had printed in the letters section a short note that was written by a girl who also happened to live in Wisconsin.

My sister's tastes were soon evolving with the era. When given the opportunity, she chose to have the walls of her bedroom painted a deep violet. Soon after gold and yellow shag carpeting was installed to complement the wild color scheme. It wasn't long before the walls were covered with the various fold-out posters of David Cassidy. One Christmas she received a great stereo—one of those portable kinds with detachable speakers, a fold-down turntable, and best of all, colored bulbs that would light up and beat to whatever music was spinning on the turntable. This may have been the same Christmas where my sister had a terrible teenage dilemma. The evening of the 4-H Christmas party had been scheduled the same night that the *Partridge Family* television show was on—and the episode being shown that night was featuring both David Cassidy and Bobby Sherman together! I vaguely remember that the party came to somewhat of a standstill as several of the girls left to watch the television show.

The Partridge Family provided a common bond for us. Mary Lou and I would go downtown to the Ben Franklin store to purchase our packs of Partridge Family bubblegum cards. We would divide the duplicate cards between us, and then take turns choosing which cards would belong to us individually. Somehow she ended up with most of the David Cassidy cards, and I ended up with most of the Susan Dey cards.

In July of 1972, three years after her first brain tumor operation, a routine medical checkup came back with bad news. The tumor had not been completely removed and had grown back again, requiring yet another stay in the hospital.

This time things were a little different. Mary Lou was taken to a closer hospital only a half-hour drive away, so my mother was able to stay home and still make daily trips to go and see her. My sister wasn't in some far away, mystical town; she was close enough for me to visit personally and observe first-hand the sights, sounds, and smells of the hospital. The seriousness of the situation was much more apparent to me. It was a very risky operation, but Mary Lou did survive this time also.

There were no handmade cards from her classmates this time. Instead, most of the get-well cards were of the commercial Hallmark variety. There may have been a party when Mary Lou came home, but if there was, I was a bit older and just not as likely to want to hang around my older sister. This second operation happened right before Mary Lou was to start her sophomore year of high school. Her thoughts with being home were not about music at all, but focused instead on having to wear a wig to school because of the loss of hair that was a result of her radiation treatments. Life had somehow gotten more serious for her. She soon found it difficult to do her schoolwork, and rather than her teaching me little facts of trivia, I found myself instead assisting Mary Lou with her math homework.

In the 25 years since then, we have each continued our separate ways. Mary Lou continues to live in our hometown, her options limited a bit by the side effects of her operations. I have moved on to a large metropolitan city, where I regularly try to see my favorite bands when they come into town. I look back though and remember and thank Mary Lou, for giving me that early exposure to music.

For myself, the peak era of bubblegum music parallels with the two times Mary Lou was in the hospital. 1910 Fruitgum Company were at their peak during her first stay, while the presence of the Partridge Family was just starting to diminish when she entered the hospital for her second stay. Who knows, perhaps the uplifting spirit associated with bubblegum music was just what was needed to keep her alive during those three years in between.

There is one more thing I must add to this story, one more piece of secrecy that I observed during Mary Lou's second hospital stay. During this stay, my five-year-old sister Becky would sleep in Mary Lou's bedroom. One evening while I was listening to some record on Mary Lou's stereo, Becky was pulling herself under the covers to go to bed. I heard Becky say "Oh, I almost forgot!" and she pulled herself out of bed, walked to a nearby wall, and kissed one of the posters of David Cassidy hanging there. She told me "Mary Lou says I have to kiss David Cassidy for her until she is well enough to come back home."

So who knows? Maybe it was bubblegum music that kept Mary Lou alive, or maybe it was the uninterrupted ritual of kissing a teen idol every night, or maybe it was just simply having sisters and brothers and other loving family members present that worked. Somehow, life seems to be more fun when I think that it was a combination of all three that did the trick.

I Hate Bubblegum! by Dennis P. Eichhorn

I'm not just stating this for its journalistic effect: I really do hate bubblegum! It's irritating, has no redeeming features, and serves only to muddy the psychic waters that normally irrigate what's left of our collective soul. And, of course, it helps line the pockets of the culture vultures who oversee the delivery of such pap: mainly the recording and broadcasting moguls, plus a few artists who shamelessly lend their expertise to the composition and creation of rhythmic drivel, aka bubblegum.

Bubblegum is a patently pale imitation of the real thing. "So, what's the real thing?" you ask? Well, back in the 1950s, the real thing was easy to spot: it consisted of Elvis Presley, Chuck Berry, Little Richard, and a few other seminal rock 'n' rollers. These harbingers of rebellion really stood out from the milquetoast minions of mediocrity whose mournful harmonies ruled the airwaves at the time.

Postwar American adolescents were rudely awakened by these perps' clarion calls for sex and good times, and the youthful countercultural revolution was underway. As it roared into the '60s, authentic rock 'n' roll established itself worldwide, and new mavens manifested themselves: Bob Dylan, the Rolling Stones, the Beatles, Cream, the Beach Boys, and lots of others. The '70s, '80s, and '90s have all generated their own crops of rockers (now including rappers and toasters; many consider rap, hip-hop and reggae to be rock 'n' roll/soul/R&B hybrids). As a musical super-genre, rock 'n' roll and its akin brethren thrive and survive on many levels, and, like Alcoholics Anonymous, will never die.

The trouble is, bubblegum music will never die either. It's been along for the ride since Day One, nestling in the belly of the rock 'n' roll beast like a tapeworm inside a tiger. It's a parasitic, not a symbiotic, relationship: rock 'n' roll could get along just fine without its ersatz fellow traveler, while bubblegum would wither and die without the true artistry of occasional rock 'n' roll genius to imitate and subvert.

You think I'm woofin'? Think Elvis. Then, think Fabian, the bubblegum Elvis. The powers-that-be had a fake Elvis ready right away; in fact, they have had a never-ending succession of fake bubblegum Elvises ever since. As David Crosby once remarked, "I never really appreciated Elvis until I caught Tom Jones' act." Jones, a bubblegum Elvis, has charisma and musical abilities of his own, and he has lent them to his presentation. But still, he's a pale imitation of the real thing.

Elvis, shaking his hips and sending out the signal that sex wasn't going to be hidden or forbidden anymore, was relevant and revolutionary. Bubblegum is never relevant, and is counter-revolutionary.

Think Beatles. Then, think Monkees. Then, think Archies.

The Beatles, evolving from tight-suited, *bon mot*-spewing British rockers to psychedelic philosophers, composers, and poets, had a powerful influence on many cultures around the world. The Beatles were revolutionary, and what they accomplished was important and still reverberates globally. But the Monkees and Archies, to name just two bubblegum bands whose careers overlap the Beatles', were not relevant or influential or by any means revolutionary. They were unimportant. In fact, in the case of the Archies, they didn't even exist as a performing group. All they did was generate a few bucks for their label and sell lots of lunchboxes, cashing in on the gullibility of the American public for catchy tunes.

That's the thing about bubblegum: there has to be a little meat to it, enough talent somewhere to think up at the very least a melody that listeners will remember. There's no substitute for a hook, a snappy stanza that implants itself in the listeners' minds and lends itself to repetition. It's what both hit recordings and effective advertising are all about.

In truth, bubblegum and commercial jingles have a lot in common, and are often served up by the same composers, producers and artists. A well-rounded or -placed composer, producer or studio musician has opportunities to work on both commercials and bubblegum. There's no real difference, and the studio musician is nothing more than a mechanic, a necessary evil as far as the money men are concerned. Because of this, bubblegum has become more and more synthetic. Fewer humans are used in recording it. Soon, it will completely be artificial, created by artificial intelligences and designed to control those who listen, even more than it does already.

As it is, bubblegum is carefully crafted to subvert the powerful cultural and political trends that threaten the power structure. For every Crosby, Stills, Nash & Young singing about the Kent State massacre and implanting the seeds of rebellion in the generational overmind, there are a dozen Cyrkles singing some crap-ass song about the sun looking like a red rubber ball or whatever, and shunting young minds into cul-de-sacs of mindless diversion. This is not an accidental process. The powers that be fear the power of rock 'n' roll, and are anxious to dilute it. And they do that with bubblegum music.

Bubblegum didn't happen overnight. It has its roots in such progenitors as Guy Lombardo and Lawrence Welk. Lombardo was a rip-off of the swing/big-band phenomenon, and served up bland fodder for the masses with the approval of the corporate bigwigs who were running things at the time. Welk took vaudeville, another original (even vulgar) American art form, cleaned it up while watering it down, and made it palatable for television viewing. These, and many other opportunists, paved the road for the bubblegum that followed.

Rock 'n' roll is the soundtrack for the revolution that could have happened. Bubblegum is the soundtrack for what actually went down.

Depressing, isn't it?

It Came Before Playboy by Jack Stevenson

Although I was never specifically a big fan of the Archies, they did have a major impact on my earliest impressions of sex. It all happened on one unforgettable afternoon . . .

The year was 1966. I was a ten-year-old kid in the fifth grade. Hamburgers were a dime, and Peter and Gordon's "Lady Godiva" played every five minutes on tinny car radios—and all the rest of the songs were by Herman's Hermits—or so it seemed.

I went to P.S. 38 grade school which was technically in Greece, a suburb next to Rochester, N.Y., but most of my schoolmates were from the working-and middle-class suburbs. There were however a few "city kids" from Rochester, and they injected a vital dose of white trash into an otherwise homogenous mix of lower-middle class kids.

My best friend that year was Danny Nelson. Danny had learning disabilities and spoke with a Deep South drawl. He told stories—with excitement in his voice—about the non-stop mad dashes his family had made across the country in various junk automobiles, like, "We made it in three and a half days in that old '56 Chevy," or "We drove straight through in that old Chrysler and didn't stop but twice to piss." I was in awe.

I would ride my bike down to his house in a ramshackle neighborhood near the polluted Genesee River. He taught me how to hop trains in the nearby rail-yards, and we'd bushwhack through abandoned, overgrown areas along the river where one was as likely as not to come across a dead body. It was great.

Danny's family moved a lot, and soon they moved out of Rochester to a more rural area about thirty minutes outside the City. My Dad drove me out there to visit one memorable afternoon, after which they moved away and I never saw Danny Nelson again.

They had what resembled a tumble-down kind of sharecropper spread. Amazing really to find such a place in the deep North. When I ventured into the back cornfield, his mom told me in her Deep South twang to be careful lest I got bit by some nasty ol' Cottonmouth. A Cottonmouth *rattlesnake* in Upstate New York, next to Lake Ontario?! I don't think so. Either she was plain stupid or she liked scaring 10-year-old boys.

Danny had a surly older brother who played an electric guitar and didn't speak much, but when he did his accent was even more Alabama than Danny's. Of course you always respect a friend's older brother. Not only could they beat you up, but they possessed a certain mysterious cool and knowledge. Me and Danny went into his bedroom that afternoon. He was layin' there on his bed with a sheet of tracing paper pressed over the pages of an *Archie* comic book, and was drawing Veronica and Betty without any clothes on. He was very good at it, an artist of sorts, the results were quite amazing. Not until I sniffed glue with Chuckie Birch a few years later did I experience anything as easy, cheap and enchanting.

And to think, I almost stepped on a non-existent Cottonmouth rattlesnake and saw my first naked woman—all in the same afternoon.

ARTIFACTS Trash & Treasures from the Golden Age of Bubblegum Marketing By Margaret Griffis

Since the beginning of time, children have had to provide their own entertainment. Whittling wooden flutes and making dolls of corn cobs and straw, the little ones bided their time until they grew up to labor alongside their parents and begin the next generation, usually long before the age of 13. In recent years, with ever-increasing leisure time and excessive amounts of pocket change, childhood has lengthened to an outrageous degree. Nevertheless, these children of all ages have adult-sized consumer appetites that haven't gone undetected by astute businessmen.

During the early 20th century, the toy market generally developed its own "superstars," like Raggedy Ann, erector sets and Lionel trains. Only occasionally would a personality like Shirley Temple cross over and become toy-worthy. The depression and WWII further limited sales. It wasn't until the 1950s and the Baby Boom that the toy market really exploded.

With the dawn of the "teenager" in the 1950s, toymakers increased the marketing of media fads, eventually creating wholesale universes around production-line teen idols and singing cartoon characters. Ultimately, this culminated in Pamela Anderson, who perhaps for the first time in history is a woman more deformed and plastic than her doll counterparts .[41]

One can argue that Elvis Presley or perhaps the Beatles kicked the music memorabilia craze into high gear. While previous aficionados were content owning long-play records, 8″×10″ glossies and sheet music, a new type of teenage SuperFan, committed to relentless gathering, arrived around 1960. Early "teen music" fans were able to buy official Beatle wigs and Elvis scarves to show off their admiration. While the music might essentially be what mattered, why not appeal to their hoarding sensibilities? Magazines like *Tiger Beat* and *16* whetted appetites and showcased new stars and products.

History's greatest marketing manipulator soon entered every home. The television age provided advertising disguised as entertainment. Media creations like the Monkees promoted many more offshoot items than did "serious" groups. The Prefab Four could be found on record albums, comic books, ugly dolls, lapel pins, posters, toy cars and much more. Music snobs might have considered them a lame Beatles knockoff, but to the retailer they were a dream come true. Moms could see in living color how much sweeter and more likable these lads were than their British counterparts. Ka-ching!!!!!

Because bubblegum was ostensibly about music, you could find many musical items on the dealer's shelf. Need a place to house your record collection? The die-cut Partridge Family Record Case could hold

---

41. Not to mention that her "toys" sell better to adults than to children.

about 150 LPs. It was a small piece of really hip furniture for the young gumster. Want to start your own band? How 'bout a Monkees guitar with their caricatures emblazoned on it? A decade later, if disco was more your thing, try the Bee Gees Rhythm Station, a low-rent Casiotone. Or should you prefer more natural beats, the Muppet Drum can provide hours of pleasure to insensitive ears. Even aspiring "stage managers" could practice with Donny and Marie. There was a *Donny and Marie Show* toy stage that came with a flexi-disc to which the dolls could lip-sync.

Bubblegum's triumph was in how it reached the youngest audiences through the boob tube. Live action gummy variety shows (*The Banana Splits*) and cartoons (*Archie*) turned small children into music fans. Maybe they were singing "Ten Little Indians" at their preschool, but they were running home to dance to "Sugar, Sugar." These two "groups" were gigantic cash cows. The Banana Splits appeared on Halloween costumes, coloring books and Dixie Cups to hold the punch at your birthday party. The Archies had dolls, toy jalopies and yet more spin-off cartoon shows. Although Archie already was a popular comic book, moving the gang to TV and making them sing was pure merchandising genius. Ka-ching-ching!!!!

With young ones clamoring for toys linked to their favorite artists, Mom could satisfy them simply by purchasing food items for the family. From cereal boxes you could get plastic spoons decorated with relief Josie and the Pussycats images, or cut the playable Bobby Sherman record off the back. Or try the Banana Split hand puppets, with their colorful images printed on thin white plastic. If your family liked jam, you could collect emptied Archies glass jars. These had color images of the Archies printed on them and the characters' bas-relief faces on the bottom. Mom could also place a sandwich in one of the many metal lunch box designs available. After breaking the glass in the thermos bottle, children could get a new box with a different featured band. By the 1980s, safer all-plastic boxes and thermoses starring the latest crop of bubblegum stars like Menudo drove the kids crazy, but left them carrying has-beens on their arm by the following school year.

The late '70s were tough for bubblegum fans. Times weren't so psychedelic, though still pretty goofy. Disco bred bizarre creatures like the Village People—who, while

appealing to children's sense of the absurd, were a bit too gay for Mom to wanna purchase their toys. Punk and new wave were too sophisticated for the little brats, but attracted childlike teens and adults to the new sounds. Think Riff Randall in *Rock 'n' Roll High School*: in pigtails and tube socks, here was a fully-grown woman bopping to bubblegummy music played by four weird guys in leather jackets, the Ramones. If their sound had been slightly more child-friendly, the Ramones would have been an obvious choice for a series of dolls, board games and cereal promotions. Instead, the closest we got was Devo and their mail-order sales of "Energy Domes" (those red flower pot hats) and uniforms.

Bubblegum came back in the '80s. With the baby boom long over, the market for Saturday morning cartoons dropped off and there went a great advertising opportunity. But MTV was hypnotizing slightly older kids with music videos.

Duran Duran had their "Into The Arena" board game, and you could buy knockoff versions of Michael Jackson's silver glove. By the '90s, dolls or action figures of nearly every artist were available. Spice Girls! Britney Spears! Even the Backstreet Boys (or was it 'N Sync?) had a video where they started out as dolls and once run over the UPC code reader came to life.

So where does this all leave us? With broken glass and chewed-up dolls? Children getting hand-me-down psychedelic cereal promotions? On the contrary, auction houses and antique malls are crammed to the rafters with our gummy detritus. Mint-in-box items bring as much if not more than a sealed LP by the same artist. Now that the first wave of gumsters have grown up and are nearing retirement with oodles of money in their 401Ks, they find they still miss their long gone "Rosebuds." Nothing will make them happier than that David Cassidy costume they wore when they were ten, or that tiny set of Mamas and Papas dolls. And it wouldn't be grand if they could just play their mail-ready Send

A Spin Record by the 1910 Fruitgum Company on a working Shaun Cassidy model record player? Here, at the turn of the Millennium there appears to be no end to the merchandising magic of bubblegum. Just like there appears to be no end to the love for that music.

Frighteningly, toy makers are creating weirder toys as we speak. (And what bizarre characters sit around dreaming up these questionable products?) Soon

science will advance beyond today's meager abilities. Will the next teen idol have a Furby-like chip implanted in her talking robotic doll? Will her lunch box cook your food? Will her concert T-shirts come with a portable MP3 player in the sleeve? Will we receive interactive hologram concerts online? Hopefully the future will bring in even weirder products than these, but I'm sure any future archaeologists studying our remnants will have a mighty job on their hands. So will future psychiatrists, for that matter. But when you see this book on your doctor's shelf 20 years from now, at least you'll know you're in good hands.

CEREAL BOX RECORDS Snap, Crackle, Rock & Roll :
Cereal Box Records by Lisa Sutton

The cereal industry has always been keenly tuned into the minds and tastebuds of Americans. Enormous amounts of research go into the packaging of boxed breakfast foods we find on the shelves of our local stores. Where adults prefer traditional and simple packaging, kids have always gone ape over flashy, colorful graphics featuring cartoon characters, animals or cowboys. Back in the '40s, it was discovered that the addition of a trinket inside the box or a mail-away offer on the package could do wonders for sales with a negligible cost to the manufacturer. Spy rings, diving submarines and character "spoon riders" all found their way into each specially marked cereal package.

In the late 1960s, rock 'n' roll was the world's greatest commodity. The cereal companies were aware of this, and came up with an ingenious way to keep teeny-boppers tugging at their mothers' skirts to buy their brands. Manufactured rock group the Monkees were the biggest-selling act in the world back then, out-selling even their real-life counterparts, the Beatles. Kellogg's was sponsoring the Monkees' TV show, and had come up with a number of clever ways to cross-promote their cereals and increase sales. They continued with standard promotions like putting Monkee rings and badges in the boxes, and with mail-away offers for mini Monkeemobiles and a guest shot on the show. When the Monkees left the prime-time line-up in 1968, Kellogg's bowed out as sponsor, though the show remained as popular as ever in reruns on Saturday mornings. Post, Kellogg's' main competitor in the cereal wars, recognized a good thing and jumped right in to pick up where Kellogg's had left off. Not to be outdone by the previous offerings, Post came up with a promotion that involved stamping a genuine record on the back of the boxes, featuring one of a selection of hit tunes by the Prefab Four.

Post wasn't the first to use a cardboard record promotion; that honor goes to Wheaties back in 1954. The Monkees were, however, the first major rock 'n' roll act to find their smiling faces used in this manner. There were three picture variations used over the course of a two-year period, with a possibility of four hot Monkee tunes encouraging obsessive cereal munchers to collect all twelve while enjoying their favorite breakfast fare.

The Archies had joined the Monkees on the Saturday morning line-up in 1969, and while kids were puttin' a little sugar on their cereal they were groovin' to the "Sugar, Sugar" records stamped onto their Alpha Bits and Honey Comb boxes. The Archies appeared on three different picture records over a slightly longer period than the Monkees, featuring the sounds and images of the colorful cartoon rockers.

Post also applied this marketing technique to one of the hottest male vocalists of the early '70s. Bobby Sherman soon found his handsome visage embossed on the back of a variety of Post cereal offerings. Bobby was selling

millions of records and making the young girls swoon as they dug into their breakfast bowls, too. Four picture variations of Bobby's five possible songs were available, making a staggering *20* possible combinations. (There were also two Canadian variations, for those who are keeping score.)

Sales of supposedly healthy (and not too appealing to kids) Raisin Bran more than tripled while Bobby's bell-bottomed picture appeared on the box.

The Jackson 5 were also huge in the early '70s preteen market, and they too were plastered on Post products from coast to coast. They had their own Saturday morning cartoon, sold-out concerts and two cereal box records gracing the aisles of every supermarket in the country. If you couldn't wait for "ABC" or "Maybe Tomorrow" to come on the radio, you could run out to the market for a box of Rice Krinkles to satisfy your hunger for Michael and his groovy brothers. The J-5 also had a variety of other cereal premiums like puffy stickers and inflatable mini-pillows for kids that weren't lucky enough to own a close-and-play phonograph.

When Post ran out of teen-idols to slap on the cereal boxes, they came up with their own imaginary band to fill in the blanks. Super Sugar Crisp was always popular with young consumers and had its own cartoon hero, Sugar Bear, on the box covers and in Saturday morning TV commercials. The Archies and Monkees were both highly successful "manufactured" groups, so why not give their cereal box icon his own band? "The Sugar Bears" got a cereal box record as well as a genuine album on Ampex-distributed label Big Tree. Cute and perky Honey Bear sported the voice of a young studio vocalist named Kim Carnes, who had also loaned her talents to David Cassidy's live act. Not surprisingly, many of the songs on the Sugar Bears LP sound remarkably like the Partridge Family.

The cereal box phenomenon was responsible for selling millions of boxes of cereal but alas, was a short lived sensation. Record manufacturers began marketing their own "picture discs" in the mid-'70s, making the cardboard variety obsolete. A few promotions followed later in the '70s, like Count Chocula and his pink friend Franken Berry, but they didn't have the same impact as real performing acts. Relegated to the same fate as defunct premiums like hi-bounce marbles, "spoon riders" and Quisp propeller beanies, the cereal box record lives on only as a sugar-frosted memory.

Discography of Known Cereal Box Records compiled by Kim Cooper with help from Don Charles, Michael Cumella, James Porter, David Smay, Vern Stoltz and especially Lisa Sutton

One of the most delightful of bubblegum artifacts is the cardboard cereal box record, cut raggedly from the back of the box by an impatient child, or carefully by a helpful adult. At the peak of the bubblegum era, it was possible to compile an excellent library of lo-fi gems by most of the major kinderpop artists, provided a kid could talk his family into eating the right cereals.

These records have interesting precedents in the annals of American marketing. Among the earliest records offered as cereal premiums was a series of six fairy tales with follow-along books put out by Post Raisin Bran in 1949. These mail-away offers included "Beauty and the Beast" and "The Golden Goose." In 1954, General Mills released a series of at least eight different 78-rpm children's songs that were actually imprinted on Wheaties cereal boxes. These included such proto-gum faves as "Take Me Out to the Ball Game, " "Three Little Fishes," and "On Top of Old Smokey." On the same boxes kids were also invited to send in a quarter to receive Wheaties-produced red-orange vinyl 78-rpm albums.

Around the same time there were at least two Walt Disney's Mouseketeer Records, cardboard cereal box 78s that featured Mickey, Donald and Goofy singing "I'd Rather Be I" and the title character performing "Donald Duck's Song." In 1964, buyers of Kellogg's Corn Flakes could mail in a quarter and a back-of-the-box coupon to receive a 7" long-playing record with the story and theme song from Hanna-Barbera's animated movie *Hey There, Yogi Bear*.

In perhaps the strangest twist of all, around 1967 the pre-bubblegum Shadows of Knight released their great "Potato Chip" single—which was only available *inside* packages of Fairmont Potato Chips!

Bubblegum-era cereal box records typically recycled the same design for between three and five possible songs in each series. The song titles appeared on the label, and a kid could pick which box they wanted by the identifying numeral stamped onto the cardboard.

The following bubblegum cereal box record discography is as complete as we could make it in a full year of research. Once a kid cut the disk off the identifying box, these babies became an archivist's nightmare.

The Archies
Archies design #1 (The Archies playing their instruments with Hot Dog panting, no track list or numbering) (Post Super Sugar Crisp/Kirshner) [Michael Cumella reports that the concept for this disk was developed by Harry Gorman of Allied Creative Services in Port Jervis, NY.] Tracks include (but may not be limited to) the following:
#. Sugar, Sugar
#. Hide 'N' Seek
#. Boys And Girls
#. Feelin' So Good (SKOOBY-DOO)
#. Bang-Shang-A-Lang
#. (Archie's Theme) Everything's Archie

Archies design #2/version A (Archie, Betty, Jughead, Hot Dog, Reggie and Veronica holding the black ring in the center of the record) (Alpha Bits?/Kirshner)
1. Archie's Party
2. You Know I Love You
3. Nursery Rhyme[s]
4. Jingle Jangle

Archies design #2/version B (Archie, Betty, Jughead, Hot Dog, Reggie and Veronica holding the black ring in the center of the record) (Alpha Bits?/Kirshner)
1. You Make Me Wanna Dance
2. Catching Up On Fun
3. Jingle Jangle
4. Love Light

Archies design #3 (Big Ethel, Dilton, Moose, Midge, Reggie, Sabrina, Archie, Veronica, Betty and Jughead dancing against a yellow background) (Honey Comb/Kirshner)
1. You Make Me Wanna Dance
2. Catchin' Up On Fun
3. Jingle Jangle
4. Love Light

Banana Splits

There were two mail-order vinyl 7" EPs offered by Kellogg's cereal; only the first track on each is taken from the band's LP.

Kellogg's 34578:
The Tra-La-La Song (One Banana, Two Banana)
That's The Pretty Part Of You b/w It's A Good Day For A Parade
The Very First Kid On My Block.

Kellogg's 34579:
Doin' The Banana Split
I Enjoy Being A Boy (In Love With You) b/w The Beautiful Calliope
Let Me Remember You Smiling

Jackson 5

Jackson 5 design #1; (Rice Krinkles/Motown)
(Photo of band standing off to the left, stacked vertically—yellow label, blue tint to grooves)
1. ABC
2. I Want You Back
3. I'll Bet You
4. Darling Dear
5. Maybe Tomorrow

Jackson 5 design #2/ version A (Alpha Bits/Motown)
(song titles on a cartoonish flower shaped background—no mention of the J5, blue tint to grooves)
1. Sugar Daddy
2. Goin' Back To Indiana
3. Who's Loving You

Jackson 5 design #2/version B (Alpha Bits/ Motown)
(song titles on a cartoonish flower-shaped background—no mention of the J-5, blue tint to grooves)
1. I'll Be There
2. Never Can Say Goodbye
3. Mama's Pearl

Josie & The Pussycats (1970)

These were mail-away 45s. Up to four were offered for 35¢ each and the coupon from the back of a box of Kellogg's Frosted Flakes.

Josie & the Pussycats Record #1
A Letter to Mama b/w Inside, Outside, Upside Down

Josie & the Pussycats Record #2
Josie (and the Pussycats) b/w With Every Beat of My Heart

Josie & the Pussycats Record #3
Voodoo b/w If That Isn't Love

Josie & the Pussycats Record #4
It's Gotta Be Him b/w I Wanna Make You Happy

The Monkees (c.1968–69)

The Monkees design #1 (Rice Krinkles/Colgems)
(Micky, Davy, Mike; green label with guitar logos between each head in spiral)
1. Monkees theme
2. Tear Drop City
3. Papa Gene's Blues
4. The Day We Fall In Love

The Monkees design #2 (Alpha Bits/Colgems)
(big Monkees logo in middle, Davy, Mike & Micky's heads around logo, black label)
1. Last Train To Clarksville
2. I Wanna Be Free
3. Forget That Girl
4. Valleri

The Monkees design #3 (Honey Comb/Colgems)
(red and white Monkees logo and musical notes, blue or purple grooves)
1. I'm A Believer
2. Pleasant Valley Sunday
3. I'm Not Your Steppin' Stone
4. Mary, Mary

H.R. Pufnstuf

There was an offer from an unknown Kellogg's brand cereal in 1970 where for 50¢ they would send you a ten-song 7" EP of songs from the show, plus a lyric sheet and a picture of H.R. Pufnstuf himself.

Bobby Sherman

Bobby Sherman design #1 (Honey Comb/
Metromedia) (blue shirt—some printed purplish—
with blue label)
1. Easy Come, Easy Go
2. La, La, La
3. July Seventeen
4. Time
5. Fun and Games

Bobby Sherman design #2(Alpha Bits/Metromedia)
(blue shirt with red label)
1. Easy Come, Easy Go
2. La, La, l a
3. Seattle
4. Love
5. Spend Some Time Lovin' Me

Bobby Sherman design #3 (Raisin Bran)
(purple shirt with orange label)
1. Little Woman
2. Hey Mr. Sun
3. I Think I'm Gonna Be Alright
4. Show Me
5. I'm Still Looking For The Right Girl

Bobby Sherman design #4 (Rice Krinkles)
(striped shirt with blue label)
1. Little Woman
2. Hey Mr. Sun
3. I'm In A Tree
4. Bubblegum and Braces
5. Make Your Own Kind Of Music

Bobby Sherman Canadian design #1
(Raisin Bran)

Lisa Sutton reports: "These are odd variations—they came flat & square inserted in the
box—each of the records has its own title with the
same art. I only have "Free To Roam" of design
#1, which has Bobby in the same picture and
pose from the Rice Krinkles box off to the left,
though they've made his pants black. The label is
red, no name on it at all, but there is a row of cartoon teenagers dancing down the right side of the
record. The background is black like a circular
record—it is orange behind that bleeding out to
the four corners of the square. There were four of
these, I've no clue what the other three were."

Bobby Sherman Canadian design #2 (cereal
unknown)
Same as Canadian design #1 except instead of the
cartoon kids on the left, there's a picture of
Canadian singer Anne Renee. There is one Bobby
song and one Anne Renee song per record. On
the back, along with playing directions, these

have a logo that says "Auravision—an activity of
Columbia Special Products"
1. *Tout Tournee Et Tout Bouge* b/w Run Away
2. *Pas De Marriage* b/w Bubblegum & Braces
3. *Toi Et Moi* b/w Bus Stop
4. *Comme Je T'aime* b/w I Think I'm Gonna
   Be Alright

The Sugar Bears

The Sugar Bears (Super Sugar Crisp)
(Sugar Bear, Honey Bear, Doobie Bear and
Shoobie Bear playing musical instruments in a
circle with a background that looks like a gold
record)
1. Love-you're a Long Time Comin'
2. You are the One
3. Feather Balloon
4. Happiness Train
5. Anyone but You

RECOMMENDED LISTENING

THE ARCHIES

Jingle, Jangle (Kirshner KES-105). One of the great pop albums of the '60s. Not a duff cut on this record—even the songs you'd normally peg as filler, like "Whoopee Tie Ai A" or "Archies Party," work splendidly. Gorgeous harmonies abound as Ron Dante multi-tracks his voice and duets with the incomparable Toni Wine. This also happens to be the Archies' most guitar-friendly record, and it sounds like they've got "Mr. Soul"-era Neil Young sitting in on "You Know I Love You." (Don't want to start any rumors—that's not Neil. Probably Hugh McCracken.) The title track was their second Top Ten single and Toni Wine's lead vocals soar. This album was her last with the Archies, but she's all over it and we're lucky to have her. "Get On The Line" should've been a hit with an unstoppable BubbleGospel groove comparable to "Mony, Mony." "Nursery Rhyme" and Ron Dante's composition "Sugar and Spice" also could've been singles. Ron also cowrote lesser-known tracks like "Everything's Alright" and "She's Putting Me Through Changes"—both lush harmony gems. If you're kicking yourself because you think you'll never find this delectable slab of vinyl, be of good cheer. Ron Dante himself has reissued this album on CD, retitled *Archies Party* (RKO 1029) with a new cover photo of Ron sporting a baseball cap and a guitar. The sound quality on this reissue is superb, by far the best the Archies have ever had on CD. Chuck Rainey's basslines pop, the guitars ring. Indispensable.

If you want an Archies Greatest Hits collection, spend a few extra bucks and get the import collection on Repertoire (with cartoon Archies on the front). Archies collections on CD have been notorious for poor tape quality, re-recordings, being mastered at the wrong speed or even being lifted straight off the vinyl. Buyer beware. If it looks too cheap to be true it probably is. Ron Dante is planning on reissuing all the original Archies LPs on CD, with *Sunshine* the next slated to come out. (David Smay)

THE BANANA SPLITS

We're The Banana Splits (Decca DL-75075): One of the best bubblegum albums ever put out. Strong contributions by Barry White, Joey Levine and Ritchie Adams. If you find it on vinyl you're either the luckiest bastard on earth or you've got a surplus of cash. A CD coupling the Splits with the Beagles is floating around out there and represents the best value for your dollar. Best cuts? So many: the theme, of course, "Don't Go Away Go-Go Girl," "Doin' The Banana Split," "I Enjoy Being a Boy," and "Wait Til Tomorrow." Hard soul and around-the-bend pop-psych. Buy it! (David Smay)

BARBIE

Beyond Pink (Sony Wonder LK63488). Brilliant bubblegum dance pop promotional tie-in for Mattel. Barbie, Christie and Teresa are credited on the cover, but Ralph Schuckett and erstwhile new wave songstress Ellen Shipley are the behind-the-scenes talent. I plucked this out of a Children's Clearance bin and was pleasantly surprised to find pop hook after pop hook. Madonna stalwart, Stephen Bray produced and co-wrote one of the standout tracks, "Wonderland." Other hits that didn't happen are "Rainbow," "Boys Will Be Boys," and "Think Pink." Sounds at different times like *True Blue*-era Madonna, the Spice Girls, Aqua and Josie & the Pussycats. Good stuff and it's still in print. (David Smay)

JEFF BARRY

The Barry production brilliance can best be heard on the albums he helmed for the Archies, Monkees and Neil Diamond. On CD, the 25-track *Sugar, Sugar* disk from Europe (Success Records, 1994) is the most complete Archies collection available, but is hard to find. Sony released a 10-cut budget package in 1992. Other even-skimpier collections abound. Ron Dante has overseen the reissue of two original Archies LPs, but they've been renamed in the process and appear as *The Archies* and *Archies Party* (both on RKO, now Boardwalk Records, 1999). The true bubblegum crisis is that straight reissues with bonus cuts taken directly from the animated show do not exist—or better yet, a box set, which would instantly form the cornerstone of every bubblegum fan's collection.

The Monkees have fared better in the digital world. All original LPs have seen reissue by Rhino with fabulous bonus cuts. For "I'm a Believer" check out *More of the Monkees*, and witness *Pisces, Aquarius, Capricorn & Jones Ltd.* for the Barry-written "She Hangs Out." Neil Diamond's early work on the Bang label can be found on *Classics: The Early Years* (Columbia, 1986).

Barry's Brill Building and girl group output spans literally hundreds of individual 45s. His biggest hits appear on *The Very Best of Red Bird/Blue Cat Records* (Taragon, 1998), which features top tunes from the Dixie Cups and Jelly Beans, and the monumental *Back to Mono* collection of Phil Spector productions, many from the pen of Barry. The best collection of Shangri-Las material is *Myrmidons of Melodrama* (RPM, 1994).

As a singer, Barry has yet to be collected on CD, although a wonderful (but possibly illegal) two-disk set has recently appeared from Europe called *Mr. Make Believe*, which rounds up rare solo singles—like "Hip Couple" on RCA—and early production work. And don't forget *The Raindrops* (Collectables, 1999), which grabs the sole Jeff and Ellie album and tacks on a few extras. (Chris Davidson)

BAY CITY ROLLERS

For years, the only Bay City Rollers collection available in the USA was the paltry ten-track *Greatest Hits* (Arista, 1977/1991), a woefully inadequate set that gathered the A-sides of the group's American singles. It was rendered permanently irrelevant by *The Definitive Collection* (Arista, 2000), a true Rollers best-of that presents 20 tracks from the original master tapes. *The Definitive Collection* includes the U.S. singles, a few tracks previously unavailable in America, the Duncan Faure-sung "Turn On The Radio" and the rockin' LP track "Wouldn't You Like It." Fans would also be well advised to investigate *Men In Plaid* (Bullseye, 2000), a Bay City Rollers tribute album that kicks off with the Flashcubes' incredible cover of "Wouldn't You Like It," and offers ace versions of Rollers tunes by the likes of Gary [Pig Gold] and the Grip Weeds, the Masticators, Chewy Marble, Ed James, Jeremy and other bright lights of the underground pop scene.

Avoid with extreme prejudice budget CDs by the '90s version of the Rollers, which have been issued under a few names, but which all . . . well, suck. (On the other hand, should you come across copies of the rare *Voxx*, *Live In Japan* or *Breakout* albums, send 'em immediately to Carl Cafarelli, c/o this publisher. You'll feel better for it.) (Carl Cafarelli)

BOYCE & HART

Presently there's no decent compendium of the duo's best material in print. Keep an eye peeled for the original LPs, especially I *Wonder What She's Doing Tonight* (A&M, LP-143/ SP-4143) and for the excellent 20-track Australian Raven compilation album from 1986, *Tommy Boyce & Bobby Hart*. (Kim Cooper)

THE BUGALOOS

Bugaloos (Capitol Records, SW-621): Tough to find this on vinyl anymore, but if you poke around on the internet . . . (hint, hint). Best cuts tend more towards Sunshine Pop with studio orchestrations like "For a Friend" and "The Senses of Our World." Relentlessly cheerful, this would clear out the Nick Cave fan club in 15 seconds or less. (David Smay)

RON DANTE

Ron Dante Brings You Up (Kirshner Records, KES-106): Ahhh, this is the stuff. Ron's first solo LP, recorded at the height of the Archies success, is essentially an extra Archies album, right down to the Barry/Kim compositions. Ron's own songwriting has never gotten the respect it deserves (he had some gorgeous cuts on *Jingle, Jangle*), but he's able to showcase it here. Pick hits: "Bring You Up," "Muddy River Water," Lovin' Lady" and "Go Where The Music Takes You." Currently available as a Japanese import CD, Ron himself has plans to re-release this domestically. (David Smay)

DEXTROSE RIDES AGAIN

For anyone who fumed "How can she leave out X, Y, and Z?" upon reading "Dextrose Rides Again," I offer a few additions. (All are in print, though a little digging via label websites or a reliable mail-order source such as Parasol <www.parasol.com> or Not Lame <www.notlame.com> may be necessary.) Those inclined towards the Teenage Fanclub brand of gum will find much to savor on the *Shoeshine Chartbusters* compilation (Shoeshine, 1997), including the BMX Bandits' deconstruction of "Where The Action Is." Listeners intrigued by Stephin Merritt's "City of the Damned" but intimidated by the *69 Love Songs* juggernaut may find happiness with the Magnetic Fields' *Holiday* (Merge, 1994) or *Get Lost* (Merge, 1995). Sloan's *Peppermint* EP (Murderecords,1992) contains two of the Halifax band's catchiest songs, "Pretty Voice" and the almighty "Sugartune." Continuing in the Canadian vein, Zumpano's *Look What The Rookie Did* (SubPop, 1994) features the Partridgesque "The Party Rages On" and the addictive "Wraparound Shades." Japanese photographer-turned-chanteuse Kahimi Karie explores the loungier aspects of gum on her self-titled American debut (Minty Fresh, 1998), including the definitive version of Momus's "Lolitapop Dollhouse." The ways to neo-gum nirvana are varied and plentiful, so dive in and enjoy! (Elizabeth Ivanovich)

EUROVISION

This is Eurovision (Virgin VTDCD 142, UK): Two CDs round up 39 assorted Songs For Europe, alternately emphasizing British entries and continental winners. You could drive a truck through the unforgivable omissions, but still, Cliff, Lulu, Clodagh, Livvy, Lynsey, the New Seekers and the Brotherhood Of Man hold up the Anglo end of things with unimpeachable aplomb, while Switzerland, Ireland, Germany, Luxembourg, Belgium, Israel, Monaco, Spain, France and the Netherlands all weigh in with their most memorable victors. All kinds of everything indeed. (Dave Thompson)

THE GO-GO'S

Beauty and the Beat (IRS 70021). Best bubblegum album of the '80s and of the new wave era. Jane Wiedlin and Charlotte Caffey wrote stellar hooks (though all the band members contribute fine songs here). The obvious hits barely hint at the pop pleasures here: "Tonite," "Lust to Love," "This Town," "Can't Stop The World" (a Kathy Valentine credit) are all perfect pop songs, and Richard Gotterher buffed them to a high gloss. (David Smay)

THE GROOVIE GOOLIES

Groovie Goolies (RCA, LSP-4420): Comparable in sound to the Hardy Boys records, though these songs were written by the Martin/Gayden team. Alternates between fine bubblegum cuts like "Save

Your Good Lovin' For Me" and "We Go So Good Together" with novelties like "Frankie" or "First Annual Semi-formal Combination Celebration Meet-the-Monster Population Party." Docked a point for not including "Chick-A-Boom." (David Smay)

THE HARDY BOYS *Here Comes the Hardy Boys* (RCA, LSP-4217) and *Wheels* (RCA, LSP-4315): These were released in connection with the Filmation cartoon, not Shaun's vehicle. Though undeniably pop, many of these cuts have a loose, almost country-rocking feel to them. Out of the RCA stable of Ed Fournier, Ricky Sheldon and Dick Monda who also worked on the Groovie Goolies record, these recordings have strong ties to Chicago's legendary garage pop label, Dunwich. The hooks and harmonies are there, but they don't have quite the snap and groove you get from the Archies. *Here Comes the Hardy Boys* is the stronger album. (David Smay)

THE HUDSON BROTHERS *Hollywood Situation* (Casablanca, NBLP 7004): "Three of Us" by the boys roars and soars on power chords and harmonies. "So You Are A Star" (covered by the Wondermints) was a bittersweet love song aimed at Goldie Hawn—a union that produced Kate Hudson. Mixed in are some crass comedy bits. But the pop stuff is cherce. (David Smay)

DANNY JANSSEN *Scooby-Doo's Snak Tracks: The Ultimate Collection* (Rhino Records, R2 75505): Danny Janssen is one of the most talented songwriters in the realm of bubblegum, but you probably wouldn't know that unless you were intimately acquainted with Partridge Family album tracks. This Scooby Doo collection sports a number of Janssen compositions, including two of the best songs in the entire genre, "Seven Days A Week" and "Recipe For My Love." Well worth lurking in the kiddie aisle of your record store to catch this when it's marked down. (David Smay)

ROBERTO Jordán Las Estrellas del Fonografo series (Bertelsmann de México, S. A. de C. V., 1995, cassette: CSC 1515, CD: CDC 0063). Look for the 2-in-1 CD on BMG Mexico (Bertelsmann), but don't be fooled by the RCA Victor logo—they put the albums out originally. This contains the two 1968 albums *Hazme una Señal* and *1-2-3 Detente!*, representing the best examples of Roberto Jordán's bubblegum recordings. 95% of the tracks are cover versions of English-language bubblegum, pop and rock hits, including songs by the 1910 Fruitgum Company, the Monkees, the Turtles, the Grass Roots and Neil Diamond. Essential tracks: "El juego de Simón" ("Simon Says") and "Como te quiero" ("Birds of a Feather"). The rest of the tracks are are a fun romp through the happening hits of the mid-to-late '60s, and

are a joy to listen to, whether you understand Spanish or not. Jordán applies enough of his own style to make them stand on their own. Note: Avoid *Ayer Y Hoy* on BMG US/Latin. It has only ten tracks, and includes some of his more recent sleepers. (Tom Walls)

JOSIE & THE PUSSYCATS *Josie & the Pussycats* (Capitol): The Holy Grail of bubblegum. The original LP is almost impossible to find, and if you could turn it up it'd cost you three figures to own. Since Capitol doesn't seem to be in any hurry to release it on CD, your best bet is a diligent internet search. You want to find not only the album, but the ultra-rare singles as well (songs like: "Voodoo," "A Letter to Mama," "Inside Outside Upside Down"). Bubblegum masters Danny Janssen & Bobby Hart wrote the songs, Patrice Holloway—sister of soul-legend Brenda Holloway—lent her vocals to the project along with Cheryl Dougher and Cherie Moor (aka Cheryl Ladd, a pre-Angel Pussycat). Janssen fought for Patrice, and booked the best soul musicians in L.A. for the sessions. That's why the Josie & the Pussycat songs sound like a great, lost Motown act. In fact, this is the nearest equivalent to a female Jackson 5 you'll ever hear. (David Smay)

KASENETZ AND KATZ PRODUCTIONS The various K-K hits have been reissued on and off in various configurations (and they're easy to find in used record stores). In 1994, Collectables went into the K-K vaults and issued the following on CD:

1910 Fruitgum Co./Ohio Express—*Golden Classics*
All the hits by K&K's two biggest bands, for those who don't have them, although the Express' "Beg, Borrow and Steal"—like Question Mark and most everything else in the Cameo-Parkway catalog—couldn't be licensed for reissue. So keep your eyes peeled for that one on 45!

Rare Breed—*The Super K Kollection*
This was a Brooklyn band that recorded for the Attack label. Includes the "doctored" version of the Ohio Express' "Beg . . ." (nothing different but the bass and drums). From early in K&K's career.

Ohio Express—*The Super K Kollection*
See, K&K recorded so much excess material under this name that some of it wasn't even released, and this is that.

Shadows of Knight—*The Super K Kollection*
Straight reissue of the band's Super K album, but in all fairness, One Way reissued this same album with four bonus tracks: "My Fire Department Needs A Fireman," "From Way Out To Way Under," "Run Run Billy Porter," and the single version of "Shake."

The Super K Kollection, Vol.1, The Super K Kollection, Vol.2

All the odds and ends from the K&K bands that didn't make it, plus rare material from the Fruitgums, Express, Shadows, etc. (James Porter)

ANDY KIM
How'd We Ever Get This Way (Steed Records, ST 37001): Jeff Barry brings out his entire arsenal of rhythm instruments to support his good friend's best album. Consistently strong hooks and arrangements on song after song make this a great listen. Love the title track, the bubble-gospel "Love That Little Woman," "You Girl," "You Got Style." One of the most underrated pop albums of its era. Elsewhere, Andy's greatest hits feature such must-haves as "Rainbow Ride" (huge, ringing guitar), the mind-boggling (yet tuneful) "Tricia Tell Your Daddy" and his biggest hit, "Baby I Love You." (A bigger hit for Andy than for the Ronettes. Or the Ramones.) (David Smay)

JONATHAN KING
The Many Faces of Jonathan King (Music Club MCCD 108, UK): 18 tracks concentrate on the master's most successful singles—which, thankfully, also sum up his most adventurous/audacious. "Everyone's Gone to The Moon" is an obvious opener, while "Johnny Reggae," "It Only Takes A Minute" and the brainlessly delicious "Loop Di Love" are unassailable highlights. However, Father Abraphart, Bubblerock and Sakkarin's heavy metallic "Sugar, Sugar" run the gems close, "Hooked On A Feeling" still packs a hookline to hang yourself from, and Nemo's rendition of "The Sun Has Got His Hat On" is as bizarrely subversive as it gets. (Dave Thompson)

KISS
Dressed To Kill (1975, in print, Uni/Mercury): Chuck Eddy called this "the most inarguable bubblemetal mixture ever" for a reason. In addition to showcasing pop-hook sensibilities, cartoonish images, and masterful marketing (all bubblegum pillars), it references the genre profoundly by subverting bubblegum's most playfully erotic convention. Instead of covertly presenting sex cloaked in the language of a 13-year-old, it overtly presents sex through the juvenile eyes and fantasies of a 13-year-old. In "Room Service" random women demand sex whenever vocalist Paul Stanley has a free moment. In "Ladies In Waiting" an orderly line of females is queued up to have sex with the boys. "C'mon And Love Me" (which opens with the unbelievable line, "She's a dancer, a romancer, I'm a Capricorn and she's a Cancer") is summarized with the offer, "Baby won't you take me down on my knees, you can do what you please." And of course, the album ends with a manifesto that, though perhaps less specifically carnal, certainly keeps up the teen fantasy-world theme, declaring, "I want to Rock and Roll All Night and Party Every Day!" (Jake Austen)

LANCELOT LINK AND THE EVOLUTION REVOLUTION
Lancelot Link and the Evolution Revolution (ABC/Dunhill, ABCS-715): Quality chimp rock from a name you can trust. Some of the hardest rocking bubblegum to come out between the Ohio Express and Shampoo. Surprisingly big guitar sound has the Evolution Revolution coming off like a simian Who—particularly on "Magic Feeling." Songwriter Steve Hoffman cranked out pure pop on "Day Dream," menacing garage rock on "Evolution Revolution," and monkey lovin' cuts like "Rolling in the Clover" and "Yummy Love." The single "Sha-La Love You" by the team of Price/Walsh has a poppier, Archies-inspired hook, but they also wrote the big-riffed "Magic Feeling." (David Smay)

THE LEMON PIPERS
Unless you care to blow big bucks in the Import or Fanatics bin, all one really requires by way of a taste of Lemon can be found on the smartly packaged, 15-song *Golden Classics* disc from Collectables. Containing all the hits, all the should-a-beens, and a healthy dose of odds 'n' sods to boot (i.e.: "Dead End Street/Half Light," "Love Beads And Meditation," plus the best of the band's several songs regarding footwear, "Shoemaker Of Leatherwear Square"), *Golden Classics* truly is the kind of compilation you needn't sit near the "skip" button whilst listening—or especially frugging—to. (Gary Pig Gold)

THE LOVIN' SPOONFUL
After a decades-long search, the original Spoonful multi-track masters have finally been found, and a total restoration of this seminal band's rich catalog is well underway at last. In the meantime, Rhino Records' authoritative-and-then-some *Lovin' Spoonful Anthology* presents all of the hits alongside a fine smattering of essential album tracks, as does Buddha's latest (and best) *Greatest Hits* collection. Also highly urged upon your ears is Razor & Tie's double-pack of the band's two film scores, *What's Up, Tiger Lily?* (Woody Allen's greatest creation ever, by the way) and *You're A Big Boy Now*, plus need I mention Zal Yanovsky's long-lost *Alive And Well In Argentina* album is well worth scouring the globe—or at least Ebay—for. (Gary Pig Gold)

LUV
Lots of Luv (2nd lp, 1978 German/Dutch Phillips 6423-117) (★★★★★ five stars) One of the five greatest pop LPs ever made . . . Abba's greatest album in all other 499 parallel universes where LUV didn't exist 'cept as a echo of forgotten memories from #500.

With Luv (1st LP, 1978 German/Dutch Phillips 6423-105) (★★★½ stars) Well over half as good as *Lots of Luv*, which is to say—a notch past half-great!

"Tingalingaling" (b/w "Billy the Kid") (1981, German Carrere 49815/Dutch Carrere 2044207) (★★★★★★★★★ more stars than I can even count) LUV's final A-side is/was their two minute plus-27-second masterpiece, everything that has been great about girlpop from the Shirelles to Britney (and the exact chronological mid-point inbetween), PLUS GREAT DANCE BEATS and gurgle-snap early synthpop noises. If you're only allowed to own one pop song in the universe—this is it! (Said Metal Mike on a bible on his deathbed, surrounded by condolence cards from all three living Spice Girls, October 2029.) (Metal Mike Saunders)

TONY MACAULEY/ COOKE & GREENAWAY "Love Grows (Where My Rosemary Goes)" by Edison Lighthouse (written by Tony Macauley and Barry Mason, produced by Tony Macaulay)

"My Baby Loves Lovin'" by White Plains (written and produced by Roger Cook and Roger Greenaway)

Taken together, these songs form the high watermark of bubblegum pop as it was practiced in Britain in the early '70s. Both were anonymous studio groups fronted by the same singer, Tony Burrows, and like all the great manufactured hits of the time, both songs use the the the imagery of the then-current counterculture to reinforce the accepted values of the day. Both songs describe the same old male fantasy, of women "liberated" enough to give themselves to a man sexually, yet satisfied with the bonds of a male-dominated relationship. The productions are sticky-sweet traps themselves, hooking the ear with dainty electric guitars, tinny string sections and lusty male vocals. The joyous, anthemic zeal with which they extol the virtues of these "wild and free" chicks who "take care of everything" will never be forgotten by those who witness it. (Derrick Bostrom)

THE MONKEES Depending upon your level of interest, there are a wide range of options available for you to satisfy your wild, rampagin' Monkees jones. Dilettantes will settle for *Greatest Hits* (Rhino, 1995), a 20-track set that includes the singles and little else. A better one-stop Monkees shop is the two-disc *Anthology* (Rhino, 1998), which gives you the hits but adds such other Monkees essentials as "Look Out (Here Comes Tomorrow)," "She," "What Am I Doing Hangin' 'Round?" and the single-that-shoulda-been, "All Of Your Toys," among many others.

Those who wish to consider the bubblegum Monkees debate firsthand can compare the two albums produced under Kirshner's aegis, *The Monkees* (Colgems, 1966/Rhino, 1994) and *More Of The Monkees* (Colgems, 1967/Rhino, 1994), to the post-Kirshner *Headquarters* (Colgems, 1967/Rhino, 1995) and *Pisces, Aquarius, Capricorn & Jones, Ltd.* (Colgems, 1967/Rhino, 1995); each of these four albums has its own merits and charm. After that, you're on your own! Rhino has reissued all of the rest of the Monkees canon—*The Birds, The Bees And The Monkees* (1968), *Head* (1968), *Instant Replay* (1969), *The Monkees Present* (1969) and *Changes*

(1970)—supplemented by a vintage live concert (*Live 1967*) and three separate *Missing Links* collections of previously-unissued '60s studio tracks. Rhino also has two Monkees reunion albums—1987's *Pool It!* and 1996's *Justus* (the latter with Michael Nesmith, the former without)—and a four-CD boxed set, *Listen To The Band* (1991).

Of course, true Monkees obsessives—like, say, for example, Carl Cafarelli and Gary Pig Gold—will need to own *Headquarters Sessions* (Rhino Handmade, 2000), a three-CD archival collection of session tapes from the recording of the only album the Monkees made as a functioning band in the '60s. And let us not forget all those rare cereal-box records, still smelling sweetly of Honey Combs and Alpha Bits all these decades later. (Carl Cafarelli)

THE POPPY FAMILY If you can't find the original LPs, you'll be pleased with *A Good Thing Lost: 1968–1973* (What Are Records, 1996), featuring a strong selection of album tracks and unreleased material by this haunting Canadian spouse act. (Kim Cooper)

TOMMY ROE *It's Now Winter's Day* (ABC Records, ABC 1088) and *We Can Make Music* (ABCS 714): You can find Tommy's greatest hits without too much trouble and we recommend that you do. These albums offer some other interesting pop thrills. *Winter's Day* features some gorgeous production by Curt Boettcher, and *We Can Make Music* is highlighted by the title cut and the gummy "Brush A Little Sunshine and Love." (David Smay)

SHAMPOO *We Are Shampoo* (IRS): Unbearably cool. Two brat-genius British teens slag off every glimmer of mid-'90s culture that falls into their gunsight. Crushing Who-like guitars ride thumping Disco-Hip-Hop-Dance beats and Jacqui Blake and Carrie Askew's sneering vocals demolish a world of pasty-faced Londoners. Best known for the hit single "Trouble," this album is wall-to-wall perfection. Own it. Love it. Regret that you weren't a 14-year-old girl when this was released in 1995. If you can't find it, splurge for an import collection of their greatest hits, because your life is incomplete without hearing "Bouffant Headbutt" with the immortal chorus: "You're dead, You're dead/Bouffant Headbutt Worthless /You're dead, You're dead/When we get you outside/ . . . You're fucking dead." Shampoo are the Sex Pistols of bubblegum. (David Smay)

SLIK AND THE QUICK Both records are long out of print; check the dollar bins. (Edwin Letcher)

P.F. SLOAN For an introduction to P.F. Sloan's solo work, watch the cutout bins for two good but sadly out-of-print compilations: Rhino's 1986 LP *The Best Of P.F. Sloan (1965–1966)—Precious Times* and *Anthology* (One Way, 1993). Less slick, but quite fascinating, is *Child of Our Times: The Trousdale Demo Sessions 1965–1967* (Varèse Sarabande, 2001), which includes the original version of "Secret Agent Man," then called "Danger Man." The Fantastic Baggys recently received an excellent retrospective on Sundazed. There are many comps of the Grass Roots' hits, most of which touch on the Sloan-Barri era before moving into their soul-pop phase. (Kim Cooper)

THE STRANGELOVES *I Want Candy: The Best of The Strangeloves* (Epic Legacy 1995-out of print): A reissue of their one and only LP, plus some pre-and post-Feldman/Gotterher/Goldstein 45s. Some duff tracks amidst the hits, but no song captures the rush of the approaching Friday 5 o'clock whistle blow like "Night Time." (Keith Bearden)

STRAWBERRY STUDIOS *Hotlegs Thinks: School Stinks* (One Way S21-17961): Not necessarily the most representative of Strawberry emissions, but one of the precious few which (a) stretched to a full album, and (b) has actually seen the light of day within the last thirty years. "Neanderthal Man" remains the archetypal one-hit-wonder and Hotlegs knew it—only "Um Wah Um Woh" comes close to the same formula, the rest of the album standing as a dry run for selected highlights of 10cc's own future career. Which, of course, means it is a magnificent effort. One can see why the kids who bought the hit weren't impressed, though. (Dave Thompson)

THE SUGAR BEARS *Presenting the Sugar Bears* (Big Tree Records, BTS-2009): Taking the bubblegum/ cereal connection to its ultimate conclusion. Upbeat pop grooves that teeter just slightly towards MOR arrangements. Kim Carnes got her start here, singing the voice of Honey Bear and contributing several songs like "Feather Balloon." "You Are the One" by Baker Knight is the pick hit here—it ought to be an oldies radio staple, but this record never took off. (David Smay)

SVENSK POP Recommended listening: The 3-CD set *Stora Popboxen: Svensk Pop 1964–69* (EMI Sweden) (Alec Palao)

THE SWEET *The Sweet* (reissued on CD by Razor and Tie #7930182189-2): Their first album was cobbled together out of their earliest singles, and Razor & Tie's expanded reissue includes all eight British A-Sides, including their hard-to-find and very bubblegum hits "Funny Funny," "Co Co," "Poppa Joe" and "Alexander Graham Bell" plus their Glam Rock thunderbolts "Blockbuster" and "Hellraiser." *Desolation Boulevard*, their first LP on Capitol, was their biggest seller with "Ballroom Blitz" and is also a worthy buy. If you decide to get *Best of Sweet* (Capitol, Price Buster series), you'll lose the early bubblegum material, but get all their glam rock hits and pick up their later Power-Pop-By-Way-Of-Queen singles "Action" and "Love is Like Oxygen." (David Smay)

THAT THING YOU DO *That Thing You Do* Soundtrack (Sony/Columbia). Everybody from Jeff Barry to the Posies was invited to submit songs for this project, but the winning entry came out from Fountains of Wayne songwriter Adam Schlesinger. But the title track isn't the only worthwhile cut on this soundtrack. The Elias/Rogness team churned out song after song of prime mid-'60s style pop-rock on songs like "Drive Faster," "Little Wild One," "She Knows It," "Dance With Me Tonight," and "I Need You (That Thing You Do)." These cuts are barely audible during the movie, but they're pure pop-rock treats waiting your discovery. All killer no filler. (David Smay)

TOOMORROW Long out-of print, the *Toomorrow* material circulates among O N-J fanatics online. (Kim Cooper)

THE TURTLES Beware the morass of lightweight, budget Best Of collections and head straight for Rhino Records' *20 Greatest Hits* when shopping for a single-disc Turtles treasury. Make note, however, that the esteemed crew over at Sundazed have now reissued the bulk of the band's original catalog as well, including the magnificent *Battle Of The Bands* album (REQUIRED LISTENING, I tell you!) True blue Turtleheads must also seek out the 1987 Rhino vinyl *Chalon Road* collection, not to mention the infamous "Rhythm Butchers" series of seven-inch EP's (which chronicle the band's post-concert motel-room shenanigans in a way the Beach Boys' *Party!* album dared only hint at). (Gary Pig Gold)

VARIOUS ARTISTS *Bubblegum Classics*, Volumes 1–3 (Varèse Sarabande): This is where you should start to build a bubblegum library. Three volumes that perfectly encapsulate the genre, from Kasenetz and Katz' most famous productions ("Yummy, Yummy, Yummy," "Indian Giver," "Simon Says"), to a fair sampling of Tony Burrows Brit-gum with White Plains and Edison Lighthouse, through the best known hits by Tommy James, Tommy Roe, the Partridge Family, the Archies and the Monkees. Each volume features some rarity that makes it worth the price of admission: Lancelot Link's only cut available on CD ("Sha-La Love You") on Vol. 3, the Fun & Games' brilliant "The Grooviest Girl in the World" on Vol. 2, or Captain Groovy's Bubblegum Army on Vol. 1. This by no means exhausts the genre, but it maps out the territory beautifully. Our Bill Pitzonka's notes are exemplary.

25 All Time Greatest Bubblegum Hits (Varèse Sarabande): And if you can really only afford one bubblegum collection, get this. Here Varèse cherry-picks their own three-volume set, and sweetens it with rare cuts by the Banana Splits and Josie & the Pussycats. (David Smay)

VITAMIN C *Vitamin C* (Elektra/Asylum). Colleen

Fitzpatrick was Debbie Harry's pretty, bitchy daughter in *Hairspray*. You remember—Ricki Lake's nemesis with the snappy footwork. Then she formed the pop rock group Eve's Plum, turned out a few classy albums that went nowhere and now she's reinvented herself again as Vitamin C. She cites her influences as coming from the "B" Bin of the records store: Beatles, Blondie, Breeders, Beastie Boys. Maybe you saw her swanning through the high school corridors on the Disney Channel with her video for "Graduation." Not unlike Beck's little sister busting a bubblegum move. Her best cut might not even be on this entirely delectable album. That would be the song "Vacation" on the first Pokémon movie soundtrack: surf guitar hook, chanting children's chorus, organ break. Pure genius. (David Smay)

WHITE WHALE RECORDS *Happy Together: The Very Best Of White Whale Records* (Varese Vintage) (Alec Palao)

Index

C

About the contributors...

Andrice Arp, a contributor to *Scram* since the first issue, does comics and illustration and resides, until further notice, in San Francisco. Information about her comic book, *Hi-Horse*, can be found at http://www.hi-horse.com.

Jake Austen, cartoonist and writer, produces the cable-access dance show *Chic-A-Go-Go* and edits *Roctober* Comics + Music magazine, in-depth explorations of dynamic, unjustly obscure music icons. $4 for sample, $10 for 3 issue subscription from 1507 E. 53rd St. #617, Chicago, IL 60615, www.roctober.com.

Peter Bagge currently writes an all-ages comic about an all-girl pop band called *Yeah!* for DC Comics, and is best known as the author of *Hate* comics. Fan website: www.peterbagge.com.

Keith Bearden is the head writer for VH1's *Where Are They Now?* He is the former editor of *Lowest Common Denominator*, the program guide of free form radio station WFMU. His work has appeared in *Slant, Fangoria, Axcess* and *Time Out NY.* He would like to thank his brother Grant for playing him "Rockaway Beach" 23 years ago.

Derrick Bostrom cut his teeth in the music biz playing drums in the legendary, decidedly non-bubblegum-influenced band the Meat Puppets. His solo outfit, Today's Sounds, plumbs the depths of pop music as the mood strikes him. Visit the Today's Sounds online at http://www.meatpuppets.com/today/

Mary Burt lives as she dreams in the dusty Los Angeles desert, where she valiantly defends her cat against the packs of coyotes that circle her shack at night. She edits *Sad* magazine, a journal to save for a rainy day, filled with sad anecdotes and other bits of sad culture. For a sample, send your top ten sad songs list and three dollars to P.O. Box 291853, Los Angeles, CA 90029.

When **Carl Cafarelli** was four, he accompanied his siblings to a drive-in screening of *A Hard Day's Night*. The rest was inevitable: Carl is a regular contributor to *Goldmine, The Syracuse New Times,* and *The Musichound Rock* books, and the co-host

(with Dana Bonn) of "This is Rock 'n' Roll Radio" on WXXE-FM in Syracuse, NY (Sundays 9pm-midnight Eastern time, online at www.wxxe.org). His wife Brenda and daughter Meghan are much cuter than Betty and/or Veronica.

Don Charles sold his soul to rock'n'roll after hearing Jeff Barry's music in September 1968 on the very first Archies cartoon. For the past 13 years, he's been singing the praises of Jeff Barry and other pop geniuses in such publications as *Goldmine, Discoveries* and *Cool & Strange Music!* magazine. He resides in Kansas City, MO.

Chinta Cooper, 12, loves to play sports. She lives in Southern California with her four brothers and parents. Her favorite bands are 'N Sync, Smashmouth, Destiny's Child, Britney Spears, Christina Aguilera and Eminem! Chinta is involved in drill team, service organizations, the math club, and volleyball. Later in life Chinta would like to work in science, probably as a Epidemiologist.

Kim Cooper is editrix of *Scram* magazine, where bubblegum is just one of the offbeat genres celebrated and dissected. A 4th generation Hollywood native, as a tyke she yearned to join the Banana Splits on their giant slide. She still does. For Scram info, visit http://www.scrammagazine.com or send $5 to P.O. Box 461626, Hollywood, CA 90046-1626 for a sample issue. email: scram@scrammagazine.com

Morgan Cooper is a 10-year-old boy. He enjoys playing football, soccer, and basketball. He also loves to swim and play water polo. His favorite band is either Blink 182 or Smashmouth. He likes to draw. When he grows up he wants to be either an artist or an astronaut. He loves his family, a lot.

Chris Davidson runs CAD Records, home to Fortune & Maltese, the Brimstones and other top combos of note. Chris has published many swingin' articles in magazines like *Cool & Strange Music!, Lounge,* and *Entertainment Weekly.* His '68 Mustang drop-top can be seen parked in front of the Driftwood Lounge on any given evening.

Katrina Dixon is a freelance journalist and pop culture addict living in Edinburgh, Scotland. In the mid-'90s she produced the *Charity Shopper*

thrifting zine (online version at www.charityshopper.co.uk), drummed in several bands and amassed way too much thrifted junk. She now writes for *The Scotsman, The Sunday Herald* and *Time Out* among other publications, but continues to covet The Partridge Family board game.

Brian Doherty is an associate editor of *Reason* magazine, publishes *Surrender* fanzine, and runs Cherry Smash Records. His rock 'n' roll youth was spent in Gainesville, Florida and he currently enjoys driving around in Los Angeles, California.

Becky Ebenkamp is a NYC-based senior editor/pop cultural anthropologist for *Brandweek* magazine, where she keeps an eye on corporate America. An L.A. native, her obsessions include Keane-style eyeballs, Polynesia, blindingly bright sitcoms and any project involving a chimp or a monkey. She has never shopped at the Gap.

Chuck Eddy is the music editor of the *Village Voice*, and the author of *Stairway to Hell: The 500 Greatest Heavy Metal Albums in the Universe* and *The Accidental Evolution of Rock 'n' Roll: A Misguided Tour Through Popular Music*. He has spent half of his life writing for *Why Music Sucks, Radio On, Creem*, and several glossier magazines whose names he forgets. He lives in Brooklyn with his pet guinea pig, Eggplant. If he had stayed in the Army, he could almost retire by now.

Dennis P. Eichhorn, a regular contributor to *Scram* and numerous other publications, is a freelance writer, editor, and videomaker who resides in the shipyard city of Bremerton, Washington.

Peter Geiberger finds writing in the third person very awkward. He shouldn't slouch so much. He should pay more attention to things. Also, he should floss more often. As of press time, he has avoided doing a number of things for this book that he had said he would. He is somewhat apologetic. Somewhat.

San Francisco's **Chas Glynn** is novelties editor of *Scram* and a regular contributor to *Gearhead*. He describes himself as a Gadabout and Bon Vivant.

Gary Pig Gold, publisher since 1975 of the legendary *Pig Paper funzine*, felt the sonic earth shift beneath him upon first encountering Tommy Roe's "Sweet Pea." Consequently, he'll be first in line for the Archies' big "Bridges Over Riverdale"

tour next year. Gary sez: "Attention! Composers and musicians alike—yep, that includes all you aspiring Boyce & Harts out there—are more than cordially invited to submit your bona fide Home Recordings to the "Unsound" Demos Only Series, an internationally-acclaimed D.I.Y. endeavor which threatens to become the Kasenetz-Katz Super Cirkus of the 21st Century! Info: PIGPROD@aol.com or http://www.unsoundonline.com/

Having chewed gum since teething, **Margaret Griffis** adored the Monkees before entering grade school in Miami Beach. A number of cavities later, her chiclelove turned to punk rock—the high octane bubblegum. Since then she's been fighting the good fight through her rantings, plunkings and doodles mostly in such rags as her self-produced *Anti-zine* (http://members.aol.com/Antizinefl/antizine.html), her slobrock band the Carbonics and through her beloved but evil Torco The Clown comic character. She also likes sargassumfish, gadgets, fire, boys and oatmeal stout. She loves to HATE!

Bill Holmes is an avid music fan and music collector whose reviews and features are published on four continents in magazines like *Pop Culture Press, Amplifier* and *Bucketful Of Brains*. He lives to widen his musical bandwidth, and hopefully yours, by believing that great music never went away, it just got harder to find. Drop him a line at bholmes_fm@msn.com.

Elizabeth Ivanovich was born after the cancellation of *Josie and the Pussycats*, but before the cancellation of *Kidd Video*. A recent graduate of Stanford University, she is thrilled to discuss a topic of earth-shattering importance in this book.

Gloria Keeley has been a rock 'n' roll lover since Elvis Presley hit the scene in 1955. She can name all of the teen stars and knows their likes and pet peeves thanks to her stash of *16s* and *Tiger Beats*. She's been published in *Blue Suede News, ROCKRGRL* and loads of poetry journals. Gloria teaches college English in San Francisco.

P. Edwin Letcher is a music freak who started collecting records as a kid. He's been in one band or another since 1978, and has been writing about music since the mid-'80s. He edits *Garage and Beat* magazine ($5 for a sample from 2754 Prewett St., Los Angeles, CA 90031) and contributes to *Flipside* as a columnist and reviewer. He currently is working on animating his cartoon strip, "Stubbo, the Cat with No Paws." See www.trigonrecords.com for Tuffies, Cheeseburger and Stubbo products, and www.garageandbeat.com for magazine.

Steve Mandich is the author of *Evel Incarnate: The Life and Legend of Evel Knievel* (Macmillan UK, 2000). He also publishes the fanzines *Heinous* and *Monorail*, covering such topics as Bob Newhart, the Human Fly, the Rolling Stones, Chick comics, and wheelies (available for $2 each from PO Box 12065, Seattle, WA 98102). Steve likes baseball, root beer, bicycling and crossword puzzles.

Mike McPadden published the zine *Happyland* under the pen(is) name Selwyn Harris. He is old and fat now and owns lots of useless dot-com stock. Visit his stupid site: www.agonizer.com.

Alec Palao: writer, musician, reissue producer, historian and rock 'n' roll know-it-all. Has worked with everyone from Ronnie Dawson through the Zombies to Faust. Fave bubblegum moment: "You Don't Have To" by the Beeds.

Partridge Family Temple: **Dan Kapelovitz** is the present incarnation of Keith Partridge. Keith Partridge is Christ. Keith is Now. Keith is Eternal. Keith is Television. Keith is Reality. Keith is Love. Kapelovitz is Keith. Dig it. **Go-Go Giddle Partridge** is the ultimate sex symbol of the Partridge Family Temple. She is also the most psychedelic cult leader that this world has ever experienced. Truth is Fun!!! Send donations to The Partridge Family Temple, P.O. Box 480775, Los Angeles, CA 90048, and visit their website www.partridgefamilytemple.com.

Robrt L. Pela is a book critic for *The Advocate* and Literary Editor for *Art & Understanding* magazine. He contributes monthly features to *Men's Fitness* magazine, and his theater reviews appear each week in *New Times* and on National Public Radio's "Morning Edition." Robrt is the author of the forthcoming book *Filthy: The Life and Times of John Waters* (Alyson Books, Spring 2001).

Bill Pitzonka produced and compiled Varèse Sarabande's *Bubblegum Classics* CD series. He has written liner notes for Varèse, Razor & Tie, RCA, Mercury, and MCA Japan. He is also a pop music reviewer for *Request* magazine.

James Porter, a resident of Chicago, has contributed to several different publications, including the *Chicago Sun-Times*, *Roctober*, *No Depression*, *Living Blues*, and *New City*, a Chicago newspaper. In addition, he is the singer/harmonica player with Hoodoo Hoedown, a local roots-rock band, and thinks the milkshakes at Jewel's Diner could cure all ills!

Domenic Priore is the author of the forthcoming *Riot on Sunset Strip: Rock 'n' Roll's Last Stand in Hollywood*, a document of 1965–'66 Los Angeles nightlife, and of *Look! Listen! Vibrate! Smile!* (Last Gasp, 777 Florida Street, San Francisco, CA 94110), devoted to Brian Wilson's smile era. He also produced *It's Happening*, a teenage rock 'n' roll TV show based on *Hollywood A GoGo*, *Ready Steady Go*, and *Shindig!*

Glenn Sadin is a musician and vinyl junkie. Soon after meeting his Japanese wife-to-be, Mariko, in 1994, Glenn developed an interest in Japanese pop culture, with special emphasis on collecting 1950s–60s Japanese pop records. He maintains a website on the subject called "Nihon no Pops" at http://home.earthlink.net/~glenn_mariko/nihon.htm. Glenn lives in San Francisco with his wife and daughter, Misa.

Metal Mike Saunders: Graduated from Hall High (Little Rock), 1969. Graduated from University of Texas/Austin, 1973. Twenty two years to date in the accounting profession. Plays/played in a punk rock band (1977–2000), cussed a lot doing it. Still a mean, big 5'6", 128 lbs. Can and will do Eurobeat dance steps to the A*Teens, Toy-Box, and all other spiritual descendents of Betty, Veronica 'n' Jughead.

Gene Sculatti is editor of *The Catalog of Cool* (Warner, 1982), *San Francisco Nights: The Psychedelic Music Trip* (St. Martin's, 1985), and *Too Cool* (St. Martin's, 1993), and co-host and producer of "The Cool & The Crazy" radio show, KCRW-FM, Santa Monica (1984–1987).

Greg Shaw is a former rock journalist/editor and whilom authority on '60s music. Nowadays he runs Bomp Records, and keeps up with contemporary bubblegum via his 8-year-old's viewing of The Disney Channel. More info@www.bomp.com.

David Smay has written for *Scram, Tiki News, Back of a Car, The Comics Journal* and *Amazing Heroes*. A graduate of Kenyon College, Mr. Smay has lavished his fine liberal arts education on subjects as varied as Spy Jazz, Jack Kirby, and, of course, bubblegum music. He currently lives in San Francisco, where his four-year-old son subjects him to unceasing requests for Dick Dale's *Greatest Hits*.

Jack Stevenson is an American film writer and film show organizer living in Denmark since 1993. Creator of the self-published *Pandemonium* book series in the late '80s, his film articles, focusing on cult, underground and exploitation, have appeared in American magazines as diverse as *Film Threat* and *Film Quarterly*, and since moving to Europe his texts have been translated into eight different languages. Visit Jack's online movie magazine at http://hjem.get2net.dk/jack_stevenson.

Vern Stoltz lives in the suburbs of Washington, D.C. His 'zine, *Cannot Become Obsolete*, features personal essays and whimsical views inspired by LPs from the 1950s and '60s. Back issues are available—inquire at itsvern@attglobal.net.

Known to many as "The Seventh Brady Kid," **Lisa Sutton** has been involved in creating dozens of pop-culture/teen-idol related CDs, handling liner notes, compilation and package design. A regular contributor to TVLand.com, Sutton has also been involved with several television projects related to music and vintage programming. Visit Mrs. Neugast's fan worship page; a place for the idol-minded at www.sunshineday.com/neugast.

Co-author (with Wreckless Eric) of THE great unfinished Eurovision entry of the mid-1980s, "Sugar Dick A Dum Dum," **Dave Thompson** has also written bestselling books on such themes as space rock, punk, death and John's Children. He is a contributor to *Mojo, Goldmine* and *Alternative Press* magazines, and his favorite record is Gary Glitter's "Rock And Roll."

Tom Walls is a travel agent, writer and website designer in Hollywood, Florida. He has a taste for vintage cars, fine wines and adventure travel. He sang in Gainesville garage bands the Jeffersons, Hey! Sasquatch, the Claude Pepper Blues Explosion and the Black Eggs, and plays the Farfisa organ. An active libertarian, Walls often writes on politics and civil liberties. See The Psychedelic Sounds of the Black Eggs at http://www.afn.org/~afn62971/eggs.html.

Glynis Ward, former love goddess of the Sunset Strip, digs all styles of '60s music and has been writing about it for 12 years. Still xeroxes her fanzine. Still wears white go-go boots. Visit *Feline Frenzy Teen 'Zine* online at http://www.mindspring.com/~felinefrenzy/.

J.R. Williams draws a lot. He draws comics, book and magazine illustrations, storyboards, and designs for animated TV programs and commercials. If it's drawable, chances are he draws it. Between projects, he's even been known to draw unemployment. Do not pity him. His work has appeared in R. Crumb's *Weirdo* magazine, on the network series *The PJs*, and, for all we know, in other dimensions.

Also available from feral House

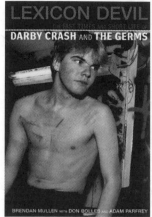

Lexicon Devil
The Fast Times and Short Life of Darby Crash and The Germs

Brendan Mullen, with Don Bolles and Adam Parfrey

This oral biography is not just a punk rock history, but a remarkable view of private lives in a surreal period of L.A. history, when est and Scientology cultists influenced children in a Los Angeles high school, when underage prostitutes, drug dealers, chickenhawks, skateboarders, gay sadomasochists, and television stars tried to find their identities while hustling one another in apocalyptic scenarios. A cast of more than 100 characters recall the most sordid, vicious and fascinating moments of their lives in this visual compendium that features 120 photographs, many never before seen. "Rock & roll, death, urine, slime, blood and pus [were] reborn on the Sunset Strip in the punk summer of '77. Darby Crash was the Christopher Columbus of horror, grotesquery, and bad behavior—of course he needs his story told. I couldn't believe the book—it brought me back in a time machine to my own brush with madness and insanity."

—Kim Fowley

Paperback original ♦ $16.95 ♦ 6 × 9 ♦ 312 pages ♦ extensively illustrated
ISBN: 0-922915-70-9

American Hardcore: A Tribal History

Steven Blush

"Encompassing and fucking interesting . . . visually and intellectually stunning. An enthralling read, this book proves interesting and insightful not just for hardcore purists, but for any avid reader. *Please Kill Me* move over—we have a new King Of The Punk Rock Publications."

—Keith Carman, *Chart Magazine*

Paperback original ♦ $19.95 ♦ 7 × 10 ♦ 336 pages ♦ extensively illustrated
ISBN: 0-922915-71-7

Tape Op The Book About Creative Music Recording

Edited by Larry Crane, Introduction by Tony Visconti

". . . cool, creative alternatives for musicians who want or need to record on a shoestring budget . . . a nice way to get up to speed on the liberating world of home recording."—Mark Watt, *Hear/Say*

"They're actually trying to help real musicians who don't have a fortune to spend on equipment figure out how to do this stuff. My kinda folks."

—Michael Goldberg

Paperback original ♦ $19.95 ♦ 8.5 × 11 ♦ 216 pages ♦ ISBN: 0-922915-60-1

To order from feral House
Domestic orders add $4.50 shipping for first item, $2 each additional item. AMEX, Mastercard, VISA, checks and money orders are accepted. (CA state residents add 8.25% tax). Canadian orders add $9 shipping for first item, $6 each additional item. Other countries add $11 shipping for first item, $9 each additional item. Non-U.S. originated orders must be international money order or check drawn on a U.S. bank only. Send orders to: Feral House ♦ P.O. Box 13067 ♦ Los Angeles, CA 90013

www.feralhouse.com